THE POLYPORACEAE OF THE UNITED STATES, ALASKA, AND CANADA

The
POLYPORACEAE
of the
UNITED STATES,
ALASKA,
and CANADA

By LEE ORAS OVERHOLTS

Prepared for Publication
by JOSIAH L. LOWE

With a New Foreword
by ALEXANDER H. SMITH

ANN ARBOR
THE UNIVERSITY OF MICHIGAN PRESS

University of Michigan Studies
Scientific Series, Volume XIX

FOREWORD
by Alexander H. Smith

E ACH group of higher fungi presents its own unique problems to the student. There is still much to be learned of the relationships of these organisms. Because of the sheer number of species, the generally imperfect specimens preserved in herbaria, and the discovery of previously unused or unrecognized features, our classification is relatively unstable. With the discovery of "new" features there must always follow a reevaluation of the position in our classification of the species showing them. Thus, it has been difficult to gain perspective in such orders as the Agaricales or Aphyllophorales to say nothing of the Hymenomycetes as a whole.

Investigators such as Overholts may be interested in many groups of fungi but are best known for their contributions in one group. Overholts worked with the nonfleshy pore fungi or Polyporaceae, as he termed them. His concept of the Polyporaceae as set forth in the first edition of his book was ultraconservative even for his time. But he had good reasons for his attitude. He could not see how the group could be divided into smaller genera with clear limits. Change for the mere sake of change was in his estimation not good science.

At the same time, the need for new generic concepts in the Polyporaceae has been recognized by all investigators working with the family from 1870 to the present day. Murrill's classification was an earlier attempt to fulfill this need. By the time Dr. Lowe assumed the tedious task of preparing the final copy of the first edition of Overholts' work for publication, the situation as regards the classification of the polypores was changing rapidly. The type of study in vogue was either a study of a cross section of the family, such as that of Bondarzew and Singer, or the description of numerous isolated genera, often based on one or very few species. Lowe, rightly, did not believe it desirable or proper to attempt a synthesis of this modern work and to use it as a framework for a classification under Overholts' name. His choice was a wise one as far as producing a treatment of

v

general use to the mycological public was concerned, though it admittedly did not suit the "splitters."

The features emphasized in modern classifications concern many hyphal characters such as the presence of clamp connections at the cross walls, thickness of the hyphal wall for hyphae of the various regions of the basidiocarp, the color of the wall as well as any irregularities in it or deposits of material on it, and the shape and size of the hyphal cells. Names have been applied to the hyphal state in the basidiocarps of the various species—being termed monomitic if only one kind (generative) of hypha is present, dimitic if two types, and so on. The recognition of these hyphal states has been of great help to our understanding of the polyporaceous basidiocarp, but has also brought in its wake a new set of difficulties.

As it is not the purpose of this Foreword to present a critical analysis of the virtues and pitfalls involving the "hyphal approach" to the taxonomy of pore fungi, one example will suffice.

The hyphal features of the polypore basidiocarp were actually recorded to a large extent in most of Overholts' descriptions, but his emphasis, following tradition, was mostly on hyphal end cells. The terminal cell of a hypha or hyphal branch has long been recognized as the most important category of the hyphal cells in the basidiocarp. The basidia, in which meiosis occurs and which produce the spores of the "sexual state," are the most important hyphal end cells in the fruiting body. Indeed, the whole basidiocarp in the Hymenomycetes has evolved about various ways of increasing number and effectiveness in producing and liberating spores. Because of their monotonous similarity morphologically, however, they furnish few taxonomic features at the generic level. Hymenial cystidia, a second type of hyphal end cell, have been emphasized in the classification of Hymenomycetes by most workers, including Overholts, throughout this century. The extensive gamut of morphological types which have evolved in this category can be seen by glancing at Plates 125–32. These and the features of the basidiospores, in addition to some hyphal features, made up the set of microscopic characters on which Overholts based his classification.

In the Agaricales hyphal end cells on the pileus (cuticle) and on the stipe are important features of taxonomic value. The same has now been found to be true for at least some of the polypores, but here they are much more difficult to demonstrate. All of these categories concern hyphal end cells which are at some exposed surface of the basidiocarp.

We have been slow to realize, however, that hyphal end cells in the interior of the basidiocarp have also evolved features constant for species and hence of taxonomic value. These have been observed and designated (or illustrated) as hyphal end cells by many workers, but because many elongate and in themselves assume more or less the shape of hyphae, they have often been termed hyphae, because they often become thick-walled and form the framework of some part of the basidiocarp. Thus, basidiocarps of some species described as dimitic (two hyphal systems), in reality may have but one system—in addition to a framework formed of hyphal-like endosetae, for instance. Classifying these structures as *hyphae* rather than *hyphal end cells,* it seems to me, opens a way of easily confusing the relationships of certain species with basidiocarps of generally similar aspect. A species with endosetae (or mycosclerids as Wright termed them) as "skeletals" is obviously more highly evolved than one in which the framework of the basidiocarp is made up entirely of hyphae rather than a category of hyphal cell. Since hyphal studies on the polypores are a tedious undertaking, making a correct hyphal analysis of a specimen on which one desires an identification, will not soon become routine in the polypores. As in the past, identification to species will most probably be made on correlated features once the basic studies have established a stable classification.

Certain neglected features of the polypores are now being studied more critically. The spore deposit color, for instance, is as important in the polypores as anywhere else in the Hymenomycetes. But for related groups one has to ascertain the spectrum—the color range for the group. This also applies to the agarics. This feature has in the past generally been unpopular with polypore students because so much of their material has been collected in a nonsporulating stage. However, it is futile to erect classifications ignoring a major character, and polypore classification will not become well stabilized until this feature is used in areas found to be critical. Spores under the microscope often appear hyaline, whereas in a deposit they will be seen to have distinctive color.

Most research in polypore taxonomy at the present time is concerned with recording the type of detail indicated here for the innumerable species, and when an odd combination of features is discovered the species usually ends up as the type of a "new genus." One cannot help but reflect that the description of "new" genera might better wait until more information about the group as a whole is available, but this is not a realistic point of view for one to take as long as an author can place his name after that of a new genus and thereby immortalize himself. It seems to me that in certain groups the natural relationships of the fungi are now being obscured by the large number of genera proposed. Genetical studies are badly needed to ascertain the behavior of critical taxonomic features. This must be done before we can make truly meaningful judgments as to the value of the characters relative to a system of classification.

In the meantime, to give the users of the Overholts manual some idea of the generic names current in the literature of this decade, a partial list of the more important genera and of their species (with page numbers) is included as a guide:

1. Albatrellus
   A. ovinus   215
   A. confluens   216
   A. Flettii   218
   A. caeruliiporus   219
   A. cristatus   221
2. Antrodia
   A. mollis   146
3. Aurantioporellus
   A. alboluteus
4. Aurantioporus
   A. croceus
5. Bjerkandera
   B. adustus
   B. fumosus
6. Boletopsis
   B. griseus   228
7. Bondarzewia
   B. montanus   237
   B. berkeleyii   238

8. Coriolus
   C. versicolor
   C. biformis
   C. hirsutus
   C. pubescens
9. Cerrena
   C. unicolor   125
9a. Climacocystis
   C. borealis
10. Coriolellus
   C. sepium   136
   C. serialis   138
   C. malicola   150
11. Coltricia
   C. cinnamomea
   C. perennis
   C. montagnei
   C. greenei
11a. Cryptoporus
   C. volvatus

PREFACE

THE first draft of this manual was written by Dr. Lee Oras Overholts in 1933, after twenty years of work at Pennsylvania State College as the foremost American specialist in the Polyporaceae. Until his death in November, 1946, at State College, he corrected the manuscript continuously as new information became known, though he made no over-all revision. For six months before his death Dr. Overholts had been actively putting the manuscript in shape for publication, and, as left, it was substantially complete. The Introduction, the keys to the genera and the species, the specific descriptions, the Glossary, the legends for the illustrations, and about two thirds of the Bibliography were written in essentially the form in which they appear here.

At the request of Dr. Frank D. Kern, formerly head of the Department of Botany at Pennsylvania State College, and of Mrs. Overholts, I undertook to prepare the manuscript for publication. Insofar as possible the original wording has been retained, and only such changes as were required for accuracy, clarity, or uniformity of style have been introduced. The text keys to the arrangement of the species present Dr. Overholts' concepts of interrelations in the Polyporaceae as nearly as could be determined from his publications and from an incomplete arrangement for the genus *Polyporus* found with the manuscript. As required by the text, some sixty titles have been added to the Bibliography, and bibliographic citations of records of hosts and of geographic distribution have been supplied in the specific descriptions. Every literature citation has been checked against the original, and cited specimens have been checked against the originals in the Overholts Herbarium.

Because, no doubt, of his poor health, Dr. Overholts did not incorporate in his manual some thirty species and varieties which have been described since 1938, most of them by Dr. W. A. Murrill. To bring the present volume up to date, these are briefly characterized at the end of the proper genera, and are also referred to in the relevant text keys. I am indebted to Dr. Murrill for the loan of the type specimens of his species.

Grateful acknowledgment is made to Dr. Kern for encouragement and financial help, to Mrs. Overholts for constant assistance—including the exacting work of retyping the manuscript—and to the administrative officers of the New York State College of Forestry for the time and the travel funds required for the completion of the work. The University of Michigan Press generously undertook to publish the manual, and particular thanks are due Miss Grace Potter for her able and constructive editorial assistance, and to Dr. Alexander H. Smith for extensive aid. Sincere thanks are also due a number of individuals who assisted in ways too various to detail here.

Over a long and extraordinarily active mycological career Dr. Overholts gave freely of his time and wide knowledge to those who turned to him for assistance. As a specialist in the same field I received more than the usual amount of help, and came to know him as a personal friend. It is a privilege, therefore, to have been able to assist in the preparation of his lifework for publication, and to present to mycologists of the world the fruit of his lifetime study in the Polyporaceae.

Josiah L. Lowe

TABLE OF CONTENTS

xiii

LIST OF PLATES

(The plates follow page 446.)

xv

INTRODUCTION

THE past fifty years have brought to the field of systematic mycology an enormously increased body of knowledge. In no group of the fungi has this increase been more manifest than in that family of higher Basidiomycetes known as the Polyporaceae. The beginning of the century presented a confusion of names and ideas seemingly in great discord in different herbaria and even in the same herbarium. Neither names nor ideas were stable, but varied with the individual. It would be too much to say that all of this has changed and that now our mycological household has been set in order with reference to this family. Erroneous ideas and conflicting opinions are still extant, and there is doubt whether complete harmony will ever be attained, and, even could it be obtained, whether it would be desirable. Even when the facts about these plants have all been learned, opinions will differ as to their evaluation. But we are at present far from any such complete information, and while we can now consolidate our position with reference to most of our species, many gaps remain to be bridged before we can point to this family as a happy example of a completely known and classified group of plants.

What we have learned has been due primarily to the work of a few individuals, among whom no names stand out with more prominence than those of C. G. Lloyd and W. A. Murrill. That these investigators represent diamétrically opposed schools of thought has been to the advantage of the subject matter. But their work would have been impossible without the co-operation of contemporary European systematic mycologists, such as Bresadola, Patouillard, and Romell, and especially without the labors of that host of American mycologists of the past few generations headed by Peck and including Curtis, Schweinitz, Ravenel, Ellis, Earle, Morgan, Everhart, Glatfelter, Lea, Commons, Kellerman, Atkinson, and numerous others, not forgetting the many lesser-known, isolated individuals who patiently collected and preserved their collections to form a substantial basis for a comprehensive knowledge of this family of fungi. It is likewise impossible to give individual credit here to the host of col-

1

lectors now in the field. Every collection bearing their names will
be a monument to their energy as long as the collections endure.

For three quarters of a century after the introduction of the binomial system of nomenclature the species at present included in
the Polyporaceae were not recognized as constituting a group distinct
from what we now consider related families.

Linnaeus himself had little conception of relationships among
the fungi. His treatment (109) of the entire group included but
eighty-six species, many of which, except in the genus *Mucor* (eleven
species), are perhaps not the usual composite Linnaean species, but
contained such anomalous fungi as are now recognized as *Amanita
muscaria* Fries, *Tricholoma equestre* Fries, *Daedalea quercina*, *Polyporus betulinus*, *Schizophyllum alneum* L. ex Schröt., *Trametes suaveolens*, *Fomes fomentarius*, *Hydnum auriscalpium* L. ex Fries, and others,
most of which are today regarded as elementary species. The entire
number of genera recognized under the group "Fungi" was ten:
Agaricus, *Boletus*, *Hydnum*, *Phallus*, *Clathrus*, *Elvella*, *Peziza*, *Clavaria*, *Lycoperdon*, and *Mucor*. In the light of present-day practices,
these are composite genera, whose boundaries coincided more nearly
with family limitations as we now know them. For example, Linnaeus' genus *Agaricus* included twenty-seven species now distributed
(with the exception of *A. quercinus*) among various genera of the
Agaricaceae; his genus *Boletus* contained twelve species, all now regarded as members of the family Polyporaceae (including Boletaceae); and all four of his species of *Hydnum* are today retained in
the family Hydnaceae. Some of the other recognized genera were
more inclusive: His genus *Phallus* contained one or more species of
the ascomycetous genus *Morchella;* *Clavaria* included such *Clavaria*-
like fungi as *Cordyceps militaris* (L. ex Fries) Link, *Xylaria digitata*
(L. ex Fries) Grev., and *X. Hypoxylon* (L. ex Fries) Grev., as well as
certain true species of *Clavaria*; his genus *Lycoperdon* included two
or more species referable either to the Tuberales or to the Hymeno-
gastrales, one species now regarded as a myxomycete (*Lycogala
epidendrum* L. ex Fries), and several species of true Lycoperdaceae;
finally, the genus *Mucor* was probably the most inclusive of all,
with five species, said to be perennial, whose identity is now somewhat in doubt, a species of powdery mildew, one or more species
of *Penicillium* and of *Aspergillus*, and perhaps two or three species

now known as Phycomycetes. This entire list includes but eight species of the family Polyporaceae (exclusive of Boletaceae). They are *Agaricus (Daedalea) quercinus, A. (Lenzites) betulinus, Boletus suberosus (Polyporus betulinus), B. (Fomes) fomentarius, B. (Fomes) igniarius, B. (Polyporus) versicolor, B. (Trametes) suaveolens,* and *B. (Polyporus) perennis.* No family or order divisions were attempted at this time, but in a later work the genera *Agaricus, Boletus, Hydnum,* and *Phallus* were grouped (110, p. 371) in a section "Pileati," and the remainder in a section "Pileo destituti." Moreover, these four genera were briefly characterized, and the first three are significant to this history: *Agaricus* was defined (110, p. 597) as "subtus lamellosus," *Boletus* (110, p. 608) as "subtus porosus," and *Hydnum* (110, p. 612) as "subtus echinatus." With these characterizations in mind, we must conclude that Linnaeus' concepts of these three genera were later to be broadened into families as we now know them, and it might be said that the family Polyporaceae had its inception at this time.

In the second half of the eighteenth century, and shortly following the work of Linnaeus, appeared Schaeffer's (191) monumental illustrations of fungi, in which a total of 330 species were portrayed. His ideas of classification are summarized in an index occupying seven (unnumbered) pages of the last of the four volumes. The only genera recognized were those already used by Linnaeus, but each genus constituted a separate tribe. These he named *Agarici, Boleti, Hydna, Elvelae, Clavariae, Pezizae, Lycoperda, Mucores, Phalli,* and *Clathri.* The Polyporaceae represented were all, with the exception of species in which the hymenium is more or less gilled, included in the *Boleti.* Schaeffer's ideas of the relationships in the fungi were no more advanced than those of Linnaeus, for *Daldinia concentrica* (L. ex Fries) Ces. & De Not. is placed in the tribe *Lycoperda,* a species of *Cyathus* and one of *Crucibulum* are in the section *Pezizae,* certain species of apparent Geoglossaceae are in the tribe *Clavariae,* one or more species of *Craterellus* are in the tribe *Elvelae,* and a species of *Morchella* is illustrated as a *Phallus.* Some familiarity with the spores of these fungi is indicated by the drawings, but undoubtedly their manner of production was unknown, and most certainly our present-day division of Ascomycetes, Basidiomycetes, and Phycomycetes, based on the manner of production of the spores, was not enunciated until three quarters of a century later.

Persoon (169), in 1825, seems to have been the first to segregate

those fungi in which the hymenium is poroid, with the basidia lining
the interior surfaces of the tubes, into a named group. In fact, in
his recognition of sections "Porodermei" (with pores) (vol. 2, p. 34),
"Odontodermei" (with teeth) (vol. 2, p. 150), and "Agaricini" (with
gills) (vol. 3, p. 1), he definitely segregated three of the now recognized families in the Hymenomycetes. He did not recognize the
Hymenomycetes as a group under that name, but included the three
sections in "Ordo tertius" of "Classis prima" of the fungi, the other
two orders constituting roughly (a) such Fungi Imperfecti as were
then known ("Ordo primus"), and (b) a curious mixture of Auricu-
lariaceae, Tremellaceae, Thelephoraceae, Clavariaceae, and genera
of the larger Ascomycetes, particularly in the Pezizales and the
Helvellales ("Ordo secundus").

In his *Systema Mycologicum* Fries divided the fungi into four
primary classes, viz., "Hymenomycetes" (vol. 1, p. 1), "Gastero-
mycetes" (vol. 2, p. 275), "Hyphomycetes" (vol. 3, p. 261), and
"Coniomycetes" (vol. 3, p. 455). The "Hymenomycetes" were segregated on the single character of the exposed hymenium. In this
group he therefore included not only the Hymenomycetes as we
know that group today, but also all Ascomycetes in which the asci
are exposed prior to the maturity of the spores. The group was
divided into six orders, one of which ("Pileati") included the genera
*Agaricus, Cantharellus, Merulius, Schizophyllum, Daedalea, Polyporus,
Boletus, Fistulina* (see Figs. 596, 625), *Hydnum, Sistotrema* (see Fig.
666, *S. confluens*), *Phlebia,* and *Thelephora,* without a recognition of
family characteristics.

GENERIC SEGREGATES IN THE FAMILY

In his earlier work Fries recognized but three genera, *Merulius*
(49, p. 326), *Daedalea* (49, p. 331), and *Polyporus* (49, p. 341). Later
he accepted the genus *Favolus* of Beauvois (161) as a subgenus of
Polyporus, raising it to generic rank in 1828 in *Elenchus Fungorum*
(50, p. 44). In 1830 Kunze (108) established the genus *Cyclomyces*
(often attributed to Kunze and Fries) on sessile plants with the
tubes breaking up to form concentric lamellae (gills). In 1836
Fries (52) established the genus *Trametes* and also recognized the genera *Cyclomyces* and *Hexagona.* In his *Epicrisis Systematis Mycologici* (51) in 1836–1838 no additional segregates were recognized
by Fries, but in *Novae Symbolae Mycologicae* in 1855 (53) the genus

Polystictus was established. Fries's conception of *Polystictus* at this time seems to have been different from his idea of a subgenus *Polysticta* (49, p. 384) in the *Systema* to which he had referred certain abnormal forms. The genus *Polystictus* was later abandoned—at least it did not appear in *Hymenomycetes Europaei* in 1874. Fries did, however, mark out under *Polyporus* the sections representing the genera *Fomes* and *Poria*, which were later raised to generic rank by others. No further segregates of generic rank were recognized by Fries at any time, so that his final concepts of generic entities within the family may be broadly stated as follows:

Lenzites—with radiating lamellae, as in *L. betulina*

Daedalea—with daedaloid hymenium, as in *D. quercina*

Cyclomyces—with concentric lamellae, as in *C. fuscus*

Favolus—primarily lamellate. but with the lamellae joined transversely to form faveolate pores, as in *F. alveolaris*

Hexagona—with large hexagonal pores, as in *H. variegata*

Trametes—daedaloid in consistency and structure, but with circular pores, as in *T. suaveolens*

Polystictus—mainly without the characteristics of the genera above, and with the pores developed in a centrifugal manner, i.e., in succession from the base or center of the pileus toward the margin; as in *P. versicolor*

Polyporus—as in *Polystictus*, but all pores developing simultaneously from above downward

It is true that in *Hymenomycetes Europaei* Fries (54) felt the necessity for grouping these genera somewhat differently, and the summation above expresses, rather, his conception of generic entities as each became apparent to him. A word of explanation as to *Favolus* and *Hexagona* seems likewise desirable, since the characters are at variance with those ascribed to them by their authors. In *Systema Mycologicum* (49, p. 342) Fries evidently regarded *Hexagona*, established by Pollini in 1816, as not sufficiently distinct from the subgenus *Favolus*, and he included species of it under *Favolus*. In *Elenchus Fungorum* (50, p. 44) the first species listed under *Favolus* is *F. brasiliensis*, which is regarded now as a synonym of *Hexagona Mori*, the type species of Pollini's genus *Hexagona*, while the type species (i.e., the species first mentioned) of *Favolus* of Beauvois (*F. hirtus*) is listed as a *Hexagona*. This explains Murrill's attempt (138g) to

restore the names to their original generic significance, with *H. Mori*
as the type of *Hexagona* and *F. hirtus* as the type of *Favolus*.

If we may take cognizance of Fries's recognition of *Fomes* and
Poria as distinct entities, we have in the eight genera (and these
two subgenera) mentioned above, all of the more important genera
recognized by conservative taxonomic mycologists since the time
of Fries. In Saccardo's *Sylloge Fungorum* and in Engler and Prantl's
Natürlichen Pflanzenfamilien the Friesian arrangement is accepted,
and it is extremely doubtful whether among the several other classifications proposed any is more practical, or perhaps even more natural, however artificial the Friesian arrangement may be. Only a
slight acquaintance with the family is necessary to make one aware
that all the Friesian genera are quite heterogeneous. But a wider
acquaintance brings an appreciation of three additional fundamental
facts, viz.: (1) a few species (e.g., *Polyporus volvatus, P. graveolens*)
stand out as distinct entities, without any near relatives; (2) a few
groups of species (e.g., the *Polyporus varius-picipes-elegans-melanopus*
group, the *P. versicolor-hirsutus-zonatus* group, the *P. sanguineus-
cinnabarinus* group, the *P. lucidus* complex) show unmistakable
evidences of close relationship within the group, but not between the
groups; (3) the bulk of the species show no close affinities, yet general
similarities are apparent. It is obvious that if the species or groups
in the first and the second categories are recognized as genera, then
they are genera of an order different from each other and different
still from those placed in the third category. In a group that varies
in as many ways as does the large share of the genus *Polyporus* it will
be found almost if not quite impossible to show relationships to any
better advantage by a multitude of generic segregates than by retaining all species in a single large genus. And if the demands of a
natural arrangement cannot be met, wherein lies the value of a multiplication of generic names? We are willing to plead guilty to the
accusation of being too conservative in generic terminology. But
to follow any principle of procedure logically and consistently in the
matter of recognizing generic segregates in *Polyporus* and *Fomes*
leads either to results that have no significance in a natural scheme
of classification, or else to the point where the conception of genera
encroaches too closely upon that of species. The result in the first
instance would in no way be an improvement over existing condi-

tions, and in the second case the main principle underlying our present method of classifying plants is set at naught. We find ourselves, therefore, unable to accept in their entirety the views of most workers in this family after 1875.

The elevation of Fries's subgenus *Poria* to generic rank by Cooke (36) and Quélet (176) was a forward step, although preceded in point of time by Gillet's establishment (57) of the genus *Physisporus* to include the same group of species. But because the species of *Poria* were recognized as distinct and segregated as early as 1794 by Persoon (166) and because of the almost universal use of the name by subsequent workers, it is felt that the name *Poria* should be conserved. The so-called "fifty-year rule" of the International Rules of Botanical Nomenclature might well be applied in this instance. Similarly, the genus *Fomes*, first recognized as a subgenus (*Perennes*) by Fries (49, p. 372) and elevated to generic rank by Gillet (57, p. 682),[1] must be accepted. But the genus *Merisma* of Gillet (57, p. 688), established to include those species with branched stems that produce large compound sporophores of the type of *Polyporus frondosus*, is rejected.

Since 1885 very few new ideas have been involved in the establishment of the multitudinous generic segregates that have been proposed. For the most part, either the tribes and sections of previous authors have been raised to generic rank, or else minor species groupings have been lopped off here and there in a more or less indiscriminate fashion. Thus, of the old genus *Polyporus*, Quélet (176) makes a total of ten genera.[2] From the hands of Karsten (93–97) the same genus emerges, not as an entity, but broken up into about seventeen genera, while *Fomes* and *Poria* suffer in similar fashion.[3]

Patouillard (162, 163) recognizes many of the segregates of Quélet and of Karsten and makes some additions.[4] Murrill (138–143) follows

[1] [But see under *Fomes*, p. 32.—J.L.L.]

[2] The genera recognized are *Caloporus, Cerioporus, Cladomeris, Coriolus, Inodermus, Leptoporus, Leucoporus, Pelloporus, Phellinus,* and *Placodes.*

[3] The genera recognized are *Polyporus, Polypilus, Polyporellus, Hapalopilus, Piptoporus, Bjerkandera, Hansenia, Fomitopsis, Pycnoporus, Tyromyces, Lenzites, Daedalea, Physisporus, Physisporinus, Xylodon, Polystictus, Onnia, Ganoderma, Ischnoderma, Inonotus, Poria, Fomes, Elfvingia, Phellinus, Antrodia, Trametes, Lenzitina, Gloeophyllum,* and *Meripilus.*

[4] Additional genera proposed by Patouillard are *Melanopus, Spongipellis,* and *Gyrophana.*

the same course, the entire number of genera[1] recognized being fifty-eight.

The work of Lloyd (111–116) was avowedly conservative, and extremely lucid and inclusive. Only in his treatment (114) of the stipitate species in 1912 is there any suggestion of new departures. Here, as he states it, "... we have employed the sectional name as the first binomial ...." From a nomenclatural standpoint, this is the height of radicalism, which he otherwise so strongly eschewed.

Miss Ames (2) attempted to reconcile the various conflicting accounts of the family. She concludes that the character and position of the stem, the annual or perennial nature of the sporophore, the diameter of the hyphae, the order of development of the pores, the uneven depths of the tubes, pore characters, color of context, presence or absence of cystidia and setae, and to a considerable extent the relation between the tube layer and the pileus are all characters of too much variation or otherwise so unsuitable that they should not be used as generic characters within the family. Further, she feels that the consistency and the surface modification of the pileus, the separable nature of the tube layer, and possibly the color of the spores are characters that can be safely used in separating genera. On the basis of these conclusions she presents a revision of the family (exclusive of the genus *Poria*) that includes sixteen genera. *Polyporus* is separated into *Bjerkandera, Ischnoderma, Cryptoporus, Piptoporus, Porodisculus, Gloeoporus, Phaeolus, Coriolus, Polystictus, Ganoderma,* and *Polyporus; Fomes* is separated into *Phellinus* and *Fomes; Trametes, Daedalea,* and *Favolus* are recognized.

It is to me a significant fact that the first six of these genera would include a total of not more than seven or eight of the species of North America; in other words, these are practically monotypic genera. And if the genus *Polyporus* cannot be broken up along more comprehensive lines, no advantage results. One might more enthusiastically embrace Miss Ames's separation of the brown-context usually stipitate species into *Polystictus* if it were not so drastic a

---

[1] The genera proposed as new (except segregates of *Poria*) are *Irpiciporus, Poronidulus, Coriolellus, Spongiporus, Tomophagus, Earliella, Rigidoporus, Porodisculus, Microporellus, Abortiporus, Aurantiporellus, Pycnoporellus, Aurantiporus, Flaviporellus, Laetiporus, Phaeolopsis, Cerrenella, Coriolopsis, Trichaptum, Pogonomyces, Nigroporus, Cycloporellus, Coltriciella, Fomitella, Pyropolyporus, Porodaedalea, Nigrofomes, Globifomes,* and *Cycloporus.*

departure from a very current concept of *Polystictus*. *Coriolus* as a genus is too much confused by species intermediate between it and the remainder of the genus *Polyporus* to permit its recognition, although she allows for it a wider range than have previous authors. *Ganoderma* might better be limited to species with a laccate pileus as in *Polyporus lucidus*. But *Fomes applanatus* is no more related to *P. lucidus* and its allies than to *F. igniarius* and its allies. *F. fomentarius* is most certainly out of place in *Ganoderma*, and its spores are not of the character predicated for that genus at all, but are cylindric and hyaline, with no wall markings whatsoever. In my opinion the genus *Ganoderma* must be limited to the species of the *P. lucidus-Curtisii* type or be dispensed with altogether.

While Miss Ames's work was a welcome step in ignoring the multitude of untenable genera that is now our heritage in this family, it is even more refreshing to consider the simple generic concepts presented in Rea's (179) work on the British members of this family. Here one finds *Polyporus*, *Fomes*, *Poria*, *Lenzites*, *Trametes*, *Daedalea*, and *Merulius* in their better-known interpretation. *Polystictus* and *Ganoderma* are both recognized, perhaps without doing too much violence to specific relationships.

Bourdot and Galzin (18) have presented the polypores of France in a very lucid and understanding account, and one which appeals to me as having much merit. They recognize about twenty genera, mostly in the sense of their compatriots Quélet and Patouillard. For those who insist that it is time for a radical revision of the polypores, yet who dislike the many small and monotypic genera of other authors, this scheme is recommended. No new generic segregates are proposed.

[The excellent studies by Donk (42) and Pilát (172) were not reviewed by Dr. Overholts, though the second of these was noted for inclusion. These authors divide the family into more genera than Bourdot and Galzin and represent the best of current mycological practice in Europe. The works cited should be consulted for greater detail.—J.L.L.]

The most recent review of the nomenclatural status of the various genera of the Polyporaceae is that of Cooke (37). He lists forty-six generic names of North American Polyporaceae that he considers valid. About 130 generic segregates of past years are excluded and nineteen are transferred to other relationships in the fungi. Cooke does not propose any new generic concepts, but apparently takes the attitude that if a name can be shown to be valid under the International Rules we are obligated to use that name, regardless of the need for it. I myself adhere to no such strictures, feeling that an author is responsible to no one for the generic units he recognizes so long as they are valid names.

As to the recent work in Europe, culminating in an article by Bondarzew and Singer (15), most of it has not been available to me except as summarized in a translation of that article, which was supplied by Mr. John A. Stevenson, but the multiplicity of "Bond. and Sing." combinations recalls the fact that other attempts of this sort have not found wide favor among mycological taxonomists, and perhaps for the present the recent proposals may be allowed to rest in a state of "innocuous desuetude."

MORPHOLOGY AND TERMINOLOGY

Importance of Exact Terminology.—No student can expect to identify plants in any group successfully without first acquiring some knowledge of the morphology of the organisms and some familiarity with the vocabulary used in the keys and in the generic and specific descriptions. Obviously, it is impossible to couch this descriptive matter in words familiar to the beginner without sacrificing conciseness and exactness. On the other hand, there is no justification for a uselessly complicated terminology. But the same terms may have a somewhat different meaning in different groups of plants or when used by different writers. As an example of the latter situation we need only refer to the words used to indicate color. When one considers the unlimited intergradation of colors it is obvious that "yellowish brown," "reddish orange," and other similar designations may be used to describe very different hues. A comprehensive Glossary at the end of this volume will make clear my use of various terms. However, some terms require illustration and perhaps a more expanded explanation than can be included in a brief definition. Consequently, a few important terms of this sort dealing with the morphology and anatomy of the fruiting body are discussed in some detail in the following paragraphs.

Sporophore.—The part of the fungus that is ordinarily visible to the collector is in reality only the fruit of the plant and has received various names. Morphologists have called it "sporophore," "fruiting body," "carpophore," "fructification," and "basidiocarp"; common terms sometimes applied to it are "conch," "punk," "bracket," and "shelf." Sometimes it is referred to as "the plant," but obviously incorrectly, since the vegetative part of the plant is in the substratum and goes by the generally accepted term *mycelium*. We shall in general use the term *sporophore* for the part commonly collected, i.e., the part on which identification is usually based; or, if the term *plant* is used in the purely descriptive matter, it is to be understood that the sporophore or fruiting body is meant. The sporophore in the Polyporaceae may be any one of three main types.

The *resupinate sporophore* is the simplest and probably also the most primitive condition, in that the entire structure lies flat on the substratum, that is, without forming a bracket-like or shelflike body. Such sporophores are typically produced on the under surface of the substratum, i.e., on the under side of logs, limbs, and fallen trees, though occasionally they are found on the vertical surface of trunks where the inequalities of the surface permit the formation of tubes that can open downward. This type of sporophore is said to be *resupinate* (Figs. 2, 18, 614), and is characteristic of the genus *Poria*. In addition, it is likely to be the form assumed by many species in all the other genera when growing in situations unfavorable for development of the characteristic form of the sporophore. For example many species of *Polyporus* develop a resupinate sporophore when growing on the under side of boards or large logs, yet no species in that genus is normally resupinate. One must therefore be constantly on guard against referring resupinate specimens to the genus *Poria* when in reality they may be resupinate only because of a situation unfavorable for developing the usual type of sporophore. There are no marks by which one can recognize an entirely resupinate specimen of *Polyporus* or *Fomes* as such; yet careful collecting of a large number of specimens at the same time and place will often show that attempts on the part of the fungus to develop a bracket (pileus) have been partly successful, and any such evidence is to be taken as an indication that the sporophore is not that of a normally resupinate species. In other words, resupinate sporophores with well-developed tubes are to be referred to *Poria* (or *Solenia* if the tubes stand isolated from each other) only in the absence of any recognizable attempt to form a pileus. Of course, one learns eventually to recognize normally pileate species even though they are growing in a resupinate condition. But such a feat is beyond the powers of the most careful beginner.

The *sessile sporophore* takes the form of a knob or bracket or shelf (Figs. 608, 626). It is the more common type outside the genus *Poria*. Sporophores vary in size from those barely recognizable as of this type to ones many inches in diameter. The bracket is usually spoken of as the *pileus*, although sometimes that term is reserved for the upper portion, and especially the upper surface, of the bracket. The sessile sporophore has no stem or stalk, and the point of attachment to the substratum is typically lateral. An approach to a stalked condition is sometimes seen when the sporophore is narrowed toward the base (Fig. 124), but such specimens are to be regarded as primarily sessile. Many species show a combination of the resupinate and the sessile form of sporophore, having a reflexed margin which forms a horizontal pileus on a sporophore that is otherwise resupinate. This type is said to be *effused-reflexed*, and is illustrated in Fig. 87.

The *stipitate sporophore*, in contrast with the resupinate and the sessile forms, is stalked or provided with a stem or stipe. All gradations of stem development are present in the family, and it is often a question whether or not a given poorly developed stemlike structure should be called a stem. In such cases the sporophore is said to be *substipitate*. The stem surface and the context tissue are usually similar to their equivalents in the pileus, and the same terms may be used in describing them. The attachment of the stem to the pileus varies from a *central* to an *excentric, lateral,* or *dorsal* position. If it is dorsal, the sporophore is *pendent*.

Stipitate specimens with isolated tubes (Figs. 596, 625) belong to the genus *Fistulina*, not treated in this manual.

Regions of the Sporophore.—The extent of the development of the different regions of the sporophore and other salient characters form the basis on which we are able to distinguish one species from another. The main regions of the pileus are the *pileus surface* (by which is meant the upper surface), *context, tube layer, pore surface,* and *hymenium.* Description of the stem presents no special terminology.

The characters of importance in connection with the *pileus surface* include the type and degree of hairiness, which varies from *glabrous* to *velvety, hispid, hirsute, tomentose, villose, fibrillose, scaly,* and all possible combinations of these, such as *velvety-tomentose* and *hirsute-tomentose*—terms which have the same significance here as in other groups of plants. When the pileus is glabrous, it is frequently *pelliculose*, i.e., covered with a very thin fragile cuticle often not discernible in fresh plants, or it may be *incrusted*, that is, covered with a more or less distinct crust, which is sometimes hard and horny and more than one millimeter thick, or is often quite thin. In the genus *Fomes*, in particular, the entire sporophore is often woody and hard throughout, and not at all incrusted. It is only when the surface is covered by a layer or crust which is distinctly harder than the underlying tissue that the pileus can be said to be incrusted.

The *context* is the inner tissue of the pileus, that is, the tissue lying between the upper surface and the tube layer (Fig. 113). It may be extremely thin and practically nonexistent or it may be several inches thick. Sometimes it is divided into two different regions, an upper soft layer and a lower firm or hard layer, in which case it is said to be *duplex*. A duplex context is usually more easily recognized in dried specimens than in fresh ones. The context is often designated as the "trama" of the pileus, but the term will not be used in that connection in this manual.

The *tube layer* (Fig. 113) is easily recognized in mature specimens as a layer of vertically placed tubes attached to the lower surface of the context and, in all but two or three species, inseparably united to that region. In mature specimens the tubes vary in length from one millimeter, or slightly less, to several centimeters. In young specimens the layer is scarcely to be recognized at all, and in identifications involving differences in tube length care must be taken to secure measurements from specimens that are more or less mature. In the perennial species of the family a new layer of tubes is added over the surface of the old layer each year. Sometimes these annual layers are quite distinct from each other and can be readily counted, as in *Fomes applanatus*, *F. connatus*, and *F. pinicola*, but more frequently the tubes are gradually extended downward year by year and the layers are indistinct, or no layering at all may be recognizable.

The *pore surface* is the lower surface of the sporophore in specimens mature enough to have a tube layer. It is the surface at which the tubes open, and whether it is a smooth, even surface or is torn and irregular depends on the diameter of the tube mouths (*pores*) and their evenness or unevenness. Very small-pored species, particularly if the walls of the tubes are relatively thick, will usually have a smooth, even, pore surface. Sporophores with larger pores appear less smooth, and often the walls of the pores are irregularly torn and lacerated, so that the pore surface is likely to look toothed or spiny. Measurements that involve the diameter of the tubes are usually best taken on the pore surface, by laying on that surface the edge of a millimeter ruler and counting the pores that appear in one millimeter. Measurements of this sort are expressed as so many per millimeter, and several readings from different places on the pore surface of one or more specimens should be made to get the range of variation. This, of course, does not give the actual diameter of the tubes, for it includes also the thickness of the walls of the tubes involved in the measurement. Therefore, tubes that average four per millimeter are considerably less than one-fourth millimeter in diameter, because the thickness of at least three separating walls is included in the measurements. Tubes whose diameters are less than a millimeter are more exactly measured under a low-power hand lens or a low-power dissecting binocular microscope.

The term *hymenium* has by some writers been used to refer to the general region bearing the basidia, that is, to the layer of tubes. But such a usage is at variance with the use of the term in most other groups of fungi, and in this manual the word will be restricted to mean the actual spore-producing layer, made up of basidia and whatever type of sterile organ may be present with them and forming a layer lining the inside of the tubes. The hymenium, in this sense, originates from a subhymenial or subbasidial layer, which, in turn, leads into the tissue forming the walls of the tubes, sometimes referred to as *tramal tissue* but more specifically designated as the *tube trama*. The appearance of the hymenial layer and its related tissues is shown in both longitudinal and cross sections of the tubes in Figures 323 and 382.

Anatomy of the Hymenium.—In studying the construction of the hymenium one must, of course, resort to microscopic sections. In an earlier paper (154) I discussed at some length the microscopic characters which are of use in identifying the higher Basidiomycetes, and for more detailed information than is offered here the reader is referred to that paper. At least for the purposes of systematic mycology the hymenium may be regarded as including, in addition to the basidia and spores, any or all of the three following types of organs: *paraphyses, cystidia,* and *setae.*

Paraphyses are sterile organs usually less conspicuous and of smaller diameter than the basidia, but not conspicuous enough to be called cystidia. But since they differ from cystidia in degree rather than in quality, only a few of the more extreme types, such as the branched paraphyses of *Daedalea confragosa* (Plate 125) are so designated here.

Cystidia, on the other hand, are more conspicuous sterile organs, almost always colorless in the Polyporaceae, yet of definite form, and distinguishable from the basidia in their usually larger size, their different shape, their projection beyond the basidial layer in many cases, and often by the fact that they are partly or entirely covered by an incrusting layer of calcium oxalate. But since large crystals of calcium oxalate or similar material are frequently present along the hymenial surface it is often necessary, and always advisable, to demonstrate that the crystalline material incrusts sterile organs rather than assuming that incrusted cystidia are present. The hymenium of *Fomes connatus* shows simple crystalline masses in many collections, but in reality these masses often cover small and inconspicuous cystidia. A potassium hydroxide solution (KOH) frequently dissolves these masses, so unless the sections are to be studied immediately it is desirable to mount them in water or in lactic acid. Cystidia conspicuous enough to be of diagnostic value are found in only a very few species of this family.

Setae are conspicuous, conical or lance-shaped, brown, sterile organs found in the hymenium of some species with brown context. Because of their color and their characteristic shape, they are always easily recognized, though their distribution is often rather erratic and their number small. In a few species *setal hyphae*, i.e., hyphae with seta-like terminations, are also present, imbedded in the walls of the tubes or in the context of the pileus, as in *Polyporus glomeratus*. Setal hyphae are best detected by making extremely thin longitudinal sections of the tubes or context, or by making crushed mounts with small bits of tissue from these regions. The crushed material should be mounted in water or in lactic acid, since the setae and setal hyphae are found only in species with brown context hyphae, which always become much darker in KOH solution.

Spores and Basidia.—The value of spore characters has, of course, long been recognized. Unfortunately, in some species spores are not present in sporophores that appear to be in good condition. But, except when dealing with certain very closely related species, spores, if obtainable, are always extremely helpful confirmatory characters. Indeed, in a number of the white species of *Polyporus*, identification cannot be made without a knowledge of spore characters. Until a species is so well known that it can be recognized at sight, cross sections of the tubes should always be made with the hope of obtaining spores. Incidentally, other hymenial characters are in this way made accessible.

Basidial characters are of less importance. Yet there is a good correlation between size of spores and size of basidia. Basidia 4 μ or less in diameter are certain to bear spores of the smallest sizes. Frequently in species with such basidia the spores are allantoid or bacilliform and measure about 3–4 $\times$ 1 μ; sometimes they are ellipsoid or subglobose and, usually, less than 4 μ in the longer dimension. *Polyporus spumeus* and *P. delectans*, with basidia 7–8 μ in diameter, are easily separated from the members of the similar *P. albellus* and *P. tephroleucus* group by the size of the basidia.

The ability of the basidial layer to produce other outgrowths than spores from the basidia has been guessed or actually described by a number of workers, especially in Europe. It was left to Bose (17) to give the fullest account of these outgrowths and to correlate them with changes in the climatic environment. Briefly, he has shown that in a number of species the basidia produce tubes that bear clamp connections and terminal spores, and that these tubes can be produced at will by controlling the moisture conditions. When a piece of the hymenium in sporulating condition is fixed to the upper part of a petri dish, the basidia that have not produced spores will gradually produce them after this fashion as the moisture evaporates and the tissue dries out. On the return of moister conditions the "germ tubes" that have not produced apical spores will become converted into basidia. How general such irregularities may be in nature is not known, nor is it known what effects they may have on the nuclear condition and processes in the basidium.

Tissues.—Tissue differentiation[1] is limited to the occasional presence of definite recognizable zones when vertical sections through the context or tubes are examined microscopically. For example, in certain species what has been termed a cuticular layer supports and gives rise to a conspicuous tomentose or hairy covering on the pileus.

[1] This subject has been more fully discussed by me in an earlier paper (154, p. 1707).

This layer is a narrow, dark-colored zone of very compact hyphae, contrasting strongly with the loose construction of the surface pubescence above it. It is well developed in such species as *Polyporus maximus* and *P. corrosus*, but is scarcely evident in strongly pubescent species like *P. hirsutus* and *P. versicolor*.

Occasionally, as in *Polyporus iodinus*, there is an additional dark zone in the context just above the tube layer. In such species, therefore, a vertical section through the pileus shows four rather well defined layers, viz., the upper tomentose layer, the cuticular layer, the main body of the context, and, finally, the dark zone just above the tubes.

The only other type of tissue differentiation likely to be met is found in *Polyporus dichrous*, where the context tissue is compactly interwoven and the tramal tissue of the tubes is highly gelatinous and will not take the eosin stain.

Hyphal Pegs.—In many species of *Polyporus* there protrude into the lumen of the tubes fascicles of closely compacted hyphae. These hyphal pegs vary considerably in form, size, and complexity in different species, but it is still somewhat uncertain what taxonomic value they have.

Hyphal Characters.—Some taxonomic use has been made, and probably more could be made, of various characters of the hyphae of the context. In making observations of this sort a small bit of tissue is taken from about the middle of the context and mounted in a drop of KOH. The material is then teased apart or crushed out with the point of a scalpel and observed microscopically. The presence or absence of branching, the type of branching if unusual, the presence or absence of cross walls and of clamp connections (see Pl. 127), the amount of thickening in the hyphal walls, and the diameter of the hyphae can then be readily ascertained. Thus *Polyporus albellus* can easily be separated from *P. tephroleucus* by the lack of extensive branching of the hyphae; *P. anceps* can be recognized by its peculiar, dendritically branched hyphae; and *P. lignosus*, with its thin-walled hyphae with cross walls, can be distinguished from *P. zonalis*, in which the hyphae are very thick-walled and contain no visible cross walls. Sometimes two very different types of hyphae are found in the context. In the *P. versicolor* section of the genus, in particular, one finds the context to be composed mainly of long, simple, thick-walled hyphae, but mixed with them are short lengths of thinner-walled hyphae with branches radiating in every direction. Such radiating hyphae I have designated *hyphal complexes*.

ECONOMIC IMPORTANCE OF THE POLYPORACEAE

The economic importance of the pore fungi lies not in any possibility of their being bought and sold as market commodities, but indirectly in the effect they have on wood, which is an article subject to barter. This article, in the crude condition, is timber, and in the finished or partly finished product, is lumber. The Polyporaceae are a wood-inhabiting group of fungi, and the presence of a single bracket or conch on a piece of wood is certain evidence that the commercial value of that wood has been reduced by the fungus. The conch indicates that the mycelium of the fungus is within the wood, and that the fungus is obtaining its food from the wood. This process cannot go on without injury to the wood, for wood is mainly, if not altogether, composed of dead, empty cells, and the mycelium of the fungus can obtain food only from the walls of the cells. To the extent that these are penetrated and dissolved, the strength, and, therefore, the value, of the wood is lessened.

The actual damage that decay fungi cause in timber of all sorts cannot be accurately evaluated. Every piece of decayed wood of merchantable size must be charged against them if it would otherwise find a market. Many other agencies are responsible for the death of trees, but only fungi can cause wood to depreciate in value through decay. It is estimated that in the hardwood forests of the eastern United States 19 per cent of the present merchantable stands is defective because of decay. This means that if these hardwood forests of merchantable size were cut tomorrow 87 million board feet of lumber would be left in the forest as unfit for marketing because of decay. In the coniferous stands of the West the loss is put at 15 per cent of the present merchantable timber, or 204 billion board feet. At a stumpage value of $3.00 per thousand board feet, the entire loss through decay in the forests of the United States at present has been placed at close to a billion dollars, and every year we are losing timber to the value of four or five million dollars on account of decay fungi.[1] But these figures do not take into account the decay in structural

[1] [It should be remembered that Dr. Overholts wrote this statement a good number of years ago, and that present values are wholly different.—J.L.L.]

timbers of all sorts, in telegraph and telephone poles, railroad ties, fencing materials, and bridge timbers, in lumber yards (88), pulp mills, and a variety of other places. When the timbers in the roof of a canning factory or under the flooring of a department store decay, it is not only the original cost of the materials that must be considered, but also the often aggravated costs of replacement under existing conditions.

Yet we should not turn from this picture without viewing it from a slightly different angle. The decay of wood in the forest not only frees new elements into the soil to be taken up again by other forms of plant life, but, were it not for the decay propensities of these fungi, every dead branch that falls to the ground, every wind-thrown trunk, and every stump left by the lumberman would lie indefinitely on the forest floor and the forests would soon be so choked with dead and down materials that they would be absolutely impenetrable. Moreover, it is permissible to look on these fungi as living organisms, seeking, as every living organism seeks, for but two things, neither of which is to perpetrate on mankind the greatest amount of mischief possible, as we are at times prone to believe. As living organisms, they are striving to obtain as best they can—handicapped by a lack of chlorophyll as no other plants are handicapped—food materials for an existence that is becoming more and more precarious as time goes on and man extends his domain. They are likewise striving continually to perpetuate their kind. Eventually some of their activities must be curbed and checked, but they have served and are serving a useful purpose in the world.

In this manual there is presented the result of thirty-two years' study of these organisms in the field and the laboratory. From the standpoint of their economic importance, too little attention has been paid them, not only taxonomically, but also morphologically, physiologically, and ecologically. No other family of comparable size is more important economically than the Polyporaceae. Of the one hundred species of fungi that might be mentioned as of more or less importance in timber decays, seventy-five at least would belong to this family, and these could probably be held responsible for 90 per cent of the important decay produced in timber. Surely no other justification for so extensive a treatise as is here presented need be advanced.

DECAY OF WOOD BY FUNGI

As indicated previously, the decay of wood by a fungus is the result of that organism's method of obtaining its food. The constituents of the woody cell walls are broken down and transformed into food by means of enzymes that the fungus secretes. All the steps in the chemistry of wood decay are not known, partly because we have no clear conception of the chemical composition of wood cells.

We do know that the mycelium does not necessarily continue to act on the walls of a cell until they are completely destroyed. Only certain substances are extracted, and when these are exhausted in the walls of one cell the mycelium invades other walls. We know that the two principal compounds that enter into the composition of wood cells are cellulose and lignin. As a matter of fact, probably neither cellulose nor lignin is a simple chemical compound, but the terms designate what are probably groups of closely related compounds. However that may be, the fact remains that of these two types of substances, some wood-inhabiting fungi seem to prefer only the cellulose compounds, and others limit themselves more or less to the lignin compounds. Since these substances differ markedly in their physical characteristics, it follows not only that the removal of either one of them affects the physical characteristics of the wood itself, but that the effect will be different depending upon which substance is removed. In general, the cellulose components of wood are light in color, while the lignin compounds are dark; cellulose has a strong affinity for water, while lignin has no such affinity; cellulose is soft but tough, while lignin is hard and brittle. Therefore, wood that has been acted upon by a lignin-dissolving fungus contains a relatively high remainder of cellulose, and will be whitened in contrast to normal wood. It will, in addition, be soft and spongy in texture, and if exposed to the elements will absorb and retain a considerable amount of water. A decay of this sort is known as a "white rot," or, more technically, as a delignifying rot or decay. Wood from which the cellulose compounds have been removed will, on the other hand, be darker than normal wood and will be dry, brittle, and of the consistency of charcoal. Decays of this sort are known as "brown rots," or carbonizing rots. If both cellulose and lignin have been removed from the wood, as occurs with a few species, a hole or hollow will be formed. It is in this way that tree trunks become hollow, although the effects of the decay may be accentuated by borers, beetles, and other small forms of animal life, such as mice and squirrels, after the wood is well decayed. In some species the action of the fungous mycelium is very much localized in wood, and as a result small pockets are decayed. The individual pockets are separated by areas of relatively sound wood, and may vary from shallow lens-shaped areas only one or two millimeters in length and width to cavities several centimeters long and broad. When the pockets are large, the wood may have the appearance of being attacked by borers, as it does in "pecky cypress" and "pecky cedar" lumber. A type of decay in which holes of this sort are characteristically formed is termed a "pocket rot."

In general, the heartwood of trees is regarded as more durable than the sapwood. But this is true, if at all, only after the tree has been converted into lumber. In living trees sapwood is almost immune to decay fungi unless it is exposed by a wound of some sort. Even then decay is not likely to progress much beyond the limits of the wounded area. The decays that infest living trees are, with this exception, always decays of the heartwood, and are called "heart rots." In dead and down timber and in lumber cut from living trees the sapwood may undergo extensive decay. Decay of the sapwood is usually designated "sap rot" and is ordinarily carried on by other species of fungi than those that decay the heartwood.

Different species of fungi may be limited not only to definite chemical constituents of the wood and to either sapwood or heartwood; they may also be limited to more or less definite horizontal areas of trees. Some decay fungi grow only at or near the base of the tree and are known as "butt rots." For example, *Polyporus Schweinitzii* is a butt-rotting fungus, and the rot never extends indefinitely up the trunk of the tree; it rarely reaches to more than ten or twelve feet above the ground, and often not nearly so far. Other species, e.g., *Fomes Pini*, are "trunk rots"; they are sometimes found on the lower portion of the trunk, but more often extend the length of the trunk. Still others, such as *Fomes roseus*, are more frequently found in the tops of trees; these are known as "top rots."

PARASITISM OF TREE-INHABITING SPECIES

Up to the present point in the discussion we have been careful to refrain from speaking of the tree-inhabiting species as parasites. A rather narrow conception of the term "parasitism" involves the idea that the mycelium of the fungus must establish an intimate contact with *living* cells of the host, from which it absorbs its food materials. According to this definition, an organism that kills the host cells by the excretion of toxic substances and then uses all or a portion of the cell content for food is not a parasite. On the other hand, if we define "parasitism" so broadly that it includes the general injurious effects that may be exercised by one organism on another, we have gone too far in the opposite direction. Even if all pathologists were agreed as to how the term should be limited, we would still be at a loss to know whether or not certain of the tree-inhabiting Polyporaceae should be regarded as parasites. This is because we have no exact knowledge of the relations that exist between these fungi and their hosts.

It is clear that the heartwood of a living tree is composed only of dead cells, and that these cells no longer function in an active manner. Therefore, a heartwood-decaying fungus is a saprophyte so long as it limits its activities to the heartwood. But what is the situation when a heartwood fungus gradually encroaches upon the cells of the sapwood, as *Polyporus sulphureus*, *P. Schweinitzii*, and *Fomes Pini* evidently do? Sapwood is also composed largely of dead cells; at least the tracheids and the tracheae are dead cells, though still functioning in water conduction. Living cells, such as wood parenchyma cells and medullary-ray cells, are present in the sapwood, though they are probably confined ordinarily to the outer annual rings. But little evidence has been brought forward to show that these fungi ever attack such living cells.

The presence of dark zones or bands near the outer limits of the decay cylinder have been supposed by White (232) to indicate true parasitism of the fungous mycelium, at least in *Fomes applanatus*. White believes the formation of these dark zones is due to the stimulating effect of the fungus on living cells of the host, and he reports also the formation of tyloses in this region, when they are absent from the surrounding tissue. According to his statements, in one case the fungus had progressed outward to the bark and had involved the cambium, which "had been attacked by the fungus and destroyed locally." Just how this was accomplished is not stated and the visible evidence that it was due to the fungus is not recorded. More positive evidence of true parasitism was obtained by Hirt

(77, p. 41) for *Polyporus gilvus* on white oak.   Here also a black zone was formed and tyloses were present, apparently because of the stimulating effect of the fungus.   But of more importance was the finding of fungous hyphae in the newly formed tyloses and in the region where living cells were still producing tyloses.   Hirt therefore regards this fungus as weakly parasitic in its mode of action.

If this is true for *Polyporus gilvus*, which is certainly one of the more innocuous of these fungi, it is likely to be true to a considerably greater degree for the important decay species.   This is in line with the recent reports of what is taken to be parasitic action in such species as *Daedalea unicolor*, *P. glomeratus*, *P. hispidus*, and perhaps *Poria obliqua* (28, 29, 30, 202).   Other investigators (32, 180), however, have expressed different opinions about the significance of the black zones in wood decays and about the parasitism of tree-inhabiting species of polypores.   Inoculation experiments designed to solve this problem have been reported (81) but are not decisive.   We must conclude that the information at hand shows clearly enough that trees are injured by the presence of heart-rotting fungi, that the life of the tree is definitely threatened by a decrease in mechanical support of the heartwood due to the effects of the fungi, and that the mycelium does, in some species at least, encroach upon and decay the cells of the sapwood to the extent that the tree may die, though the manner of bringing about the injury is not entirely known. Some pathologists will doubtless continue to consider the evidence strong enough to convict the fungi of parasitic propensities, but others will prefer to await further investigations on the subject.

INFORMATION FROM PURE CULTURES

There is gradually being built up in this country a body of information derived from the growth of wood-decaying fungi in pure cultures, for almost every species of fungus—if not every species— will produce in culture a set of characters that is not repeated in entirety by any other species.   Furthermore, the experience of many individuals indicates that the characters shown by a fungus in nature can be expected to be exhibited by the same species when grown in culture.   Dr. Irene Mounce (135) has reported on such duplications. Work with cultures has now reached a point where experts are often able to identify an unknown species of wood-destroying organism by comparing its cultural characteristics with those of a series of fungi whose characteristics have been already tabulated, or by comparing such an unknown directly with cultures that are growing in the laboratory.

The usefulness of the method depends to a great extent on having available a fairly large set of cultures. Thus, if one had a complete set of cultures of all the known species of wood-decay fungi it would be possible to identify unknown cultures with almost as great accuracy as can be achieved when comparing a specimen with the usual correctly named, dried sporophore collections in a herbarium. And if one had an idea of the identity of a species, he could verify or reject his tentative identification rather easily and quickly.

The cultures intended for this use are grown under identical conditions throughout, with each species in a petri dish, so that they can be put side by side and compared macroscopically and microscopically. The fungi are usually easily obtained in pure culture; malt agar and potato-dextrose agar have been found to be the most suitable substrata. Some of the more important of the characters exhibited by the cultures and used in comparisons are: (1) rate of growth; (2) color of mycelium produced; (3) characters of the growth; (4) production of color in the agar; (5) production of spores, either of primary basidiospores or of secondary spores of the type known as oidia, conidia, chlamydospores, and so on; (6) presence or absence of cross walls and of clamp connections; (7) diameter and other characteristics of the hyphae produced; and (8) production of setae or other types of organs. Any other characters typically produced under culture may also be useful.

Undoubtedly this method of attack is capable of greater expansion, and probably we will eventually have keys based entirely on cultural characters.[1] Work looking toward this is now going on in several laboratories, especially in that of the Division of Forest Pathology at Beltsville, Maryland, in the United States Forests Products Laboratory at Madison, Wisconsin, in the Forests Products Laboratory of Canada, at Ottawa, Canada, and in my own laboratory at Pennsylvania State College. Workers at these laboratories have not infrequently been able, on the basis of their cultures, to establish definitely the identity of poorly developed specimens of which I

[1] [See R. W. Davidson, W. A. Campbell, and Dorothy B. Vaughn, *U. S. Dept. Agr. Tech. Bul.* 785. 1942; and Mildred K. Nobles, *Canad. Jour. Res.*, C, 26: 281–431. 1948.—J.L.L.]

could make only a tentative disposition, and occasionally I have been able to make similar identifications for them.

Identification by means of cultures is of particular value in problems of the decay of timber in the woods or of timbers in construction work where sporophores may not be present or may not be produced at sufficiently brief intervals to permit recognition of the fungus responsible.

AIMS OF THIS MANUAL

This manual is an attempt to present a complete and satisfactory account of the pileate Polyporaceae (comprising 8 genera, 235 species, and 12 varieties[1]) of North America north of Mexico and southern Florida. It has been my intention to maintain a conservative nomenclatorial attitude so that the species may be presented in so far as possible under names well established by common usage. Certain names more or less current in European literature might well be substituted for names used here if such changes did not carry with them the implication that I had personally verified the synonymy. Verification of this type can rarely be made from the literature; it can only be made after a comparison of authentic specimens. The same conservative attitude has been adopted with regard to synonyms in general. No names are here reduced to synonymy except where I have been able to examine the specimens personally. Consequently, long lists of synonyms that might have been copied from the literature, and so have given the manual a more learned appearance, have been omitted. While in general I have attempted to follow the International Rules of Botanical Nomenclature, I have made few, if any, wild guesses as to the correct interpretation of earlier and indefinite names, leaving that to those who might guess with more dexterity than myself. Pilát (171, vol. 52, p. 51) has well expressed my attitude, in the following words: "Der Hauptbeweis für diesen unseren Standpunkt besteht darin, das wir es für wertlos und eines Naturforschers wenig würdig halten, in alten Folianten und Archiven zu wühlen und aus diesen alte, unpassende und seit langer Zeit ganz

---

[1] [The nomenclature of taxa below the rank of species is that of Overholts, and not that approved at the International Botanical Congress at Stockholm in 1950. Consequently, references to "the species," where Overholts is comparing the type variety to another variety (or other varieties), should be interpreted as referring to the type variety, i.e., *Fomes pini* var. *pini*, and so on.—J.L.L.]

vergessene Namen zu entnehmen, und dies alles nur auf Grund zweifelhafter Priorität. Diese alten Namen sind grösstenteils nur nomina nuda." The result is a list of names most of which are well known wherever the species occur.

The descriptions are concise, couched in technical terms, and nearly or quite comparable, character for character, throughout the work. Where it was thought necessary to be exact in the matter of color designations, Ridgway's colors (185) were used, and names taken from that source are always in quotation marks. Other color names represent only my own conception of color values.

In connection with each species I have given a host range that is as comprehensive as the various collections studied would allow. Obviously, there are errors in host determinations in every herbarium, and such errors may account for some of the unusual hosts and substrata here recorded. Often not enough of the substratum is attached to a specimen to enable one to substantiate or refute statements accompanying the specimen. Host range is given in terms of genera of hosts. Most polypores are not sufficiently specific in their range within a host genus to make precise citation necessary. No such comprehensive host ranges as are included here have previously appeared in the literature dealing with American polypores; only a few local lists have been published (101, 130, 181, 182, 183, 209, 222, 223, 226, 227, 230, 236).

The geographical range is likewise made as inclusive as the data with the various collections permit. This range is given by states and provinces, which are always arranged in the same sequence. Indication of the geographical range has, similarly, not been attempted before on so large a scale. The present study includes, as well, a relatively few extensions of range taken from what are believed to be authoritative sources in the literature. These are definitely indicated. However, the omission of a particular published record does not necessarily imply that it is not considered reliable. No extended search of the literature has been made to discover outlying stations or host ranges reported for any species. And it is obvious that even if such an exhaustive search had been made, a list of species or hosts so compiled would be far from authoritative, or desirable.

It has been my intention in this manual to illustrate each species as extensively as space will permit, but I have made a conscious endeavor to devote more space to illustrations of the less-known species than to those well known. Illustrations in the literature are cited only where the reproduction is of unusual excellence or to be regarded as authentic. Many illustrations in the European literature are too inaccessible to warrant citation. Many scattered ones in the American literature have undoubtedly been overlooked.

Notes generally follow the technical descriptions. These call attention to the salient features of the species, discuss synonymy, or are otherwise critical in character. Some attention has been paid to recording the type of decay produced by species of lignicolous habit, and this should be of value to those accustomed to making such observations.

ACKNOWLEDGMENTS

It would not have been possible to accumulate the information contained in the following pages without the assistance and co-operation of various individuals and institutions. Visits were made to the following herbaria and libraries, and acknowledgment is due them for the many courtesies received: New York Botanical Garden Herbarium and Library, New York City; Missouri Botanical Garden Herbarium and Library, St. Louis, Missouri; Mycological Collections of the Bureau of Plant Industry, including the Forest Pathology series and the C. G. Lloyd Mycological Herbarium of the Smithsonian Institution, Beltsville, Maryland; New York State Museum, Albany, New York; Philadelphia Academy of Sciences, Philadelphia, Pennsylvania; the herbarium of the Brooklyn Botanical Garden, Brooklyn, New York; and the herbarium of Columbia University, New York City. Many individuals have liberally contributed specimens that have extended the geographical or host range of the various species, and every such contribution has been gratefully received. Finally, I am much indebted to the trustees of the Elizabeth Thompson Science Fund for a generous contribution to further the preparation of the illustrations.

KEYS AND DESCRIPTIONS

Family POLYPORACEAE

Tube-bearing basidiomycetous fungi with annual or perennial manner of fruit-body growth; fruiting bodies stipitate, sessile, effused-reflexed, or entirely resupinate; consistency varying from woody to leathery or fleshy-tough; tube layer inseparable from pileus with rare exceptions; wood-inhabiting or, rarely, terrestrial; occasionally pore walls breaking up to give appearance of a hydnaceous hymeno-phore or tubes radially elongated to give a lamellate hymenophore.

The family Polyporaceae of the order Agaricales has been made by some authors to include two rather diverse elements, viz., the boletes and the true polypores. The treatment here excludes the first of these, so that the family is limited to those tube-bearing fungi in which the consistency is fleshy-tough to woody and comparatively persistent, rather than soft-fleshy and soon putrescent, and in which, with the exception of two or three coriaceous or corky species, the layer of tubes is inseparably united to the flesh of the pileus. Com-paratively few of the species are terrestrial, and many of those that seem so are in reality attached to buried wood, so that the family is prevailingly lignicolous. A glance at the key to the genera (pp. 30–31) will reveal my conception of the limits of the family for the pur-pose of this treatment. It is seen to include resupinate, sessile, and stipitate members, genera in which well-developed tubes with circular to irregular pores are present, and others in which the hymenial configuration is distinctly toothed or distinctly gilled. Concerning this last character, the justification for including such forms in this family lies in the fact that in *Lenzites*, for example, the hymenial configuration is sometimes distinctly poroid, sometimes truly gilled, and even, at times, may vary from poroid to gilled in a single species. If more warrant is desired, it may be said that the texture of those gilled species here included is unlike that in any of the typical gilled fungi (family Agaricaceae), being leathery to corky. Moreover, their importance as timber-destroying agents allies them with the present family rather than with other gilled forms. Numerous preceding authors have followed the same course, so that it may be taken as all but the universal conception that the genus *Lenzites* is more closely related to the Polyporaceae than to the Agaricaceae.

In recognition of Dr. Burt's monograph (26) of the genus *Merulius*, that group of species is omitted. Unfortunately, the genus *Poria* is still largely in a chaotic state. But three papers have appeared on that genus (38, 126, 158), exclusive of the unfinished work of Murrill (144, 147), and these have treated only the members of the genus as found in three separate states, viz., Oregon, New York, and Pennsylvania, although Baxter (9, 10, 11) has given us much information about species over a wider range.

The family as treated here includes only the common genera well known, in their concept at least, to every student of systematic mycology, and embraces all normally pileate mostly lignicolous fungi that have the hymenial layer lining the inner surfaces of tubes, however irregular. A few gilled forms in *Lenzites* and *Daedalea* are included because of their obvious similarity in other respects. It must be remembered, also, that if the walls of the tubes split at maturity, a toothed condition may be attained, but in practically all such cases indications of a tubular or poroid condition will be retained in the younger tubes at the margin of the pileus, and such a condition always indicates that the specimen is truly polyporoid and is referable to this family.

KEY TO THE GENERA

1. Sporophores growing on the ground 2
   Sporophores growing on wood or around stumps 3
2. Hymenial region composed of gill-like plates arranged concentrically (Fig. 465) .... *Cyclomyces*, p. 116
   Hymenial region showing pores rather than concentric gills
   .... *Polyporus*, p. 163
3. Sporophore always entirely resupinate, i.e., lying flat on the substratum; no pileus formed 4
   Sporophore sessile, effused-reflexed, or stipitate; always pileate to some extent 5
4. Pores very shallow in mature sporophores and reduced to shallow pits separated by narrow ridges or reticulations over which the basidial layer is continuous .. *Merulius*[1]

---

[1] The genus *Merulius* is not included in this manual.

Pores deeper in mature specimens than in *Merulius* and apparent as the openings into definite tubes, or, if rather shallow, then the basidial layer not continuous over the folds .... *Poria*[1]

5. Sporophore perennial, the tube region consisting of several or many distinct or indistinct layers,[2] to which additions are made each year (Fig. 371) .... *Fomes*, p. 32

Sporophore annual, the tubes in but a single layer or, rarely, in two or three layers 6

6. Hymenial region daedaloid (Fig. 464) or verging toward lamellate; sporophore coriaceous to corky but never soft and fleshy; context usually white or light-colored
Daedalea, p. 118

Hymenium lamellate (Fig. 518) or, if somewhat daedaloid, then context decidedly brown; always sessile *Lenzites*, p. 107

Hymenium poroid or, if verging toward daedaloid, then sporophore soft and watery when fresh; sessile or stipitate .. 7

7. Sporophore sessile; pores large and hexagonal (Fig. 528);[3] subtropical species only................ *Hexagona*, p. 131

Sporophore stipitate or substipitate; pores hexagonal and arranged in rows that radiate outward from the stem (Fig. 576) .... *Favolus*, p. 155

Sporophore stipitate or sessile, but pores not arranged in radiating rows 8

8. Sporophore stipitate or substipitate .... *Polyporus*, p. 163

Sporophore sessile 9

9. Tubes not in a distinct stratum but sunken to unequal depths into the context, so that their bases do not form a straight line[4] .... *Trametes*, p. 133

Tubes in a distinct stratum, their bases forming an unbroken, straight line .... *Polyporus*, p. 163

---

[1] The genus *Poria* is not included in this manual.

[2] Cut the sporophore in two vertically to observe this. Refer very hard and woody sporophores here, even though the tube layers are not apparent.

[3] In the Polyporaceae the pores vary in size from those 2–3 mm. in diameter down to those 8 or 9 per mm.

[4] No one realizes better than I how difficult, even impossible, it is to recognize a species of *Trametes* on the basis of this character. The sporophores are all more or less dry and tough or corky, with cylindric spores 6–15 μ long, and the hymenial surface is never daedaloid or lamellate.

Genus 1. FOMES (Fries) Kickx[1]

Fl. Crypt. Flandres, 2: 236. 1867

Polyporus ***** (*Fomes*) Fries, Summa Vegetab. Scand., p. 321. 1846–1849.
Ganoderma Karst. pro parte, Rev. Mycol. 3: 17. 1881.
Elfvingia Karst., Finl. Basidsv., p. 333. 1889.
Mucronoporus Ell. & Ev. pro parte, Jour. Mycol. 5: 28. 1889.
Pyropolyporus Murr., Torrey Bot. Club Bul. 30: 109. 1903.
Porodaedalea Murr., Torrey Bot. Club Bul. 32: 367. 1905.
Elfvingiella Murr., Northern Polypores, p. 52. 1914.
Fulvifomes Murr., Northern Polypores, p. 49. 1914.

Plants truly perennial, typically persisting for several to many years, the new growth of each season adding to the outward extension of the margin of the pileus and the downward extension of the hymenial region, sometimes rather tough and watery the first year, but typically soon hard and woody in texture or with a hard, horny surface and a softer (punky to corky) context, often becoming rimose in age, varying from thin and applanate to decidedly ungulate, often strongly zonate or furrowed by the irregular marginal growth of successive years; context white to dark brown, fibrous or punky to hard and woody; tubes often in definite annual layers, sometimes extended downward from the growth of the previous year without definite layering; spores white to dark brown, variable in shape from globose to cylindric; cystidia present or absent; setae present in some brown species.

TYPE SPECIES: *Fomes marginatus* (Pers. ex Fries) Gill.

Fomes differs typically from all other genera in the truly perennial habit of growth. Specimens persisting from fifty to seventy years have been recorded. Sometimes the tubes are definitely layered, as in *F. connatus*, *F. applanatus*, and *F. pinicola*, but in many species their downward extension from year to year is not well marked, as in *F. igniarius* and *F. fomentarius*. In such cases, and in the first year's growth of many other species, one must often rely on the woody consistency of the sporophore for a generic determination. But in spite of all precautions, in the first year's growth such species as *F.*

[1] [Dr. Overholts attributed this genus to Gillet, *Champ. France*, vol. 1, p. 682. 1878. *Fomes marginatus* is Dr. Overholts' selection of the type species for the genus.—J.L.L.]

connatus and *F. Meliae*, with their softer consistency and white coloration, are almost certain to be referred to *Polyporus* until the species are so well known as to be recognized at sight. A separation of such reviving species of *Trametes* as *T. serialis* and *T. americana*, and of such species of *Polyporus* as *P. gilvus* (at times), is likewise almost impossible for the beginner. On the other hand, a few species, such as *F. scutellatus*, *F. roseus*, and the thin form of *F. Pini* (var. *Abietis*) may with equal propriety be referred to *Polyporus*. Even though they persist for two or more years, their perennial nature is quite difficult to recognize because of the small size of the specimens or the limited growth after the first year.

Though the hymenium is typically poroid, with circular to angular pores, variations to a daedaloid condition (e.g., in *Fomes Pini*) are sometimes met. No typically resupinate species are included in the genus, for they are referred to the genus *Poria*, and no truly perennial stipitate forms are present in our flora.

The recognition of the genus *Ganoderma* does not seem to be justifiable, particularly since that segregate is based largely on a spore character. Some of the generic segregates recognized by Murrill and to some extent those proposed by European workers also seem unjustified. The frequent absence of spores from the hymenium of these species renders such treatment unsatisfactory. A better segregation could be made on the color of the context, and that character serves just as well in breaking the genus into sections.

Although the concept of the genus *Fomes* dates from pre-Friesian authors, it was not formally recognized until 1867.

KEY TO THE SPECIES OF FOMES

Context white or bright-colored, including whitish, wood color, pinkish, pinkish red, flesh color, reddish orange, or rusty orange . . . . Section I
Context umber to dark yellowish brown or dark rusty brown, not bright-colored, black where touched with KOH solution
Section II, p. 36

SECTION I

1. Context white, whitish, or not darker than wood-colored . . . 2
   Context flesh color, pinkish or pinkish red, or olivaceous 7
   Context reddish orange or rusty orange; on living *Juniperus* only . . . . 36. *F. juniperinus*

2. Sporophores fitting well into one of the following groups:
   a. Context chalky in dried specimens, very bitter to the taste; on conifers only; sporophore large, more than 5 cm. in shortest diameter; from Michigan to Arizona and northward .... 6. *F. officinalis*
   b. On *Shepherdia* only, from the Dakotas to New Mexico, Montana, and Saskatchewan; pileus strongly radiate-rugose, soon grayish black to blackish and rimose; spores somewhat truncate at one end and 5.5–8 × 3.5–5 μ .... 5. *F. Ellisianus*
   c. Sporophore small, usually less than 2 × 3 × 1 cm.; never on living trees; cystidia none 3
  Sporophores not fitting well into any of the groups above ... 4
3. Usually on *Alnus*, rarely on other hardwoods; spores cylindric, 8–9 × 2.5–3.5 μ; basidia 6–8 μ in diameter; context hyphae considerably branched; sometimes persisting for two or three years .... 8. *F. scutellatus*
  Never on *Alnus*, usually on *Fagus*, but sometimes on other hardwoods; spores ovoid with a truncate apex, 9–12 × 6–7 μ; basidia 9–12 μ in diameter; context hyphae unbranched; truly perennial .... 3. *F. ohiensis*
  Never on *Alnus* or *Fagus*, usually on conifers; spores subglobose, 3.5–5 × 3–4 μ; basidia 5–6 μ in diameter; context hyphae simple or nearly so .... 1. *F. annosus*
4. Mouths of tubes averaging 2–3 per mm. 5
  Mouths of tubes averaging 4 or more per mm. 6
5. Pileus brown (finally blackish) on upper surface, not rimose, with thin crust at maturity; spores subglobose, 3.5–5 × 3–4 μ; usually on wood of coniferous trees, rarely on hardwoods .... 1. *F. annosus*
  Pileus white, then blackening, soon rimose, not incrusted; spores ellipsoid to ovoid, usually truncate at one end, 6–9 × 5–6 μ; usually on living *Fraxinus*, never on conifers .... 4. *F. fraxinophilus*
6. Context hyphae with cross walls; tubes very distinctly stratified in old sporophores; incrusted cystidia present; usually on *Acer* or *Carya* north of the Gulf States
                                               9. *F. connatus*

Context hyphae with cross walls; tubes not distinctly stratified; no cystidia, or cystidia not incrusted; on a variety
of hardwoods in the Gulf States . . . .   10. *F. geotropus*
Context hyphae without cross walls   7

7. Largest context hyphae at least 8 μ in diameter; tubes very
distinctly stratified in old sporophores; pileus usually
with a dark resinous crust, red to black, but sometimes
this color discernible only on margin or only at base of
pileus, rarely entirely absent; on both hardwoods and
conifers . . . .   2. *F. pinicola*
Largest context hyphae at least 8 μ in diameter; tubes never
distinctly stratified; pileus sometimes slightly incrusted
but crust not resinous; on hardwoods only   11
Largest context hyphae not more than 6 μ in diameter   8

8. Pileus incrusted with a thick horny crust; tubes very definitely stratified after the first year; pileus 10 cm. or more
broad and long; spores brown; producing a white rot of
the wood . . . .   37. *F. applanatus*
Pileus somewhat incrusted; tubes not definitely stratified;
pileus usually less than 10 cm. long; spores hyaline; producing a white rot of the wood . . . .   1. *F. annosus*
Pileus not incrusted or only slightly so; tubes not definitely
stratified; pileus usually less than 10 cm. long; spores
hyaline; producing a brown rot of the wood   9

9. Usually on wood of coniferous trees; sporophores with some
trace of pink, rosy, or pinkish brown in context, pileus,
or hymenium; cosmopolitan   12
Usually on hardwoods; sporophores without a trace of pink
or rose color; from Indiana to Missouri and southward   10

10. Pileus plane or somewhat convex; margin acute; context gray
or very pale wood color . . . .   11. *F. Meliae*
Pileus very convex or somewhat ungulate; margin very ob-
tuse; context pale umber . . . .   See *F. avellaneus* (p. 105)

11. Context olivaceous below, paler above; spores cylindric,
9–10 × 3 μ . . . .   See no. 126, *Polyporus supinus*
Context uniformly pallid, not at all olivaceous; spores ovoid,
6–7 × 5–6 μ . . . .   7. *F. fraxineus*

12. Spores elongate-ellipsoid, not curved, 5–7 × 2.5–3.5 μ; context usually silvery pinkish . . . .   12. *F. roseus*

Spores cylindric, slightly curved, 4–7 × 1.5–2 μ; context usually pinkish cinnamon to pinkish brown

13. *F. subroseus*

Section II

A. *Pileus incrusted, i.e., covered by a distinct crust (at least in old specimens), under which the context is of softer consistency (for sporophores with unincrusted pilei see AA, p. 37)*

[1] Not known from the mainland of the United States.

Spores cylindric, smooth, hyaline, usually not obtainable by
scraping the tubes 21

19. Context practically obsolete; pileus steep and annulate in
front; tubes hard and horny, not stratified   39. *F. annularis*

Context well developed, distinct; tubes not hard, usually distinctly stratified 20

20. Spores 9–12 × 7–9 μ; from California only . . . .   40. *F. Brownii*

Spores 6–9 × 4.5–6 μ; cosmopolitan . . . .   37. *F. applanatus*

21. From North Carolina southward; pileus convex to somewhat
ungulate . . . .   33. *F. marmoratus*

From North Carolina northward; pileus usually strongly
ungulate . . . .   32. *F. fomentarius*

AA. *Pileus not incrusted though often hard and woody throughout*

  B. *Setae present in hymenium* (for sporophores without setae see
  BB, p. 39)

22. Pileus applanate to somewhat convex, sometimes largely
resupinate, usually less than 5 cm. thick 23

Pileus strongly convex to ungulate, not partially resupinate,
usually more than 5 cm. thick 33

23. On wood of coniferous trees only 24

On wood of deciduous trees only 27

24. Hymenium poroid or daedaloid, the pores averaging 2–4 per
mm. 25

Hymenium always poroid, the pores averaging 4–7 per mm.   26

25. Setae narrow lance-shaped, projecting 25–60 μ, 5–9 μ in
diameter; spores cylindric . . . .   17. *F. tenuis*

Setae with a broader base, tapering rapidly to a sharp point,
projecting but 15–30 μ, 7–15 μ in diameter
                                        22. *F. Pini* var. *Abietis*

26. Spores ellipsoid or subglobose; setae not abundant, often rare,
projecting up to 20 μ and rather inconspicuous; no black
line in context . . . .   20. *F. repandus*

Spores cylindric; setae rather numerous, projecting 12–20 μ,
quite conspicuous; with a narrow black line dividing context into unequal layers . . . .   21. *F. nigrolimitatus*

27. Spores pale brownish as seen in unstained sections of tubes,
subglobose, 3–3.5 μ in diameter or 3 × 2.5 μ; sporophore
almost entirely resupinate, the pores averaging 7–10 per
mm. . . . .   23. *F. densus*

Spores hyaline, cylindric, 5–8 × 1.5–2 μ; sporophore often
  resupinate, the pores averaging 2–4 per mm. .   17. *F. tenuis*
Spores hyaline or tinted, ellipsoid to globose; pileus sometimes
  resupinate, the pores averaging 3–8 per mm.   28

28. Pileus at first strongly tomentose, and remaining so on the
  growing margin   29
  Pileus glabrous or nearly so from the first   30

29. Context bright yellow-brown, 0.5–2 cm. thick; some context
  hyphae with cross walls . . . .   19. *F. torulosus*
  Context yellowish brown or darker, less than 0.5 cm. thick;
  hyphae without cross walls . . . .   18. *F. conchatus*

30. Context hyphae with cross walls   31
  Context hyphae without cross walls   32

31. On *Prunus* only; spores subglobose; setae 6–8 μ in diameter
                                                      15. *F. pomaceus*
  On a wide variety of substrata; spores oblong-ellipsoid; setae
  3–6 μ in diameter . . . .   See no. 145, *Polyporus gilvus*

32. Setae often with curved apices . . . .   28. *F. extensus*
  Setae straight, 4–6 μ in diameter, projecting only slightly;
  spores 3.5–4.5 × 3–4 μ; pores 3–7 per mm.
                                      14. *F. igniarius* var. *laevigatus*
  Setae straight, usually 6–9 μ in diameter, projecting up to
  18 μ; spores 4–5 × 3.5–4.5 μ; pores 5–7 per mm.
                                                      18. *F. conchatus*
  Setae straight, 12–14 μ in diameter; spores 4.5–6 μ in diameter; pores 3–4 per mm. . . . .   16. *F. occidentalis*

33. Pores averaging 2–3 per mm., occasionally smaller, often
  daedaloid; nearly always on wood of coniferous trees;
  setae 7–15 μ in diameter . . . .   22. *F. Pini*
  Pores averaging 4 or more per mm., never daedaloid; nearly
  always on hardwoods; setae usually smaller   34

34. Old tubes stuffed with a rather conspicuous white mycelium,
  as seen when pileus is cut vertically . . . . . .   14. *F. igniarius*
  Old tube layers not so stuffed   35

35. Spores hyaline, 6–8 μ in diameter; tubes in distinct annual
  layers . . . .   29. *F. robustus*
  Spores brown, 4–6 μ in diameter; tubes usually not distinctly
  layered   36

36. From Florida only; pileus usually attached by vertex and pendent; setae 4–6 μ in diameter; context hyphae without cross walls .... **27.** *F. dependens*
    From Ontario to Georgia and westward; pileus laterally attached; setae 5–12 μ in diameter; some context hyphae with cross walls **37**
37. Widely distributed in the eastern United States; pore surface brown; spores chestnut-brown .... **25.** *F. Everhartii*
    From the Southwest only; pore surface yellowish brown; spores bright golden yellow .... **26.** *F. praerimosus*

BB. *Setae absent from hymenium*

38. Pore surface smoke-colored; pores averaging 5–7 per mm.
    See no. 126, *Polyporus supinus*
    Pore surface brown; pores averaging 4 or more per mm. ... **39**
39. Sporophores quite small and strongly ungulate, less than 3 × 3 × 4 cm.; pileus rimose; on *Arctostaphylos* and *Adenostoma* in Arizona and California.. **14.** *F. igniarius*
    Sporophores larger, or, if about the same size, then with other hosts and a different range **40**
40. Pileus not more than 2 cm. thick, not rimose; spores pale yellowish brown as seen in unstained mounts and less than 4 μ in diameter; basidia 3–5 μ in diameter **41**
    Pileus more than 2 cm. thick, in age more or less rimose; spores hyaline or brown, 4–10 μ in diameter; basidia 8–10 μ in diameter or larger **42**
41. Pileus narrowly multizonate at least on margin, becoming blackish and woody with age; from Louisiana only
    24. *F. Langloisii*
    Pileus broadly zonate or azonate, not becoming blackish; context hyphae with some cross walls; from Canada to Maryland and westward .... **34.** *F. Ribis*
42. Spores brown, 4–6 μ in diameter; mostly on living trees, usually on *Robinia* .... **35.** *F. rimosus*
    Spores hyaline[1] **43**
43. Spores 5–6 μ in diameter; on *Quercus* and perhaps other hosts, usually in the Gulf States; tubes not distinctly layered; pores 6–8 per mm. .... **31.** *F. Calkinsii*

[1] If no spores can be found on the hymenium it may usually be safely assumed that they are hyaline.

Spores 6–8 μ in diameter; on standing snags or on fallen
trunks, especially of *Quercus* and *Betula* but also on a few
other hosts; tubes very distinctly layered 29. *F. robustus*
Spores 7–10 μ in diameter; on *Juniperus* in Texas, Arizona,
and New Mexico .... 30. *F. texanus*

1a. *Context white or somewhat darker, or pinkish; not permanently*
   blackening in KOH solution
2a. *Context white or somewhat darker*
3a. *Pores usually averaging 4 or less per mm.*

1. FOMES ANNOSUS (Fries) Cooke

Grevillea 14: 20. 1885

(Figs. 353–354, 426, 460, and Plate 125)

Polyporus annosus Fries, Syst. Myc. 1: 373. 1821.
Polyporus irregularis Underw., Torrey Bot. Club Bul. 24: 85. 1897.

Sporophore sessile or more often effused-reflexed or entirely resupinate, tough or corky when fresh, rigid and hard on drying; pileus
applanate, 0–15 × 2–25 × 0.5–7 cm., at first pallid, then gray-brown
or uniform light brown to coffee-brown, dark brown, or with a tinge
of red, sometimes turning blackish with age, at first compactly villose-
tomentose, finally more glabrous and more or less incrusted, the
crust appearing as a dark thin line at the surface of vertical sections
of the pileus, often somewhat zonate and sometimes furrowed; context white to isabelline, corky or hard-corky, 0.2–1 cm. thick; pore
surface white or yellowish, the tubes 2–10 mm. long, sometimes longer
in old specimens, indistinctly stratified and often in a single layer,
the mouths subcircular to angular, rather thick-walled and entire,
averaging 2–3(–4) per mm.; spores subglobose, apiculate, hyaline,
3.5–5 × 3–4 μ; basidia 5–6 μ in diameter; cystidia none, but in a
few cases some hyaline, weak, cystidia-like hairs about 3 μ in diameter
projecting slightly beyond the basidia; hyphae hyaline, simple or
sparingly branched, mostly with completely thickened walls, with no
cross walls or clamps, 2.5–5(–6) μ in diameter, a few with very thin
walls, 3–4 μ in diameter.

HABITAT: Usually on stumps and trunks of coniferous trees,
especially at their bases, occasionally on logs and structural timbers,

noted on *Abies, Cupressus, Juniperus, Picea, Pinus, Pseudotsuga, Thuja,* and *Tsuga*; sometimes on hardwoods, noted on *Acer, Carya, Castanea, Kalmia, Quercus,* and *Ulmus*; reported on *Larix* and *Populus* (Mont., Weir [227]).

DISTRIBUTION: Specimens have been examined from Me., N.H., Vt., Mass., Conn., N.Y., Pa., N.J., Del., Md., D.C., Va., W. Va., N.C., Ga., Fla., Ala., La., Miss., Tenn., Mo., N. Mex., Colo., Idaho, Ore., Wash., Calif., and Alaska; in Canada from Quebec and British Columbia; reported from Mich. (Kauffman [101]).

ILLUSTRATIONS: Boyce, Forest Path., fig. 30; Fries, Icones Sel. Hym., pl. 186, fig. 2 (as *Polyporus*); Hubert, Outline Forest Path., fig. 103; Lloyd, Synop. Fomes, fig. 573; Shope, Mo. Bot. Gard. Ann. 18: pl. 36; Spaulding, Important Tree Pests Northeast, p. 170, figs. A–B.

Usually specimens of this fungus are found without a basidial layer and are, therefore, sterile. The fungus is a common one on mine timbers and, curiously enough, sporulates freely in that location, but the fruiting bodies are often of abnormal shapes, though rather easily recognized by the nearly white context and hymenium and a brown upper surface that is finely tomentose.

The species is easily confused with *Trametes serialis*, but can be readily separated by the presence of a thin crust at the surface of the pileus. This crust is most evident if the pileus is cut vertically, when it appears as a narrow black line at the upper surface.

A peculiar type of conidium production occurs in this species. The spores are produced on short sterigmata covering a stalked globose head. This stage has been referred to the genus *Oedocephalum* of the Fungi Imperfecti. The character renders the species easy to identify when grown in pure culture.

The types of *Polyporus irregularis* are preserved at New York. *Trametes radiciperda* Hartig is undoubtedly synonymous. The specimen labeled *P. annosus* in the Schweinitz Herbarium is *Fomes robustus*.

The rot produced by this fungus is known as "spongy sap rot," and involves both sapwood and heartwood. In the early stages of decay a pinkish or violaceous color of the wood is said (22, pp. 35–36; 87, pp. 370–374) to be recognizable; the late stages include the formation of irregular, elongated white pockets, often with a black center, appearing first in the springwood of the annual ring. As a result, the annual rings easily separate, and the wood becomes soft and spongy. Usually the decay is a butt or root rot and, where it occurs in living trees, is accompanied by a copious resin flow. Sporophores in such cases are formed at the ground line or on exposed roots. The fungus is regarded as having parasitic tendencies, especially as a root rot, but is probably of less importance in this country than in Europe.

2. FOMES PINICOLA (Swartz ex Fries) Cooke

Grevillea 14: 17. 1885

(Figs. 352, 383, 396, and Plate 126)

Boletus pinicola Swartz, Svenska Vetensk.-akad. Handl. 1810, p. 88. 1810.
Polyporus pinicola Swartz ex Fries, Syst. Myc. 1: 372. 1821.
Fomes ungulatus Schaeff. ex Sacc., Syll. Fung. 6: 167. 1888.
(*Fomes*) *Polyporus ponderosus* von Schrenk, U. S. Dept. Agr. Pl. Ind. Bul. 36: 30. 1903.

Sporophore sessile or decurrent on the substratum, hard-corky to woody; pileus applanate to convex or ungulate, 4–30 × 6–40 × 2.5–22 cm., at first usually covered at least in part with a resinous crust that varies from red to brown or blackish, later hardening and varying in color from grayish to black, sulcate with age, the margin frequently rounded and obtuse; context pallid to wood color, sometimes lemon-yellow in young specimens, turning pinkish where wounded in growing plants and dark .cherry-red changing to dark reddish brown when touched with KOH solution, corky to woody, 0.5–2 cm. thick; pore surface white to umber or sometimes light yellow, yellow when bruised in fresh specimens, sometimes with a lilac tint where wounded, the tubes 3–5 mm. long each season, [very distinctly stratified—J.L.L.], the mouths averaging 3–5 per mm., the walls rather thick and entire, showing a color change with KOH similar to that in the context; spores ovoid to subglobose, hyaline, 5–7 × 4–5 μ; basidia 6–8 μ in diameter; typical cystidia absent, but fine hairs 2–3.5 μ in diameter often projecting above the basidial layer; hyphae mostly simple, hyaline to pale-colored in KOH, with partially or entirely thickened walls, with no cross walls or clamps, 4–9 μ in diameter; hyphal complexes composed of hyaline hyphae 3–4 μ in diameter, present in considerable numbers; all parts much darker in KOH solution, sometimes becoming cherry-red before darkening.

HABITAT: Usually on dead trees, or on stumps or logs, of both deciduous and coniferous species, occasionally on living trees, noted on *Abies, Acer, Alnus, Betula, Fagus, Larix, Picea, Pinus, Populus, Prunus, Pseudotsuga, Quercus, Salix, Sequoia,* and *Tsuga*; reported on *Carya* (Wis., Neuman [148]), on *Castanea* (N.Y., Murrill), on *Libocedrus* (Calif., Boyce [19]), and on *Pyrus* (Weir [222]).

DISTRIBUTION: Specimens have been examined from Me., N.H., Vt., Mass., N.Y., Pa., Va., W. Va., N.C., Tenn., Ohio, Mich., Wis., Minn., S. Dak., Mo., N. Mex., Ariz., Utah, Colo., Wyo., Mont., Idaho, Ore., Wash., Calif., and Alaska; in Canada from Quebec, Ontario, Manitoba, Alberta, and British Columbia; reported from New Brunswick (Mounce [134]) and Saskatchewan (Mounce).

ILLUSTRATIONS: Atkinson, Cornell Agr. Exp. Sta. Bul. 193: fig. 81 (as *Polyporus*); Boyce, Forest Path., fig. 200; Duggar, Fungous Dis. Plants, fig. 231; Farlow, Icones Farl., pl. 94; Clements, Minn. Mushrooms, fig. 59; Hard, Mushrooms, fig. 348; Meinecke, Forest Tree Dis. Calif. Nev., pl. 14; Mounce, Canada Dept. Agr. Bul., N.S. 111: pl. 1; Overholts, Wash. Univ. Studies 3: pl. 5, fig. 27; Owens, Prin. Plant Path., fig. 151; Schaeffer, Fung. Bavar., pls. 137, 270; von Schrenk, U. S. Dept. Agr. Veg. Phys. Path. Bul. 25: pls. 4–5 (as *Polyporus*); Shope, Mo. Bot. Gard. Ann. 18: pl. 34, figs. 1–2.

Schweinitz' plant preserved under this name is *Fomes applanatus*. He has the present species, *F. pinicola*, however, under the name *Polyporus marginatus*.

Frequently in the KOH reaction noted above, a red color does not show, but the treated areas immediately become dark. If this reaction is allowed to take place slowly (without wetting the dried specimen with alcohol), the red is more likely to be apparent.

The extent of the incrustation of the pileus is very variable. In certain forms on conifers the pileus may be uniformly covered with a thick red, brown, or shining-black crust so resinous in consistency that, when cut with a knife, the resin adheres to the blade. Quite frequently there is a broad reddish resinous band on the margin which appears to have weathered down, at the rear of the pileus, to a dark inconspicuous layer, sometimes scarcely crustlike.

Except in the South and in the hardwood regions of the Middle West this species is very common in our forests and causes large amounts of decay in dead standing and down timber, destroying both the heartwood and the sapwood.   Among hardwoods, birch and maple are its favorite hosts.   On living trees it works slowly and never assumes the importance, as a decay-producing agent, of such species as *Fomes Pini* and *F. officinalis*.   The decay is of the general carbonizing type, which renders the wood brown and causes it to fracture extensively (43, pp. 78–79 and pl. 36; 83, pp. 45–48; 87, pp. 382–384; 215, pp. 24–31; 229, pp. 28, 31, 39, 40).   In the fractures rather extensive mycelial mats are formed that rival or surpass those of *Polyporus sulphureus*, but usually do not equal those of *F. officinalis*.   The decay is generally known as "brown crumbly rot."   Dr. Mounce (134) deals in detail with various phases of the life history of this fungus and gives a list of ninety-one host species.   Schmitz (195) discusses some physiological aspects, and Mounce and Macrae (137) report on interfertility phenomena.

Var. marginatus (Pers. ex Fries) Overh., comb. nov.

Boletus marginatus Pers., Obs. Myc. 2: 6. 1799.
Polyporus marginatus Pers. ex Fries, Syst. Myc. 1: 372. 1821.

Pileus differing from that of type variety in being at first entirely white or smoky and in rarely if ever having the reddish crust, becoming blackish with age; context of very young specimens conspicuously bright yellow.

HABITAT: Usually on dead standing trunks of *Populus*, occasionally on coniferous hosts such as *Pseudotsuga*, *Abies*, and *Pinus*.

DISTRIBUTION: Probably that of the species.

ILLUSTRATIONS: Lloyd, Myc. Notes 54: fig. 1168.

This *Populus* form is likely to be referred to *Fomes applanatus* at first sight, although it uniformly lacks the heavy crust of that species. It is not uncommon in central Pennsylvania, growing most frequently at the base of dead *Populus* snags.

3. FOMES OHIENSIS (Berk.) Murr.

Torrey Bot. Club Bul. 30: 230. 1903
(Figs. 404, 523, and Plate 126)

Trametes ohiensis Berk., Grevillea 1: 66. 1872.

Sporophore sessile or attached by the vertex, leathery when fresh, hard and rigid when dry; pileus circular or dimidiate, convex to un-

gulate, 0.5–3 × 0.5–5 × 0.2–2 cm., young specimens entirely white
or drying yellowish, older specimens becoming black at the base, the
margin remaining white or pallid, often zonate or sulcate, at first very
finely tomentose, soon glabrous; context corky or woody, white to
wood color, 1–3 mm. thick; pore surface white, the tubes 1–7 mm.
long, the mouths subcircular, rather thick-walled, entire, averaging
3–5 per mm.; spores ovoid with a truncate apex, 9–12 × 6–7 μ;
basidia 9–12 μ in diameter; cystidia none, but large fusoid crystals
40–60 × 24–30 μ sometimes present; hyphae unbranched, the walls
partially thickened, with no cross walls or clamps, 2.5–4 μ in diameter;
pileus becoming dark red-brown or blackish in KOH. (Compare no.
8, *Fomes scutellatus*.)

HABITAT: On dead wood of deciduous trees, noted on *Crataegus*,
Fagus, *Ostrya*, *Quercus*, *Robinia*, and *Ulmus*; reported on *Acer* (Mich.,
Kauffman [101]).

DISTRIBUTION: Specimens have been examined from Mass., N.Y.,
Pa., N.J., Va., W. Va., N.C., Tenn., Ky., Ohio, Ind., Ill., Mich., Wis.,
Minn., N. Dak., Iowa, Mo., Kans., and Okla.; in Canada from On-
tario.

ILLUSTRATIONS: Coker, Elisha Mitchell Sci. Soc. Jour. 43: pl. 14
(as *Ganoderma*); Overholts, Mo. Bot. Gard. Ann. 2: pl. 25, fig. 22.

In the Ohio River Valley this species is usually found on dead
branches of beech; occasionally it occurs on fence posts and fence rails.
In Pennsylvania it has been collected only on *Robinia*. Its relations to
Fomes scutellatus were discussed by me in an earlier paper (150, pp.
719–721).

The idea recently advanced by Coker (35, p. 133) and earlier by
Romell (186) that this species should be classed in *Ganoderma* simply
because the wall of the spore is thick though smooth and colorless and
the base (really the apex) truncate, adds another foreign element to
that genus as originally described by Karsten and emended first by
Patouillard and later by Murrill. It is difficult to decide why these
authors omit *Fomes fraxinophilus*, *F. juniperinus*, and *F. Ellisianus*.
In all of these, either constantly or at times, the spores have a truncate end, though they are not thick-walled. The genus was first
described on the basis of the laccate pileus surface; then the character
of truncate, brown spores was added; now Coker says the punctate
wall and the color are of little concern, but the thickness of the wall

must be considered. It is not a much greater step to include species in which the wall is neither punctate nor thickened, but only truncate, and not always that.

4. FOMES FRAXINOPHILUS (Peck) Sacc.

Syll. Fung. 6: 172. 1888

(Figs. 413–414)

Polyporus fraxinophilus Peck, N. Y. State Mus. Ann. Rept. 35: 136. 1882.

Sporophore sessile or decurrent on the substratum, hard and woody in texture; pileus convex to somewhat ungulate, usually single, 2–25 × 3.5–40 × 1.5–10 cm., at first white, soon grayish black or black, remaining white or pale brown at the margin, not rugose, somewhat rimose with age, usually sulcate, glabrous or nearly so, the margin thick and rounded and usually white; context woody, pale wood-colored to yellow-brown, 0.5–1.5 cm. thick; pore surface white to brownish, the tubes 2–4 mm. long each season, indistinctly stratified, the older layers white-stuffed, the mouths circular, thick-walled, entire, averaging 2–3 per mm.; spores ellipsoid to ovoid, usually truncate at the apex, hyaline, 6–9 × 5–6 μ; basidia 8–12 μ in diameter; cystidia none; hyphae simple, pale brownish in KOH, the walls partially thickened, with no cross walls or clamps, 2.5–5 μ in diameter.   (Compare no. 7, *Fomes fraxineus*.)

HABITAT: Usually on living or dead *Fraxinus*, noted also on *Platanus*, *Quercus*, and *Ulmus*; reported on *Salix* (N.Y., Kauffman [99]).

DISTRIBUTION: Specimens have been examined from Conn., N.Y., Pa., Va., W. Va., Tenn., Ky., Ohio, Ind., Ill., Mich., Wis., N. Dak., S. Dak., Iowa, Mo., Kans., Nebr., N. Mex., and Ariz.; in Canada from Quebec, Ontario, and Manitoba; reported from Ark. (Swartz [212]) and Mont. (Weir [227]).

ILLUSTRATIONS: Hard, Mushrooms, fig. 350; McDougall, Mushrooms, opp. p. 117; von Schrenk, U. S. Dept. Agr. Pl. Ind. Bul. 32: pl. 1 (as *Polyporus*).

The species is particularly common in the Ohio and the Mississippi River Valleys, fruiting well above the ground on either the trunk or the main branches.   In this character it is very different from *Fomes fraxineus*.

The fungus produces an extensive heart rot of living trees. The decay is of the general delignifying type, the wood eventually being reduced to a whitish or straw-colored fibrous mass (7; 87, pp. 379–381; 216; 219, pp. 46–47). In the earlier stages the annual rings separate easily.

5. FOMES ELLISIANUS Anderson

Bot. Gaz. 16: 113. 1891

(Figs. 421–423, 602–604, and Plate 126)

Polyporus circumstans Morgan, Cincinnati Soc. Nat. Hist. Jour. 18: 37. 1895.

Sporophore sessile, woody; pileus convex to ungulate, 3–10 × 3–15 × 1.5–8 cm., at first nearly white, becoming grayish black or blackish, radiate-rugose and with a reddish tinge when young, black and usually somewhat rimose or imbricate-rimose with age, often sulcate, glabrous or practically so; context pallid to wood-colored, punky to corky or woody, 0.5–2 cm. thick; pore surface white to isabelline, the tubes 2–6 mm. long each season, not distinctly stratified, the mouths averaging 2–3 per mm.; spores oblong-ellipsoid to broadly ellipsoid, smooth, hyaline, in age often somewhat truncate at the apex, 5.5–8 × 3.5–5 μ; basidia 7–9 μ in diameter; cystidia none; hyphae simple, hyaline, with thickened walls, with no cross walls or clamps, 2.5–5 μ in diameter; all parts becoming considerably darker but not black in KOH solution, sometimes a dirty reddish-brown color developing first, then darker.

HABITAT: Known only on *Shepherdia*.

DISTRIBUTION: Specimens have been examined from N. Dak., S. Dak., N. Mex., Utah, Colo., and Mont.; in Canada from Saskatchewan; reported from Wis. (?) (Neuman [148]) and Wyo. (Baxter [7]).

ILLUSTRATIONS: Overholts, Mo. Bot. Gard. Ann. 2: pl. 25, fig. 23; Shope, Mo. Bot. Gard. Ann. 18: pl. 37, fig. 3 (as *Fomes fraxinophilus* f. *Ellisianus*).

That this species is closely related to *Fomes fraxinophilus* cannot be doubted. It seems to me sufficiently distinct, in spite of Lloyd's assertion to the contrary and Baxter's (7) more recent attempt to assign it the rank of a form of that species.

6. FOMES OFFICINALIS (Vill. ex Fries) Faull

Roy. Canad. Inst. Trans. 11: 185. 1916

(Figs. 355, 360, 605, and Plate 126)

Boletus officinalis Vill., Hist. Plant. Dauph. 3: 1041. 1789.
Polyporus officinalis Vill. ex Fries, Syst. Myc. 1: 365. 1821,
Fomes albogriseus Peck, Torrey Bot. Club Bul. 30: 97. 1903.
Fomes Laricis Jacq. ex Murr., Torrey Bot. Club Bul. 30: 230. 1903.

Sporophore sessile, cheesy when fresh, drying rigid; pileus at first convex and knoblike, finally becoming ungulate, 5–15 × 4–20 × 5–30 cm., white or yellowish, sometimes slightly incrusted, finally sulcate, sometimes somewhat rimose;.context white or whitish, cheesy when fresh, in mature plants friable, bitter to the taste, with farinaceous odor, 2–5 cm. thick; pore surface white or discolored on drying, the tubes 3–20 mm. long each season, often quite distinctly stratified, the mouths angular, rather thick-walled, entire, averaging 3–4 per mm.; spores ellipsoid or ovoid, hyaline, 4–5 × 3–4 μ; basidia 4–6 μ in diameter; cystidia none; hyphae long and flexuous, hyaline, simple or sparingly branched, with no cross walls or clamps, 2.5–6 μ in diameter; reaction with KOH various, sometimes yellowish, sometimes quite dark, at times with a bright red tinge and sometimes a dark dirty red.

HABITAT: On trunks of living or dead coniferous trees, noted on *Abies, Larix, Picea, Pinus, Pseudotsuga,* and *Tsuga.*

DISTRIBUTION: Specimens have been examined from Mich., Ariz., Colo., Mont., Idaho, Ore., Wash., Calif., and Alaska; in Canada from Ontario and British Columbia; reported from Wis. (Neuman [148]), S. Dak. (Brenckle [25]), and Nev. (Meinecke).

ILLUSTRATIONS: Boyce, U. S. Dept. Agr. Bul. 1163: pl. 6 (as *Fomes Laricis*); *idem,* Osborn Bot. Lab. Bul. 1: fig. 18 (as *F. Laricis*); *idem,* U. S. Dept. Agr. Tech. Bul. 286: pl. 8, fig. B (as *F. Laricis*); *idem,* Forest Path., fig. 196 (as *F. Laricis*); Faull, Roy. Canad. Inst. Trans. 11: pls. 18–20; Hubert, Outline Forest Path., fig. 119 (as *F. Laricis*); Meinecke, Forest Tree Dis. Calif. Nev., pl. 7 (as *F. Laricis*); Neuman, Wis. Geol. and Nat. Hist. Survey Bul. 33: pl. 10; Weir, in Idaho Voc. Ed. Bul. 5, 5: figs. 11–12.

This species is not uncommon in the coniferous forests of the Rocky Mountains and westward, but it is almost unknown in the eastern and southern United States, although it occurs in southern Canada from Ontario to the Pacific Ocean. The fungus is often reported in the literature as *Fomes Laricis*. If the names are synonyms (and they probably are), *F. officinalis* has priority.

The very bitter taste of the fungus is similar to that of quinine, and it is said to have been used as a substitute for that substance by the American Indians and the early settlers. From its taste it has received the name of the "chalky quinine fungus." Neuman (148) illustrates an elongated specimen said to be 65 cm. long, with 70 strata. Faull (46) records a specimen 2 feet long, showing 45 tube layers. He also reports the formation of chlamydospores, 2–7 $\times$ 2–6 μ, in chains on the surface of the pileus. Chlamydospores are formed in profusion in pure cultures.

The fungus causes extensive rot in standing coniferous timbers, producing a general carbonizing decay of the heartwood. It is practically always a trunk rot, extending upward in later stages to the limits of heartwood formation. Very extensive mats of mycelium, sometimes several feet in length and as much as half an inch in thickness, develop in the wood fractures (20, pl. 4), and this character suggests the name "felted heart rot" for the decay. It has also been designated "reddish brown heart rot," "brown trunk rot" (22, p. 24; 83, pp. 33–37), and "red rot." *Fomes pinicola* and *Polyporus sulphureus* are the only other important decay species that form mycelial mats comparable to those produced by this species. Faull (46) has pointed out that when examined under the microscope the hyphae making up the mats of *F. officinalis* are uniformly 1.5–2 μ in diameter and infrequently branched, with the branches given off at right angles; in contrast, those in the mats of *P. sulphureus* vary in size up to 6.5 μ, the larger threads branching at acute angles to give rise to narrower threads of about the same size as those of *F. officinalis*. Meinecke (132, p. 44) reports *F. officinalis* as one of the serious menaces to sugar pine (*Pinus Lambertiana* Dougl.), and Hedgcock (66, p. 78) reports it as causing a "common heart rot of larches" in northwestern United States and says that in northern Arizona "*Pinus ponderosa* is diseased more often with this than any other fungus." Boyce (21) reports that it causes 2.7 per cent loss of the gross volume in the Douglas fir stands in Oregon and that it is second only to "conk rot" in importance on that host. Over its entire range, it is probably to be ranked with *F. Pini* and *P. Schweinitzii* as one of the three most important sources of defect in standing coniferous timber.

3b. *Pores averaging 4 or more per mm.* (see also *Fomes avellaneus*,
        p. 105; *Oxyporus nobilissimus*, p. 106; and *Polyporus
        lignosus*, p. 427)

7. FOMES FRAXINEUS (Bull. ex Fries) Cooke

Grevillea 14: 21. 1885

(Figs. 433, 559, and Plate 126)

Boletus fraxineus Bull., Herb. France 2, pl. 433, fig. 2. 1789.
Polyporus fraxineus Bull. ex Fries, Syst. Myc. 1: 374. 1821.
Polyporus induratus Lloyd, Letter 68, p. 11. 1918.

Sporophore sessile or decurrent on the substratum, corky and
somewhat watery to firm and rigid; pileus plane to convex, 3–10 ×
3–20 × 0.5–6 cm., often imbricate, usually light-colored with reddish
or reddish-brown stains, rarely altogether cinereous or altogether
reddish, glabrous or at first with a fine scurfy tomentum, becoming
darker with age, finally incrusted with a thin, hard, though not very
distinct crust, sometimes somewhat zonate, frequently rough and
uneven on the surface; context punky to corky, 0.4–3 cm. thick,
somewhat flesh-colored when fresh, often fading out to pallid, pale
wood color, or somewhat olivaceous in drying; pore surface whitish
to flesh color or somewhat cinereous to brownish, the tubes 2–10 mm.
long, often in a single layer, the mouths subcircular to subangular,
rather thin-walled, barely visible to the unaided eye, averaging 4–6
per mm.; spores broadly ovoid, smooth, hyaline, 6–7 × 5–6 μ; basidia 6–10 μ in diameter; cystidia none or represented at times by
slightly projecting, hyaline bodies about 4 μ in diameter; hyphae
hyaline, simple, with walls partially or entirely thickened, with no
cross walls or clamps, 5–10 μ in diameter; context and hymenium
dark with KOH.   (Compare no. 4, *Fomes fraxinophilus*.)

HABITAT: Usually on stumps or trunks of *Fraxinus* close to the
ground line, also noted on *Acer*, particularly *A. negundo*, and on *Nyssa*,
Quercus, and *Ulmus*.

DISTRIBUTION: Specimens have been examined from N.Y., N.J.,
Fla., Ala., La., Ohio, Ill., and Mich.; in Canada from Quebec and
Ontario; reported from Iowa (Wilson [233]) and Ark. (Swartz [212]).

ILLUSTRATIONS: Baxter, Mich. Acad. Sci. Arts and Letters Papers
4, 1: pl. 3; McDougall, Ill. State Acad. Sci. Trans. 12: fig. 6 (as *Polyporus induratus*).

This species is in every way distinct from *Fomes fraxinophilus.* The reddish coloration usually present in fresh specimens, together with the leathery or corky rather than woody consistency, the non-rimose pileus, the small pores, and the habit of fruiting at the ground line rather than higher on the trunk are all decisive characters.

I have a fine specimen of the present species from the type locality of *Polyporus induratus,* collected on box elder in Illinois. Specimens so determined in the New York State Museum at Albany are in error, being thick forms of *P. fumosus.* Schweinitz' record, if based on the specimen preserved in the Philadelphia Academy of Natural Science, is incorrect, for that specimen is *Fomes conchatus.*

The fungus produces a soft white heart rot of its hosts, and usually fruits at or near the ground line. It is of little importance as a decay organism, and is infrequently met. Baxter (8) has described its characteristics in culture.

8. FOMES SCUTELLATUS (Schw.) Cooke

Grevillea 14: 19. 1885

(Figs. 364–365 and Plate 126)

Polyporus scutellatus Schw., Amer. Phil. Soc. Trans. II, 4: 157. 1832.

Sporophore typically attached by the vertex and pendent, sometimes laterally attached, larger specimens sometimes appearing resupinate with strongly reflexed margins, corky when fresh, hard on drying; pileus dimidiate to circular in outline, convex to ungulate, 0.5–1.5 × 0.5–2.5 × 0.3–1 cm., at first white, soon entirely dark brown or black or with the margin remaining white, rarely with alternating brown and blackish zones, at first very minutely tomentose but soon glabrous, slightly sulcate and rugose; context corky, wood color to umber, 1–3 mm. thick; pore surface white to isabelline, the tubes 1–2 mm. long each season but not always reviving, not distinctly stratified, the mouths subcircular, thick-walled, entire, usually pulverulent, averaging 4–5 per mm., visible to the unaided eye; spores cylindric, smooth, hyaline, 8–9 × 2.5–3.5 μ; basidia 6–8 μ in diameter; cystidia none or not noteworthy; hyphae considerably branched, nearly hyaline, with no cross walls or clamps, 2–3 μ in diameter; all parts becoming slowly blackish in KOH solution.

HABITAT: Usually on dead *Alnus,* also noted on *Acer, Amelanchier, Cornus, Crataegus, Liquidambar, Pyrus,* and *Quercus*; reported by Bisby *et al.* (12) on *Celastrus.*

DISTRIBUTION: Specimens have been examined from Me., N.H., Vt., Conn., N.Y., Pa., Del., W. Va., Ga., Fla., Tenn., Ohio, Ind., N. Dak., and Idaho; in Canada from Quebec, Ontario, Manitoba, and British Columbia; reported from N.C. (Coker [35]), Mich. (Kauffman [105]), Iowa (Wolf [234]), and Mont. (Weir [227]).

ILLUSTRATIONS: Overholts, Mo. Bot. Gard. Ann. 2: pl. 25, fig. 24.

In form, size, and color this species approaches *Fomes ohiensis* but may usually be distinguished by the very different spores, the smaller basidia, the more abundantly branched hyphae of the context, and the fact that it usually occurs on dead alders (150, p. 719). It is a common species in the New England States and the Appalachian Mountains, where *F. ohiensis* is rarely found. Neuman's record of it as "quite common on old fence rails and posts" is certainly erroneous, probably referring to *Trametes sepium* or *F. ohiensis*.

9. FOMES CONNATUS (Weinm.) Gill.

Champ. France 1: 684. 1878

(Figs. 420, 446–448, 483–484, and Plate 126)

Polyporus connatus Weinm., Florae Ross., p. 332. 1836.
Fomes populinus (Schum. ex Fries) Cooke, Grevillea 14: 20. 1885.

Sporophore sessile, watery, tough or corky when fresh, firm and rigid on drying; pileus usually somewhat imbricate, convex, 2–12 × 3–18 × 0.5–4 cm., white to gray or ochraceous when fresh, sometimes black behind with age, compactly villose-tomentose or occasionally with a short strigose tomentum on the margin, even, never rimose, rarely sulcate; context soft-corky, white to ochraceous, 0.3–1 cm. thick; pore surface white to cream color or yellowish when fresh, often yellowish and glistening on drying, the tubes 2–5 mm. long each season, very distinctly stratified, the mouths rather thin-walled, subcircular to angular, entire or denticulate, averaging 4–5 per mm.; spores ellipsoid to globose, [hyaline—J.L.L.], 4.5–5 × 3–4 μ or 3–5 μ in diameter; basidia 5–6 μ in diameter; cystidia abundant in most specimens as protruding hyphae heavily incrusted at the ends, incrustations often more or less dissolved after long periods in KOH, sometimes quite rare or inconspicuous, or not projecting, 7–11 μ in diameter; hyphae nearly simple, hyaline, thin-walled, with abundant and conspicuous cross walls but no clamps, 3–5 μ in diameter; pore surface usually darkening strongly where touched with KOH solution.

HABITAT: Usually near the ground on living trunks of *Acer*, occasionally on *Aesculus, Betula, Carya, Fagus, Fraxinus, Liquidambar, Liriodendron, Nyssa, Ostrya, Quercus, Tilia,* and *Ulmus*; frequently covered with moss.

DISTRIBUTION: Specimens have been examined from Me., N.H., Vt., Mass., Conn., N.Y., Pa., N.J., Del., Md., Va., W. Va., N.C., Ga., Tenn., Ky., Ohio, Ind., Ill., Mich., Wis., Minn., Iowa, Mo., and Nebr.; in Canada from Nova Scotia, Quebec, and Ontario; reported from Kans. (Bartholomew [4]), Ark. (Swartz [212]), and from Manitoba (Bisby *et al.* [12]).

ILLUSTRATIONS: Fries, Icones Sel. Hym., pl. 185, fig. 2 (as *Polyporus*); Overholts, Wash. Univ. Studies 3: pl. 6, fig. 29.

During the first few years of its development this species is likely to be taken for a species of *Polyporus* because of the white watery pileus and the hyphae of the context.   After it develops far enough to produce the typically stratified tubes, it is a highly distinctive species.   *Acer* is the usual host, but it is not uncommon on *Carya*. The cystidia may on first examination appear to be only crystalline masses along the hymenium, but further examination will show that this material incrusts the ends of hyphae.   Sections to show cystidia should be mounted in lactic acid rather than KOH.

Schweinitz' record (198, p. 156) of *"Polyporus populinus"* was apparently based on a specimen of *Trametes malicola*.   At any rate, such is the identity of the single specimen preserved in his herbarium under this name.

The fungus produces a poorly characterized heart rot of living trees, in which the decayed wood becomes soft and straw-colored to yellowish brown and may eventually disappear, leaving a hollow. The species has proved difficult to isolate either from sporophore or from wood tissue because of the prevalence of contaminating organisms.   Campbell (27) has secured and described isolations from multiple spore cultures.

10. FOMES GEOTROPUS Cooke

Grevillea 13: 119. 1885

(Figs. 416, 418, and Plate 126)

Polyporus (Fomes) geotropus Cooke, Grevillea 13: 32. 1884.

Sporophore sessile to effused-reflexed, corky when fresh, hard and rigid when dry; pileus applanate or strongly convex, 6–15 × 7–25 ×

1–8 cm., white when fresh, drying ochraceous to pale tan or pale bay, slightly fibrillose or subtomentose to glabrous, usually azonate, often pitted and tubercular, the margin rather thick, often deflexed in drying; context white or cream color in fresh plants, ochraceous on drying, 0.5–7 cm. thick, homogeneous, firm-corky to almost woody when dry; pore surface pinkish salmon when fresh, grayish isabelline to smoky isabelline or sordid flesh color on drying, usually glistening, the tubes not stratified, 5–15 mm. long each season, sordid flesh color or dull chestnut within, the mouths angular, thin-walled, entire, averaging 5–8 per mm.; spores globose, smooth, hyaline, 6–7 μ in diameter; basidia 8–9 μ in diameter, isolated at time of sporulation; cystidia present in the sporulating hymenium, bulbous, with mucronate or beaded apex, 6–9 μ in diameter, disappearing from the old hymenial region; hyphae closely compacted, thin-walled, often collapsed, nearly simple, with occasional cross walls but no clamps, 3–7 μ in diameter; context of old herbarium specimens spotting black where touched with KOH solution. (Compare no. 81, *Polyporus zonalis*, and no. 84, *P. robiniophilus*.)

HABITAT: On dead wood or from wounds in living trees, noted on *Acer, Broussonetia, Carya, Celtis, Liquidambar, Magnolia, Persea, Populus,* and *Ulmus*; reported on *Taxodium* (Long [119] and Murrill).

DISTRIBUTION: Specimens have been examined from Ga., Fla., La., Miss., Ark., and Texas; reported from Mo. (Maneval [131]).

I would refer here all specimens with flesh-colored hymenium as in *Polyporus lignosus* but with much thicker context and much longer tubes. The color of the pileus and the context is usually a uniform ochraceous, and the hymenium loses its color (or does not develop it) more than in *P. lignosus*. *P. lignosus* of the tropics is thin and applanate with thin context. *Fomes geotropus* is thick, usually convex, and with thick context. The hyphae in the two species are identical. I had hoped, when I first discovered it, that the black spotting with KOH—always pronounced in *F. geotropus*—would serve as an easy means of differentiating the two species. Tests show, however, that some specimens which I have referred to *P. lignosus* are more or less blackened following the application of the reagent. In others there is no reaction.

The species may be responsible for a limited amount of heart rot in southern hardwood trees, especially cottonwood, but little information is at hand. Johnson and Edgerton (91) describe it as a heart-rotting fungus on magnolia in Louisiana. Long (119) reported finding sporophores of this fungus on cypress in eight swamps in Florida, Louisiana, and Arkansas, in some cases directly associated with the typical "pecky" defect of that tree. I failed to find it on cypress in an entire summer in the Mississippi River Delta region in Louisiana and Arkansas, although I collected it a few times on hardwoods. I do not believe "pecky" cypress can be attributed to this fungus.

11. FOMES MELIAE (Underw.) Murr.

Torrey Bot. Club Bul. 30: 232. 1903

(Figs. 350, 356–358, and Plate 126)

Polyporus Meliae Underw., Torrey Bot. Club Bul. 24: 85. 1897.
Trametes subnivosa Murr., North Amer. Flora 9: 43. 1907.

Sporophore sessile or decurrent on the substratum, corky when fresh, hard and rigid when dry; pileus convex or plane, usually imbricate, 1–5 × 3–10 × 0.7–5 cm., isabelline or dirty white to smoky, glabrous or very compactly tomentose, azonate, usually more or less roughened, the margin acute; context cinereous to pale wood color, 0.3–1.5 cm. thick, corky when fresh, hard when dry; pore surface isabelline to dark-colored, the tubes 2–6 mm. long, sometimes in 2 or 3 layers, the mouths subcircular, thick-walled, entire, averaging 4–5 per mm.; spores cylindric, smooth, hyaline, 6–8 × 2–3 μ; cystidia none; hyphae hyaline, flexuous, often thick-walled, with no cross walls or clamps, 3–6 μ in diameter, the smaller ones considerably branched; context darkening but not black in KOH solution. (Compare no. 60, *Polyporus submurinus*.)

HABITAT: On dead wood, usually of deciduous trees, especially *Fraxinus* and *Melia*, noted also on *Acer, Gleditsia, Platanus, Prunus, Pyrus, Quercus*, and *Taxodium*.

DISTRIBUTION: Specimens have been examined from Fla., Ala., La., Tenn., Ind., Mo., Nebr., Ark., and Texas.

The species is characterized by the general smoky-gray color, by the trametoid consistency, with the tubes typically in separate strata, and by the year's increment being conspicuously marked in the context. It is easily separated from *Polyporus submurinus* on these points and by the uniform nature of the context hyphae. *Trametes subnivosa* does not seem to be specifically distinct. The specimens are nearly always entirely sterile. One collection on *Fraxinus* at the New York Botanical Garden, made by Earle and Baker in Alabama in 1910, is fertile; the types of *Fomes Meliae* are also fertile, with spores 6–7 × 2–3 μ.

Frequently there is a considerable amount of crystalline material along the hymenium, as is seen in sections made through that region, and some of these crystalline masses look like incrusted cystidia. More often, they are definitely not incrusted cystidia, and I have not been able to satisfy myself that they ever are.

The species occurs abundantly in Louisiana, especially on *Fraxinus* logs and stumps. The fungus causes an extensive brown crumbling rot of the sapwood.

2b. *Context pinkish to rose* (see also no. 7, *Fomes fraxineus*)

12. FOMES ROSEUS (Alb. & Schw. ex Fries) Cooke

Grevillea 14: 19. 1885

(Figs. 375, 380–381, and Plate 126)

Boletus roseus Alb. & Schw., Consp. Fung., p. 251. 1805.
Polyporus roseus Alb. & Schw. ex Fries, Syst. Myc. 1: 372. 1821.
Trametes arctica Berkeley, in herb.

Sporophore sessile or effused-reflexed, corky to somewhat woody, drying hard, rigid; pileus convex to somewhat ungulate, 1–6 × 1.5–10 × 1–3 cm., brownish pink or pinkish red at first and sometimes remaining so on the margin, becoming smoky brown or dark gray, then blackish with age, at first very minutely tomentose, soon glabrous, sometimes rugulose, the surface finally hardening and darkening to give an incrusted appearance and then likely to be inconspicuously rimose, usually azonate, but furrowed or sulcate in old specimens, especially on the acute or rounded margin; context silvery pinkish or pale rose-colored, soft-corky to rather hard, 2–10 mm. thick; pore surface pinkish brown at first, soon avellaneous or smoky brown, the tubes 0.5–3 mm. long each season, rather distinctly stratified in old specimens, the mouths circular or subangular, rather thick-walled, entire, averaging 3–5 per mm.; spores ellipsoid-cylindric or oblong-cylindric, hyaline, 5–7(–8) × 2.5–3.5 μ; cystidia none; hyphae pale brown in

KOH solution, long and flexuous, simple, with no cross walls or clamps, 2.5–5 μ in diameter; context quickly changing to blackish where touched with KOH solution, other parts usually changing less rapidly.

HABITAT: On dead wood, usually of coniferous trees, noted on *Abies, Picea, Pseudotsuga,* and *Tsuga*; rarely on hardwoods, noted on *Platanus.*

DISTRIBUTION: Specimens have been examined from Me., N.H., Vt., N.Y., N. Mex., Utah, Colo., Wyo., Mont., Idaho, Ore., and Calif.; in Canada from British Columbia; reported from Iowa (Wilson [233]).

ILLUSTRATIONS: Lloyd, Synop. Fomes, fig. 576; Shope, Mo. Bot. Gard. Ann. 18: pl. 29, figs. 4–6.

The spores seem the best character on which to differentiate this species from *Fomes subroseus,* as is explained under that species. Specimens of more or less ungulate form sometimes have the narrow spores of *F. subroseus* and sometimes the broader spores of *F. roseus.*

As a timber-decaying organism this species is of only minor importance in most regions. The decay is a brown rot of the carbonizing type similar to that produced by *Lenzites saepiaria.* Mycelial mats are formed to some extent in the wood fractures. Boyce (21) reports it as a top rot in Douglas fir in the Northwest, where it occurs especially in connection with trees with dead tops. He suggests the name "yellow-brown top rot" for this defect. The effects produced on red cedar, as described by von Schrenk (214), include considerable localization of the activity of the fungus, resulting in the formation of cavities in the wood not unlike those made by *Polyporus amarus* in incense cedar. The cavity is surrounded by carbonized material fractured into small cubes. I have never observed this type of decay in connection with this species.

13. FOMES SUBROSEUS (Weir) Overh.

Pa. Agr. Exp. Sta. Tech. Bul. 316: 11. 1935
(Figs. 376–379 and Plate 126)

Trametes carnea American authors, not *T. carnea* Nees.
Trametes subrosea Weir, Rhodora 25: 217. 1923.

Sporophore sessile or effused-reflexed, leathery to corky when fresh, drying subflexible or rigid; pileus applanate or occasionally somewhat convex or ungulate, 1–7 × 3–12 × 0.3–2 cm., pinkish red at first, but soon pinkish brown, dirty rufescent, grayish brown, grayish, or in old specimens becoming blackish, finely and compactly tomentose, finally nearly or quite glabrous or becoming radiately fibrillose or rugulose, not incrusted in any stage and never rimose, often zonate, the margin usually acute; context rosy pink to pinkish cinnamon or pinkish brown, floccose to soft-corky, 2–15 mm. thick; pore surface pinkish red, becoming pinkish brown, finally reddish brown in age, the tubes 1–3 mm. long each season, not definitely stratified and apparently not reviving for more than two or three years, the mouths circular to subangular, rather thick-walled, entire, averaging 4–5 per mm.; spores narrow-cylindric, slightly curved, hyaline, 4–7 × 1.5–2 μ, occasionally 5 × 1 μ; cystidia none; hyphae pale brown in KOH solution, long and flexuous, simple, with no cross walls or clamps, 2.5–5 μ in diameter; context quickly changing to black where touched with KOH solution.

HABITAT: On dead wood, usually of coniferous trees, noted on *Abies, Juniperus, Larix, Picea, Pinus, Pseudotsuga,* and *Tsuga*; rarely on hardwoods, noted on *Betula, Populus,* and *Prunus*; reported on *Arbutus* (Ore., Weir [223] and on *Thuja* (Mich., Kauffman [105]).

DISTRIBUTION: Specimens have been examined from Me., N.H., Vt., Mass., Conn., N.Y., Pa., N.J., Md., Va., W. Va., N.C., Ga., Fla., Ala., Tenn., Ky., Ind., Mich., Wis., Minn., Nebr., Ark., N. Mex., Ariz., Colo., Wyo., Mont., Idaho, Ore., Wash., and Calif.; in Canada from Quebec, Ontario, Manitoba, Alberta, and British Columbia; reported also from S. Dak. (Brenckle [25]) and Iowa (Wilson).

ILLUSTRATIONS: Lloyd, Synop. Fomes, fig. 577 (as *Trametes carnea*); Shope, Mo. Bot. Gard. Ann. 18: pl. 32, fig. 1 (as *Trametes*); Zeller, Jour. Agr. Res. 33: 688, fig. 1.

Considerable controversy has raged around the autonomy of this species and its relation to *Fomes roseus*. As treated here it is in general the fungus formerly known in this country as *Trametes carnea*. Because of the ambiguous use of that name, Weir proposed in 1923 the name *T. subrosea* and marked out certain differences he believed to exist between *T. subrosea* and *F. roseus*. I cannot concede, however, that any such differences prevail to the extent indicated by him. In general, the context of *F. roseus* becomes a silvery white and contrasts to a greater or less degree with the more deeply tinted context of *F. subroseus.* Yet this fact is not always correlated with a significant difference in spore size, as is shown in my herbarium No. 8030, in which the spores are allantoid, 5–6 × 2 μ, and the context nearly "pale vinaceous pink," but in which the tubes are rather distinctly stratified and a slightly rimose crust is present on the pileus. As I have previously pointed out (157) and as Mounce and Macrae have verified (136, p. 158), the significant difference between the two species lies in the size and the shape of the spores. In *F. subroseus* they are narrow-cylindric and slightly curved, measuring 4–7 × 1.5–2 μ; in *F. roseus* they are elongate-ellipsoid to oblong or short-cylindric, not at all curved, and measure 5–7(–8) × 2.5–3.5 μ. I do not find in any specimen (and I have examined also the *F. roseus* specimens at Beltsville, Maryland) spores that average 8–10 μ in length (as stated by Weir), or that even reach a length of 10 μ.

Snell *et al.* (205) report a significant difference in growth rate at 30° C. in cultures of these two species, by which they can be differentiated "with absolute reliability" (p. 283). They also discuss the relation of these plants to moisture, and find that *Fomes roseus* occurs in drier situations, showing a preference for hewn timbers in exposed places. *F. subroseus,* on the other hand, usually fruits on logs in moist or damp locations.

Mounce and Macrae have recently (136) applied the mating test to two groups of collections exhibiting the spore differences pointed out above. They find that whereas monosporous cultures of the narrow-spored type are completely interfertile and cultures of the broader-spored type are likewise completely interfertile, there is a total lack of interfertility between the narrow-spored group and the broad-spored group. Thus the contention that these two species are not to be covered by a single species name is substantiated from three angles.

As a decay organism this species has been too much confused in the literature with *Fomes roseus* to permit reliable conclusions. It is undoubtedly much more common than is that species. Zeller (238) describes a carbonizing pocket rot of stone-fruit trees from California to British Columbia as being produced by this species. This characterization seems to agree well with von Schrenk's description (214) of the decay produced in *Thuja.* See also the notes on decay due to *F. roseus,* above.

Snell (204) discusses the relation of this species to the decay of timbers in textile mills in New England.

1b. *Context reddish orange, yellowish brown or darker, permanently*
    darkening in KOH solution
  2a. *Setae present*
    3a. *Spores hyaline*
      4a. *Pores 2–5(–6) per mm.*

14. FOMES IGNIARIUS (L. ex Fries) Kickx

Fl. Crypt. Flandres, 2: 237. 1867

(Figs. 359, 424, 430, 435–438, 583, and Plate 126)

Boletus igniarius L., Sp. Plant., p. 1176. 1753.
Polyporus igniarius L. ex Fries, Syst. Myc. 1: 375. 1821.
Pyropolyporus igniarius (L. ex Fries) Murr., Torrey Bot. Club Bul. 30:
   110. 1903.
Fomes Arctostaphyli Long, N. Mex. Chapt. Phi Kappa Phi Papers 1: 2. 1917.

Sporophore sessile or somewhat decurrent on the substratum, very hard and woody; pileus plane to convex or ungulate, 3–15 × 5–20 (–30) × 2–12 cm., young specimens and the growing margins of older specimens usually brown and finely tomentose, becoming grayish black or black and glabrous with age, usually somewhat rimose with age, usually not incrusted but sometimes developing a slight crust, often furrowed; context hard and woody, brown, 0.5–1 cm. or rarely several centimeters thick; pore surface gray-brown to brown, the tubes 2–5 mm. long each season, the older layers conspicuously white-stuffed with narrow hyaline hyphae 1–2 μ in diameter, the mouths subcircular, rather thick-walled, entire, averaging 4–5 (rarely 3–4) per mm.; spores globose or subglobose, smooth, hyaline, 5–6.5 × 4–5 μ or 4.5–5.5 μ in diameter; basidia 5–7 μ in diameter; setae sometimes rare, sometimes rather abundant, sharp-pointed, not projecting strongly, 12–18 × 4–6 μ; hyphae simple, brown, the walls partially thickened, with no clamps or cross walls, 3–5 μ in diameter; all parts black in KOH solution. (Compare no. 25, *Fomes Everhartii*, and no. 29, *F. robustus*.)

HABITAT: On trunks of living or deciduous trees, noted on *Acer, Adenostoma, Alnus, Arbutus, Arctostaphylos, Betula, Carpinus, Castanopsis, Cornus, Fagus, Fraxinus, Juglans, Ostrya, Populus, Pyrus, Quercus, Rhamnus, Salix,* and *Ulmus*; one collection (Colo., Bartholomew) said to be on *Picea*; reported on *Prunus* and *Sambucus* (Weir [226, 227]), on *Sassafras* (Mich., Kauffman [101]), and on *Xanthoxylon* (Hedgcock [66]).

DISTRIBUTION: Specimens have been examined from Me., N.H., Vt., Mass., Conn., R.I., N.Y., Pa., Md., Va., W. Va., Tenn., Ohio, Ind., Mich., Wis., Minn., N. Dak., S. Dak., Iowa, Mo., Nebr., N. Mex., Ariz., Utah, Colo., Wyo., Mont., Idaho, Ore., Wash., Calif., and Alaska; in Canada from Newfoundland, Quebec, Ontario, Manitoba, and British Columbia; reported from Kans. (Bartholomew [4]) and Ark. (Swartz [212]).

ILLUSTRATIONS: Atkinson, Cornell Agr. Exp. Sta. Bul. 193: figs. 73–74 (as *Polyporus*); Boyce, Forest Path., figs. 173–174; Fries, Icones Sel. Hym., pl. 184, fig. 2 (as *P. nigricans*); Gillet, Champ. France 2: pl. 290 (45); Hard, Mushrooms, fig. 349; Hepting, Civil. Cons. Corps Forestry Publ. 2: fig. 2; Hubert, Outline Forest Path., fig. 116; Lloyd, Myc. Notes, Polyp. Issue No. 1: figs. 209–210 (as *Fomes nigricans*); Meinecke, Forest Tree Dis. Calif. Nev., pl. 15; Neuman, Wis. Geol. and Nat. Hist. Survey Bul. 33: pl. 8, fig. 29 (as *F. nigricans*); Overholts, Mo. Bot. Gard. Ann. 2: pl. 25, figs. 18, 20, and 21 (as var. *nigricans*); Rankin, Man. Tree Dis., figs. 58–60; von Schrenk and Spaulding, U. S. Dept. Agr. Pl. Ind. Bul. 149: pls. 1, 6 (as *F. nigricans*); Shope, Mo. Bot. Gard. Ann. 18: pl. 35; Sowerby, Col. Fig. English Fungi, pl. 132 (as *Boletus*); Stevens, Fungi Plant Dis., fig. 307; Verrall, Minn. Agr. Exp. Sta. Tech. Bul. 117: figs. 1–3.

This is a very common species in New England and New York and in most of the Pacific Northwest. Southward it is less abundant. For example, it is quite abundant in the northern part of Pennsylvania, but is almost lacking from the central and southern parts of the state and from points southward, although it is occasionally found as far south as Tennessee and Missouri. Its range in the eastern half of the United States approximates that of *Betula lutea*, one of its favorite substrata, and in general its range over North America, north of Mexico, is approximately that of *Populus tremuloides*, which is also one of its favorite hosts.

The setae are always comparatively small and do not project prominently, protruding scarcely beyond the level of the spores on the basidia. In some specimens they are absent from all the pores of any ordinary-sized cross section; in others one may find a dozen or more per pore, and sometimes they are quite numerous. Schweinitz' record of this species, if based on the specimen now in his herbarium, is in error, the sporophore there being that of *Fomes rimosus*.

Verrall (213) has studied the variations shown by this species both in morphological and in cultural characters.   He prefers to recognize three groups within the species.   These groups are characterized as follows: (1) a group limited to *Populus*, with small sporophores and the pore surface often at a wide angle from the horizontal, with longer setae (the average lengths of the three groups differ at most by 2.7 μ), and with wider hyphae (greatest difference 1.27 μ), in culture showing a slower growth rate and producing a wintergreen odor on malt agar; (2) a birch group with larger, more applanate sporophores, with shorter setae and narrower hyphae, in culture showing a faster growth rate and, except rarely and less distinctly, producing no wintergreen odor on malt agar; (3) a group miscellaneous as to host but growing quite often on *Betula*, with large sporophores of the type of those on birch but more ungulate and often rimose, with larger pores (approximately 50 μ greater in average diameter), with shorter setae and narrower hyphae than the aspen group, but not always separable from the birch group culturally. I am inclined to believe that there is a group restricted to aspen, which Neuman (148, p. 81) called var. *populinus*.   I would, however, attach the variety name to *Fomes igniarius* rather than, as Neuman does, to *F. nigricans*, which is a name of doubtful significance even as a variety.

Specimens of *Fomes Arctostaphyli* are exact duplicates, except in point of size, of small specimens of the Eastern form of the species, and are quite similar to the form on *Populus tremuloides*.   One collection examined seemed to be without setae, but sections of the sporophores of *F. igniarius* occasionally show no setae.   Romell (187) reports a collection from Lapland without setae.

Sometimes black cinder-like knobs are found on *Betula* that are evidently aborted sporophores of some fungus, and it has been frequently stated that these are sterile growths of *Fomes igniarius*. For example, Verrall has stated (213) that cultures of such sterile conks on birch in Minnesota are definitely *F. igniarius*.   He cites no microscopic evidence, however.   These cinder-like growths have also appeared in the literature as "*F. nigricans*."   Early observations by Dr. Irene Mounce, confirmed in my laboratory, revealed that when some of these bodies are cultured they produce basidiospores that are quite different from those of *F. igniarius* and, in fact, unlike the spores of any species of *Fomes*.   Campbell and Davidson, working with these sterile conks in the Eastern states, found (29) that after infected trees died, a species of *Poria* fruited abundantly on the dead snags. This species of *Poria*, I believe, is *P. obliqua* (Pers. ex Fries) Karst., and the idea is substantiated by comparing specimens with a series of sporophores of that species received from Pilát. Further confirmation comes from a paper by Škorić (201), who describes somewhat similar finds. It is possible, however, that *P. obliqua* (Pers. ex Fries) Karst. as it is known in Europe today is a species complex rather than a single species. I do not intend to convey the idea, however, that all sterile conks of this type are caused by *P. obliqua*. Campbell and Davidson were concerned only with the appearance of these structures on *Betula*, and the conks are brought into the discussion at this point because of the earlier assumption that they belonged to *F. igniarius*.

This species causes a destructive heart rot of many of its hardwood hosts. The decay (87, pp. 388–395; 219, pp. 25–37) is a delignifying rot of the generalized type, as a result of which the interior of the trunk or of the larger branches is reduced to a soft, spongy, whitened mass. This decayed area is bounded on the outside by conspicuous dark zones or black lines. The relation of this fungus to forest management of aspen stands is discussed by Schmitz and Jackson (196) and by Meinecke (133). Hopp (79) gives some hitherto unreported facts concerning the variability of the species in pure culture.

Var. LAEVIGATUS (Fries) Overh.

Mycologia 23: 126. 1931

(Fig. 409)

Polyporus laevigatus Fries, Hym. Eur., p. 571. 1874.
Fomitiporella betulina Murr., North Amer. Flora 9: 12. 1907.

Sporophore entirely resupinate or with merely a suggestion of a reflexed condition, up to 3 cm. thick; pores 3–7 per mm., but usually of the smaller size; characters otherwise as in the species except for the spores being somewhat smaller, 3.5–4.5 × 3–4 μ, and the basidia measuring 4–5 μ in diameter.

HABITAT: On old logs or on erect dead trunks of deciduous trees, especially *Betula*, noted also on *Acer*, *Alnus*, *Carya*, *Fagus*, *Gleditsia*, *Ostrya*, *Populus*, *Prunus*, and *Quercus*.

DISTRIBUTION: Specimens have been examined from Me., N.H., Vt., N.Y., Pa., Md., W. Va., N.C., La., Tenn., Ill., Mich., Wis., Mo.,

Idaho, Wyo., and Wash.; in Canada from Quebec, Ontario, Manitoba, and British Columbia.

ILLUSTRATIONS: Baxter, Mich. Acad. Sci. Arts and Letters Papers 17: pl. 50, fig. 2.

The specimens referred to the variety do not conform well to the original description of Fries, which calls for a thinner plant, but European investigators seem to have followed the present concept, though maintaining our variety as a species of *Poria*. Romell (187) remarks that "typical P[olyporus] laevigatus [referring to Fries's conception of the species] appears quite distinct from typical *P. igniarius*," and says that after more than twenty years of study of the plant, including the thicker form as it occurs in Lapland, he is "still in doubt as to whether their identity should be admitted or not." The plants I refer here occur only on old logs or on dead snags, very rarely show any indication of a pileus, and have a range not entirely coincident with that of the species. For example, this variety occurs throughout the Ohio and the Mississippi River Valleys, where *Fomes igniarius* is almost unknown. The old tube layers have the white-stuffed appearance typical of the species, and I have noted no microscopic differences except for the definitely smaller spore size. At any rate, the situation seems to be that we have a common, perennial, resupinate variety of *F. igniarius*; but perhaps some other name should be used for it if it is to be maintained.

15. FOMES POMACEUS (Pers.) Lloyd

Myc. Notes 35: 469. 1910

(Figs. 427–429 and Plate 126)

Polyporus pomaceus Pers., Myc. Eur. 2: 84. 1825.
Boletus fulvus Scop., Flora Carn., 2d ed., vol. 2: 469. 1772.
Polyporus fulvus Scop. ex Fries, Epicr. Syst. Myc., p. 466. 1836–1838.
Fomes fulvus (Scop. ex Fries) Gill., Champ. France 1: 687. 1878.
Pyropolyporus fulvus (Scop. ex Fries) Murr., Torrey Bot. Club Bul. 30: 112. 1903.

Sporophore sessile or, more often, attached to the lower side of branches and subcircular or elongate in form with both margins reflexed, often effused-reflexed; pileus plane to convex, 0–6 $\times$ 4–10 $\times$

0.5–3 cm., glabrous except for the finely tomentose margin, brown or gray on the margin, gray or grayish black or blackish behind, scarcely rimose though somewhat so at times, not incrusted; context woody, brown, 3–8 mm. thick; pore surface brown, the tubes 1–4 mm. long each season, the older tubes often stuffed with white mycelium as in *Fomes igniarius*, the mouths brown, subcircular, rather thick-walled, entire, averaging 4–6 per mm.; spores subglobose, smooth, hyaline, 3.5–5 × 3–4.5 μ; basidia 5–7 μ in diameter; setae sharp-pointed, not projecting conspicuously, 16–25 × 6–8 μ; hyphae simple, brown, the walls only slightly thickened, with rather abundant cross walls but no clamps, 3–6 μ in diameter; all parts black in KOH solution. (Compare no. 14, *F. igniarius*, and no. 23, *F. densus*.)

HABITAT: Growing only on trunks or branches of species of *Prunus*; reported on *Crataegus* (Mich., Baxter [7]).

DISTRIBUTION: Specimens have been examined from Me., Pa., Md., D.C., Va., W. Va., N.C., S.C., Ga., Ala., Tenn., Ky., Ohio, Ind., Mich., Minn., N. Dak., Iowa, Mo., Kans., Nebr., N. Mex., Colo., and Wyo.; in Canada from Ontario; reported from Vt. (Spaulding [209]), Mont. (Weir [227]), and from Manitoba (Bisby *et al.* [12]).

ILLUSTRATIONS: Lloyd, Synop. Fomes, fig. 588; Overholts, Wash. Univ. Studies 3: pl. 7, fig. 35 (as *Fomes fulvus*); Shope, Mo. Bot. Gard. Ann. 18: pl. 34, figs. 4–6 (as *F. fulvus*).

Baxter (7) describes a form that he deems worthy of recognition on the basis of its entirely resupinate habit and its occurrence on *Crataegus*, *Prunus americana*, and *P. persica*. *Fomes pomaceus* is likely to be confused with *F. igniarius*, but has smaller spores and basidia and rather abundant cross walls in the context hyphae. It should be pointed out that the European homologue of the American plant has spores that are somewhat larger than those given above. In the European collections they measure 6–7 × 4–5 μ (or 5–6.5–7.5 × 4–5–7 μ, according to Bourdot and Galzin). The American plant should perhaps be designated as a distinct variety.

The fungus causes an extensive heart rot in living trunks of *Prunus*, especially the wild species. The decay is of the delignifying type, the wood becoming soft and stringy, though discolored brownish, with flecks and streaks.

16. Fomes occidentalis Overh.

Mycologia 33: 101. 1941

(Fig. 667)

Sporophore perennial, largely resupinate, but where best developed showing a pileus 1–2 × 4–5 × 0.5–1 cm., hard and woody, the growing margin light-colored and finely tomentose, the older pileus surface becoming black, only indistinctly and narrowly subzonate or not at all zonate, not incrusted, not cracked, rather even; context dark brown, black with KOH, woody, only about 1 mm. thick; pore surface dark cinnamon-brown or darker, the tubes becoming as much as 8 mm. long, not layered, gray within, the mouths circular, thick-walled, entire, averaging 3–4 per mm.; spores globose or subglobose, smooth, hyaline, 4.5–6 μ in diameter; setae very occasional, sometimes apparently absent, 36–48 × 12–14 μ; context hyphae brown, sparingly branched, the walls somewhat thickened, with no cross walls or clamps, 3–4 μ in diameter.

HABITAT: On dead and living trees of *Crataegus Douglasii* Lindl.

DISTRIBUTION: Specimens have been examined only from Idaho.

ILLUSTRATIONS: Overholts, Mycologia 33: 99, fig. 8.

Nothing more can be added to the information given with the original description.

The types of this species include two mixed collections in one box in the herbarium of the Division of Forest Pathology at Beltsville, Maryland, the numbers being 9484 and 11109. No. 9484 was collected at St. Maries, Idaho, September 18, 1911, No. 11109, at Priest River, Idaho, August 17, 1911, both by G. G. Hedgcock and J. R. Weir. The two collections cannot now be separated. Portions of these collections are also in the Overholts Herbarium, as No. 21572.

Superficially, the species resembles *Fomes Pini*. It is apparently not closely allied to *F. pomaceus* f. *Crataegi* as described by Baxter, though this might be inferred from the host and a certain superficial resemblance to that species. The pileus is not incrusted, yet when cut vertically with a sharp knife, there is a thin black cuticular layer. This character serves to separate the species from the closely allied *F. conchatus*, which has a definite black line underlying the tomentum and which, moreover, has a much more tomentose pileus, slightly smaller spores, and pores about half the size of those in the present species. Weir apparently recognized this fungus as an undescribed species when he studied it, but did not suggest a name.

17. FOMES TENUIS Karst.

Soc. Fauna Flora Fenn. Meddel. 14: 81. 1887
(Figs. 361, 363, 382, and Plate 127)

Trametes gilvoides Lloyd, Myc. Notes 38: 520. 1912.
Trametes setosus Weir, Jour. Agr. Res. 2: 164. 1914.
[*Poria isabellina* (Fries) Overh., Pa. Agr. Exp. Sta. Bul. 418: 57. 1942.—
J.L.L.]

Sporophore often entirely resupinate, occasionally pileate, flexible when fresh, somewhat rigid on drying; pileus 0–2 × 1–4 × 0.5–1 cm., applanate, occasionally laterally connate into larger fruiting bodies, rusty brown, tobacco-brown or becoming blackish brown and finally entirely black behind, at first softly hirsute-tomentose, eventually compactly tomentose and in old specimens nearly or quite glabrous, rather narrowly zonate where best developed; context rusty yellow or dark brown, rather soft or punky, often very thin or nearly obsolete, sometimes 1–3 mm. thick; pore surface gray-brown to dark brown, the tubes grayish within, 2–5 mm. long and in pileate specimens usually quite long in proportion to the narrow context, occasionally in two or three layers, the mouths subcircular to subangular, rather thin-walled, entire, averaging 2–3 or 3–4 per mm.; spores cylindric, hyaline, 5–8 × 1.5–2 μ; setae present, always abundant and frequently extremely so, narrow lance-shaped, typically projecting 25–60 μ, 5–9 μ in diameter; imbedded setal hyphae absent; context hyphae flexuous, thin-walled, simple, with no cross walls or clamps, 2–4(–5) μ in diameter.

HABITAT: On dead wood of both coniferous and deciduous trees, noted on *Acer, Alnus, Asimina, Betula, Castanea, Hamamelis, Larix, Picea, Pinus, Populus, Pseudotsuga, Quercus, Rhododendron, Salix, Taxodium, Thuja, Tsuga,* and *Vitis.*

DISTRIBUTION: Specimens have been examined from Me., N.H., Conn., N.Y., Pa., Md., Va., W. Va., N.C., Fla., Tenn., Ky., Ohio, Ill., Mich., S. Dak., Mo., Colo., Mont., Idaho, Ore., Wash., and Calif.; in Canada from Ontario, Manitoba, and British Columbia; reported from N. Dak. (Brenckle [25]).

ILLUSTRATIONS: Karsten, Icones Sel. Hym. Fenn., fig. 58; Lloyd, Synop. Apus, figs. 686–687 (as *Polyporus setosus*); *idem*, Myc. Notes 38: fig. 516 (as *Trametes gilvoides*); Shope, Mo. Bot. Gard. Ann. 18: pl. 30, figs. 1–2 (as *T. isabellina*); Weir, Jour. Agr. Res. 2: pl. 10 (as *T. setosus*).

This is a very common species, usually entirely resupinate and therefore often referred to the genus *Poria*. Of the sixty-five collections in my herbarium only about ten are at all pileate. The species differs from all other related pileate species in the long slender setae, which are sometimes extremely abundant but at other times only rather numerous. *Fomes nigrolimitatus* differs in its setae and in the black line or lines in the context, in the hyphae of larger diameter, and in the smaller pores. The resupinate form of *F. tenuis* approaches *Poria ferruginosa* (Schrad. ex Fries) Karst., but may be separated by the slender spores (4–6 × 3 μ in *P. ferruginosa*) and the longer setae, usually projecting more than 20 μ beyond the basidia.

The further synonymy is in question. There is little doubt that both *Poria superficialis* (Schw.) Cooke and *P. viticola* (Schw.) Cooke were based on the form of this species on hardwoods, but the type specimens of both are sterile, though the setae are like those found in *Fomes tenuis*. Romell studied the types of *P. contigua* (Pers. ex Fries) Karst. and says that they, too, are sterile, and that Fries's idea of *P. contigua* involves a different plant. *Trametes isabellina* Fries is said to be this species also. All of these specific names antedate Karsten's name for the species. Romell, who communicated his conception of these species to me several years ago, regarded all these names as applicable to the same plant.

Some variation exists in the size of the pores in different collections. Specimens on *Vitis* exactly like the type of *Poria viticola*, and on some other hosts as well and even on coniferous substrata, have pores that consistently average only 2 per mm. In other collections they average 3–4 per mm., but all intermediates are found. The color of the pore surface varies from a tan or yellowish brown to dark brown or sometimes almost purplish brown. There is also some variation in the setae; typically, they are long and slender and 5–7 μ in diameter at the broadest portion, and project 25–60 μ beyond the basidia. But it seems impossible to use these dimensions as a criterion of species. In some collections that are alike in all other characters the setae are comparatively short and about the length of those of *P.*

ferruginosa; in some the diameter, measured over the broadest portion, is up to 9 or perhaps 10 μ. Whether it may prove feasible to separate out some of these as different specific units I cannot say, but these variations seem not to be correlated with variations in other characters, so that I am inclined to ascribe them to the great variability of the species. It cannot be denied that my treatment of the species is rather comprehensive. On receipt of a specimen from Romell labeled *P. contigua* Pers., I attempted to segregate from my *Fomes tenuis* collections those with somewhat shorter and broader setae, as in Romell's specimen, where they were uniformly 8–11 μ in diameter. I was not satisfied with my results, however, since intergrading dimensions were found.

Trametes gilvoides seems somewhat different at first sight, but I think it is correctly referred to synonymy here. The setae are long and slender and project 25–50 μ, though they are not so numerous as is usual with this species. The types are sterile, and I think Lloyd's spore record is an error. The hyphae are 2.5–4 μ in diameter.

4b. *Pores averaging 5–8 per mm.* (see also *Pyropolyporus Taxodii*, p. 106)

18. FOMES CONCHATUS (Pers. ex Fries) Gill.

Champ. France, p. 685. 1878

(Figs. 440–442 and Plate 126)

Boletus conchatus Pers., Obs. Myc. 1: 24. 1796.
Polyporus conchatus Pers. ex Fries, Syst. Myc. 1: 376. 1821.
Pyropolyporus conchatus (Pers. ex Fries) Murr., Torrey Bot. Club Bul. 30: 117. 1903.

Sporophore often mostly resupinate, sometimes entirely so, sometimes sessile and then thin and conchate or very rarely ungulate, always hard and woody; pileus 0–7 × 4–12 × 0.2–1.5 cm., grayish brown, yellowish brown, or blackish, sulcate, often moss-covered, not incrusted, rimose only with extreme age, usually uneven, the margin compactly tomentose and rusty yellow or yellowish brown, the tomentum becoming thrown into zones and eventually disappearing; context yellowish brown or darker, 1.5–3 mm. thick, usually showing a narrow black line under the tomentum or in the context;

pore surface yellowish brown (near "clay color" in growing specimens) to dark brown, the tubes 1–2 mm. long each season, indistinctly or not at all stratified, becoming slightly gray within in age, the mouths circular, thin-walled, entire, invisible to the unaided eye, averaging 5–7 per mm.; spores subglobose, smooth, hyaline, rarely brown with age, 4–5(–6) × 3.5–4.5 μ or more globose and about 4.5 μ in diameter; setae sharp-pointed, (4–)6–9(–12) μ in diameter at the base, projecting rather conspicuously to about 18 μ; hyphae simple, brown, the walls only partially thickened, with no cross walls or clamps, 2.5–4 μ in diameter; all parts becoming black in KOH solution.

HABITAT: On dead wood of deciduous trees, rarely on living trees, noted on *Acer, Amelanchier, Betula, Carya, Crataegus, Cydonia, Evonymus, Fagus, Fraxinus, Gleditsia, Juglans, Lonicera, Ostrya, Physocarpus, Populus, Prunus, Pyrus, Rhus, Quercus, Ulmus,* and *Viburnum*; one collection (Ohio, Leeper) said to be on *Tsuga*; reported on *Alnus* (Wis., Dodge [40]) and on *Salix* and *Tilia* (Mich., Kauffman [101]).

DISTRIBUTION: Specimens have been examined from Me., N.H., Vt., Mass., R.I., N.Y., Pa., N.J., Md., W. Va., N.C., Fla., Ohio, Ind., Ill., Mich., Wis., Minn., N. Dak., Iowa, Mo., and Texas; in Canada from New Brunswick, Quebec, Ontario, and Manitoba; reported from Tenn. (Kauffman [100]), Ark. (Swartz [212]), and Mont. (Weir [227])

ILLUSTRATIONS: Fries, Icones Sel. Hym., pl. 185, fig. 1 (as *Fomes salicinus*); Karsten, Icones Sel. Hym. Fenn., fig. 5 (as *F. salicinus*); Overholts, Wash. Univ. Studies 3: pl. 6, fig. 33.

Considerable variation exists in the setae of this species. In adjoining tubes one may find slender setae not more than 4 μ in diameter and larger ones as much as 9 μ in diameter. However, the larger ones predominate, and most of them measure 6–9 μ. In abundance they vary from 3 or 4 to many per pore section. On this point the species can be distinguished from a resupinate condition of *Polyporus gilvus*, since there the setae are more abundant and all of narrow diameter, not more than 6 μ. The spores are more globose, also. That species, furthermore, has larger hyphae in the context, measuring 3–5 μ in diameter. *Fomes densus* is quite similar, too, but attains much greater thickness, is hard and woody, and has pores that average 8–10 per mm. and spores that are smaller and pale brownish. The validity of that species was not recognized until recently, and it is possible that a few of the hosts and distributions recorded above refer to it. *F. pomaceus* may be easily distinguished by the rather numerous cross walls in the context hyphae, as well as by the much more completely imbedded setae and of course, usually, by the substratum.

If *Polyporus salicinus* Fries is adequately represented by Fries's illustration, then it is synonymous with the present species.

I have a single collection in which the spores from marginal tubes are entirely hyaline, whereas those from older tubes are distinctly brown.

In the Allegheny region *Fraxinus* is the more common host. The fungus produces a general delignifying decay of the sapwood. The wood has a rusty appearance as though shot through with brown mycelium, but the general coloration is yellowish. No black lines are present.

19. Fomes torulosus (Pers.) Lloyd

Myc. Notes, Polyp. Issue No. 3: 48. 1910

(Fig. 657 and Plate 127)

Polyporus torulosus Pers., Myc. Eur. 2: 79. 1825.
Polyporus fusco-purpureus Boudier, Soc. Bot. France Bul. 28: 92. 1881.
Trametes rufi-tincta (Berk. & Curt.) Bres., Ann. Mycol. 18: 62. 1920.

Sporophore sessile or somewhat decurrent, corky to somewhat woody in texture; pileus convex or applanate, 2–10 × 2–10 × 0.5–3 cm., yellowish brown to rusty brown or becoming grayish black in age, with a conspicuous though compact rusty tomentum that eventually more or less weathers away, usually irregular though with a velvety feel as long as the tomentum persists; context bright yellow-brown in young plants, darkening with age, soft-corky to firm, 0.5–2 cm. thick; pore surface at first purplish brown, then dark brown, with a smooth velvety feel, the tubes up to 2.5 mm. long, finally in several indistinct layers, decidedly gray within where best developed, the mouths circular, thick-walled, entire, invisible to the unaided eye, averaging 6–8 per mm.; spores ellipsoid to oblong-ellipsoid, often appearing subglobose, smooth, hyaline, 3–4 × 2–3 μ; basidia 4–5 μ in diameter; setae rather abundant, lanceolate, 20–30 × 5–8 μ, projecting up to 20 μ; hyphae mainly brown, simple or nearly so, with somewhat thickened walls, with occasional cross walls but no clamps, 3–4.5 μ in diameter; all parts black in KOH.

HABITAT: On wounded or dying deciduous trees, noted on *Fraxinus*, *Melia*, *Prosopis*, *Quercus*, and *Sassafras*.

DISTRIBUTION: Specimens have been examined from La., Miss., Mo., Ark., and Texas.

ILLUSTRATIONS: Boudier, Icones, pl. 156 (as *Polyporus fuscopurpureus*).

The microscopic characters of this species are exactly those of *Polyporus licnoides* in all points. The species is rare and not well known, and I take it in the sense of Lloyd's determination (115, p. 243) of Edgerton's plants on live oak from Louisiana. In agreement with these microscopically are the larger and thicker specimens of at least three collections made at the base of *Sassafras* trees in the vicinity of St. Louis, Missouri, which were originally determined by Peck as *Fomes Ribis* and described by Spaulding (*Science*, N.S. 26: 479–480. 1907) as causing a destructive heart rot of *Sassafras*. These collections were reported again by Maneval (131, p. 36).

The true identity of the plant has always been a mystery to me. I sent specimens of Missouri plants on *Sassafras* to Bresadola, who eventually referred them to *Trametes rufi-tincta* (by error stating that the substratum was *Gymnocladus dioica*) and redescribed (*Ann. Mycol.* 18: 62. 1920) that species on the basis of my specimens. The same collections have also been otherwise referred. In the Lloyd Herbarium they were filed as *Fomes salicinus*. In my treatment of the Middle Western Polyporaceae (151, p. 50) I referred them to *Polyporus licnoides*. I am not yet satisfied as to the proper specific name. That they are *F. torulosus* cannot be questioned if Edgerton's plants are correctly named. Yet along with thicker specimens that agree in all respects there are thin specimens, almost glabrous, and almost referable to *P. licnoides*. I can only express the hypothesis, therefore, that *F. torulosus* may be a thick form of *P. licnoides*. *P. licnoides* is a common saprophyte in subtropical America. Apparently the plants referred to *F. torulosus* bear a different relation to the host.

The hymenium is the same color as in *Polyporus gilvus*, showing in young specimens the purplish tint so frequently seen in the hymenium of that species.

20. FOMES REPANDUS Overh.

Mycologia 44: 224. 1952

(Figs. 660–661, 670, and Plate 126)

Sporophore perennial, hard and woody, effused-reflexed or more usually nearly or quite resupinate and then broadly effused with a bright rusty-ochraceous margin that may become tumid, black, receding, never more than narrowly reflexed to a pileus length of 1–3 cm.; pileus with surface black and rough from the annual increments, not truly incrusted but the surface layer becoming blackish and hardened, becoming as much as 3 cm. thick where best developed, glabrous, the growing margin narrowly brown; context scanty, less than 0.5 cm. thick, brown, hard and woody; pore surface dark brown to smoky brown, even, the tubes indefinitely stratified to a thickness of 2.5 cm., brown within, hard and woody, the mouths circular, thick-walled, entire, averaging 5–7 per mm.; spores ellipsoid or subglobose, smooth, hyaline, 3–5 μ in diameter; setae few, inconspicuous, projecting up to about 20 μ, short and blunt or at times broadly or narrowly conic, 7–10 μ in diameter; [hyphae rarely branched, thick-walled, with inconspicuous cross walls, 3–5 μ in diameter—J.L.L.].

HABITAT: On dead wood of coniferous trees, noted on *Larix*, *Pinus*, and *Pseudotsuga*.

DISTRIBUTION: Type collected at Upper Priest River, Idaho, July, 1925, by Dr. C. Epling (No. 1751), Overholts Herb. No. 11648; also from Priest River, Idaho, Weir Nos. 8036 and 9547, and Overholts Herb. Nos. 3878 and 4491; from Nordman, Idaho; from Roberts Creek, British Columbia, Mounce (No. 3588); and from Cowichan Lake Forest Exp. Station, British Columbia, Overholts Herb. No. 16592.

Of the five collections at hand, the type collection is the only one with well-developed pileate tendencies. Apparently some investigators regard this species as properly referred to *Fomes spongiosus* Pers. ex Cooke. Romell (187, p. 18) indicates that Persoon, Fries, and Secretan had three different conceptions of *F. spongiosus*, and each idea has some adherents. It seems best, therefore, for the present, to think of that name as a permanent source of confusion and to rename our plant. Specimens at the New York Botanical Garden determined by Bresadola as *F. spongiosus* represent our species, but Romell says Bresadola's conception of *F. spongiosus* is erroneous.

The species differs from *Fomes nigrolimitatus* in the very different setae and spores, as well as in other characters. Where resupinate specimens have been separated from the substratum, the sporophore surface is typically a bright yellow-red or rusty red because of a thin spongy subiculum of that color. Weir distributed specimens of our plant under the name *F. putearius*, although his type collection of that species is not this. See further under *F. nigrolimitatus*, below.

21. FOMES NIGROLIMITATUS (Rom.) Egeland

Magazin for Naturvidenskaberne (Nyt) 52: 135. 1914

(Figs. 399–401, 620, and Plate 126)

Polyporus nigrolimitatus Rom., Arkiv för Bot. 11, 3: 18. 1912.
Fomes putearius Weir, Jour. Agr. Res. 2: 163. 1914.

Sporophore sessile, effused-reflexed or resupinate, soft-corky and flexible when fresh, rigid when dry; pileus applanate or convex, usually quite irregular and with semiconfluent pilei that only partly renew their growth in successive seasons, very light in weight, 0–6 × 2–10 × 0.5–3(–5) cm., tawny brown to tobacco-brown, finally blackish brown or grayish black, soft and tomentose or the rusty tomentum finally weathering more compact and thrown into furrows and ridges, the margin frequently very obtuse; context tawny to dark tawny, soft and spongy in fresh plants, becoming punky or soft-corky in drying, 0.3–1(–3) cm. thick, with one or more very narrow black lines separating the context (or the subiculum) into two or more layers; pore surface gray-brown or pale tan to dark brown in age, the tubes 2–6 mm. long each season, never markedly stratified and apparently only infrequently perennial, whitish or isabelline within the older layers, the mouths circular to subangular, rather thick-walled, entire, averaging 5–6 per mm., scarcely visible to the unaided eye; spores cylindric, hyaline, straight, 6–7 × 2–2.5 μ; setae rather numerous but not abundant, 5–9 μ in diameter, projecting 12–20 μ, slender-pointed; hyphae brown, with walls only partly if at all thickened, with occasional cross walls but no clamps, 3–4.5 μ in diameter; imbedded setal hyphae absent from both trama and context. (Compare no. 17, *Fomes tenuis*, and no. 20, *F. repandus*.)

HABITAT: On dead wood of coniferous trees, noted on *Abies*, *Larix*, *Picea*, *Pseudotsuga*, *Taxus*, and *Tsuga*.

DISTRIBUTION: Specimens have been examined from Colo., Mont., Idaho, Ore., Wash., Calif., and Alaska; in Canada from British Columbia and Vancouver Island.

ILLUSTRATIONS: Baxter, Mich. Acad. Sci. Arts and Letters Papers 17: pl. 45; Weir, Jour. Agr. Res. 2: pl. 9 (as *Fomes putearius*).

This species was only rather recently recognized as occurring in our American flora, but it seems to be not uncommon in the northern Rocky Mountains. It is sent with nearly every collection which comes from that region. Because of the poorly developed specimens usually found, it is likely to be easily confused with *Poria Weirii* Murr., *P. ferrugineo-fusca* Karst., and *Fomes tenuis*. The first two of these have imbedded in their context and trama brown setal hyphae, which are best observed in longitudinal sections of the tubes mounted in lactic acid. The setal hyphae in *P. Weirii* are very conspicuous, reaching a diameter of 8–9 μ, and are often somewhat incrusted. In *P. ferrugineo-fusca* they are much less conspicuous, and are best recognized by the nature of the hymenial setae, which are easily seen to be the ends of such hyphae. The species differs from *F. tenuis* in having a conspicuous context (subiculum in resupinate specimens), in producing a well-marked pocket rot rather than a general delignifying decay of the wood, and in the fact that one or more definite, often quite irregular, black lines, visible under a lens, separate the context into two or more unequal layers. Romell says in his original description that the name "alludes to the fact that each new stratum of the subiculum is separated from the older one by a thin, black layer, which appears as a fine sharp black line on a vertical section of the fungus." Such successive lines are not present in any collections I have seen.

The relation of this species to *Fomes spongiosus* (Pers.) Cooke is uncertain. Romell states that his species is not *Polyporus spongiosus* Pers. according to a specimen in the Persoon Herbarium, and, as is noted in the discussion under *F. repandus*, he believes that Bresadola's conception of *F. spongiosus* is erroneous. Bresadola's specimens sent to Murrill (145, p. 21) are here referred to *F. repandus*. Murrill's remark that Weir's *F. putearius* agrees with Bresadola's specimens of *F. spongiosus* seems to be true, for at Beltsville, Maryland, a fragment of a resupinate sporophore marked as from the type collection of *F. putearius* is another species, *F. repandus,* as noted under that species. For the present, therefore, I prefer to retain Romell's name, although if it should be shown that *F. nigrolimitatus* and *F. spongiosus* are synonymous, and there is little in Persoon's description to indicate that they may not be, the Persoonian name would of course have precedence.

Weir's material of *Fomes putearius,* both the types at Beltsville and specimens distributed by him to the New York Botanical Garden and to myself, is a mixture of species. The resupinate fungus (in my herbarium) yields ellipsoid or subglobose hyaline spores 4–5 × 3–4 μ, and this is the basis of my report (155, p. 127) on the spores of that species. Shope (200, p. 381) correctly reports *F. nigrolimitatus* as producing a pocket rot of the wood, but was misled by my erroneous spore record for *F. putearius* into disregarding Hubert's previously expressed opinion (82, p. 528, legend for pl. 1; 87, p. 381) that *F. putearius* and *F. nigrolimitatus* are synonyms. A specimen in another box at Beltsville, labeled as containing the type of *F. putearius,* is identical with *F. nigrolimitatus* as far as one can judge, though it is entirely sterile. Black lines are present in the context.

The typical decay stages produced by this fungus show the formation of conspicuous pockets 1–2 cm. long and 0.3–0.6 cm. wide in the heartwood. These pockets are lined with white cellulose fibers, so that the appearance is much like that produced by *Fomes Pini,* except that the pockets are much larger (221).

3b. *Spores sometimes or always brownish to brown* (see also no. 18, *Fomes conchatus,* and *F. senex,* p. 106)

22. Fomes Pini (Thore ex Fries) Karst.

Bidr. Finl. Nat. Folk 37: 79. 1882

(Figs. 392–395 and Plate 126)

Boletus Pini Thore, Chloris Dept. Landes, p. 487. 1803.
Boletus Pini Brot., Flora Lusit. 2: 468. 1804.
Daedalea Pini Brot. ex Fries, Syst. Myc. 1: 336. 1821.
Trametes Pini Thore ex Fries, Epicr. Syst. Myc., p. 489. 1836–1838.
Porodaedalea Pini (Thore ex Fries) Murr., Torrey Bot. Club Bul. 32: 367. 1905.
Daedalea vorax Harkness, Pacific Rural Press 17ᐧ 49. 1879.

Sporophore sessile or decurrent on the substratum, hard and woody; pileus applanate to convex or more typically ungulate, 6–15 × 4–25 × 1–15 cm., at first tawny and with elevated zones of appressed tomentum, becoming glabrous and blackish, the surface cracking or becoming rough and irregular though remaining tomentose and rusty brown toward the margin; context not more than 5 mm. thick, tawny or ochraceous tawny, woody; pore surface ochraceous orange to brown, the tubes 2–6 mm. long each season, the mouths rounded or angular to sinuous and daedaloid, rather thick-walled, entire, averaging 2–3 per mm. or in poroid forms 4–5 per mm.; spores globose or subglobose, hyaline or pale brown, 4–6 × 3.5–5 μ; basidia 5–6 μ in diameter; setae abundant, sharp-pointed, brown, extending 15–30 μ beyond the basidia, 7–15 μ in diameter; hyphae simple, brown, the walls thin or only partially thickened, with no cross walls or clamps, 3–6 μ in diameter; all parts black in KOH solution.

HABITAT: Usually on living or fallen trunks of coniferous trees, noted on *Abies, Larix, Picea, Pinus, Pseudotsuga, Thuja*, and *Tsuga*; recorded also on *Chamaecyparis* and *Libocedrus*; rarely on hardwoods, noted on *Betula* and *Crataegus*; reported on *Acer* (Vt., Percival [165]).

DISTRIBUTION: Specimens have been examined from Me., N.H., Vt., Mass., N.Y., Pa., N.J., Del., Md., Va., N.C., Fla., Ala., Miss., Tenn., Ky., Ohio, Ind., Minn., Iowa, N. Mex., Utah, Colo., Wyo., Mont., Idaho, Ore., Wash., Calif., and Alaska; in Canada from New Brunswick, Quebec, Ontario, Manitoba, Alberta, and British Columbia; reported from Ga. (Graves [61]), La. and Ill. (Owens [160]), Mich. (Kauffman [105]), Wis. (Dodge [40]), Minn. and W. Va. (Percival [165]), S. Dak. (Brenckle [25]), Kans. (Bartholomew [4]), and Ark. (Swartz [212]).

ILLUSTRATIONS: Abbot, Vermont Agr. Exp. Sta. Bul. 191: pl. 3 (as *Trametes*); Boudier, Icones, pl. 161 (as *Trametes*); Lloyd, Synop. Fomes, figs. 608–609; Meinecke, Forest Tree Dis. Calif. Nev., pls. 4–5 (as *Trametes*); Percival, N. Y. State Coll. Forestry Tech. Pub. 40: fig. 6.; Pilát, Soc. Mycol. France Bul. 49: pl. 23 (as *Xanthochrous*).

This is the fungus well known in the literature of forest pathology as *Trametes Pini*. Without doubt, it causes a greater timber loss through decay of the heartwood of living trees than does any other fungus. It grows on nearly every species of conifer important as a lumber tree (except the cedars and the cypress), and in only a few of its host species are its ravages equalled or excelled by any other fungus. For example, Boyce (21) remarks that if the Douglas fir of the Pacific Northwest were free from this one defect "it would take its place with the pines as a sound tree." The decay produced is best known as "conch rot" (22, pp. 21–24; 83, pp. 13–20; 215, pp. 31–40) and is a delignifying decay of the pocket-forming type, the small elliptical pockets, 3–10 × 1–3 mm., being lined with white cellulose fibers that give the decayed wood a speckled appearance (1; 20, pl. 2 [as *Trametes*]; 22; 23, pp. 23–26; 43, p. 74 and pl. 30 [as *Trametes*]; 56; 87, pp. 399–411). Usually it is confined to the heartwood of the tree, but in the less resinous hosts it occurs also in the sapwood. It may at times be only a butt rot, but typically it is a trunk rot. Abbott (1) is of the opinion that in Vermont 2 per cent of the timber that reaches the mill is rendered worthless and 9 per cent of milled timber is reduced in value one half by the presence of this defect. There is no distinction to be made between the decays produced by this species and its variety.

Percival (165) discusses at length the biology of the species. Owens treats this fungus in two recent papers (159, 160). His first paper deals with the gross morphology of the sporophores, in an attempt to discover differences that might be correlated with host. Concerned only with the species as it occurs in the Pacific Northwest, he finds that on *Abies grandis* Lindl. the sporophores are nearly always of the thin, shell-shaped type that I have consistently referred to var. *Abietis*, although that variety is by no means confined to *Abies* hosts, as I have previously shown (150). I have treated other points relating to Owens' first paper in the same article. His second paper deals with the cultural characteristics of the species, and he finds that the growth rate of the western form of the species on *Abies* also differs from that of cultures originating from other hosts. Since here again the form is evidently var. *Abietis*, my contention that this variety may be recognized as a taxonomic unit is supported. Owens is apparently of the opinion, however, that the recognition should be by cultural characters, which would exclude from the variety many forms which, morphologically, are duplicates of the slow-growing form but which occur on other hosts. I am quite convinced that such a separation is not defensible. To be of any value taxonomically in this group the variants must be named, if at all, on morphological grounds. There is no objection, of course, to attempts to correlate morphological and physiological characters. Even though the variety as here recognized is not constant in gross characters, and grades into the more robust type, it may oftentimes be desirable to have a designation for it.

My earlier statement (150) that var. *Abietis* is usually an annual form of the species is erroneous. It perennates (ordinarily, at least) for several years, but does not reach the advanced ages often shown in the more robust form. Owens does not appear to have been familiar with my article, nor with a statement made many years previously by Meinecke (132, p. 43) that the host seems to exercise an effect on the shape of the sporophores of this species.

Hepting and Chapman (70) discuss the importance of this fungus in shortleaf and loblolly pine stands in Arkansas and Texas, and Haddow (63) discusses the history of the species, its host range, and its other features. In another paper Haddow (64) gives an extended description of various phases of the disease. He remarks also on the scarcity of sporophores on living infected trees and finds that this species fruits much more abundantly on dead and down trees and on the larger slash. This comment agrees with my own observations, especially on spruce. When the sporophores are on living trees they are usually, if not always, of the larger and more perennial type—at least they are not typical of var. *Abietis*.

Var. Abietis (Karst.) Overh.

Wash. Univ. Studies 3: 63. 1915

(Fig. 387)

Fomes Abietis Karst., Bidr. Finl. Nat. Folk 37: 242. 1882.
*Tr[ametes] Pini *Tr. Abietis* Karst., Finl. Basidsv., p. 336. 1889.
Polyporus piceinus Peck, N. Y. State Mus. Ann. Rept. 42: 25. 1889.

Sporophore typically effused-reflexed, sometimes sessile, rather thin and applanate or entirely resupinate; pileus 1–5 × 1–7 × 0.3–1 cm., tawny or russet tawny, the immediate margin sometimes brighter-colored, zonate with elevated ridges of tomentum, grayish black or brownish black with age toward the base; context colored as in the species, 1–3 mm. thick, separated from the tomentum by a narrow black line (as seen with a hand lens) that later becomes the cuticular layer when the tomentum disappears; pore surface typically ochraceous tawny; spores, setae, and hyphae as in the species. (Compare no. 17, *Fomes tenuis*.)

HABITAT AND DISTRIBUTION: About that of the species, with a collection recorded on *Taxus* and with Conn., D.C., and Mich. as additional stations.

ILLUSTRATIONS: Lloyd, Synop. Fomes, fig. 610 (as *Trametes piceina*); von Schrenk, U. S. Dept. Agr. Veg. Phys. Path. Bul. 25: pl. 12 (as *T. Pini* f. *Abietis*).

The relationships of the variety to the species have been discussed by me in a previous paper (150, pp. 721–724) and under the species, above. The narrow black line separating tomentum from context is less evident in the species than in the variety because of the fact that a more persistent tomentum is present in the variety. As the sporophores age the pubescence becomes thinner, and in the species it soon weathers away entirely, whereupon the black line becomes the cuticular layer of the pileus.

23. FOMES DENSUS Lloyd[1]

Synop. Fomes, p. 245. 1915

(Figs. 431–432 and Plate 126)

Sporophore largely or entirely resupinate, occasionally narrowly reflexed, very hard, heavy, and woody; pileus usually scarcely more than the result of receding growth from year to year as the fruiting body grows downward on the underside of the substratum, never reflexed more than 2.5 cm., glabrous, becoming blackish, not incrusted, the margin usually bright ochraceous orange or orange-yellow and somewhat tomentose, zonate or furrowed, rough and irregular; context practically none, the entire inner brown substance composed of the tubes, which attain a total depth of 0.5–5 cm.; pore surface yellow-brown to dark brown (near "Sudan brown"), the tubes 2–4 mm. long each season, rather indistinctly stratified, sometimes in 20 layers or more, dark yellow-brown within, the mouths circular, thick-walled, entire, averaging 7–10 per mm., invisible to the unaided eye; spores minute, subglobose or broadly ellipsoid, pale brownish at maturity, 3–3.5 μ in diameter or 3 $\times$ 2.5 μ; basidia 4–5 μ in diameter; setae projecting conspicuously, 16–20 $\times$ (4–)6–7 μ; hyphae brown, simple, with no cross walls or clamps, 3 μ in diameter; all parts black with

[1] [For another interpretation of this species see *Mycologia* 44: 231. 1952.—J.L.L.]

KOH solution. (Compare no. 14, *Fomes igniarius* var. *laevigatus*, and no. 18, *F. conchatus*.)

HABITAT: On the lower side of old logs, noted on *Aesculus*, *Carya*, *Fagus*, *Fraxinus*, *Quercus*, and *Ulmus*.

DISTRIBUTION: Specimens have been examined from Va., La., Tenn., Ohio, Ind., and Mo.; reported from Iowa by Lloyd.

This species is likely to be mistaken for a thick form of *Fomes conchatus*, which it resembles in coloration but from which it differs markedly in the spores, the thickness attained by the fruiting body, and the somewhat more slender setae. It is a very hard, heavy species. I have about a dozen collections, with one sporophore reaching a thickness of 5 cm., the others somewhat less. It grows on the lower surface of old logs, and in most cases the pileus is scarcely more than the accumulated thicknesses of successive years' growth laid down one beneath the other, the whole structure pendent from the lower side of the log. In one collection, however, there is a definitely reflexed pileus about 2.5 cm. long, so that I feel that the species belongs in *Fomes*, although it has probably been described in *Poria*.

24. FOMES LANGLOISII (Murr.) Sacc. & D. Sacc.

Syll. Fung. 17: 118. 1905
(Fig. 406 and Plate 126)

Pyropolyporus Langloisii Murr., Torrey Bot. Club Bul. 30: 118. 1903.

Sporophore sessile, very hard and woody; pileus thin, applanate, often partially overgrown with moss, 4–12 × 5–12 × 0.2–1.5 cm., at first brown and compactly tomentose, in age becoming glabrous and blackish except perhaps on the growing margin, not incrusted, strongly but narrowly zonate-furrowed on the very thin margin; context very thin, 1–10 mm. thick, golden brown; pore surface yellowish brown, the tubes 2–4 mm. long each season, the mouths minute, invisible to the unaided eye, subcircular, thin-walled, entire, averaging 6–8 per mm.; spores minute, subglobose, smooth, pale yellowish brown in KOH, 2.5–3 μ in diameter or 3 × 2.5 μ; basidia 3–5 μ in diameter; setae none; hyphae brown, simple, the walls partially thickened, some with occasional cross walls but no clamps, 3–5 μ in diameter. (Compare no. 18, *Fomes conchatus*, and no. 34, *F. Ribis*.)

HABITAT: On dead or dying *Crataegus*, perhaps also on other hosts.

DISTRIBUTION: Specimens have been examined only from La.

It scarcely seems possible that this can be different from *Fomes densus*, in spite of the very thin pileus, the strictly sessile habit, and the absence of setae. Points in favor of the identity of the two species are the hard, indurated character of the plant, the very thin context, and the highly characteristic spores, entirely unlike those of any other species. Murrill reported the spores as hyaline, but, as was correctly observed by Lloyd, there is a slight but distinct rusty-yellow tinge to them when seen under the microscope. I have not made an exhaustive search for setae, but in view of the considerable variation in setae in other species, e.g., *F. igniarius*, it would not be surprising if they were shown to be present.

Lloyd's record (115, p. 282) that this species is identical with *Fomes Ribis* does not seem probable, although the two are not always easily separated.

25. FOMES EVERHARTII (Ell. & Gall.) von Schrenk & Spaulding

U. S. Dept. Agr. Pl. Ind. Bul. 149: 48. 1909

(Figs. 402–403, 425, 593, 597, and Plate 127)

Mucronoporus Everhartii Ell. & Gall., Jour. Mycol. 5: 141. 1889.
Pyropolyporus Everhartii (Ell. & Gall.) Murr., Torr. Bot. Club Bul. 30: 114. 1903.

Sporophore sessile, very hard and woody; pileus convex or ungulate, 2–15 × 4–36 × 2–15 cm., at first uniformly brown, becoming grayish black or black behind but remaining brown on the slightly tomentose margin, not incrusted, sulcate, rough and rimose with age; context rusty brown, woody, 1–4 cm. thick; pore surface brown, the tubes 3–6 mm. long each season, the mouths subcircular to subangular, rather thin-walled, entire, averaging 4–6 per mm.; spores subglobose to globose, chestnut-brown in KOH, 4–6 × 3.5–4.5 μ or 4–5 μ broad; setae sometimes quite abundant, projecting 10–22 μ, 15–35 × 5–12 μ; hyphae brown, simple, straight, with cross walls in the lighter-colored ones but no clamps, 2–5 μ in diameter. (Compare no. 14, *Fomes igniarius*; no. 27, *F. dependens*; and no. 35, *F. rimosus*.)

HABITAT: Usually on living trunks of *Quercus*, occasionally on logs, also recorded on *Carya, Fagus, Juglans, Liriodendron, Oxydendron*, and *Ulmus*; reported on *Betula* and *Prosopis* (Hedgcock [66]), on *Populus* (Mont., Weir [227]), and on *Pyrus* (Mo., Maneval [131]).

DISTRIBUTION: Specimens have been examined from N.H., Mass., Conn., R.I., N.Y., Pa., N.J., Del., Md., Va., W. Va., N.C., Ga., Ala., Tenn., Ky., Ohio, Ind., Ill., Mich., Wis., Minn., Iowa, Mo., Kans., and Nebr.; in Canada from Ontario; reported from Ark. (Swartz [212]) and Mont. (Weir [227]).

ILLUSTRATIONS: Hirt, Mycologia 22: pl. 25; Neuman, Wis. Geol. and Nat. Hist. Survey Bul. 33: pl. 7, fig. 26; Overholts, Wash. Univ. Studies 3: pl. 6, fig. 34.

In the Eastern and Middle Western states *Quercus* is the usual host, although one collection is recorded from New Jersey and one from New York on *Fagus*, as well as one from Ohio on *Liriodendron*.

Old specimens become very thick, ungulate, and rimose and look somewhat different superficially from the browner and more applanate or convex young specimens. Perhaps larger sizes than are indicated here are attained at times.

As in *Fomes dependens*, the setae vary considerably. In some specimens they are short and almost conical, all individuals being less than 20 μ long and greatly enlarged at the bases; in others they are larger and longer, up to 35 μ long and in exceptional cases up to 12 μ in diameter.

Fomes Everhartii is a heart-rotting organism in the trunks of living trees, and is of considerable importance. The decay produced is extensive and of the delignifying type, with well-developed broad brown zones indicating the limits of serious rot (6; 219, p. 48).

26. FOMES PRAERIMOSUS (Murr.) Sacc. & D. Sacc.

Syll. Fung. 17: 117. 1905
(Fig. 391 and Plate 126)

Pyropolyporus praerimosus Murr., Torrey Bot. Club Bul. 30: 115. 1903.

Sporophore sessile, ungulate, hard and woody; pileus 7–12 × 10–20 × 8–12 cm., brown and even the first year, blackish and very rimose with age, sometimes furrowed, glabrous except for the compact tomentum on the growing obtuse margin; context rusty brown or dark

yellowish brown, very thin and practically disappearing in old sporophores, always less than 1 cm. thick, hard and woody, sometimes with
a small central core of differently textured tissue somewhat similar to
the core of *Polyporus dryophilus*; pore surface "honey yellow" then
"tawny-olive," the tubes finally occupying the entire thickness of the
sporophore, indistinctly stratified, 2–7 mm. long each season, finally
yellowish-stuffed, the mouths circular to subangular, thick-walled,
entire, barely visible to the unaided eye, averaging 5–6 per mm.;
spores broadly ellipsoid or subglobose, smooth, bright golden yellow
in KOH, 4.5–5.5 × 3.5–4.5 μ; basidial layer bright rusty orange in
KOH; setae scattered, narrow-conic or with a bulbously enlarged
base, 24–40 × 8–12 μ; context hyphae brown, the walls partially
thickened, with cross walls in a few lighter-colored ones but no
clamps, 2–5 μ in diameter.

HABITAT: Growing from wounds in living trees, noted on *Juglans*
and *Quercus*.

DISTRIBUTION: Specimens have been examined from Texas, N.
Mex., and Ariz.

Although later listed by Murrill (145, p. 14) and regarded by
others as synonymous with *Fomes Everhartii*, this species is certainly
distinct enough to warrant a designation of some sort.   Superficially,
it may be hard to separate from *F. Everhartii* except by its lighter-
colored pore surface.   Internally, the much paler spores and the
bright-colored basidial layer are distinct aids.   The pore surface of
F. Everhartii is a rich dark brown, near "warm sepia" or "bister,"
the spores are chestnut-brown in KOH, and the basidial layer is
colorless.

27. FOMES DEPENDENS (Murr.) Sacc. & Trott.

Syll. Fung. 21: 292. 1912

(Figs. 434, 443, and Plate 126)

Pyropolyporus dependens Murr., North Amer. Flora 9: 106. 1908.
Fulvifomes dependens Murr., Tropical Polypores, p. 89. 1915.

Sporophore sessile or attached by the vertex, very hard and
woody; pileus dimidiate to irregular, ungulate or more rarely applanate, 2–8 × 3–13 × 2–10 cm., early becoming very black and very
rimose, marked with many narrow furrows; margin thick, often

rounded; context dark sordid brown ("argus brown"), 0.5–2 cm. thick, hard and almost horny; pore surface deep rich brown, often with a silky luster, 1–8 cm. thick, the tubes concolorous with the context within, not distinctly stratified, adding 2–3 mm. each year, the mouths circular, thick-walled, entire, barely visible to the unaided eye, averaging 5–7 per mm.; spores broadly ellipsoid or subglobose, smooth, brown, 3.5–4.5 × 3–3.5 μ or 4–6 μ in diameter; setae usually present, not abundant but readily demonstrated, sharp-pointed, 4–6 μ in diameter; context hyphae brown, thick-walled, simple, with no cross walls or clamps, 3–5 μ in diameter. (Compare no. 25, *Fomes Everhartii*, and no. 35, *F. rimosus*.)

HABITAT: On dead wood or from wounds in living trees, noted only on *Lysiloma*, but undoubtedly occurring on other hosts.

DISTRIBUTION: Specimens have been examined only from Fla.

ILLUSTRATIONS: Lloyd, Synop. Fomes, fig. 597.

Spore characters of brown-spored species of *Fomes* are likely to be confusing, and specific lines must not be drawn too closely. For example, the type of *F. dependens* shows spores that are very pale brown and subglobose, 3.5–4.5 × 3–3.5 μ. In another collection, surely referable here, they are dark brown (as in *F. rimosus*), globose, and 5.5–6.5 μ in diameter. In yet another, otherwise similar, they are dark brown and 3.5–4.5 μ in diameter. Murrill apparently met the same difficulty. In his original description of this species in *North American Flora* he says "spores . . . 3 μ," but in his *Tropical Polypores* (142) he gives them as 4–7 μ. The species is very close to *F. praerimosus*, in which the spores are golden brown in KOH and the setae 8–12 μ in diameter. The single collection from Florida has spores 6–7 × 4.5–6 μ.

When specimens of *Fomes dependens* are carefully compared with specimens of *F. Everhartii* on *Quercus* in the United States, it seems hardly possible that the present species can be more than a tropical form of *F. Everhartii*. However, some collections, apparently without setae, are extremely difficult to separate from *F. rimosus*. *F. dependens* seems, therefore, to be properly regarded as an intermediate. Although it was originally published as asetulose, and stated to be so by Lloyd, the type collection, as well as others, contains setae, which are sometimes fully as abundant as in *F. Everhartii*. In other collections I have failed to see them in the sections I have made.

The essential characters of the species appear to be the very black and very rimose pileus, usually growing pendent, the horny nature of the context tissue, the chestnut-brown spores, and the few, small setae, only 15–22 μ long.

28. FOMES EXTENSUS (Lév.) Cooke[1]

Grevillea 14: 18. 1885

(Figs. 367–368, 595, and Plate 126)

Polyporus (Apus) extensus Lév., Ann. Sci. Nat. Bot. III, 5: 129. 1846.

Sporophore sessile, very hard and rigid; pileus thin and applanate, dimidiate to irregular, 4–20 × 5–20(–30) × 0.4–3 cm., tawny brown to dark brown or blackish, zonate or furrowed, at first short velvety-tomentose, later becoming glabrous on the older portions, at maturity the surface layers sometimes much hardened and indurated but scarcely incrusted, the margin thin, entire; context yellow-brown to rusty, woody, 3–10 mm. thick; pore surface yellow-brown, smooth, often velvety, perennial, becoming 3 cm. thick or perhaps more, the tubes in fairly distinct or quite indistinct layers, 1–2.5 mm. long each year, the mouths circular, very thick-walled and entire, averaging 6–8 per mm., invisible to the unaided eye; spores broadly ellipsoid or subglobose, hyaline or distinctly tinted, smooth, 3.5–5 μ in diameter or 4–5 × 3.5–4 μ; setae present, conspicuous, rather abundant, many or most with hooked or curved tips, 25–40 × 8–11 μ; context hyphae brown, thick-walled, simple, with no cross walls or clamps, 3.5–4 μ in diameter.

HABITAT: On dead wood or from wounds in living trees, noted only on *Quercus* and *Castanea*.

DISTRIBUTION: Specimens have been examined only from Fla. and Tenn.

It should perhaps be noted that none of my specimens agree microscopically, especially with reference to the setae, with a fragment said to be of the type that I examined in the Lloyd Herbarium many years ago. The setae there were shorter, broader, and definitely did not have curved tips.

In all the specimens I refer here a considerable proportion of the setae have curved or hooked apices, and in this character *Fomes*

[1] [For another interpretation of this species see *Mycologia*, 44: 232. 1952.—J.L.L.]

extensus differs from all species from the United States with which it is likely to be confused. In one collection I find only colorless spores, but in all others both colorless and brown-tinted spores are present. There is a fine lot of sporophores of this fungus at the New York Botanical Garden, although apparently it is not at all abundant on the mainland of the United States. Dr. Hesler sent me two collections from Tennessee that I cannot otherwise refer. One collection was made at Gatlinburg and the other in Cades Cove, in the Great Smoky Mountains National Park.

According to Long (122) this fungus occurs on *Exothea, Lysiloma,* and *Taxodium* in Florida. In these hosts it produces a white pocket rot of the heartwood, the pockets being 5–20 mm. long or, in *Taxodium,* as much as 4–8 cm. long.

2b. *Setae absent*
3a. *Spores hyaline*

29. FOMES ROBUSTUS Karst.

Finl. Basidsv., p. 467. 1889
(Figs. 362, 371–373, 669, and Plate 126)

Fomitiporia dryophila Murr., North Amer. Flora 9: 8. 1907.
Fomitiporia tsugina Murr., North Amer. Flora 9: 9. 1907.
Pyropolyporus Bakeri Murr., North Amer. Flora 9: 104. 1908.
Pyropolyporus Abramsianus Murr., Western Polypores, p. 26. 1915.

Sporophore small and nodulose-sessile or larger and sessile but not imbricate, often resupinate, woody; pileus 1–13 × 3–20 × 2–12 cm., convex, ungulate or hemispherical, not incrusted, at first even, in age considerably rimose, gray-brown or yellow-brown on the margin, becoming grayish black or blackish behind with age, applanate specimens often furrowed, the margin rounded and smooth, at first very compactly tomentose, elsewhere glabrous; context shining bright yellow-brown (between "cinnamon-buff" and "clay color"), drying hard and woody, somewhat zonate, 1–4 cm. thick; pore surface yellowish brown or grayish brown, the tubes in old specimens becoming distinctly layered, each year's growth 3–10 mm. long, whitish-stuffed with age, the mouths circular, thick-walled, entire, averaging 4–6 per mm., scarcely or barely visible to the unaided eye; spores globose or nearly so, smooth, hyaline, 6–8 μ in diameter or 6–7.5 × 5–6 μ;

basidia 8–12 μ in diameter; setae none, or rare in occasional specimens; context hyphae simple, brown, with walls slightly or partially thickened, with no cross walls or clamps, 3–6 μ in diameter; tramal hyphae with rather strongly thickened walls, 3–4.5 μ in diameter; all parts quickly black in KOH solution.

HABITAT: On dead snags or on living trunks of deciduous trees, noted on *Acer, Betula, Cereus, Eucalyptus, Juglans, Opuntia, Pittosporum, Quercus, Salix,* and *Syringa*; also on wood of coniferous trees, noted on *Abies, Picea, Pinus, Pseudotsuga, Taxus, Thuja,* and *Tsuga.*

DISTRIBUTION: Specimens have been examined from Me., N.H., Vt., N.Y., Pa., N.J., Del., Md., D.C., Va., W. Va., N.C., S.C., Fla., La., Ohio, Wis., Minn., Mo., Texas, Ariz., Colo., Idaho, Ore., Wash., Calif., and Alaska; in Canada from Quebec and British Columbia; reported from Mich. (Povah) and Iowa (Wolf [234]).

ILLUSTRATIONS: Lloyd, Synop. Fomes, fig. 589; Neuman, Wis. Geol. and Nat. Hist. Survey Bul. 33: pl. 7, fig. 27 (as *Fomes Bakeri*); Overholts, Mycologia 12: pl. 9 (as *F. Bakeri*); Pilát, Soc. Mycol. France Bul. 49: pl. 16, fig. 1 (as *Phellinus*).

The characteristic features of this species consist of the bright-colored and shining context, the definitely stratified tubes, the large globose hyaline spores, the large basidia, and the absence, usually, of setae. In one American collection a few isolated setae were seen, and I have a small specimen from Romell in which they can be found, but ordinarily I have failed to find them. *Fomes Calkinsii* is a closely related species, but it differs in the more reddish pileus with some incrustation, the indefinitely layered tubes, the smaller pores, and so on.

Fomes igniarius and *F. Everhartii* are somewhat similar, but both have setae, the tubes are not definitely layered, and, in addition, *F. Everhartii* has brown spores.

The inclusion of the two cactus genera (*Cereus* and *Opuntia*) as hosts for this fungus is possible through the kindness of R. W. Davidson. It certainly was a surprise to have them, but the fungus present cannot be otherwise referred.

The specimens I have seen from the Pacific Coast are less developed and usually nodulose-sessile, as in the types of *Pyropolyporus Abramsianus*, but in all other respects they resemble the plant as we find it in the Middle West and in the East, especially on *Betula lenta* L. and *B. nigra* L., which are its usual hosts. On all its coniferous substrata it usually grows nearly or entirely resupinate, and occasionally does so when it occurs on *Quercus*. I described and illustrated this species in an earlier paper (*Mycologia* 12: 136–137 and pl. 9. 1920) under the name *Fomes Bakeri*.

I am now quite satisfied that *Fomes Hartigii* (Allesch.) Sacc. & Trav., as the name has been used in this country, is the same species. I have two or three collections from the Pacific Northwest that are sterile, and members of the Division of Forest Pathology in that section have been designating such plants *F. Hartigii*. These collections are not sufficiently different in any of their characters to warrant separation. And this in spite of Lohwag's recent paper (*Ann. Mycol.* 35: 339–349. 1937) in which he attempts to show that they are different. Perhaps he is dealing with another fungus. Hartig's definite opinion that the two are different need carry no weight, for, as Lohwag brings out, Hartig did not know *F. robustus*, but referred all his specimens of that species to *F. igniarius*.

The decay produced is a whitish or pale-yellowish delignifying rot, apparently of both heartwood and sapwood.

30. FOMES TEXANUS (Murr.) Hedgcock & Long

Mycologia 4: 112. 1912
(Figs. 369–370 and Plate 127)

Pyropolyporus texanus Murr., North Amer. Flora 9: 104. 1908.

Sporophore sessile, rather woody; pileus dimidiate, ungulate, 3–6 × 4–10 × 2–10 cm., very young specimens yellowish brown with a very short tomentum, soon dark brown and glabrous but remaining yellow-brown and tomentose on the rounded growing margin, in age dark brown then dark wood-brown or somewhat blackish and eventually quite imbricate-rimose, not incrusted, more or less irregularly furrowed by the annual growth; context rather bright yellow-brown and subshining in younger plants, somewhat darker in old ones, 0.7–2.5 cm. thick, woody; pore surface gray-brown to dark brown, the tubes 2.5 mm. long each season, rather distinctly stratified in several to many layers, the mouths subcircular to subangular, rather thick-walled, entire, averaging 4–6 per mm., barely visible to the unaided eye; spores globose at maturity, ovoid when young, thin-walled, hyaline, 7–10 μ in diameter; basidia inflated, 10–12 μ in diameter; setae none; hyphae red-brown in KOH solution, with only slightly thickened walls, with no cross walls or clamps, 4–6 μ in diameter.

HABITAT: On living trunks of *Juniperus*.

DISTRIBUTION: Specimens have been examined from Texas, N. Mex., and Ariz.

ILLUSTRATIONS: Hedgcock and Long, Mycologia 4: pl. 64, figs. 2–3, and pl. 65, figs. 1, 4, 7.

Lloyd (115, p. 242) likens this species to *Fomes igniarius* and *F. pomaceus*, but I see little resemblance to either. It is much more similar to *F. robustus* and, indeed, may be only a small, much more rimose form of that species. The spore records (Lloyd and Murrill) previously published are in error. I was unable to find spores in the type collection, but obtained them from specimens sent me by Dr. W. H. Long. The mature basidia I have certainly seen are in all cases only bisterigmate. They are unusually large and inflated and generally have a large oil globule.

The fungus produces a soft yellowish stringy rot in the heartwood of the living trees. The springwood is mostly affected, exhibiting a marked "cup-shake" type of decay in which the annual rings easily separate (67).

31. FOMES CALKINSII (Murr.) Sacc. & D. Sacc.

Syll. Fung. 17: 119. 1905
(Figs. 439, 445, and Plate 125)

Pyropolyporus Calkinsii Murr., Torrey Bot. Club Bul. 30: 113. 1903.

Sporophore sessile, hard and woody; pileus convex to ungulate, dimidiate, 3–13 × 3–13 × 3–7 cm., typically reddish coated over with black, but sometimes grayish black except for some reddish stains and glabrous except for the yellow-brown, rather obtuse, finely tomentose margin, the covering becoming hard and horny to form a rather indistinctly marked crust, becoming considerably furrowed at times and smooth or in some cases somewhat rimose; context hard, yellow-brown, 1–3 cm. thick; pore surface brown or yellow-brown, the tubes indistinctly stratified, 2–6 mm. long each season, the mouths circular, thick-walled, entire, invisible to the unaided eye, averaging 6–8 per mm.; spores globose, smooth, hyaline, 5–6 μ in diameter; basidia 8–10 μ in diameter; setae none; hyphae straight, brown, the walls partially thickened, with no cross walls or clamps, 3–4.5 μ in diameter; all parts black in KOH solution.

HABITAT: On living deciduous trees, noted only on *Fagus* and *Quercus*; perhaps sometimes on dead wood.

DISTRIBUTION: Specimens have been examined from N.C., Fla., Ala., La., Miss., and Tenn.

This seems to be a good species, characterized by the hard and horny pileus surface (which does not form, however, a well-marked crust as in *Fomes applanatus*), the rather bright-brown hard context, the globose hyaline spores, the large basidia, and the absence of setae. The spores do not attain the sizes given by Lloyd (5–6 $\times$ 10 μ). Neither was I able to detect any coloration in the spore wall such as was described by Murrill. The context color is almost as bright as in *F. robustus* and in several other points the species is similar, but the pileus is smoother, more distinctly incrusted, and with more red in its coloration, the tubes are not as definitely layered, and the pores are of considerably smaller diameter. This species differs most decidedly from *F. Everhartii*, which commonly inhabits the same hosts, in the hyaline and larger spores and the lack of setae.

Fomes Calkinsii is of some importance as a heart-rotting organism of the southern oaks, and this seems to be another point of distinction between it and *F. robustus*. It produces a general whitish or pale-rusty decay similar to that caused by *Polyporus hispidus*. The medullary rays remain almost intact.

32. FOMES FOMENTARIUS (L. ex Fries) Kickx

Fl. Crypt. Flandres 2: 237. 1867

(Figs. 351, 407–408, 417, 582, and Plate 126)

Boletus fomentarius L., Sp. Plant., p. 1176. 1753.
Polyporus fomentarius L. ex Fries, Syst. Myc. 1: 374. 1821.
Elfvingia fomentaria (L. ex Fries) Murr., Torrey Bot. Club Bul. 30: 298. 1903.

Sporophore sessile, externally hard and horny; pileus typically ungulate, sometimes more convex, 3–15 $\times$ 6–20 $\times$ 2–15 cm., typically

gray or grayish black, younger specimens pale brown to grayish
brown, finally becoming gray or grayish black, at first with a thin
velvety villosity, finally glabrous, with a horny and very distinct crust
that is often more than 1 mm. thick, zonate or sulcate, the zones often
darker brown or blackish; context punky or soft-corky, dark tan or
brown, 0.3–3 cm. thick; pore surface gray to brown (typically near
"wood brown" or "buffy brown"), the tubes with a total depth of
0.5–6 cm., not distinctly stratified and often appearing continuous,
the mouths circular, thick-walled, entire, averaging 3–4 per mm.,
visible to the unaided eye; spores cylindric, hyaline, smooth,
12–18 $\times$ 4–5 μ;[1] basidia 8–10 μ in diameter; cystidia none; hyphae
mostly simple, golden brown (close to "buckthorn brown") in KOH,
with no cross walls or clamps, 5–10 μ in diameter; some hyphal complexes present, composed of hyphae about 3 μ in diameter. (Compare no. 14, *Fomes igniarius*.)

HABITAT: Usually on trunks or logs of dead deciduous trees,
sometimes from wounds in living trees, noted on *Acer, Alnus, Betula,
Carya, Fagus, Populus*, and *Prunus*; one collection (N.C., Graves)
on *Tsuga*; reported on apple (*Pyrus*) from Mont. (Weir [224]).

DISTRIBUTION: Specimens have been examined from Me., N.H.,
Vt., Mass., Conn., N.Y., Pa., Va., W. Va., N.C., Tenn., Ohio, Mich.,
Wis., Minn., S. Dak., Iowa, Texas, Mont., Idaho, Wash., and Alaska;
in Canada from Newfoundland, Quebec, Ontario, Manitoba, Saskatchewan, and British Columbia; reported from N. Dak. (Brenckle
[25]).

ILLUSTRATIONS: Gillet, Champ. France 2: pl. 289 (44); Hepting,
Civil. Cons. Corps Forestry Pub. 2: fig. 6; Hilborn, Maine Agr. Exp. Sta.
Bul. 409: pls. 1–2; Kellerman, Jour. Mycol. 9: pl. 3 (as *Elfvingia
fomentaria*); Lloyd, Synop. Fomes, fig. 584; McKenny, Mushrooms
Field and Wood, fig. 39; Neuman, Wis. Geol. and Nat. Hist. Survey
Bul. 33: pl. 9, fig. 30; Overholts, Wash. Univ. Studies 3: pl. 6, fig.
32; von Schrenk and Spaulding, U. S. Dept. Agr. Pl. Ind. Bul. 149:
pl. 8.

The unusual length of the tubes in proportion to the thickness of
the context provides a striking contrast in old specimens. I have

---

[1] See Hilborn's measurements below.

seen specimens with a total tube length of 6 cm., divided into 4 or 5 zones or apparent layers by as many dark lines, yet the tubes, under a lens, are distinctly continuous across these lines.   How many years' growth is involved is difficult to determine, unless one relies on the furrows on the external surface of the pileus.

Spores are rarely obtained in sections of the hymenium.   I have found them most often in the very young tubes of small, young specimens.   The sporulating basidia, as I have seen them, are very scattered; there are rarely more than 2 or 3 per pore in tranverse sections, and sometimes they project scarcely enough to be recognizable. The spores retain their position on the basidia quite well, and there is no difficulty in seeing their attachment, once a sporulating hymenium is located.

Schweinitz' record of this species was apparently based on a specimen of *Fomes applanatus.*

Hilborn and Linder (75) have brought out the fact that Kickx was responsible for locating the species in *Fomes*, whereas Gillet had previously been given credit for this. Hilborn (74) studied the species rather extensively.   His spore measurements exceed those usually cited for the species, being essentially 20–27 $\times$ 7–11 μ.   I recall distinctly that some of my own measurements were of spores on basidia and these could easily have been immature.   Hilborn's data on spore discharge are interesting, but lack the weight they might have if they were more extensive both as regards time and numbers.   Hilborn also gives considerable cultural data, and concludes that strains, as far as could be discerned by gross observations, do not exist.

The species is common in New England, New York, and the northern Rocky Mountains.

The fungus causes extensive decay (87, p. 379; 219, pp. 50–51) in dead and down timbers, and sometimes grows from large wounded areas on living trees, but it is probably of little importance as a decay-producing organism of living trees, although occasionally recorded. It may attack both heartwood and sapwood of dead timber, producing a general delignifying decay.   In the early stages of advanced decay a peculiar white checkerwork is evident, perhaps due to the alternation of areas in advanced stages of decay with areas of more sound wood. Later the wood becomes whitish or somewhat straw-colored, and if fissures occur in it extensive mats of straw-colored mycelium are developed.

33. FOMES MARMORATUS (Berk. & Curt.) Cooke
Grevillea 14: 18. 1885
(Figs. 397–398)

Polyporus marmoratus Berk. & Curt., Amer. Acad. Arts and Sci. Proc. 4: 122. 1860.
Elfvingia fasciata (Swartz ex Fries) Murr., Torrey Bot. Club Bul. 30: 298. 1903.

Sporophore sessile, hard and horny; pileus convex to somewhat ungulate, 7–15 × 6–20 × 2.5–10 cm., heavily covered with a horny gray or blackish crust, often marked with dark narrow zones, becoming somewhat cracked at times but usually even, more or less furrowed, the margin rather thick, acute or obtuse; context 1–5 cm. thick, tough and fibrous to hard-corky, cinnamon-brown or bright yellowish brown; pore surface cinnamon-brown or dull grayish brown, the tubes grayish brown within, indistinctly or not at all stratified, apparently 1–5 cm. long each season, the mouths circular, averaging 4–5 per mm., the walls thick and entire; spores not found, probably about 12–15 × 4–5 μ; cystidia and setae none; hyphae mostly simple, rather thick-walled, with no cross walls or clamps, 4–6(–9) μ in diameter. (Compare no. 29, *Fomes robustus*; no. 32, *F. fomentarius*; and no. 37, *F. applanatus*.)

HABITAT: On dead wood or on living trees, noted on *Carya, Celtis, Diospyros, Gleditsia, Liquidambar, Magnolia, Platanus, Quercus, Tsuga,* and *Ulmus.*

DISTRIBUTION: Specimens have been examined from N.C., Ga., Fla., Ala., La., Miss., Ark., and Texas; reported from Tenn. (Hesler [71]).

Though usually considered to be the southern and tropical analogue of *Fomes fomentarius* of temperate regions, specimens are usually not so ungulate, the tubes are shorter, and the pileus is whiter.

The fungus seems to be especially common on species of *Carya.*

3b. *Spores brown*
  4a. *Spores smooth* (see also no. 23, *Fomes densus*; no. 24, *F. Langloisii*; and *F. pseudosenex*, p. 106)

34. FOMES RIBIS (Schum. ex Fries) Gill.

Champ. France 1: 685. 1878
(Figs. 388–390 and Plate 126)

Boletus Ribi[s] Schum., Enum. Plant. Saell. 2: 386. 1803.
Polyporus Ribis Schum. ex Fries, Syst. Myc. 1: 375. 1821.
Pyropolyporus Ribis (Schum. ex Fries) Murr., Torrey Bot. Club Bul. 30: 118. 1903.

Sporophore sessile or effused-reflexed, somewhat flexible to woody and rigid; pileus thin and applanate where best developed, 1–3 × 1–4 × 0.2–0.5 cm., sometimes imbricate-confluent and then often larger, 3–10 × 3–8 × 0.5–1.5 cm., yellow-brown or rusty brown, sometimes grayish black with age, slightly if at all incrusted after weathering, decidedly rusty-tomentose at first, later more glabrous, zoned or sulcate; context apparently duplex before the thick tomentum constituting its upper layer wears off and in this stage a narrow dark line frequently marking the boundary between tomentum and the lower, harder context, brown, 2–6 mm. thick; pore surface gray-brown to dark brown, the tubes not more than 3 mm. long, the mouths angular, rather thick-walled, entire, invisible to the unaided eye, averaging 7–8 per mm.; spores ellipsoid to globose, pale rusty, 3–4 × 2.5 μ; basidia 3–4 μ in diameter; setae none; hyphae brown, simple or sparingly branched, the walls thin or partially thickened, with some cross walls but no clamps, 2.5–4 μ or rarely 3–6 μ in diameter; all parts black in KOH solution.

HABITAT: At the bases of living stems of *Chionanthus, Lonicera, Maclura, Ribes, Rosa,* and *Symphoricarpos.*

DISTRIBUTION: Specimens have been examined from R.I., N.Y., Pa., N.J., Md., Ohio, Ind., Minn., N. Dak., Kans., and Mont.; in Canada from Ontario and Manitoba; reported from Ore. (Zeller [237]).

ILLUSTRATIONS: Lloyd, Synop. Fomes, fig. 594; Overholts, Wash. Univ. Studies 3: pl. 6, fig. 30; Rostkovius, in Sturm, Deutsch. Flora, Abt. 3, Bd. 4: pl. 53 (as *Polyporus*); Stewart, N. Y. State Agr. Exp. Sta. Geneva Bul. 463: pl. 7.

Three other species have been described with the unusually small pale-rusty spores and the small basidia characteristic of *Fomes Ribis*. *F. densus* is a thick, mostly or entirely resupinate plant with setae; *F. Langloisii* more nearly approaches *F. Ribis* and in fact may not be distinct, differing mainly in the almost entire lack of a context, which in *F. Ribis* occupies about half the total thickness of the pileus; *F. pectinatus* (Klotzsch) Cooke is also similar, but is not known to occur on the mainland of the United States. Among the more widely distributed species of *Fomes*, *F. conchatus* is a close relative, but has larger, hyaline spores and setae. The fungus earlier described on *Sassafras* as belonging here is a different species (*F. torulosus*).

The illustration given by Stewart (*loc. cit.*) is especially good of the general habit of the fungus on the crowns of *Ribes*.

35. FOMES RIMOSUS (Berk.) Cooke

Grevillea 14: 18. 1885

(Figs. 384–386)

Polyporus rimosus Berk., London Jour. Bot. 4: 54. 1845.
Pyropolyporus Robiniae Murr., Torrey Bot. Club Bul. 30: 114. 1903.
Fulvifomes Robiniae Murr., Northern Polypores, p. 49. 1914.

Sporophore sessile, hard and woody; pileus dimidiate, applanate to ungulate, 3–20 × 5–30(–43) × 1.5–15 cm., young specimens and the growing margins of old ones a beautiful rich brown ("snuff brown") and compactly tomentose, soon becoming blackish and very rimose or at times woody-scaly, sometimes with two or three broad shallow furrows, more often with many narrow concentric furrows, the margin thick, often rounded; context woody, yellowish brown, 0.5–2 cm. thick; pore surface yellow-brown to deep rich brown, the tubes attaining lengths of 2–9 cm., though added at the rate of 2–5 mm. per year, sometimes in rather distinct strata but often not, the mouths thick-walled, circular, entire, averaging 4–6 per mm.; spores broadly ellipsoid to globose, smooth, light brown to chestnut-brown, 4–6 μ in diameter or 4.5–6 × 3.5–5 μ; setae none; context hyphae brown, the walls partly thickened, with no cross walls or clamps, 4–7 μ in diameter.

HABITAT: On living trees or on dead wood usually of the family Leguminosae, in temperate regions mostly on *Robinia*, noted also on *Acacia, Castanea, Coccolobis, Juglans*, and *Prosopis*; reported on *Quercus* (Wis., Neuman [148]).

DISTRIBUTION: Specimens have been examined from N.Y., Pa., N.J., Md., D.C., Va., W. Va., N.C., Fla., Ala., La., Tenn., Ky., Ohio, Ind., Iowa, Mo., Texas, N. Mex., Ariz., and Calif.

ILLUSTRATIONS: Hard, Mushrooms, fig. 347; Hepting, Civil. Cons. Corps Forestry Publ. 2: fig. 3; Overholts, Wash. Univ. Studies 3: pl. 7, fig. 38; Rankin, Man. Tree Dis., fig. 35; von Schrenk, Mo. Bot. Gard. Ann. Rept. 12: pls. 1–2 (as *Polyporus*).

The fungus causes extensive decay in living trees of black locust.[1] The decay is of the delignifying type, in which the wood is reduced to a soft spongy yellowish or pale-brownish mass. Usually it is localized in large pockets in the heartwood, but it may involve the entire width of that region.

36. FOMES JUNIPERINUS (von Schrenk) Sacc. & Syd.

Syll. Fung. 16: 151. 1902

(Figs. 410–412 and Plate 126)

Polyporus juniperinus von Schrenk, U. S. Dept. Agr. Veg. Phys. Path. Bul. 21: 9. 1900.
Pyropolyporus juniperinus (von Schrenk) Murr., Torrey Bot. Club Bul. 30: 116. 1903.
Pyropolyporus Earlei Murr., Torrey Bot. Club Bul. 30: 116. 1903.

Sporophore sessile, corky to woody; pileus more or less ungulate, 3–10 × 4–15 × 2–14 cm., at first entirely yellowish orange and compactly tomentose, later brownish orange to grayish black or black and glabrous, the margin often remaining yellowish, smooth, then furrowed, very rough and rimose in age; context reddish orange or rusty orange, soft-corky to corky, 0.5–1 cm. thick; pore surface yellowish to brownish, the tubes 5–10 mm. long each season, the mouths subcircular to slightly irregular, thick-walled, entire, averaging 2–3 per mm.; spores ellipsoid to subglobose, truncate at one end or somewhat quadrangular, brown to slightly colored or almost hyaline, smooth, 6–9 × 4.5–7 μ; basidia 5–8 μ in diameter; setae none; hyphae simple, brown, the walls slightly thickened, with no

[1] See von Schrenk, *Mo. Bot. Gard. Ann. Rept.* 12: 21–31. 1901; and von Schrenk and Spaulding (219).

cross walls or clamps, 2.5–4 μ in diameter; all parts wine-red then black where touched with KOH solution.

HABITAT: On living trunks of *Juniperus*.

DISTRIBUTION: Specimens have been examined from Pa., Md., Tenn., Ky., Texas, N. Mex., Ariz., Utah, Colo., Ore., and Calif.; reported from Mo. (von Schrenk) and Mont. (Weir [227]).

ILLUSTRATIONS: Boyce, Forest Path., fig. 161; Hedgcock and Long, Mycologia 4: pl. 64, figs. 1, 4–6 (as *Fomes Earlei*), pl. 65, figs. 2, 5, 6, 8 (as *F. Earlei*), and 9; Overholts, Wash. Univ. Studies 3: pl. 8, fig. 40; von Schrenk, U. S. Dept. Agr. Veg. Phys. Path. Bul. 21: pls. 1–4.

The spores of this species remind one of those of *Fomes fraxino-philus* and of *F. Ellisianus*. Mature basidia occur at irregular intervals in the youngest tubes of the specimens I have examined, often mixed with young cylindric or finger-like basidia. As is not true of most other brown species, a wine-red color first slowly develops if dried specimens are touched with KOH solution, then changes to black. If the KOH is preceded on the specimen by a drop of alcohol the color is immediately black, the change occurring so rapidly that the red is not noticeable. *F. Demidoffii* (Lév.) Sacc. & Syd. is said (145) to be an older name for this species.

Von Schrenk (214) and Hedgcock and Long (67) described the decay caused by this fungus in red cedar. An initial whitening of the wood indicates a delignifying organism; in the later stages of decay, cavities one to several inches in diameter and length are formed, lined with white cellulose fibers.

4b. *Spores echinulate, truncate at the apex* (see also *Ganoderma subtuberculosum*, p. 106)

37. FOMES APPLANATUS (Pers. ex Wallr.) Gill.

Champ. France 1: 686. 1878

(Figs. 419, 449–452, 587, 590, and Plate 125)

Boletus applanatus Pers., Obs. Myc. 2: 2. 1799.
Polyporus applanatus Pers. ex Wallr., Flora Crypt. Germ. 4: 591. 1833.
Ganoderma applanatum (Pers. ex Wallr.) Pat., Soc. Mycol. France Bul. 5: 67. 1889.

Polyporus megaloma Lév., Ann. Sci. Nat. Bot. III, 5: 128. 1846.
Elfvingia megaloma (Lév.) Murr., Torrey Bot. Club Bul. 30: 300. 1903.

Sporophore sessile, rarely effused-reflexed, hard and woody; pileus plane or convex or, when more or less pendent, steep and ungulate, 3–30 × 5–50 × 1.5–10 cm., the surface often tuberculate, usually grayish or grayish black, sometimes brown, covered with a crust which is usually hard and horny but which may at times be thin enough to be indented with the thumbnail and may be cracked and furrowed, or the margin may be indistinctly zonate; context punky to soft-corky, brown (occasionally whitish), 0.5–5 cm. thick; pore surface white in fresh plants, quickly darker where bruised or handled, often becoming yellow or umber or with a slight olivaceous tinge in dried plants, the tubes 4–12 mm. long each season, becoming distinctly stratified and the strata separated by distinct layers of context, the mouths circular, rather thick-walled, entire, averaging 4–6 per mm.; spores ovoid, smooth or appearing somewhat echinulate under greater magnification, slightly truncate at one end, [brown—J.L.L.], 6–9 × 4.5–6 μ; basidia 9–12 μ in diameter; cystidia rarely seen but present in the very young hymenium as projecting hyaline flask-shaped organs 6–10 μ in diameter; hyphae mostly brown, nearly simple or sparingly branched, thin-walled, with no cross walls or clamps, up to 6 μ in diameter, mostly tapering out to hyaline branched whiplike extremities 2–4 μ in diameter; some hyaline branched hyphal complexes present.

HABITAT: Usually on old logs or stumps of deciduous trees, often from wounds in living trees, noted on *Acer, Aesculus, Ailanthus, Alnus, Betula, Carpinus, Carya, Castanea, Crataegus, Fagus, Fraxinus, Gleditsia, Hovenia, Liriodendron, Lonicera, Magnolia, Morus, Platanus, Populus, Prunus, Pyrus, Quercus, Robinia, Sabal, Salix, Tilia, Ulmus,* and *Umbellularia*; occasionally on wood of conifers, noted on *Abies, Picea, Pseudotsuga,* and *Tsuga*; reported on *Acacia, Eucalyptus,* and *Schinus* (Calif., Rhoads [183]), on *Coccolobis* (Fla., Humphrey and Leus [89]), on *Pinus* (Canada, White [232]), and on *Thuja* (Wash., Boyce, U. S. Dept. Agr. Tech. Bul. 104: 25. 1929).

DISTRIBUTION: Specimens have been examined from every state in the Union except R.I., W. Va., S.C., Ga., Ala., Miss., S. Dak., Okla., Texas, Ariz., Nev., and Wyo.; in Canada from Newfoundland,

Quebec, Ontario, Manitoba, and British Columbia; reported from W. Va. (Gould [58]).

ILLUSTRATIONS: Atkinson, Cornell Agr. Exp. Sta. Bul. 193: fig. 82 (as *Polyporus*); *idem*, Ann. Mycol. 6: pls. 2–4 (as *Polyporus*); Clements, Minn. Mushrooms, fig. 58; Gillet, Champ. France 2: pl. 287 (42); Hepting, Civil. Cons. Corps Forestry Publ. 2: fig. 5; Hesler, Tenn. Acad. Sci. Jour. 4: fig. 4; Krieger, Natl. Geog. Mag. 37: 409 (as *Polyporus*); Lloyd, Myc. Notes 62: fig. 1729; Neuman, Wis. Geol. and Nat. Hist. Survey Bul. 33: pl. 9, fig. 31; Overholts, Wash. Univ. Studies 3: pl. 7, fig. 37; Shope, Mo. Bot. Gard. Ann. 18: pl. 32, fig. 4 (as *Ganoderma*).

Humphrey and Leus (89) give an exhaustive treatise on this species and its (so-called) variants. They would refer (among others of Oriental distribution) *Fomes Brownii* and *F. australis* (= *F. tornatus*) as varieties of the base species, *F. applanatus*.

I have examined sections from the tubes of more than twenty collections of this species without finding spores on the basidia. The very young hymenium consists of large inflated cells 9–12 μ in diameter, which are probably the basidia, and some flask-shaped cells 6–10 μ in diameter with attenuate projecting apices. These flask-shaped cells are entirely hyaline, and both they and the basidia quickly disappear from the mature hymenium. One form of the species has a soft but distinct brown crust; another, a very hard and horny whitish or gray crust. The second of these has been known as *Fomes leucophaeus* (described from Ohio by Montagne [*Syll. Crypt.*, p. 157. 1856]) and has been referred in synonymy to the present species (90, p. 168). The southern and tropical form of the species, often known as *F. australis* (Fries) Cooke, does not seem to be specifically distinct. The spores are peculiar in having one end slightly truncated and, as seen under an oil-immersion lens, a wall that is apparently roughened. The structure of these spores has been explained by Atkinson in the article cited above under Illustrations. The truncated end of the spore is said to be the apex, which it probably is, also, in *Polyporus lucidus* and its allies. Largely on the basis of spore characters, all these species would be combined by some investigators into the genus *Ganoderma*.

The pileus is frequently covered by a brown pulverulence, due to the presence of myriads of spores of the same type as the basidiospores.

Various mycologists have believed these to be conidia (Schulzer von Müggenberg, *Oesterr. bot. Zeitschr.* 30: 321–323. 1880; Murrill [139, p. 114]; Lloyd [115, p. 263]). Dodge (40, p. 830) tells of covering the surface of a pileus free of such spores with white paper and, after a few days, of finding a thin brown spore deposit on the upper surface of the paper, but none on the pileus beneath the paper. This and other observations indicate that these spores are basidiospores, carried upward from the hymenium by air currents and settling at length on the pileus surface. White (232) records his failure to obtain conidia in cultures of this species, and several cultures in my own collection have uniformly failed to produce any type of secondary spore. Bose, however, describes (16) an interesting case of spore formation in the tubes of this species and in *Polyporus lucidus.* At the end of the rainy season in India, Bose found that hyphal projections each bearing two conjugate nuclei were observabie between the basidia. These projections each bear a terminal spore of the form and color of mature basidiospores, and they may be so abundant as to obscure the basidia completely. The spores are asymmetrically placed on the tip of the hyphae, and are to be regarded as basidiospores. This interpretation is borne out by the fact that when Bose studied the cytology of these structures he found that the two nuclei of the terminal cell of these outgrowths fuse, and then the fusion nucleus "fragments" into four or five pieces. These fragments pass out of the hypha into the spore and there seem to be reorganized into the spore nucleus. He believes this fragmentation is a form of amitosis. No mitotic figures were seen. It might be remarked that if these bodies are basidiospores they should not be called "secondary spores," as Bose calls them, because of the confusion that results between them and such secondary spore types as conidia.

Occasionally one finds what is probably a parasitized condition of the context and old tube layers of this species, in which that region is nearly white. Zeller (236, p. 181) reports this condition as common in Oregon specimens, but is inclined to attribute it to other causes. Humphrey and Leus (89, p. 517) speak of this bleaching as a changing to a "light buff" or "pinkish buff," and express the opinion "that it is [due to] an autodigestive process, since the hyphae are much smaller in diameter and with thin walls as if they had been subjected to gradual uniform fermentation."

Hopp (80) describes a method of developing sporophores in cultures of this species.

In hardwood regions this is probably the most common species of *Fomes*. White (232) says that "a list of its hosts includes practically all the [tree] species of our local flora." Hedgcock (66) gives a list of forty-three species of trees or woods attacked by it. The white hymenial surface of fresh plants, turning dark immediately where wounded, provides a fine surface for etching, and has earned the name "artist's fungus" for the species. The fruiting bodies are usually found near the ground on old stumps or dead snags, though occasionally they occur at heights of thirty feet or more.

This species produces a general white or straw-colored, mottled, delignifying decay of sapwood and heartwood in which the wood remains for a long time rather firm, though light in weight, but eventually becomes very soft and watery. Some investigators (183; 232) are of the opinion that it may at times be parasitic in its action.

38. FOMES LOBATUS (Schw.) Cooke

Grevillea 14: 18. 1885
(Figs. 405, 415)

Polyporus lobatus Schw., Amer. Phil. Soc. Trans. II, 4: 157. 1832.
Elfvingia lobata (Schw.) Murr., North Amer. Flora 9: 114. 1908.
Ganoderma lobatum (Schw.) Atk., Ann. Mycol. 6: 190. 1908.
Polyporus reniformis Morgan, Cincinnati Soc. Nat. Hist. Jour. 8: 103. 1885.

Sporophore sessile or appearing substipitate, usually reviving for only two or three years and producing pilei each of which comes out below the one of the preceding year, corky when fresh, rigid when dry; pileus plane or depressed, 4–12 × 4–15 × 1–4 cm., yellowish brown to rusty brown, dark reddish brown, or umber, the margin long remaining whitish, with a thin but distinct, easily indented crust; context soft and punky, brown, 0.3–1 cm. thick; pore surface white, yellowish, or umber-brown, darker where bruised, the tubes 0.4–1 cm. long, the mouths circular and thick-walled, then angular and thin-walled, entire, averaging 4–5 per mm.; spores pale brown to dark brown, ovoid, truncate at the apex, appearing minutely echinulate, 8–9(–10) × 4.5–6 μ; cystidia none; hyphae simple, pale brown to dark brown, with walls partially thickened, with no cross walls or clamps, 3–7 μ in diameter; all parts black in KOH solution. (Compare no. 37, *Fomes applanatus*.)

HABITAT: On or about old logs and stumps of deciduous trees, noted on *Acer, Carya, Castanea, Liriodendron, Morus, Populus*, and *Quercus*; reported on *Citrus* (Fla., Humphrey and Leus [89]).

DISTRIBUTION: Specimens have been examined from Vt., N.Y., Pa., N.J., Md., D.C., Va., W. Va., N.C., Ga., Fla., Ala., La., Miss., Tenn., Ky., Ohio, Ind., Ill., Iowa, Mo., Ark., Texas, Ariz., and Utah; reported from Kans. (Bartholomew [4]).

ILLUSTRATIONS: Humphrey and Leus, Philippine Jour. Sci. 45: pl. 36, figs. 7–11 (spores only); Overholts, Wash. Univ. Studies 3: pl. 7, fig. 36.

Though this species is usually distinct enough from *Fomes applanatus* in the thinner and softer crust and the reviving manner of growth, yet occasionally the crust of that species is fairly soft, and young specimens of the two species may sometimes be confused. As in that species, I have not seen spores on basidia of *F. lobatus*, but it is not unusual to observe them in distinct groups of 3 or 4 along the lining of the tubes, each with the truncated end outermost and very likely all attached to the same basidium. The explanation of the apparent roughness of the spores is said to be the same as for the spores of *F. applanatus*.

39. FOMES ANNULARIS (Fries) Lloyd

Synop. Fomes, p. 268. 1915

(Fig. 374)

Polyporus annularis Fries, Nov. Symb. Myc., p. 52. 1855.
Polyporus tornatus Pers., in Gaudichaud-Beaupré, Voy. Freyc. Bot. 1: 173. 1826.

Sporophore sessile, very hard and rigid; pileus 5–10 × 7–12 × 10–14 cm., vertically elongate and steep in front, very heavily incrusted, with the crust 1 mm. or more thick, the steep margins of the annual layers gray, the upper surface grayish black to blackish, glabrous or brown-pulverulent, becoming slightly cracked, strongly concentrically ridged and furrowed on the steep margin; context none beneath the hard crust; pore surface grayish, the tubes unstratified and the tube region attaining a total depth of as much as 12 cm., very hard and horny, the tubes soon whitish-stuffed, the mouths very smooth and even, circular, very thick-walled, entire, averaging 3.5–4 per mm.; spores ovoid with truncate apex, apparently echinulate, pale brown, 10–12 × 6–8 μ; cystidia none; hyphae brown, sparingly branched, the walls completely thickened, with no cross walls or clamps, up to 9 μ in diameter, the branches tapering down to about 2 μ in diameter.

HABITAT: On dead wood of deciduous trees, noted on *Quercus, Umbellularia*, and "laurel."

DISTRIBUTION: Specimens have been examined only from Calif.

ILLUSTRATIONS: None, unless Lloyd's figure of *Fomes annularis* (Synop. Fomes, fig. 604) is referable here.

There are three collections of this species at the New York Botanical Garden and many in the Lloyd Herbarium. It is obviously distinct from *Fomes applanatus*, not only in the form of the sporophore, which is occasionally simulated to a slight extent in that species, but also in the absence of layering of the tubes, in the consistently larger spores, and in the lack of a context in old sporophores. The tubes begin just under the pileus crust and extend, without separation into layers, the full thickness of the sporophore. Sporophores of this species are very hard and heavy. It is a rare species of limited range.

Fomes Brownii has spores comparable in size to those of *F. annularis*, but has, also, a well-developed context layer and a less heavily incrusted pileus.

40. FOMES BROWNII (Murr.) Sacc. & Trott.

Syll. Fung. 23: 394. 1925

(Fig. 444 and Plate 125)

Elfvingia Brownii Murr., Western Polypores, p. 29. 1915.
Ganoderma applanatum (Pers. ex Wallr.) Pat. var. *Brownii* (Murr.) Humphrey and Leus, Philippine Jour. Sci. 45: 531. 1931.

Sporophore sessile; pileus convex to somewhat ungulate, 7–12 × 10–25 × 3–8 cm., covered with a hard horny crust that becomes somewhat cracked, grayish to brownish, pruinose to glabrous, somewhat furrowed and uneven, the margin obtuse and rounded, sometimes yellowish; context punky-corky to hard-corky but decidedly softer than the incrusting layer, 3–8 cm. thick, dark rusty brown; pore surface gray or perhaps more constantly pale yellow, dark where bruised, the tubes 5–15 mm. long each season, probably distinctly stratified in age, the mouths circular, thick-walled, entire, averaging 4–5 per mm., visible to the unaided eye; spores ovoid or ellipsoid, strongly truncate at one end, distinctly brown, the epispore hyaline and appearing verrucose, $9–12 \times 7–9 \mu$; cystidia none; main hyphae long and flexuous, chestnut-brown, somewhat branched, with no cross walls or clamps, $3–8 \mu$ in diameter; a few hyphae hyaline, forming much-branched hyphal complexes, the branches with attenuate tips.

HABITAT: On dead wood of deciduous trees, noted on *Hakea, Quercus, Schinus,* and *Umbellularia.*

DISTRIBUTION: Specimens have been examined only from Calif.

The relationships of this species are very close to *Fomes applanatus.* It differs not so much in the yellow pore mouths, as was emphasized by Murrill, but, more fundamentally, in the larger spores. The spores of *F. applanatus* rarely reach a length of 9μ and a width of 6μ. Here they are constantly larger and of a darker brown, while the context is much thicker than in *F. applanatus.* Yellow pore mouths are found in *F. applanatus* and that variation Lloyd once described as *F. oroflavus,* but he himself states that the plant from California with this character is not to be included under his species. Possibly the California plants had been named prior to Murrill's designation of the species, but the history of the older names based on forms of *F. applanatus* is confusing.

In my herbarium are three collections of this species, two from the type locality on the type substratum, *Umbellularia,* and another from the same region on *Hakea.* All of these are thicker specimens than the types, but otherwise they agree.

OMITTED SPECIES

(Entries not in brackets were included by Dr. Overholts, but were not fully described; those in brackets have been added to cover species recently proposed.—J.L.L.)

Fomes avellaneus (Murr.) Overh. This species was included by Dr. Overholts in the *Fomes* key. It has been described from Nicaragua by Murrill (139, p. 116), but no other collections are recorded. The species was not known to Lloyd (114, p. 108).

[*Oxyporus nobilissimus* W. B. Cooke, *Mycologia* **41**: 444. 1949. This is a massive plant on conifers in the Pacific Northwest, somewhat resembling *Fomes connatus*, but with a deep surface layer of interwoven fibers and with spores 6–7 × 3.5–4 μ.]

Fomes pseudosenex (Murr.) Sacc. & Trott. This species was included in the *Fomes* key by Dr. Overholts. It is known from Mexico, Nicaragua, and Cuba, and has been described by Lloyd (115, p. 255) and by Murrill (139, p. 107).

Fomes senex (Nees & Mont.) Cooke. This species was included in the *Fomes* key by Dr. Overholts. It is a widely distributed tropical species and has been described by Lloyd (115, p. 259).

[*Ganoderma subtuberculosum* Murr., *Lloydia* **7**: 326. 1944. According to its author, this species is related to *G. tuberculosum* Murr., but the upper surface is not tuberculate and the spores are much larger, being 10–12 × 7–8 μ.]

[*Pyropolyporus Taxodii* Murr., *Torrey Bot. Club Bul.* **65**: 651. 1938. This species resembles *Fomes conchatus*, but occurs on cypress in Georgia and Florida and has more slender spores, 4.5–5 × 2.5–3 μ.]

Genus 2. LENZITES Fries

Gen. Hym., p. 10. 1836

Gloeophyllum Karst., Bidr. Finl. Nat. Folk 37: x and 79. 1882.

Plants annual or persisting for several years, sessile, leathery and flexible when fresh, usually drying more or less rigid, applanate, dimidiate, of rather small size, color variable; context white to brown, fibrous to corky; hymenium typically lamellate or strongly inclined to a lamellate condition, but in some specimens almost entirely poroid, the gills when present rather thick and coriaceous, frequently branched or anastomosing, white to brown; spores cylindric, hyaline; cystidia usually absent, never very conspicuous; setae none.

Type species: *Lenzites betulina* (L. ex Fries) Fries.

The present genus is based on the lamellate hymenium, and the genus *Daedalea* is based to the same extent on the daedaloid hymenium. Here again we have a character that is more or less variable. *Lenzites trabea* is about as frequently poroid or daedaloid as it is lamellate, and *L. betulina*, our commonest species on hardwoods, is sometimes poroid. At one time all species of *Lenzites* were contained in the genus *Daedalea*. Fries, in his earlier work, so referred them, but he separated them into *Lenzites* in 1836. Karsten proposed the separation of the brown species into the genus *Gloeophyllum*, and was followed in this by Murrill. There is no question but that this would be the logical separation to make were the genus in serious need of being divided.

The genus is often included in the Agaricaceae on account of its hymenial configuration. But because of the more leathery consistency, the evident relationships to *Daedalea*, and the importance of some of its species in timber decays, it finds a logical position in the Polyporaceae.

KEY TO THE SPECIES OF LENZITES

1. Context and gills white or light-colored 2
   Context and gills umber to rusty brown 3
2. Pileus strongly pubescent .... 1. *L. betulina*
   Pileus finely pubescent to glabrous   See no. 1, *Daedalea confragosa*

3. Context not more than 1 mm. thick 4
   Context 1–3(–4) mm. thick 5
   Context 3–7 mm. thick; usually from the Gulf States; on
     wood of coniferous trees ...... See no. 6, *Daedalea Berkeleyi*
4. Spores 7–10 × 2.5–4 μ; common and cosmopolitan; pileus
     cinnamon, finely tomentose .... 2. *L. trabea*
   Spores 8–10.5 × 2.5–3 μ; found only at one station in the
     Rocky Mountains; pileus "hair brown," strigose-tomen-
     tose or becoming velvety .... 5. *L. abietinella*
   Spores 4–6 × 1.5–2.5 μ; cosmopolitan and common; pileus
     gray to blackish, strigose to villose or tomentose
                  See no. 97, *Polyporus abietinus* var. *Abietis*
5. Entire sporophore umber or cinnamon without and within ... 6
   Entire sporophore bright rusty brown or darker, the margin
     alone often of brighter color .... 3. *L. saepiaria*
6. Hymenium imperfectly gilled, more or less poroid; common
     throughout except in the Rocky Mountain region
                                            2. *L. trabea*
   Hymenium completely gilled; mostly from the Gulf States;
     inconspicuous cystidia present in the hymenium
                                            4. *L. striata*

1. Lenzites betulina (L. ex Fries) Fries

Epicr. Syst. Myc., p. 405. 1836–1838
(Figs. 517–518, 525, and Plate 127)

Agaricus betulinus L., Sp. Plant., p. 1176. 1753.
Daedalea betulina L. ex Fries, Syst. Myc. 1: 333. 1821.
Lenzites ochraceus Lloyd, Myc. Notes 66: 1130. 1922.
Lenzites variegata Lloyd, Myc. Notes 72: 1273. 1924.

Sporophore sessile or effused-reflexed, coriaceous and very flexible
when fresh, more or less rigid when dry; pileus 2–8 × 2–12 × 0.3–
1.5 cm., prevailingly grayish to brownish, zonate, often with many
narrow, multicolored zones, hirsute or tomentose; context white,
0.5–3 mm. thick; pore surface white or whitish, sometimes poroid,
usually lamellate, but frequently with the lamellae branched or anastomosing at least toward the margin of the pileus, coriaceous, about
1 mm. apart, 0.3–1 cm. broad; spores short-cylindric, hyaline, 4–7 ×
1.5–3 μ; cystidia present as hyaline, sharp-pointed or blunt cylindric

organs, 24–40 × 4–7 μ, projecting 10–20 μ; hyphal pegs none; hyphae hyaline, mostly with completely thickened walls but some thin-walled, simple or sometimes branched and mostly 4–9 μ in diameter, with a tendency for the ultimate branches to be attenuated to 2–3 μ in diameter, with no cross walls or clamps except, rarely, on the hyphae of smaller diameter; hyphal complexes present but not abundant.

HABITAT: On dead wood, usually of deciduous trees, noted on *Acer, Aesculus, Amelanchier, Betula, Carpinus, Carya, Castanea, Cornus, Fagus, Fraxinus, Liquidambar, Liriodendron, Nyssa, Paulownia, Persea, Platanus, Quercus, Robinia, Salix, Tilia,* and *Ulmus*; occasionally on wood of coniferous trees, noted on *Pinus, Thuja,* and *Tsuga*; reported also on *Pyrus* (Mich., Kauffman [101]).

DISTRIBUTION: Specimens have been examined from Me., N.H., Vt., Mass., Conn., N.Y., Pa., N.J., Md., D.C., Va., W. Va., N.C., S.C., Ga., Fla., Ala., La., Miss., Tenn., Ky., Ohio, Ind., Ill., Mich., Wis., Minn., S. Dak., Iowa, Mo., Kans., Nebr., Ark., Texas, Mont., Ore., and Calif.; in Canada from Nova Scotia, Quebec, Ontario, Manitoba, Alberta, and British Columbia; reported from N. Dak. (Brenckle [25]).

ILLUSTRATIONS: Hard, Mushrooms, figs. 184–185; Humphrey, U. S. Dept. Agr. Bul. 510: pl. 7, figs. 2–3; Lloyd, Myc. Notes 59: fig. 1427; *ibid.*, 74: fig. 3114; Michael, Führ. f. Pilzfr. 3: fig. 43; Sowerby, Col. Fig. English Fungi, pl. 182 (as *Agaricus betulinus*); Stevens, Fungi Plant Dis., fig. 313.

This is a very common and widespread species, not likely to be confused with any other if the strongly tomentose, zoned pileus, the white context, and the white lamellate hymenium are considered. The cystidia and spores are also highly characteristic. It is most similar, perhaps, to gilled forms of *Daedalea confragosa*. The variation in the color of the pileus is as great as, and simulates more or less, that in *Polyporus versicolor*, but uniformly gray or ochraceous specimens are more likely to recall *P. hirsutus*. A green algal growth is not uncommon on the pileus as it ages.

The fungus produces a general delignifying decay of the sapwood, in which the wood is often straw-colored.

2. Lenzites trabea Pers. ex Fries

Epicr. Syst. Myc., p. 406. 1836–1838
(Figs. 366, 537–538, and Plate 127)

Agaricus trabeus Pers., Synop. Meth. Fung., Addenda, p. 29. 1801.
Daedalea trabea Fries, Syst. Myc. 1: 335. 1821.
Gloeophyllum trabeum (Pers. ex Fries) Murr., North Amer. Flora 9, 1: 129. 1908.
Lenzites vialis Peck, N. Y. State Mus. Ann. Rept. 26: 67. 1872.

Sporophore sessile or effused-reflexed, frequently reviving for more than one season, coriaceous and leathery when fresh, more rigid on drying; pileus applanate to somewhat convex, often laterally connate, 1–5 × 2–8 × 0.2–0.8 cm., gray to cinnamon-brown or pale rusty brown, blackish with age if persisting for more than a year, at first compactly tomentose, weathering to nearly glabrous, the surface often rugose or furrowed; context umber-brown or pale yellowish brown, 1–4 mm. thick; lower surface more or less poroid or daedaloid, rarely lamellate, the pores or lamellae brown, rather thick-walled, entire, averaging 2–3 per mm., the tubes or lamellae 1–3 mm. deep; spores cylindric or cylindric-elliptic, smooth, hyaline, perhaps brownish in extreme age, 7–10 × 2.5–4 μ; cystidia rare, cylindric, hyaline, 3–5 μ in diameter, projecting but slightly beyond the basidia; hyphae for the most part rarely branched, cinnamon-brown in KOH, flexuous, the walls partially thickened, with no cross walls or clamps, 3–5(–6) μ in diameter, other hyphae hyaline in KOH, branched, with clamps, 2.5–4 μ in diameter; tissues darkening in KOH solution.

Habitat: On dead wood, usually of deciduous trees, noted on *Acer, Betula, Castanea, Fagus, Fraxinus, Juglans, Liriodendron, Platanus, Populus, Prunus, Pyrus, Quercus, Tilia,* and *Ulmus*; occasionally on wood of coniferous trees, noted on *Abies, Cupressus, Juniperus, Picea, Pinus, Pseudotsuga, Taxodium, Thuja,* and *Tsuga.*

Distribution: Specimens have been examined from Me., Vt., Mass., Conn., R.I., N.Y., Pa., N.J., Md., Va., W. Va., N.C., S.C., Ga., Ala., La., Miss., Tenn., Ky., Ohio, Ind., Ill., Wis., Minn., N. Dak., Iowa, Mo., Kans., Nebr., Ark., Okla., Colo., Mont., Ore., and Calif.; in Canada from Quebec, Ontario, and Manitoba; reported from Mich. (Povah [174]).

ILLUSTRATIONS: Humphrey, U. S. Dept. Agr. Bul. 510: pl. 7, fig. 1; Overholts, Wash. Univ. Studies 3: pl. 8, fig. 46 (as *Lenzites vialis*); Shope, Mo. Bot. Gard. Ann. 18: pl. 38, fig. 1.

This species differs from *Lenzites saepiaria* in the duller color and less tomentose surface of its pileus and in its occurrence, usually, on wood of deciduous trees. There are no microscopic characters available for the separation of the brown species of *Lenzites*. It differs from *L. betulina* primarily in the uniform brownish color of the fresh plants, the umber-brown context, and the lack of cystidia in the hymenium.

Both oidia and chlamydospores have been reported as secondary spore forms in this species by Snell (204).

The decay produced by this fungus is of the general carbonizing type, similar to that of *Lenzites saepiaria*. The species is usually regarded as of less significance than *L. saepiaria* from an economic standpoint, but when the importance of the various timber-decaying fungi is finally evaluated, *L. trabea* will stand near the head of the list. It seems to be common on *Taxodium* in the Southern states, but northward it is more closely limited to hardwoods. This is usually the species found decaying and fruiting on the woodwork of automobiles. Snell (204) discusses its relation to decay conditions in textile and paper mills in New England.

3. LENZITES SAEPIARIA (Wulf. ex Fries) Fries
Epicr. Syst. Myc., p. 407. 1836–1838
(Figs. 533–536, 567, and Plate 127)

Agaricus sepiarius Wulf., in Jacquin, Collect. ad Bot. 1: 339. 1786.
Daedalea sepiaria Wulf. ex Fries, Syst. Myc. 1: 333. 1821.
Gloeophyllum hirsutum Schaeff. ex Murr., Torrey Bot. Club Bul. 32: 370. 1905.

Sporophore sessile or effused-reflexed, probably reviving for several seasons, coriaceous to rigid; pileus dimidiate, 1–7 × 2–10 × 0.3–1 cm., bright yellowish red to tobacco-colored or dark ferruginous, the growing margin often white, yellow, or orange, hirsute-tomentose to fibrillose-tomentose or nearly glabrous or with a very compact tomentum at maturity, zonate; context yellowish brown or rusty brown, 1–3 mm. thick, soft-corky; pore surface brown, sometimes daedaloid, poroid, or even toothed, but usually lamellate, the lamellae 0.5–1 mm. apart, 2–5 mm. broad; spores cylindric, smooth, hyaline, 6–10 × 2–4 μ; cystidia rare, cylindric, pointed, hyaline, 3–5 μ in diameter, projecting but slightly beyond the basidia; hyphae mostly pale chestnut, rarely branched, thick-walled, with no cross walls or clamps, 3–5 μ in diameter, a few hyphae paler or nearly hyaline, with clamps; all parts black in KOH solution.

HABITAT: On dead wood, usually of coniferous trees, noted on *Abies, Cupressus, Juniperus, Larix, Picea, Pinus, Pseudotsuga, Taxodium*, and *Tsuga*; occasionally on hardwoods, noted on *Alnus, Betula, Crataegus, Populus, Prunus*, and *Salix*; frequent on railroad ties and structural timbers; reported on *Acer* (Weir [222]) and on *Libocedrus* (Calif., Boyce [19]).

DISTRIBUTION: Specimens have been examined from Me., N.H., Vt., Mass., Conn., N.Y., Pa., N.J., Md., Va., W. Va., N.C., S.C., Ga., Fla., Ala., La., Miss., Ohio, Ind., Mich., Wis., Minn., S. Dak., Nebr., Ark., Texas, N. Mex., Ariz., Utah, Colo., Wyo., Mont., Idaho, Ore., Wash., and Alaska; in Canada from Nova Scotia, Newfoundland, Quebec, Ontario, Manitoba, and British Columbia; reported from fourteen other states (Spaulding [207]), from Tenn. (Hesler [71]), Iowa (Wolf [234]), and Kans. (Bartholomew [4]).

ILLUSTRATIONS: Humphrey, U. S. Dept. Agr. Bul. 510: pl. 6, figs. 5–6; Michael, Führ. f. Pilzfr. 3: fig. 44; Overholts, Wash. Univ. Studies 3: pl. 8, fig. 47; Schaeffer, Fung. Bavar., pl. 76; Shope, Mo. Bot. Gard. Ann. 18: pl. 37, fig. 1; Spaulding, U. S. Dept. Agr. Pl. Ind. Bul. 214: pls. 1–4.

The surface of the pileus is quite variable with regard to pubescence, but the species is usually easily distinguished from *Lenzites trabea*, its only close relative, by the more rusty or tobacco-colored pileus and the more highly colored context, as well as the more lamellate hymenium and the fact that the plants are most often found on wood of coniferous trees. The fresh, growing margin of *L. trabea* never shows the bright color found in this species.

Microscopically the species cannot be separated from either *Lenzites trabea* or *L. striata*. The only measurable variable is the extent of the development of the narrow, pointed cystidia; these are seen more abundantly in *L. striata* than in either of the others, yet their abundance, or at least their easy recognition, seems to be dependent on the degree of development of the basidial layer.   In a sporulating hymenium they are scarcely discernible.

Both chlamydospores and oidia are known as secondary spore forms in this species.

The fungus causes a brown, checked, carbonizing decay of both sapwood and heartwood, especially in structural timbers, railroad ties, and the like.   It is one of the most important of the timber-decaying species, producing a rot similar to that of *Polyporus Schwein-itzii*.   It rarely occurs as a heart rot on living trees.   Snell (204) discusses it in relation to decay of timbers in position in the weave sheds of cotton mills in New England.   Many phases of the decay the fungus produces and of its life history are illuminated by the extensive researches of Falck, in A. Möller's *Hausschwammforschungen in amtlichen Auftrage* (Heft 3, pp. 1–234. 1909).

4. Lenzites striata (Swartz ex Fries) Fries

Epicr. Syst. Myc., p. 406. 1836–1838

(Figs. 526–527, 539–540, and Plate 127)

Agaricus striatus Swartz, Nov. Gen. Sp. Plant. Prodromus, p. 148. 1788.
Daedalea striata Swartz ex Fries, Syst. Myc. 1: 334. 1821.
Gloeophyllum striatum (Swartz ex Fries) Murr., Torrey Bot. Club Bul. 32: 370. 1905.

Sporophore sessile, rarely effused-reflexed, quite thin and flexible in both fresh and dried condition, annual; pileus dimidiate to flabelli-form, 2–6 × 4–10 × 0.1–0.6 cm., rich umber-brown or tobacco-brown when fresh and growing, weathering to gray-brown or gray with age, with a fine soft tomentum that eventually mats down to a compact even surface, usually azonate behind, sometimes with several unicolorous zones toward the margin, rarely multizonate, the margin very thin; context umber-brown or darker, soft, 0.5–3 mm. thick; lower surface always gilled, with radiating, or nearly parallel, leathery or coriaceous gills spaced 0.5–1 mm. apart, rarely anasto-mosing or forked, 1–3 mm. wide; spores ellipsoid-cylindric, smooth, hyaline, 6–8 × 2–4 μ; basidia 5–6 μ in diameter; cystidia scarcely noteworthy in the sporulating hymenium, but present as numerous, slightly or scarcely projecting, narrow, hyaline organs 3–6 μ in diameter; hyphae in part brown, simple or nearly so, with no cross walls or clamps, 3–6 μ in diameter, and in part hyaline, somewhat branched, with numerous inconspicuous cross walls and clamps, 2–4 μ in diameter, these hyphae with age becoming pale brownish and often collapsed.

HABITAT: On dead wood of coniferous trees, noted on *Juniperus* and *Taxodium*.

DISTRIBUTION: Specimens have been examined from Ga., Fla., and Ariz.

This species appears to be rather common in tropical America. It seems quite closely related to *Lenzites abietina*, having the same type of inconspicuous cystidia in the hymenium. The spores I have seen are much shorter and more robust than in that species, but this difference may depend on the maturity of the specimens. There are no microscopic differences between this species, *L. trabea*, and *L. saepiaria*.

5. LENZITES ABIETINELLA (Murr.) Sacc. & Trott.

Syll. Fung. 21: 126. 1912

(Plate 127)

Gloeophyllum abietinellum Murr., North Amer. Flora 9: 129. 1908.

Sporophore sessile, leathery when fresh, somewhat flexible when dry; pileus 2–3.5 × 4–6 × 0.2–0.5 cm., uniformly brown (close to "hair brown"), strigose-tomentose or becoming velvety with age, zonate, the margin thin; context dark umber-brown, 0.5–1 mm. thick; pore surface gray-brown to umber-brown, the gills simple and distinct, 1–2 mm. broad, averaging 1–2 per mm., the edges nearly entire, finely pubescent, as are also the sides; spores cylindric, hyaline, smooth, 8–10.5 × 2.5–3 μ; cystidia present, not well represented in the sporulating hymenium but more abundant in the older hymenium, very slightly incrusted at times, 4–7 μ in diameter; hyphae uniformly pale brown, thin-walled, flexuous, nearly simple, with no cross walls or clamps, 4–6 μ in diameter.

HABITAT: On dead wood of coniferous trees, said to occur also on *Alnus* (Kauffman [102]).

DISTRIBUTION: Specimens have been examined only from the "Rocky Mountains" (no precise locality given); reported from Colo. (Kauffman [102]).

ILLUSTRATIONS: Lloyd, Myc. Notes 72: fig. 2806.

This is a true lenzitoid plant, not related to a lamellate condition of *Polyporus abietinus* var. *Abietis*, as has been suggested. Spores are abundant, both free and on basidia in one specimen from the type collection, and they, too, are typically lenzitoid. The fungus is a thin brown species of *Lenzites* without relationship to other species of the genus in America, though with considerable resemblance to the southern *L. striata* and to *L. abietina* (Bull. ex Fries) Fries of Europe.

Macoun collected the fungus in the Rocky Mountains in 1885, and his collection was made the type of the species by Murrill.

Genus 3. CYCLOMYCES Kunze

In Fries, Linnaea 5: 512. 1830

Cycloporus Murr., Torrey Bot. Club Bul. 31: 423. 1904.

Plants annual in our species, terrestrial and stipitate or substipitate, the pileus coriaceous when fresh and growing, rusty brown; context brown; pore surface brown; tubes in a single layer, the mouths at first poroid but at maturity more or less broken up into concentric gill-like or platelike structures; spores pale brown; setae none.

Type species: *Cyclomyces fuscus* Kunze.

The genus is represented in America by but a single species, which is widely distributed in the eastern United States.   The concentric arrangement of the gill-like plates that constitute the hymenium is the decisive character on which the genus is based.

Murrill held that since the genus *Cyclomyces* was originally based on a sessile wood-inhabiting species, our American stipitate terrestrial plant should be segregated.   For this segregate he proposed the name *Cycloporus*.   The basic character of the genus is, however, the concentric gills, and, as defined in that sense, the genus is no more heterogeneous than are the other genera of the family recognized here.   Besides, the genus is a small one, and the multiplication of generic names is neither necessary nor desirable.

Cyclomyces Greenei Berk.

London Jour. Bot. 4: 306. 1845

(Fig. 465 and Plate 125)

Cycloporus Greenei (Berk.) Murr., Torrey Bot. Club Bul. 31: 424. 1904.

Sporophore centrally stipitate, rarely two or more sporophores confluent, coriaceous, drying rigid; pileus circular or irregular in outline, usually centrally depressed, 2.5–17 cm. broad, 0.5–2 cm. thick, yellowish brown to rusty brown or purplish brown, at first densely velvety-tomentose but becoming more glabrous, sometimes zonate; context fulvous to cinnamon-brown or rusty brown, soft and spongy,

116

5–10 mm. thick; pore surface brown, the tubes 5–8 mm. long, soon breaking up to form brownish, concentric, coriaceous lamellae; stem central, velvety, fulvous to rusty brown, 2–7 cm. long, 0.7–2 cm. thick; spores elongate-ellipsoid, smooth, brownish under the microscope, 9–15 × 5–7 μ; basidia 7–9 μ in diameter; cystidia none; hyphae brown, thin-walled, sparingly branched, with cross walls but no clamps, 5–10(–12) μ in diameter; all parts of the sporophore quickly black where touched with KOH solution.

HABITAT: On the ground in woods, rare.

DISTRIBUTION: Specimens have been examined from Mass., Conn., N.Y., Pa., N.J., Del., Md., D.C., W. Va., N.C., Tenn., Ky., Ohio, and Iowa; reported from Mich. (Mains [129]).

ILLUSTRATIONS: Clements, Minn. Mushrooms, fig. 68; Farlow, Icones Farl., pl. 95; Hard, Mushrooms, figs. 360–361; Lloyd, Myc. Notes, figs. 380, 382, 902.

This species is easily recognized by the rusty-brown color throughout and by the fact that the hymenium at maturity shows lamellate plates arranged concentrically around the stem on the lower side of the pileus. At the margin of the pileus the poroid condition is usually retained. The spores are hyaline until after their discharge from the basidia, but eventually appear pale brown under the microscope. I have seen only two-spored basidia in the hymenium.

Genus 4. DAEDALEA Pers. ex Fries

Syst. Myc. 1: 331. 1821

Daedalea Pers., Synop. Meth. Fung., p. 499. 1801.

Plants annual, or reviving for several seasons in some species, wood-inhabiting, sessile or effused-reflexed or, in some species, sometimes narrowed into a stemlike point of attachment, coriaceous to corky or very firm-corky, white to wood color or brown; context white to brown; tubes never layered, homogeneous with the substance of the pileus and not forming a distinct stratum, the mouths typically elongated or sinuous (daedaloid) in outline, sometimes verging to poroid and sometimes nearly or quite lamellate, usually entire, sometimes toothed; spores oblong or oblong-ellipsoid to cylindric, never globose, hyaline; cystidia never conspicuous, usually absent; setae none.

TYPE SPECIES: *Daedalea quercina* L. ex Fries.

This is a small genus of half a dozen species, for the most part easily recognized by the daedaloid hymenium. In *Daedalea unicolor*, however, the hymenium at maturity often becomes very much toothed; occasionally in *D. confragosa* and more rarely in *D. quercina* it is distinctly poroid, and both of these species, but particularly the first, often show a lamellate condition as well-developed as in any species of *Lenzites*. Therefore toothed or lamellate species serve to confuse the Polyporaceae with each of the two large families Hydnaceae and Agaricaceae, though obviously unrelated to either. To make the confusion worse, various species of *Polyporus* and at least one of *Fomes* show a daedaloid hymenium, either as a regular feature or as an occasional variation. It does not seem feasible to attempt the removal of these species to *Daedalea* since their other characters are generally at variance with those of this genus. Some species of other genera frequently found with a daedaloid hymenium have been included for convenience in the key to the species of *Daedalea*. Structurally, since the tissue of the context descends unaltered between the tubes to form the trama, the species of this genus resemble coriaceous species of *Polyporus* and species of *Trametes* with daedaloid pore surface.

118

KEY TO THE SPECIES OF DAEDALEA

1. Pileus surface decidedly villose, hirsute, or tomentose 2
   Pileus surface mostly glabrous or only finely tomentose 6
2. Sporophore soft and white when fresh, drying reddish
   See no. 54, *Polyporus fragilis*
   Sporophore spongy or tough or leathery, not drying reddish . 3
3. Context practically none; pileus surface covered by a thick
   layer of stiff brownish or blackish fibers; from southern
   Florida only .... See no. 102, *Polyporus trichomallus*
   Context white; pileus surface white or gray, sometimes drying yellowish; on hardwoods 5
   Context rusty brown or darker; pileus surface brown to
   blackish 4
   Context brownish; pileus surface gray or grayish black; on
   conifers only . See no. 97, *Polyporus abietinus* var. *Abietis*
4. Pileus thin and flexible; pore surface more or less toothed and
   usually with a greenish tinge; setae none; on hardwoods
   only .... 7. *D. farinacea*
   Pileus more or less woody and nearly inflexible; pore surface
   not toothed, but only daedaloid; setae present
   See no. 22, *Fomes Pini* and var. *Abietis*
5. Pileus 1 cm. or more thick; tubes 1 cm. or more long
   See no. 90, *Polyporus obtusus*
   Pileus not more than 0.5 cm. thick; tubes less than 0.5 cm.
   long .... 4. *D. unicolor*
6. Pores or interspaces (i.e., between the gills) 1 mm. or more
   broad, the walls thick and obtuse; producing a brown,
   carbonizing decay of the wood 7
   Pores mostly 1–3 per mm., or the gills (if present) less than 1
   mm. apart, the walls thin; producing a white decay of
   the wood 9
7. On living or dead *Juniperus* only .... 3. *D. juniperina*
   On other coniferous substrata 8
   On hardwood substrata .... 2. *D. quercina*
8. Context brown; mostly confined to the Gulf States
   6. *D. Berkeleyi*
   Context white or light-colored; distribution more general
   See no. 4, *Trametes heteromorpha*

9. Context and surface of pileus white in fresh specimens, at
    least in part; southern in distribution **10**
    Context and surface of pileus usually not white, but pallid
    or wood-colored; cosmopolitan . . . .   1. *D. confragosa*
10. Pileus typically 1 cm. or more thick; hymenial region rarely
    lamellate; ranging north to West Virginia and Illinois
    5. *D. ambigua*
    Pileus typically less than 1 cm. thick; hymenial region fre-
    quently lamellate; from subtropical areas only .   *D. elegans,*
    see under no. *5, D. ambigua*

1. DAEDALEA CONFRAGOSA Bolt. ex Fries

Syst. Myc. 1: 336. 1821

(Figs. 467–472 and Plate 125)

Boletus confragosus Bolt., Hist. Fung., Appendix, p. 160. 1791.
Daedalea albida Schw., Schr. Nat. Ges. Leipzig 1: 93. 1822.
Daedalea zonata Schw., Schr. Nat. Ges. Leipzig 1: 94. 1822.

Sporophore sessile or effused-reflexed, leathery and watery when
fresh, rigid and firm on drying; pileus plane or slightly convex,
2–10 × 3–15 × 0.2–2(–3) cm., grayish, cinereous, smoky umber or
brownish, sometimes blackish in extreme age, occasionally somewhat
rosy when handled fresh, unchanged on drying, finely pubescent to
glabrous or nearly so, sometimes radiately rugose, often multizonate
at least toward the margin, and frequently drying rough, the margin
thin, acute; context whitish to wood-colored or pale brown, zonate,
floccose to corky, 0.2–1(–2) cm. thick; pore surface whitish to avellaneous, isabelline, or pale brown, sometimes pinkish flesh color
where handled, poroid, daedaloid, or lamellate, the tubes 0.1–1.5 cm.
long, the mouths subcircular to elongate, daedaloid, or lamellate,
0.5–1.5 mm. broad, the walls sometimes thick and regular, but often
becoming lacerate and sometimes toothed; spores cylindric, smooth,
hyaline, 7–9 × 2–2.5 μ; cystidia none, but hyaline or slightly colored,
branched, inconspicuous, paraphysis-like hyphae 2–3 μ in diameter
present between the basidia, sometimes abundant but usually only
occasional and often not easily located; main hyphae simple, with the
walls completely thickened, with no cross walls or clamps, 5–12(–15) μ
in diameter; other smaller hyphae 4–6 μ in diameter, considerably
branched to form a simple type of hyphal complex.

HABITAT: On dead wood or occasionally from wounds in living deciduous trees, noted on *Acer, Alnus, Betula, Carya, Castanea, Cornus, Crataegus, Fagus, Fraxinus, Gleditsia, Ilex, Liquidambar, Liriodendron, Magnolia, Nyssa, Ostrya, Platanus, Populus, Pyrus, Quercus, Salix, Tilia,* and *Ulmus*; very rarely on wood of coniferous trees, noted on *Picea* and *Tsuga*; reported on *Abies* (Wash., Weir [223]), on *Juglans* (Mo., Maneval [131]), and on *Prunus* and *Sassafras* (Mich., Kauffman [101]).

DISTRIBUTION: Specimens have been examined from Me., N.H., Vt., Mass., Conn., N.Y., Pa., N.J., Del., Md., D.C., Va., W. Va., N.C., S.C., Ga., Fla., Ala., La., Miss., Tenn., Ky., Ohio, Ind., Ill., Mich., Wis., Minn., N. Dak., S. Dak., Iowa, Mo., Kans., Nebr., Ark., Texas, Mont., and Wash.; in Canada from Nova Scotia, Quebec, Ontario, Manitoba, Alberta, and British Columbia.

ILLUSTRATIONS: Hard, Mushrooms, figs. 351–352 (as *Trametes rubescens*), 358; Lloyd, Myc. Notes 72: fig. 2792; McDougall, Mushrooms, opp. p. 118; Moffatt, Chicago Acad. Sci. Nat. Hist. Survey Bul. 7: pl. 18; Neuman, Wis. Geol. and Nat. Hist. Survey Bul. 33: pl. 3, fig. 12; Overholts, Pa. Agr. Exp. Sta. Bul. 316: figs. 1–12; White, Conn. State Geol. and Nat. Hist. Survey Bul. 3: pl. 34.

One form of this highly polymorphic species is said to have been designated *Daedalea (Trametes) rubescens* Alb. & Schw. ex Fries. It shows a beautiful pinkish-red color on the pore surface where handled and is usually poroid, or the pores are only slightly elongated. Other synonyms, based on some of the many variations, are said to be *D. corrugata* Klotzsch, *Lenzites Klotzschii* Berk., *L. Crataegi* Berk., *L. Cookei* Berk., and *L. proxima* Berk. I have seen authentic specimens of none of these, but, as interpreted by American mycologists, all of them belong here.

Considerable collecting is necessary before the relationship of all the forms of this species becomes clear. The hymenium varies from forms entirely poroid, with angular pores, to ones with the pores merely elongated in a radial direction, to distinctly daedaloid forms, and even to completely lamellate ones. These variations are all well shown in the Overholts' illustrations cited above. *Salix* and *Betula* seem to be the most common hosts.

Evidently the narrow, branched paraphyses cannot be considered of much aid in identifying the species. Where they are present they are diagnostic enough, but often they are absent. Apparently, as in species of *Stereum* and *Corticium*, they may be abundant in the earlier stages of hymenial development, but later enlargement of the basidia renders them less conspicuous, and there is some evidence that they partially gelatinize at maturity and are then not demonstrable.

Chlamydospores have been reported by Patouillard (*Rev. Mycol.* 4: 37. 1882 [as *Trametes rubescens*]) as a secondary spore form in this species. I have not been able to verify this observation in the numerous cultures of the species in my collection.

The fungus produces a white delignifying decay of the sapwood, in some hosts associated with the formation of black lines in the decayed wood.

2. DAEDALEA QUERCINA L. ex Fries

Syst. Myc. 1: 333. 1821

(Figs. 479–480 and Plate 125)

Agaricus quercinus L., Sp. Plant., p. 1176. 1753.

Sporophore sessile, rigid or hard-corky, persisting for several years; pileus applanate or young specimens convex, 4–15 × 4–20 × 1–8 cm., whitish to umbrinous or black with age, at first finely and compactly tomentose, soon glabrous, uneven, finally rimose when very old, eventually zonate or furrowed, the margin often thick and obtuse; context pallid or light brown (not pure white), corky, 0.2–1.5 cm. thick; pore surface whitish to umber or avellaneous, the tubes 0.5–3 cm. long, the mouths rarely poroid, usually daedaloid, sometimes lamellate, 1 mm. or more broad, the walls thick (nearly 1 mm.) and obtuse; spores cylindric, hyaline, 5–6 × 2–3 μ; basidia 4–6 μ in diameter; cystidia none; hyphae pale brown in KOH, simple or in some specimens sparingly branched, with walls partially thickened, with no cross walls or clamps, 3–6 μ in diameter; all parts becoming dark or blackish in KOH solution.

HABITAT: Usually on logs, stumps, or trunks of *Castanea* and *Quercus*, noted also on *Fagus*, *Fraxinus*, *Juglans*, *Populus*, *Prunus*, and *Ulmus*; rarely from wounds in living trees.

DISTRIBUTION: Specimens have been examined from Me., Vt., Mass., Conn., N.Y., Pa., N.J., Del., Md., D.C., Va., W. Va., N.C., Ohio, and Iowa.

ILLUSTRATIONS: Ames, Ann. Mycol. 11: pl. 13, fig. 68; Boyce, Forest Path., fig. 203; Clements, Minn. Mushrooms, fig. 67; Gillet, Champ. France 2: pl. 266 (39); Hard, Mushrooms, fig. 357; Marshall, Mushroom Book, opp. p. 114; Meinecke, Forest Tree Dis. Calif. Nev., pl. 2; Michael, Führ. f. Pilzfr. 3: fig. 45; Schaeffer, Fung. Bavar., pl. 231; von Schrenk and Spaulding, U. S. Dept. Agr. Pl. Ind. Bul. 149: pl. 10; Sowerby, Col. Fig. English Fungi, pl. 181 (as *Agaricus*); Stevens, Fungi Plant Dis., fig. 312.

Sporophores of this species are unquestionably perennial, the pores being extended downward year by year and renewed growth usually taking place also at the margin of the pileus. As a result, the older surface of the pileus soon becomes furrowed and blackish. The hymenium is less variable than in *Daedalea confragosa*, though partially poroid forms, as well as those more or less lamellate, are found. Within its range this is one of the most common pore fungi, but it is practically limited to the Allegheny region and the Atlantic seaboard, although Murrill records it from "temperate North America." I have seen no specimens from west of the Mississippi River, except one sent from Iowa by Dr. G. W. Martin, who reports it as "extremely rare in that state."

The decay produced by this fungus is of the general brown carbonizing type usually affecting only the heartwood. It seems to be largely a butt rot and progresses very slowly, the rotted wood remaining firm for a long period. The rot is scarcely to be distinguished from that caused by *Polyporus Spraguei* and is very similar to that of *P. sulphureus*. Both of these are not infrequent, however, as trunk rots rather than butt rots. *Daedalea quercina* does sometimes occur at considerable heights on the tree and was on one occasion observed on a large branch stub forty feet from the ground.

3. DAEDALEA JUNIPERINA Murr.

North Amer. Flora 9: 125. 1908

(Figs. 473–474 and Plate 125)

Agaricus juniperinus Murr., Torrey Bot. Club Bul. 32: 85. 1905.

Sporophore sessile, decurrent, or resupinate, rigid and corky; pileus 1–7 × 2–8 × 1–4 cm., gray to cinnamon or ochraceous, finally somewhat blackish at the base, distinctly but compactly tomentose, the margin rather thick; context white or pallid, punky to soft-corky, 0.5–1 cm. thick; pore surface white or pallid to isabelline, daedaloid or approaching lamellate, the interspaces 1 mm. broad or more, the walls thick and obtuse; spores cylindric, hyaline, 6–8 × 2.5–3.5 μ; cystidia none; hyphae hyaline, quite flexuous, nearly simple, with partially or completely thickened walls, with no cross walls or clamps, 3–6 μ in diameter. (Compare no. 2, *Daedalea quercina*, and *D. Westii*, p. 130.)

HABITAT: On living trees, structural timbers, or stumps of *Juniperus virginiana* L.

DISTRIBUTION: Specimens have been examined from Pa., N.J., Md., D.C., Va., N.C., Fla., Miss., Ky., Mo., Kans., Nebr., Ark., and Ariz.; reported from N.Y. (Lowe [125]).

The erratic distribution of this species is interesting, and in no wise correlated with the distribution or prevalence of its host. Though a specimen from Pennsylvania is in the Lloyd Herbarium and though the host is extremely common throughout the state, I have never collected the species there in a period of more than thirty years. Moreover, though it occurs abundantly in a restricted area near Great Falls, Virginia, it is not otherwise known from that state. Its similarity in pileate condition to *Daedalea quercina* is very marked, and the resupinate form could easily be confused with *Trametes heteromorpha*. *D. quercina* and *D. juniperina* are quite distinct in culture.

The relationship of *Trametes kansensis* Cragin to this species cannot be decided at the present time, and may always be an unsolved problem. Murrill (139) listed *T. kansensis* as a possible synonym of *Daedalea quercina*. But I have seen no specimen of *D. quercina* from Kansas, nor from any state (except Iowa) west of the Mississippi River, although Murrill (139) records it as occurring in "temperate North America." If *T. kansensis* were in reality synonymous with *D. juniperina*, its occurrence in Kansas would not be remarkable, for *D. juniperina* has been collected from that and nearby states. *T. kansensis* is, of course, a much earlier name.

4. DAEDALEA UNICOLOR Bull. ex Fries

Syst. Myc. 1: 336. 1821

(Figs. 475–478, 554, and Plate 125)

Boletus unicolor Bull., Herb. France, pl. 408. 1788.
Cerrena unicolor (Bull. ex Fries) Murr., Jour. Mycol. 9: 91. 1903.

Sporophore sessile or effused-reflexed, thin, coriaceous when fresh, more or less rigid or somewhat flexible when dry, usually imbricate; pileus rarely entirely resupinate, 0.5–6 × 2–8 × 0.15–0.5 cm., white to cinereous, olivaceous, ochraceous, or brownish, black behind with age, densely villose or hirsute, strongly zonate, often covered with a growth of green algae; context white or light-colored, 1 mm. or less thick, sometimes almost obsolete, a thin dark line separating the context from the pubescence; pore surface white to cinereous or smoky, the tubes 0.5–4 mm. long, the mouths at first daedaloid and averaging 2–3 per mm., often breaking up into *Irpex*-like teeth, in rare cases poroid throughout; spores oblong or oblong-ellipsoid, smooth, hyaline, 4.5–5.5 × 2.5–3.5 μ; cystidia scarcely noteworthy, but sometimes present as subcylindric or clavate hyaline bodies in the hymenium and projecting slightly, 3–7 μ in diameter, rather blunt-pointed at the apex; hyphal pegs occasionally present, more or less spreading at the tips; hyphae hyaline, the larger ones simple or nearly so, the smaller ones considerably branched, with some unmistakable evidence of clamp connections and cross walls but these rarely seen, 2–5 μ in diameter.

HABITAT: Usually on dead wood of deciduous trees, noted on *Acer, Aesculus, Ailanthus, Alnus, Amelanchier, Betula, Carpinus, Carya, Castanea, Celtis, Cornus, Crataegus, Fagus, Fraxinus, Ilex, Liriodendron, Magnolia, Populus, Prunus, Pyrus, Quercus, Salix, Tilia,* and *Ulmus*; rarely on wood of coniferous trees, noted on *Juniperus* and *Tsuga*; reported on *Abies* (Idaho, Weir [223]) and on *Ostrya* (Mich., Kauffman [101]).

DISTRIBUTION: Specimens have been examined from Me., N.H., Vt., Mass., Conn., R.I., N.Y., Pa., N.J., Del., Md., D.C., Va., W. Va., N.C., La., Tenn., Ky., Ohio, Ind., Ill., Mich., Wis., Minn., N. Dak., S. Dak., Iowa, Mo., Kans., Nebr., Texas, Colo., Wyo., Mont., Idaho, Ore., and Wash.; in Canada from Nova Scotia, Quebec, Ontario, Manitoba, Alberta, and British Columbia; reported from Ark. (Swartz [212]).

ILLUSTRATIONS: Campbell, Jour. Forestry 37: p. 976; Moffatt, Chicago Acad. Sci. Nat. Hist. Survey Bul. 7: pl. 17, fig. 2; Murrill, Mycologia 10: pl. 6, fig. 6 (as *Cerrena*); Overholts, Wash. Univ. Studies 3: pl. 8, fig. 45.

In well-developed specimens the tomentose layer is seen to arise from a rather definite cuticular layer, which appears as a dark line just beneath the tomentum in lateral view of a vertical section of the pileus, but which is not conspicuous under the microscope. The cystidia seem to be prominent enough to be of distinct aid in identifying this species only if the hymenium is well developed. Young specimens usually show a distinctly daedaloid pore surface, as does the growing margin of more mature specimens. But in age the older tubes become so irpiciform that the fungus is likely to be referred to *Hydnum* or *Irpex*.

The decay produced by this fungus is of the general delignifying type, whitening the wood and rendering it brittle, so that it flakes easily when rubbed between thumb and fingers. No black lines are formed, but brown water-soaked flecks have been noted. The fungus gives rise to large cankers on the face of living *Acer rubrum* L. and *Acer saccharum* Marsh., and Campbell (28) is of the opinion that it is parasitic. He holds that it gains entrance to the tree through dead or cut companion sprouts, first decaying the heartwood and then working out through the sapwood. When the cambium is reached a canker is produced, the outline of which is often marked by prominent callusing.

5. DAEDALEA AMBIGUA Berk.

London Jour. Bot. 4: 305. 1845

(Figs. 463–464, 481–482, and Plate 125)

Boletus Aesculi-flavae Schw., Schr. Nat. Ges. Leipzig 1: 96. 1822.
Daedalea Aesculi (Schw.) Murr., North Amer. Flora 9: 126. 1908.

Sporophore sessile though sometimes appearing substipitate or tuberculate-sessile, corky or flexible when fresh, rigid and hardcorky when dry; pileus 3–20 × 5–35 × 0.3–3 cm., white or whitish, often umber to purplish black at the base, drying white, gray, smoky, or somewhat yellowish, often zonate at the margin, minutely velvety to glabrous, usually quite smooth and velvety to the touch, the margin thin; context milk-white to light wood color, floccose-punky to hard-corky, 0.2–2 cm. thick; pore surface white, usually yellowish to pale brown on drying, the tubes 2–4 mm. long, the mouths circular to daedaloid or more or less lamellate, averaging 2–3 per mm., the walls thick and entire; spores cylindric, smooth, hyaline, 5–7 × 1.5–2.5 μ; cystidia none; inconspicuous simple or forked paraphyses present, about 2 μ in diameter; hyphae mostly simple, thick-walled, with no cross walls or clamps, 3–7 μ in diameter; sometimes much-branched hyphal complexes present. (Compare no. 84, *Polyporus robiniophilus.*)

HABITAT: On stumps, logs, and trunks of deciduous trees, occasionally from wounded areas in living trees, noted on *Acer, Ailanthus, Carya, Celtis, Diospyros, Magnolia, Nyssa, Populus, Quercus, Salix,* and *Ulmus*; reported on *Carpinus* and *Juglans* (Mo., Maneval [131]).

DISTRIBUTION: Specimens have been examined from W. Va., N.C., S.C., Ga., Fla., Ala., La., Miss., Tenn., Ky., Ohio, Ind., Ill., Mo., Kans., Ark., Okla., and Texas; reported from Wis. (Dodge [40]) and Iowa (Wolf [234]).

ILLUSTRATIONS: Hard, Mushrooms, figs. 355–356.

The species was reported by Miss M. M. Wolf from Iowa (234) only on the basis of MacBride's record. She says there is no specimen in the State University of Iowa Herbarium at present. Dodge's record from Wisconsin (40) is doubtful. Lowe's record in the first edition of his New York paper (124, p. 103) was an error.

In some specimens the hymenium is distinctly daedaloid, in others, entirely poroid.

I do not deem it advisable to replace the name under which this species has been known so long with the Schweinitzian name, although an examination of the specimen purporting to be the Schweinitz type shows they are unquestionably synonymous. *Daedalea glaberrima* Berk. & Curt., described from South Carolina, *Trametes Berkeleyi* Cooke, from Ohio, and *T. lactea* Fries, from Carolina, have been recorded as synonyms. *D. elegans* Spreng. ex Fries of all tropical regions is only a thin, more lamellate form of this species, and the name is an older one. This form is rarely if ever found on the United States mainland. *Lenzites (Daedalea) repanda* (Pers.) Fries is the same form. Lloyd (*Letter* 62: 7. 1916) agreed to this interpretation.

The decay produced by this species seems to be confined to the sapwood, and is of the general delignifying type.

6. Daedalea Berkeleyi Sacc.

Syll. Fung. 6: 381. 1888

(Figs. 530–532)

Gloeophyllum Berkeleyi (Sacc.) Murr., Torrey Bot. Club Bul. 32: 370. 1905.

Sporophore sessile, apparently perennial, sometimes laterally confluent, leathery to corky; pileus 2–5 × 2.5–10 × 0.7–2.5 cm., convex or nearly plane, rusty brown to dark rusty brown, weathering finally to grayish or blackish, at first compactly tomentose, soon glabrous or nearly so, somewhat zoned or furrowed, the margin rather thick or almost obtuse; context dark rusty brown, 3–7 mm. thick, punky, or soft-corky; pore surface nearly concolorous with margin of pileus, poroid to daedaloid or somewhat lamellate, the tubes attaining lengths up to 2 cm., but usually 4–6 mm., the mouths subcircular in poroid forms and averaging 1–2 per mm., in daedaloid and lamellate forms 0.5–2 mm. broad, thick and entire; spores cylindric, smooth, hyaline, 7–8 × 2.5–3 μ; cystidia none; hyphae long and flexuous, simple or nearly so, nearly hyaline to chestnut-brown in KOH, with clamps and cross walls occasional or rare on the lighter-colored hyphae, 3–6 μ in diameter.

HABITAT: On the dead wood of coniferous trees, noted on *Pinus*.

DISTRIBUTION: Specimens have been examined from Va., S.C., Fla., Ala., La., Miss., Tenn., and Texas.

ILLUSTRATIONS: Humphrey, U. S. Dept. Agr. Bul. 510: pl. 6, fig. 7 (as *Lenzites*).

This fungus is frequently referred to as *Lenzites Berkeleyi*, but apparently it is not *L. Berkeleyi* Lév., which is said to be a synonym of *L. betulina*.

7. Daedalea farinacea (Fries) Overh.

Torrey Bot. Club Bul. 65: 174. 1938

(Figs. 461–462 and Plate 125)

Irpex farinaceus Fries, Linnaea 5: 523. 1830.
Cerrenella farinacea (Fries) Murr., North Amer. Flora 9: 74. 1908.
Irpex cinerascens Schw., Synop. Fung. Amer. Bor., p. 164. 1832.
Irpex coriaceus Berk. & Rav., Grevillea 1: 101. 1873.

Sporophore sessile, effused-reflexed, or largely resupinate, thin and flexible and remaining so in dried specimens; pileus 0–1 × 1–4 ×

0.1–0.2 cm., dimidiate or conchate, dark rusty brown or umber-brown, tomentose, with the tomentum finally thrown into folds or zones and eventually becoming much compacted or entirely disappearing, the margin thin and flexible; context about 1 mm. thick, rusty brown, soft and fibrous; pore surface typically olivaceous or yellowish green, finally becoming more gray or somewhat brownish, the tubes not more than 1 mm. long, the mouths angular to sinuous and irregular and sometimes becoming entirely lacerate and toothed, the edges thin and fimbriate, averaging about 2 per mm.; spores cylindric, smooth, hyaline, 5–6 × 2–2.5 μ; cystidia none; hyphae mostly simple, brown, rather thin-walled, with no cross walls or clamps, 3–6 μ in diameter, with some smaller and more hyaline hyphae interspersed; all parts black in KOH.

HABITAT: On dead wood of deciduous trees, noted on *Liriodendron*, *Quercus*, and *Ulmus*.

DISTRIBUTION: Specimens have been examined from D.C., W. Va., S.C., Ala., La., Tenn., Ohio, Ill., Iowa, and Mo.; reported also from Fla. (Murrill).

Like *Irpex Tulipiferae* Schw., this species is properly classed with the polypores in my estimation. Both species may exhibit a decidedly *Irpex*-like hymenium at times, but this is a condition of advanced age, after the tubes have split. The margin of the pileus of *Daedalea farinacea* shows well-formed pores. In *I. Ravenelii* Berk., which was originally described in *Daedalea*, pores are not formed. There, very plainly in the specimens I have examined, the lower surface is from the first irpiciform, the teeth being, in reality, often more *Radulum*-like than *Irpex*-like. Therefore I do not consider that species to belong to this family. Though of the same habit of growth and similar in size, the two species can be differentiated by the color of the pore surface as well as by its configuration. *I. Ravenelii* is a bright yellow-brown on the pore surface; *D. farinacea* is greenish yellow. While discussing these *Irpex*-like species, I may add that, to me, *I. cinnamomeus* Fries (*Hydnoporia fuscescens* (Schw.) Murrill) has no polyporoid characters, but belongs in the genus *Irpex* as originally described by Fries.

I have not examined the types of *Irpex coriaceus* Berk. & Rav., but the specimens distributed in Ravenel's Fungi Carol. Exsic. 3: 21 under that name are referable in synonymy here.

OMITTED SPECIES

[*Daedalea Westii* Murr., *Torrey Bot. Club Bul.* 65: 649. 1938. The type material of this species agrees with the concept of *D. juniperina* in this manual.   It should be noted, however, that Dr. W. A. Murrill specifically states that "this species shows no resemblance to *D. juniperina*, which is ungulate in form and much larger, although the descriptions sound much alike."—J.L.L.]

Genus 5. HEXAGONA Pollini emend. Fries

Epicr. Syst. Myc., p. 496. 1836–1838

Hexagona Pollini, Horti Prov. Pl. Nov., p. 35. 1816.

Plants annual, sessile, typically subcircular or reniform, growing on wood, pliant, thin, and flexible, the surface strongly zoned; context avellaneous to umber, thin; tubes shallow, the mouths hexagonal to subcircular, usually 1 mm. or more in diameter, often more or less radiately arranged; spores cylindric, hyaline; cystidia none in our species.

TYPE SPECIES: *Hexagona Wrightii* Klotzsch.

The genus differs from *Favolus* as here treated in the strongly zoned, sessile, pubescent pileus of leathery consistency, the brown context, and the weaker tendency of the tubes to be radially arranged. In general, these are the characters (except for the sessile nature of the pileus) that distinguish the genus from certain species of *Polyporus*. However, such species as *P. pinsitus* are scarcely to be separated on these or any other points.

Only a single species is known to enter our southernmost limits, although *Hexagona tenuis* Fries may be looked for in the extreme South.

HEXAGONA VARIEGATA Berk.

Ann. and Mag. Nat. Hist. II, 9: 196. 1852
(Figs. 528–529 and Plate 127)

Favolus variegatus (Berk.) Murr., Torrey Bot. Club Bul. 32: 101. 1905.

Sporophore sessile; pileus quite pliant and flexible when fresh, somewhat flexible when dry, dimidiate to reniform, 3–6 × 4–10 × 0.1–0.4 cm., dark-colored and strongly zonate, the predominating color chestnut or hazel but the alternate zones often brownish or inclining to olivaceous, strongly short-pubescent when young, becoming gradually glabrous on the hazel zones, usually somewhat radiate-striate under the pubescence, the margin usually of lighter color, quite thin; context avellaneous to umber-brown, about 1 mm.

thick, fibrous; pore surface avellaneous to pale umber, the tubes less than 1 mm. long, the mouths hexagonal to subcircular, averaging 1–1.5 per mm., the walls rather thick and entire; spores cylindric and 12–15 × 4–6 μ when mature, often oblong-ellipsoid in earlier stages and 8–10 μ long, hyaline; basidia 9–12 μ in diameter; cystidia none; hyphae pale brown in KOH, long and flexuous, simple or nearly so, mostly with partially thickened walls, with no cross walls or clamps, 4–6 μ in diameter.

HABITAT: On dead wood of deciduous trees.

DISTRIBUTION: Specimens have been examined only from Fla.

ILLUSTRATIONS: Lloyd, Synop. Hexagona, fig. 287.

This species, when well-developed, is an elegant one, easily recognized by the thin, pliant, velvety pileus with predominating chestnut or reddish color and strongly zonate surface, the umber-brown context, and the large but very shallow hexagonal to subcircular pores. *Hexagona tenuis* Fries is somewhat similar in form and texture, but the color is decidedly lighter, without reddish tints, and the zones are more uniformly colored. Our species differs from species of *Favolus* in the sessile habit, the brown context, the more leathery consistency, and the strongly zoned pileus.

Genus 6. TRAMETES Fries

Gen. Hym., p. 11. 1836

Antrodia Karst., Soc. Fauna Flora Fenn. Meddel. 5: 40. 1879.
Funalia Pat. pro parte, Essai Tax. Hym., p. 95. 1900.
Pogonomyces Murr., Torrey Bot. Club Bul. 31: 609. 1904.
Coriolellus Murr., Torrey Bot. Club Bul. 32: 481. 1905.
Coriolopsis Murr. pro parte, Torrey Bot. Club Bul. 32: 358. 1905.

Plants typically annual, sometimes persisting for a few years, leathery to corky, sessile or some species varying to resupinate at times (no truly resupinate species are included); context white to brown, punky to corky, descending unchanged into the walls of the tubes, hence the pores typically extending to uneven depths into the context so that their upper terminations do not form a continuous straight line; pore mouths circular to angular, usually quite regular and entire, never strongly daedaloid or lamellate; spores cylindric, hyaline; cystidia none; setae rarely present.

TYPE SPECIES: *Trametes suaveolens* (L. ex Fries) Fries.

No genus of the family is provocative of more confusion and uncertainty than the present one. It seems impossible to delimit it so that it can be readily recognized. One eventually, after much experience, acquires a more or less practical concept of its typical characters. That mycologists have always found it a stumbling block is evidenced by the fact that many species of *Polyporus* (especially of the *Polystictus* type) and some species of *Fomes* and *Daedalea* have at one time or another been transferred to it. Indeed, one must conclude that the classification of the family was not especially enriched by its establishment. In common with what one finds in *Lenzites* and *Daedalea*, the tissue of the context of the pileus descends unchanged into the walls of the tubes, but the application of this criterion to the genus *Polyporus* would necessitate the inclusion in *Trametes* of many species of that genus, especially of the thin, coriaceous (*Polystictus*-type) species. In order to avoid as much confusion as possible, the species more usually referred to *Trametes* have been retained (with such notable exceptions as *Fomes Pini*), while many whose positions are more or less debatable have been referred to *Polyporus*. Moreover, most of the species here retained are keyed out also in that genus, and some species from the other genera have been included in the *Trametes* key. Practically, it may be the best identification procedure for the beginner to disregard this genus until the specimen at hand has been run through the *Polyporus* key.

KEY TO THE SPECIES OF TRAMETES

1. Context white or not darker than pale wood color or ochraceous 2
   Context pinkish, pinkish brown, or rose-colored
                  See no. 13, *Fomes subroseus*
   Context distinctly brown to dark rusty brown 14
2. Pileus strongly pubescent, fibrillose to hirsute or hispid 3
   Pileus slightly villose, finely tomentose, or glabrous 4
3. Pileus thin and coriaceous, less than 0.5 cm. thick; from the
   District of Columbia and Tennessee southward; usually
   on hardwoods .... 10. *T. rigida*
   Pileus thin and coriaceous, less than 0.5 cm. thick; from
   Colorado to Manitoba and westward; on conifers only
             See no. 109, *Polyporus cuneatus*
   Pileus thicker and more leathery, more than 0.5 cm. thick;
   from Maryland to California and northward; on hardwoods only .... 5. *T. Trogii*
4. Pileus small and shield-shaped, usually measuring less than
   0.5 × 1.5 cm., sometimes larger, sessile, soon blackish
   on top; usually on dead *Alnus* .. See no. 8, *Fomes scutellatus*
   Pileus not characterized as above 5
5. Pileus brown, often almost entirely resupinate 6
   Pileus white to yellowish, reddish, or pale wood color, sometimes black with age 7
6. Pileus thin, less than 0.6 cm. thick; usually on hardwoods; a
   narrow black line separating the short tomentum from
   the context; pores 1–3 per mm.; spores cylindric
             8. *T. mollis*
   Pileus thin, less than 0.3 cm. thick; on conifers only; no black
   line under the scanty tomentum; pores 1–2 per mm.;
   spores cylindric .... 3. *T. variiformis*

Pileus thicker and more triangular in section, usually 0.5 cm.
or more thick; on both hardwoods and conifers; no black
line and no tomentum; pores averaging 3 per mm.;
pileus without evident crust; spores more or less cylindric .... 2. *T. serialis*
Pileus as in the last; usually on wood of coniferous trees;
pores about 3 per mm.; pileus with a thin crust evident
as a narrow black line at the surface of vertical sections;
spores subglobose .... See no. 1, *Fomes annosus*
7. Pileus up to 20 cm. long, 5–35 cm. broad 8
Pileus 0–3 cm. long, 1–6 cm. broad 12
8. Pores averaging 4–6 per mm. 9
Pores averaging 1–4 per mm. 10
9. Hyphae of context 6–12 μ in diameter; on living trees,
especially *Robinia*; rare or absent in the Gulf States
See no. 84, *Polyporus robiniophilus*
Hyphae of context 4–7 μ in diameter; on dead wood; from
Florida and Louisiana .... 7. *T. cubensis*
10. Pileus odorous when fresh; spores 3–4 μ wide. . 6. *T. suaveolens*
Pileus inodorous; spores 1.5–2.5 μ wide 11
11. Context and surface of pileus white in fresh specimens at
least in part; ranging from West Virginia and Illinois
southward .... See no. 5, *Daedalea ambigua*
Context and surface of pileus usually not white but pallid or
wood-colored; cosmopolitan. See no. 1, *Daedalea confragosa*
12. Pores typically large and rather irregular or daedaloid, 1 mm.
or more in diameter; tubes 3–10 mm. long; usually on
wood of coniferous trees, occasionally on hardwoods
4. *T. heteromorpha*
Pores smaller and more regular, never daedaloid, measuring
less than 1 mm. in diameter; usually on hardwoods,
occasionally on conifers 13
13. Context 2–5 mm. thick; pileus, pores, and context not white
but rather pale wood color; spores 7–9 μ long
11. *T. malicola*
Context 1.5 mm. or less thick; pileus, pores, and context
white or nearly so; spores 9–11 μ long....... 1. *T. sepium*
14. Pores averaging 3–5 per mm.; pileus with a thick mat of
black stiff hairs; from the Gulf States
See no. 141, *Polyporus hydnoides*

Pores larger than above; pileus often pubescent but not as
above; ranging northward 15

15. Pileus 2.5 cm. or less long 16
Pileus becoming more than 2.5 cm. long 18

16. On hardwoods only; setae none; context more than 1 mm.
thick .... 11. *T. malicola*
Usually on hardwoods; setae none; context 1 mm. or less
thick .... 8. *T. mollis*
On hardwoods only; setae present .... See no. 17, *Fomes tenuis*
On conifers only; setae none .... 13. *T. carbonaria*
On conifers only; setae present 17

17. Setae 5–9 μ in diameter; spores cylindric; pileus and hymenium dark rusty brown .... See no. 17, *Fomes tenuis*
Setae 7–15 μ in diameter; spores subglobose to globose; pileus
and hymenium typically bright tawny
See no. 22, *Fomes Pini* var. *Abietis*

18. Context light brown or umber-brown; setae none; spores
cylindric, 12–15 × 4–5 μ; pores averaging 1–2 per mm.;
usually on *Salix* .... 9. *T. hispida*
Context tawny or ochraceous tawny; setae present; spores
globose; pores averaging 3–4 per mm.; on conifers only
See no. 22, *Fomes Pini* var. *Abietis*
Context rusty brown or darker; setae none; spores cylindric,
9–12 × 3–5 μ; pores averaging 2–3 per mm.; on conifers
only .... 12. *T. americana*

1a. *Context white or whitish*
2a. *Context not over 1.5 mm. thick*

1. TRAMETES SEPIUM Berk.
London Jour. Bot. 6: 322. 1847
(Figs. 506–507 and Plate 125)

Coriolellus sepium (Berk.) Murr., Torrey Bot. Club Bul. 32: 481. 1905.

Sporophore annual, sessile, effused-reflexed, or resupinate, often
imbricate, flexible when fresh, corky when dry; pileus 0–1 × 1–2.5 ×
0.2–0.7 cm., typically isabelline or pale wood color, sometimes white
or whitish, zonate or azonate, at first finely tomentose or short-

pubescent, then nearly or quite glabrous, occasionally with a short, erect, and somewhat agglutinated tomentum in mature specimens; context white, watery when fresh, tough, less than 1.5 mm. thick; pore surface white or pallid, the tubes 1–5 mm. long, the mouths at first circular, finally likely to become angular or slightly sinuous, averaging 1–2 per mm.; spores cylindric or cylindric-ellipsoid, hyaline, maximum size 9–11 $\times$ 3–4.5 μ, but often 7–10 $\times$ 3.5–4 μ; basidia usually 6–8 μ in diameter, occasionally 8–10 μ; cystidia none; hyphae in part nearly simple, hyaline, the walls usually completely thickened, but the thickening not conspicuous, mostly with few or no cross walls or clamps, 3–6 μ in diameter, but usually intermixed with some considerably branched hyphae, with walls only partly thickened and with rather numerous but quite inconspicuous clamps.

HABITAT: On dead wood, usually of deciduous trees, often on fence posts and structural timbers, noted on *Acer, Arbutus, Azalea, Betula, Castanea, Diospyros, Fagus, Fraxinus, Ostrya, Quercus, Rhus, Salix, Ulmus,* and *Viburnum*; occasionally on wood of coniferous trees, noted on *Abies, Cupressus, Juniperus, Pinus, Pseudotsuga,* and *Taxodium*; reported on *Carpinus, Sassafras,* and *Tilia* (Mich., Kauffman [101]), on *Catalpa* (Kans., Stevens [210]), and on *Thuja* (Mich., Kauffman [105]).

DISTRIBUTION: Specimens have been examined from N.H., Mass., Conn., N.Y., Pa., N.J., Del., Md., D.C., Va., W. Va., N.C., Ga., Fla., Ala., La., Miss., Tenn., Ky., Ohio, Ind., Ill., Wis., Iowa, Mo., Kans., Nebr., Ark., Texas, N. Mex., Ariz., and Calif.; in Canada from Quebec and Ontario; reported from Vt. (Spaulding [209]), Mich. (Kauffman [105]), Mont. (Weir [227]), and Ore. (Kauffman [106]).

ILLUSTRATIONS: Lloyd, Myc. Notes 59: figs. 1420–1421 (as *Trametes minima*); Overholts, Wash. Univ. Studies 3: pl. 7, fig. 39; *idem*, Mycologia 15: pl. 22, fig. 5.

The small, strictly pileate form has been known as *Trametes minima*. To some extent the species appears to intergrade with *T. heteromorpha* and *T. malicola*. Several collections of a rather strongly pubescent variation have been noted from the Far West.

Trametes sepium produces a general brown carbonizing decay in which the wood fractures into cubical blocks.

2. TRAMETES SERIALIS Fries

Hym. Eur., p. 585. 1874

(Figs. 508–510, 610, and Plate 125)

Polyporus serialis Fries, Syst. Myc. 1: 370. 1821.
Coriolellus serialis (Fries) Murr., North Amer. Flora 9: 29. 1907.

Sporophore often resupinate and usually only slightly reflexed, leathery when fresh, rigid when dry; pileus 0–1 × 1–4 × 0.3–0.8(–2) cm., often laterally connate, at first nearly white, soon of a uniform brown color ("tawny-olive" to "buckthorn brown"), zonate where best developed, at first slightly tomentose, soon glabrous or with a short brown tomentum; context white, fibrous, not more than 1 mm. thick; pore surface white or nearly so, sometimes isabelline, the tubes usually 2–5 mm. long but frequently perennial and elongating to as much as 1 cm. but not distinctly stratified, the mouths circular to angular, rather thick-walled and entire, averaging 3 per mm., visible to the unaided eye; spores cylindric-elliptic or cylindric, often with pointed ends, hyaline, 5–8 × 2–3 μ; basidia 5–6 μ in diameter; cystidia none; hyphae long and flexuous, mostly simple with thickened walls, many without clamps but others with scattered inconspicuous clamps, also some thin-walled hyphae with clamps, all 2–4 μ in diameter.

HABITAT: On dead wood, usually of coniferous trees, noted on *Abies, Larix, Picea, Pinus, Pseudotsuga, Sequoia, Taxodium, Thuja,* and *Tsuga*; occasionally on hardwoods, noted on *Arbutus, Betula, Fraxinus, Populus,* and *Quercus*; reported on *Alnus* (Wis., Neuman [148]), on *Juniperus* (Baxter [11k]), and on *Salix* (Colo., Kauffman [102]).

DISTRIBUTION: Specimens have been examined from Me., N.H., Vt., Mass., N.Y., Pa., N.J., Md., W. Va., N.C., Ala., La., Tenn., Ohio, Ill., Mich., Wis., Mo., Kans., Ark., N. Mex., Ariz., Colo., Idaho, Ore., Wash., and Calif.; in Canada from Ontario and British Columbia; reported from Fla. (Murrill), Iowa (Wolf [234]), N. Mex. and Mont. (Weir [223; 227]), Manitoba (Bisby *et al.* [12]), and from Conn., R.I., Va., Ga., Ky., Minn., Texas, Wyo., Alaska, Newfoundland, Alberta, Yukon Territory, and Northwest Territory (Baxter [11k]).

ILLUSTRATIONS: Baxter, Mich. Acad. Sci. Arts and Letters Papers 27: pl. 1, figs. 1 and 9; Fries, Icones Sel. Hym., pl. 191, fig. 2; Lloyd, Myc. Notes 69: fig. 2393; Nobles, Canad. Jour. Res. C, 21: figs. 39–41; Shope, Mo. Bot. Gard. Ann. 18: pl. 30, fig. 3; Snell, Mycologia 15: pl. 16, figs. 1–3.

This species often occurs in a resupinate condition, and its identification is likely to be sought in *Poria*. In its resupinate condition *Trametes rigida* is sometimes quite similar to *T. serialis*, but may be separated by the slightly larger pores and the pale brown subiculum, which, under the microscope, is seen to be composed entirely of pale brown hyphae. In the pileate condition the two species are not at all similar, for they differ in the pubescence and in the color of the pileus. Care must often be exercised in distinguishing *T. serialis* from *Fomes annosus*, especially in the resupinate condition. If the specimen be sporulating, this separation is easily made on the basis of the spores, and pileate conditions present little difficulty because of the incrusted layer, often quite thin, over the pileus of *F. annosus*— a character that is always lacking in *T. serialis*. *T. serialis* causes a brown carbonizing type of decay, whereas *F. annosus* causes a delignifying decay. Furthermore, the context is thicker in *F. annosus*, and the hyphae lack clamp connections.

Chlamydospores are known as a secondary spore form in pure cultures of *Trametes serialis*.

Mildred K. Nobles has recently (*Canad. Jour. Res.* C, 21: 211–234. 1943) attempted to throw much-needed light on the *Trametes serialis* complex, especially as it pertains to the resupinate fungi closely related to *T. serialis*. Baxter (11k) prefers to treat the complex as a unit. Thus he reduces *Poria Sequoiae* to synonymy here, and at the same time admits failure to explain satisfactorily why *T. serialis* (in the broad sense) is an important factor in living trees of *Sequoia* but not in its other coniferous hosts.

Trametes serialis is of considerable importance as a decayer of structural timbers—in fact, it is more frequently met on such timbers, at least in the eastern United States, than in other situations. Snell (204) describes its effects on timbers of weave sheds and cotton mills. It appears commonly on flooring timbers and bridge timbers and in many similar places, where it causes a carbonizing cubical decay.

3. TRAMETES VARIIFORMIS Peck

N. Y. State Mus. Ann. Rept. 54: 170. 1901

(Figs. 504–505 and Plate 125)

Polyporus variiformis Peck, N. Y. State Mus. Ann. Rept. 42: 26. 1889.

Sporophore often resupinate, sometimes narrowly effused-reflexed, rarely sessile, thin and flexible when fresh, somewhat flexible on drying; pileus 0–1 × 1–5 × 0.1–0.3 cm., cinnamon-brown or tawny rufescent, fibrillose-tomentose, weathering to glabrous, zonate; context white, less than 1 mm. thick; pore surface white, whitish, or pale isabelline, the tubes 1–3 mm. long, the mouths sometimes somewhat daedaloid, elongate or rather irregular, averaging 1–2 per mm. but sometimes more elongated; spores cylindric, hyaline, 7–10 (–12) × 3–3.5 μ; basidia 5–6 μ in diameter; cystidia none, in nonsporulating hymenium often with capitate-incrusted narrow hyphae, the incrustations 5–6 μ in diameter; hyphae hyaline, not much branched, with no or very few cross walls or clamps, 2.5–4.5 μ in diameter.

HABITAT: On dead wood of coniferous trees, noted on *Abies*, *Larix*, *Picea*, *Pinus*, and *Tsuga*; reported on *Betula* (Wash., Weir [223]).

DISTRIBUTION: Specimens have been examined from Me., N.H., Vt., N.Y., Minn., and Colo.; in Canada from Newfoundland, Quebec, and Ontario; reported from Mich. (Povah [174]) and from Mont. and Wash. (Weir [227; 223]).

ILLUSTRATIONS: Baxter, Mich. Acad. Sci. Arts and Letters Papers 21: pl. 39; *ibid.* 27: pls. 8–9; Lloyd, Myc. Notes 61: figs. 1521–1522; *ibid.* 62: fig. 1698; Shope, Mo. Bot. Gard. Ann. 18: pl. 30, fig. 4.

In some fruit bodies not in sporulating condition the narrow, cystidium-like hyphae with rather conspicuous incrustations are very numerous, but where the hymenium is sporulating they are rarely seen. Similar incrusted hyphae are sometimes observed in *Trametes serialis*, into which small-pored forms of this species grade and to which this species has been referred in synonymy. *T. variiformis* differs typically in the thin pileus and the much larger pores, which often present a sublamellate condition.

The decay produced is of the brown carbonizing type.

2b. *Context usually 1.5 mm. or more thick* (see also *Trametes alaskana, T. corrugata,* and *T. subcubensis,* p. 154)

4. TRAMETES HETEROMORPHA (Fries) Bres.

In Neuman, Wis. Geol. and Nat. Hist. Survey Bul. 33: 40. 1914
(Figs. 488, 501–503, 612, and Plate 125)

Daedalea heteromorpha Fries, Obs. Myc. 1: 108. 1815.
Lenzites heteromorpha Fries, Epicr. Syst. Myc., p. 407. 1836–1838.
Coriolus hexagoniformis Murr., North Amer. Flora 9: 20. 1907.
Trametes lacerata Lloyd, Myc. Notes 43: 604. 1916.

Sporophore often entirely resupinate, sometimes shortly reflexed and occasionally definitely sessile or somewhat decurrent on the substratum, leathery and watery when fresh, drying rigid; pileus 0–3 × 2–6 × 0.5–1 cm., white or becoming straw color or wood color with age and on drying, usually rather distinctly radiate-striate or rugose and inconspicuously zoned, finely tomentose when young, more glabrous and rougher at maturity; context white, soft-corky or punky, 1–3 mm. thick; pore surface white, sometimes becoming yellowish on drying, the tubes 3–10 mm. long, the mouths often oblique and gaping, sometimes regular and hexagonal and measuring 1–2 mm. broad, sometimes nearly circular and about 1 mm. in diameter, but more frequently daedaloid and irregular, the walls rather thin, ciliate-pubescent to nearly glabrous, entire or dentate; spores cylindric when mature, oblong-ellipsoid in young stages, hyaline, 7–11(–14) × 4–6 μ; basidia 7–8 μ in diameter when sporulating; cystidia none; hyphae long and flexuous, simple, with walls partially or nearly completely thickened, with no cross walls or clamps except on some hyphae of small diameter, 4–7 μ in diameter. (Compare no. 1, *Trametes sepium*; no. 2, *T. serialis*; and *T. alaskana* Baxter, p. 154.)

HABITAT: Usually on dead wood of coniferous trees, noted on *Abies, Larix, Picea, Pinus, Pseudotsuga,* and *Tsuga*; occasionally on hardwoods, noted on *Alnus, Betula,* and *Quercus*; reported on *Juniperus* (Baxter [11e]).

DISTRIBUTION: Specimens have been examined from Me., N.H., Vt., Mass., N.Y., Pa., Ala., Mich., S. Dak., N. Mex., Colo., Wyo., Mont., Idaho, Ore., Wash., Calif., and Alaska; in Canada from

Nova Scotia, Quebec, Ontario, and British Columbia; reported from Va., Wis., Minn., Mo., Alberta, and Yukon Territory (Baxter [11e]).

ILLUSTRATIONS: Baxter, Mich. Acad. Sci. Arts and Letters Papers 21: pl. 36; *ibid.* 27: pls. 10–11; Lloyd, Myc. Notes 43: fig. 854 (as *Trametes lacerata*); *ibid.* 59: figs. 1415–1419; Weir, Mycologia 9: pl. 6 (as *Lenzites heteromorpha*).

The large irregular pores usually readily distinguish this species from any other found on wood of coniferous trees except *Trametes alaskana*, but the circular-pored form grades toward *T. sepium.*

The decay produced is of the brown carbonizing type, with small mycelial mats developed in the fractures.

5. TRAMETES TROGII Berk.

In Trog, Schweiz. Schwämme, Suppl. 2: 52. 1850

(Figs. 499–500, 524, and Plate 125)

Sporophore sessile, effused-reflexed, or resupinate, tough and flexible when fresh, rigid and firm when dry; pileus 0–6 × 1–12 × 0.7–2 cm., with a dense ochraceous, brownish, tan, or somewhat tawny hirsute pubescence, sometimes weathering to gray but never becoming blackish, azonate or inconspicuously zonate, the margin usually thin and acute; context white or nearly so, fibrous, drying rather hard at times, 2–5 mm. thick; pore surface whitish to isabelline, often with a flesh-gray or somewhat lavender tint when growing, the tubes 3–7 mm. long, rarely in 2 layers, the mouths subcircular to angular and irregular, rather thick-walled and entire, averaging 3 per mm.; spores cylindric, often slightly curved, hyaline, 8–9(–10) × 2–3 μ; basidial layer not more than 15 μ thick, the basidia 7–8 μ in diameter; hyphal pegs present, about 30 × 20 μ; hyphae hyaline, mostly thick-walled, many simple, but many very much branched and forming hyphal complexes, 3–7 μ in diameter; all parts darker but not black in KOH.

HABITAT: On dead wood, usually of *Populus* and *Salix*, also noted on *Acer, Betula*, and *Fagus.*

DISTRIBUTION: Specimens have been examined from Me., N.H., Vt., Mass., Conn., N.Y., Pa., Md., Mich., Wis., N. Mex., Colo., and Calif.; in Canada from Nova Scotia and Ontario; reported from Manitoba (Bisby *et al.* [12]).

Plants of this species have often been referred to *Trametes hispida*. They differ in being usually somewhat thinner, with a thinner context that is definitely white or whitish and that contains no brown hyphae, in having smaller pores with light-colored mouths, and especially in having much smaller spores. Neuman (148) seems to have correctly interpreted this species from Wisconsin. Dried plants have the pale bay color characteristic of *Polyporus biformis*, but the pores are smaller and the pubescence more dense and erect.

The relation of the present species to *Trametes Morgani* Lloyd is uncertain. Lloyd gave only fragmentary information about the type in the original description (*Letter* 69: 15. 1919), and when I last visited the Lloyd Herbarium no collection was found that could be considered the type. Lloyd, however, states that Fungi Columbiani No. 5094 is *T. Morgani*. My conception of Lloyd's species is based on this plant, and it is the plant long referred by Peck to *T. Trogii* Berk. and earlier considered by Murrill, myself, and many others to be a thin, light-colored, often resupinate condition of *T. hispida*.

Still other species are involved. Ravenel's Fungi Americani No. 429, issued as *Poria Beaumontii* Berk. & Curt., is evidently this species. Lloyd himself states that Romell's *Polyporus albo-carneo-gilvidus* is *Trametes Morgani*, but this seems doubtful, since a fragmentary specimen from Romell in my collection has spores 11–13 × 6 μ, markedly larger than those of *T. Trogii*. *T. salicina* Bres. is probably the present species.

A specimen under the name *Trametes Morgani* at the New York Botanical Garden was sent by Morgan to Ellis from Ohio. It is possible that this collection represents Lloyd's type. If so, I am in error regarding the synonymy of that species, for the specimen is a resupinate form of *T. serialis*.

6. TRAMETES SUAVEOLENS (L. ex Fries) Fries

Epicr. Syst. Myc., p. 491. 1836–1838

(Figs. 485–486, 563, 568, and Plate 125)

Boletus suaveolens L., Sp. Plant., p. 1177. 1753.
Polyporus suaveolens L. ex Fries, Syst. Myc. 1: 366. 1821.

Sporophore sessile or rarely effused-reflexed, soft-corky and somewhat watery when fresh and growing, firm and corky when dry;

pileus 1–10 × 5–16 × 1–4 cm., plane or convex, white, grayish or isabelline when fresh, sometimes drying yellowish, villose-tomentose to glabrous, azonate; context white or whitish, 0.5–2 cm. thick, tough or corky, anise-scented in fresh plants; pore surface white then dark-colored, drying yellowish if collected when light-colored, the tubes 0.3–1.5 cm. long, sometimes layered, the mouths circular, rather thick-walled, entire, averaging 1–3 per mm.; spores cylindric when mature, ellipsoid, oblong, or oblong-ellipsoid when young, smooth, hyaline, 7–11 × 3–4 μ; cystidia none or not noteworthy; hyphal pegs not abundant, conoidal to cylindric in form; hyphae sparingly branched, with thickened walls, with no cross walls or clamps, 6–12 μ in diameter, a few hyphae considerably smaller, about 3–4 μ in diameter. (Compare no. 84, *Polyporus robiniophilus*.)

HABITAT: Usually on dead or diseased willows (*Salix*), occasionally on *Betula* and *Populus*; reported on *Abies* (Idaho, Weir [222]).

DISTRIBUTION: Specimens have been examined from Me., N.H., Vt., Mass., Conn., N.Y., Pa., N.J., Ga., Ohio, Minn., Mo., Utah, Wyo., and Mont.; in Canada from Ontario and Alberta; reported from S. Dak. (Brenckle [25]), Iowa (Wolf [234]), Kansas (Bartholomew [4]), Idaho (Weir [222]), and Manitoba (Bisby *et al.* [14]).

ILLUSTRATIONS: Boudier, Icones, pl. 163; Hirt, N. Y. State Coll. Forestry Tech. Publ. 37: pl. 7, fig. 68.

Fresh specimens of this plant are pleasantly anise-scented, especially on the margin. As in typical *Trametes* species, spores are to be found only on the young, short tubes at the growing margin of the pileus.

The rot produced is a white mottled rot of the heartwood.

7. TRAMETES CUBENSIS (Mont.) Sacc.

Syll. Fung. 9: 198. 1891

(Figs. 519–520 and Plate 125)

Polyporus cubensis Mont., Ann. Sci. Nat. Bot. II, 8: 364. 1837.

Sporophore sessile or decurrent, flexible and leathery when fresh, rigid on drying; pileus applanate or somewhat triquetrous, dimidiate,

3–8 × 5–15 × 0.5–2.5 cm., at first uniformly covered with a soft, short, villose tomentum, finally glabrous except on the growing margin, white to ochraceous, with age becoming reddish, bay, or hazel behind, usually somewhat zonate and often radiate or radiate-rugose, the margin quite thin or sometimes quite thick and rounded; context white or pallid to ochraceous, soft-corky or fibrous, 0.4–1 cm. thick; pore surface white or cream-colored when fresh, usually drying yellowish, ochraceous, or tan, the tubes 1–7 mm. long, the mouths circular to angular, rather thick-walled, entire, averaging 4–6 per mm., barely visible to the unaided eye; spores not found, probably cylindric, hyaline; cystidia abundant, where basidia are present, as narrow, sharp-pointed organs 3–4 μ in diameter; hyphae long and flexuous, many with walls considerably thickened, simple except for an occasional hyphal complex, with no cross walls or clamps, 4–7 μ in diameter.

HABITAT: On dead wood of deciduous trees, noted on *Liquidambar* and *Quercus*.

DISTRIBUTION: Specimens have been examined only from Fla. and La.

ILLUSTRATIONS: Montagne, Plant Cell. Cuba, pl. 16, fig. 3 (as *Polyporus*).

Old specimens of this species are easily recognized by the reddish color at the base of the pileus. Sporophores, though quite trametoid, are of very light weight when dried. The only specimens I have seen from the mainland of the United States are in a collection made at New Smyrna, Florida, by Beardslee in 1926 and in one made by myself at Deer Park, Louisiana, in 1931. Another Louisiana collection, by Kaufert, is referred here with some misgivings.

When basidia are present, this species can be recognized by the characteristic narrow, sharp-pointed cystidia that project slightly and are 3–4 μ in diameter. Specimens without basidia seem to lack these structures.

1b. *Context pale brown or darker but not true brown, that is, not perma-
    nently darkening in KOH* (see also *Trametes corrugata* and
    Coriolopsis Tisdaleana, p. 154)

8. TRAMETES MOLLIS (Sommerf.) Fries

Hym. Eur., p. 585. 1874

(Figs. 491–495 and Plate 125)

Daedalea mollis Sommerf., in Wahlenberg, Flora Lapp., Suppl., p. 271. 1826.
Antrodia mollis (Sommerf.) Karst., Soc. Fauna Flora Fenn. Meddel. 5: 40.
1879.

Sporophore effused-reflexed or entirely resupinate, coriaceous-
flexible when fresh, firm and nearly rigid when dry; pileus 0–2.5 ×
1–6 × 0.1–0.6 cm., umber-brown to tobacco-brown or blackish, at
first velvety-tomentose, finally nearly glabrous, zonate, usually with
darker zones; context light brown, less than 1 mm. thick, with a
narrow black line separating it from the tomentum; pore surface
grayish to brown, the tubes 2–3 mm. long or longer in oblique situations, the mouths subcircular to angular and sinuous, sometimes
toothed or somewhat lamellate, averaging 1–3 per mm.; spores cylindric, hyaline, 8–11 × 3–4 μ; basidia 6–8 μ in diameter; cystidia
represented by narrow, lanceolate, hyaline organs 3–4 μ in diameter,
scarcely projecting beyond the basidia; hyphae simple or sparingly
branched, hyaline to pale brown, with no cross walls or clamps, 2–4 μ
in diameter.

HABITAT: On dead wood of deciduous trees, noted on *Acer,
Alnus, Betula, Carya, Fagus, Ostrya, Prunus, Salix, Sambucus, Tilia,*
and *Ulmus*; recorded also on *Abies, Picea,* and *Thuja*; reported on
Populus (Mont., Weir [227]).

DISTRIBUTION: Specimens have been examined from Me., N.H.,
Vt., N.Y., Pa., D.C., W. Va., N.C., Tenn., Ky., Ohio, Ind., Ill.,
Mich., Minn., Colo., Wyo., Idaho, Ore., and Wash.; in Canada from
Nova Scotia, Quebec, Ontario, and British Columbia; reported from
Wis. (Neuman [148]), Iowa (Wolf [234]), and Mont. (Weir [227]).

ILLUSTRATIONS: Overholts, Wash. Univ. Studies 3: pl. 8, fig. 42;
Pilát, Soc. Mycol. France Bul. 49: pl. 12, fig. 4; Shope, Mo. Bot.
Gard. Ann. 18: pl. 31, fig. 1 (as *Trametes stereoides*).

Ordinarily the species grows nearly or entirely resupinate. The large pores, the brown to blackish pileus, and the pale brown•context separated from the overlying tomentum by a narrow black zone are sufficient to identify it.

The species produces a general whitish or straw-colored delignifying decay of the sapwood. In some regions it seems to be not uncommon on wood of coniferous trees. Neuman (148) reports it as "quite abundant" in southern Wisconsin on fallen hemlock or spruce.

I am inclined, however, to doubt the coniferous substrata referred to above. Lowe (125, p. 90) says that Kauffman's report of a coniferous substratum should be discarded, and, considering the number of plants that resemble this species, the other records are probably misdeterminations also.

9. TRAMETES HISPIDA Bagl.

Erb. Crittog. Ital. No. 1356. 1866

(Figs. 487, 490, 511, and Plate 125)

Trametes Peckii Kalchbr., apud Peck, in Bot. Gaz. 6: 274. 1881.
Funalia stuppea (Berk.) Murr., Torrey Bot. Club Bul. 32: 356. 1905.

Sporophore sessile and occasionally decurrent on the substratum, flexible when fresh, drying rigid; pileus 1–6(–10) $\times$ 2.5–12(–25) $\times$ 0.5–2(–4) cm., covered with a dense yellowish-brown hirsute or strigose pubescence, sometimes weathering to grayish; context light brown or umber-brown, 2–10 mm. thick, the upper part grading by degrees into the erect pubescence; pore surface grayish brown to smoky brown or blackish, the tubes 3–10(–30) mm. long, the mouths angular, thick-walled, entire, averaging 1–2 per mm. or in exceptional specimens 2 mm. or more in diameter; spores hyaline, cylindric, 12–15 $\times$ 4–5 μ; basidial layer 20 μ or more thick, the basidia 7–8 μ in diameter; cystidia none; hyphal pegs 45–55 $\times$ 30–35 μ; hyphae of two kinds, the first brown, simple, thick-walled, 5–7(–9) μ in diameter, and the second hyaline, very much branched, with no cross walls or clamps, 3–5 μ in diameter; all parts blackish in KOH solution.

HABITAT: On dead wood of deciduous trees, especially *Populus* and *Salix*, but also noted on *Acer*, *Fraxinus*, *Pyrus*, and *Schinus*;

reported on *Quercus* (Wis., Neuman [148]) and on *Pseudotsuga* (Wash., Weir [223]).

DISTRIBUTION: Specimens have been examined from Mass., N.Y., La., Ohio, Ind., Ill., Wis., Minn., N. Dak., Iowa, Mo., Kans., Nebr., Ark., Texas, N. Mex., Utah, Colo., Wyo., Mont., Idaho, Ore., Wash., and Calif.; in Canada from Manitoba, Alberta, and British Columbia; reported from Mich. (Kauffman [101]).

ILLUSTRATIONS: Shope, Mo. Bot. Gard. Ann. 18: pl. 31, fig. 3; Smith, Mycologia 22: pl. 26.

The typical form assumed by this species has the following characters: sessile sporophores with densely hirsute pilei less than 10 cm. broad and 2 cm. thick; pore surface more or less smoky or dark, with pores averaging 1 mm. in diameter. Variations occur as indicated in the description above. From Washington and Oregon I have received unusually large specimens, up to 25 cm. broad and 4 cm. thick, with pores as much as 2 mm. or even 3 mm. in diameter. Intergrading specimens are known, so that it is impossible to keep these variations distinct. Throughout the range of the species thinner forms are collected, with pores averaging 2 per mm. Occasionally the pore surface is light brown, scarcely darker than pale cinnamon, and when this variation occurs in thin, mostly resupinate specimens with quite small pores the connection with *Trametes Trogii* is clearly apparent, although the two can be distinguished readily enough. *T. hispida* has a distinctly brown context, in which there are brown hyphae 5–9 μ in diameter, and the entire context region is thicker, the spores are large, usually 14–15 $\times$ 4–5 μ, and the basidial layer is 20–25 μ thick. The context of *T. Trogii* is thin and white, all the hyphae are hyaline and not over 6–7 μ in diameter, while the spores are very much smaller, never over 10 μ long and usually 8–9 μ, and only 2–3 μ in diameter, and the basidial layer is not more than 15 μ thick. The pore surface is never smoky, and the tubes are small, averaging 3 per mm.

Trametes hispida produces a general delignifying decay of the sapwood, the decayed wood being nearly white and easily separating at the annual rings. Smith (203) reports that in Colorado it occurs on living *Populus*, and also that it causes a heart rot in apple trees that eventually leads to the death of many trees.

10. TRAMETES RIGIDA Berk. & Mont.

Ann. Sci. Nat. Bot. III, 11: 240. 1849

(Figs. 496–497 and Plate 125)

Coriolopsis rigida (Berk. & Mont.) Murr., North Amer. Flora 9: 75. 1908.

Sporophore annual, varying from sessile to resupinate, thin and applanate, very flexible when fresh, rather rigid when dry; pileus 0–3 × 1–6 × 0.1–0.3 cm., cinereous to tan or light brown, pubescent to hirsute-tomentose or coarsely fibrillose or hispid, zonate or subzonate and with a tendency to become glabrous in narrow zones that reveal the underlying bay-colored cuticular layer; context light brown or golden cinnamon, 0.5–3 mm. thick; pore surface whitish or more typically isabelline or pale brown, the tubes 1–4 mm. long, the mouths circular to angular, thick-walled and entire, averaging 2–3 per mm.; spores hyaline, cylindric, 7–12 × 3–5 μ; basidia 7–8 μ in diameter; cystidia none; hyphal pegs present; hyphae pale cinnamon in KOH solution, flexuous, the larger ones simple, the smaller ones considerably branched, with no cross walls or clamps, 2.5–6 μ in diameter.

HABITAT: Usually on dead wood of deciduous trees, especially *Fraxinus*, noted also on *Acer, Carpinus, Carya, Platanus, Quercus,* and *Salix*; occasionally on wood of coniferous trees, noted on *Pinus*.

DISTRIBUTION: Specimens have been examined from D.C., S.C., Fla., Ala., La., Tenn., Mo., and Texas.

The species is a common one in the Gulf States and in tropical America, often in a mostly resupinate condition. I have seen no specimens from the more northern ranges cited by Murrill. A functional hymenium is usually absent from the tubes. In the bottom of a few of the oldest tubes in two collections I found basidia with spores.

Neuman's record (148) from Wisconsin is probably erroneous, and the distribution given by me earlier (151) was also probably confused.

The fungus produces a soft white general decay of the sapwood.

11. Trametes malicola Berk. & Curt.

Acad. Nat. Sci. Phila. Jour. II, 3: 209. 1856

(Figs. 334, 498, and Plate 125)

Coriolellus malicola (Berk. & Curt.) Murr., Mycologia 12: 20. 1920.

Sporophore sessile, effused-reflexed, or entirely resupinate, flexible and soft-corky when fresh, rigid on drying; pileus 0–2 × 1–5 × 0.3–1.5 cm., pale cinnamon to wood color or becoming blackish with age, finely tomentose to glabrous or nearly so, sometimes somewhat scrupose-tomentose, azonate; context light brown or wood color, 2–5 mm. thick; pore surface pallid to pale brownish, the tubes 2–5 mm. long, rarely in 2 or 3 layers, the mouths circular, angular, or sinuous, thick-walled, entire, averaging 1.5–2 per mm.; spores cylindric, hyaline, 7–9 × 2.5–3.5 μ; basidia 5–8 μ in diameter; hyphae hyaline or nearly so, simple or nearly so, with no cross walls or clamps, 3–5 μ in diameter.

Habitat: On dead wood of deciduous trees, noted on *Acer*, *Ailanthus*, *Betula*, *Carya*, *Fagus*, *Gleditsia*, *Juglans*, *Liquidambar*, *Liriodendron*, *Populus*, *Prunus*, *Pyrus*, *Quercus*, *Salix*, and *Ulmus*.

Distribution: Specimens have been examined from Vt., Conn., N.Y., Pa., N.J., D.C., W. Va., N.C., Ga., La., Tenn., Ky., Ohio, Ind., Ill., Mich., Wis., S. Dak., Iowa, and Mo.; in Canada from Quebec, Ontario, Manitoba, and Alberta; reported from Mont. (Weir [227]).

Illustrations: Overholts, Wash. Univ. Studies 3: pl. 8, fig. 43.

This species is rather closely related to, and occasionally intergrades with, *Trametes sepium*, from which it can usually be distinguished by the smaller pores with thicker walls and by the more wood-colored and thicker pileus, that is typically triangular in section. Occasionally specimens are perennial for two or three years.

I have not studied the types of this species, but Berkeley and Curtis, in their commentaries on Schweinitz' North American fungi (*Acad. Nat. Sci. Phila. Jour.* II, 3: 209. 1855–1858) refer Schweinitz' No. 366, published as *Polyporus populinus* Fries, to *Trametes malicola*. This Schweinitzian specimen is a nice pileate condition of what I have regarded as *T. malicola*.

Acer and *Carya* are the more usual hosts of this species.   The decay is of a light-brown carbonizing type, indistinguishable from that produced by *Trametes sepium* and very similar to that caused by *Daedalea quercina*.

1c. *Context dark brown, permanently darkening in KOH solution*

12. TRAMETES AMERICANA Overh.

Pa. Agr. Exp. Sta. Bul. 316: 15. 1935
(Figs. 513–516 and Plate 125)

Trametes odorata American authors, not *T. odorata* (Wulf. ex Fries) Fries.
Trametes protracta American authors, not *T. protracta* Fries.
Lenzites sepiaria β *porosa* Peck, in Porter and Coulter, Synop. Flora Colo., U. S. Geol and Geog. Survey Misc. Publ. 4: 164. 1874.

Sporophore typically sessile, occasionally mostly or entirely resupinate, leathery when fresh, drying rigid; pileus 0–6 × 3–12 × 0.5–3 cm., sometimes thin and applanate, but typically thicker and often triangular in section, at first finely and compactly tomentose, but very soon the tomentum wearing away or becoming agglutinated into a smooth, seared surface or in thin specimens appearing fibrillose-striate under a lens, at first rusty yellow, usually weathering to whitish gray and sometimes becoming blackish, sometimes gradually becoming a dark rusty yellow or dark brown, and finally in old specimens entirely blackish except on the margin, which remains more or less rusty and tomentose and may be either thin and acute or rather broadly obtuse; context corky or soft-corky, dark rusty brown, occasionally 1–2 mm. thick but usually 0.5–2 cm.; pore surface buff to rusty yellow and finally dark brown, the tubes 2–10 mm. long, apparently continuing growth for at least two or three seasons but not stratified, conspicuously gray within, the mouths circular to angular or radially elongate, averaging 2–3 per mm. in strictly poroid forms, larger and more irregular and up to 1 × 5 mm. in daedaloid forms, the walls always thick and entire; spores cylindric or cylindric-ellipsoid, smooth, hyaline, 9–12 × 3–5 μ; basidia 6–8 μ in diameter; setae none; hyphae long and flexuous, hyaline and brown ones present in the same mount, nearly simple or sparingly branched, with no cross walls or clamps except in some of the hyaline ones, 3–6 μ in diameter.

HABITAT: On dead wood of coniferous trees, noted on *Abies, Larix, Picea, Pinus, Pseudotsuga,* and *Thuja;* not infrequent on structural timbers, bridge beams, and railroad ties.

DISTRIBUTION: Specimens have been examined from Me., N.H., Vt., R.I., N.Y., Pa., N.J., Del., Va., W. Va., Fla., Mich., Wis., Minn., N. Mex., Ariz., Colo., Wyo., Mont., Idaho, Ore., Wash., Calif., and Alaska; in Canada from Newfoundland, Ontario, Manitoba, Alberta, and British Columbia; reported from Tennessee (Hesler [71]).

ILLUSTRATIONS: Shope, Mo. Bot. Gard. Ann. 18: pl. 31, fig. 4 (as *Trametes odorata*).

Snell *et al.* (205) record that this species, sometimes considered a poroid form of *Lenzites saepiaria,* can be easily distinguished by its less rapid growth rate in pure culture, especially at temperatures between 28° and 36° C.

When growing on charred wood, in particular, the pileus is likely to weather gray.

Neuman (148) remarks, of a species which he calls *Trametes odorata,* that "on drying the odor becomes stronger and sweetish," but most authors make no reference to such an odor in American collections, although the European *T. odorata* is described as anisescented. Neuman's photograph (pl. 2, fig. 10) is probably not of our species, although his description would seem to apply. The European *T. odorata* is said to be thicker and to be definitely a species of *Fomes,* with spores 6–7.5 × 3–5 µ (Bourdot and Galzin [18]). In a European specimen so labeled in the Lloyd Herbarium I found spores 6–8 × 2.5–3.5 µ.

13. TRAMETES CARBONARIA (Berk. & Curt.) Overh.

Mycologia 23: 126. 1931

(Fig. 512 and Plate 125)

Hexagona carbonaria Berk. & Curt., Grevillea 1: 68. 1872.
Trametes Sequoiae Copeland, Ann. Mycol. 2: 507. 1904.
Coriolellus Sequoiae (Copeland) Murr., North Amer. Flora 9: 29. 1907.

Sporophore usually resupinate, often covering a foot or more of the substratum, sometimes nodulose-effused on less horizontal substrata, and occasionally sessile, soft and flexible even in dried plants; pileus when present 0–1 × 1.5–8 × 0.1–0.5 cm., or perhaps larger at times, compactly tomentose and of a uniform umber-brown without and within, somewhat zonate; context or subiculum less than 1 mm. thick, brown, soft and fibrous; pore surface at first grayish, then gray-brown to smoky or umber-brown, the tubes 1–5 mm. long, decidedly gray or whitish within, the mouths subcircular to angular, rather thin-walled, entire, averaging 1–2 per mm.; spores cylindric, sometimes slightly curved, hyaline, 7–9 × 2–3 μ; sterigmata 4 μ long; basidia 5–7 μ in diameter; setae none; hyphae long and flexuous, nearly hyaline to pale brownish, simple, with no cross walls or clamps,[1] 2.5–4 μ in diameter.

HABITAT: On dead charred wood of coniferous trees, especially on *Sequoia*, noted also on *Chamaecyparis*, *Larix*, *Pinus*, *Thuja*, and *Tsuga*; reported on *Pseudotsuga* (Mont., Weir [227]).

DISTRIBUTION: Specimens have been examined from N.Y., Tenn., Mo., Idaho, Ore., Wash., and Calif.; in Canada from Ontario and British Columbia; reported from Mich. (Povah [175]) and Mont. (Weir [227]); type from S.C.

Two collections (New York, Van Hook, 1901, on charred *Tsuga*; Washington, 1910, on charred *Thuja*) are in pileate condition. Identification of specimens will usually be mistakenly attempted in the genus *Poria*. All of the several collections I examined are definitely on charred wood, so that the fungus is undoubtedly limited to that sort of substratum. With three exceptions, all collections I have seen are sterile. Spores as much as 11 μ in length are recorded in my notes on a specimen at the New York Botanical Garden collected in Indiana by Van Hook, but I have not observed any as large as this in other specimens.

Care must be exercised in distinguishing this species from resupinate forms of *Polyporus versatilis* in southern stations. *P. versatilis* usually does not grow on charred wood, abundant cystidia are present in the hymenium, and the mouths of the tubes are quite uneven.

---

[1] [Clamp connections occur, a fact that was demonstrated to and acknowledged by Dr. Overholts.—J.L.L.]

OMITTED SPECIES

(Entries not in brackets were included by Dr. Overholts,
but were not fully described; those in brackets have been
added to cover species recently proposed.—J.L.L.)

Trametes alaskana Baxter.   According to the original description
(11k, p. 150), this species differs distinctly from *T. heteromorpha* in
culture, but its morphological characters' appear to intergrade with
those of that species.

Trametes corrugata (Pers.) Bres.   This species was included by
Dr. Overholts in the key to the species of *Polyporus* (at key nos.
147 and 175) and is illustrated in Fig. 324.   A full description is
given by Murrill (139, p. 45).   The species may occur in the area
covered by this manual.

[*Trametes subcubensis* Murr., *Torrey Bot. Club Bul.* 65: 656. 1938.
This species is very similar to *T. cubensis*, differing, according to its
author, in having much longer tubes, an anoderm surface, and
elongate spores.]

[*Coriolopsis Tisdaleana* Murr., *Torrey Bot. Club Bul.* 65: 656. 1938.
The type material of this species is very similar to *Trametes mollis*,
but the black line is absent from the context.]

Genus 7. FAVOLUS Beauv. emend. Fries

Elench. Fung., p. 44. 1828

Favolus Palisot de Beauvois, Fl. d'Oware et Benin 1: 1. 1804.

Fruiting body annual, wood-inhabiting, more or less stipitate, the stipe at times much reduced, often lateral, fleshy-tough to somewhat leathery when fresh, thin and applanate, never more than 1 cm. thick and usually considerably thinner, white to bay or somewhat brownish; context white, thin; tubes short, the mouths typically hexagonal or radially elongate, sometimes verging toward lamellate, usually rather large and nearly 1 mm. in diameter, sometimes smaller; stem usually lateral or excentric, short, slender, often reduced to a short lateral extension of the pileus; spores cylindric (except in *Favolus Rhipidium*), hyaline; cystidia none (except in *F. Rhipidium*); setae none.

TYPE SPECIES: *Favolus europaeus* Fries.

The original significance of the genus *Favolus* has been more or less lost since the time of Fries, but attempts to revert to the limitations originally prescribed would result only in endless confusion. In some respects its species intergrade with the Agaricaceae. For example, in *F. brasiliensis*, in particular, the radial walls of the tubes are often in radiating lines between stem and pileus margin, while the tangential walls are less conspicuous and, at times, are even more or less wanting, which gives a true gilled structure to the hymenium. All species are thin and pliant when fresh, and all (except *F. Rhipidium*) have the same general habit, with large, and typically hexagonal, radiating pores. However, a few species in *Polyporus* approach this pore character. For example, *P. arcularius* and even *P. squamosus* might well be admitted to the genus on the basis of this character alone. *F. Rhipidium*, on the other hand, has at times been placed in *Polyporus*, and a small-pored form of *F. alveolaris* might be thought to belong in *Polyporus*. As a rule, the stem is laterally, or at least excentrically, placed in species of this genus, whereas in those thin forms of species of *Polyporus* most likely to cause confusion, the stem is typically centrally placed. The genus

155

Hexagona often has similar pores, but its species are leathery rather than fleshy-tough, their context is distinctly brown, and their pilei partake of the nature of the pilei of such species of *Polyporus* as *P. versicolor*.

Outside of the Gulf States, only a single species is commonly met, viz., *Favolus alveolaris*. *F. Rhipidium* is widely scattered, but, on account of its very small size, is rarely collected.

KEY TO THE SPECIES OF FAVOLUS

1. Pores scarcely visible to the unaided eye, averaging 3–4 per mm.; spores ellipsoid to subglobose, 3–4 × 2–3 μ; fruiting bodies small, rarely more than 2 cm. in diameter
                                         6. *F. Rhipidium*
    Pores always easily visible to the eye, averaging 2 or less per mm.; spores cylindric or elongate-ellipsoid 2
2. Pileus pubescent, with inconspicuous white hispid hairs, especially toward the base 3
    Pileus densely hirsute-tomentose . . See no. 93, *Polyporus pinsitus*
    Pileus glabrous or nearly so 4
3. Stem not more than 2 mm. thick . . . . 5. *F. floridanus*
    Stem 3–5 mm. thick . . . . 4. *F. reniformis*
4. Sporophore centrally stipitate . . See no. 52, *Polyporus arcularius*
    Sporophore excentrically or laterally stipitate 5
5. Pores usually equally hexagonal; spores 14–20 × 5–8 μ; tropical only . . . . 3. *F. cucullatus*
    Pores radially elongate; spores 8–11 × 3–4 μ 6
6. Pileus typically reniform, at first reddish; ranging north into Canada . . . . 1. *F. alveolaris*
    Pileus reniform to flabelliform, never reddish; limited to the Gulf States . . . . 2. *F. brasiliensis*

1. FAVOLUS ALVEOLARIS (DC. ex Fries) Quél.

Ench. Fung., p. 185. 1886

(Figs. 453, 575–576, and Plate 125)

Merulius alveolaris DC., Flora France 6: 43. 1815.
Cantharellus alveolaris DC. ex Fries, Syst. Myc. 1: 322. 1821.
Hexagona alveolaris (DC. ex Fries) Murr., Torrey Bot. Club. Bul. 31: 327. 1904.

Favolus canadensis Klotzsch, Linnaea 7: 197. 1832.
Favolus striatulus Ell. & Ev., Amer. Nat. 31: 339. 1897.
Hexagona micropora Murr., Torrey Bot. Club Bul. 31: 328. 1904.
Favolus Kauffmanii Lloyd, Myc. Notes 44: 614. 1916.
Favolus Whetstonei Lloyd, Myc. Notes 44: 615. 1916.

Sporophore more or less stipitate, fleshy-tough when fresh, rigid and brittle when dry; pileus 1–8 × 1–10 × 0.1–0.7 cm., typically reniform, sometimes flabelliform, at first reddish yellow to pale brick-red and innately fibrillose or fibrillose-scaly, later weathering to cream color or white and squamulose to glabrous; context white, 0.5–2 mm. thick; pore surface white, drying yellowish, the tubes 1–5 mm. long, the mouths decurrent on the stem, angular, hexagonal, usually in radiating lines and radially elongate, rarely somewhat lamellate, variable in size, 0.5–3 mm. long, 0.5–2 mm. broad; stem often only a lateral tubercle, never more than 1 cm. long, 1.5–7 mm. thick; spores cylindric, hyaline, 9–11 × 3–3.5 μ; basidia 6–8 μ in diameter; cystidia none; hyphal pegs present but not abundant, cylindric, 70 × 25 μ; hyphae hyaline, somewhat branched, with thickened walls, with no cross walls or clamps, attenuate at the extremities, up to 7 μ in diameter.

HABITAT: On dead branches of deciduous trees, noted on *Asimina, Carpinus, Carya, Castanea, Fagus, Fraxinus, Juglans, Populus, Prunus, Quercus, Rosa, Salix, Sorbus,* and *Ulmus*; reported also on *Acer* and *Betula* (Mich., Kauffman [101]).

DISTRIBUTION: Specimens have been examined from Me., N.H., Vt., Conn., N.Y., Pa., N.J., Del., Md., D.C., Va., W. Va., N.C., Ga., Ala., Tenn., Ohio, Ind., Ill., Mich., Wis., Mo., Kans., Nebr., Ark., Colo., and Mont.; in Canada from Quebec, Ontario, and Manitoba; reported from Ky. (Kauffman [100]) and Iowa (Wolf [234]).

ILLUSTRATIONS: Ames, Ann. Mycol. 11: pl. 13, fig. 67; Clements, Minn. Mushrooms, fig. 66 (as *Favolus canadensis*); Hard, Mushrooms, fig. 359 (as *F. canadensis*); Lloyd, Myc. Notes, Polyp. Issue No. 2: figs. 256 (as *F. europaeus*) and 257 (as *F. microporus*); *idem*, Myc. Notes 44: fig. 869 (as *F. Kauffmanii*); Shope, Mo. Bot. Gard. Ann. 18: pl. 38, fig. 5; Stevens, Fungi Plant Dis., fig. 311 (as *F. europaeus*).

This is the common species of *Favolus* of temperate North America. It is one of the first polypores to come into fruit in early summer. Dead branches of hickory are its favorite habitat. It is probably identical with *F. europaeus*. The microscopic characters are similar to those of *Polyporus fagicola*, from which it can usually be distinguished by the less prominent stem development and the colored pileus. *P. fagicola*, *P. squamosus*, *P. decurrens*, and *F. brasiliensis* seem to represent a group with a common ancestry, and these may be related to *F. alveolaris*.

The fungus produces a white delignifying decay of the sapwood.

2. FAVOLUS BRASILIENSIS Fries

Elench. Fung., p. 44. 1828

(Figs. 457–458 and Plate 125)

Daedalea brasiliensis Fries, Syst. Myc. 1: 332. 1821.
Hexagona Daedalea Link ex Murr., Torrey Bot. Club Bul. 31: 328. 1904.
Favolus caespitosus Lloyd, Myc. Notes 58: 821. 1919.

Sporophore stipitate or attached by a narrowed stemlike base, tough when fresh, rigid and brittle when dry; pileus reniform to flabelliform or unequally crateriform, often clustered, white when fresh, white, cream-colored, ochraceous, or pale tan in herbarium specimens, 4–8 cm. broad and long, 1–3(–5) mm. thick, short hispid-pubescent at the base or entirely glabrous, azonate, more or less striate and occasionally tessellate; margin thin, usually deflexed on drying, entire to fimbriate-ciliate; context white, rather soft, up to 2.5 mm. thick; pore surface white to cream color, yellowish or light bay on drying, poroid to sublamellate, the tubes 1–3 mm. long, radially arranged, the mouths at first elongate-hexagonal, coalescing radially at times, 1–3.5 × 0.5–2 mm., thin-walled, sometimes denticulate or fimbriate; stem distinct and central to indistinct and lateral, 1–3 cm. long, 2–10 mm. thick, marked with the decurrent tubes, pubescent to tomentose; spores short-cylindric, smooth, hyaline, 8–11 × 3–4 μ; cystidia none; hyphal pegs present; hyphae forming a homogeneous tissue except for many vesicle-like openings 15–26 μ in diameter, extremely sinuous and irregular, rather thin-walled, sparingly branched, with no cross walls or clamps, mostly 3–7 μ in diameter, the branches attenuate to narrow diameters (2 μ or less).

HABITAT: On dead wood of deciduous trees, noted on *Carya*, *Celtis*, *Quercus*, and *Vitis*.

DISTRIBUTION: Specimens have been examined from Fla. and La.

ILLUSTRATIONS: Lloyd, Myc. Notes, Polyp. Issue No. 2: fig. 258; *idem.*, Myc. Notes 58: fig. 1372 (as *Favolus caespitosus*); *ibid.* 64: figs. 1818–1819.

This is the common species of *Favolus* of the Gulf States and tropical America.

3. FAVOLUS CUCULLATUS Mont.
Plant Cell. Cuba, p. 378. 1838–1842
(Fig. 466 and Plate 125)

Hexagona cucullata (Mont.) Murr., Torrey Bot. Club Bul. 31: 332. 1904.
Hexagona Taxodii Murr., Torrey Bot. Club Bul. 31: 332. 1904.

Sporophore attached by a lateral or dorsal point or disk, scarcely substipitate, tough and flexible when fresh, rigid when dry; pileus dimidiate to reniform, 2–6 × 2–10 × 0.1–0.3 cm., pinkish cinnamon to pale tan or bay in dried specimens, probably more or less ochraceous or whitish when fresh, glabrous, sometimes more or less radiate-striate or rugose, the margin thin, entire; context white or pallid, 0.5–1 mm. thick; pore surface white or pallid, becoming yellowish or reddish on drying, the tubes up to 2 mm. long, the mouths not strongly radiating, quite regularly hexagonal and radially elongate, denticulate, sometimes compound, averaging 1–2 per mm.; spores elongate-ellipsoid, smooth, hyaline, 14–20 × 5–8 μ; sterigmata large, 5–7 μ long, 2–3 μ in diameter at base; basidia 8–12 μ in diameter, 4-spored; cystidia none; hyphal pegs well-developed; hyphae extremely branched, regular in outline and with thickened walls, the branches of the main hyphae attenuate to whiplike extremities, with no cross walls or clamps, up to 5.5 μ in diameter.

HABITAT: On dead wood, noted on *Persea* and *Taxodium.*

DISTRIBUTION: Specimens have been examined from Ga. and Fla.; also supposed to occur in S.C.

ILLUSTRATIONS: Lloyd, Myc. Notes, Polyp. Issue No. 2: fig. 259 (as *Hexagona cucullata*); *idem*, Synop. Hexagona, fig. 324 (as *Hexagona*).

The only collections I have examined from the mainland are one from Georgia on *Persea*, made by R. M. Harper in 1903, and two from Florida on cypress, one made in 1904 and one in 1915. *Favolus curtipes* Berk. & Curt. is said to be a synonym, and if it is, this extends the range into South Carolina. The attachment of the pileus is much like that in the smaller forms of *F. alveolaris*. Nothing that can be called a stem is present. On drying, the color varies from that typical of *F. brasiliensis* to a bay about like that in herbarium specimens of *Mycobonia flava* (Berk.) Pat. An important diagnostic character is the almost equally hexagonal pores. Spores and hyphae are also highly characteristic, the former in their size and the latter because of their thickened walls and consequent regularity of outline.

4. FAVOLUS RENIFORMIS (Murr.) Sacc. & Trott.

Syll. Fung. 21: 356. 1912

Hexagona reniformis Murr., North Amer. Flora 9: 50. 1907.

Sporophore laterally stipitate, tough when fresh, rigid when dry; pileus reniform to broadly flabelliform, 1.5–3 × 1.5–5 × 0.2–0.4 cm., pallid when fresh, drying ochraceous to yellowish brown, more or less tessellate, pubescent with short white hispid hairs that eventually become fewer toward the more or less ciliate-fimbriate margin; context paper-thin; pore surface concolorous with pileus, the tubes 1–3 mm. long, radiately arranged, the mouths somewhat radially elongate, very thin-walled, minutely denticulate, 1–1.5 × 2–2.5 mm.; stem lateral, more densely hispid-pubescent than the pileus, 3–7(–15) mm. long, 3–5 mm. thick; spores cylindric, smooth, hyaline, 8–10 × 3–4 μ; cystidia none; hyphal pegs abundant, subcylindric, visible in the tubes under a good hand lens, 70–85 × 20–25 μ; hyphae very much branched, the branches attenuate to whiplike extremities, with no cross walls or clamps, up to 8 μ in diameter, or some deeply staining, inflated hyphae up to 12 μ or more in diameter.

HABITAT: On dead wood.

DISTRIBUTION: Specimens have been examined only from the type locality, Fla.

The conspicuous feature about this species seems to be the white hispid pubescence on the pileus. Murrill refers to the surface of the pileus as "densely tomentose," but the surface covering is not a tomentum. The large size of the hyphal pegs is also unusual. It seems to be a good species.

5. FAVOLUS FLORIDANUS (Murr.) Sacc. & D. Sacc.

Syll. Fung. 17: 144. 1905

(Fig. 454)

Hexagona floridana Murr., Torrey Bot. Club Bul. 31: 330. 1904.

Sporophore stipitate or substipitate, fleshy-tough when fresh, rigid when dry; pileus broadly flabelliform to reniform in outline, 1–2 × 1–3 × 0.2–0.3 cm., white when fresh, ochraceous-tan on drying, with a short white hispid pubescence scattered toward the margin and more distinct at the base, inconspicuously radiate-striate or slightly tessellate, the margin slightly ciliate-fringed or entire; context paper-thin; pore surface concolorous with pileus, the tubes up to 2 mm. long, radiately arranged, the mouths radially elongate, fimbriate-denticulate, 0.5–1 × 1.5–3 mm.; stem definite, lateral, 3–5 × 2 mm.; spores cylindric, smooth, hyaline, 8–10 × 3–3.5 μ; cystidia none; hyphal pegs present, cylindric; hyphae much branched, the branches attenuate into whiplike extremities, with no cross walls or clamps, up to 6(–8) μ in diameter.

HABITAT: On dead wood of deciduous trees.

DISTRIBUTION: Known only from the type collection, made at Miami, Fla.

Probably this is only a small, regular form of *Favolus brasiliensis*. All the microscopic characters agree with those of that species. The main difference is in the white hispid pubescence of the pileus.

6. FAVOLUS RHIPIDIUM (Berk.) Sacc.

Syll. Fung. 6: 397. 1888

(Figs. 455–456, 459, and Plate 125)

Polyporus Rhipidium Berk., London Jour. Bot. 6: 319. 1847.

Sporophore excentrically or laterally stipitate, fleshy-tough when fresh, rigid when dry; pileus reniform to spathulate, 0.3–1.5(–2.5) cm. broad, 0.5–4 mm. thick, white or cream color when fresh, white to clay color or brick-red when dry, usually brick-red in herbarium specimens, zonate or azonate, minutely squamulose or mealy; context not more than 1 mm. thick, white, the taste peppery; pore surface white, becoming brick-red in dried plants, pruinose, the tubes 0.5–2 mm. long, the mouths somewhat though not conspicuously faveolate, averaging 3–4 per mm., the walls at first very thick and even, rather thin and somewhat denticulate in old specimens; stem well-developed or reduced, typically nearly lateral, pruinose, 0.3–2.5 cm. long, 1–4 mm. thick, colored like the pileus; spores ellipsoid to subglobose, smooth, hyaline, 3–4 × 2–3 μ; cystidia represented by projecting hyaline hairs that occur singly or in groups of three or four, 2.5–3 μ in diameter, projecting 10–15 μ; hyphae very irregular, thin-walled and often collapsed, with occasional cross walls and very occasional clamps, mostly 4–8 μ in diameter; much-branched botryoid hyphae, resembling conidiophores, probably sporiferous, present on swollen mouths of tubes.

HABITAT: On dead wood of deciduous trees, noted only on *Acer*, *Carpinus*, *Liquidambar*, and *Quercus*.

DISTRIBUTION: Specimens have been examined from N.Y., Va., S.C., Ga., Fla., Ala., La., Tenn., Ky., Ohio, Wis., and Ark.; reported from Iowa (Wolf [234]).

ILLUSTRATIONS: Lloyd, Myc. Notes, Polyp. Issue No. 2: fig. 260 (as *Polyporus*); Neuman, Wis. Geol. and Nat. Hist. Survey Bul. 33: pl. 1, fig. 7.

Fresh specimens are light in color, but after several years in the herbarium the hymenium and often the pileus become brick-red, deep rusty red, or pinkish red. Usually the plants are quite small, less than 1 cm. in diameter, but a collection in the Lloyd Herbarium from the mainland of the United States has some pilei as much as 2.5 cm. in diameter and stems of about the same length. The general appearance of the plant is similar to that of *Panus stipticus* Fries.

Genus 8. POLYPORUS[1] Micheli ex Fries

Syst. Myc. 1: 341. 1821

Polyporus Micheli, Nov. Plant. Gen., p. 129. 1729.

Plants typically annual, but occasionally reviving for two or three years as in *Fomes* or sometimes reviving by new marginal growth only; stipitate, sessile, or effused-reflexed; terrestrial or epixylous; fleshy to tough, leathery or woody; color and surface various; context white to bright-colored or dark brown; tubes typically in a single layer, usually sunken into the context to equal depths so that their bases form a straight line, the mouths circular to angular or, in a few species, somewhat daedaloid, the walls even and entire or lacerate and more or less toothed; stem when present central or lateral, simple or branched; spores white to brown, smooth or rough, variable in shape; cystidia present or absent; setae present or absent.

[TYPE SPECIES: *Polyporus tuberaster* Jacq. ex Fries.—J.L.L.]

This is the large, central genus of the Polyporaceae, differing from *Fomes* only in the annual habit, which is of course reflected in a general way in a variety of characters, including consistency, roughness of surface, and thickness of pileus. The identity of individuals that do persist a second or a third year, adding to the downward growth of the tubes each year, is certain to be looked for in the genus *Fomes*, while species of *Fomes* in their first year's growth are often likely to be referred to this genus. The genus *Trametes* has never been delimited from *Polyporus* in a practical way, so that

---

[1] The following genera are segregates from the genus *Polyporus* either wholly or in part and are not recognized here: *Abortiporus* Murr., *Aurantiporellus* Murr., *Aurantiporus* Murr., *Cerrenella* Murr., *Coltricia* S. F. Gray, *Coltriciella* Murr., *Coriolopsis* Murr., *Coriolus* Quél., *Cryptoporus* Shear, *Cycloporellus* Murr., *Flaviporellus* Murr., *Fomitella* Murr., *Funalia* Pat., *Ganoderma* Karst., *Globifomes* Murr., *Gloeoporus* Mont., *Grifola* S. F. Gray, *Hapalopilus* Karst., *Inonotus* Murr., *Irpiciporus* Murr., *Ischnoderma* Karst., *Laetiporus* Murr., *Microporellus* Murr., *Mucronoporus* Ell. & Ev., *Nigroporus* Murr., *Phaeolus* Pat., *Piptoporus* Karst., *Pogonomyces* Murr., *Polystictus* Fries, *Porodisculus* Murr., *Poronidulus* Murr., *Pycnoporellus* Murr., *Pycnoporus* Karst., *Rigidiporus* Murr., *Scutiger* Paulet, *Spongipellis* Pat., *Trichaptum* Murr., and *Tyromyces* Quél. Many other such segregates have appeared in the European literature.

163

confusion is sure to occur. Nearly all species of *Trametes* are, for this reason, included in the key to the species of *Polyporus*.

The large size of the genus has caused it to be regarded as a fair subject for the operations of those who profess to believe in the expediency of small genera, forgetting, it seems, that the characters used for separating such genera can be used as well in the delimitation of groups within a larger genus. None of the schemes so far presented seems workable in its entirety. Certain sharp segregates, involving a few species each, can be recognized, but the number of species disposed of is too small to allow consideration of these segregates. A primary division of the genus either on the basis of context color or spore color would be the only alternative. But spores are too often absent and are always difficult for the beginner to find, while the context colors intergrade to a considerable extent and are frequently different in the growing plant and in the dried specimen.

KEY TO THE SPECIES OF POLYPORUS[1]

Context white, whitish, very light yellow, or very pale brown; spores hyaline .... Section I
Context pinkish, yellowish red, orange, yellow, or saffron; spores hyaline .... Section II, p. 198
Context yellowish brown to umber-brown or darker; spores hyaline or brown .... Section III, p. 200

SECTION I

A. *Sporophore stipitate or substipitate,*[2] *erect or pendent* (for sessile or effused-reflexed sporophores see AA, p. 175)
  B. *Sporophore terrestrial or growing from buried wood or from an underground sclerotium* (for stipitate sporophores growing on wood above ground see BB, p. 168)
    C. *Pilei 2 to many on the branches of a common stem*[3] (for solitary pilei see CC, p. 166)

[1] The terms "broad," "long," and "thick" as used in this key are defined in the Glossary.

[2] Care should be taken not to include in the substipitate section plants that by virtue of their position on top of a log or a similar substratum may become laterally united into a funnel-shaped or cup-shaped mass and have more or less the appearance of being centrally stemmed, as in Figs. 132 and 606. Include here pendulous species like that illustrated in Fig. 545.

[3] See Figs. 180 and 264.

1. Pilei few, often only 2 or 3 2
   Pilei many, usually 25 or more 5
2. Spores strongly echinulate, 6–8 μ broad; pileus finely tomentose to glabrous .... 25. *P. Berkeleyi*
   Spores smooth or nearly so, 9–12 × 8–9 μ; pileus with a
   dense mat of fibrils or becoming somewhat scaly
                                          23. *P. sylvestris*
   Spores smooth, subcylindric, 10–16 × 4–6 μ; sporophore
   developing from a definite compact underground sclerotium .... 26. *P. tuberaster*
   Spores different from above; pilei different.............. 3
3. Pore surface blackish on drying, especially toward the
   margin of the pileus .... 27. *P. giganteus*
   Pore surface not blackish on drying 4
4. Spores ovoid, 5–6 × 4–5 μ; pileus yellowish green when
   fresh and becoming areolate; growing on the ground
                                          10. *P. cristatus*
   Spores ellipsoid to ovoid, 5–7 × 3.5–4.5 μ; pileus salmon
   color when fresh; growing from buried roots of living
   trees .... 28. *P. sulphureus* var. *cincinnatus*
   Spores 3–4.5 × 2.5–3 μ; pore surface drying brick-red or
   becoming so in the herbarium .... 6. *P. confluens*
   Spores 3–4.5 × 2.5–3 μ; pore surface drying only yellowish,
   never red .... 8. *P. Peckianus*
5. Spores globose, strongly echinulate, 6–8 μ in diameter
                                          25. *P. Berkeleyi*
   Spores cylindric, smooth, 7–9.5 × 3–4 μ .. 30. *P. umbellatus*
   Spores ellipsoid to ovoid or globose, smooth, smaller than
   in either of the above 6
6. Pileus white, fibrous, not more than 2 or 3 mm. thick, the
   entire cluster scarcely exceeding 10 cm. in diameter;
   pores poorly developed, often appearing only as scattered plates or ridges; spores 4.5–5.5 × 3.5–4 μ
                                          43. *P. fimbriatus*
   Pileus salmon-colored, much thicker, the entire cluster
   always more than 10 cm. in diameter; pores well developed in mature plants; spores 5–7 × 3.5–4.5 μ
                                  28. *P. sulphureus* var. *cincinnatus*
   Pileus pallid to grayish, fuscous, or pale mouse color, not

white, fleshy-tough rather than fleshy, forming large clusters 20–60 cm. in diameter; cosmopolitan 7

Entire sporophore brick-red on drying or in the herbarium; pores well developed; spores 4–5 × 3.5–4 μ 31. *P. illudens*

7. Pore surface blackish where bruised and on drying; spores nearly globose, 5–7 μ in diameter; hyphae of context 4–8 μ in diameter; pores 4–7 per mm.. . 27. *P. giganteus*

Pore surface not becoming blackish; spores ovoid or ellipsoid, 5–7 × 3.5–5 μ; hyphae of context 6–15 μ in diameter; pores 1–3 per mm. . . . . 29. *P. frondosus*

CC. *Pileus single; stem simple, unbranched*[1]

8. Sporophore showing all the characters in one of the following sets:

   a. Stem black at the base or on the lower part of the · above-ground portion, but not with a black root .. 9

   b. Stem not black on the above-ground portion, but with a well-developed black radicating portion below ground;[2] spores subfusiform, 12–15 × 6–8 μ

   18. *P. radicatus*

   c. Stem not at all black but with an ochraceous or red varnish that forms a distinct crust; spores ovoid, with a truncate apex, apparently echinulate, light brown, 9–13 × 5–7 μ . . . . 4. *P. Curtisii*

   d. Stem not at all black above ground and not varnished; spores globose, echinulate, hyaline, 5–9 μ in diameter 11

   Sporophore not showing all the characters in any of the groups above 12

9. Pileus white or gray . . . . 33. *P. albiceps*

   Pileus tan, mouse color, brown, or darker 10

10. Pores averaging 5–7 per mm.; spores 6–8 × 3–4 μ; pileus typically tan to chestnut, glabrous or essentially so

    44. *P. picipes*

    Pores averaging 2–4 per mm.; spores 8–12 × 3.5–4 μ; pileus brown, velvety-scurfy or almost scaly.. 19. *P. melanopus*

11. Pileus brown; from California, Idaho, Montana, and British Columbia . . . . 24. *P. montanus*

[1] See Figs. 170, 172, and 188.   [2] See Fig. 172.

Pileus pallid or pale-colored; widely distributed
25. *P. Berkeleyi*

12. Context consisting of a soft upper layer and a very firm
layer next the tubes, especially in dried plants; or
sporophore much aborted and nearly the entire surface
covered with pores .... 13. *P. biennis*
Context not conspicuously duplex as in the above 13

13. Pileus multizonate .... 12. *P. dealbatus*
Pileus azonate or nearly so 14

14. Pileus, tubes, and stem bluish gray or pale indigo-blue
when fresh, drying brownish or reddish, not distinctly
pubescent; spores subglobose, 4–6 μ in diameter or
4–6 × 3–5 μ; from east of the Alleghenies
9. *P. caeruleoporus*
Pileus more or less brown in fresh specimens, very much
darker on drying, distinctly tomentose .. 11. *P. persicinus*
Pileus whitish, yellowish, greenish, or grayish in fresh
plants, sometimes smoky on drying but usually not
reddish and not conspicuously pubescent 15
Pileus yellow to yellowish green, orange, reddish, or brown
in fresh plants, scarcely changing on drying, glabrous,
pubescent, or scaly 18

15. Pileus 2–5 cm. broad; spores 6–10 × 3–4 μ; context hyphae
2.5–4.5 μ in diameter; growing on the ground in pastures; ranging from Kansas northward and westward
21. *P. cryptopus*
Pileus and hyphae as above; growing from buried wood
33. *P. albiceps*
Pileus more than 5 cm. broad 16

16. Sporophore tough and leathery, not discoloring on drying;
largest context hyphae not more than 5 μ in diameter
33. *P. albiceps*
Sporophore fleshy and likely to be mistaken for a specimen
of *Boletus*, discoloring on drying; largest context hyphae
often 10 μ or more in diameter 17

17. Spores tuberculate or angled, 5–6.5 μ in diameter or
5–6 × 4–5 μ; context hyphae without cross walls
15. *P. griseus*
Spores smooth, ellipsoid to subglobose, 3.5–4 × 2.5–3.5 μ;
context hyphae with cross walls .... 5. *P. ovinus*

Spores and hyphae as in *P. ovinus* but pileus greenish blue
   when young .... 7. *P. Flettii*
Spores smooth, cylindric, 4–6 × 2–2.5 μ; context hyphae
   without cross walls .... 14. *P. osseus*
18. Spores less than 12 μ long, tear-shaped to ellipsoid, ovoid-
   elliptic, or cylindric 19
Spores more than 12 μ long, subcylindric or somewhat
   fusoid 21
19. Pileus yellow, yellowish green, pale tan, or yellowish brown 20
Pileus brown or reddish brown; spores 8–11 × 5–6 μ
   16. *P. Pes-Caprae*
Pileus brown; spores 7–11 × 2–3 μ .... 52. *P. arcularius*
20. Pileus nearly glabrous, never areolate; spores 3–4.5 ×
   2.5–3 μ .... 8. *P. Peckianus*
Pileus with large fasciculate or imbricate scales, not areolate; spores 8–9 × 5–7 μ .... 17. *P. Ellisii*
Pileus with small brown scales and a ciliated margin; spores
   7–11 × 2–3 μ .... 52. *P. arcularius*
Pileus compactly tomentose to glabrous, soon areolate;
   spores 5–6 × 4–5 μ .... 10. *P. cristatus*
Pileus fibrillose or otherwise pubescent 22
21. Pileus fibrillose-scaly or with wartlike scales .. 20. *P. decurrens*
Pileus covered with short, stiff, erect hairs.... 51. *P. hirtus*
22. Spore wall canaliculate, giving it a rough appearance; from
   Tennessee and North Carolina ..... 22. *P. canaliculatus*
Spore wall smooth or nearly so and not canaliculate; from
   the far Northwest .... 23. *P. sylvestris*

BB. *Sporophore growing on wood, above ground; not terrestrial*
   D. *Pileus white, gray, or pallid in fresh plants, not definitely
   colored and scarcely changing color on drying or only
   becoming yellowish* (for sporophores with definitely colored pilei see DD, p. 172)

23. Sporophore definitely pendent, i.e., attached by a dorsal
   stemlike prolongation of the pileus[1] 24

[1] See Figs. 149 and 577.

Sporophore with a central, excentric, or lateral stem, or a
 stemlike base 25

24. Sporophore very small, less than 1 cm. broad and long; on
 dead branches of coniferous trees .... 34. *P. subpendulus*
 Sporophore much larger; on *Betula* only .... 50. *P. betulinus*

25. Pilei 2 to many on the branches of a common stem, or
 growing more or less confluent, forming a compound
 sporophore[1] 26
 Pilei single; stem simple, unbranched[2]................. 30

26 Spores minute, 2–3 × 1.5–2 μ .... 75. *P. canadensis*
 Spores larger, 3 μ or more in the longer dimension 27

27. Pilei not exceeding 2 or 3 mm. in thickness; sporophore
 usually less than 10 cm. in diameter 28
 Pilei thicker than in the above; sporophore usually 20–60
 cm..in diameter 29

28. From the Gulf States .... 43. *P. fimbriatus*
 From more northern stations .... 42. *P. scrobiculatus*

29. Pore surface blackish where bruised and on drying; spores
 nearly globose, 5–7 μ in diameter; hyphae of context
 4–8 μ in diameter; pores 4–7 per mm.; cystidia none;
 pileus finely tomentose or fibrillose ...... 27. *P. giganteus*
 Pore surface not becoming blackish; spores ovoid or ellipsoid, 5–7 × 3.5–5 μ; hyphae of context 6–15 μ in diameter; pores 1–3 per mm.; cystidia none; pileus
 glabrous or finely scabrous .... 29. *P. frondosus*
 Pore surface not becoming blackish; spores ovoid or ellipsoid, 4.5–7 × 3.5–5 μ; hyphae of context 4.5–9 μ in
 diameter; pores 2–3 per mm.; cystidia present; pileus
 hispid to tomentose .... 83. *P. borealis*

30. Stem definitely lateral in position or not well developed and
 only present as a stemlike base to the pileus[3] 31
 Stem central or subcentral, distinct and well developed .. 42

31. Context composed of a soft upper layer and a firm or hard
 lower layer, best observed in dried plants 32
 Context uniform or nearly so in texture 34

[1] See Figs. 180 and 264. [2] See Figs. 170 and 172. [3] See Fig. 225.

32. Context 0.5–2 mm. thick; pores 4–5 per mm.; cystidia none

                              36. *P. fractipes*

    Context 2–20 mm. thick; pores 1–3 per mm.; inconspicuous

       cystidia present 33

33. Surface of pileus drying rough-tomentose; usually on wood

       of coniferous trees . . . . **83.** *P. borealis*

    Surface of pileus drying smooth or velvety; usually on wood

       of deciduous trees . . . . **13.** *P. biennis*

34. Growing only on wood of coniferous trees 35

    Growing only on hardwoods 36

35. Pileus 1–5 mm. thick, radiately fibrillose, not spotted;

       spores ellipsoid, 3–4 × 2–2.5 μ . . . . . . **35.** *P. floriformis*

    Pileus 5–15 mm. thick, glabrous or practically so, marked

       with circular depressed spots; spores oblong or short-

       cylindric, 3–4.5 × 2–2.5 μ . . . . **63.** *P. guttulatus*

    Pileus 3–20 mm. thick, silky to glabrous, not spotted; spores

       allantoid or cylindric-oblong, 4–6 × 2–2.5 μ **14.** *P. osseus*

36. Sporophore showing all the characters in one of the following

       sets:

    a. Pileus thin and conchiform, bearing a cup-shaped

         sterile body at its base;[1] pores averaging 2–3 per

         mm.; found only on dead elm branches

                          107. *P. conchifer*

    b. Pileus strongly convex, the margin projecting down-

         ward 5 mm. or more beyond the level of the pore

         surface; tubes separating smoothly from the con-

         text in fresh specimens; found only on birches in

         north-temperate regions . . . . **50.** *P. betulinus*

    c. Pileus with scattered, depressed, circular spots; thin

         and applanate, drying yellowish. . . **63.** *P. guttulatus*

    d. Stem black at base; pileus scaly; pores usually 1 mm.

         or more wide . . . . **39.** *P. squamosus*

    Sporophore not showing all the characters in any of the

       groups above 37

37. Sporophore not more than 2.5 cm. long or broad 38

    Sporophore larger 39

38. Stem distinct, usually terete; pileus not drying resinous or

       cartilaginous . . . . See no. 6, *Favolus Rhipidium*

---

[1] See Figs. 33 and 34.

Stem only the lateral prolongation of the pileus; pileus
drying resinous or horny-cartilaginous

127. *P. semisupinus*

39. Pores averaging 2–5 per mm.; pilei usually 1 cm. or more
thick, azonate **40**

Pores averaging 5–8 per mm.; pilei less than 1 cm. thick .. **41**

40. Pileus corky or leathery, drying hard; context firm; ranging
from southern Ohio southward

See no. 5, *Daedalea ambigua*

Pileus somewhat fleshy, drying soft and of very light weight;
from South Carolina and the Gulf States

79. *P. amygdalinus*

Pileus fleshy-tough or leathery, drying firm; from Pennsylvania, New York, and New England . 32. *P. admirabilis*

41. Spores allantoid, 3–5 × 1–1.5 μ; pileus drying ochraceous
orange; context hyphae 3–4 μ in diameter

115. *P. ochrotinctellus*

Spores ellipsoid, 5–6 × 4–5 μ; pileus drying gray to brownish; context hyphae 3–8 μ in diameter... 12. *P. dealbatus*

Spores ellipsoid, 3–4.5 × 2.5–3 μ; pileus drying gray to
brownish; context hyphae 4–6 μ in diameter

37. *P. mutabilis*

42. Pileus conspicuously scaly; pores 1–2.5 mm. broad

39. *P. squamosus*

Pileus not or only slightly scaly; pores less than 1 mm.
broad **43**

43. Pileus conspicuously multizonate; ranging from Delaware
to Missouri and southward **44**

Pileus not at all zonate; not limited to a southern range .. **45**

44. Spores ellipsoid, 5–6 × 4–5 μ; context hyphae 3–8 μ in
diameter .... 12. *P. dealbatus*

Spores ellipsoid, 3–4.5 × 2.5–3 μ; context hyphae 4–6 μ in
diameter .... 37. *P. mutabilis*

45. Context composed of a soft upper layer and a firm or hard
lower layer, best observed in dried plants **46**

Context uniform or nearly so in composition **47**

46. Context 0.5–2 mm. thick; pores 4–5 per mm.; cystidia
none..................................... 36. *P. fractipes*

Context 2–10 mm. thick; pores 1–3 per mm.; cylindric
cystidia present .... 13. *P. biennis*
47. Pileus up to 4 cm. broad, the margin strongly ciliated with
coarse hairs .... 38. *P. Tricholoma*
Pileus less than 4 cm. broad, the margin not ciliated
See no. 6, *Favolus Rhipidium*
Pileus more than 4 cm. broad, the margin not ciliated ... 48
48. Pores averaging 1–2 per mm.; sporophore soft and almost
fleshy, drying yellow, often with a sweet odor
41. *P. fagicola*
Pores averaging 3–5 per mm.; sporophore tough or leathery,
drying white or gray; without characteristic odor 49
49. Pileus less than 10 cm. broad; tubes 1–3 mm. long
33. *P. albiceps*
Pileus up to 35 cm. broad; tubes 3–7 mm. long
32. *P. admirabilis*

DD. *Pileus definitely colored when fresh, yellow, salmon, drab, tan,
brown, red, black, and so on, not changing color on
drying*

50. Pileus and stem, or at least the stem, covered with a reddish,
yellowish, or mahogany-colored varnish, usually shining
and forming a thin crust 51
Pileus and stem not both varnished, and not shining 54
51. Pileus at least partly ochraceous or tan when mature; spores
9–13 × 5–7 μ; ranging from Massachusetts to Nebraska southward .... 4. *P. Curtisii*
Pileus and stem red or blackish; not limited to a southern
range 52
52. Context brownish throughout, though paler above; on or
about stumps or trunks of hardwood trees.. 1. *P. lucidus*
Context pallid or nearly white throughout, slightly brownish
on the lower half; usually on wood of coniferous trees .. 53
53. Spores 9–11 × 6–8 μ; pileus never more than 5 cm. thick;
ranging west to Wisconsin............... 2. *P. Tsugae*
Spores 10–16 × 7.5–9 μ; pileus typically 7–12 cm. or more
thick; ranging from the Rocky Mountains westward
3. *P. oregonensis*
54. Sporophore small and pendent, less than 1 cm. high
49. *P. pocula*

Sporophore larger or, if approaching the size above, not
  pendent 55
55. Pilei 2 to many on the branches of a common tubercular
  stem[1] 56
Pilei single; stem simple, unbranched 58
56. Spores 9–12 × 8–9 μ; pileus with a dense mat of fibrils or
  becoming scaly; from Washington and British Columbia .... **23.** *P. sylvestris*
Spores 5–7 × 3.5–5 μ; pileus not conspicuously scaly or
  fibrillose 57
57. Pileus salmon color to yellow or orange in fresh plants,
  fading on drying   **28.** *P. sulphureus* and var. *cincinnatus*
Pileus gray to fuscous or pale mouse color, unchanged on
  drying .... **29.** *P. frondosus*
58. Sporophore showing all the characters in one of the following
  sets:
  a. Context consisting of a soft upper layer and a very
    firm layer next the tubes, especially in dried
    plants; spores narrowly ovoid, 5–7.5 × 3–5 μ
                                   13. *P. biennis*
  b. Pileus strongly convex, the margin projecting down-
    ward 5 mm. or more beyond the level of the pore
    surface; tubes separating in a smooth layer from
    the context in fresh specimens; found only on
    birches in north-temperate regions.. **50.** *P. betulinus*
  c. Stem entirely black or black on the lower half 59
Sporophore not showing all the characters in any of the
  groups above 61
59. Pores large, 1–2.5 mm. broad .... **39.** *P. squamosus*
Pores small or minute, averaging 3–8 per mm. 60
60. Pileus tan or ochraceous, 1.5–7 cm. broad ..... **45.** *P. elegans*
Pileus bay or chestnut, 4–20 cm. broad; spores 6–8 × 3–4 μ
                                   44. *P. picipes*
Pileus usually tan, rarely chestnut, 5–12 cm. broad; spores
  7–12 × 3–4 μ .... **46.** *P. varius*
Pileus tan to chestnut or vinaceous black, 1–5 cm. broad;
  probably in Florida only .... **47.** *P. Blanchetianus*
61. Growing only on wood of coniferous trees; pileus nearly or
  quite glabrous but usually marked with circular de-

[1] See Figs. 180 and 264.

pressed spots; context not drying unusually hard;
spores 3–4.5 × 2–2.5 μ .... 63. *P. guttulatus*
Growing only on wood of coniferous trees; pileus nearly or
quite glabrous, not spotted; context usually drying hard
and horny; spores 4–6 × 2–2.5 μ .... 14. *P. osseus*
Growing only on wood of coniferous trees; pileus with short
stiff erect hairs, not spotted; context not drying hard;
spores 12–17 × 4.5–6 μ .... 51. *P. hirtus*
Growing on wood of deciduous trees, or with different
characters than above 62
62. Pores medium-sized or large, averaging not more than 4
per mm. 63
Pores minute, averaging 4–8 per mm. 68
63. Tubes long-decurrent on the stem; spores 10–17 μ long 64
Tubes slightly or not at all decurrent on the stem, or stem
nearly obsolete; spores mostly 8–10 μ or less long 65
64. Pileus decidedly scaly with erect scales, yellowish brown;
from California only .... 40. *P. McMurphyi*
Pileus glabrous or not markedly scaly; ranging from Maine
to Michigan .... 41. *P. fagicola*
65. Pores averaging 1 mm. or more in the longest dimension,
usually radiating outward somewhat from the stem .. 66
Pores smaller and not markedly radiating 67
66. Stem well developed, usually central .... 52. *P. arcularius*
Stem very short or rudimentary, usually lateral
See no. 1, *Favolus alveolaris*
67. Pileus drying blackish, more than 2.5 cm. in diameter; stem
central or excentric; of wide distribution . 53. *P. brumalis*
Pileus drying reddish, usually less than 2.5 cm. in diameter;
stem usually lateral; of wide distribution
See no. 6, *Favolus Rhipidium*
Pileus drying cinnamon-brown to chestnut, more than 2.5
cm. in diameter; stem subcentral; from Florida only
48. *P. virgatus*
68. Margin of pileus ornamented with coarse ciliate hairs
38. *P. Tricholoma*
Margin of pileus not ciliated as above 69
69. Sporophore with a central or subcentral stem............ 70
Sporophore with a lateral stem or with only a stemlike
base 72

70. Pileus zonate .... 12. *P. dealbatus*
     Pileus azonate 71
71. Pileus smoky or blackish; of wide distribution   53. *P. brumalis*
     Pileus reddish or chestnut; from Florida only .   48. *P. virgatus*
72. Stem cylindric, well developed but small, the pileus less
          than 2.5 cm. broad .... See no. 6, *Favolus Rhipidium*
     Stem not well developed and present only as a stemlike
          base to the pileus, or cylindric and sporophore larger .   73
73. Sporophore more than 1 cm. thick ...... 79. *P. amygdalinus*
     Sporophore less than 1 cm. thick...................... 74
74. Largest context hyphae not exceeding 4 μ in diameter;
          pileus drying more or less ochraceous or ochraceous
          tan; from the Gulf States .... 115. *P. ochrotinctellus*
     Largest context hyphae 6–8 μ in diameter; pileus not drying
          bright-colored 75
75. Stem indistinct; pileus with only a stemlike base; growing
          only in the northern states, or south, in the mountains
          only, to Tennessee .... 127. *P. semisupinus*
     Stem distinct, cylindric; ranging from Delaware to Missouri
          and southward 76
76. Spores ellipsoid, 5–6 × 4–5 μ; context hyphae 3–8 μ in
          diameter .... 12. *P. dealbatus*
     Spores ellipsoid, 3–4.5 × 2.5–3 μ; context hyphae 4–6 μ in
          diameter .... 37. *P. mutabilis*

AA. *Sporophore sessile or effused-reflexed, not stipitate and not pendent*
  E. *Plants inhabiting wood of coniferous trees* (for hardwood-in-
          habiting species see EE, p. 184)
    F. *Pileus definitely colored in fresh plants, salmon, orange, red,
          brown, black, and so on, usually the same on drying* (for
          sporophores with white, pallid, wood-colored, or gray
          pilei see FF, p. 178)

77. Sporophore showing all the characters in one of the follow-
          ing sets:
    a. Pileus salmon or orange in fresh specimens, usually
          fading on drying, 10 cm. or more broad when
          mature, fleshy, drying brittle; spores ovoid or
          ellipsoid, 5–7 × 3.5–4.5 μ; associated with a
          cubical brown heart rot
                    28. *P. sulphureus* and var. *cincinnatus*

    b. Found usually on incense cedar on the Pacific Coast; sporophores convex to ungulate, pallid to brownish, up to 10 cm. or more thick; associated with a pin rot[1] of the heartwood of living trees

62. P. amarus

    c. Found only on *Cupressus* in California; sporophore thin and applanate; associated with a brown carbonizing butt rot of living trees ..   91. *P. basilaris*

    d. Pileus red or blackish, covered by a thin varnish of the same color that forms a thin crust; spores pale brown, apparently echinulate   78

  Sporophore not fitting well into any of the groups above ..   79

78. Spores 9–11 × 6–8 μ; pileus never more than 5 cm. thick; ranging west to Wisconsin . . . .   2. *P. Tsugae*

  Spores 10–16 × 7.5–9 μ; pileus typically 7–12 cm. or more thick; ranging from the Rocky Mountains westward

3. P. oregonensis

79. Sporophore 1 cm. or more thick   80

  Sporophore less than 1 cm. thick   83

80. Pileus seal-brown to blackish brown, densely velvety

74. P. resinosus

  Pileus not at all brown when fresh, sometimes reddish brown on drying   81

81. Pileus very soft and watery when fresh; pore surface discolored where handled and entire sporophore discolored rufescent or darker on drying   82

  Pileus tough and leathery when fresh; pore surface not discolored where handled and sporophore not darker on drying . . . .   See no. 1, *Daedalea confragosa*

82. Pileus permanently pubescent or with a mat of soft fibers; hyphae with abundant and conspicuous clamps

54. P. fragilis

  Pileus becoming glabrous; hyphae with a few inconspicuous cross walls . . . .   56. *P. mollis*

83. Sporophore soft and fleshy-watery or cartilaginous when fresh   84

  Sporophore tough and coriaceous or leathery when fresh ..   85

---

[1] See Fig. 186.

84. Pore surface yellowish where handled and entire sporophore
    rufescent or darker on drying; pores 2–4 per mm.,
    usually somewhat daedaloid; clamps abundant and
    conspicuous on the context hyphae; spores allantoid
                                                 54. *P. fragilis*
    Pore surface not discoloring where handled and sporophore
    not rufescent, but pileus sometimes bay on drying;
    pores 4–5 per mm., never daedaloid; clamps few and
    inconspicuous on the context hyphae; spores oblong-
    ellipsoid or cylindric, not curved . . . . . . 67. *P. cutifractus*

85. Pileus distinctly and uniformly brown or blackish brown,
    particularly in fresh plants 86
    Pileus gray, cinereous, or tinged with brown or other colors,
    but not uniformly brown or blackish 90

86. Sporophore 1–8 mm. thick 87
    Sporophore rarely more than 1 mm. thick . . . . 93. *P. pinsitus*

87. Pileus 1 cm. or less long; sporophore mostly resupinate . . . 88
    Pileus more than 1 cm. long; sporophore not mostly resupi-
    nate 89

88. Pores averaging 1–2 per mm.; tubes 1–3 mm. long
                                    See no. 3, *Trametes variiformis*
    Pores averaging 3 per mm.; tubes 2–5 mm. long
                                    See no. 2, *Trametes serialis*

89. Pileus fibrillose, drying radiate-striate; cystidia present,
    4–7 μ in diameter, not conspicuous; clamps present on
    the context hyphae . . . . 112. *P. balsameus*
    Pileus hirsute-tomentose, not drying striate; cystidia none;
    clamps absent . . . . 104. *P. hirsutus*

90. Pileus nearly or quite glabrous . See no. 1, *Daedalea confragosa*
    Pileus velvety to hirsute, fibrillose, or tomentose 91

91. Pores averaging 2 or less per mm. 92
    Pores averaging 3 or more per mm. 93

92. Pileus multizonate; cystidia none; context less than 1 mm.
    thick . . . . 93. *P. pinsitus*
    Pileus not multizonate; cystidia small, capitate-incrusted;
    context more than 1 mm. thick . . . . 92. *P. versatilis*

93. Pileus with an inconspicuous tomentum, with unicolorous
    zones; tubes soon breaking up into teeth
                                              98. *P. pargamenus*

Pileus strongly pubescent but scarcely tomentose, typically multizonate with multicolored zones; tubes not becoming toothed . . . .   103. *P. versicolor*

FF. *Pileus white, pallid, or gray in fresh specimens, not definitely colored, on drying sometimes yellowish, more rarely reddish, often unchanged*

G. *Context 1 mm. or less thick* (for sporophores with thicker context see GG, p. 180)

94. Pileus strongly pubescent[1]   95
    Pileus less markedly pubescent or glabrous[2]   104
95. Pores averaging 1–2 or less per mm. . . . . , ...   96
    Pores averaging 2–4 per mm.   99
96. Pileus strongly multizonate . . . .   93. *P. pinsitus*
    Pileus not multizonate   97
97. Pileus soft and watery-fleshy; pores shallow, flesh-colored to reddish, cosmopolitan; spores allantoid, 3–4 × 1 μ
                                      See *Merulius tremellosus*[3]
    Pileus not at all fleshy; pores not shallow nor reddish; spores not allantoid   98
98. Pileus soft and spongy; cystidia present; context hyphae with cross walls; ranging from Colorado to Idaho and British Columbia . . . .   109. *P. cuneatus*
    Pileus firm and rigid; cystidia none; context hyphae usually without cross walls, cosmopolitan
                                   See no. 1, *Trametes sepium*
99. Pileus drying very soft and floccose, less than 1 cm. long; from the Pacific Northwest . . . .   69. *P. perdelicatus*
    Pileus drying rigid or at least leathery; of wider distribution   100
100. Pileus coriaceous; hyphae with clamps . . .   114. *P. amorphus*
    Pileus tough and leathery when fresh; hyphae without clamps   101
101. Pileus multizonate, usually 2 cm. or more long; usually on hardwoods   102
    Pileus with 1 or 2 (or occasionally more) zones, usually less than 2 cm. long; usually on conifers . . . .   97. *P. abietinus*

---

[1] That is, with pubescence as marked as that of *Polyporus abietinus* or *P. hirsutus*.
[2] As in *Trametes sepium* or *Polyporus pargamenus*.   [3] See Burt (26).

111. Pileus watery when fresh, drying somewhat rufescent
                                 113. *P. subcartilagineus*
    Pileus dry, not rufescent . . . .   See no. 2, *Trametes serialis*

  GG. *Context more than 1 mm. thick*

112. Sporophore showing all the characters in one of the follow-
      ing sets:
    a. Sporophore globose or compressed-globose, 1–3.5 cm.
        thick; pore surface covered and concealed by a
        thick persistent membrane with a single circular
        opening . . . . 108. *P. volvatus*
    b. Growing on incense cedar on the Pacific Coast; sporo-
        phore ungulate, up to 10 cm. or more thick and
        associated with a pin rot[1] of the heartwood of
        living trees . . . . 62. *P. amarus*
    c. Growing on *Cupressus* on the Pacific Coast; sporo-
        phore thin and applanate and associated with a
        brown carbonizing butt rot . . . . . . 91. *P. basilaris*
    d. Pileus with scattered depressed circular spots, thin
        and applanate, drying strongly yellowish, gla-
        brous or nearly so; spores oblong or short-cylin-
        dric, 3–4.5×2–$2.5\ \mu$ . . . . 63. *P. guttulatus*
    e. Pore surface orange to brick-red or reddish purple in
        fresh plants, the tubes waxy or fleshy-gelatinous.   113
    f. Entire sporophore becoming pinkish, reddish, or tawny
        on drying; spores allantoid or cylindric 114
    Sporophore not showing all the characters in any of the
      groups above 116
113. Pore surface pale bay to reddish purple or purplish black;
      pores 5–8 per mm., not reduced to shallow pits
                               116. *P. dichrous*
    Pore surface pinkish red, or orange to brick-red; pores
      2–4 per mm.; tubes of appreciable length, not shallow
      pits . . . . 114. *P. amorphus*
    Pore surface fleshy red to cinnabar-red; pores 1–2 per mm.,
      irregular, shallow, merulioid
                          Compare *Merulius tremellosus*[2]

---

[1] See Fig. 186.   [2] See Burt (26).

114. Pileus with an erect, short, hispid pubescence; spores cy-
    lindric, 7–11 μ long .... 55. *P. lapponicus*
    Pileus not hispid; spores allantoid, 3–6 μ long 115
115. Pileus permanently pubescent or with a mat of soft fibers,
    less than 1.5 cm. thick; hyphae with abundant and
    conspicuous clamps .... 54. *P. fragilis*
    Pileus becoming glabrous, more than 1.5 cm. thick; hyphae
    with a few inconspicuous cross walls ..... 56. *P. mollis*
116. Pores averaging 1–3 per mm. 117
    Pores averaging 3 or more per mm. 120
117. Pileus soft and spongy, strongly tomentose, less than 0.5
    cm. thick; incrusted cystidia in the hymenium; spores
    3.5–5 × 3–4 μ; context hyphae with cross walls
                                        109. *P. cuneatus*
    Pileus soft and spongy, strongly tomentose, more than 0.5
    cm. thick; spores 4.5–7 × 3.5–5 μ; context hyphae with
    occasional cross walls and clamps .... 83. *P. borealis*
    Pileus very soft, more than 0.5 cm. thick; spores 4–5 ×
    1–1.5 μ .... 65. *P. leucospongia*
    Pileus coriaceous; cystidia none; spores 6–8 × 2–2.5 μ;
    hyphae with cross walls and clamps ..... 94. *P. biformis*
    Pileus firm and leathery or corky, not strongly pubescent;
    cystidia none; spores more elongate; hyphae without
    cross walls 118
118. Pore surface white, the pores irregular and elongated
                            See no. 4, *Trametes heteromorpha*
    Pore surface pallid but not white, the pores regular though
    sometimes elongated 119
119. Pileus less than 2.5 cm. long; associated with a brown car-
    bonizing rot of the wood; context less than 2 mm. thick
                                See no. 1, *Trametes sepium*
    Pileus more than 2.5 cm. long; associated with a soft white
    rot of the wood; context 2–10 mm. thick
                            See no. 1, *Daedalea confragosa*
120. Pileus glabrous or only inconspicuously pubescent........ 121
    Pileus definitely and usually strongly pubescent or tomen-
    tose under a lens 129
121. Pore surface smoke-colored or blackish ...... 118. *P. adustus*
    Pore surface white or whitish and becoming only yellowish
    on drying 122

122. Tubes 2 mm. long; pileus not more than 1 cm. long, pendent
     by a short, dorsolateral, stemlike base   34. *P. subpendulus*
     Tubes longer; pileus typically larger (except in no. 58, *P.
     anceps*) and never attached by a dorsal, stemlike base   123
123. Pileus narrowly attached by an attenuated base   124
     Pileus always broadly attached, not attenuate to a narrow
     base   125
124. Pileus less than 0.5 cm. thick . . . .   35. *P. floriformis*
     Pileus 0.5 cm. or more thick . . . .   14. *P. osseus*
125. Sporophore very soft and watery; spores allantoid, 3–5 ×
     0.7–2 μ   126
     Sporophore cartilaginous to tough and firm when fresh;
     spores not allantoid   127
126. Tubes typically 5–15 mm. long; context hyphae simple or
     nearly so; odor never fragrant; associated with a brown
     carbonizing decay . . . .   72. *P. tephroleucus*
     Tubes typically 1.5–3 mm. long; context hyphae very much
     branched; odor usually fragrant; associated with a soft
     white rot . . . .   73. *P. albellus*
127. Pileus 1–4 cm. long   128
     Pileus usually 5–10 cm. or more long . . . .   59. *P. palustris*
128. Spores cylindric, 7–10 × 2–3 μ; some context and tramal
     hyphae with antlered branching . . . .   58. *P. anceps*
     Spores short-cylindric, 4–5 × 2–3 μ; hyphae not with
     antlered branching . . . .   67. *P. cutifractus*
129. Pileus distinctly zonate   130
     Pileus azonate   132
130. Pileus very thin, usually less than 2 mm. thick; tubes soon
     becoming torn and lacerated . . . .   98. *P. pargamenus*
     Pileus typically more than 2 mm. thick; tubes never
     toothed   131
131. Pileus fibrillose, soft or cartilaginous when fresh; pore
     surface white or yellowish; context hyphae with clamps
                                           112. *P. balsameus*
     Pileus velvety-tomentose, leathery when fresh; pore sur-
     face black or blackish; context hyphae with clamps
                                           118. *P. adustus*

Pileus hirsute-tomentose, leathery when fresh; pore surface usually whitish, sometimes smoky; context hyphae without clamps .... 104. *P. hirsutus*

132. Pileus surface drying soft cottony-spongy with a very thick tomentum; spores cylindric, 4–5 × 1–1.5 μ; from high altitudes in the Rocky Mountains and westward
65. *P. leucospongia*

Pileus surface drying firm and sometimes rough........ 133

133. Spores cylindric, 6–8 × 2–3.5 μ; cystidia none; from the southeastern United States .... 59. *P. palustris*

Spores ellipsoid or ovoid, 4.5–7 × 3.5–5 μ; cystidia 7–10 μ in diameter, sometimes rare; ranging from Virginia and Tennessee northward and westward ..... 83. *P. borealis*

Spores broadly ellipsoid or subglobose, 2–3 × 1.5–2.5 μ .. 134

Spores ellipsoid or cylindric, 3–5 μ long 135

134. Context hyphae with clamps, 4–6 μ in diameter
75. *P. canadensis*

Context hyphae without clamps, 2–3 μ in diameter
76. *P. abieticola*

135. Spores short-cylindric or allantoid, 3–5 × 0.7–2 μ; sporophore broadly attached; pileus tomentose or pubescent 136

Spores oblong-ellipsoid or ellipsoid, not allantoid, 3–4 × 2–2.5 μ; sporophore narrowly attached by the attenuate base of the pileus; pileus fibrillose ..... 35. *P. floriformis*

136. Pileus surface drying rough .... 64. *P. immitis*

Pileus surface drying smooth or only fibrillose 137

137. Pileus slightly villose-tomentose, never strigose, the margin glabrous; pileus usually drying with a thin yellowish pellicle; context hyphae very much branched
73. *P. albellus*

Pileus strongly villose-tomentose all over and usually strigose at the base; pileus without a pellicle on drying; context hyphae only sparingly branched .. 68. *P. caesius*

Pileus tomentose at the base, radiate-fibrillose on the margin; context hyphae sparingly branched.. 111. *P. lineatus*

[Pileus becoming cartilaginous in appearance; on charred wood only .... 71. *P. carbonarius*—J.L.L.]

EE. *Plants inhabiting wood of deciduous trees* (*i.e., hardwoods*)
  H. *Pileus more than 1 cm. thick* (for pilei less than 1 cm. thick
    see HH, p. 189)

138. Sporophore showing all the characters in one of the following
    sets:
    a. Pileus with a red or mahogany-colored varnish; spores
        pale brown, truncate at one end, apparently echin-
        ulate, and always present in mature sporophores
                                                1. *P. lucidus*
    b. Pileus bright yellow to salmon-colored or orange in
        fresh plants, usually fading on drying; pore surface
        sulphur-yellow when fresh; spores hyaline, 5–7 $\times$
        3.5–4.5 μ; sporophore 10–30 cm. or more broad
        when mature, usually with imbricate pilei
                                                28. *P. sulphureus*
    c. Pileus strongly convex, the sterile margin projecting
        downward 5 mm. or more beyond the level of the
        pore surface; tubes separating in a smooth layer
        from the context in fresh specimens; spores 3.5–5
        $\times$ 1–2 μ; found only on birches in north-tem-
        perate regions .... 50. *P. betulinus*
    d. Pileus with scattered, depressed, circular spots, rather
        thin and applanate, drying yellowish; spores
        short-cylindric, 3–4.5 $\times$ 2–2.5 μ .. 63. *P. guttulatus*
    e. Pileus covered with a dense mat of erect hairs, yellow-
        brown to black, easily discernible without a lens   139
    Sporophore not showing all the characters in any of the
        groups above 140
139. Hairs of pileus yellow to brown; pore surface whitish to
        isabelline, the pores angular; spores 8–10 $\times$ 2–3 μ;
        context hyphae up to 7 μ in diameter; cosmopolitan
                                    See no. 5, *Trametes Trogii*
    Hairs of pileus black or blackish; pore surface smoky to
        blackish, the pores elongate in one direction; spores
        5–7 $\times$ 3–3.5 μ; context hyphae up to 4.5 μ in diameter;
        from Florida only .... 102. *P. trichomallus*
140. Pileus nearly uniform seal-brown to blackish brown or
        blackish .... 74. *P. resinosus*
    Pileus usually white or gray, occasionally reddish tan, pale

[1] Very old specimens, of course, often weather blackish.

larger; largest context hyphae 5 μ or more in diameter;
pores often partly or entirely daedaloid
        See no. 1, *Daedalea confragosa*, and no. 5, *D. ambigua*
Sporophore usually not at all resupinate, the pileus usually
    more than 2 cm. long; context hyphae 6–12 μ in
    diameter; pores circular; anise-scented when fresh
                    See no. 6, *Trametes suaveolens*
149. Pileus not more than 1.5 cm. thick, usually strongly ap-
    pressed-fibrillose, occasionally finely tomentose; spores
    cylindric, 6–8 $\times$ 2–2.5 μ .... **94.** *P. biformis*
Pileus more than 1.5 cm. thick, usually tomentose; spores
    ellipsoid to subglobose, 4.5–8 $\times$ 3.5–6 μ **150**
150. Hyphae of the upper part of the context thin-walled, of the
    lower part thick-walled; pores 0.5–1 mm. in diameter;
    pileus applanate, with a thin margin; often on logs, but
    usually not on *Quercus* .... **88.** *P. delectans*
Hyphae of the context thick-walled throughout; pores usu-
    ally 1 mm. or more in diameter; pileus convex, with an
    obtuse margin; usually on living *Quercus* .. **90.** *P. obtusus*
151. Context white or nearly so **153**
Context not entirely white, but pale flesh color, pale buff,
    or somewhat umber............................. **152**
152. Context pale flesh color when fresh, soft and watery; growing
    only on living trees; context hyphae much agglutinated,
    with clamps; of wide distribution .... **89.** *P. fissilis*
Context pale flesh color or pinkish, corky; usually growing
    on stumps and trunks of *Fraxinus*; context hyphae
    not agglutinated, without clamps; of wide distribution
                    See no. 7, *Fomes fraxineus*
Context pale buff, soft and watery; growing only on *Castanea*
    and *Quercus*; context hyphae much agglutinated, with
    clamps; of wide distribution .... **133.** *P. croceus*
Context pale umber, corky; usually not on *Fraxinus* and
    never on living trees; context hyphae not at all ag-
    glutinated, without clamps; ranging from North Car-
    olina along the coast to Texas and in Arkansas
                        126. *P. supinus*
153. Context hyphae without clamps, or these rare **154**
Context hyphae with frequent to abundant clamps **160**

162. Pores averaging 4–6 per mm.; spores ellipsoid, minute,
2.5–3 × 2–2.5 μ; sporophore with a pleasant odor when
fresh .... 86. *P. galactinus*
Pores averaging 2–5 per mm.; spores larger; no pleasant
odor 163
163. Context uniform in consistency, drying hard; spores ovoid
to subglobose, 4.5–7 × 4–5 μ; usually on *Castanea,*
Quercus, or *Fagus* .... 82. *P. Spraguei*
Context with a hard layer next the tubes, softer above;
spores ellipsoid or ovoid, 4.5–7 × 3.5–5 μ; rarely on
hardwoods, reported only on *Acer* and *Populus*
83. *P. borealis*
Context duplex as in the last, drying firm but not hard next
the tubes; spores broadly ellipsoid to subglobose, 6–10
× 4.5–6 or 5–7 μ in diameter; on a variety of hardwoods but not on chestnut or oak ..... 87. *P. spumeus*
Context duplex but less conspicuously so; spores 4–5 ×
3.5–4 μ; especially common on living apple trees
87. *P. spumeus* var. *malicola*
164. Tube layer separated from the context by a narrow dark
line .... 119. *P. fumosus*
Tube layer not so separated from the context 165
165. Sporophore poorly developed, nodulose, with a disagreeable
odor in both fresh and dried condition. 78. *P. compactus*
Sporophore well developed, not nodulose; odor not disagreeable 166
166. Context yellow where touched with KOH solution; spores
narrow-ellipsoid or narrow-ovoid, 3–3.5 × 1.5–2 μ;
from South Carolina and the Gulf States only
79. *P. amygdalinus*
Context not yellow with KOH 167
167. Spores globose, 3.5–4 μ; from Florida only . 85. *P. Calkinsii*
Spores cylindric, 6–8 × 2.5–3.5 μ; southern . 60. *P. submurinus*
Spores allantoid, 3–5 × 0.7–2 μ; of wide distribution 168
Spores oblong or short-cylindric, 5–7 × 3–3.5 μ; northern in
distribution .... 57. *P. transmutans*
168. Context hyphae very much branched; tubes usually only
1.5–3 mm. long; fresh plants with a sweet odor; no
bluish tinge; associated with a white rot .. 73. *P. albellus*

Context hyphae nearly or entirely unbranched; tubes usually 5–15 mm. long; fresh plants without a sweet odor; no bluish tinge; associated with a brown carbonizing rot
72. *P. tephroleucus*

Context hyphae sparingly branched; tubes 2–8 mm. long; fresh plants with a sweet odor and often with a bluish tinge; associated with a brown rot . . . . . 68. *P. caesius*

HH. *Pileus not more than 1 cm. thick*

I. *Pores large, averaging not more than 2 per mm.* (for sporophores with smaller pores see II, p. 190)

169. Pileus fleshy-tough when fresh; pore surface reddish or becoming so on drying; tubes reduced to shallow pits separated by obtuse ridges . . . . See *Merulius tremellosus*[1]

Pileus tough to woody; pore surface not reddish or only slightly pinkish where rubbed; tubes of appreciable length 170

170. Pileus glabrous or only inconspicuously pubescent or tomentose 171

Pileus conspicuously fibrillose, hirsute, or tomentose. 176

171. Pileus always less than 3 cm. long, often mostly resupinate 172

Pileus more than 3 cm. long, usually not partly resupinate 175

172. Pileus dark brown or blackish . . . . . . See no. 8, *Trametes mollis*

Pileus lighter in color 173

173. Pores typically large and irregular or daedaloid, 1 mm. or more in diameter; rare on hardwoods
See no. 4, *Trametes heteromorpha*

Pores smaller and more regular, 1 mm. or less in diameter 174

174. Context 1.5 mm. or less thick; pileus, pores, and context white or nearly so; spores 9–11 μ long
See no. 1, *Trametes sepium*

Context 2–5 mm. thick; pileus, pores, and context not white but rather pale wood color; spores 7–9 μ long
See no. 11, *Trametes malicola*

Context 1.5 mm. or less thick; pileus, pores, and context white when fresh; spores 4–6 × 1–1.5 μ 96. *P. undosus*

175. Pileus at least in part red or reddish; subtropical in range and expected to occur in southern Florida
See *Trametes corrugata*, p. 154

[1] See Burt (26).

Pileus not at all reddish; cosmopolitan and common
        See no. 1, *Daedalea confragosa*, and no. 5, *D. ambigua*
176. Pileus less than 1 mm. thick .... 93. *P. pinsitus*
     Pileus more than 1 mm. thick 177
177. Pileus with a suberect hispid or hirsute pubescence easily
     visible without a lens; southern in distribution, mainly
     from the Gulf States 178
     Pileus with a more appressed tomentum 180
178. Context distinct from the covering of coarse matted fibrils;
     pores averaging 1 per mm. 179
     Context not to be differentiated from the covering of coarse
     fibrils; pores averaging somewhat smaller   92. *P. versatilis*
179. Pileus not more than 2 mm. thick .... 93. *P. pinsitus*
     Pileus more than 2 mm. thick .... 92. *P. versatilis*
180. Incrusted cystidia present in the hymenium; context hyphae
     without clamps .... 95. *P. Tulipiferae*
     Small capitate-incrusted cystidia present in the hymenium;
     context hyphae with clamps .... 98. *P. pargamenus*
     Cystidia absent; clamps present at least on the smaller
     hyphae 181
181. Pileus up to 1 cm. long; spores 9–11 × 3–4.5 μ; basidia 6–8 μ
     in diameter; tubes not breaking up into teeth; causing
     a brown cubical rot of the wood   See no. 1, *Trametes sepium*
     Pileus usually more than 1 cm. long; spores 6–8 × 2–2.5 μ;
     tubes usually soon breaking up into teeth; causing a
     soft white rot of the wood .... 94. *P. biformis*

   II. *Pores smaller, averaging more than 2 per mm.*
    J. *Pores averaging 2–4 per mm.* (for sporophores with pores
     more than 4 per mm. see JJ, p. 194)

182. Sporophore very watery and somewhat fragile when fresh,
     not capable of much bending without breaking, dried
     specimens becoming soft and spongy or sodden when
     soaked; context friable, not fibrous................ 183
     Sporophore tough to leathery when fresh, bending nearly
     double without breaking, dried specimens changing to
     this condition when soaked; context fibrous, stringy   192
183. Sporophore 1–2 mm. thick; tubes less than 1 mm. long
                       43. *P. fimbriatus*

191. Pileus glabrous but with a gelatinous cuticle that often
 dries rough; context 2–5 mm. thick; mouths of the
 tubes entire . . . . 67. *P. cutifractus*
 Pileus silky-tomentose, becoming glabrous in zones, no
 gelatinous cuticle; context less than 1 mm. thick;
 mouths of the tubes strongly lacerate . . 66. *P. cerifluus*
 Pileus soft-tomentose, strongly discolored on drying; context 5 mm. or more thick; spores 5–7 × 3–3.5 μ
 57. *P. transmutans*
192. Pileus covered with a red varnish forming a thin crust;
 spores ovoid, pale brown, apparently echinulate
 1. *P. lucidus*
 Pileus not varnished and usually not at all red; spores
 different 193
193. Tubes separated from the context by a narrow dark line as
 seen when the pileus is cut vertically . . . . 119. *P. fumosus*
 Tubes not so separated from the context 194
194. Pileus nearly or quite glabrous when mature 195
 Pileus with stiff erect hydnoid processes; from Florida only
 101. *P. aculeifer*
 Pileus velvety to hirsute, hispid, fibrillose, or tomentose, at
 least in part 200
195. Pileus arising from a cup-shaped sterile structure that
 remains for some time on the upper surface of the
 mature sporophore near the base; found usually on
 dead branches of *Ulmus* . . . . 107. *P. conchifer*
 Pileus not as above; usually on other hosts 196
196. Pileus 2 mm. or less thick; from the Gulf States
 43. *P. fimbriatus*
 Pileus usually 2 mm. or less thick; northern in distribution
 127. *P. semisupinus*
 Pileus more than 2 mm. thick 197
197. Sporophore mostly resupinate; pileus not more than 1 cm.
 long, brown . . . . See no. 2, *Trametes serialis*
 Sporophore not mostly resupinate; pileus usually more than
 1 cm. long 198
198. Pileus drying yellow; from Florida only . . . . . 85. *P. Calkinsii*
 Pileus drying white, gray, reddish, or brownish 199

199. Pileus smooth and velvety to the touch, usually 5 cm. or
more long and 1 cm. or more thick
See no. 5, *Daedalea ambigua*
Pileus not particularly smooth and not velvety, usually
radiate-striate or rugose, less than 5 cm. long and 1 cm.
thick .... 105. *P. pubescens* var. *Grayii*

200. Pileus entirely white when fresh, sometimes yellowish on
drying 201
Pileus distinctly gray, cinereous, smoky, brownish, and so
on, but not entirely white when fresh, unchanged on
drying 202

201. Context usually more than 5 mm. thick, composed of a soft
upper layer and a firm layer next the tubes, best observed in dried plants; spores ellipsoid to ovoid, 4.5–7 ×
3.5–5 μ; rare on hardwoods .... 83. *P. borealis*
Context less than 5 mm. thick, cartilaginous; spores ellipsoid, 4.5–6.5 × 2–3 μ .... 113. *P. subcartilagineus*
Context less than 5 mm. thick, uniform in consistency;
spores cylindric, 5–8 × 2–2.5 μ; common on hardwoods .... 105. *P. pubescens*

202. Pileus usually azonate, covered with grayish to brownish
hirsute pubescence .... See no. 5, *Trametes Trogii*
Pileus azonate, covered with erect, stiff, black, coarse hairs;
from Florida only .... 102. *P. trichomallus*
Pileus zonate, the pubescence hirsute-tomentose to velvety-
tomentose, but not composed of erect hispid or hirsute
hairs 203

203. Context 1 mm. or less thick 204
Context more than 1 mm. thick 209

204. Pileus with many zones, often of contrasting colors 205
Pileus zonate but with unicolorous zones 206

205. Pileus villose to velvety-pubescent; pore surface never
strongly toothed.................... 103. *P. versicolor*
Pileus villose to velvety; pore surface soon strongly toothed
98. *P. pargamenus*
Pileus densely villose or hirsute; pore surface becoming
strongly toothed .... See no. 4, *Daedalea unicolor*

206. Pore surface breaking up into teeth 207
Pore surface not becoming toothed 209

207. Pore surface isabelline to somewhat dark; with small
capitate-incrusted cystidia in the hymenium; ranging
from South Carolina to Texas and southward

          100. *P. sector*

  Pore surface more or less smoky as above; no cystidia;
cosmopolitan .... 104. *P. hirsutus*

  Pore surface white, whitish, or lavender-tinted 208

208. Pileus 1–7 cm. long; cystidia slightly capitate-incrusted at
the apex .... 98. *P. pargamenus*

  Pileus less than 1.5 cm. long; cystidia heavily incrusted
over a considerable portion of the distal end

         95. *P. Tulipiferae*

209. Tomentum of the pileus underlaid with a thin, hard, bay
or chestnut layer which eventually becomes exposed in
zones or all over 210

  Tomentum not underlaid as above 211

210. Pore surface uneven and toothed; pileus often 10 cm. or
more long and broad; subtropical ..... 106. *P. maximus*

  Pore surface even; pileus less than 10 cm. long and broad;
cosmopolitan .... 103. *P. versicolor*

211. Pileus velvety-tomentose; without cystidia . 110. *P. velutinus*

  Pileus villose-tomentose; with small capitate-incrusted cystidia .... 99. *P. subchartaceus*

  Pileus hirsute-tomentose 212

212. Pileus definitely radiate-striate .... 105. *P. pubescens*

  Pileus not at all radiate-striate .... 104. *P. hirsutus*

   JJ. *Pores averaging more than 4 per mm.*

213. Pore surface flesh color to pinkish, rosy, reddish, or purplish 214

  Pore surface white to smoke color or blackish in fresh plants,
sometimes yellowish on drying, never bright-colored . 219

214. Context hyphae reaching diameters of 8 μ or more 215

  Context hyphae not exceeding 6 μ in diameter 217

215. Pores 4–6 per mm.; context hyphae without cross walls;
pileus usually azonate, drying corky

       See no. 7, *Fomes fraxineus*

  Pores 6–9 per mm.; context hyphae with cross walls; pileus
zonate, drying very hard and rigid 216

216. Sporophore largely resupinate; pileus distinctly pubescent; ranging north to Missouri, Ohio, and New Jersey
80. *P. rigidus*

Sporophore usually sessile, scarcely pubescent; from the Gulf States only .... 81. *P. zonalis*

217. Context hyphae with clamps; tube layer waxy, pale buff to reddish purple .... 116. *P. dichrous*

Context hyphae without clamps; tube layer waxy, pinkish or flesh color .... 117. *P. conchoides*

Context hyphae without clamps; tube layer not waxy, flesh color to pale rosy 218

218. Context hyphae with cross walls; pores averaging 7–9 per mm. .... See *P. lignosus*, p. 427

Context hyphae without cross walls; pores averaging 4–6 per mm. .... 125. *P. modestus*

219. Sporophore when fresh soft, fleshy-fragile, watery, not bending without breaking, dried specimens changing to a similar condition when soaked 220

Sporophore when fresh tough and flexible, bending nearly or quite double without breaking, or somewhat corky 226

220. Sporophore usually narrowly attached by a basal attenuation of the pileus, usually with scattered circular depressed spots; spores oblong or short-cylindric, 3–4.5 × 2–2.5 μ .... 63. *P. guttulatus*

Sporophore broadly attached, without circular depressed spots 221

221. Odor sweet and pleasant when fresh; context drying soft .. 222

Odor not characteristic; context drying hard 224

222. Taste bitter in both fresh and dried sporophores
64. *P. immitis*

Taste mild 223

223. Spores ellipsoid or subglobose, 2.5–3.5 × 2–2.5 μ; pileus gray, unchanged on drying .... 77. *P. fumidiceps*

Spores allantoid, 3–5 × 0.7–1 μ; pileus white or slightly gray, sometimes drying yellowish; context hyphae nearly simple .... 72. *P. tephroleucus*

Spores and colors about as in the last above; context hyphae very much branched .... 73. *P. albellus*

224. Pileus glabrous but with a gelatinous pellicle that usually
        dries bay .... 67. *P. cutifractus*
     Pileus more or less tomentose, not drying bay 225
225. Spores 3–4 × 1.5–2 μ; context hyphae with clamps
                                    64. *P. immitis*
     Spores 4.5–7 × 1.5–2.5 μ; context hyphae without clamps
                                    61. *P. durescens*
226. Pileus conspicuously pubescent or tomentose, scarcely re-
        quiring the use of a hand lens for detection 227
     Pileus minutely and inconspicuously pubescent or gla-
        brous 234
227. Pore surface black or blackish 228
     Pore surface not at all black 229
228. Tube layer waxy and separable in a smooth elastic layer
        from the context in fresh plants or when wet; spores
        3–4.5 × 0.5–1 μ .... 116. *P. dichrous*
     Tube layer not at all waxy and entirely inseparable from
        the context; spores 3.5–5 × 2–3 μ ...... 118. *P. adustus*
229. Pileus azonate; context hyphae with cross walls
                             See no. 9, *Fomes connatus*
     Pileus zonate; context hyphae without cross walls 230
230. Sporophore mostly resupinate; pileus definitely brown and
        with a narrow black line underlying the pubescence;
        context hyphae not over 4.5 μ in diameter
                                    128. *P. planellus*
     Sporophore usually not mostly resupinate and pileus not
        definitely brown, or, if so, not with a black line under
        the pubescence; context hyphae reaching 7 μ or more
        in diameter 231
231. Pileus becoming glabrous only in zones, these usually multi-
        colored.......................... 103. *P. versicolor*
     Pileus not becoming glabrous or becoming more or less
        entirely glabrous, the zones usually unicolorous 232
232. Pileus up to 2 mm. thick, permanently villose-tomentose
                                    122. *P. pavonius*
     Pileus 3 mm. or more thick, finally nearly glabrous 233
233. Pileus white to straw color or ochraceous tan; context 1–2
        mm. thick .... 123. *P. subectypus*
     Pileus isabelline to reddish or bay; context 2–5 mm. thick
                                    124. *P. ectypus*

POLYPORUS

197

234. Pileus more than 0.5 cm. thick 235
Pileus 0.5 cm. or less thick 244
235. Context hyphae with clamps 236
Context hyphae without clamps 238
236. Tubes 2–8 mm. long; spores globose, 3.5–4 μ in diameter;
pileus drying yellowish; known from Florida only, but
may occur in other Gulf States .... 85. *P. Calkinsii*
Tubes 5 mm. or less long; spores cylindric, 6–8 $\times$ 2.5–3.5 μ;
pileus not drying yellowish; from North Carolina and
Louisiana .... 60. *P. submurinus*
Tubes 4 mm. or less long; spores oblong or oblong-ellipsoid,
3.5–6 $\times$ 2–3 μ; pileus not drying yellowish; cosmopolitan 237
237. Pores averaging 5–7 per mm. .... 118. *P. adustus*
Pores averaging 3–5 per mm. .... 119. *P. fumosus*
238. Context hyphae 2–3 μ in diameter, much branched
See no. 8, *Fomes scutellatus*
Context hyphae attaining 4–10 μ in diameter, simple or
nearly so 239
239. Pore surface white or cream color. See no. 7, *Trametes cubensis*
Pore surface smoky, avellaneous, or discolored 240
240. Largest context hyphae reaching diameters of only 4–6 μ;
associated with a dry crumbling rot of the wood 241
Largest context hyphae reaching diameters of 8 μ or more;
rot not dry and crumbling 242
241. Pore surface smoky or blackish; usually on *Melia* or *Fraxinus* .... See no. 11, *Fomes Meliae*
Pore surface pallid or discolored but not blackish
60. *P. submurinus*
242. Pores averaging 5–7 per mm.; growing on logs and stumps . 243
Pores averaging 4–6 per mm.; growing on living trees
See no. 7, *Fomes fraxineus*
243. Pileus zonate; context nearly white .... 124. *P. ectypus*
Pileus azonate; context umber to olivaceous or brownish
126. *P. supinus*
244. Pore surface gray to brownish, smoky, or blackish 245
Pore surface white or whitish, sometimes drying yellowish 248
245. Context hyphae with clamps 246
Context hyphae without clamps 247

246. Pores averaging 3–5 per mm. . . . .   119. *P. fumosus*
     Pores averaging 5–7 per mm. . . . .   118. *P. adustus*
247. Pores averaging 4–6 per mm.; growing on living trees
                                   See no. 7, *Fomes fraxineus*
     Pores averaging 5–7 per mm.; growing on logs and stumps
                                   126. *P. supinus*
248. Pileus soon black on the older portions, the margin remain-
     ing white . . . .   See no. 8, *Fomes scutellatus*
     Pileus drying white, yellowish, bay, or ochraceous orange,
     never becoming blackish   249
249. Context hyphae usually with clamps; widely distributed
     northward   250
     Context hyphae usually without clamps; from the Gulf
     States   251
250. Hyphal pegs broadly conoidal; spores 2.5–3 $\times$ 2–2.5 μ;
     pileus more or less zonate . . . .   127. *P. semisupinus*
     Hyphal pegs narrow and subcylindric; spores allantoid,
     2.5–3.5 $\times$ 0.5 μ; pileus azonate . . . . .   70. *P. semipileatus*
251. Sporophore 2–4 mm. thick; context hyphae 3–4 μ in di-
     ameter . . . .   115. *P. ochrotinctellus*
     Sporophore 3–5 mm. thick; context hyphae up to 8 μ or
     more in diameter . . . .   123. *P. subectypus*
     Sporophore 2 mm. or less thick; context hyphae up to 8 μ
     or more in diameter   252
252. Pileus and pore surface brown and the pileus strongly
     zonate on drying . . . .   121. *P. Drummondii*
     Pileus and pore surface pallid on drying . . . .   120. *P. tenuis*

SECTION II

253. Pileus and pore surface deep cinnabar-red (but pileus some-
     times fading)   254
     Pileus and pore surface not deep cinnabar-red (rosy, buff,
     or orange in some species)   255
254. Pileus very thin, less than 5 mm. thick, never zonate; tubes
     less than 5 mm. long; cystidia none; on hardwoods;
     from New York and Nebraska southward
                                   130. *P. sanguineus*
     Pileus thicker, usually more than 5 mm. thick, often zonate;

tubes less than 5 mm. long; cystidia none; usually on
hardwoods; cosmopolitan .... 129. *P. cinnabarinus*
Pileus thicker, never zonate; tubes 1 cm. or more long;
cystidia present; on logs of coniferous trees; from
alpine and subalpine stations in the western mountains
and rarely from Quebec, New York, and Michigan
132. *P. alboluteus*
Pileus thicker; tubes 2–6 mm. long; cystidia present; on
wood of coniferous trees in the northern states and
Canada .... 131. *P. fibrillosus*
255. Pore surface bright sulphur-yellow in fresh plants; pileus
orange or salmon-colored, glabrous .... 28. *P. sulphureus*
Pore surface bright rusty yellow; pileus rusty brown or
rusty red, hirsute 256
Pore surface not bright sulphur-yellow nor rusty yellow .. 257
256. Pileus 2 cm. or more thick; spores brown .. 161. *P. hispidus*
Pileus less than 3 cm. thick; spores hyaline .. 131. *P. fibrillosus*
257. On the wood of coniferous trees only; spores cylindric .. 258
On the wood of hardwood trees only; spores ellipsoid to
globose 259
258. Pileus orange-red or orange-brown, rather soft; tubes 0.2–
0.6 cm. long; pores 1.5–2 per mm.; spores 5–9 × 2.5–4 μ
131. *P. fibrillosus*
Pileus orange or fading, very soft and spongy; tubes 1–3 cm.
long; pores 1–3 mm. broad, soon toothed; spores
7–10 × 3–4 μ.................... 132. *P. alboluteus*
Pileus rose-colored or pinkish brown, fading to gray or
blackish, leathery to woody; tubes 0.1–0.3 cm. long;
pores 4–5 per mm.; spores 4–7 × 1.5–2 μ
See no. 13, *Fomes subroseus*
Pileus white; upper context white, lower context red; tubes
0.05–0.2 cm. long; pores 2–4 per mm.; spores 3–4 ×
0.7–1 μ .... 114. *P. amorphus*
259. Growing at the bases or from the roots of living trees
28. *P. sulphureus* var. *cincinnatus*
Growing in other situations 260
260. Pileus buff or orange, rather firm; context uniform; tubes
0.5–2 cm. long; pores 2–4 per mm.; spores 5–7 × 4–5 μ;
on dead wood of *Castanea* and *Quercus* .. 133. *P. croceus*

Pileus pinkish brown or buffy umber, soft and spongy when
fresh; context uniform; tubes 2–7 mm. long; pores
2–4 per mm.; spores 3–4 × 2–3 μ; on the wood of
various deciduous trees .... 142. *P. nidulans*
Pileus white to somewhat flesh-colored; context duplex;
pores 1–3 per mm.; otherwise as in *P. croceus* but
growing from wounds in living trees .. 89. *P. fissilis*
Pileus slightly reddish, firm and corky; tubes 0.2–1 cm.
long; pores 4–6 per mm.; spores broadly ovoid, 6–7 ×
5–6 μ; usually on trees or stumps of *Fraxinus*
See no. 7, *Fomes fraxineus*

Section III

A. *Sporophore stipitate or substipitate* (for sessile or effused-reflexed
sporophores see AA, p. 201)

268. Context not darker than cinnamon; hyphae extensively branched; stem about 1 cm. thick; from Florida only
48. *P. virgatus*

Context yellow-brown or darker; hyphae not much if at all branched **269**

269. Context of dried plants decidedly duplex; setae present; spores hyaline or pale brown .... 137. *P. tomentosus*

Context only slightly if at all duplex; cystidia present; spores hyaline .... 140. *P. Schweinitzii*

Context usually not duplex; neither cystidia nor setae present; spores dilutely colored; hyphae 7–15 μ in diameter; pores 0.5–2 mm. broad .... 138. *P. Montagnei*

Context not duplex; neither cystidia nor setae present; spores colorless or nearly so; hyphae 4–6 μ in diameter; pores averaging 2–4 per mm. .... 135. *P. perennis*

AA. *Sporophore sessile or effused-reflexed, sometimes narrowed to a stemlike base but not stipitate*

   B. *Pileus with a distinct firm crust under which the context is distinctly softer or of a different color* (for nonincrusted pilei see BB, p. 202)

270. Sporophore consisting of many closely overlapping pilei, forming a subglobose or cylindric mass with a central solid core,[1] the individual pilei less than 1 cm. thick
158. *P. graveolens*

Sporophore not entirely as above **271**

271. Pileus covered by a thin red varnish .... 1. *P. lucidus*

Pileus not red-varnished, rarely of reddish-brown color .. **272**

272. Context ochraceous, cinnamon, or umber **273**

Context rust-brown or darker **274**

273. Context less than 0.5 mm. thick; pileus less than 4 cm. long; from the northern states and Canada
128. *P. planellus*

Context 4–10 mm. thick; pileus 3–8 cm. long; from the Gulf States .... See no. 7, *Trametes cubensis*

274. Growing only at the bases of living oak trees or on stumps of recently felled trees, or on conifers in the Pacific

[1] See Fig. 636.

Northwest; context 1.5–4 cm. thick; spores globose, smooth, hyaline; setae present but often not abundant
149. *P. dryadeus*

Growing only on logs and stumps; context less than 1 cm. thick; spores subglobose, smooth, yellow, 4.5–6 × 3.5–4.5 μ; setae present . . . . 160. *P. glomeratus*

Growing on or around old dead stumps; context 1 cm. or less thick; spores ovoid, apparently echinulate, brown; setae none . . . . See no. 38, *Fomes lobatus*

BB. *Pileus not at all incrusted*
    C. *Sporophore growing on or about stumps or trunks of coniferous trees* (for sporophores on hardwoods see CC, p. 203)

275. Spores rough-walled; pileus not exceeding 1.5 cm. in diameter . . . . 139. *P. dependens*
    Spores smooth; pileus larger 276

276. Found usually on *Libocedrus* from Idaho to Oregon and California; producing a large pocket rot in the heartwood of living trees . . . . 62. *P. amarus*
    Found on other coniferous hosts and producing a different kind of decay 277

277. Pileus not more than 1 mm. thick, very flexible when fresh 278
    Pileus always more than 1 mm. thick, somewhat flexible to brittle 279

278. Pileus brown on drying, radiate-striate; on *Taxodium* in Florida and Louisiana . . . . 121. *P. Drummondii*
    Pileus grayish or whitish on drying, not radiate-striate; on other substrata and of wider distribution   97. *P. abietinus*

279. Context pale brown to cinnamon-brown; pore surface nearly white when fresh . . . . 74. *P. resinosus*
    Context rusty brown or darker; pore surface not white when fresh 280

280. Clavate or cylindric cystidia present in the hymenium; spores 5.5–8 × 4–5 μ; on various conifers
140. *P. Schweinitzii*

    Brown sharp-pointed setae present in the hymenium 281
    Neither cystidia nor setae present in the hymenium; spores globose, 6–8 μ in diameter; known only from Texas on *Juniperus* . . . . 153. *P. juniperinus*

Neither cystidia nor setae present in the hymenium; spores
9–12 × 3–5 μ; widely distributed and on wood of
other coniferous trees . . .   See no. 12, *Trametes americana*

281. Setae 5–16 μ in diameter; hyphae of the context usually
with some cross walls; pileus 4–10 cm. or more broad
and long 282
Setae and hyphae as above; pileus 0.5–10 cm. broad and
long   See no. 17, *Fomes tenuis*, and no. 21, *F. nigrolimitatus*
Setae 7–15 μ in diameter; hyphae without cross walls
See no. 22, *Fomes Pini* var. *Abietis*

282. Context distinctly duplex, soft above and firm below;
pileus tomentose but hardly hispid; spores hyaline or
pale-colored, 4–6 × 3–5 μ .... 137. *P. tomentosus*
Context not duplex; pileus hispid; spores dark brown,
7.5–10 × 6.5–9 μ .... 161. *P. hispidus*
Context not duplex; pileus glabrous or nearly so; spores
hyaline or pale-colored, 6–8 × 5–6 μ .. 149. *P. dryadeus*

CC. *Sporophore growing on wood of hardwood trees, often on
living trunks*
  D. *Context ochraceous or very pale brown* (for darker context
see DD, p. 204)

283. Pileus 0.5 cm. or more thick when mature 284
Pileus less than 0.5 cm. thick 287

284. Pileus hirsute or strigose; pores averaging 1–2 per mm.
See no. 9, *Trametes hispida*
Pileus covered by a dense mat of forked, stiff, brownish-
black hairs; pores averaging 2–3 per mm.; from Florida
only .... 102. *P. trichomallus*
Pileus velvety to glabrous; pores averaging 2–7 per mm. . 285

285. Pores 2 per mm. or larger .... See no. 1, *Daedalea confragosa*
Pores 4–7 per mm. 286

286. Pileus whitish or becoming reddish; from the Gulf States
only .... See no. 7, *Trametes cubensis*
Pileus often reddish or blackish at the base; southern in
distribution .... 126. *P. supinus*
Pileus brown or blackish, large; more northern in distribu-
tion .... 74. *P. resinosus*
Pileus black in age but margin pale
See no. 8, *Fomes scutellatus*

287. Pores averaging 5–6 per mm.; pileus only 1–2 mm. thick

128. *P. planellus*

Pores 6 per mm.; pileus concolorous with context

143. *P. crocatus*

Pores averaging 1–4 per mm.; pileus usually 2–5 mm. thick 288

288. In the northern United States and Canada, ranging from Kentucky northward; on a variety of substrata, more often on *Acer* and *Fagus* .... See no. 8, *Trametes mollis*

Commonly in South Carolina and the Gulf States 289

289. Pileus less than 3 cm. long ...... See no. 10, *Trametes rigida*

Pileus more than 3 cm. long 290

290. Pileus 3–15 mm. thick, nearly glabrous ..... 126. *P. supinus*

Pileus 1–3 mm. thick, short velvety-tomentose 100. *P. sector*

    DD. *Context yellowish brown or darker*

      E. *Context usually less than 7 mm. thick; sporophore small or medium-sized* (for thicker and larger sporophores see EE, p. 206)

        F. *Setae present in the hymenium* (for setae absent see FF, p. 205)

291. Setae imbedded in the pore tissue and in the context as well as between the basidia; pores greenish yellow when fresh .... 160. *P. glomeratus*

Setae found only between the basidia 292

292. Largest hyphae of the context 2.5–7 μ in diameter 294

Largest hyphae of the context 6–12 μ in diameter 293

293. Spores 5.5–8 × 4–5 μ; pileus with no evidence of a central core; usually on hosts other than *Populus*

152. *P. cuticularis*

Spores 4.5–7 × 3.5–4.5 μ; pileus with some slight evidence of a central core as in *P. dryophilus*; on *Populus* only

157. *P. dryophilus* var. *vulpinus*

294. Pileus distinctly tomentose or hispid 295

Pileus nearly glabrous or only inconspicuously pubescent or fibrillose 298

295. Pileus 3 mm. or less thick, thin and flexible; with a black zone separating the tomentum from the context; from Florida and Louisiana .... 147. *P. iodinus*

Pileus more than 3 mm. thick, rather rigid; usually no
black zone separating context from tomentum 296
296. Pores averaging 4–5 per mm.; pileus somewhat flexible
and radiate-fibrillose or radiate-rugose . 148. *P. radiatus*
Pores averaging 5–8 per mm.; pileus woody and not at all
radiate 297
297. Context 0.5–2 cm. thick; on wounded areas on living trees
from Missouri southward; spores 3–4 × 2–3 μ
See no. 19, *Fomes torulosus*
Context less than 0.5 cm. thick; on dead wood over most of
our range; spores 4–6 × 3.5–4.5 μ
See no. 18, *Fomes conchatus*
298. Pileus very thin, narrowly zonate . . . . 146. *P. licnoides*
Pileus of medium thickness, not narrowly zonate, though
often sulcate 299
299. Setae scarcely projecting beyond the basidia, 6–12 μ in
diameter; spores 4–6 × 3–4 μ; pileus tomentose to
fibrillose or glabrous; pores averaging 4–5 per mm.; in
temperate regions south to North Carolina; usually on
Alnus and *Betula* . . . . 148. *P. radiatus*
Setae projecting rather conspicuously, 3–6 μ in diameter;
spores 4–5 × 2.5–3.5 μ; pileus glabrous or soon becoming so; pores averaging 5–8 per mm.; in temperate
and tropical regions on all kinds of hardwoods
145. *P. gilvus*
As in the last above, but pileus becoming weather-beaten
and disintegrating on the upper surface, becoming
darker; tubes in several indistinct layers; from the
Gulf States . . . . 146. *P. licnoides* var. *sublilacinus*

FF. *Setae absent from the hymenium*

300. Pileus covered with a thick mat of stiff, erect, black or
brownish-black hairs; from the Gulf States only
141. *P. hydnoides*
Pileus not as above and range not always limited to the
Gulf States 301
301. Spores minutely rough-walled . . . . : 139. *P. dependens*
Spores smooth 302
302. Context dark vinaceous brown . . . . 144. *P. vinosus*
Context yellowish brown or rusty brown 303

303. Sporophore becoming purple or red where touched with
  KOH solution 304
  Sporophore only darker with **KOH** 305
304. Plants soft and watery; context not separated from tomentum by a dark line; usually growing on *Betula,*
  Carya, or *Quercus* wood; common from North Carolina
  northward .... 142. *P. nidulans*
  Plants more firm and not watery; context separated from
  the tomentum by a dark line; growing on wood of
  deciduous trees in the Gulf States ...... 150. *P. corrosus*
305. Pileus drying soft, thin, flexible, less than 0.5 cm. thick;
  pore surface brown, the mouths entire; from the Gulf
  States .... 143. *P. crocatus*
  Pileus drying as above but 2 mm. or less thick; pore surface
  olivaceous or yellowish green, the mouths becoming
  lacerate or toothed .... See no. 7, *Daedalea farinacea*
  Pileus drying firm to rigid, usually 0.5 cm. or more thick .. 306
306. Context distinctly duplex; spores 3–5 $\times$ 2–3.5 μ 307
  Context not duplex; spores 7–10 $\times$ 5–7 μ ... 156. *P. texanus*
  Context not duplex; pileus thin and applanate; spores
  4–7 μ in longest dimension....................... 308
307. Pores averaging 6–8 per mm.; context separated from the
  tomentum by a black line .... 150. *P. corrosus*
  Pores averaging 2 per mm.; context without black lines
             151. *P. fruticum*
308. Plants growing on *Populus,* in temperate regions; spores
  oblong-ellipsoid, 4.5–7 $\times$ 3.5–4.5 μ
       157. *P. dryophilus* var. *vulpinus*
  Plants on other substrata, in the Gulf States; spores globose, 4–5 μ in diameter .... 155. *P. porrectus*

  EE. *Context more than 7 mm. thick; sporophore large, 8–30*
   cm. broad

309. Setae present, but only in the basidial layer 310
  Setae present in the basidial layer and also in the tissue
  of the pore walls and in the context .. 160. *P. glomeratus*
  Setae absent 311

310. Spores brown,[1] 7.5–10 × 6.5–9 μ; pileus hirsute; growing on various diseased deciduous trees; without a central core

161. *P. hispidus*

Spores brown,[1] 7–8 × 5–7 μ; pileus fibrillose-tomentose or glabrous; usually growing on wood or trees of *Quercus*; pilei with a central core[2] .... 157. *P. dryophilus*

Spores brown,[1] 5.5–8 × 4–5 μ; pileus fibrillose-tomentose; rarely growing on *Quercus*; without a central core

152. *P. cuticularis*

Spores brown,[1] 6.5–8 × 4.5–6 μ; pileus velvety-tomentose; without a central core; from Arizona and nearby states

162. *P. Munzii*

About as in *P. Munzii* but pileus hispid .... 159. *P. Farlowii*

Spores hyaline[1] or a very dilute brown; pileus glabrous, with a thin, brown crust; growing on *Quercus* only; without a central core .... 149. *P. dryadeus*

Spores hyaline;[1] pileus soon glabrous, not incrusted; growing on a great variety of hardwoods but not usually on living trees; without a central core .... 145. *P. gilvus*

Spores hyaline,[1] 3–4 × 2–3 μ; usually perennial

See no. 19, *Fomes torulosus*

311. Context cherry-red in KOH solution .... 142. *P. nidulans*

Context black or at first red and then black in KOH solution 312

312. Pileus with a more or less central or basal solid core permeated by white fibrils as seen in vertical section[2]

157. *P. dryophilus* and var. *vulpinus*

Pileus without such a core 313

313. Pileus not more than 5 cm. long and 2.5 cm. thick; spores ellipsoid, 4–7 × 3–4.5 μ; tubes less than 0.5 cm. long .. 314

Pileus more than 5 cm. long and 2 cm. thick; spores dark brown, ellipsoid to globose, 7.5–10 × 6.5–9 μ; tubes more than 0.5 cm. long .... 161. *P. hispidus*

Pileus and tubes as in *P. hispidus*; spores dark brown, 6.5–8 × 4.5–6 μ .... 162. *P. Munzii*

---

[1] In the species under no. 310 it is easy to ascertain whether or not spores are brown simply by crushing a bit of the tube tissue in KOH on a slide. If no spores are obtained from well-developed plants by this process, assume that they are hyaline.

[2] See Fig. 303.

Pileus and tubes as in *P. hispidus*; spores 5–6 × 3.5–4 μ;
    southern in distribution . . . .   154. *P. ludovicianus*
314. Spores pale brown; from the Gulf States . . . .   151. *P. fruticum*
    Spores dark brown; more generally distributed
                      157. *P. dryophilus* var. *vulpinus*

1a. *Context white, whitish, or very light yellow when fresh; spores hya-*
    line
  2a. *Sporophore stipitate or substipitate*
    3a. *Pileus laccate*

1. POLYPORUS LUCIDUS Leys. ex Fries

Syst. Myc. 1: 353. 1821

(Figs. 335–338, 611, and Plate 130)

Boletus lucidus Leys., Flora Halensis, p. 300. 1783.
Ganoderma sessile Murr., Torrey Bot. Club Bul. 29: 604. 1902.
Polyporus polychromus Copeland, Ann. Mycol. 2: 507. 1904.
Ganoderma subperforatum Atk., Bot. Gaz. 46: 337. 1908.
Polyporus incrustans Lloyd, Synop. Stip. Polyp., p. 102. 1912.
Polyporus metallicus Lloyd, Myc. Notes 65: 1099. 1921.

Sporophore sessile or stipitate, often imbricate when sessile, leathery to corky when fresh, rigid on drying; pileus circular to reniform or
dimidiate, 2–20 × 3–35 × 0.5–8 cm., covered by a thin coat of a
subshining varnish-like substance chiefly dark red but varying to
blood-rèd, mahogany color, or reddish black and frequently ochraceous on the margin, drying as a thin crust, glabrous except for a
powdery coating of brown spores at times, usually with a few zones or
furrows and often radially wrinkled on drying, the margin thin or
rather thick; context pallid or isabelline, or more frequently isabelline
above and hair-brown next the tubes, or sometimes entirely deep
rich umber-brown throughout, soft or soft-corky varying to hard,
usually zonate in thick specimens, 0.2–3 cm. thick; pore surface
whitish to yellowish or dull brown, the tubes rarely in two distinct
layers, 2–18 mm. long, the mouths circular to angular, rather thin-
walled, entire, averaging about 4 per mm.; stem when present usually
lateral, sometimes subcentral, varnished and incrusted to a greater
degree than the pileus, up to 10 cm. (rarely more) long, 0.5–4 cm.
thick; spores ellipsoid or ovoid, the wall apparently faintly to strongly

punctate or roughened, or apparently smooth, pale brown to rather dark brown, sometimes truncate at the apex, 10–12 × 6–9 μ; cystidia none; context hyphae hyaline to brown, more or less branched, the branches of the largest hyphae sometimes attenuated, with no cross walls or clamps, up to 12 μ in diameter, usually 5–10 μ, hyphae of the lower context more branched than those of the upper.

HABITAT: At the base of living deciduous trees or on stumps or roots, noted on *Acer, Celtis, Citrus, Fraxinus, Gleditsia, Gymnocladus, Liquidambar, Nyssa, Planera, Quercus, Robinia, Salix, Schinus, Ulmus,* and *Umbellularia.*

DISTRIBUTION: Specimens have been examined from N.Y., Pa., N.J., Del., Md., D.C., Va., W. Va., Fla., Ala., La., Miss., Tenn., Ky., Ohio, Ind., Ill., Mich., Wis., Minn., Mo., Ark., Okla., Texas, Ore., and Calif.; reported from Tenn. (Kauffman [100]), Iowa (Wolf [234]), and Kans. (Bartholomew [4]).

ILLUSTRATIONS: Batsch, Elench. Fung., pl. 41, fig. 225 (as *Boletus nitens*); Dufour, Atl. Champ. Comest. Vén., pl. 49, fig. 116; Haddow, Arnold Arboretum Jour. 12: pl. 29, figs. 4–5, and pl. 30, figs. 12–15 (as *Ganoderma sessile*); Jaccottet, Champ. Nature, pl. 57 (*pars*); Lanzi, Funghi Mang., pl. 22, fig. 2 (as *Fomes*); Michael, Führ. f. Pilzfr. 3: fig. 38 (as *Fomes*); Overholts, Wash. Univ. Studies 3: pl. 4, fig. 20; Sowerby, Col. Fig. English Fungi, pl. 134 (as *Boletus*).

Many forms of this species have been described in both Europe and America, and much controversy has raged over the limits of the various names that are accepted. After more than thirty years' familiarity with *Polyporus lucidus* and *P. Tsugae*, I believe they can be distinguished almost invariably by their hosts; moreover, they can be distinguished without knowing the hosts. The context of *P. Tsugae* is white except next the tubes; in *P. lucidus* the context is not pure white in any portion and is considerably deeper-colored toward the tubes. The degree of varnishing is much greater in *P. Tsugae* than in *P. lucidus*, and the stem exhibits a higher gloss. Both species lose much of their glossiness as they dry, particularly if they have not reached maturity at the time of collection.

These two entities may be regarded as distinct species, or one may be treated as a variety of the other. I prefer to call the form associated with hardwoods *Polyporus lucidus* and that associated with coniferous trees *P. Tsugae*, even though the authors of these species may not have had the same concept (see Haddow [62]).

There frequently occurs on the pilei of these species a brown pulverulence, which, when examined, proves to be made up of spores exactly like the basidiospores of the species. They have been said to be conidial, but Romell (*Svensk Bot. Tidskr.* 10: 340–348. 1916) has shown them to be in part, at least, deposited by air currents, though that would not preclude the possibility—expressed by Patouillard as the explanation for their occurrence in *"Polyporus fulvus"* and *Fomes igniarius* var. *nigricans*—that they are partly produced *in situ* by superficial basidia on the surface of the pileus. The presence of the varnish layer may be thought of, however, as making such an explanation extremely unlikely.

In 1920 Murrill (145, p. 15) conceded that his species *Ganoderma sessile* was not distinct from *Polyporus lucidus* of Europe. The relations of these species have been discussed by me (150, pp. 709–715). *P. incrustans* is a form of *P. lucidus* with a very heavy crust. *P. polychromus* is only a large thick form of *P. lucidus* that often loses much of its varnish. Schweinitz' record of this species is incorrect, the specimen preserved at Philadelphia being *P. Curtisii*.

Var. zonatus (Murr.) Overh., comb. nov.

(Figs. 339–340)

Ganoderma zonatum Murr., Torrey Bot. Club Bul. 29: 606. 1902.
Ganoderma sulcatum Murr., Torrey Bot. Club Bul. 29: 607. 1902.

Characters generally as in the species, but spores 10–12 × 5–6 μ (hence narrow- or oblong-ellipsoid) and the pileus strongly furrowed and usually more ochraceous tan.

HABITAT: On palmetto and *Cocos*.

DISTRIBUTION: Specimens have been examined only from Georgia and Florida.

2. POLYPORUS TSUGAE (Murr.) Overh.

Mo. Bot. Gard. Ann. 2: 714. 1915
(Figs. 341–345, 489, 585, and Plate 132)

Ganoderma Tsugae Murr., Torrey Bot. Club Bul. 29: 601. 1902.

Sporophore stipitate, or sessile by a narrowed base; pileus watery or soft-corky when fresh, rigid and corky when dry, reniform or flabelliform, 5–20 × 6–30 × 1–5 cm., with a mahogany-colored, brownish orange (typically near "Morocco red" except for a white or "xanthine-orange" margin in young specimens), or almost black, shining, incrusted surface, paler on the margin when growing, glabrous but sometimes pulverulent because of a brown coating of spores, azonate or somewhat zonate or sulcate on the margin; context white or nearly so throughout but usually slightly brownish next the tubes, 0.5–3 cm. thick, tough and watery when fresh, punky when dry; pore surface white to brown, discoloring where handled when fresh, the tubes 0.3–1 cm. long, the mouths rather thick-walled, entire, averaging 4–6 per mm.; stem when present usually lateral, sometimes central in plants growing on the top of logs or stumps, with color and context as in the pileus or more shining, 3–15 cm. long, 1–4 cm. thick; spores ovoid with a truncate apex, apparently echinulate, the outer wall very pale, the inner light brown, 9–11 × 6–8 μ; cystidia none; hyphae hyaline to pale brown, very irregular and much branched, the branches usually smaller in diameter and attenuate at the apex, with no cross walls or clamps, up to 6–9(–15) μ in diameter.

HABITAT: On or about stumps and dead trunks of coniferous trees, noted on *Picea, Pinus,* and *Tsuga*; reported rarely on *Acer* and *Betula.*

DISTRIBUTION: Specimens have been examined from Me., N.H., Vt., Mass., N.Y., Pa., N.J., Va., W. Va., N.C., Tenn., Ohio, Ind., Mich., and Wis.; in Canada from Nova Scotia, Quebec, and Ontario.

ILLUSTRATIONS: Atkinson, Bot. Gaz. 46: 323, fig. 1 (as *Ganoderma pseudoboletum*); *idem*, Mushrooms, fig. 188 (as *Polyporus lucidus*); Güssow and Odell, Mushrooms and Toadstools, pl. 100, fig. 2 (as *G. lucidum*); Overholts, Wash. Univ. Studies 3: pl. 5, fig. 23.

This species can usually, if not always, be separated from *Polyporus lucidus* and *P. Curtisii* (see Overholts, *Mo. Bot. Gard. Ann.* 2: 709–714. 1915) by the coniferous substratum, the rougher spores, the more shining and usually darker mahogany color, the nearly white context, and the greater degree of branching in the context hyphae. In *P. lucidus* the markings on the spore wall are scarcely discernible under the high-power dry objective; in *P. Tsugae* they are very evident under this magnification. Reports of the occurrence of this species growing on hardwoods are badly in need of confirmation.

The species is a beautiful one. The pileus first appears as a small knob, nearly or quite white, and gradually takes on color and varnish from the base outward as the plant matures. If collected and dried before reaching maturity, the pileus is likely to wrinkle and to lose its luster.

Haddow's recent discussion (*Arnold Arboretum Jour.* 12: 25–46. 1931) of the relationships of this species has tended to confuse rather than to clarify the situation, though he finally arrives at the same conclusion as is held by Murrill and myself, that *Polyporus Tsugae* is a species distinct from the form usually found on hardwoods and called *Ganoderma sessile* by Murrill and *P. lucidus* by me.

The distinction to be accorded to *Polyporus oregonensis* is largely a matter of opinion. In its best-developed condition it attains a thickness and a tube length never reached by specimens of *P. lucidus* and *P. Tsugae* collected in the East. Collections no thicker than Eastern collections of these two species are at hand, but they have the larger spore sizes of the Western species. The difference between average spore lengths in *P. lucidus* and *P. Tsugae* and in *P. oregonensis* is less significant than the difference between the maximum lengths.

Polyporus Tsugae produces a soft wet whitish or straw-colored cellulose-destroying decay of the wood, but attacks the lignin elements in the later stages. A network of cracks filled with white mycelium characterizes the advanced stages, and there are numerous small black dots throughout the wood, as described by West (*Mycologia* 11: 262–266. 1919).

3. POLYPORUS OREGONENSIS (Murr.) Kauffman

Mich. Acad. Sci. Arts and Letters Papers 5: 121. 1926

(Figs. 346–347 and Plate 131)

Ganoderma oregonense Murr., North Amer. Flora 9: 119. 1908.
Ganoderma Sequoiae Murr., North Amer. Flora 9: 119. 1908.

Sporophore stipitate or tuberculate-sessile; pileus soft-corky when fresh, firm-corky when dry, convex, reniform to dimidiate, 5–28(–80)

× 5–40(–100) × 2–10(–20) cm., covered with a varnish-like crust typically reddish mahogany or blackish mahogany in color, the margin sometimes lighter, glabrous; context soft and punky, white or straw-colored throughout or pale brownish next the tubes, not duplex, 1.5–8 cm. thick; pore surface whitish, discoloring brownish on drying or when wounded, the tubes 0.6–2 cm. long, the mouths subcircular, thick-walled, entire, averaging 3 per mm.; stem lateral or reduced to a tuberculate point, with color and surface as in the pileus; spores ovoid with a truncate apex, apparently echinulate, brown, mostly 10–16 × 7.5–9 μ; basidia inflated, 10–12 μ in diameter; cystidia none; hyphae nearly or quite hyaline, much branched, with attenuate branches, with no cross walls or clamps, 4–9 μ in diameter.

HABITAT: On dead wood of coniferous trees, noted on *Abies*, *Picea*, *Pinus*, *Pseudotsuga*, and *Tsuga*.

DISTRIBUTION: Specimens have been examined from N. Mex., Idaho, Ore., Wash., Calif., and Alaska; in Canada from British Columbia.

The essential difference between this species and *Polyporus Tsugae* lies in the larger spores of *P. oregonensis*. Typically, specimens are much thicker and reach at times enormous sizes, but this is a variable character. For a further discussion of this and related species see *P. lucidus* and *P. Tsugae*.

4. POLYPORUS CURTISII Berk.

Hooker's Jour. Bot. 1: 101. 1849

(Figs. 348–349, 573, and Plate 129)

Ganoderma Curtisii (Berk.) Murr., North Amer. Flora 9: 120. 1908.

Sporophore stipitate; pileus corky or soft-corky, reniform to flabelliform, rarely subcircular, 3–12 × 3–20(–30) × 0.7–3 cm., covered with a thin crust or varnish that may be entirely ochraceous when young, or partly ochraceous and partly dull red in mature plants, rarely entirely dull red, becoming zonate or occasionally furrowed, glabrous, the margin usually truncate or obtuse; context soft and nearly white above, brown and firm next the tubes, usually with one or more hard resinous lines in the lower portion, 0.5–1.5 cm.

thick; pore surface white to brownish or pale sulphureous, immediately brownish where wounded when fresh, the tubes 0.3–1.2 cm. long, the mouths circular to subcircular, thick-walled, entire, barely visible to the unaided eye, averaging 4–5 per mm.; stem lateral or rarely subcentral, occasionally connate, rarely nearly obsolete, incrusted, with color and context as in the pileus or darker, 2–10 cm. long, 0.5–2 cm. thick; spores ovoid with a truncate apex, apparently echinulate, light brown, 9–11(–13) × 5–7 μ; cystidia and hyphal pegs none; hyphae hyaline or brown, somewhat branched and the tips of the branches attenuate and wavy-walled, with no cross walls or clamps, up to 8 μ in diameter; lower part of context and the tubes black with KOH solution.

HABITAT: Usually on stumps or trunks of deciduous trees or attached to buried roots, noted on *Acer*, *Gleditsia*, *Liquidambar*, *Magnolia*, *Prunus*, and *Quercus*; very rarely on wood of conifers, recorded on *Pinus*.

DISTRIBUTION: Specimens have been examined from Mass., N.Y., Pa., N.J., Del., Md., Va., W. Va., N.C., S.C., Ga., Fla., Ala., La., Miss., Tenn., Ky., Mo., Nebr., Ark., Okla., and Texas; reported from Iowa (Wolf [234]) and Kans. (Bartholomew [4]).

ILLUSTRATIONS: Atkinson, Bot. Gaz. 46:327, fig. 3 (as *Ganoderma*); Haddow, Arnold Arboretum Jour. 12: pl. 29, fig. 6, and pl. 30, figs. 18–20 (all as *Ganoderma*); Overholts, Wash. Univ. Studies 3: pl. 4, fig. 21.

The context of young, growing specimens may be almost concolorous throughout, but usually it is pale above and decidedly brown next the tubes. The pileus, the context, and the interior of the tubes of herbarium specimens become permanently black where touched with KOH solution. Occasionally the resinous crust of the pileus is scarcely evident in old specimens, and frequently it is minutely areolate.

This species differs from *Polyporus lucidus* mainly in the bright ochraceous color of the pileus in young, growing specimens; the pileus becomes darker as the specimen ages. The sporophores are always stipitate, in which character the species differs from many specimens of *P. lucidus*. A single collection has been noted as occurring on *Pinus* stumps in Louisiana.

3b. *Pileus not laccate*
  4a. *Sporophore terrestrial or on buried wood*
    5a. *Pileus typically simple; stem simple*
      6a. *Spores rarely more than 8 μ long*
        7a. *Spores small, 3–4.5 × 2.5–3.5 μ* (see also *Scutiger subrubescens*, p. 428)

5. POLYPORUS OVINUS Schaeff. ex Fries

Syst. Myc. 1: 346. 1821
(Figs. 170, 179, and Plate 131)

Boletus ovinus Schaeff., Fung. Bavar. 4: 83. 1774.

Sporophore stipitate, sometimes caespitose-confluent; pileus usually circular and regular, convex, fleshy, 4–12(–15) cm. broad, the surface white or dirty white when fresh, becoming smoky, pale tan, or pinkish buff with age, rufescent or with an olivaceous tinge on drying, finely silky-tomentose to glabrous, even or in large thick specimens areolate-scaly with age, the margin thin; context white, drying yellowish or olivaceous, taste mild; pore surface white to sordid lemon-yellow in fresh plants, drying usually pale olivaceous or sordid, rarely with a reddish tinge in the herbarium, the tubes 1–2 mm. long, irregularly decurrent on the stem, the mouths angular, thin-walled, sometimes entire, sometimes minutely dentate, averaging 2–4 per mm.; stem central or subcentral, enlarged downward but pointed at the base, whitish, discoloring on handling and on drying, sometimes with pinkish or reddish traces in the herbarium, 3–8 cm. long, 1–3 cm. thick at the base; spores ellipsoid to ovoid or subglobose, smooth, hyaline, 3.5–4 × 2.5–3.5 μ; cystidia none; hyphae of context irregular, inflated, thin-walled, with cross walls but no clamps, 5–20 μ in diameter, hyphae of the dissepiments very small, about 3–4 μ in diameter, with cross walls but no clamps. (Compare no. 6, *Polyporus confluens*, and no. 10, *P. cristatus*.)

HABITAT: On the ground, probably always under or near coniferous trees, noted under *Picea* and *Pinus*.

DISTRIBUTION: Specimens have been examined from Me., Vt., Mass., N.Y., Tenn., Wis., Colo., Mont., Ore., Wash., and Calif.; in Canada from Quebec, Ontario, and Manitoba.

ILLUSTRATIONS: Bresadola, Funghi Mang., pl. 94; Dufour, Atl. Champ. Comest. Vén., pl. 48, fig. 113; Gillet, Champ. France 3: pl. 565 (68); Lloyd, Synop. Ovinus, fig. 497; Michael, Führ. f. Pilzfr. 1: fig. 18; Pilát, Bot. Centbl. Beih. 48: 414, fig. 2, and pl. 15 (as *Caloporus*); Schaeffer, Fung. Bavar., pls. 121–122; Shope, Mo. Bot. Gard. Ann. 18: pl. 24, fig. 2.

This species seems to have been variously confused by a number of authors. It differs from *Polyporus confluens* in the color of the fresh plants and in not becoming decidedly reddish or, most often, not becoming at all reddish on drying. The spores and other microscopic features are about the same as in that species, though the spores in *P. confluens* seem to be more constantly ellipsoid or oblong-ellipsoid and of slightly smaller size. The species is readily distinguished from *P. griseus* by the smooth spores. The colors of the fresh plants, particularly of the pileus, would seem sufficient to distinguish it from *P. cristatus* and *P. Peckianus*.

6. POLYPORUS CONFLUENS Alb. & Schw. ex Fries

Syst. Myc. 1: 355. 1821

(Figs. 176–177 and Plate 129)

Boletus confluens Alb. & Schw., Consp. Fung., p. 244. 1805.
Scutiger laeticolor Murr., Torrey Bot. Club Bul. 30: 428. 1903.
Scutiger Whiteae Murr., Torrey Bot. Club Bul. 30: 432. 1903.

Sporophore stipitate, single or in clusters with stem bases somewhat fused; pileus subcircular to irregular, convex to depressed, 3–20 cm. broad, fleshy, yellow, ochre, pale orange, or reddish when fresh, changing little or becoming more red on drying, sometimes in clusters and the individuals confluent, slightly scaly to glabrous or nearly so, at least when mature; context white or yellow, changing color with the pileus and more or less saffron or pale cinnabar in dried plants, taste mild; pore surface white, yellow, or yellowish, becoming saffron-red or cinnabar-red on drying or after many years in the herbarium, the tubes 1–3 mm. long, decurrent, the mouths angular, thin-walled, entire, averaging 2–4 per mm.; stem excentric or irregular, never well developed, 3–6 cm. long, 1–3 cm. thick, white to pale buff, becoming red on drying; spores oblong-ellipsoid to broadly ellipsoid, smooth, hyaline, 3–4.5 × 2.5–3 μ; cystidia none; hyphae of context thin-walled, inflated, with cross walls but no clamps, 3–9 μ

in diameter, hyphae of the dissepiments about 3 μ in diameter. (Compare no. 5, *Polyporus ovinus*; no. 9, *P. caeruleoporus*; and no. 10, *P. cristatus*.)

HABITAT: On the ground in woods.

DISTRIBUTION: Specimens have been examined from Me., Vt., Mass., N.Y., N.J., W. Va., N.C., S.C., Ala., Colo., Ore., Wash., and Calif.; in Canada from the Gaspé Peninsula and British Columbia; reported from Tenn. (Kauffman [100]).

ILLUSTRATIONS: Barla, Champ. Nice, pl. 29, figs. 2–3; Bresadola, Funghi Mang., pl. 96; Dufour, Atl. Champ. Comest. Vén., pl. 49, fig. 115; Fries, Sverig. Ätliga, pl. 24; Kauffman, Mich. Acad. Sci. Arts and Letters Papers 1: pl. 34; Michael, Führ. f. Pilzfr. 1: fig. 17; Pilát, Bot. Centbl. Beih. 48: pl. 13 (left half); Schaeffer, Fung. Bavar., pls. 109–110; Shope, Mo. Bot. Gard. Ann. 18: pl. 28, fig. 1.

The entire plant, at least after a time in the herbarium, has the color of a faded specimen of *Hypomyces lactifluorum* on *Lactarius*. The species differs from *Polyporus ovinus* in the color of fresh plants and in the red color developed on drying or after a time in the herbarium. The appearance of the fresh plants is much like that of *Hydnum repandum*. Kauffman (102, pp. 119–122) describes collections from Colorado that he refers to this species and states that after a year in the herbarium there is only a trace of red in the plants. However, his plants are described as white or nearly so when fresh. Concerning the coloration of *P. confluens*, Fries writes (54, p. 539): "Colore fallax, nunc carneus, nunc paleaceus, in rufum et ochraceum vergens (aurantium non vidi), sed facile dignotus pileis subcircinantibus, in massam amorpham, siccitate rigidam, confluentibus."

Polyporus caeruleoporus, *P. ovinus*, and *P. confluens* have, in general, similar microscopic characters. The first has larger and more nearly subglobose spores, measuring 4–6 × 3–5 μ. The last two have spores of almost the same size, not exceeding 4.5 × 3.5 μ, but generally of somewhat different shape, usually more or less ellipsoid in *P. confluens* and often ovoid to subglobose in *P. ovinus*.

Polyporus laeticolor (Murr.) Sacc. & D. Sacc. is in no wise distinct; the spores of the type specimens are ellipsoid to broadly ovoid, smooth, hyaline, 3–4.5 × 2.5–3 μ. It is described as coming from Alabama.

7. Polyporus Flettii Morse
Mycologia 33: 507. 1941

Sporophore stipitate, solitary to caespitose; pileus circular or somewhat irregular, 10–20 cm. in diameter, 1–2 cm. thick, at first convex, then plane or depressed at the center, color when young greenish blue, paler at the margin, finally dingy ochraceous, glabrous; context subfleshy to fleshy-tough, up to 1.5 cm. thick, white, with farinaceous odor and taste; tubes 1–7 mm. long, the mouths at first white, then apricot to salmon and staying so on drying, decurrent on the stem, angular, thin-walled, becoming lacerate or fimbriate, averaging 1–4 per mm.; stem white, solid, smooth below the reticulations, drying dingy ochraceous, usually excentric, 6–14 cm. long, 2–3.5 cm. thick; spores ellipsoid to subglobose, smooth, hyaline, 3.5–4 × 2.5–3 μ; basidia clavate, 12–16 × 4–6 μ, 4-spored; cystidia none; context hyphae thin-walled, sparingly branched, hyaline, probably with clamps but no clamps seen, 4–8 μ in diameter.

Habitat: On ground in mixed forest.

Distribution: Specimens have been examined only from the vicinity of Bremerton, Wash.

Illustrations: Morse, Mycologia 33: 508.

The species is well illustrated by Miss Morse. I have not seen fresh material. The specimens in my herbarium (two collections) have not retained the farinaceous taste or odor. Now (1943) the pore surface and stem have become red—a change that often occurs in specimens of this section of the genus. The description above is drawn mostly from notes made by Mr. Flett and Miss Morse on specimens in the fresh condition. The validity of the species rests largely, if not entirely, on the blue coloration of the fresh plants. I have never seen a description of *Polyporus confluens* that contained the terms "blue" or "greenish blue."

8. Polyporus Peckianus Cooke
Bot. Soc. Edinburgh Trans. and Proc. 13: 148. 1879
(Figs. 171, 195, 221, and Plate 131)

Polyporus flavidus Peck, N. Y. State Mus. Ann. Rept. 26: 68. 1874. (Not *P. flavidus* Berk. 1852.)

Sporophore stipitate, sometimes with two or more pilei, fleshy-tough when fresh, drying rigid and rather fragile; pileus circular.

depressed or infundibuliform, 3–12 cm. broad, 2–5 mm. thick, yellow to cinnamon-buff when fresh, drying pale tan or tan, glabrous or practically so; context white, 1–2 mm. thick; pore surface white, pale yellowish, or barium-yellow, the tubes strongly decurrent, 1–3 mm. long, the mouths angular, averaging 4–5 per mm.; stem central or excentric, sometimes branched, pallid, glabrous, 2–5 cm. long, 0.5–1.5 cm. thick; spores ellipsoid or broadly ellipsoid, hyaline, 3–4.5 × 2.5–3 μ; cystidia none; hyphae very irregular and with wavy walls, much inflated, somewhat branched, thin-walled, hyaline, with cross walls and clamps, up to 15 μ in diameter at the inflations. (Compare no. 5, *Polyporus ovinus*; no. 6, *P. confluens*; and no. 10, *P. cristatus*.)

HABITAT: On the ground or attached to buried wood, noted only on *Fagus*; reported on *Tilia* (Lowe [125]).

DISTRIBUTION: Specimens have been examined from Vt., N.Y., Wis., and Minn.; in Canada from Quebec and Manitoba; reported from Tenn. (Hesler [71]).

This species is collected only occasionally. It is paler than *Polyporus hirtus*, *P. cristatus*, and *P. radicatus*, and not white like *P. fractipes*, which is also of tougher consistency. *P. cristatus* differs in its yellowish-green and areolate pileus and its somewhat larger spores. There is no color change to red in *P. Peckianus*, as there is in *P. confluens*, though the spores are about the same.

7b. *Spores larger, up to 8 μ long* (see also *Polyporus Arnoldae*, *Grifola cristatiformis*, and *P. Gratzianus*, p. 426; *P. Stewartae*, p. 428; and *Scutiger Tisdalei*, p. 429)

9. POLYPORUS CAERULEOPORUS Peck

N. Y. State Mus. Ann. Rept. 26: 68. 1874

(Plate 128)

Scutiger caeruleoporus (Peck) Murr., Torrey Bot. Club Bul. 30: 429. 1903.
Polyporus holocyaneus Atk., Jour. Mycol. 8: 117. 1902.

Sporophore stipitate, single or caespitose; pileus soft and watery when fresh, drying rigid, nearly circular, convex, more or less uniformly pale indigo-blue, bluish gray, or smoky indigo in fresh plants, reddish yellow or darkening and becoming brownish in age and on drying, sometimes red in herbarium specimens, 2–7(–15) × 0,3–2 cm., glabrous or subtomentose, dry, slightly rugose or smooth, the margin lobed, deflexed; context white, sometimes red in herbarium specimens, 1–8 mm. thick, taste mild or becoming acid; pore surface pale indigo-blue, becoming darker on drying, often red in herbarium specimens, the tubes 2–5 mm. long, pale blue within, the mouths thin-walled, entire, averaging 1–2 per mm. or up to 5 per mm., decurrent on the stem; stem central or excentric, equal, pitted from the decurrent tubes, deep indigo-blue, discoloring or becoming red on drying, pallid within, glabrous, 2.5–7 cm. long, 0.5–2 cm. thick; spores subglobose, hyaline, 4–6 μ in diameter or 4–6 × 3–5 μ; cystidia none; hyphae thin-walled, hyaline, considerably branched, with cross wall but no clamps, very irregular, 4–10(–15) μ in diameter; context and pore walls red in KOH solution. (Compare no 5, *Polyporus ovinus*, and no. 6, *P. confluens*.)

HABITAT: On the ground in damp woods.

DISTRIBUTION: Specimens have been examined from Me., Vt., N.Y., Pa., and N.C.; in Canada from New Brunswick and Ontario.

This is a rare plant, of which perhaps not a dozen collections are known in America. In most collections I have seen the hymenium has become almost cinnabar-red in the herbarium. In a Pennsylvania collection made in 1920 the pore surface discolored brown on drying, but now shows some cinnabar-red, and the context is deep cinnabar. An ample collection made in Pennsylvania in 1931 has dried nearly uniformly pale smoky or smoky brown, and the dried context shows no red. Fresh spores are rather prominently apiculate.

Large dried specimens of *Polyporus caeruleoporus* unaccompanied by notes as to color when fresh are likely to be confused with *P. ovinus* and *P. confluens*. In all three species the tubes may eventually become red in the herbarium. The best separating character in such collections seems to be the spores, although comparative studies may be necessary even there. The spores of *P. ovinus* are distinctly more ellipsoid than those of *P. caeruleoporus*, which are much more rounded (care must always be taken to study spores that show the apiculus). Furthermore, the spores of *P. caeruleoporus* are slightly larger than those of *P. ovinus*, being 4–6 × 3–5 μ as compared with

3.5–4 × 2.5–3.5 μ. The spores of *P. confluens* and of *P. ovinus* are scarcely distinguishable, for they correspond very closely in measurements, though they are more often ovoid to subglobose in *P. ovinus* and usually more or less ellipsoid in *P. confluens*.

Polyporus holocyaneus Atk. is described by Coker (35, p. 132) as viscid when fresh and as having pores that average 4–5 per mm. His description would apply to a collection made in Pennsylvania in 1920 in which the entire sporophore is blue or bluish gray. Peck's original account describes the pileus as brown, and this agrees with my 1931 collection. Perhaps my 1920 collection should be referred to *P. holocyaneus* and my 1931 collection to *P. caeruleoporus*, but I have combined my notes in the composite description above on the supposition that Peck may have had specimens in which the pileus had lost its original color.

10. POLYPORUS CRISTATUS Pers. ex Fries

Syst. Myc. 1: 356. 1821
(Figs. 178, 185, 194, and Plate 129)

Boletus cristatus Pers., Synop. Meth. Fung., p. 522. 1801.
Polyporus flavovirens Berk. & Rav., in Berkeley and Curtis, Ann. and Mag. Nat. Hist. II, 12: 431. 1853.
Grifola poripes (Fries) Murr., Torrey Bot. Club Bul. 31: 335. 1904.

Sporophore stipitate, standing singly or with several united in their growth; pileus fleshy, circular or irregular, plane or somewhat convex, 4–20 cm. broad, 0.3–2.5 cm. thick, yellowish green, yellowish brown, or tan, sometimes almost entirely yellow in the center and entirely brown on the margin, becoming cracked and areolate, compactly tomentose or velvety to glabrous; context white, yellowish green where worm-eaten or long exposed, 2–20 mm. thick; pore surface white, yellowish, or greenish yellow, rarely reddish on drying, the tubes 1–5 mm. long, decurrent, the mouths entire, averaging 1–3 per mm.; stem simple, 3–6 cm. long, 1–2.5 cm. thick; spores ovoid or subglobose, apiculate, guttulate, smooth, hyaline, 5–6 × 4–5 μ; cystidia none; hyphal pegs lacking; hyphae simple or sparingly branched, thin-walled and sometimes collapsed, with occasional cross walls but no clamps, 3–6(–9) μ in diameter or with a few inflations up to 25 μ in diameter; context and tubes of herbarium specimens changing slowly to light cherry-red with KOH solution. (Compare no. 5, *Polyporus ovinus*, and no. 6, *P. confluens*.)

HABITAT: On the ground in deciduous or coniferous woods.

DISTRIBUTION: Specimens have been examined from Vt., Mass., Conn., N.Y., Pa., N.J., Del., Md., D.C., Va., W. Va., N.C., S.C., Ala., Tenn., Ohio, Ind., Wis., Mo., and Ark.; in Canada from Ontario.

ILLUSTRATIONS: Hard, Mushrooms, fig. 327 (as *Polyporus flavovirens*); Lloyd, Synop. Ovinus, fig. 501; Michael, Führ. f. Pilzfr. 2: fig. 33; Overholts, Wash. Univ. Studies 3: pl. 1, fig. 5.

At maturity the pileus of this species becomes areolate. In two collections from Pennsylvania, one from Indiana, and one from West Virginia the hymenium has taken on a reddish tinge in drying; otherwise the plants are typical. Occasionally, in additional collections, the bases of the tubes in some specimens are reddish, though the mouths have not changed color. This variation to a reddish hymenium was designated as var. *decolorans* by Lloyd. The hymenium and the freshly growing margin of the pileus are likely to stain yellowish green where handled, and sometimes the hymenium becomes nearly egg-yellow in drying. Potassium hydroxide solution turns the context and usually the hymenium of herbarium specimens light cherry-red.

Schweinitz' report of this species is doubtful. The single specimen preserved in the Schweinitz Herbarium (No. 338), at Philadelphia, is scarcely determinable.

11. POLYPORUS PERSICINUS Berk. & Curt.
Grevillea 1: 37. 1872
(Plate 131)

Scutiger persicinus (Berk. & Curt.) Murr., Torrey Bot. Club Bul. 30: 431. 1903.

Sporophore centrally stipitate, simple or multiplex-caespitose and 30 cm. in diameter, with stem bases fused, soft and fleshy-spongy when fresh, drying brittle and light of weight; pilei 10–25 cm. in diameter, up to 3 cm. thick, light buffy brown or pinkish brown when fresh, becoming sordid rufescent brown to blackish brown with age or where handled or on drying, covered with a short hispid tomentum, obscurely or not at all zoned; context soft, watery white changing to brownish flesh color where exposed, friable and pale brown on drying, 1–2 cm. thick, the taste slightly bitter; pore surface nearly white at first, creamy at maturity, in age and where injured or when dried becoming dark and sordid, the tubes 5–8 mm. long, the mouths angular, thin-walled, averaging 3–4 per mm.; stem short, simple or fused together at the base, sordid in color, 5–7 cm. long, 2–2.5 cm. thick, brown within in dried plants; spores broadly ellipsoid or subglobose, smooth, hyaline, 5–8 × 4–5 μ; cystidia none; hyphae hyaline to pale brown, thin-walled, simple or nearly so, with no cross walls or clamps except in some of the larger ones and then hyphae filled with brown material and up to 16 μ in diameter, mostly 5–8 μ in diameter; all parts black-spotted in KOH.

HABITAT: On the ground, probably always attached to buried wood, noted under trees of *Pinus* and *Quercus*.

DISTRIBUTION: Specimens have been examined from N.C. and Ark.; the type was collected in S.C.

This species is not too well known and has been collected only two or three times. Murrill studied the types at the Royal Botanic Gardens, Kew, England, and reported that the specimens do not agree with the description. Coker collected the fungus twice at Chapel Hill, North Carolina. His specimens are at the New York Botanical Garden. I collected the species at Eudora, Arkansas, in 1931.

12. POLYPORUS DEALBATUS Berk. & Curt.

Ann. and Mag. Nat. Hist. II, 12: 432. 1853
(Figs. 306–307, 326, and Plate 129)

Sporophore centrally or laterally stipitate, tough when fresh, drying rigid and hard; pileus circular to reniform or flabelliform, 2–10 cm. broad, the surface avellaneous to livid brown, minutely velutinous or gray scurfy-tomentose, multizonate; context white, 1–2 mm. thick, drying very hard; pore surface somewhat flesh-colored in fresh plants, darker on drying, the tubes 1–4 mm. long, the mouths angular, rather thin-walled, entire, averaging 6–7 per mm.; stem central or lateral, 5–7 cm. long, 0.5–1 cm. thick, colored like the pileus, drying hard and rigid; spores ellipsoid to broadly ellipsoid, smooth, hyaline, rather strongly apiculate, 5–6 × 4–5 μ; basidia 7–8 μ in diameter; cystidia none; hyphae a mixture of small and large types, the small ones thin-walled, 3–5 μ in diameter, the large ones with walls partly thickened, 5–8 μ in diameter.

HABITAT: On the ground, probably attached to buried wood.

DISTRIBUTION: Specimens have been examined from N.C. and S.C.

ILLUSTRATIONS: Lloyd, Synop. Stip. Polyp., fig. 422.

The identity of this species has been somewhat in dispute, mainly because adequate collections have not been made. At present there are three good collections at the New York Botanical Garden and one at Beltsville, Maryland. Lloyd claims that the specimen distributed by Ravenel (178, no. 10) is not *Polyporus dealbatus* but *P. mutabilis*. Though the original description makes this a terrestrial species, in all probability the fungus was growing attached to buried wood. The flesh-colored pore surface and the distinctly stipitate form of the plant, with strongly zoned pileus and minute pores, make it fairly easy to recognize. *P. mutabilis* is less distinctly stipitate, and the pore surface is not flesh-colored. Neither does that fungus dry hard like *P. dealbatus*.

13. POLYPORUS BIENNIS (Bull. ex Fries) Fries

Epicr. Syst. Myc., p. 433. 1836–1838

(Figs. 190–193, 606–607, and Plate 128)

Boletus biennis Bull., Herb. France, pl. 449, fig. 1. 1790.
Daedalea biennis Bull. ex Fries, Syst. Myc. 1: 332. 1821.
Boletus distortus Schw., Schr. Nat. Ges. Leipzig 1: 97. 1822.
Abortiporus distortus (Schw.) Murr., Torrey Bot. Club Bul. 31: 422. 1904.
Polyporus abortivus Peck, Bot. Gaz. 6: 274. 1881.
Polyporus Balloui Lloyd, Myc. Notes 69: 1191. 1923.

Sporophore stipitate or substipitate, tough to coriaceous when fresh, rigid on drying; when well developed having a circular pileus 2–20 cm. broad and 0.5–1.5 cm. thick or composed of two or three overlapping pilei from the same stem, more often wholly distorted and having almost the entire surface covered with the tubes, white to tan or rufescent, conspicuously villose-tomentose or occasionally more strigose; context white, duplex in well-developed specimens (best seen in dried sporophores), 0.2–1 cm. thick; pore surface whitish, or rufescent when bruised, the tubes 1–6 mm. long, the mouths angular to daedaloid, entire or slightly dentate, averaging 1–3 per mm.; stem central, lateral, or wanting, rarely well developed and up to 6 cm. long, more often rudimentary and tubercular, villose-tomentose; spores oblong-ellipsoid to broadly ellipsoid or ovoid, or some spores very narrowly ovoid, smooth, hyaline, 5–7.5(–10) × 3–5 μ; chlamydospores often present in distorted forms, thick-walled, more or less globose, 5–7 μ in diameter or 7–9 × 6–7 μ; cystidia occasionally present but never abundant, inconspicuous, scarcely projecting beyond the basidia, hyaline, cylindric, usually blunt, 5–10 μ in diameter, sometimes with forked tips; hyphae of upper context rather thin-walled, sparingly branched, with numerous cross walls and clamps, 3–6 μ in diameter, those of lower context a mixture of large simple thick-walled hyphae with no cross walls or clamps, 4–8 μ in diameter, and of many very thin-walled hyphae with clamps and cross walls, 3–6 μ in diameter. (Compare no. 8, *Polyporus Peckianus*, and no. 11, *P. persicinus*.)

HABITAT: Usually about stumps and trunks of deciduous trees, noted on *Acer, Ailanthus, Castanea, Fraxinus, Juglans, Nyssa, Platanus, Pyrus, Quercus, Salix*, and *Ulmus*; occasionally in connection with coniferous hosts, noted on *Pinus*.

DISTRIBUTION: Specimens have been examined from Mass., Conn., N.Y., Pa., N.J., Del., Md., D.C., N.C., Ga., Fla., Ala., La., Tenn., Ky., Ohio, Ind., Ill., Mich., Wis., Iowa, Mo., Nebr., Ark., Texas, Ore., and Wash.; in Canada from Quebec, Ontario, and British Columbia.

ILLUSTRATIONS: Bulliard, Herb. France 2: pl. 449, fig. 1 (as *Boletus*); Lloyd, Myc. Notes 40: fig. 753 (as *Polyporus distortus*); *ibid.* 69: fig. 2395 (as *P. Ballouii*); *idem*, Synop. Stip. Polyp., fig. 456 (as *P. rufescens*) and fig. 458 (as *P. distortus*); Overholts, Wash. Univ. Studies 3: pl. 1, fig. 3 (as *P. distortus*); Pilát, Bot. Centbl. Beih. 52: pls. 11–12 (as *Phaeolus*).

The abnormal or distorted form of this species is more easily recognized than the centrally stipitate, pileate form, which is not often collected. It is easily distinguished from such stipitate species as *Polyporus fractipes* and *P. Peckianus* by the thicker and strongly duplex context, the cystidia, and the larger spores. The variation in the number and form of the cystidia is unusual. Some collections show only small and relatively inconspicuous cystidia; others have this type and, in addition, a very conspicuous type, often with forking tips. In general, the microscopic characters are those of *P. borealis.*

The centrally stipitate, well-developed form of this species is often referred to *Polyporus rufescens* Pers. ex Fries. Additional synonyms are given by Pilát (171, vol. 52, pp. 69–70).

A ptychogastric form is known in Europe under the name *Ceriomyces terrestris* Schulzer. This form does not produce external pores but is divided internally into lacunae in which conidia, measuring 6–9 × 5–8 μ, are produced. They are identical with the chlamydospores often found in the tramal tissue of pileate forms of the species.

Graff (*Mycologia* 31: 466–484. 1939) has recently studied this species. He would retain for a darker form the species name that I am using here, and would refer to varieties the other forms mentioned above.

14. POLYPORUS OSSEUS Kalchbr.

Matem. Term. Közlem. 3: 217. 1865

(Figs. 225, 263, 566, and Plate 131)

Polyporus Zelleri Murr., Western Polypores, p. 13. 1915.

Sporophore usually attenuate to a narrow stemlike base or a distinct excentric or lateral stalk, sometimes nearly sessile, fleshytough and watery when fresh, very rigid and firm when dry; pilei usually somewhat imbricate but not always so, 1–6 × 2–11 × 0.3–2 cm., white, gray, light brown, or "mouse gray," often pale tan in herbarium specimens, nearly glabrous or finely silky-pubescent; context white, soft when fresh, hard when dry, 3–10 mm. thick, odor pleasant, taste somewhat bitter; pore surface white or whitish when fresh, yellowish on drying, the tubes 1–3 mm. long, the mouths minute, angular, even or finely denticulate, averaging 3–5 per mm.; spores allantoid or cylindric-oblong, smooth, hyaline, 4–6 × 2–2.5 μ; basidia 3.5–4 μ in diameter; hyphae extremely irregular, of short lengths in crushed mounts, thick-walled, nonstaining, clamps and cross walls not readily discernible, often with many short branches, 6–24 μ in diameter.

HABITAT: Usually on dead wood of coniferous trees, noted on *Larix, Pinus, Pseudotsuga,* and *Tsuga;* rarely on hardwoods, noted on *Betula;* reported on *Picea* (Colo., Kauffman [102]) and on *Quercus* (Iowa, Wolf [234]).

DISTRIBUTION: Specimens have been examined from N.H., Mass., N.Y., Pa., Mich., Wis., Minn., Colo., Mont., Idaho, Wash., and Calif.; in Canada from Ontario and British Columbia; reported from Iowa (Wolf [234]) and Manitoba (Bisby *et al.* [12]).

ILLUSTRATIONS: Kalchbrenner, Icones Sel. Hym. Hung., pl. 34, fig. 2; Lloyd, Synop. Stip. Polyp., fig. 496; Pilát, Bot. Centbl. Beih. 52: pls. 9–10 (as *Grifola*); Shope, Mo. Bot. Gard. Ann. 18: pl. 29, fig. 3.

This species is found infrequently, but is easily distinguished by the habitat, the grayish pileus, the reduced stemlike point of attachment, and the fact that the context dries hard. It is northern in its range. *Polyporus Zelleri* Murr., described from Washington, is a drab-colored form of the species.

Occasionally one finds plants of this species in which the stem is absent and the attachment is lateral. Sometimes such specimens on drying resemble *Polyporus albellus*, but usually they dry with a much harder context, and the hyphae of the context are very different.

A complete transition from nearly white to drab or "mouse gray" is shown in specimens in my herbarium. At first sight the drab form (*Polyporus Zelleri*) seems distinct enough, but the intergradations are too confusing. I have specimens of this form exactly matching the color of the types of *P. Zelleri*, from Pennsylvania, and Epling has sent me a still darker form, "mouse gray" in color, from Idaho.

Polyporus osseus was published and described in 1865 by Kalchbrenner in a Magyar paper issued by the Hungarian Academy of Sciences, as cited in the heading above. The next year specimens accompanied by a description were distributed in Rabenhorst's Fungi Europaei as No. 706. The Magyar paper is consistently cited by all previous authors in referring to this species as "Enum."[1] and "Enumerat. Hung.,"[2] but the title as well as the text is in Magyar, not in Latin. The "p. 160" accompanying these citations is an error, but the species listed were numbered, and *P. osseus* is No. 160 in this list. I am indebted to Dr. Barnhart, of the New York Botanical Garden, for this information.

Not much is known about the rot produced by this fungus.

[1] See Saccardo, P. A., *Syll. Fung.* 6: 101. 1888; Kalchbrenner, C., *Icones Sel. Hym. Hung.* 4: 54. 1877; Fries, E., *Hym. Eur.*, p. 541. 1874.
[2] See Oudemans, C., *Enum. Syst. Fung.* 1: 382. 1919.

Specimens have come to me associated with a brown carbonizing decay.

15. POLYPORUS GRISEUS Peck
N. Y. State Mus. Ann. Rept. 26: 68. 1874
(Fig. 168 and Plate 130)

Scutiger griseus (Peck) Murr., Torrey Bot. Club Bul. 30: 431. 1903.
Polyporus Earlei Underw., Torrey Bot. Club Bul. 24: 84. 1897.

Sporophore stipitate; pileus circular to irregular, 4–12 cm. in diameter, fleshy or fleshy-tough when fresh, ivory-white or with a darker center when young and growing, but soon becoming gray and then smoky umber and darkening even more on drying (especially in old sporophores), sometimes with streaks of purple when changing color and sometimes drying smoky greenish, glabrous or nearly so, azonate; context white, nearly concolorous with pileus on drying; pore surface white to discolored, often with an olivaceous tinge on drying, the tubes 0.5–4 mm. long, the mouths angular, thin-walled but entire, averaging 2–4 per mm.; stem 4–8 cm. long, 1–2.5 cm. thick, concolorous with pileus, the tubes somewhat decurrent; spores irregular, tuberculate or obtusely angled, hyaline, 5–6.5 μ in diameter or 5–6 $\times$ 4–5 μ; cystidia none; hyphae very irregular and variable, thin-walled and often collapsing, without apparent cross walls or clamps, 2–12 μ in diameter. (Compare no. 5, *Polyporus ovinus*, and no. 6, *P. confluens*.)

HABITAT: On the ground in coniferous or deciduous woods, reported on decaying *Pinus* (Mont., Weir [227]).

DISTRIBUTION: Specimens have been examined from N.H., Mass., N.Y., Pa., N.J., N.C., Ala., Tenn., Mich., Mo., Mont., and Wash.

ILLUSTRATIONS: Lloyd, Synop. Ovinus, figs. 499–500.

The very decidedly tuberculate spores constitute *the* character of this species. It is to be distinguished further from *Polyporus ovinus* by the darker color on drying, and from *P. confluens* by the absence of all reddish tints in herbarium specimens. Perhaps if the specimens are dried rapidly they do not become so dark as they do otherwise. The colors are similar to those of *Boletus griseus* Frost.

Polyporus subsquamosus Fries is a synonym, according to Lloyd.

The types of *Polyporus Earlei* Underw. are in the New York Botanical Garden. *P. leucomelas* should also be compared, since the spores are tuberculate and tuberculate spores are extremely rare in polypores. Pilát (172, p. 21) refers *P. griseus* to synonymy under *Caloporus leucomelas* f. *subsquamosus* (L.) Pilát.

6b. *Spores usually 8 μ or more long* (see also *Polyporus Westii*, p. 429)

16. POLYPORUS PES-CAPRAE Pers. ex Fries
Syst. Myc. 1: 354. 1821
(Figs. 173–175, 562, and Plate 131)

Polyporus Pes-Caprae Pers., Traité Champ. Comest., p. 241. 1819.
Polyporus retipes Underw., Torrey Bot. Club Bul. 24: 85. 1897.
Scutiger retipes (Underw.) Murr., Torrey Bot. Club Bul. 30: 428. 1903.
Scutiger oregonensis Murr., Mycologia 4: 93. 1912.

Sporophore stipitate, more or less broadly turbinate, single or somewhat confluent, probably from an underground sclerotium; pileus subcircular or irregular, 3–10(–20) cm. or more broad, fleshy-tough or brittle when fresh, rigid when dry, at first sordid gray, then pinkish brown to brown or blackish brown, or brown tinged with red in herbarium specimens, at first covered with fine soft fibrils that soon become arranged into definite scales or a sort of plush at least at the center of the pileus, azonate; context white, pink on exposure to the air, 0.5–2 cm. thick, taste mild; pore surface white to isabelline, yellowish or greenish yellow, sometimes becoming pinkish, the tubes 2–5 mm. long, the mouths thin-walled, entire, angular, large, 1–2 mm. in diameter or larger by confluence; stem simple or branched, lateral or excentric, pallid or with yellowish base, becoming darker, enlarged or bulbous below, with strongly decurrent tubes, 3–8 cm. long, 1–4 cm. thick; spores ovoid, broadly ellipsoid, or ovoid-elliptic, with a single large oil globule, rather strongly apiculate, smooth, hyaline, 8–11 × 5–6 μ; cystidia none, hyphae very irregular, branched, thin-walled, with no cross walls or clamps, with irregular inflations up to 40 μ in diameter, other hyphae as small as 6–8 μ in diameter. (Compare no. 17, *Polyporus Ellisii*, and no. 51, *P. hirtus*.)

HABITAT: On the ground in woods.

DISTRIBUTION: Specimens have been examined from N.J., N.C., Ala., Tenn., Ore., and Calif.

ILLUSTRATIONS: Gillet, Champ. France 3: pl. 566 (69); Lloyd, Synop. Ovinus, fig. 504; *idem*, Myc. Notes 35: fig. 332; Lucand, Fig. Peint. Champ. France, pl. 150; Michael, Führ. f. Pilzfr. 2: fig. 34; Pilát, Bot. Centbl. Beih. 48: pl. 13 (right half).

I refer here as synonyms both *Polyporus retipes* and *Scutiger oregonensis.* If *P. Ellisii* is different, it must be largely in the yellowish-green color ascribed to the pileus of that species. Persoon records *P. Pes-Caprae* as edible. The large spores and pores, densely tomentose to scaly pileus, reddish to brown coloration, and terrestrial habit are the diagnostic characters.

17. POLYPORUS ELLISII Berk.
Grevillea 7: 4. 1878
(Fig. 243 and Plate 129)

Scutiger Ellisii (Berk.) Murr., Torrey Bot. Club Bul. 30: 427. 1903.
Polyporus flavo-squamosus Underw., Torrey Bot. Club Bul. 24: 84. 1897.

Sporophore stipitate; pileus 12–15 cm. broad, sulphur-yellow or with a greenish tinge when fresh, not changing much in drying, with large fasciculate or imbricate scales; context white, usually yellowish green after exposure, otherwise drying white and firm; pore surface white, then becoming yellowish, discolored greenish on handling, the tubes 2–5 mm. long, the mouths angular, averaging 1–2 per mm., becoming lacerate in age; stem excentric, somewhat reticulate, yellow or dark yellow, 7–8 cm. long, 4–5 cm. thick; spores ovoid or ovoid-elliptic, rather conspicuously apiculate, hyaline, 8–9 × 5–7 μ; cystidia none. (Compare no. 16, *Polyporus Pes-Caprae.*)

HABITAT: On the ground in woods.

DISTRIBUTION: Specimens have been examined from N.J., Ala., and Calif.

ILLUSTRATIONS: Lloyd, Myc. Notes, Polyp. Issue No. 2: fig. 264.

This species seems to be different from *Polyporus Pes-Caprae*, although the spores are almost exact duplicates of those in that species, even to the conspicuous apiculus. But the pileus and, indeed, the whole plant are yellowish green rather than brown in the few specimens available. *P. flavo-squamosus*, which both Murrill and Lloyd refer here, is synonymous.

18. POLYPORUS RADICATUS Schw.

Amer. Phil. Soc. Trans. II, 4: 155. 1832

(Figs. 172, 622, and Plate 131)

Scutiger radicatus (Schw.) Murr., Torrey Bot. Club Bul. 30: 430. 1903.
Polyporus Morgani Peck, N. Y. State Mus. Ann. Rept. 32: 34. 1879.
Polyporus kansensis Ell. & Barth., Erythea 4: 1. 1896.

Sporophore stipitate; pileus fleshy-tough when fresh, drying rigid or somewhat flexible, circular, convex to depressed, 3.5–25 cm. broad, 0.3–1(–2.5) cm. thick, yellowish brown to sooty brown, fibrillose-scaly, velvety-scabrous, or scurfy, nearly glabrous at center at maturity; context white, 3–10 mm. thick; pore surface white or yellowish, the tubes decurrent, 1–5 mm. long, the mouths angular or sinuous, averaging 2–3 per mm.; stem central, scurfy to squamulose, with a long black root, 6–13(–17) cm. long, 0.5–2.5 cm. thick; spores ovoid-elliptic or subfusiform, 12–15 × 6–8 μ; basidia 8–12 μ in diameter; cystidia none; hyphae variable in different collections, always a preponderance of thin-walled ones, often collapsing, with occasional clamps and cross walls or some semblance of these, 5–10 μ in diameter, sometimes with larger, deeply staining hyphae 9–15 μ in diameter, and sometimes with some thick-walled hyphae 6–12 μ in diameter, these without clamps.

HABITAT: On the ground, usually around stumps and probably always attached to buried wood of deciduous trees.

DISTRIBUTION: Specimens have been examined from Vt., Mass., N.Y., Pa., Md., Ala., Tenn., Ohio, Ind., Mo., Kans., and Nebr.; in Canada from Ontario; reported from Wis. (Neuman [148]) and Iowa (Wolf [234]).

ILLUSTRATIONS: Hard, Mushrooms, fig. 329; Lloyd, Synop. Ovinus, fig. 508; *idem*, Synop. Stip. Polyp., fig. 465 *bis*; Neuman, Wis. Geol. and Nat. Hist. Survey Bul. 33: pl. 15, fig. 54.

Polyporus radicatus is to be regarded as rather an uncommon species, found most abundantly through the Ohio and Mississippi River Valleys, as well as in the states of Wisconsin and Michigan.

In coloration it approaches *P. brumalis*, but otherwise it is entirely distinct from that species. The scabrous-scurfy radicating stem is the outstanding character of the species.

19. POLYPORUS MELANOPUS Fries

Syst. Myc. 1: 347. 1821

(Figs. 188–189 and Plate 130)

Scutiger subradicatus Murr., Torrey Bot. Club Bul. 30: 430. 1903.

Sporophore stipitate, fleshy-tough when fresh, rigid and brittle or hard when dry; pileus 4–10 cm. broad, convex to somewhat depressed or almost infundibuliform, circular to reniform or irregular, isabelline to hair-brown or somewhat reddish brown, azonate, with a fine velvety scurfiness or appearing almost scaly, glabrate with age, more or less wrinkled on drying, the margin thin; context white, 1–5 mm. thick; pore surface white or yellowish, the tubes 1–3 mm. long, the mouths angular to irregular, thin-walled, entire to somewhat dentate, averaging 2–4 per mm.; stem irregular, central to excentric (rarely lateral), rarely confluent, black on the lower half or entirely black, finely velvety-villose, 1.5–7 cm. long, 0.5–2.5 cm. thick; spores cylindric with ends more or less pointed, hyaline, 8–12 × 3.5–4 μ; cystidia none; hyphae hyaline, flexuous, much branched, with no cross walls or clamps, 3–8 μ in diameter or some of the branches attenuate to diameters of 1.5 μ. (Compare no. 18, *Polyporus radicatus*; no. 46, *P. varius*; and no. 51, *P. hirtus*.)

HABITAT: On the ground, attached to buried wood of deciduous trees, noted on wood of *Ostrya*.

DISTRIBUTION: Specimens have been examined from N.Y., Mich., Wis., Minn., Idaho, Wash., and Alaska; in Canada from Prince Edward Island, Quebec, Ontario, Manitoba, Saskatchewan, and Alberta.

ILLUSTRATIONS: Neuman, Wis. Geol. and Nat. Hist. Survey Bul. 33: pl. 14, fig. 53 (as *Polyporus subradicatus*).

There are some intergrading forms between *Polyporus melanopus* and *P. varius* that are difficult to refer, yet in general the species are distinct. The pileus of *P. melanopus* is rather definitely villose at first, but more glabrate with age.   There is an irregularity and lack of smoothness on both pileus and hymenium that is quite at variance with *P. picipes* and *P. varius*, in which the pileus and the hymenium are always even.   In addition, the stem of *P. varius* is glabrous, whereas that of *P. melanopus* is definitely velvety above the black underground portion, which is probably always attached to buried wood of deciduous trees.   *P. varius* grows on wood above ground. *P. radicatus* grows on buried wood, and it is always buried several inches, so that the underground portion of the stem is distinctly longer and radicating.   There is no question but that *Scutiger subradicatus* is referable here, though the types are sterile.   The pileus color of *P. melanopus* is typically that of *P. radicatus*, but the stem is short, the pores and spores smaller, and the consistency tougher, though not so leathery as in *P. varius* and *P. picipes*.   Lloyd's report (111, p. 908) of *P. cyathoides* Fries from Ohio is said to be based on a small form of this species.

Schweinitz' record of this species is not correct.   A specimen preserved in his herbarium at Philadelphia is only a small form of *Polyporus picipes*.

20. POLYPORUS DECURRENS Underw.
Torrey Bot. Club Bul. 24: 83. 1897
(Figs. 629–630 and Plate 129)

Scutiger decurrens (Underw.) Murr., Torrey Bot. Club Bul. 30: 428. 1903.

Sporophore stipitate; pileus circular, convex to slightly depressed, fleshy-tough, 4–6 cm. broad, 4–8 mm. thick, dull orange, drying yellowish brown or reddish brown, with tuberculate or finally fibrillose-appressed scales; context white, 4–5 mm. thick; pore surface white, drying yellowish or brownish, the tubes 2–3 mm. long, long-decurrent on the stem, the mouths angular, rather thin-walled, entire, averaging 1–2 per mm.; stem central or nearly so, whitish to brownish, 3–5 cm. long, 0.5–1.5 cm. thick, reticulated from the decurrent pores; spores cylindric or elliptic cylindric, smooth, hyaline, 13–18 × 4–6 μ; basidia 6–8 μ in diameter; cystidia none; hyphae flexuous, somewhat branched, rather thin-walled, with occasional cross walls and clamps, mostly 4–7 μ in diameter but some irregularly inflated up to 20 μ in diameter.

HABITAT: On the ground in woods.

DISTRIBUTION: Specimens have been examined only from Calif.

The microscopic characters of this species are so strikingly similar to those of *Polyporus McMurphyi* that the two species may eventually have to be united. The types of *P. McMurphyi* are said to have grown on the wood of *Alnus*, and no other collections of it on a woody substratum are known. A collection by Epling at Carmel Highlands, California, in 1924 (Epling Herbarium), grew on the ground under pine trees; a collection by Harper in 1911 is also said to have been on the ground; and there is no indication in the type of *P. decurrens* that it had a different substratum. However, all of these specimens may have been attached to buried wood, and if they were, I doubt that there is a specific difference between them.

21. POLYPORUS CRYPTOPUS Ell. & Barth.

Erythea 4: 79. 1896

(Fig. 184 and Plate 129)

Scutiger cryptopus (Ell. & Barth.) Murr., Torrey Bot. Club Bul. 30: 428. 1903.

Sporophore stipitate; pileus fleshy-tough when fresh, drying rigid, circular, 2–5 cm. broad, 2–3 mm. thick, grayish white or isabelline; context 1–2 mm. thick, white; pore surface white or yellowish, the tubes less than 2 mm. long, decurrent, the mouths angular, entire, averaging about 3 per mm.; stem central, partially inserted in the ground, equal or tapering upward, 1–2 cm. long, 3–7 mm. thick, concolorous with the pileus or darker at the base; spores elongate, the ends somewhat pointed, smooth, hyaline, 6–10 × 3–4 μ, obliquely apiculate at times; cystidia none; hyphal pegs present but rare; hyphae thin-walled, somewhat branched, with inconspicuous cross walls and clamps, 2.5–4.5 μ in diameter.

HABITAT: On the ground in sandy pastures, attached to dead grass roots.

DISTRIBUTION: Specimens have been examined from N. Dak., Kans., Colo., and Wash.; reported from Mont. (Weir [227]).

This is a species apparently very limited in its range and only rarely collected. The peculiar habitat will easily identify it, although

Weir's record from Montana states that it grew at the base of a dead tree of *Pinus*, slightly attached to the bark. The color of the pileus is about that of the pileus of *Clitocybe vilescens* Peck or *Clitopilus abortivus* Peck.

22. POLYPORUS CANALICULATUS Overh.[1]

Mycologia 33: 100. 1941

Sporophore single; pileus 9–18 cm. broad, convex-plane or depressed, near "dark purplish gray" but after prolonged rains "cinnamon-buff" to "tawny-olive," the surface provided with conspicuous "olive-ocher" hairs which are arranged in hirsute reticulations, older specimens more or less glabrous; context 1–2.5 cm. thick next the stem, homogeneous, subfloccose-fragile, whitish or grayish, odor and taste mild; tubes not separable, decurrent on the stem, 8–12 mm. long, the mouths mostly about 1 mm. in diameter but up to 3 mm., the dissepiments thin, lacerated, circular to elongate, "wood brown" to "avellaneous"; stem central to almost lateral, equal or tapering upward, not radicating, solid, marked with aborted tubes and coarse reticulations, concolorous with pileus, 5–10 cm. long, 2.5–5 cm. in diameter; spores ovoid to subglobose, slightly apiculate, apparently minutely verrucose but actually with the inner spore wall channeled with short tubes, 8–12 × 8–10 μ; cystidia none.

HABITAT: On the ground under *Rhododendron*.

DISTRIBUTION: Specimens have been examined from N.C. and Tenn.

The diagnostic feature of this species is the canaliculate spore wall, which is similar to that described by Atkinson for *Fomes applanatus* and for the species in the *Polyporus lucidus* complex. *P. canaliculatus* differs from both *P. sylvestris* and *P. Pes-Caprae* on this point, and from the second of these, further, in the larger spores, which are not strongly apiculate.

[1] [Dr. D. P. Rogers calls attention to an earlier homonym, *Polyporus canaliculatus* Pat., *Soc. Myc. France Bul.* 14: 153. 1898; and Dr. L. R. Hesler writes that Coker (*Elisha Mitchell Sci. Soc. Journ.* 64: 288. 1948) has placed this species in synonymy with *Polyporoletus sublividus* Snell. The valid name would be *Polyporus sublividus* (Snell) Lowe, comb. nov.—J.L.L.]

5b. *Pilei more than one; stem branched or the bases fused*
  6a. *Pilei few to several* (see also *Abortiporus subabortivus*,
      p. 428)

23. POLYPORUS SYLVESTRIS Overh.

Mycologia 33: 94. 1941
(Fig. 327 and Plate 132)

Sporophore stipitate, composed of three or four confluent pilei with the stems also partially united, the entire mass 10–15 cm. in diameter; pilei slightly greenish blue around margin where bruised, apparently fleshy-tough when fresh, drying rigid, olive-ochraceous when fresh, sordid yellowish green to bright tan in dried plants, covered with a mat of short coarse yellowish-green fibrils that separate slightly into inconspicuous scales or form a more or less minutely tufted plush over the surface; context umber in dried plants, probably pallid when fresh, thin, taste mild; pore surface smoky olivaceous or smoky black, the tubes 1–5 mm. long, the mouths angular, thin-walled, entire, distinctly velvety-pubescent, slightly greenish where bruised, averaging 1–2 per mm., long-decurrent on the stem; stems subcentral or excentric, confluent, concolorous with the pileus at the base, 4–6 cm. long, 2–3 cm. thick; spores broadly ellipsoid, broadly ovoid or subglobose, at first smooth, finally somewhat verrucose, hyaline, 9–12 × 8–9 μ; basidia 10–12 μ in diameter, with prominent sterigmata up to 10 μ long; cystidia none.

HABITAT: Apparently growing on the ground, but perhaps growing from buried roots.

DISTRIBUTION: Specimens have been examined from Wash.; in Canada from British Columbia.

ILLUSTRATIONS: Overholts, Mycologia 33: 94, fig. 5.

This species has the manner of growth and the form shown by most illustrations of *Polyporus confluens*, from which it differs in every other particular, although belonging in the same section of the genus. The salient characters seem to be the growth habit, the yellowish-green pileus with its covering of coarse short fibrils, the smoky-black pore surface of dried plants, and the distinctly verrucose spores.

The fungus differs from similar species in the verrucose spores.

Polyporus Peckianus and *P. cristatus* have much smaller spores and lack the pileus covering of this species. *P. Ellisii* has a very similar pileus covering, but its spores are smooth, measure only 8–9 × 5–7 μ, and are very strongly apiculate—in fact the base of the spore is strongly narrowed to the apiculus, so that a tear-shaped spore results. *P. Pes-Caprae* is perhaps more nearly related, but its pores are 1–2 mm. in diameter, its pore surface is not darkened on drying, and its spores are entirely smooth and more pointed (hence less globose) than those of this plant. Moreover, the pileus is drab or brown. The same objections apply to Murrill's *Scutiger oregonensis*, which I have carefully compared with this; in addition, the spores of that specimen are entirely smooth. In *P. decurrens* the spores are elongate and entirely smooth. The spore walls of *P. sylvestris* are so distinctly roughened that the character is easily recognized under the ordinary high power of the microscope. The type collection was made by Mr. G. C. Riley and turned over to Dr. Irene Mounce, of the Dominion Experimental Farm, at Ottawa. A second collection was received from Dr. A. H. Smith, who found the fungus in the Olympic Mountains, in Washington.

24. POLYPORUS MONTANUS (Quél.) Ferry
Rev. Mycol. 19: 144. 1897
(Figs. 581, 598, and Plate 130)

Cerioporus montanus Quél., Assoc. Française 16, 2: 589. 1888.

Sporophore stipitate or substipitate, fleshy-tough, drying rigid, simple or somewhat merismoid; pileus irregular, 6–25 cm. broad, dark rich brown because of a covering of short, plushlike velvety pubescence; context white, spongy, drying hard; pore surface whitish, drying darker, the tubes 1–6 mm. long, the mouths rather irregular and angular, rather thick-walled, averaging 1–2 per mm.; stem short and thick above ground, developed into a tuberous, irregular rootlike portion below ground, 6–12 cm. long, 2–4 cm. thick, externally covered like the pileus; spores globose, somewhat echinulate, hyaline, 5–7 μ in diameter; cystidia none. (Compare no. 25, *Polyporus Berkeleyi*, and no. 51, *P. hirtus*.)

HABITAT: On the ground under conifers, probably attached to buried wood, one collection under pine trees, one under *Abies*, one under *Picea*, and another attached to rotted wood of *Pseudotsuga*.

DISTRIBUTION: Specimens have been examined from Mont., Idaho, and Calif.; in Canada from British Columbia.

ILLUSTRATIONS: Imazeki, Jour. Jap. Bot. 15: figs. 10–11; Lloyd, Myc. Notes 67: fig. 2203; Pilát, Bot. Centbl. Beih. 52: pl. 5 (as *Grifola*).

Recent mycologists have elaborated but little on Quélet's original description. This seems to be a very rare species. Bourdot and Galzin (18, p. 523) include it and record it as growing at the base of pine trunks in mountain forests, but they note that they had not seen any specimens. Rea does not include it for Britain. Lloyd's earlier opinion was that it was the European representative of *Polyporus Berkeleyi*, and the European descriptions would seem to bear this out. But Lloyd's later concept of the fungus seems to agree better with California plants that differ conspicuously from *P. Berkeleyi* in the rich dark-brown coloration of the pileus, the type of pubescence, and the slightly smaller and less echinulate spores, though in other points the species seem to be very similar. The macroscopic appearance and the coloration are somewhat similar to those of *P. hirtus*, but the spores are quite different. Pilát has more recently described and illustrated the species (171, vol. 52, pp. 62–66), and so (presumably) has Imazeki (*Jour. Jap. Bot.* 15: 442–444. 1939).

25. POLYPORUS BERKELEYI Fries

Nov. Symb. Myc., p. 56. 1851

(Figs. 156, 160, 167, and Plate 128)

Grifola Berkeleyi (Fries) Murr., Torrey Bot. Club Bul. 31: 337. 1904.
Polyporus Beatiei Banning, apud Peck, in N. Y. State Mus. Ann. Rept. 31: 36. 1879.
Polyporus lactifluus Peck, Torrey Bot. Club Bul. 8: 51. 1881.

Sporophore stipitate and composed of from one to five broad pilei, or simple with but one large centrally depressed pileus; pilei fleshy-tough when fresh, rigid and brittle when dry, 6–25 cm. broad, 0.5–2 cm. thick, whitish or grayish to yellowish or avellaneous, finely and compactly tomentose, weathering to nearly glabrous or with a fibrillose appearance, often radiately rugose or pitted, sometimes obscurely zoned; context white, 0.3–2 cm. thick; pore surface white or whitish, discoloring on drying, the tubes 2–10 mm. long, decurrent, the mouths angular, unequal and sometimes much lacerated and toothed, large, 0.5–2 mm. broad; stem short and thick, more or less tubercular, sometimes (perhaps always) arising from an underground sclerotium or tuber, the portion above ground 4–10 cm. long, 3–5 cm. thick; spores globose or nearly so, hyaline, strongly echinulate, body of spore 6–8 μ broad; basidia 9–12 μ in diameter; cystidia none; hyphae flexuous, hyaline, nearly simple, mostly thin-walled and with a staining content, with no cross walls or clamps, 3–9 μ in diameter. (Compare no. 24, *Polyporus montanus*; no. 27, *P. giganteus*; and no. 29, *P. frondosus*.)

HABITAT: Growing around trees and stumps, usually of deciduous trees, especially *Castanea* and *Quercus*, noted also on *Prunus*; occasionally on or about coniferous trees in the Northwest, noted on *Abies, Larix, Picea,* and *Pinus.*

DISTRIBUTION: Specimens have been examined from Mass., N.Y., Pa., N.J., Md., D.C., Va., W. Va. N.C., S.C., Ga., Ala., La., Tenn., Ky., Ohio, Ind., Ill., Mich., Mo., Ark., Texas, Idaho, Ore., Wash., and Calif.; in Canada from Ontario and British Columbia; reported from Conn. (Murrill), Iowa (Wolf [234]), Kans. (Bartholomew [4]), and Mont. (Weir [227]).

ILLUSTRATIONS: Boyce, Forest Path., fig. 168; Hard, Mushrooms, figs. 323–324; Lloyd, Photographs, Issue Nos. 23, 24; *idem*, Polyp. Issue No. 3: figs. 362–363; Long, Jour. Agr. Res. 1: pl. 8, figs. 2–3; Overholts, Wash. Univ. Studies 3: pl. 2, fig. 6; Weir, Phytopathology 3: pl. 9.

The strongly echinulate spore is the best character by which to identify this species. The echinulations are easily visible under the high magnifications of the ordinary compound microscope. The pilei are much thicker than in *Polyporus giganteus*, and the species may be distinguished from *P. frondosus* by the smaller number of pilei. Hard's photographs, cited above, are quite characteristic.

The history of *Polyporus anax* Berk. is given by Lloyd (111, p. 342). Both he and Murrill (139, p. 69) regard it as a synonym of *P. Berkeleyi. P. subgiganteus* Berk. & Curt. is likewise referred here. The type of the former is from Ohio; of the latter, from Connecticut.

The fungus causes a serious butt rot of the heartwood of living trees (117).   The wood is first whitened (delignified), and eventually is completely broken down, so that hollow butts result, although before this stage the rot is easily recognized by the persistent medullary rays.   These persistent rays interwoven with the stringy wood remnants have given the name "string and ray rot" to the decay.

26. POLYPORUS TUBERASTER Jacq. ex Fries

Syst. Myc. 1: 347. 1821

(Fig. 659 and Plate 132)

Boletus tuberaster Jacq., Collect. ad Bot. Suppl., pls. 8–9. 1796.
Grifola Tuckahoe Güssow, Mycologia 11: 109. 1919.

Sporophore stipitate, simple or somewhat compound; pileus fleshy, circular or subcircular, somewhat convex to plane, depressed or somewhat infundibuliform, 5–15 cm. broad, 0.5–1 cm. or more thick, ochraceous tan to ochraceous tawny, with small scattered tan or umber-brown scales, otherwise even and glabrous; context pallid, nearly concolorous with the surface, fleshy-tough, 3–10 mm. thick; pore surface pale tan or yellowish brown, the tubes 1–3 mm. long, somewhat decurrent on the stem, the mouths rather irregular and sometimes compound, varying from circular to angular or somewhat elongate, rather thick-walled, entire or somewhat dentate, averaging 1.5–2 per mm.; stem central or excentric, cylindric, sometimes branched, 2.5–7 cm. long, 1–2.5 cm. thick; spores subcylindric or ellipsoid-cylindric, smooth, hyaline, 10–16 × 4–6 μ; cystidia none; hyphae of two kinds, one conspicuous, thick-walled, rapidly attenuate at one or both ends, 5–10(–15) μ in diameter, the other thin-walled, collapsed, indefinite, 5–8 μ in diameter, with no cross walls or clamps in either type.

HABITAT: On the ground in deciduous woods, growing from large black sclerotia.

DISTRIBUTION: Probably widely distributed in the northern United States and Canada; fruiting bodies have been reported from Manitoba (Bisby *et al.* [12]).

ILLUSTRATIONS: Badham, Escul. Fung. England, 1st ed., pl. 14, fig. 3; Lanzi, Funghi Mang., pl. 31, fig. 1; Lloyd, Synop. Ovinus, fig. 509; Viviani, Funghi d'Italia, pl. 55.

The range of this species is uncertain.   Sclerotia somewhat similar but perhaps not identical with those of this fungus have been found on several occasions in the eastern United States. Güssow reports twenty or more collections of the sclerotium from Saskatchewan and Manitoba. He reports that he was able to grow a sporophore from but a single one of these. Dr. Irene Mounce sent me for examination a small sporophore produced in 1928–1929 from an inoculation of a malt-agar substratum containing poplar twigs. The sclerotium from which this sporophore was grown was obtained from Alberta, Canada. No one has studied the large underground sclerotia of our several polypore species that produce them; hence identifications made on the sclerotia alone are questionable. The sclerotia are all of considerable size and have a black and irregularly roughened exterior; internally they are at first waxy or rubbery, but on drying become exceedingly hard. The color inside varies from white to gray or blackish.

The sclerotium of *Polyporus tuberaster* contains a considerable amount of soil and sand debris and after drying looks like black loam penetrated by white mycelial strands and cords. From references to the sclerotium of this species as it grows in Italy I do not conclude that it is the sclerotium which is edible, but rather the sporophore (113). From the earliest times, however, references are found in the American literature to the use of "tuckahoe" as a food by the Indians. Güssow believes the present fungus, or rather its sclerotium as it is found in the western prairie provinces of Canada, is the authentic tuckahoe, and he has named the fungus *P. Tuckahoe*. Lloyd (111, p. 954) is just as firmly convinced that it is not. It is difficult to understand how the sand- and dirt-containing sclerotium of *P. tuberaster* could possibly be used as food. In fact, the internal structure of the sclerotium is similar to a form of "pseudosclerotium" I have found associated with sporophores of *P. sulphureus* growing from old roots at the surface of the ground. The sclerotia of *P. umbellatus* and those of the Australian *P. Mylittae* Mass., on the other hand, seem to be internally free of debris of this sort, and might be more desirable as food. I am much indebted to Dr. Güssow for forwarding specimens of the sclerotia of this fungus, and particularly for giving me an opportunity to examine the specimens grown from these sclerotia at the Department of Agriculture laboratory at Ottawa, as well as a portion of the type specimen of *P. Tuckahoe*. This type specimen is preserved in alcohol, but spores were obtained resembling those of *P. tuberaster*, and the hyphae of the context are the same. I am thoroughly convinced that his species is referable here.

27. Polyporus giganteus Pers. ex Fries
Syst. Myc. 1: 356. 1821
(Figs. 313, 570, 600, and Plate 130)

Boletus giganteus Pers., Synop. Method. Fung., p. 521. 1801.
Grifola Sumstinei Murr., Torrey Bot. Club Bul. 31: 335. 1904.

Sporophore stipitate, compound, 15–40 cm. or more broad, composed of a number (sometimes two or three, sometimes twelve to fifteen or more) of broad, fleshy-tough pilei 6–15 cm. in diameter and less than 1 cm. thick, dimidiate to flabelliform or spathulate, grayish to drab, becoming smoky brown or, more usually, blackish, at least on the margin, when dried, radiately rugose, finely tomentose or fibrillose, the margin thin and acute, involute on drying; context white, 1–10 mm. thick; pore surface white or whitish, blackish where bruised and on drying, the tubes 1–3 mm. long, the mouths angular or irregular, becoming lacerate, averaging 4–7 per mm.; stem short and thick; spores broadly ovoid to subglobose, with a very small apiculus, smooth, hyaline, $6–7 \times 4.5–6$ μ or 5–7 μ in diameter; cystidia none; hyphae nearly simple, thin-walled, with very occasional cross walls but no clamps, 4–8 μ in diameter. (Compare no. 25, *Polyporus Berkeleyi*, and no. 29, *P. frondosus*.)

Habitat: On the ground around stumps or trees, usually in deciduous woods of *Fagus* and *Quercus*; reported on conifers (Idaho, Weir [222]); perhaps always attached to buried wood.

Distribution: Specimens have been examined from Mass., N.Y., Pa., N.J., Md., D.C., Va., W. Va., N.C., Ala., La., Tenn., Ohio, Ind., Wis., Iowa, and Mo.; reported from Ill. (McDougall [128]), and Idaho (Weir [222]).

Illustrations: Boudier, Icones, pl. 153; Bresadola, Fungi Trid. II: pl. 134; Gillet, Champ. France 3: pl. 559 (62); McDougall, Mushrooms, opp. p. 114; *idem*, Ill. State Acad. Sci. Trans. 12: fig. 4; Michael, Führ. f. Pilzfr. 3: fig. 240; Pilát, Bot. Centbl. Beih. 52: fig. 2 (as *Grifola sulphurea* f. *conglobata*); Rostkovius, in Sturm's Deutsch. Flora, Abt. III, Bd. 4: pl. 19.

Polyporus frondosus is the closest relative of this species, but the spores of *P. giganteus* are a bit more globose and have a very small apiculus, whereas those of *P. frondosus* are distinctly ovoid or ellipsoid, though, of course, they appear globose from the end view. The pilei of *P. giganteus* are usually fewer and broader, and considerable blackening takes place, especially on the margin, in drying. But occasionally the pilei are as numerous as in *P. frondosus*. These two species probably hold the record for size in this family. Dr. F. J. Seaver recently sent me a photograph of a specimen of *P. giganteus* that measured thirty-three inches across and weighed thirty-six pounds.

My specimens agree in all essentials with those received from Bresadola and with the descriptions and figures more recently published by Pilát (171, vol. 52, pp. 35–39).

Not much is known regarding the importance of this species from the standpoint of forest pathology. Probably it has often been mistaken for *Polyporus frondosus*. Pilát (*op. cit.*, p. 39) says of it as it occurs in Europe: "Wahrscheinlich ist dieser Pilz mehr Saprophyt als Parasit. Er infiziert fast nur alte und kranke Bäume."

28. POLYPORUS SULPHUREUS Bull. ex Fries

Syst. Myc. 1: 357. 1821

(Figs. 166, 181, 238, 591, and Plate 132)

Boletus sulphureus Bull., Herb. France, pl. 429. 1789.
Laetiporus speciosus Batt. ex Murr., Torrey Bot. Club Bul. 31: 607. 1904.

Sporophore sessile or attenuate at the base and appearing substipitate, or more frequently in large rosette-like or imbricate clusters 20–60 cm. broad, fleshy and watery to rather firm when fresh, drying rigid and brittle; pileus 5–25 × 4–30 × 0.5–2.5 cm., salmon, sulphur-yellow, or bright orange, weathering to almost white with age, nearly glabrous; context white, light yellow, or pale salmon, 0.4–2 cm. thick; pore surface bright sulphur-yellow or fading with age, the tubes 1–4 mm. long, the mouths angular, thin-walled, entire or slightly dentate, averaging 2–4 per mm.; spores ellipsoid to broadly ellipsoid or ovoid, smooth, hyaline, 5–7 × 3.5–4.5 μ; cystidia none; hyphae thin-walled, sparingly branched, hyaline, with cross walls but no clamps, mostly 5–10 μ in diameter, but some inflated to 20 μ. (Compare no. 79, *Polyporus amygdalinus*.)

HABITAT: Growing on stumps, trunks, and logs of both deciduous and coniferous trees, noted on *Abies, Acer, Castanea, Eucalyptus, Fraxinus, Gleditsia, Juglans, Larix, Liriodendron, Picea, Pinus, Pru-*

nus, Pseudotsuga, Quercus, Robinia, Schinus, Tamarix, Tsuga, and *Ulmus*; reported on *Celtis* and *Juglans* (Hedgcock [66]) and on *Fagus* (Mich., Kauffman [101]).

DISTRIBUTION: Specimens have been examined from Me., N.H., Vt., Mass., Conn., R.I., N.Y., Pa., N.J., Del., Md., D.C., Va., W. Va., N.C., Fla., Ala., La., Tenn., Ky., Ohio, Ind., Ill., Minn., Iowa, Mo., Nebr., Ark., Okla., Idaho, Ore., Wash., Calif., and Alaska; in Canada from Ontario; reported from Mich. (Kauffman [101]), Wis. (Dodge [40]), Kans. (Bartholomew [4]), Mont. (Weir [227]), Quebec (Odell [149]), and Manitoba (Bisby *et al.* [12]).

ILLUSTRATIONS: Atkinson, Mushrooms, figs. 184–185; *idem,* Cornell Agr. Exp. Sta. Bul. 193: figs. 64–65; Barla, Champ. Nice, pl. 30, figs. 1–3 (as *Polyporus Ceratoniae*); Boyce, U. S. Dept. Agr. Tech. Bul. 286: pl. 9; *idem,* Forest Path., fig. 197; Fries, Sverig. Ätliga, pl. 88; Güssow and Odell, Mushrooms and Toadstools, pl. 101; Hard. Mushrooms, figs. 326, 328 (as *P. heteroclitus*); Jaccottet, Champ. Nature, pl. 56 *(pars)*; Lanzi, Funghi Mang., pl. 23, fig. 2; Meinecke, Forest Tree Dis. Calif. Nev., pl. 9; Michael, Führ. f. Pilzfr. 2: fig. 31 (as *P. caudicinus*); Pilát, Bot. Centbl. Beih. 52: pls. 2–4, 6–7 (as *Grifola*); Schaeffer, Fung. Bavar., pls. 131–132; Sowerby, Col. Fig. English Fungi, pl. 135 (as *Boletus*).

The species is common throughout the region covered by this manual. Old specimens fade out to white on both the pileus and the hymenium. When the plant first appears after a warm summer rain it is one of the best of the edible fungi, and is about the only species of the family that is tender enough to be eaten. *Polyporus casearius* Fries, as far as American records are concerned, belongs here. *Agaricus speciosus* Batt. (*Laetiporus speciosus* Batt. ex Murr.) is also said to be a synonym.

DeSeynes long ago reported conidia (probably chlamydospores) as a secondary spore form in this species, and I find them to be a constant feature of cultures, forming a deep powdery mass over the surface of the mycelium. In nature, a ptychogastric form has been designated *Ceriomyces aurantiacus* Pat. I have not met it.

The species causes a destructive red-brown heart rot of the carbonizing type, in which the wood becomes very much checked and cracked, and thin sheets of white mycelium appear in the cracks (215, pp. 40–49; 219, pp. 37–39).

Var. CINCINNATUS (Morgan) Overh.[1]

Pa. Agr. Exp. Sta. Tech. Bul. 298: 27. 1933
(Figs. 165, 226, 613)

Polyporus cincinnatus Morgan, Cincinnati Soc. Nat. Hist. Jour. 8: 97. 1885.
Polyporus sulphureus var. *Overholtsii* Rosen, Mycologia 19: 194. 1927.

Like the species, but pileus salmon-colored or occasionally very pale pinkish ochraceous; pore surface white, late in growing.

HABITAT: Occurring at the bases or on the roots of *Quercus* and perhaps of other trees, growing from a pseudosclerotium and with a rootlike prolongation of the central stem.

ILLUSTRATIONS: Rosen, *Mycologia* 19: pl. 16.

Var. *cincinnatus* is the only variation of the species constant enough to warrant a distinct designation. Its characters were first noticed in recent years by Rosen (189), who gave it a varietal name. Since he first called my attention to it I have observed it in Pennsylvania, and find the variety to be more common than the species. The variety grows from the roots or bases of trees or stumps (never from the trunks) and is associated with a pseudosclerotium. That is, the rotted wood, and sometimes the ground around the infected root, is tied together into a solid mass by numerous strands of mycelium. From this mass there arises a blackish rootlike structure that leads to the surface of the ground. When this rootlike structure is broken it exudes a milky, watery fluid. Morgan recorded the fungus as occurring at the base of trees, and though I think no specimens of his species are preserved, there can be no doubt that he was dealing with this plant. He described the pileus as yellowish red and the hymenium as white. No other form of *Polyporus sulphureus* ever shows a white hymenium. I have never observed the species to have a white hymenium when growing from the side of a tree or on an old log, and I believe we have here a well-defined and constant variation from the species, one worthy of varietal designation. Peck (*N. Y. State Mus. Bul.* 105: 34. 1906) noted a form with a white hymenium which he designated var. *semialbinus* Peck. This also is referable to the variety *cincinnatus*. Peck re-

---

[1] [Dr. A. H. Smith observes that the valid name for this variety would be *semialbinus*. The error was discovered in galley proof, and expensive alterations in the text appeared unwarranted.—J.L.L.]

marks that the hymenium is often composed of closed cells, which might indicate a parasitized condition. Rosen, however, observes that the hymenium is generally slow in developing. Herbarium specimens of the variety are probably usually unrecognizable unless exceptionally well dried.

It is impossible to state either the geographical or the host range of the variety. The fact that it occurs in Pennsylvania, Ohio, and Arkansas indicates a distribution perhaps as wide as that of the species. Miss Margaret Wolf's report (234) of *Polyporus heteroclitus* Bolt. ex Fries from Iowa may represent a form between the species and the variety, since she describes her specimens as arising from a radical tubercle, but as having a yellow pore surface. A variety designated *albolabyrinthiporus* by Rea has a white pore surface but has larger, irregular and labyrinthiform pores, and would not seem to be the same.

6b. *Pilei typically many*

29. POLYPORUS FRONDOSUS Dicks. ex Fries
Syst. Myc. 1: 355. 1821
(Figs. 182, 264, 588, 617, and Plate 130)

Boletus frondosus Dicks., Plant Crypt. Brit., fasc. 1: 18. 1785.
Grifola frondosa (Dicks. ex Fries) S. F. Gray, Nat. Arr. British Plants 1: 643. 1821.

Sporophore stipitate or substipitate, the stem branching many times and giving rise to numerous overlapping pilei, the whole plant forming a more or less globose mass, often as much as 60 cm. in diameter; pilei fleshy to fleshy-tough, flabelliform or spathulate, 2–7 cm. broad, 2–7 mm. thick, grayish, drab, or pale "mouse gray," nearly glabrous or finely fibrillose, scabrous to strongly scabrous-tomentose; context white, not more than 5 mm. thick; pore surface white to yellowish, the tubes 2–3 mm. long, decurrent, the mouths angular, unequal, averaging 1–3 per mm.; stem compound, short and thick; spores ovoid or ellipsoid, smooth, hyaline, 5–7 × 3.5–5 μ; cystidia none; hyphal pegs lacking; hyphae thin-walled, branched, with cross walls but no clamps, mostly 6–15 μ in diameter. (Compare no. 25, *Polyporus Berkeleyi*, and no. 27, *P. giganteus*.)

HABITAT: Growing around stumps or trunks, usually of deciduous trees, noted on *Nyssa*, *Quercus*, and *Ulmus*; occasionally around coniferous trees, noted under *Larix* and *Pinus*; reported on *Acer* (Mo., Maneval [131]) and *Pseudotsuga* (Mont., Weir [227]).

DISTRIBUTION: Specimens have been examined from Mass., N.Y., Pa., N.J., Md., D.C., W. Va., N.C., La., Tenn., Ohio, Ind., Ill., Wis., Minn., Iowa, Mo., and Idaho; reported from Va. and Canada (Long [117]), Ark. (Swartz [212]), Mont. (Weir [227]), and Wash. (Weir [222]).

ILLUSTRATIONS: Atkinson, Mushrooms, figs. 181–182; Badham, Escul. Fung. England, 1st ed., pl. 15, fig. 3; Barla, Champ. Nice, pl. 29, fig. 1; Bresadola, Funghi Mang., pl. 97 *bis*; Cordier, Champ. France, pl. 39, fig. 1; Hard, Mushrooms, fig. 321; Krieger, Natl. Geog. Mag. 37: 408; Lanzi, Funghi Mang., pl. 24, fig. 2; McDougall, Mushrooms, opp. p. 113; *idem*, Ill. State Lab. Nat. Hist. Bul. 11: pl. 135; McIlvaine, Amer. Fungi, pl. 128; McKenny, Mushrooms Field and Wood, fig. 39 (*pars*); Michael, Führ. f. Pilzfr. 2: fig. 35; Neuman, Wis. Geol. and Nat. Hist. Survey Bul. 33: pl. 12, fig. 43.

The pilei do not turn black on drying and they are much more numerous than in *Polyporus giganteus*, which differs further in having a more globose type of spore. *P. frondosus* is distinguished from *P. umbellatus* by its larger size, the spathulate or flabelliform pilei with compressed stem bases, and the ellipsoid spores. It is very common in the Allegheny region.

The fungus produces a soft, wet, general delignifying butt rot of its hosts (117). It may grow at the bases of living trees, especially oaks, or around stumps and roots of dead trees.

30. POLYPORUS UMBELLATUS Pers. ex Fries
Syst. Myc. 1: 354. 1821
(Fig. 180 and Plate 132)

Boletus umbellatus Pers., Synop. Meth. Fung., p. 519. 1801.
Grifola ramosissima Scop. ex Murr., Torrey Bot. Club Bul. 31: 336. 1904.

Sporophore stipitate, compound, fleshy, 7–20 cm. in diameter, the stem branching repeatedly and giving rise to many centrally attached, imbricate pilei which are orbicular, 1–4 cm. broad, less than 5 mm. thick, whitish to smoky brown, fibrillose or glabrous; context white, usually not more than 1 mm. thick; pore surface white or drying yellowish, the tubes less than 2 mm. long, decurrent, the mouths angular, thin-walled, entire or somewhat uneven, averaging

2–4 per mm.; stem arising from an underground tuber or sclerotium of irregular shape, compound, the stem branches cylindric, central or subcentral, white, entirely covered with the decurrent tubes; spores cylindric, smooth, hyaline, 7–9.5 × 3–4 μ; cystidia none; hyphae mostly quite irregular, thin-walled, often inflated up to 25 μ in diameter, some of the smaller ones considerably branched, with no cross walls or clamps, mostly 4–15 μ in diameter.

HABITAT: On the ground about stumps or trees or in connection with buried wood of deciduous trees; reported on *Picea* (Mont., Weir [227]).

DISTRIBUTION: Specimens have been examined from Mass., Conn., N.Y., Pa., Tenn., Ky., and Ohio; in Canada from Ontario; reported from Iowa (Wolf [234]), Kans. (Bartholomew [4]), Idaho and Wash. (Weir [222]), and Manitoba (Bisby *et al.* [12]).

ILLUSTRATIONS: Atkinson, Mushrooms, fig. 183; Clements, Minn. Mushrooms, fig. 61; Güssow and Odell, Mushrooms and Toadstools, pl. 102; Hard, Mushrooms, fig. 320; Lanzi, Funghi Mang., pls. 26–27; Lloyd, Synop. Stip. Polyp., fig. 450; Overholts, Wash. Univ. Studies 3: pl. 2, fig. 7; Schaeffer, Fung. Bavar., pl. 111.

The species is at once distinguished by the small regular pilei with cylindric stem bases, as well as by the elongate spores. It is infrequently collected in most regions. Schweinitz' record is an error, his plants being either *Polyporus frondosus* or *P. giganteus.* Coker (35, p. 131) reports the species from North Carolina, but is somewhat doubtful of the identity of his collection because of the larger pilei (4–9 cm. broad).

The species is collected so infrequently that there are no records concerning its importance as a tree parasite, but it would not be surprising to learn that it causes losses through its wood-decaying propensities, and the decay might be assumed to be more or less similar to that produced by *Polyporus frondosus.*

31. POLYPORUS ILLUDENS Overh.
Mycologia 33: 95. 1941
(Fig. 183 and Plate 130)

Sporophore stipitate, multiplex-imbricate, about 10 cm. broad; pilei numerous, 1.5–4 cm. broad and long, 1–3 mm. thick, fleshy-tough, irregular, more or less spathulate or petaliform, concave to depressed, color of fresh plant unknown, everywhere brick-red on drying or at least so colored in the herbarium, glabrous, not areolate; context white, watery, 1–2 mm. thick, finally tinted rusty red in the herbarium, changing to cherry-red with KOH solution; tubes about 1 mm. long, the mouths subangular to radially elongate, entire, rather thick-walled, averaging about 2 per mm.; spores minute, ellipsoid to subglobose, smooth, hyaline, 4–5 × 3.5–4 μ; basidia 5 μ in diameter; cystidia none; hyphae thin-walled, much inflated, branched, almost always very irregular, with no cross walls or clamps, 4–35 μ in diameter.

HABITAT: On the ground in coniferous woods.

DISTRIBUTION: Known only from the type collection, made at Bovill, Idaho.

ILLUSTRATIONS: Overholts, Mycologia 33: 96, fig. 6.

The sporophore is much like that of *Polyporus umbellatus* in form, but it differs microscopically in many points, especially in the much smaller spores, and macroscopically in the general brick-red coloration in the dried condition. The spores are likewise smaller than those of *P. cristatus*, and the strongly multiplex habit with small pilei is distinctly different. There is no indication that the sporophore grew from a tuberoid sclerotium, as it does in a few other species of this section.

4b. *Sporophore growing on wood, above ground*
   5a. *Pileus white, gray, or pallid*
      6a. *Pores averaging 3 or more per mm.*

32. POLYPORUS ADMIRABILIS Peck
Torrey Bot. Club Bul. 26: 69. 1899
(Fig. 223 and Plate 128)

Polyporus Underwoodii Murr., in Peck, N. Y. State Mus. Bul. 105: 27. 1906.

Sporophore stipitate or substipitate, fleshy-tough or cheesy when fresh, firm and rigid when dry; pileus 7–35 cm. broad, 0.5–3 cm. thick, centrally depressed or infundibuliform with a raised wavy or lobed margin at maturity, white or cream color or drying more yellowish, nearly glabrous or finely tomentose, typically very smooth and even; context white, 0.5–2 cm. thick, at first subfleshy, then tough when mature, soft-corky when dry; pore surface white, somewhat blackish where handled when fresh, the tubes 3–7 mm. long, the mouths white, minute, regular and angular or somewhat irregular and lacerate, averaging 3–5 per mm.; stem short and thick, central or excentric, white or more usually black at the base, solid, 2–4 cm. long, 1–3 cm. thick; spores elongate, somewhat pointed at the ends, hyaline, 7.5–9 × 2.5–3.5 μ; cystidia none; a few hyphal pegs present; hyphae with walls somewhat or completely thickened, with no cross walls or clamps, usually 5–6 μ in diameter, considerably branched with the branch tips tapering to about 2 μ in diameter.

HABITAT: On wounds in living deciduous trees or on or about stumps and roots, noted on *Acer, Betula, Fraxinus, Juglans, Pyrus, Quercus*, and *Salix*, perhaps occasionally on other hosts.

DISTRIBUTION: Specimens have been examined from N.H., Vt., Mass., Conn., N.Y., and Pa.

ILLUSTRATIONS: Dodge, Mycologia 8: pls. 173–174.

This species has not been widely collected, although there are a number of specimens at the New York Botanical Garden and in the herbarium of Columbia University. Apparently it is much restricted in its range, rarely being found outside of New England and New York. The distinguishing characters are the rather large size and the smooth white pileus (but compare *Polyporus albiceps*). Its most frequent habitat in New England is wounds or hollows in living apple trees, in which it produces a serious heart rot.

33. POLYPORUS ALBICEPS Peck

Torrey Bot. Club Bul. 27: 19. 1900

(Figs. 224, 627–628)

Sporophore stipitate, fleshy-tough or coriaceous when fresh, drying rigid; pileus circular or subcircular, 3–10 cm. broad, 0.3–0.6 cm. thick, convex to depressed, probably white when fresh, gray to cream-colored or ochraceous on drying, glabrous or very finely velvety, covered more or less with a smooth pellicle, azonate, margin fairly thick; pore surface white or becoming decidedly yellowish, the tubes 1–3 mm. long, the mouths thin-walled, angular, entire, averaging 3 per mm.; stem central or excentric, terete, usually but not always black or smoky at the base, 2–5 × 0.5–1.5 cm.; spores not found; main context hyphae long and flexuous, hyaline, the walls slightly thickened, somewhat branched, with few or no cross walls or clamps, 3–5 μ in diameter. (Compare no. 32, *Polyporus admirabilis*.)

HABITAT: Attached to buried wood.

DISTRIBUTION: Specimens have been examined from N.H., N.Y., Pa., Minn., and Iowa; in Canada from Manitoba and the "Rocky Mountains."

The specimens studied appear to represent only a depauperate condition of *Polyporus admirabilis*, but until the microscopic characters are better known it seems best to keep them separate. I have been unable to find a good hymenium in any of the specimens I have examined. In addition to the characteristics of apparently growing from buried wood, of small size, and of thin pileus, the hyphae of the context are somewhat different. The walls are only slightly thickened, and the narrow hyphae about 2 μ in diameter that arise from the attenuations of the larger main hyphae, and are so characteristic of *P. admirabilis*, are nearly absent here. Narrow hyphae that stain readily and that bear a few clamps are present.

34. POLYPORUS SUBPENDULUS Atk.

Ann. Mycol. 6: 61. 1908

(Fig. 149 and Plate 132)

Sporophore short-stipitate and pendent from a dorsolateral point of attachment; pileus chalk-white or drying yellowish bay, 0.4–1 cm. broad, 0.3–0.5 cm. long, 0.3–0.5 cm. thick, finely tomentose to glabrous, smooth or slightly radiate-rugose; context white, fragile, 0.5–2 mm. thick; pore surface whitish or yellowish, the tubes 2 mm. long, the mouths averaging 6–8 per mm.; stem gradually expanding into the pileus; spores subcylindric, flattened on one side or slightly curved, apiculate, smooth, hyaline, 4–5 × 2 μ; cystidia none; hyphae 3–5 μ in diameter except for some scattered inflated cells up to 10 μ in diameter.

HABITAT: On dead branches of *Tsuga canadensis*.

DISTRIBUTION: Known only from the type collection, made at Coy Glen, Ithaca, N.Y.

Dr. H. M. Fitzpatrick kindly allowed me to study the type collection at Ithaca, New York. No other collection has ever been made. The form of the sporophore is that in *Polyporus pocula* or *P. betulinus*; this, together with its coniferous habitat, should make the species easy to recognize.

35. POLYPORUS FLORIFORMIS Quél.
In Bresadola, Fungi Trid. I: 61. 1881
(Fig. 112 and Plate 129)

Sporophore substipitate or attenuate to a lateral stemlike base, sometimes in the form of a rosette and with a central stemlike point of attachment, sometimes sessile, tough, watery, and very flexible when fresh, drying rigid, reviving; pileus 1–2(–4) × 1–1.5(–5) × 0.1–0.5 cm., white or grayish, not changing color much in drying, usually azonate, appressed silky and minutely radiate-fibrillose; context white, fibrous, hard on drying, 0.5–4 mm. thick, taste intensely bitter in herbarium specimens; pore surface whitish or yellowish, the tubes 0.5–3 mm. long, the mouths angular, thin-walled, entire or nearly so, averaging 3–6 per mm.; stemlike base occasionally developed, 1–2.5 cm. long, 3–5 mm. thick; spores oblong-ellipsoid or ellipsoid, smooth, hyaline, 3–4 × 2–2.5 μ; basidia 10–12 × 4–6 μ; cystidia none; hyphal pegs not abundant; main hyphae simple or somewhat branched, hyaline, with only partially thickened walls and a staining content, 4–7 μ in diameter, with rather frequent cross walls and clamps on all hyphal types. (Compare no. 112, *Polyporus balsameus*, and no. 127, *P. semisupinus*.)

HABITAT: Usually on dead wood of coniferous trees, noted on *Abies*, *Larix*, *Pinus*, *Thuja*, and *Tsuga*; rarely on wood of deciduous trees, reported on *Acer* (Ore., Zeller [236]).

DISTRIBUTION: Specimens have been examined from N.H., Mass., N.Y., Pa., N.C., Tenn., and Mich.; in Canada from Ontario and Nova Scotia; also reported from Ore. (Zeller [236]) and Manitoba (Bisby *et al.* [12]).

ILLUSTRATIONS: Bresadola, Fungi Trid. I: pl. 68; Lowe, Mich. Acad. Sci. Arts and Letters Papers 19: pl. 15, fig. 1.

There is little variation in the spores of the collections I have referred to *Polyporus floriformis*. In specimens from Bresadola and in some American collections they are strictly oblong, measuring scarcely more than 3 μ in length; in other American collections they are more ellipsoid, measuring 3–4 × 2.5–3 μ.

The species seems fairly well characterized by the small, elongate spores, the absence of cystidia, and the lack of a color change (at most becoming only slightly yellowish) on drying. Lowe (123, p. 144) discusses this species, suggesting that it is not distinct from *Polyporus semisupinus*, but the specimens, both fresh and dried, that I have referred here have an intensely bitter taste that is unmistakable when the tissue is well chewed far back in the mouth. *P. semisupinus* is similar, but it can be readily distinguished. It has a mild taste and a more cartilaginous texture, and dries harder and more bay-colored; the spores are broadly ellipsoid and of unusually small size, $2.5-3 \times 2 \mu$. In addition, some of the hyphae of *P. semisupinus* have completely thickened walls, are entirely unstaining in eosin, and show practically no clamps, although some of the hyphae of small diameter stain with eosin and have occasional clamps. *P. floriformis* is usually confined to coniferous substrata, and *P. semisupinus* generally occurs on hardwoods.

Polyporus balsameus is closely related, but has rather conspicuous cystidia in the hymenium, the pileus is less inclined to be stipitate and dries brownish and zonate, and the spores are apparently more cylindric.

More collections of these closely related species need to be made. Unfortunately all three species seem not to occur abundantly, although nearly always the hymenial region is in sporulating condition.

36. POLYPORUS FRACTIPES Berk. & Curt.

Grevillea 1: 39. 1872

(Figs. 207–208, 220, and Plate 129)

Polyporus humilis Peck, N. Y. State Mus. Ann. Rept. 26: 69. 1874.

Sporophore stipitate, soft and flexible but tough when fresh, drying rigid; pileus flabelliform to reniform or orbicular, 1–6 cm. broad, 1–3 mm. thick, white, drying ochraceous or straw color, finely tomentose; context white, 0.5–2 mm. thick, duplex, with a thin soft upper layer and a firm hard lower layer next the hymenium; pore surface white, the tubes 0.5–1.5 mm. long, the mouths angular, thin-walled, entire, averaging 4–5 per mm.; stem lateral, sometimes confluent, 2–4 cm. long, 3–10 mm. thick, white, soft, minutely tomentose; spores ovoid to globose, smooth, hyaline, $4-5 \times 3.5-4.5 \mu$; basidia short and thick, $9-12 \times 6-8 \mu$; cystidia none; hyphae variable, long and flexuous, sparingly branched, with very few cross walls and clamps, 3–5 μ in diameter. (Compare no. 13, *Polyporus biennis*, and no. 37, *P. mutabilis*.)

HABITAT: Attached to dead wood of deciduous trees either above or below ground, known only on *Betula* and *Fagus*.

DISTRIBUTION: Specimens have been examined from N.H., N.Y., Tenn., Minn., and Mo.

ILLUSTRATIONS: Lloyd, Myc. Notes 56: fig. 1252 (as *Polyporus humilis*); Overholts, Wash. Univ. Studies 3: pl. 1, fig. 4 (as *P. humilis*).

The species is not often collected. *Polyporus Bartholomaei* Peck is apparently somewhat similar and may be but a form of this species. Except for it, no other pure-white, wood-inhabiting species of *Polyporus* of this section is likely to be met. *P. mutabilis* is similar in some respects, but lacks the duplex context. The upper context of *P. fractipes* is really only the heavy tomentose layer of the pileus. The basidia are characteristic in their length and diameter.

Polyporus delicatus Berk. & Curt. is given as a synonym of this species by Lloyd (114, p. 146), and the description certainly bears out this disposition of the name.

37. POLYPORUS MUTABILIS Berk. & Curt.

Ann. and Mag. Nat. Hist. II, 12: 433. 1853

(Figs. 231–232, 242, and Plate 131)

Sporophore laterally stipitate or attached by a narrowed stemlike base, spathulate to flabelliform, very rarely centrally stipitate; pileus thin and coriaceous when fresh, very rigid on drying, 1–12 × 1–6 × 0.1–0.3 cm., white or whitish when fresh, gray or straw color to light bay or brownish on drying, minutely silky-pubescent to glabrous or fibrillose-striate, sometimes hispidulous at the base, conspicuously zonate with slightly darker zones when fresh, these more inconspicuous on drying, the margin thin, entire to lobed, deflexed on drying; context thin, white, up to 2 mm. thick; pore surface white, becoming yellowish or isabelline on drying, sometimes with a silky luster, the tubes up to 1.5 mm. long, the mouths barely visible to the unaided eye, angular, thin-walled, entire, averaging 6–8 per mm.; stem usually lateral, usually distinct, finely pubescent or tomentose, concolorous, up to 4 cm. long, 1–6 mm. thick; spores ellipsoid to broadly ellipsoid, smooth, hyaline, 3–4.5 × 2.5–3 μ; cystidia none; hyphae closely compacted, thin-walled, flexuous, with very occasional cross walls and conspicuous clamps, mostly 4–6 μ in diameter or a few narrower.

HABITAT: On dead wood, noted on *Nyssa, Quercus, Salix,* and *Taxodium.*

DISTRIBUTION: Specimens have been examined from Del., Ga., Fla., Ala., La., Tenn., Ky., Ind., Ill., Mo., and Ark.

ILLUSTRATIONS: Lloyd, Synop. Stip. Polyp., fig. 446.

In general appearance this species sometimes approaches *Polyporus Drummondii,* but it is more distinctly stipitate; the hyphae seem to offer an excellent diagnostic feature. *P. Ravenelii* Berk. & Curt. is given as a synonym by Lloyd (114, p. 147).

38. POLYPORUS TRICHOLOMA Mont.
Ann. Sci. Nat. Bot. II, 8: 365. 1837
(Figs. 209–211 and Plate 132)

Sporophore centrally stipitate, tough when fresh, rigid when dry; pileus circular, 1–4 cm. broad, 0.5–3 mm. thick, convex and umbilicate, white or yellowish when fresh, straw color to ochraceous or ochraceous bay on drying, glabrous, sometimes slightly radiate-lineate on drying, azonate, the margin thin, beautifully and densely ciliate with hairs up to 2 mm. long or becoming glabrous, usually inflexed on drying; context white, up to 1.5 mm. thick; pore surface white to yellowish, the tubes up to 1 mm. long, the mouths angular, thin-walled, entire, averaging 3–6 per mm., visible to the unaided eye, somewhat decurrent on the stem; stem central, isabelline or pale brown, glabrous or minutely pubescent, 1–5 $\times$ 0.1–0.2 cm.; spores cylindric, straight, hyaline, 6–9 $\times$ 2.5–3.5 μ; cystidia none; hyphal pegs present; hyphae very irregular, some large ones 5–8 μ in diameter, collapsed, thin-walled, with attenuate branches, and many smaller ones 2.5–4 μ in diameter, with cross walls and clamps very rare, a few very large irregular hyphae with short cells, up to 20 μ in diameter. (Compare no. 52, *Polyporus arcularius.*)

HABITAT: On dead wood of deciduous trees.

DISTRIBUTION: Specimens have been examined only from Texas.

ILLUSTRATIONS: Lloyd, Synop. Stip. Polyp., fig. 466.

The pileus is usually the color of that of *Pholiota marginella* Peck and *P. marginata* Batsch ex Fries on drying, but is occasionally paler. Sometimes the cilia completely disappear from the margin of the pileus. The plants in general resemble *Polyporus arcularius*, but are typically smaller and have much smaller pores. *Polyporus Tricholoma* is a common species in tropical America and probably occurs in all the Gulf States.

6b. *Pores averaging less than 3 per mm.*

39. POLYPORUS SQUAMOSUS Micheli ex Fries

Syst. Myc. 1: 343. 1821

(Figs. 204–205 and Plate 132)

Agaricus squamosus Micheli, Nov. Plant. Gen., p. 118. 1729.
Agaricus squamosus Huds., Flora Angl., 2d ed., p. 614. 1778.
Polyporus caudicinus Scop. ex Murr., Jour. Mycol. 9: 89. 1903.

Sporophore short-stipitate or almost sessile, single or in imbricate clusters, somewhat fleshy-tough and watery when fresh, rigid when dry; pileus 6–30 cm. broad, 0.5–4 cm. thick, subcircular to reniform, plane to somewhat centrally depressed, whitish to dingy yellowish or brownish, clothed with small imbricate or larger appressed brownish scales or scalelike spots; context white, 0.5–3.5 cm. thick, soft-corky on drying; pore surface white or yellowish, the tubes 2–8 mm. long, decurrent, the mouths large and angular, 1–2.5 mm. wide or, rarely, much smaller and less than 1 mm., thin-walled and entire; stem lateral or occasionally subcentral, often rudimentary, black at the base where well developed, reticulate above, 1–5 cm. long, 1–4 cm. thick; spores elongate, smooth, hyaline, 10–15(–18) × 4–6 μ; basidia 45–55 × 6–8 μ; cystidia none; hyphae highly characteristic, non-staining, having a central enlarged section with very thick walls and tapering strongly (and often branched) at both ends, with no cross walls or clamps, 10–21 μ in diameter in the middle region, 3–10 μ in diameter in the tapering portion. (Compare no. 41, *Polyporus fagicola.*)

HABITAT: Growing from wounds in living deciduous trees or, rarely, on logs or stumps, noted on *Acer, Aesculus, Betula, Celtis, Liriodendron, Populus, Salix, Tilia, Ulmus,* and *Umbellularia.*

DISTRIBUTION: Specimens have been examined from Me., Vt., Mass., Conn., N.Y., Pa., N.J., Md., N.C., Ky., Ohio, Ill., Mich., Wis., Iowa, Nebr., and Colo.; in Canada from Quebec, Ontario, and

Manitoba; also reported from Tenn. (Hesler [71]), Kans. (Bartholo-mew [4]), Ark. (Swartz [212]), and W. Va., Mo., and Mont. (Graff [59]).

ILLUSTRATIONS: Bresadola, Fungi Trid. II: pl. 133; Clements, Minn. Mushrooms, fig. 60; Duggar, Fungous Dis. Plants, figs. 223–224; Hard, Mushrooms, fig. 325; Hesler, Tenn. Acad. Sci. Jour. 4: fig. 2; Jaccottet, Champ. Nature, pl. 56 (*pars*); Lloyd, Photo. Amer. Fungi, pl. 5; Neuman, Wis. Geol. and Nat. Hist. Survey Bul. 33: pl. 14, fig. 51, and pl. 15, fig. 51a; Schaeffer, Fung. Bavar., pls. 101–102; Shope, Mo. Bot. Gard. Ann. 18: pl. 29, figs. 1–2; Stevens, Fungi Plant Dis., fig. 301.

This species is easily recognized by the habit, the habitat, the large scales on the pileus, and the large pores. The hyphae that are described above seem to occur only in the large robust specimens of this species. Sporophores of smaller stature, intermediate be-tween the large ones of this species and those of *Polyporus fagicola*, have hyphae of an intermediate type. *P. caudicinus* Scop. ex Murr. is said to be an earlier name for the species. Clements (34) gives a secondhand report of specimens growing on the ground in Minnesota and attaining a width of seven feet and a weight of forty pounds. Graff (59) discusses the synonymy and points out that Micheli rather than Hudson was the originator of the specific name. He also reduces *P. pennsylvanicus* and *P. fagicola* to the status of varieties of *P. squamosus*, but treats them as separate varieties. I can see no sufficient grounds for keeping these two American species separate from each other, even as varieties. Whether one considers them jointly as a variety of *P. squamosus* or keeps them as a separate species (*P. fagicola*), as is done here, is a matter of personal choice. In either event, the relationship is probably close.

40. POLYPORUS McMURPHYI Murr.

Western Polypores, p. 12. 1915

(Fig. 317 and Plate 130)

Sporophore centrally or excentrically stipitate; pileus circular, convex, 5–7 × 0.5–1 cm., yellowish brown, the center scaly with erect fibrillose scales that may become appressed as the pileus weath-ers, the margin appressed-scaly; context white, 3–8 mm. thick; pore surface white, the tubes decurrent on the stem, 3–6 mm. long, the mouths angular or faveolate, decidedly denticulate-fimbriate, averaging 1–2 per mm.; stem central or excentric, terete, equal, solid, white or whitish, pitted-reticulate with the decurrent pores, 2–4 cm. long, 1–1.5 cm. thick; spores cylindric or cylindric-elliptic, smooth, hyaline, 10–15 × 4.5–6 μ; basidia 7–8 μ in diameter; cystidia none; hyphae flexuous, considerably branched, some with thickened walls, with no cross walls or clamps, 2.5–8 μ in diameter. (Compare no. 20, *Polyporus decurrens*, and no. 41, *P. fagicola*.)

HABITAT: On dead wood of deciduous trees (*Alnus*) or on the ground and probably growing from buried wood.

DISTRIBUTION: Specimens have been examined only from Calif.

The hymenial characters are exact counterparts of those of *Polyporus fagicola*, but the species differs in being decidedly scaly, with erect scales. *P. decurrens* is also a close relative. My drawings of the spores of *P. McMurphyi* are from a specimen preserved for a time in alcohol, then dried. Some of the spores have a rough, reticulated appearance that was probably brought on by this treatment.

41. POLYPORUS FAGICOLA Murr.

Torreya 6: 35. 1906

(Figs. 325, 560, and Plate 129)

Polyporus pennsylvanicus Sumstine, Jour. Mycol. 13: 137. 1907.

Sporophore stipitate; pileus soft and fleshy, or fleshy-tough, drying rigid and fragile, circular, depressed or umbilicate, 4–12(–20) cm. broad, 0.2–0.5 cm. thick, pale tan or ochraceous buff, glabrous, or with small tufts of hairlike scales, or more rarely with more conspicuous appressed scales, often slightly radiate-rugose; context white, rather fragile when dry, 2–4 mm. thick, with a sweet odor or odorless; pore surface white, yellowish in age or on drying, the tubes decurrent or long-decurrent on the stem, 2–4 mm. long, the mouths angular, about 1 mm. long, not quite so broad, denticulate; stem central or excentric, pallid, somewhat short-hispid, becoming glabrous, 2–5 cm. long, 0.4–1 cm. thick; spores oblong-elliptic or cylindric, smooth, hyaline, 10–14 × 4–5.5 μ; cystidia none, but with large peglike tufts of hyphae projecting into the pores from the walls of the tubes, 60–100 × 30 μ; hyphae nearly simple, thin-walled, often contorted, with some cross walls and clamps, 4–8(–12) μ in diameter. (Compare no. 1, *Favolus alveolaris*, and no. 39, *Polyporus squamosus*.)

HABITAT: On old logs of deciduous trees, noted on *Acer, Fagus,* and *Platanus.*

DISTRIBUTION: Specimens have been examined from Me., Vt., N.Y., Pa., Ohio, and Mich.; in Canada from Nova Scotia and Quebec.

ILLUSTRATIONS: Lowe, Mich. Acad. Sci. Arts and Letters Papers 9: pl. 15, figs. 3–4.

Some investigators (Graff [59] and Lowe [125]) have held that this plant is a form or variety of *Polyporus squamosus* and, moreover, that it is distinct from *P. pennsylvanicus.* But, as usually collected, it is much smaller and thinner and lacks the scaliness of *P. squamosus.* However, in the herbarium of Columbia University there is a collection from Edgewater, New York, on *Celtis occidentalis,* made by Orton and Thurston in 1917, which consists of one large well-developed specimen typical of *P. squamosus* and one small specimen typical of *P. fagicola.* In another box there is a large specimen fairly typical of *P. fagicola;* it is practically glabrous, though with a slightly appressed scaliness just at the center, and 20 cm. in diameter, and it has the thin pileus and the fragile pores of *P. fagicola.* This specimen was collected by E. L. Nixon in New York, in 1917.

Polyporus Boucheanus (Klotzsch) Fries seems to be a similar species—in fact, it would appear to be identical, but I have seen no specimens. A number of other species are described as having the large spores and the large pores of *P. squamosus,* but as differing in stature, the amount of scaliness on the pileus, the presence of black on the stem, the hairiness of the stem, and so on; all are probably in this species complex, and their interpretation is a matter of personal opinion.

The American species has sometimes been referred to *Polyporus pallidus* Schul. & Kalchbr., but Kalchbrenner's illustration (92, pl. 38, fig. 2) shows a plant with a black stem and larger, longer, and more irregular tubes, so that I am not certain as to its relationship. *P. Rostkowii* Fries is even more distinct in my opinion, not only in the black stem but also in the size, having the dimensions of a well-developed specimen of *P. squamosus.* However, in view of the intergrading specimens mentioned above, it might represent one form of the present species. There is a possibility that our plants should be referred to *P. lentus* Berk., which seems not to be a well-known species in Europe.

Polyporus fagicola is evidently a rare species, usually growing singly or in twos. The fleshy-tough texture, the small size, and the large spores and pores are its distinctive characteristics. Dried specimens have some resemblance to *P. arcularius*, from which they may be separated by the strongly decurrent tubes. Small specimens can be confused with *Favolus alveolaris*, but the stem is more central and better developed and the pileus never has the red coloration characteristic of that species. The relation of *P. McMurphyi* of the Pacific Coast to this species and to its forms that grade toward *P. squamosus* needs to be investigated.

42. POLYPORUS SCROBICULATUS Overh.

Mycologia 33: 91. 1941
(Figs. 645–646)

Sporophore substipitate; pileus 2–4 cm. in diameter or confluent to 7 cm., thin and pliant, bending double without breaking, the individual pilei varying from circular to flabelliform, white, becoming slightly yellowish on drying, the surface uneven and more or less radiately ridged, glabrous or finely velutinous, the margin thin, sometimes drying cartilaginous or resinous; context white, scarcely more than 1 mm. thick, drying rather fragile, not fibrous; pore surface white, drying somewhat yellowish, the tubes 1–2 mm. long, the mouths angular, thin-walled, quite uneven and irregular, averaging 1.5–4 per mm.; stems not well developed, usually coalesced at the base, white, glabrous, not more than 1 cm. long, tapering downward and expanding upward into the pileus; spores ellipsoid or somewhat elongate-ellipsoid, smooth, hyaline, 4–6 × 3–4 μ; cystidia none; hyphae rather flaccid, mainly thin-walled, with occasional cross walls but no clamps, 3–5 μ in diameter.

HABITAT: On dead areas in living root of *Quercus*.

DISTRIBUTION: Specimens have been examined only from the type locality, Huntington Co., Pa.

ILLUSTRATIONS: Overholts, Mycologia 33: 92, figs. 2–3.

This rather striking species seems to have no near relatives. One can duplicate the external appearance of the sporophore in a number of species, but in each instance the spores are a distinctive factor. Perhaps the closest resemblance is to a substipitate form of

Polyporus pubescens. The stem is too well developed for the plant to be a substipitate form such as one occasionally finds in normally sessile species growing on the top surface of their substratum. The texture is more that of the *P. pargamenus–P. pubescens* group than of the more fragile species of the *P. albellus* group. The plant has some resemblance to unusually well-developed specimens of *P. semi-supinus,* but the texture and, especially, the spores are different.

43. POLYPORUS FIMBRIATUS Fries

Linnaea 5: 520. 1830

(Fig. 169 and Plate 129)

Sporophore caespitose-multiplex in rosette-like clusters up to 10 cm. broad but usually smaller, with a central point of attachment, or growing more sessile and imbricate; pilei spathulate or flabelliform, 0.8–3 cm. broad, 1–2 mm. thick, white or whitish when fresh, yellow or isabelline on drying, sometimes somewhat zonate, with a few darker zones, very finely pubescent or becoming glabrate and some-what lineate-striate, the margin typically fimbriate but sometimes entire; context white, fibrous, less than 0.5 mm. thick; pore surface white to yellowish, usually hydnoid but poroid where best developed, the tubes more or less linearly arranged, always less than 1 mm. long, the mouths radially elongate, dentate, averaging 2–3 per mm., or in hydnoid specimens the teeth varying from almost cylindric to strongly flattened and linearly arranged; spores broadly ellipsoid or subglobose, smooth, hyaline, 4.5–5.5 × 3.5–4 μ; cystidia none; hyphae of the suprahymenial tissue loosely interwoven, considerably branched, thin-walled, with rather frequent cross walls but no clamps, 3.5–7 μ in diameter.

HABITAT: On dead wood.

DISTRIBUTION: Specimens have been examined from Ala. and La.

ILLUSTRATIONS: Lloyd, Synop. Stip. Polyp., fig. 453.

Collections of this species have been referred in the past to *Polyporus Drummondii* and *P. armenicolor.* From these it can be separated in its poroid form by the lighter color of the pileus, by the lack of zonation, and, microscopically, by the hyphae, which are septate and somewhat branched. In *P. Drummondii* the hyphae are aseptate, and practically simple; in addition, their walls are thickened, often to the exclusion of the cell lumen. *P. fimbriatus* differs from *P. tenuis* in its spores and in the tendency of the hymenium to show a hydnoid appearance, even in the best-developed specimens.

Generally the hymenial configuration is hydnoid, and this species has been variously referred to *Polyporus, Hydnum,* and *Thelephora.* Sometimes, though rarely, the teeth are practically cylindric; most often they are flattened as in *Irpex*; in but one collection have I seen a distinctly poroid hymenium.

Hydnum multifidum (Klotzsch) Henn. is this species, as is revealed by the excellent description given by Hennings (*Bot. Jahrb.* **17:** 493. 1893) when he transferred the species from *Thelephora,* where it was originally described by Klotzsch.

5b. *Pileus colored*
    6a. *Pores averaging 3 or more per mm.* (see also *Polyporus Rhoadsii,* p. 428)

44. POLYPORUS PICIPES Fries

Epicr. Syst. Myc., p. 440. 1836–1838
(Figs. 196–197, 601, 650–655, and Plate 131)

Polyporus fissus Berk., London Jour. Bot. **6:** 318. 1847.

Sporophore stipitate, leathery when fresh, rigid on drying; pileus thin, usually circular or subcircular, convex to depressed or infundibuliform, 4–20 cm. broad, 1–8 mm. thick, glabrous, chestnut-brown, hazel, or reddish brown or becoming entirely black in old specimens, the center usually darker-colored than the very thin, often lobed margin; context white or pallid, usually pale brown in dried specimens, 1–7 mm. thick; pore surface white to brownish or tan, the tubes up to 2 mm. long, somewhat decurrent, the mouths very minute, circular to somewhat angular, averaging 5–7 per mm., the walls rather thick and entire; stem central or excentric, black throughout or on the lower half, glabrous, 1–6 cm. long, 0.4–1.5 cm. thick; spores cylindric-elliptic or short-cylindric, smooth, hyaline, 6–8 $\times$ 3–4 μ; cystidia none; hyphal pegs present, rather rare, very short conoidal; hyphae much branched, some of the branches attenuate, some of the main hyphae wavy-walled and slightly thickened, with no cross walls or clamps, 5–7(–12) μ in diameter, but most not more than 4 μ in diameter. (Compare no. 45, *Polyporus elegans,* and no. 46, *P. varius.*)

Habitat: On stumps and logs, usually of deciduous trees, noted on *Acer, Alnus, Betula, Fraxinus, Juglans, Liriodendron, Populus, Pyrus, Quercus, Salix,* and *Ulmus*; occasionally on wood of coniferous trees, noted on *Abies, Picea, Pinus,* and *Thuja*; reported also on *Fagus* (Vt., Spaulding [209]).

Distribution: Specimens have been examined from Me., N.H., Vt., Mass., Conn., N.Y., Pa., D.C., W. Va., N.C., Ala., Tenn., Ky., Ohio, Ind., Ill., Mich., Iowa, Mo., Mont., Idaho, Ore., Wash., Calif., and Alaska; in Canada from Nova Scotia, Quebec, Ontario, Manitoba, and British Columbia; reported from Md. (Stevenson and Ermold [211]), Wis. (Dodge [40]), Kans. (Bartholomew [4]), and Ark. (Swartz [212]).

Illustrations: Batsch, Elench. Fung., pl. 25, fig. 129 (as *Boletus perennis*); Hard, Mushrooms, fig. 319; Moffatt, Chicago Acad. Sci. Nat. Hist. Survey Bul. 7, 1: pl. 12, fig. 2; Neuman, Wis. Geol. and Nat. Hist. Survey Bul. 33: pl. 14, fig. 52.

As is pointed out under *Polyporus elegans*, no difficulty should be experienced in distinguishing that species from *P. picipes*. The spores of *P. picipes* are consistently shorter and broader and the hyphal pegs smaller; the sporophore is usually larger and dark bay to chestnut in color. The pores are so minute as to be almost or entirely invisible to the unaided eye. *P. varius*, though usually given specific rank, is closely related to this species and even more closely to *P. elegans*. It is thicker and smaller than *P. picipes* and usually has a shorter stem; the pores are somewhat larger, the pileus is not quite so glabrous and is typically more radiate-lineate, and the spores are considerably larger.

Polyporus picipes var. *castaneus* Lloyd is described from Oregon as a small chestnut-brown variety of this species. *P. fissus* Berk. is said to be a synonym.

45. Polyporus elegans Bull. ex Fries
Epicr. Syst. Myc., p. 440. 1836–1838
(Figs. 217–219, 233, and Plate 129)

Boletus elegans Bull., Herb. France, pl. 46. 1783/1784.

Sporophore stipitate, leathery when fresh, drying rigid; pileus circular to reniform, 1.5–7 cm. broad, 0.2–0.5(–1) cm. thick, pale tan to dull tan, weathering at times to almost white, pruinose to glabrous, often radiate-striate; context white or pallid, usually pale cinnamon in herbarium specimens, 1–3 mm. thick, homogeneous; pore surface gray to light bay, the tubes 1–3 mm. long, decurrent, the mouths angular, thin-walled, entire, averaging 4–5 per mm.; stem central to lateral, black at the base or on the lower half, pruinose or glabrous, 0.5–5(–8) cm. long, 0.2–0.6 cm. thick; spores cylindric, smooth, hyaline, 6–10 × 2.5–3.5 μ; cystidia none; hyphal pegs present, broadly conoidal; hyphae much branched, the tips considerably attenuate, thick-walled, with no cross walls or clamps, 2.5–4.5 μ in diameter. (Compare no. 44, *Polyporus picipes*, and no. 46, *P. varius*.)

HABITAT: On dead wood, usually of deciduous trees, noted on *Acer, Alnus, Betula, Carpinus, Fagus, Prunus, Quercus, Ribes, Salix,* and *Tilia*; rarely on wood of coniferous trees, noted on *Pinus*; reported on *Amelanchier* (Mont., Weir [227]), on *Populus* (Colo., Kauffman [102]), and on *Tsuga* (Idaho, Weir [223]).

DISTRIBUTION: Specimens have been examined from Me., N.H., Vt., Mass., Conn., N.Y., Pa., N.J., Del., Va., W. Va., N.C., Ala., Tenn., Ohio, Mich., Wis., Minn., N. Dak., Iowa, Nebr., Ariz., Utah, Colo., Mont., Idaho, Ore., Wash., Calif., and Alaska; in Canada from Nova Scotia, Quebec, Ontario, Manitoba, Alberta, and British Columbia; reported from Ky. (Kauffman [100]) and Ark. (Swartz [212]).

ILLUSTRATIONS: Bulliard, Herb. France, pl. 46; Lloyd, Myc. Notes 64: figs. 1833–1835; Overholts, Wash. Univ. Studies 3: pl. 1, fig. 1; Patouillard, Tab. Anal. Fung., fig. 137.

Figure 1835 of Lloyd's *Notes*, cited above, represents one extreme of the species, being too large to be at all typical. *Polyporus elegans* is a common species in the Eastern hardwood region, usually growing on small dead branches or twigs, whereas its relative, *P. picipes*, usually grows on logs and stumps. *P. elegans* ordinarily has a lighter-colored pileus, and is generally smaller than well-developed specimens of *P. picipes*. Usually the pileus is only 1–3 cm. in diameter. *P. elegans* and *P. varius* differ but little, except in size (see, however, the discussion under the description of *P. picipes*). The color of *P. elegans* is typically about "cinnamon-buff." In the Allegheny region birch is the most common substratum.

Polyporus trachypus Berk. & Mont., described from Ohio, is said to be referable here.

46. POLYPORUS VARIUS Fries

Syst. Myc. 1: 352. 1821

(Figs. 199–200, 222, and Plate 132)

Sporophore centrally to laterally stipitate, leathery when fresh, drying firm and rigid; pileus subreniform to subcircular, 5–12 cm. broad, 0.3–1 cm. thick, depressed or nearly plane, glabrous or young specimens slightly scurfy-tomentose, a shade of tan, golden tan, sordid tan, or very rarely chestnut-brown, fading somewhat lighter with weathering, azonate, usually with radiate narrow streakings or fleckings of a lighter color; context white or more often pale ochraceous, 2–10 mm. thick; pore surface white or yellowish to pale bay, the tubes 1–2 mm. long, the mouths angular, rather thin-walled at maturity, always entire, averaging 3–4 per mm.; stem lateral or subcentral, subequal or tapering down, often short and rudimentary, finely velvety to glabrous, entirely black or black below or in reduced forms black only at the point of attachment, 1–6 cm. long, 0.5–1.5 cm. thick; spores cylindric, smooth, hyaline, 7–12 × 3–4 μ; cystidia none; hyphal pegs present, rather conspicuous and well developed, conical; hyphae much branched, the branches attenuate, with no cross walls or clamps, the larger hyphae 3–6 μ in diameter. (Compare no. 44, *Polyporus picipes*, and no. 45, *P. elegans*.)

HABITAT: On dead wood of deciduous trees, noted on *Acer*, *Fagus*, *Populus*, *Prunus*, *Quercus*, and *Salix*; rarely on wood of coniferous trees, noted on *Abies* and *Picea*.

DISTRIBUTION: Specimens have been examined from N.H., Vt., Mass., N.Y., D.C., W. Va., N.C., Tenn., Mich., Minn., Mo., Utah, Colo., Wyo., Ore., Wash., and Calif.; in Canada from Nova Scotia, New Brunswick, Ontario, Manitoba, and Alberta; reported from Iowa (Wolf [234]).

ILLUSTRATIONS: Gillet, Champ. France 3: pl. 569 (72); Lucand, Fig. Peint. Champ. France, pl. 50 (as *Polyporus picipes*).

This species is closely related both to *Polyporus picipes* and to *P. elegans*. In size it is intermediate between the two or, most often, approaches the size of *P. elegans*. It differs from *P. picipes* in the thicker pileus and context, the pale bay or tan coloration rather than dark bay or chestnut, and the more pronounced hyphal pegs. It can usually be separated from *P. elegans* by the larger size, the thicker context, and, often, the peculiarly streaked pileus. The spores and other details of microscopic structure are as in *P. elegans*.

The species differs from *Polyporus melanopus* Fries in growing on wood above ground or just at the surface of the ground and in being of a more leathery consistency with a bay or chestnut pileus, whereas in that species the pileus is more fleshy-tough and avellaneous or hair-brown. *P. calceolus* Fries, as usually determined in herbaria, seems to belong here rather than with *P. elegans*.

47. Polyporus Blanchetianus Berk. & Mont.

Ann. Sci. Nat. Bot. III, 11: 238. 1849

(Fig. 198)

Sporophore laterally stipitate, rarely attached by a lateral point, very rigid and brittle when dry; pileus reniform to broadly spathulate, 1–5 cm. long and broad, 0.5–3(–5) mm. thick, tan to bright chestnut or dark vinaceous black, azonate, even or faintly striate, entirely glabrous or very minutely scabrous-pubescent at the base, the margin thin, entire; context white or cinnamon, with a black cuticular layer, 1–4 mm. thick; pore surface at first white, becoming gray to smoky black on drying, the tubes 0.5–2 mm. long, the mouths circular to subangular, powdery with age, rather thick-walled, averaging 6–7 per mm.; stem up to 1.5 cm. long, 1.5–4 mm. thick, blackish, glabrous or nearly so; spores cylindric, straight, hyaline, 6–8 × 2.5 μ; cystidia none; hyphal pegs present but rare, short conoidal; hyphae rather thick-walled, hyaline, the larger ones characteristically branched at wide angles, with no cross walls or clamps, 2–5 μ in diameter.

Habitat: On dead wood.

Distribution: Specimens have been examined only from Fla.

In rare instances the hymenium revives a second season. The species seems to be a thin, chestnut-colored, extreme variant of *Polyporus picipes*. Its uniformly small size and brighter-colored pileus render it rather distinct.

48. Polyporus virgatus Berk. & Curt.

Linnean Soc. Bot. Jour. 10: 304. 1868
(Fig. 212)

Sporophore stipitate, rigid, brittle, of light weight when dry; pileus more or less depressed at the center, subcircular, 3.5–10 cm. broad, the dried specimens rufous or chestnut in color, the cuticle separating into radial fibrillose lines exposing the context, glabrous over the unbroken cuticle; context cinnamon or pale brown, 4–10 mm. thick, punky when dry; pore surface discoloring on drying, the tubes 1–3 mm. long, the mouths angular, thin-walled, entire, averaging 3–4 per mm.; stem subcentral, equal, concolorous with pileus but darkening where handled, firm, 2.5 cm. long, about 1 cm. thick; spores not found; hyphae of short lengths, nearly hyaline, with no cross walls or clamps, much branched, the branches rapidly attenuate at their tips, the main hyphae 5–9 μ in diameter, the branches 3–5 μ in diameter at their bases; all parts of the dried plant quickly dark red then blackish where touched with KOH solution.

HABITAT: On dead wood of deciduous trees.

DISTRIBUTION: Specimens have been examined from Fla.

ILLUSTRATIONS: Lloyd, Synop. Stip. Polyp., fig. 468.

The description above is based on a specimen that was collected at Hogtown, Florida, by F. M. O'Byrne in 1911 and sent to me, and on three tropical collections in the New York Botanical Garden. No other than the Florida collection is known from the mainland of the United States. The specimens are entirely sterile, but the species is extremely well marked in the virgate chestnut-colored pileus, the pale-brown, soft (dry) context, the highly characteristic hyphae, and the color change in KOH. Its relations are with the *Polyporus picipes* group.

49. Polyporus pocula (Schw.) Berk. & Curt.

Amer. Acad. Arts and Sci. Proc. 4: 122. 1860
(Figs. 153, 545, 584, and Plate 131)

Sphaeria pocula Schw., Acad. Nat. Sci. Phila. Proc. 4, N.S.: 189. 1832.
Polyporus cupulaeformis Berk. & Curt., Grevillea 1: 38. 1872.
Porodisculus pendulus (Schw.) Murr., North Amer. Flora 9: 47. 1907.

Sporophore short-stipitate and pendent from dead branches or on the lateral surfaces of fallen trunks, coriaceous when fresh, rigid when dry; pileus 1–5 mm. broad, 1–3 mm. thick, whitish to brown, pruinose or mealy; context white, less than 1 mm. thick; pore surface whitish or brownish, the tubes not more than 0.5 mm. long, the mouths at first pruinose, circular, very minute, averaging 5–6 per mm.; stem dorsally attached, expanding into the pileus, pruinose, not more than 5 mm. long; spores allantoid, smooth, hyaline, 3–4 $\times$ 1 μ; basidia 2.5–4 μ in diameter; cystidia none; hyphae nearly simple, with much-thickened and highly gelatinized nonstaining walls and narrow staining lumina, with no cross walls or clamps, 3–5 μ in diameter.

HABITAT: Usually on branches or fallen trunks of dead chestnut (*Castanea*) or oak (*Quercus*), noted also on *Carya*, *Juglans*, *Prunus*, and *Rhus*; one collection on *Pinus Strobus*; reported by Murrill as "occasionally on red cedar."

DISTRIBUTION: Specimens have been examined from Mass., Conn., N.Y., Pa., N.J., Del., Va., W. Va., N.C., Ga., Fla., Ala., Tenn., Ohio, and Mo.; reported from S.C. (types of *Polyporus cupulaeformis*) and Iowa (Wolf [234]).

ILLUSTRATIONS: Lloyd, Myc. Notes, Polyp. Issue No. 3: fig. 369; *idem*, Myc. Notes 41: fig. 777; *idem*, Synop. Stip. Polyp., fig. 443.

This species looks like a small stipitate ascomycete, and in fact was originally described as a species of *Sphaeria*. It is our smallest polypore, easily recognized by its size, habit, and habitat. *Peziza pendula* Schw. is said to be an earlier name for the species. *Polyporus cupulaeformis* var. *leucotrophus* Peck is *Polyporus pocula* weathered white. I have never seen the collections on red cedar referred to by Murrill, but I once collected the species on a fallen white-pine branch. In the autumn of 1942 it was extremely common in the vicinity of Pennsylvania State College, in a wooded area where lumbering had been done the previous winter. Literally bushels of it could have been collected. It fruited in the greatest abandon on oak slash left by the lumbering operation, growing on everything, from branches four inches in diameter up to cull logs as much as eight and ten inches through.

50. POLYPORUS BETULINUS Bull. ex Fries

Syst. Myc. 1: 358. 1821

(Figs. 161–164, 577, and Plate 128)

Boletus betulinus Bull., Herb. France, pl. 312. 1787.
Piptoporus suberosus L. ex Murr., Jour. Mycol. 9: 94. 1903.

Sporophore sessile or attached by a lateral stemlike umbo or, rarely, pendent, fleshy-tough or corky when fresh, rigid and firm when dry; pileus 3–15 × 3–25 × 1–5(–10) cm., covered with a whitish, tan, brown, or smoky pellicle that often shows distinct pitting or reticulation, this pellicle disappearing with age and leaving the pileus white, smooth and glabrous or the pellicle slightly scurfy, the margin deflexed, inrolled and projecting downward beyond the pore surface; context white, 1–3.5 cm. thick, watery-tough when fresh, corky when dry; pore surface white, avellaneous with age, the tubes 2–8 mm. long, separating without difficulty in a smooth layer from the context in fresh specimens, the mouths circular or subangular, rather thick-walled, averaging 3–4 per mm., occasionally becoming quite dentate, but usually very smooth and entire; spores cylindric or allantoid, smooth, hyaline, 3.5–5 × 1–2 μ; cystidia and hyphal pegs none; hyphae somewhat branched, hyaline and nonstaining, a few of the smaller ones with cross walls and clamps, 2.5–5(–6) μ in diameter.

HABITAT: Growing only on living or dead birch trees.

DISTRIBUTION: Specimens have been examined from Me., N.H., Vt., Mass., Conn., N.Y., Pa., N.J., W. Va., N.C., Tenn., Mich., Wis., Minn., Iowa, and Wash.; in Canada from Nova Scotia, Quebec, Ontario, Manitoba, Alberta, and British Columbia; reported from Kans. (Bartholomew [4]) and from Mont. (Weir [227]).

ILLUSTRATIONS: Boyce, Forest Path., fig. 202; Hard, Mushrooms, fig. 337; Hubert, Outline Forest Path., fig. 91; Lloyd, Synop. Sect. Apus, figs. 631–632; Rankin, Man. Tree Dis., fig. 13; von Schrenk and Spaulding, U. S. Dept. Agr. Pl. Ind. Bul. 149: pl. 9; Sowerby, Col. Fig. English Fungi, pl. 212 (as *Boletus*); White, Conn. State Geol. and Nat. Hist. Survey Bul. 3: pl. 37.

The species reaches its best development in the cooler climate of New England and across the continent to Wisconsin and Minnesota.

Though it is common in the vicinity of New York City, it rarely occurs in central and southern Pennsylvania, even where the birches appear to thrive. It is one of the easiest of the pore fungi to identify because of the pale-brown upper surface of the pileus and the obtuse margin that projects downward beyond the general level of the pore surface. Occasionally oddities appear. At Albany there is a collection from Minnesota made by Mrs. M. W. Hill in 1913 in which the sporophores are pendulous and lack a pore surface, one specimen being bell-shaped, the other cucumber-shaped (see Fig. 163).

Boletus suberosus L. has been indicated as an earlier name for this plant.

Von Schrenk and Spaulding (219, pp. 51–52) imply that they have found this species on living birch trees, but I am convinced that it much more frequently inhabits trees already dead. In dead trees it causes a yellowish- or reddish-brown carbonizing decay that usually, if not always, begins in the sapwood and extends eventually into the center of the tree, although the trees in which the center is affected are likely to be ones that have not yet formed heartwood.

6b. *Pores averaging 3 or less per mm.*

51. POLYPORUS HIRTUS Quél.

Champ. Jura Vosg., p. 356. 1873

(Figs. 201–203, 574, and Plate 130)

Polyporus hispidellus Peck, N. Y. State Mus. Bul. 5, 25: 649. 1899.
Scutiger hispidellus (Peck) Murr., Western Polypores, p. 16. 1915.

Sporophore stipitate or substipitate, single, fleshy, drying rigid; pileus 4–15 cm. broad, or sometimes deformed and undersized, convex, 0.5–2 cm. thick, grayish brown or dark isabelline to smoky brown or seal-brown, clothed with short, stiff, erect hairs or these becoming compacted into a short stiff tomentum; context white, bitter, 0.3–2 cm. thick; pore surface white or cream-colored, drying yellowish; tubes 2–6 mm. long, the mouths subrotund, then angular or irregular, averaging 1–2 per mm., the dissepiments thin and becoming dentate or lacerate; stem typically lateral, occasionally nearly central, often irregular, short-hispid like the pileus when well-developed, 2–8 cm. long, 7–20 mm. thick; spores subfusiform or *Euglena*-shaped, smooth, hyaline, 12–17 × 4.5–6 μ; basidia 8–12 μ in diameter; cystidia none or not noteworthy; context hyphae irregular, flexuous, often contorted, and with irregular swellings, thin-walled, with cross walls and clamps, mostly 4–10 μ in diameter but up to 15 μ at the swellings; tramal hyphae 2–3 μ in diameter.

HABITAT: Around trees or stumps, attached to buried wood of coniferous trees, or on the roots of uptorn trees, noted on *Abies*, *Picea*, *Pseudotsuga*, and *Tsuga*; reported on *Thuja* (Mich., Kauffman [101]).

DISTRIBUTION: Specimens have been examined from N.Y., Mich., Colo., Idaho, Ore., Wash., and Calif.; in Canada from Quebec and British Columbia; reported from Wis. (Neuman [148]).

ILLUSTRATIONS: Lloyd, Synop. Stip. Polyp., fig. 426; Shope, Mo. Bot. Gard. Ann. 18: pl. 27, fig. 3.

This is a rare plant, of which a total of about a dozen collections have been examined. The spores are quite variable in size and shape; in immature stages they are short and broad. In dried specimens the bitter taste remains but usually cannot be detected until the material reaches the back of the mouth. Then it is as bitter as is *Fomes officinalis*.

The type specimen of *Polyporus hispidellus* Peck is well preserved at Albany and shows all the features of the European species. Murrill at first referred it in questionable synonymy with *P. radicatus*.

52. POLYPORUS ARCULARIUS Batsch ex Fries
Syst. Myc. 1: 342. 1821
(Figs. 206, 215–216, 553, and Plate 128)

Boletus arcularius Batsch, Elench. Fung., p. 97. 1783.
Polyporus arculariformis Murr., Torreya 4: 151. 1904.

Sporophore stipitate, fleshy-tough, drying rigid, reviving well after drying; pileus circular, convex to umbilicate or infundibuliform, 1–8 cm. broad, 1–4 mm. thick, golden brown, yellowish brown, or dark brown, squamulose, the margin often ciliate, involute on drying; context white, less than 2 mm. thick; pore surface white or yellowish, the tubes 1–2 mm. long, sometimes decurrent, the mouths angular, large, averaging about 0.5 × 1 mm.; stem central, yellowish brown or dark brown, fuscous-squamulose to glabrous, sometimes hispid at the base, 2–6 cm. long, 2–4 mm. thick; spores cylindric, smooth, hyaline, 7–11 × 2–3 μ; cystidia none; walls of the tubes provided with scattered columnar tufts of hyphae, 30–40 × 16–20 μ; hyphae very much branched and quite irregular, mostly 2–8 μ in diameter, the branches attenuate to whiplike extremities, often quite irregular and collapsed, apparently without clamps. (Compare no. 1, *Favolus alveolaris*, and no. 53, *Polyporus brumalis*.)

HABITAT: On dead wood of deciduous trees, occasionally growing from buried wood, noted on *Acer, Alnus, Carya, Castanea, Populus, Quercus,* and *Ulmus;* reported on *Betula, Carpinus, Fagus,* and *Tilia* (Mich., Kauffman [101]).

DISTRIBUTION: Specimens have been examined from Conn., N.Y., Pa., N.J., Del., D.C., Va., W. Va., N.C., S.C., Ga., Fla., Ala., La., Miss., Tenn., Ky., Ohio, Ind., Ill., Wis., S. Dak., Iowa, Mo., Kans., Nebr., Okla., Texas, N. Mex., Colo., Idaho, and Ore.; in Canada from Manitoba; reported from Md. (Stevenson and Ermold [211]), Mich. (Kauffman [101]), and Mont. (Weir [227]).

ILLUSTRATIONS: Hard, Mushrooms, fig. 336; McDougall, Mushrooms, opp. p. 116; Overholts, Wash. Univ. Studies 3: pl. 1, fig. 2; Shope, Mo. Bot. Gard. Ann. 18: pl. 24, figs. 5–6.

The diagnostic characters of this species include the small size, the centrally stipitate pileus that is brown and more or less squamulose, and the habit of fruiting in the spring months. The fungus seems to be typically a plant of the hardwood regions and occurs sparingly or not at all in mixed stands of deciduous and coniferous trees. Consequently it is most abundant through the Ohio and the Mississippi-Missouri River Valleys, seemingly without exhibiting much preference as to species among deciduous hosts. Collectors have not usually recorded substrata for this species, however, and the list above can certainly be greatly increased. Depauperate forms are sometimes found on small twigs and chips; these forms were designated *Polyporus arculariformis* by Murrill. The plant usually appears much earlier in the season than most of the epixylous pore fungi, and may be expected after the warm rains of May and June. The large angular or hexagonal pores, the yellowish-brown color, and the ciliate margin of the pileus separate it from *P. brumalis.* In addition, it is usually thinner and more umbilicate than that species.

Favolus Curtisii Berk. was described from North Carolina. Since the specific name was preoccupied in *Polyporus*, Murrill [138f] changed the name to *P. arculariellus*. The species has not been recognized since its original discovery, and Lloyd (114, p. 176) says that it is the late summer form of *P. arcularius*. *P. alveolarius* Bosc. ex Fries, described from South Carolina, is said by Lloyd to belong here.

The fungus is of little or no importance as a decay species.

53. POLYPORUS BRUMALIS Pers. ex Fries

Syst. Myc. 1: 348. 1821

(Figs. 213–214, 668, and Plate 128)

Boletus brumalis Pers., Mag. Bot. (Neues) 1: 107. 1794.
Polyporus Polyporus (Retz) Murr., Torrey Bot. Club Bul. 31: 33. 1904.

Sporophore stipitate, tough to somewhat leathery when fresh, drying rigid; pileus circular, convex or umbilicate, 1.5–5(–10) cm. broad, 0.2–0.4 cm. thick, sometimes subzoned, yellowish brown to dark brown, dark red-brown, or almost black, sometimes fading to very pale tan, in very early stages usually densely hirsute-hispid with short hairs, finally minutely hispid, scabrous, or punctate-scabrous to nearly glabrous; margin involute when young and on drying, only occasionally ciliate-fimbriate; context white, 2 mm. or less thick; pore surface whitish, the tubes 1–3 mm. long, usually slightly decurrent, the mouths circular and thick-walled, then angular and the walls thinner, averaging 2–3 per mm.; stem central or excentric, grayish or brownish, minutely hispid to glabrous, 2–3(–6) cm. long, 0.2–0.6 cm. thick; spores short-cylindric, smooth, hyaline, sometimes obliquely apiculate, 5–7 × 1.5–2.5 μ; cystidia none; walls of the tubes with occasional scattered columnar tufts of projecting hyphae; hyphae somewhat branched and the branches greatly attenuate (down to 2–3 μ in diameter), the walls partially thickened, with only occasional cross walls or clamps, 4–9 μ in diameter. (Compare no. 45, *Polyporus elegans*, and no. 52, *P. arcularius*.)

HABITAT: On dead wood, usually of deciduous trees, noted on *Acer, Alnus, Betula, Carpinus, Carya, Castanea, Fagus, Fraxinus, Ostrya, Populus, Prunus, Pyrus, Quercus, Robinia, Sassafras*, and *Tilia*; also noted on *Tsuga*; reported on *Ailanthus* (N.Y., Fairman [45]).

Distribution: Specimens have been examined from Me., N.H., Vt., Mass., Conn., N.Y., Pa., N.J., Del., D.C., W. Va., Tenn., Ky., Ohio, Ind., Wis., Iowa, and Minn.; in Canada from Nova Scotia, Newfoundland, Ontario, and Manitoba; reported from Mich. (Kauffman [105]), Kans. (Bartholomew [4]), Ark. (Swartz [212]), and Mont. (Weir [227]).

Illustrations: Atkinson, Mushrooms, fig. 186; Hard, Mushrooms, fig. 335; Murrill, Mycologia 10: pl. 6, fig. 3 (as *Polyporus Polyporus*); Neuman, Wis. Geol. and Nat. Hist. Survey. Bul. 33: pl. 13, fig. 47.

Throughout the birch region the plant is probably most abundant on that host, although it may be expected on dead wood of all kinds of deciduous trees. It may be found almost throughout the year, for it persists through the winter in good condition. Only rarely does the color approach that of *Polyporus arcularius*, its closest relative, and even then the specimens are usually easily distinguished by their smaller and less hexagonal pores. Well-developed specimens are generally dark because of the short hispid pubescence, but often, as this disappears, the pileus becomes lighter, approaching the light tan of *P. elegans*, which is glabrous at all stages. Dark livid-red specimens appear to have been segregated as *P. luridus* Berk. & Curt.; they can be separated from *P. picipes* by the hairiness of the pileus and the absence of black from the lower part of the stem. *P. dibaphus* Berk. & Curt. is given as a synonym by Lloyd, and the description bears out this disposition. Var. *reticulatus* Peck is a form with the stem apex slightly reticulated by the decurrent pores.

2b. *Sporophore sessile or effused-reflexed*
  3a. *Pileus usually rather thick, corky or fragile*
    4a. *Sporophore rufescent on bruising or drying* (see also *Tyromyces Newellianus*, p. 427)

54. Polyporus fragilis Fries

Elench. Fung., p. 86. 1828

(Figs. 142–143, 635, and Plate 130)

Spongipellis fragilis (Fries) Murr., Southern Polypores, p. 61. 1915.
Spongipellis sensibilis Murr., Mycologia 4: 93. 1912.

Sporophore sessile or broadly effused and narrowly reflexed, sometimes imbricate, soft and watery when fresh, in age somewhat tough and coriaceous, drying rigid and brittle; pileus 0–6 × 1–10 × 0.3–1.5 cm., at first white, becoming rufescent or pinkish red at maturity, discolored yellowish then rusty red where handled and sordid discolored or dark rufescent on drying, or, rarely, young specimens drying with the pileus only slightly discolored, covered with soft white fibers that become matted in age; context white, soon reddish yellow where exposed, discolored on drying, soft, fragile to firm in dried specimens, 2–12 mm. thick, no color change in KOH, taste mild; pore surface pure white but quickly yellow then rusty where handled, discolored on drying, the tubes 2–8 mm. long, the mouths angular to sinuous or daedaloid, rather thin-walled, entire or lacerate, averaging 2–4 per mm.; spores allantoid, smooth, hyaline, 4–5 × 1–1.5 μ; cystidia none; hyphal pegs not definite; hyphae flexuous, with thickened walls and very small staining lumina and with conspicuous clamps and cross walls, 3–6 μ in diameter. (Compare no. 55, *Polyporus lapponicus*, and no. 56, *P. mollis*.)

HABITAT: On dead wood of coniferous trees, noted on *Abies, Picea, Pinus, Pseudotsuga*, and *Tsuga*.

DISTRIBUTION: Specimens have been examined from Me., N.H., Mass., Conn., N.Y., Pa., D.C., Va., N.C., Tenn., Mich., Colo., Idaho, Ore., Wash., and Calif.; in Canada from Nova Scotia, New Brunswick, Quebec, Ontario, and British Columbia; reported from Wis. (Neuman [148]) and Mont. (Weir [227]).

ILLUSTRATIONS: Fries, Icones Sel. Hym., pl. 182, fig. 2; Lloyd, Synop. Apus Polyp., fig. 661 (pore surface); Shope, Mo. Bot. Gard. Ann. 18: pl. 24, fig. 4.

Though somewhat similar to *Polyporus mollis*, *P. fragilis* is distinct, notwithstanding the synonymy by Baxter (11h, p. 175) to the contrary, in having a permanently pubescent pileus and in having clamps on the context hyphae. In addition, *P. mollis* is often a much larger species. *P. fragilis* differs from *P. lapponicus* in the allantoid and smaller spores and in the covering of the pileus, as well as in the entire absence of cystidia. All three of these species grow only on wood of coniferous trees and become rufescent where handled and on drying. From my studies of the types of *Spongipellis sensibilis* Murr. and of specimens sent by S. M. Zeller I do not feel inclined to recognize it as distinct from *P. fragilis*. The only difference that I have yet seen is in the very soft tomentose covering of the pileus as opposed to the more silky-fibrillose covering in *P. fragilis*. Hyphal pegs are abundant in the type specimens of *S. sensibilis*.

Fresh sporophores of *Polyporus fragilis* are very sensitive to contact, especially on the pore surface, changing to yellowish brown almost immediately where touched. In 1933 I watched an extensive imbricate series of sporophores develop on an old *Tsuga* stump in central Pennsylvania. Appearing about September 1 as a soft watery mass distilling drops of water from the surface, the pileus became slightly rufescent in about two weeks and readily discolored where handled, the pore surface changing to a dirty yellowish. By October 8 the sporophores were fully matured and some had begun to disintegrate because of the attacks of insects. At this stage the pore surface was still nearly white, and it discolored yellowish brown or yellowish red where handled, while the pileus had naturally become entirely rusty red. These specimens were brought into the laboratory and left exposed in the collecting basket overnight. The next day a distinctly sweet odor was noticeable, similar to that of *Polyporus albellus* and *P. galactinus*.

Peck's determinations of *Polyporus Weinmanni* are referable here.

The fungus is responsible for a brown carbonizing decay of the wood substratum.

55. POLYPORUS LAPPONICUS Rom.
Arkiv för Bot. 11, 3: 17. 1912
(Figs. 139–141 and Plate 130)

Polyporus ursinus Lloyd, Synop. Apus, p. 319. 1915. (Not *P. ursinus* Link.)

Sporophore sessile, dimidiate or laterally connate, heavy and watery-tough when fresh, rigid and hard on drying; pileus 2–10 × 2–14 × 0.7–3 cm., sometimes steep in front, at first with a very distinct, upright, short, strigose-tomentose covering that dries rough, sometimes costate-ribbed on the margin or, rarely, to the base, white or grayish when fresh, rufescent where handled, and uniformly fawn-colored to cinnamon, very pale tawny, or red-brown in age or on drying, azonate, the margin often deflexed; context soft, watery, white, sometimes drying with a pinkish tinge, 0.5–2.5 cm. thick, in well-developed specimens becoming quite hard on drying; pore surface white or flesh-colored, or discolored reddish when old or in handling, darkening on drying, the tubes 2–5 mm. long, the mouths angular to somewhat sinuous, rather thin-walled, entire or lacerate and frequently ciliate, averaging 2–3 per mm., sometimes seriately arranged; spores elongate, slightly pointed at the ends, hyaline, 7–11 × 2.5–3.5 μ; cystidia present, sometimes rather abundant and sometimes rare, cylindric and obtuse or somewhat flask-shaped and slightly pointed at the end, sometimes slightly capitate-incrusted at the apex, sometimes heavily incrusted, the incrustation dissolving in KOH, thick-walled, 4–9 μ in diameter, projecting up to 20 μ; hyphal pegs present but rare, cylindric; hyphae very thick-walled, flexuous, hyaline, with conspicuous clamps and cross walls, mostly 5–10 μ in diameter. (Compare no. 54, *Polyporus fragilis*, and no. 56, *P. mollis*.)

HABITAT: On dead wood of coniferous trees, noted on *Larix*, *Picea*, *Pinus*, *Pseudotsuga*, *Thuja*, and *Tsuga*.

DISTRIBUTION: Specimens have been examined from N.H., Vt., N.Y., Mich., Minn., Colo., Wyo., Mont., Idaho, and Ore.; in Canada from Quebec, Ontario, Manitoba, and British Columbia.

ILLUSTRATIONS: Lloyd, Synop. Apus, figs. 659–660; Shope, Mo. Bot. Gard. Ann. 18: pl. 19, figs. 5–8 (as *Polyporus ursinus*).

This species is distinct from *Polyporus fragilis* and *P. mollis* in the more hispid pubescence, the usually larger size, the very different spores, and the cystidia. In addition, the hyphae of the context are larger and more irregular. The species has no other near relatives. Though long unrecognized, it seems to be a rather common fungus in the northern forests and in the higher altitudes of the Rocky Mountains.

56. POLYPORUS MOLLIS Pers. ex Fries

Syst. Myc. 1: 360. 1821

(Figs. 137–138 and Plate 130)

Boletus mollis Pers., Obs. Myc. 1: 22. 1796.
Tyromyces Smallii Murr., North Amer. Flora 9: 32. 1907.
Polyporus Pini-ponderosae Long, N. Mex. Chapt. Phi Kappa Phi Papers 1: 3. 1917.

Sporophore typically sessile and decurrent on the substratum, sometimes nearly resupinate on vertical surfaces, fleshy-tough and watery when fresh, rigid when dry; pileus dimidiate to laterally elongate, 3–10 × 3–8 × 1.5–4 cm., triangular in section, white when young and fresh, becoming pinkish or rufescent with age or where handled, apparently at times pinkish red from the first, and often blackish and resinous on drying, azonate, sparingly tomentose at first, finally nearly or quite glabrous with age and sometimes almost pelliculose; context concolorous with pileus, corky or soft-corky or somewhat rubbery when dry, 0.5–2 cm. thick; pore surface rufescent in mature plants and sordid-rufescent or dark pinkish brown on drying, the tubes 3–10 mm. long, the mouths angular, thin-walled, entire or somewhat dentate, averaging 3–4 per mm.; spores allantoid, smooth, hyaline, 4–6 × 1.5–2 μ; cystidia none; hyphal pegs lacking; hyphae thick-walled, hyaline, sparingly branched, with a few inconspicuous cross walls but no clamps, 3–8 μ in diameter. (Compare no. 54, *Polyporus fragilis*, and no. 55, *P. lapponicus*.)

HABITAT: On dead wood of coniferous trees, noted only on *Abies*, *Picea*, *Pinus*, and *Pseudotsuga*.

DISTRIBUTION: Specimens have been examined from N.H., Fla., Ala., La., Mich., Ark., Texas, N. Mex., Colo., Wyo., Idaho, Ore., Wash., and Calif.; in Canada from Quebec; reported from N.Y. (Lowe [124]).

ILLUSTRATIONS: Fries, Icones Sel. Hym., pl. 182, fig. 3.

This species has been much discussed, but I am now convinced that we have in this country the plant portrayed in Fries's *Icones*, although the color of the pileus is too bright in that publication. The pileus is glabrous with age and the hyphae lack clamps. Sometimes in crushed mounts the hyphae are mixed with dark resinous matter, which is separate, however, from the hyphae themselves. These characters distinguish the species quite well from *Polyporus fragilis*, its close relative. In addition, the pileus is thicker, more triangular in section, and less fragile. The pore surface regularly dries rufescent and usually pinkish brown; in old plants it dries somewhat darker. The color assumed by the pileus varies still more. If young plants are dried without handling there may not be much color change, only an ashen color developing, except perhaps on the margin; older plants become decidedly rufescent. There is little question but that the species named by Murrill and by Long belong here.

Polyporus mollis has been found in association with a brown carbonizing decay of the wood.

57. Polyporus transmutans Overh.

Mycologia 44: 226. 1952

Sporophore sessile; pileus 2.5–5 × 3–6 × 1–2 cm., soft and spongy when fresh, not bending without breaking, drying firm but more or less waxy and not brittle, the upper surface azonate, white to very pale buff, drying dark rufescent brown and discoloring dark rufescent on handling, soft-tomentose; context 0.5–1 cm. thick, white, soft, drying discolored but not hard, zonate in both fresh and dried condition, the odor strongly fungoid, the taste bitter; pore surface creamy to very pale buff, the tubes 3–5 mm. long, the mouths rufescent or brownish with a tinge of reddish or lavender where handled and in drying, rather thick-walled, subangular, 2–2.5 per mm.; spores oblong or short-cylindric, smooth, hyaline, 5–7 × 3–3.5 μ; cystidia none; [hyphae thin-walled, rarely branched, with clamp .connections, 4–6 μ in diameter—J.L.L.].

HABITAT AND DISTRIBUTION: On dead *Prunus serotina*. Type collected near Westline, McKean Co., Pa., Aug. 9, 1940 (Overholts Herbarium No. 22971).

This species has some of the characters of *Polyporus fissilis*, but is a smaller species with different spores. The cultural characters are almost identical with those of *P. subcartilagineus*, but the species is more definitely pileate and the context is much thicker.

4b. *Sporophore not rufescent*
    5a. *Spores cylindrical to ellipsoid*
        6a. *Spores straight*
            7a. *Spores usually 5 μ or more long*

58. Polyporus anceps Peck

Torrey Bot. Club Bul. 22: 207. 1895

(Figs. 87, 662, and Plate 128)

Tyromyces anceps (Peck) Murr., North Amer. Flora 9: 35. 1907.
Tyromyces Ellisianus Murr., North Amer. Flora 9: 34. 1907.
Polyporus Ellisianus (Murr.) Sacc. & Trott., Syll. Fung. 21: 281. 1912.

Sporophore sessile and often somewhat imbricate or more often effused-reflexed or entirely resupinate, watery-tough to corky when fresh, compact and rigid when dry, reviving; pileus 0–2 × 1–7 × 0.5–2 cm., white, concolorous on drying or becoming pale tan or brownish discolored, glabrous or very finely velvety-tomentose, rarely with a slight evidence of a thin cuticle on drying, azonate; context white, tough when fresh, firm and hard on drying, 4–10 mm. thick, bitter; pore surface white, or drying gray or yellowish, the tubes 2–7 mm. long, the mouths angular, rather thin-walled but entire, averaging 4–5 per mm.; spores cylindric, smooth, hyaline, 7–10 $\times$ 2–3 μ; basidia 7–9 μ in diameter; cystidia none; hyphal pegs occasional, short-conoidal; hyphae dendritically branched (especially in the walls of the tubes), the larger ones 4–7.5 μ in diameter and abruptly terminating in a number of smaller ones that rapidly narrow down to whiplike extremities, the walls completely thickened throughout, non-staining, with clamps present but rare.

HABITAT: On dead wood of coniferous trees, noted on *Abies*, *Picea*, *Pinus*, *Pseudotsuga*, *Thuja*, and *Tsuga*; reported on *Larix* (Mont., Weir [227]).

DISTRIBUTION: Specimens have been examined from Me., N.H., Mass., Conn., N.Y., Pa., N.J., Md., Va., La., Miss., Mich., Wis., Minn., S. Dak., Nebr., N. Mex., Ariz., Colo., Mont., Idaho, Ore., Wash., and Calif.; in Canada from Quebec, Ontario, and British Columbia; reported from Vt. (Spaulding [209]) and Manitoba (Bisby *et al.* [12]).

ILLUSTRATIONS: Kauffman, Mycologia 18: pl. 5.

Demonstration of the dendritically branched hyphae of the tube walls and context is the only safe criterion for this species.

Tyromyces Ellisianus Murr. was described from specimens collected in New Jersey on dead pine trunks. Comparison of the descriptions of the two species as given by Murrill would indicate a conspicuous difference in the matter of zonation of the pileus, but a comparison of the type specimens scarcely substantiates such a view, and no other characters seem available for purposes of separation. Though the types of *Polyporus anceps* are nearly pure white, whereas traces of almost bay appear in those of *T. Ellisianus*, that is a question of age and of drying, and this difference is not borne out by other collections. The spores of the two species are identical (but not globose, 4 or 5 μ, as stated by Murrill [139]), and the peculiar branching of the hyphae, best seen in mounts from the walls of the tubes but usually distinct in the context also, is the same and not exactly matched by any other white species. This character is duplicated in the hyphae of pure cultures, so that *P. anceps* is easily distinguished in culture. Weir's determinations of *P. stypticus* Fries belong here.

This species produces a decay of both heartwood and sapwood that has been designated "western red rot" and "red ray rot." Long (120), Hubert (83, pp. 29, 32–33; 87, pp. 333–340), and Boyce (22, p. 38) describe the rot in more or less detail. It is a sap rot in dead and down material and a heart rot of living trees. The heartwood first becomes reddish or brownish and frequently shows radiating discolored arms. Small mottled areas appear on the faces of the annual rings, and decay becomes localized in these spots, with the result that white pockets are eventually formed, especially in the springwood. These pockets are similar to those produced by *Fomes Pini* but have blunter ends. *Polyporus palustris* is a species sometimes quite similar to this one; the two may best be distinguished by the dendritic hyphae of *P. anceps* and the type of rot produced.

59. POLYPORUS PALUSTRIS Berk. & Curt.

Grevillea 1: 51. 1872

(Fig. 86 and Plate 131)

Tyromyces palustris (Berk. & Curt.) Murr., North Amer. Flora 9: 31. 1907.

Sporophore sessile, watery-tough to corky when fresh, hard and rigid when dry; pileus 2–10 × 2–20 × 0.6–3 cm., white or slightly yellowish in fresh plants, usually yellowish or sordid ochraceous orange on drying, azonate, very compactly tomentose to glabrous, on drying almost pelliculose but usually with a rough surface, the margin rather thick and somewhat rounded; context 0.5–2 cm. thick, white, corky as in *Trametes* or quite hard on drying; pore surface white to yellowish or somewhat smoky, the tubes 5–10 mm. long, the mouths angular, rather thin-walled, entire to somewhat dentate, averaging 4–5 per mm.; spores cylindric, hyaline, 6–8 × 2–3.5 μ; cystidia and hyphal pegs none; hyphae mostly flexuous, heavy-walled, simple or sparingly branched, with some evidence of cross walls or clamps, 4–6(–9) μ in diameter, but some hyphae small, 3–4 μ in diameter, branched and with cross walls and clamps. (Compare no. 58, *Polyporus anceps*.)

HABITAT: On dead wood of coniferous trees, noted on *Pinus*.

DISTRIBUTION: Specimens have been examined from S.C., Ga., Fla., La., and Miss.; reported from Ark. (Long [121]).

Typically, plants of this species dry quite rigid or hard, becoming decidedly yellowed and, usually, rough. The hyphae do not present the peculiar branching characteristic of *Polyporus anceps*, and that species is smaller and whiter; but otherwise there is some similarity. Miss E. M. Wakefield very kindly compared specimens from my herbarium with the types of *P. palustris* at the Royal Botanic Gardens at Kew, England, and reports that they are almost exactly the same, and not related to *P. albidus*, as was maintained by Lloyd. Lowe's New York record (125, p. 77), based in part on Lloyd's record of Burnham's collection, is likewise evidently in error. The Burnham specimen appears to be *P. anceps*. One could be quite certain that *P. palustris* does not occur in New York.

The decay produced is a brown carbonizing rot of the heartwood.

60. POLYPORUS SUBMURINUS (Murr.) Lloyd

Synop. Apus, p. 307. 1915

(Figs. 227–228 and Plate 132)

Trametes submurina Murr., North Amer. Flora 9: 43. 1907.

Pileus sessile or more frequently decurrent, dimidiate, imbricate, rigid when dry, more or less laterally connate, $0.5–4 \times 1–8 \times 0.3–1.5$ cm., more or less murinous or becoming so on drying, minutely and finely villose-tomentose or villose-pubescent under a lens, azonate, surface sometimes rough and uneven, the margin thin or rather thick; context white or pallid, 2–10 mm. thick, corky; pore surface white or somewhat discolored but not smoky, the tubes 1–5 mm. long, the mouths circular or subangular, rather thick-walled, entire, averaging 4–5 per mm.; spores cylindric, smooth, hyaline, $6–8 \times 2.5–3.5$ μ; basidia 4–6 μ in diameter; cystidia none; hyphae in part simple, nonstaining, with walls completely or partially thickened, with no cross walls or clamps, 3–6(–8) μ in diameter, and in part staining, with numerous cross walls and clamps, 2.5–4 μ in diameter. (Compare no. 11, *Fomes Meliae*.)

HABITAT: On dead wood of deciduous trees, noted on *Fraxinus* and *Populus*.

DISTRIBUTION: Specimens have been examined only from N.C. and La.

I take the species largely in the sense of the type collection at the New York Botanical Garden, with which four or five other tropical collections agree beyond doubt, though a number, mostly from Jamaica, are not so certain.

The unusually well marked dual hyphae of the context seem to be a distinctive feature of the species and may serve nicely to separate it from *Fomes Meliae.* No information is at hand as to the type of rot produced.

61. POLYPORUS DURESCENS Overh.

Mycologia 33: 98. 1941

(Figs. 89, 144, and Plate 129)

Sporophore sessile, sometimes in imbricate clusters 10 cm. or more broad, tough or corky and watery when fresh, drying very hard and rigid; pileus dimidiate, $4–12 \times 5–15 \times 1–4$ cm., white or grayish when fresh, unchanged on drying or discoloring to somewhat bay or yellowish, azonate, compactly spongy-tomentose and usually drying rough, the margin rather thin; context white, tough and watery when fresh, typically drying very hard and almost horny, 1–3 cm. thick; pore surface white or gray, sometimes somewhat isabelline or discolored on drying, the tubes 0.2–1 cm. long, the mouths subangular, rather thin-walled, entire, averaging 3–5 per mm.; spores cylindric, hyaline, $4.5–7 \times 1.5–2.5$ μ, often attenuate at one end, sometimes slightly curved; basidia 4–5 μ in diameter; cystidia none; main context hyphae simple or somewhat branched, with completely thickened walls, with no cross walls or clamps, 4–6 μ in diameter, other hyphae considerably branched, with no cross walls or clamps, of smaller diameter, about 3 μ, all hyphae nonstaining.

HABITAT: On logs and stumps of deciduous trees, noted on *Acer*, *Fagus*, *Fraxinus*, and *Quercus.*

DISTRIBUTION: Specimens have been examined from N.Y., Pa., La., Tenn., Ky., Ohio, and Ind.

ILLUSTRATIONS: Overholts, Mycologia 33: 99, figs. 9–10.

This species is a segregate from plants previously referred by all recent American mycologists to *Polyporus Spraguei*, to which the resemblance is so strong, at least in sporophores that have been dried, that I have thus far not been able to separate them without recourse to the microscope. The spores are entirely different in the two species, the basidia of *P. Spraguei* are much larger than those of this species, and clamps seem to be entirely absent from the context hyphae of *P. durescens*, so that the distinction is ample. The blackening of the edge of the pilei that is characteristic of *P. Spraguei* on drying has not been seen in *P. durescens*, but the context becomes even harder in the present species than in dried specimens of *P. Spraguei*. Specimens of *P. palustris* sometimes appear quite similar, but that species occurs only on wood of coniferous trees and is entirely southern in distribution. From the dozen collections of *P. durescens* in my herbarium, it seems likely that the species is most common in the Ohio River Valley.

Since I have not collected fresh specimens of this species in recent years, I am not yet certain about its odor when fresh. Most of the sporophores I collected frequently in southwestern Ohio many years ago (determined as *Polyporus Spraguei* by all who saw them) were malodorous. Some of these now prove to be the present species, but no notes on odor are attached to any particular collection. On the other hand, I collected *P. Spraguei* in 1933 and again in 1934, and at least some collections were pleasantly scented. Specimens of *P. durescens* were submitted to Miss E. M. Wakefield, at the Royal Botanic Gardens at Kew, England, who was unable to give me a name for them. At the same time she reported that the types of *P. Spraguei* are not in good condition, so that it is entirely within the realm of possibility that my usage of that name is erroneous. In other words, *P. Spraguei* may be the proper name for *P. durescens*, and if it is, the globose-spored species here designated *P. Spraguei* should bear another name. I am of the present opinion that *P. Spraguei* will prove to be pleasantly scented, or else without odor, and *P. durescens* always malodorous.

I have referred here a few specimens in which the hyphae do not quite reach the sizes typical of the species and in which scattered clamps are present on some of the smaller hyphae.

In the single collection where a part of the wood substratum was preserved with the sporophores, the decay seems similar to that produced by *Polyporus Spraguei*.

62. Polyporus amarus Hedgcock

Mycologia 2: 155. 1910

(Figs. 186–187)

Polyporus Libocedris von Schrenk, Science, N.S. 16: 138. 1902 (nomen nudum).

Sporophore sessile, convex to ungulate, soft and watery when fresh, very hard and rigid when dry; pileus 7–12 × 7–20 × 4–15 cm., pubescent when young, drying rough or wrinkled and more glabrous, at first pallid or buff, becoming brownish or brownish black on drying, azonate, the margin thick and rounded; context yellow to wood color or pale brown, soft when fresh, drying very hard; pore surface yellowish when fresh, discolored on handling and on drying, the tubes 0.5–1.5 cm. or more long, yellow within, the mouths angular, rather thin-walled, entire, averaging 2–3 per mm.; spores ellipsoid or narrow-ellipsoid, smooth, hyaline, 6–7.5 × 3.5–5 μ; cystidia none; hyphae very thick-walled, somewhat branched, irregular, and breaking into short lengths, with an occasional, usually distorted clamp, 5–9 μ in diameter; sections of the hymenium and sections of the surface of the context becoming pale lemon-yellow in KOH solution.

Habitat: On living or fallen coniferous trees, usually on *Libocedrus*, noted on *Abies*, also.

Distribution: Specimens have been examined from Idaho, Ore., and Calif.

Illustrations: Boyce, U. S. Dept. Agr. Bul. 871: pl. 1; Meinecke, Forest Tree Dis. Calif. Nev., pl. 11; von Schrenk, Mo. Bot. Gard. Ann. Rept. 11: pl. 2 (rot only).

Few sporophores of this fungus have ever been collected. Half a dozen good collections are preserved at Beltsville, Maryland. Apparently the species fruits infrequently, and the sporophores are soon destroyed by insects. It is confined practically to *Libocedrus*, but at the Brooklyn Botanical Garden there is a specimen from Idaho on *Abies grandis*, collected by Hubert.

The fungus is known to cause a destructive heart rot of incense cedar. The rot is a local carbonizing one, resulting in the formation of tunnels in the wood that are often one centimeter or more in diameter and several centimeters long. The wood within these pockets is a brown, carbonized, friable, checked mass that eventually disappears.

The decay is known as "pecky cedar" or "pin rot" and is the chief defect in incense cedar. Various phases of the decay are discussed by Boyce (19; 22, pp. 39–41).

7b. *Spores not over 5 μ long* (see also *Polyporus albidus*, p. 426)

63. POLYPORUS GUTTULATUS Peck
In Saccardo, Syll. Fung. 6: 106. 1888
(Figs. 123–125, 641, 643–644, and Plate 130)

Tyromyces guttulatus (Peck) Murr., North Amer. Flora 9: 31. 1907.
Polyporus maculatus Peck, N. Y. State Mus. Ann. Rept. 26: 69. 1874.
  (Not *P. maculatus* Berk. 1848.)
Tyromyces tiliophila Murr., North Amer. Flora 9: 33. 1907.
Tyromyces substipitatus Murr., Mycologia 4: 96. 1912.

Sporophore sessile or attenuate to a narrowed lateral base (rarely distinctly stipitate); pileus rather thin and applanate, firm and sub-fleshy, cheesy, drying rigid, 3–12 × 5–15 × 0.5–1.5 cm., white to yellowish, becoming reddish or brownish where bruised in fresh plants, and usually sordid yellow on drying, glabrous or practically so, usually marked with rounded depressed spots and often rugose-rivulose or radiately wrinkled when dry; context white, 0.4–1 cm. thick, rather firm, very bitter in both fresh and dried plants; pore surface white to yellowish, the tubes 1–5(–10) mm. long, the mouths angular, thin-walled, entire, averaging 4–5 per mm.; spores oblong or short-cylindric, usually uniguttulate, smooth, hyaline, 3–4.5 × 2–2.5 μ; cystidia not noteworthy, though small pointed sterile bodies 3–4.5 μ in diameter sometimes discernible between the basidia; main hyphae nearly simple, hyaline, thick-walled, with small staining lumina, the walls indistinct as though partly gelatinized, with some cross walls and clamps, 5–8 μ in diameter.

HABITAT: Usually on dead wood of coniferous trees, noted on *Abies, Larix, Picea, Pinus, Pseudotsuga, Thuja,* and *Tsuga;* occasionally on hardwoods, noted on *Fagus, Liriodendron, Rhamnus,* and *Tilia.*

DISTRIBUTION: Specimens have been examined from Me., N.H., Vt., Mass., N.Y., Pa., Va., N.C., Tenn., Ky., Ohio, Ind., Mich.,

Wis., Minn., Ariz., Idaho, Ore., Wash., and Calif.; in Canada from Newfoundland, Prince Edward Island, Quebec, Ontario, Manitoba, and British Columbia.

Fresh plants are somewhat watery, though decidedly leathery or cheesy in texture, and usually quite thin and applanate. All collections of fresh specimens that I have seen have shown the rounded depressed spots on the pileus. Usually the plants grow singly. The taste of dried specimens is as bitter as is *Fomes officinalis*.

On first examination, *Polyporus tiliophilus* (Murr.) Sacc. & D. Sacc., described from a collection made by Macoun at Ottawa, Canada, on *Tilia*, seemed different from the present species. Lloyd suggested that it was probably only a form of *P. guttulatus*, and, after thorough study, I agree with him in regarding it as an extremely well-developed form of this species, with longer tubes and thicker flesh than usual. Microscopically, the two plants are essentially alike except that in the context of *P. tiliophilus* there are many enlarged hyphae that stain deeply in eosin and that appear to be of the order of latex hyphae. At the cross walls these hyphae are often much enlarged, being up to 20 μ in diameter. In the first two collections of *P. guttulatus* that I examined for this, I found no such hyphae. But a third collection (at the New York Botanical Garden, made by Murrill in Washington in 1911) showed their presence in limited numbers, as did other collections later, as well as other species of this group. A number of polypores have been described as exuding watery or milky drops in certain stages of growth, and the phenomenon is known in *P. guttulatus* itself; it may be that these hyphae have a physiological connection with the weeping habit.

I have not attempted to determine the relation of this species to *Polyporus alutaceus* Fries of Europe. Several writers have indicated their synonymy, and Saccardo in a late volume of *Sylloge Fungorum* (23: 379. 1925) accepted it. In one of his last papers Romell (188, pp. 3, 4, 6) could not agree with this conclusion, and Pilát (171, vol. 52, p. 51) does not accept it.

At one time I was of the opinion that *Polyporus substipitatus* (Murr.) Sacc. & Trott. was referable to *P. floriformis*, but I am now convinced that this can scarcely be so. I take it now to be a small form of the present species. Young sporophores of *P. guttulatus* are likely to be rather distinctly laterally stipitate, and so they simulate *P. floriformis* to some extent. Microscopically *P. floriformis* is quite similar, as are also *P. balsameus* and *P. immitis*. In fact, *P. immitis* intergrades considerably with *P. guttulatus*, which is best distinguished by the thin, applanate, and typically spotted pileus. *P. immitis* dries with rough tomentose points or nodules and, typically, is thicker and nearly triangular in section and tougher and more leathery when fresh. I have seen no specimens of *P. guttulatus* which have quite the narrowly oblong spores of the types of *P. immitis*. *P. guttulatus*, *P. immitis*, and *P. floriformis* are very bitter to the taste in dried specimens; *P. balsameus* is not.

The decay produced by this species is a brown carbonizing rot, much checked in drying, that is, a typical cubical rot.

64. POLYPORUS IMMITIS Peck

N. Y. State Mus. Ann. Rept. 35: 135. 1884

(Figs. 111, 546, 549, 561, 569, 615, and Plate 130)

Sporophore sessile, dimidiate, cheesy and watery when fresh, not bending without breaking, drying hard and rigid; pileus 1.5–8 × 2–15 × 0.4–2.5 cm., white throughout but often drying more or less yellowish, with a rather coarse, compact tomentum agglutinated into nodules because of which the pileus dries rough or radiately rugose, not zonate, the margin thin, entire; context somewhat or not at all duplex, white, cheesy, drying rather firm or even resinous, with a somewhat pleasantly rancid odor in fresh specimens and a very bitter taste in both fresh and dried condition, 5–15 mm. thick; pore surface white when fresh, yellowish and somewhat glistening on drying, the tubes 2–12 mm. long, the mouths angular, thin-walled, entire, 3–5 or 4–6 per mm., visible to the unaided eye; spores short-cylindric or oblong, sometimes slightly curved, smooth, hyaline, 3–4 × 1.5–2 μ; cystidia none; hyphae flexuous, simple or somewhat branched, the walls highly thickened, with narrow staining lumina, with some cross walls and clamps, 3–8 μ in diameter, often gelatinized considerably when sporophores are badly weathered. (Compare no. 63, *Polyporus guttulatus*; no. 82, *P. Spraguei*; no. 86, *P. galactinus*; and *P. albidus*, p. 426.)

HABITAT: On dead wood of both coniferous and deciduous trees, noted on *Acer*, *Fraxinus*, *Picea*, *Thuja*, and *Tsuga*; reported on *Betula* (Kauffman [104]).

DISTRIBUTION: Specimens have been examined from N.H., Vt., Mass., N.Y., Pa., Tenn., Ohio, and Idaho; in Canada from Ontario, Manitoba, and British Columbia; reported from Mich. (Kauffman [104]).

ILLUSTRATIONS: Lowe, Mich. Acad. Sci. Arts and Letters Papers 19: pl. 14, figs. 1–3 (as *Polyporus albidus*).

Dried specimens resemble *Polyporus galactinus* to some extent, but the sporophores are more brittle, the tomentum is different, and the spores are distinct from those of that species, as well as from those of *P. guttulatus* and *P. spumeus*. Kauffman (104) first noticed that this was a separate species from *P. galactinus*, to which the name had previously been referred in synonymy. He collected it on *Fraxinus* and on *Betula*, and the types are said to have been on *Fraxinus*. There are, however, three other collections, at the New York State Museum at Albany, New York, two of them from *Tsuga*, which I must refer here. They constitute Peck's conception of *P. epileucus* and *P. epileucus* var. *candidus*. A number of other collections at Albany, determined as *P. epileucus* or as *P. immitis*, are in error. The taste of dried plants, both the type specimens and all the specimens in my herbarium, is as bitter as is *Fomes officinalis*.

The fungus is always associated with a brown crumbling rot of the substratum.

65. POLYPORUS LEUCOSPONGIA Cooke & Harkness

Grevillea 11: 106. 1883

(Figs. 130, 664, and Plate 130)

Spongiporus leucospongia (Cooke & Harkness) Murr., Torrey Bot. Club Bul. 32: 474. 1905.

Sporophore sessile or more often effused-reflexed, soft and watery when fresh, rigid but with a very soft upper surface on drying; pileus dimidiate to elongate, convex, 1–5 × 2–10 × 0.5–2.5 cm., retaining a soft layer of cottony tomentum often 1 cm. thick over the upper surface or, rarely, this drying more or less firm and with a thin papery cuticle, pure white to somewhat discolored, the margin often deflexed or with a cottony roll of tomentum; context pure white, up to 1.5 cm. thick, tough when fresh, drying firm and very different in texture from the overlying cottony tomentum; pore surface white, nearly always discoloring on drying, the tubes 2–6 mm. long, discolored within on drying, the mouths angular, thin-walled, nearly even or becoming markedly lacerate-dentate, averaging 2–3 per mm.; spores cylindric, curved, hyaline, 4–5 × 1–1.5 μ; basidia 4–5 μ in diameter; cystidia none; hyphal pegs present, narrow, pointed, composed of only a few hyphae; hyphae mostly flexuous, thick-walled, simple or sparingly branched, with some cross walls and clamps, 4–7 μ in diameter.

HABITAT: On old logs or stumps of coniferous trees at elevations of 5000 feet or more, noted on *Abies, Larix, Picea, Pinus, Pseudotsuga,* and *Tsuga.*

DISTRIBUTION: Specimens have been examined from Utah, Nev., Colo., Wyo., Mont., Idaho, Ore., Wash., and Calif.

ILLUSTRATIONS: Lloyd, Synop. Apus, fig. 665; Shope, Mo. Bot. Gard. Ann. 18: pl. 17, figs. 1–2.

This is a very well marked species, especially characteristic in its thick, soft, cottony-tomentose covering, the strong discoloration of the tubes on drying, and the alpine or subalpine habitat. Sporophores are extremely light in weight when dried. Specimens that have been snow-covered through the winter often persist in good condition. It is a common species at elevations of 8000 feet to timber line in the Rocky Mountains and westward.

The rot produced is of the brown carbonizing cubical type, quite similar to that caused by *Lenzites saepiaria.* Apparently the decay may be present in both sapwood and heartwood.

66. POLYPORUS CERIFLUUS Berk. & Curt.

Grevillea 1: 50. 1872

Tyromyces cerifluus (Berk. & Curt.) Murr., North Amer. Flora 9: 33. 1907.

Sporophore sessile, dimidiate, fleshy-tough when fresh, rigid when dry; pileus 1.5–2.5 × 1.5–4 × 0.3–0.5 cm., silky-tomentose, becoming glabrous in broad bands, white, more or less reddish especially on the glabrous bands on drying, somewhat guttulate toward the margin, the margin thin, acute; context very thin, less than 1 mm. thick, white; pore surface white, discolored on drying, the tubes several times longer than the thickness of the context, 3–5 mm. long, the mouths thin-walled, markedly lacerate-fimbriate, angular, averaging 3–4 per mm.; spores short-cylindric or oblong, 4–5 × 2–2.5 μ; cystidia none; hyphal pegs lacking; hyphae somewhat branched, hyaline, mostly with very gelatinous walls so that the central medulla shows up plainer than the gelatinized exterior, with some inconspicuous walls and clamps, 4–7 μ in diameter.

HABITAT: On dead wood of deciduous trees, reported on *Populus* (Mont., Weir [227]).[1]

DISTRIBUTION: Specimens have been examined only from S.C.; reported from Mont. (Weir [227]).

There are no specimens at the New York Botanical Garden except the Ravenel collection from South Carolina. The important characters of the species seem to be the oblong spores (not globose as reported), the highly gelatinized hyphal walls, and the very thin context with long tubes whose mouths are much lacerated (though not deeply enough to be irpiciform), so that when the hymenium is viewed laterally the appearance is that of a hydnaceous plant. The pileus has dried more or less latericeous and is peculiarly guttate toward the margin. Lloyd says the flesh is peppery to the taste. It is practically an unknown species, and more collections are very desirable.

67. POLYPORUS CUTIFRACTUS Murr.

Mycologia 4: 217. 1912
(Fig. 98 and Plate 129)

Tyromyces cutifractus Murr., Mycologia 4: 94. 1912.

Sporophore sessile, fleshy-tough or somewhat cheesy when fresh, hard and very rigid when dry, reviving; pileus 2–4 × 2–6 × 0.4–1 cm., whitish or decidedly grayish when young, the upper surface becoming gelatinous-cartilaginous and with a brownish cuticle that may in part disappear in patches as the pileus expands, azonate or nearly so, glabrous though more or less roughened in age by a gelatinized upper-surface layer; context white, watery, 2–5 mm. thick, drying hard; pore surface white, yellowish or discoloring on drying, the tubes 2–4 mm. long, the mouths angular, rather thin-walled, entire, averaging 4–5 per mm.; spores oblong-ellipsoid or short-

---

[1] [This collection should be referred to *Polyporus fragilis*.—J.L.L.]

cylindric, smooth, hyaline, 4–5 × 2–3 μ; cystidia absent from sporulating parts of the hymenium, present in younger parts as lance-
shaped or fusoid, rather conspicuous, hyaline organs 20–25 × 5–8
μ, projecting up to 12 μ; hyphal pegs rare; hyphae simple or sparingly
branched, hyaline, with greatly thickened and partly gelatinized
walls and very narrow lumina, with a few inconspicuous cross walls
and clamps, 4–8(–10) μ in diameter.   (Compare no. 113, *Polyporus
subcartilagineus*.)

HABITAT: On dead wood of deciduous and coniferous trees,
noted on *Abies, Acer, Betula, Picea, Pinus, Pseudotsuga, Quercus,
Thuja*, and *Tsuga*; reported on *Cupressus* (Calif., Rhoads [183]).

DISTRIBUTION: Specimens have been examined from Mont., Ore.,
Wash., and Calif.; in Canada from British Columbia.

Cystidia are not easily seen in sections of a sporulating hymenium,
and the species may thus be distinguished from *Polyporus balsameus*; the gelatinous tomentum on the pileus and the more gelatinized hyphae of the context are additional points of difference.
After a few minutes in KOH and eosin the hyphal walls become indistinct, while the contents of the lumina take the eosin stain readily.
Sometimes the pileus dries somewhat rufescent or tawny as it does in
P. fragilis, but the spores differ in not being allantoid and the sporophores dry harder than in that species.   *P. lapponicus* differs in the
larger spores, the more conspicuous cystidia, and the more truly
rufescent color on drying.
A brown cubical decay has accompanied a few specimens, but
nothing is known about the importance of the rot.

6b. *Spores allantoid, in part at least* (see also *Tyromyces
leucomallellus*, p. 427)

68. POLYPORUS CAESIUS Schrad. ex Fries

Syst. Myc. 1: 360. 1821

(Figs. 103–105 and Plate 128)

Boletus caesius Schrad., Spic. Flora Germ., p. 167. 1794.
Tyromyces caesius (Schrad. ex Fries) Murr., North Amer. Flora 9: 34. 1907.
Tyromyces caesiosimulans Atk., Ann. Mycol. 6: 61. 1908.

Sporophore sessile or effused-reflexed, soft and watery or at least spongy when fresh, breaking easily on the hymenial surface; pileus typically triangular in section, sometimes thin and applanate, 1–5 × 1–4(–8) × 0.2–1(–2) cm., white or gray, often bluish gray or stained bluish, or with a bluish marginal band, drying white, gray, or yellowish, uniformly villose-pubescent or strigose-pubescent at the base and villose on the margin; context white, 1–10 mm. thick, taste mild, odor usually sweet; pore surface white, cinereous, or grayish blue, sometimes light blue where handled, the tubes 2–8 mm. long, the mouths unequal, angular or sinuous, averaging 2–4 per mm., the walls thin, even or torn and lacerated; spores cylindric or allantoid, smooth, hyaline under the microscope, pale ashen blue in mass, 3–5 × 0.7–1.5 μ; cystidia none; hyphal pegs rather abundant, cylindric, usually with adhering spores; hyphae simple or nearly so, hyaline, with greatly thickened nonstaining walls and small central lumina, with rather conspicuous cross walls and clamps, 4–8 μ in diameter. (Compare no. 72, *Polyporus tephroleucus*; no. 73, *P. albellus*; no. 77, *P. fumidiceps*; and no. 86, *P. galactinus*.)

HABITAT: On dead wood of both deciduous and coniferous trees, noted on *Abies, Acer, Carya, Fagus, Liriodendron, Magnolia, Oxydendron, Pinus, Platanus, Populus, Pseudotsuga, Quercus, Rhododendron, Tsuga*, and *Ulmus*; reported on *Betula* and *Larix* (Idaho, Weir [222]) and on *Picea* (Calif., Rhoads [183]).

DISTRIBUTION: Specimens have been examined from Me., Conn., N.Y., Pa., N.J., Del., D.C., Va., W. Va., N.C., Ala., Tenn., Ohio, Mich., Wis., Mo., Idaho, Ore., Wash., and Calif.; in Canada from Quebec, Ontario, Manitoba, and British Columbia; reported from Ky. (Kauffman [100]), Iowa (Wolf [234]), Colo. (Kauffman [102]), and Mont. (Weir [227]).

ILLUSTRATIONS: Gillet, Champ. France 3: pl. 558 (61); Overholts, Wash. Univ. Studies 3: pl. 2, fig. 8; Shope, Mo. Bot. Gard. Ann. 18: pl. 28, fig. 3.

Dried specimens often have a peculiar cinereous tinge that makes the species easily recognized. Fresh specimens do not always show a bluish color, but usually there is a trace of blue or ashy blue, at least on the pore surface, and sometimes the pileus shows a beautiful marginal band of that hue. There is a very small and thin form of the species and a larger, thicker form. There is likewise a short silky-villose form and a more strigose-pubescent form. The pores are larger than those of *Polyporus albellus* and *P. tephroleucus*, and the walls are usually soon torn and lacerate. The nearly simple hyphae of the context also distinguish the plant from *P. albellus*. The species differs from *P. fumidiceps* and *P. galactinus* in having allantoid spores.

The situation in regard to *Polyporus caesiosimulans* Atk. is well summed up by Lowe (125, p. 74). The minute, globose spores described by Atkinson are very abundant in mounts of sections of the hymenial region, but I was never able to demonstrate them on basidia. Lowe's discovery of spores like those of *P. caesius*, but still not on basidia, brings the evidence one step nearer the conclusion that this fungus is only *P. caesius* parasitized by a hyphomycete.

Although Shope reports *Polyporus caesius* as associated with a white spongy rot, I find that a number of my collections are definitely accompaned by a brown carbonizing decay.

69. POLYPORUS PERDELICATUS Murr.

Mycologia 4: 217. 1912
(Fig. 674 and Plate 131)

Tyromyces perdelicatus Murr., Mycologia 4: 95. 1912.

Sporophore sessile, effused-reflexed, or sometimes pendent; pileus dimidiate or circular, 0.5–1 × 0.5–2 × 0.1–0.3 cm., pure white or with an ashy tinge when fresh, very slightly if at all yellowish on drying, soft floccose-tomentose, the margin usually decurved; context pure white, soft even in dried plants, less than 1 mm. thick; pore surface white, usually drying yellowish, the tubes 1–2 mm. long, the mouths angular, rather thin-walled, entire or slightly dentate, averaging 3–4 per mm.; spores very narrow-cylindric or allantoid, smooth, hyaline, 4–5 × 1 μ; cystidia none or not noteworthy; hyphal pegs rather abundant, narrow-conical; some hyphae thin-walled, others with walls partially thickened, hyaline, sparingly branched, with rather numerous but not conspicuous cross walls and clamps, 2.5–5 μ in diameter. (Compare no. 68, *Polyporus caesius*.)

HABITAT: On dead wood of coniferous trees, noted on *Abies*, *Pseudotsuga*, and *Tsuga*.

DISTRIBUTION: Specimens have been examined from Idaho, Ore., and Wash.; in Canada from British Columbia.

The small size and the soft, pure-white or ashy pileus should render easy the identification of this species. It could be mistaken for a thin white form of *Polyporus caesius*, from which it differs in degree rather than in quality, for it is scarcely more than a small, thin condition of that species; it often lacks, however, the bluish or ashen tint usually found in *P. caesius*, has a thinner context and shorter tubes, and is never so villose as that species. In addition, the spores may be a trifle longer and more slender.

70. POLYPORUS SEMIPILEATUS Peck
N. Y. State Mus. Ann. Rept. 34: 43. 1881
(Figs. 70–71, 79, and Plate 132)

Tyromyces semipileatus (Peck) Murr., North Amer. Flora 9: 35. 1907.

Sporophore occasionally sessile, more often effused-reflexed and largely resupinate, coriaceous or somewhat cartilaginous, spongy or watery when fresh, rigid on drying; pileus 0–1.5 × 0.7–3.5 × 0.1–0.5 cm., white or cinereous when fresh, gray to yellowish or somewhat bay when dry, finely villose-tomentose to glabrous, azonate; context white, 1–4 mm. thick, usually with a sweet odor in fresh plants; pore surface usually white, sometimes greenish or somewhat violaceous, drying white or yellowish, the tubes less than 2 mm. long, the mouths angular, thin-walled but entire, averaging 5–8 per mm.; spores allantoid, smooth, hyaline, 2.5–3.5 × 0.5 μ; basidia 3 μ in diameter; cystidia none; small hyphal pegs composed of a few hyaline projecting hairs rather abundant; main hyphae simple, with few cross walls and clamps, 2–5 μ in diameter, in the context ending in dichotomously branched, close hyphal complexes. (Compare no. 58, *Polyporus anceps*, and no. 73, *P. albellus*.)

HABITAT: On old branches and rotten wood of deciduous trees, noted on *Acer, Ailanthus, Alnus, Betula, Carya, Cornus, Fagus, Fraxinus, Gleditsia, Liquidambar, Liriodendron, Populus, Prunus, Quercus, Salix, Sambucus, Tilia*, and *Ulmus*; a collection on *Picea* (Ontario), one on *Pinus* (Ontario), and several on *Thuja* (Idaho and British Columbia) seem referable here.

DISTRIBUTION: Specimens have been examined from Me., N.H., Vt., Mass., Conn., N.Y., Pa., N.J., Del., D.C., Va., N.C., Ga., Fla., Ala., La., Tenn., Ky., Ohio, Ind., Ill., Mich., Wis., Minn., Iowa, Mo.,

Nebr., Idaho, Wash., and Calif.; in Canada from Quebec, Ontario, Manitoba, and British Columbia.

ILLUSTRATIONS: Lloyd, Synop. Apus, figs. 654–655 (as *Polyporus semisupinus*); Overholts, Wash. Univ. Studies 3: pl. 5, fig. 18.

Bourdot and Galzin (18, p. 544) interpret *P. chioneus* of Quélet as this species. In fresh specimens the pileus is pure white or slightly stained with latericeous color. The pore surface only occasionally has other than a white or creamy coloration. These aberrant colors may be the signs of the presence of another fungus, or even of bacteria. The spores are more minute than in most pileate polypores, and only the most favorable material yields decisive spore characters. The form and color of the sporophore recalls *P. anceps*, from which *P. semipileatus* differs, however, in every other character.

This species produces a white to straw-colored general delignifying decay of the sapwood. Wilson (233) reports it as a wound parasite on *Salix* in Iowa.

71. POLYPORUS CARBONARIUS Murr.

Mycologia 4: 217. 1912

Tyromyces carbonarius Murr., Mycologia 4: 94. 1912.

Sporophore sessile or effused-reflexed, rather soft when fresh, hard and rigid when dry; pileus 1×1.5–3×0.5–1 cm., white or slightly yellowish, with a roughish suberect tomentum that gradually wears away, leaving the pileus more smooth and cartilaginous in appearance, azonate, the margin pale rose (?); context white, 3–5 mm. thick, not fragile; pore surface white (or pale rose ?), the tubes 2–4 mm. long, the mouths more or less lacerate, averaging 2–4 per mm.; spores cylindric or somewhat allantoid, smooth, hyaline, 4–5×2 μ; cystidia none; hyphae hyaline, considerably branched, with very conspicuous cross walls and clamps, the clamps apparently easily torn from the hyphae and often found floating in mounts, 4–7 μ in diameter.

HABITAT: On charred logs, noted on *Abies*; reported on *Cupressus* and *Pinus* (Calif., Rhoads [183]).

DISTRIBUTION: Specimens have been examined only from Wash.; reported from Calif. (Rhoads [183]).

The collection on which this species is based is very fragmentary. The fungus is close to *Polyporus balsameus* of the East, but the spores and the hyphae seem quite different. It must not be confused with *Trametes carbonaria*. I have seen none but the type collection.

72. POLYPORUS TEPHROLEUCUS Fries

Syst. Myc. 1: 360. 1821

(Figs. 551, 558, and Plate 132)

Sporophore sessile, soft and watery when fresh, rather fragile, sometimes rather subgelatinous, rigid and friable when dry; pileus typically triangular in section, 1–8 × 1–14 × 0.7–4 cm., white to gray, often becoming yellowish in age or on drying, very finely villose or sometimes slightly hispid-tomentose at the base, often glabrous with age and covered with a thin pellicle that is more evident in dried specimens but sometimes disappears in patches, leaving the pileus with a soft villose appearance under a lens, often drying somewhat rugose in young specimens; context white, soft and friable when dry, 0.4–3 cm. thick, no odor when fresh, taste mild; pore surface white or drying yellowish, somewhat glistening, the tubes 5–15 mm. long, typically longer than the thickness of the context, the mouths angular, thin-walled, entire or only slightly lacerate, averaging 3–5 per mm.; spores cylindric or allantoid, smooth, hyaline, 3–5 × 0.7–1 μ; cystidia none; hyphal pegs present but not abundant; hyphae unbranched or nearly so, mostly thick-walled and with narrow staining lumina, clamp connections prominent and usually rather abundant, 4–8 μ in diameter. (Compare no. 73, *Polyporus albellus*; no. 77, *P. fumidiceps*; and no. 86, *P. galactinus*.)

HABITAT: Usually on dead wood of deciduous trees, noted on *Acer, Betula, Crataegus, Fagus, Fraxinus, Liriodendron, Nyssa, Platanus, Populus, Pyrus, Quercus, Salix*, and *Ulmus*; occasionally on wood of coniferous trees, noted on *Abies, Pinus*, and *Tsuga*; one collection said to have been on *Picea*.

DISTRIBUTION: Specimens have been examined from Vt., Conn., N.Y., Pa., N.J., Del., Md., D.C., W. Va., N.C., Tenn., Ohio, Ind., Mo., Kans., Nebr., Idaho, and Mont.; in Canada from Quebec, Ontario, Manitoba, and British Columbia; reported from Iowa (Wolf [234]).

ILLUSTRATIONS: Rostkovius, in Sturm's Deutsch. Flora, Abt. 3, Bd. 4: pl. 26.

The best distinction between this species and *Polyporus albellus* is a microscopic one, i.e., the nearly simple, parallel hyphae in the context here as contrasted with the much-branched and interwoven hyphae in the context of *P. albellus*. The hyphae of the two species must be seen side by side in mounts for this comparison to be appreciated, but it is a very decisive one. In addition, *P. tephroleucus* does not have the sweet odor of *P. albellus* when fresh, and the decay produced is of the brown, carbonizing type. Dried specimens of *P. tephroleucus* are likely to present variations in the character of the upper surface and the length of the tubes, depending on the age of the fungus when collected. Specimens that have not reached maturity will nearly always dry with a rather rough upper surface, whereas those that are more mature may be entirely smooth, and, on drying, a definite though very thin pellicle may be in evidence. Mature sporophores are typically gray, but less so than in *P. fumidiceps*, which is further distinguished by the very different spores. In mature and well-developed sporophores of *P. tephroleucus* the tubes are longer than the thickness of the context, whereas sporophores of *P. albellus* of the same degree of maturity have shorter tubes.

I regret that in my earlier determinations of specimens of this fungus for correspondents and in my treatment of them in previous studies I referred them to *Polyporus albellus*. This disposition was based on what I supposed could be taken as authentic specimens determined by Peck in Dr. E. A. Burt's herbarium. My conception of the species as a unit remains the same, but further study of the types of *P. albellus* at the New York State Museum at Albany, New York, leads me to the only possible conclusion, namely, that Peck's species is synonymous with my previous conception of *P. chioneus*. The types show the much-branched hyphae of that species, and the sporophores are smaller, with short tubes. My previous contention (150, pp. 697–701) that two closely related species are involved here still holds. Sporophores with the much-branched hyphae are referable to *P. albellus*. Those with parallel and simple hyphae I would now refer to *P. tephroleucus*. There are no "confusing intermediates" (125, p. 74) where these two species are concerned. I have given up the use of the name *P. chioneus* because of the disagreement in Europe as to the characters of that species, and the sporophores I previously referred to it are here described as *P. albellus*.

Though the original description of *Polyporus tephroleucus* calls for a gray, villose pileus, Romell admits collections only slightly gray toward the margin, and Lloyd remarks that he has seldom seen sporophores with the characters exactly as outlined by Fries. I am inclined to believe that these variations can be satisfactorily included within the confines of a single species. What is more natural than that in young sporophores the upper surface should be more or less pubescent and that in age this pubescence should wear away, leaving, in some specimens, a very thin pellicle, which in turn should wear off or be broken after drying and so reveal the underlying context, with a more villose appearance? I believe the pellicle does not become apparent until the fungi are dried, and not then unless they are fully mature. In substantiation of this view, I made notes on Missouri collections of fresh specimens in 1926, observing in particular that no pellicle was evident in the fresh sporophores. But in the dried specimens the pellicle is very evident, in fact it is as well shown in these collections as in any others in my herbarium.

Lloyd (111, p. 885) has described and illustrated a var. *scruposus* on *Picea canadensis* from Montana that should, however, be compared with *Polyporus guttulatus*.

P. tephroleucus produces a brown carbonizing rot of the wood.

73. POLYPORUS ALBELLUS Peck

N. Y. State Mus. Ann. Rept. 30: 45. 1878

(Figs. 110, 647–648, and Plate 128)

Tyromyces chioneus (Fries) Karst. sensu Murrill, North Amer. Flora 9: 35. 1907.

Sporophore sessile or effused-reflexed, soft and watery when fresh, sometimes somewhat flexible but breaking when bent at a sharp angle, drying rigid and usually friable; pileus applanate or convex, 2–7 × 1–12 × 0.5–3 cm., pure white or watery white when fresh, grayish or more usually yellowish on drying, slightly villose to nearly glabrous, usually drying with a thin grayish or yellowish pellicle; context white, fragrant and soft and watery when fresh, friable when dry, 2–15 mm. thick; pore surface white or yellowish, the tubes

1.5–3(–7) mm. long, the mouths angular, averaging 3–4(–5) per mm., the walls thin but nearly or quite entire; spores cylindric or allantoid, smooth, hyaline, 3.5–5 × 1–2 μ; basidia 4 μ in diameter; cystidia none; hyphal pegs present; hyphae hyaline, much branched, with some rather conspicuous cross walls and clamps, 4–8 μ in diameter. (Compare no. 72, *Polyporus tephroleucus*; no. 77, *P. fumidiceps*; no. 86, *P. galactinus*; and no. 87, *P. spumeus.*)

HABITAT: Usually on dead wood of deciduous trees, noted on *Acer*, *Alnus*, *Betula*, *Carya*, *Castanea*, *Fagus*, *Liquidambar*, *Ostrya*, *Platanus*, *Populus*, *Prunus*, *Pyrus*, *Quercus*, *Salix*, and *Sassafras*; occasionally on wood of coniferous trees, noted on *Abies*, *Picea*, *Pinus*, and *Tsuga*; reported on *Fraxinus* (Vt., Spaulding [209]) and *Thuja* (Mont., Weir [227]).

DISTRIBUTION: Specimens have been examined from Me., N.H., Vt., Mass., Conn., N.Y., Pa., N.J., Md., Va., N.C., Fla., Tenn., Ohio, Ind., Mich., Wis., Minn., Mo., Mont., Idaho, Ore., and Wash.; in Canada from Nova Scotia, Newfoundland, Quebec, Ontario, Manitoba, and British Columbia; reported from Ky. (Kauffman [100]) and Iowa (Wolf [234]).

ILLUSTRATIONS: Lloyd, Synop. Apus, fig. 638 (as *Polyporus trabeus*).

The soft watery-white pileus with little pubescence, the sweet odor, the much-branched hyphae of the context, and the minute, allantoid spores are the diagnostic characters. The favorite habitat in the Allegheny region is small dead branches of *Betula* lying on the ground. In drying, the pileus is likely to become quite yellowed. In the field, specimens do not usually persist through the winter. My earliest record for a collection is July 6.

Most records of *Polyporus chioneus* and *P. lacteus*, as they have appeared in American literature and as they are commonly found in American herbaria, belong here. It is doubtful if the true *P. lacteus* occurs in this country—at least anything that answers to the description left by Fries. My previous recognition (150, pp. 697–701) of *P. albellus* as distinct from *P. chioneus* was based on specimens in Burt's herbarium, determined by Peck. However, the types of *P. albellus* are in no wise distinct from what has passed as *P. chioneus* in this country. Plants previously referred by me to *P. albellus* will be found described here under *P. tephroleucus*. The distinctions discussed in the previous paper are valid, but what is there said regarding *P. albellus* can be transferred to *P. tephroleucus*, and *P. albellus* in the present sense replaces *P. chioneus*. This leaves us, of course, with nothing to refer to *P. chioneus*. But so many different opinions have been expressed (see 18, p. 544; 105, p. 214; 116, pp. 294 and 301; 187, p. 15; 188, pp. 4, 9) about the identity of that species that perhaps it is as well to use some other name.

My contention that *Polyporus albellus* can always be separated from *P. tephroleucus* by the much-branched hyphae of the context is still maintained. The "confusing intermediates" that Lowe discusses (125, p. 74) indicate to me, always, that the specimen in question belongs to neither of these species and that its identity should be sought elsewhere. That these two species may actually represent "extremes of only one species" is entirely untenable, since *P. albellus* produces a white rot and *P. tephroleucus* produces a brown cubical decay. *P. albellus* has a fragrant odor when fresh, whereas *P. tephroleucus* is quite odorless. *P. albellus*, furthermore, is usually a larger and thicker species. Both *P. galactinus* and *P. fumidiceps* have a sweet odor when fresh. If sterile specimens are in question, with basidia present, this species and its allies can be distinguished from *P. spumeus* and related species by the much smaller diameter of the basidia, as well as by the shorter tubes.

Polyporus albellus produces a wet, stringy, delignifying decay of the sapwood.

74. POLYPORUS RESINOSUS Schrad. ex Fries

Syst. Myc. 1: 361. 1821

(Figs. 279, 318, and Plate 131)

Boletus resinosus Schrad., Spic. Flora Germ., p. 171. 1794.
Ischnoderma fuliginosum (Scop. ex Fries) Murr., Torrey Bot. Club Bul. 31: 606. 1904.

Sporophore sessile or effused-reflexed, watery and fleshy or tough when young, corky when mature and rigid on drying; pileus 3–15 × 7–25 × 0.8–4 cm., dark brown to seal-brown or blackish brown (close to "Prout's brown"), at first densely velvety-tomentose, becoming more glabrous at maturity, sometimes shallowly furrowed or with blackish metallic zones, often radiately rugose, the margin usually rather thick, exuding drops of water when young and growing; context straw-colored and slightly darker next the tubes in fresh plants, very light brown or umber when dry, becoming dark in KOH, 0.5–2 cm. thick; pore surface white to pallid, darker where bruised and on drying, the tubes 1–10 mm. long, the mouths averaging 4–6 per mm., the walls rather thick, entire or becoming thin and slightly dentate; spores cylindric or allantoid, smooth, hyaline, 4–7 × 1.5–2 μ; cystidia and hyphal pegs none; hyphae simple, sparingly branched, with walls greatly thickened, with occasional conspicuous cross walls and clamps, 4–6(–8) μ in diameter.

HABITAT: On old logs and stumps of deciduous and coniferous trees, noted on *Abies, Acer, Betula, Carya, Fagus, Larix, Liriodendron, Picea, Populus, Pseudotsuga, Pyrus, Quercus, Salix, Tilia, Tsuga,* and *Ulmus*; reported on *Pinus* (N.Y., Rhoads [181]).

DISTRIBUTION: Specimens have been examined from Me., N.H., Vt., Mass., Conn., N.Y., Pa., Md., D.C., Va., W. Va., N.C., Fla., Tenn., Ky., Ohio, Ind., Ill., Mich., Wis., Minn., Iowa, Mo., Kans., Nebr., Idaho, Ore., Wash., Calif., and Alaska; in Canada from Quebec, Ontario, Manitoba, and British Columbia; reported from Ark. (Long [121]), Colo. (Kauffman [102]), and Mont. (Weir [227]).

ILLUSTRATIONS: Fries, Icones Sel. Hym., pl. 183, fig. 2 (as *Polyporus benzoinus*); Hard, Mushrooms, fig. 331; Kalchbrenner, Icones Sel. Hym. Hung., pl. 36, fig. 1 (as *P. benzoinus*); Moffatt, Chicago Acad. Sci. Nat. Hist. Survey Bul. 7, 1: pl. 15, fig. 1; Shope, Mo. Bot. Gard. Ann. 18: pl. 22, fig. 2.

Spores are found only on the young margin of the hymenium, where the tubes are short, 2–3 mm. long, or only near the mouths of tubes that are considerably longer, indicating that spore production is the function of the newly formed hymenial region, as in *Trametes*.

In my study of the Middle Western Polyporaceae (151) I reported that I was unable to find good distinguishing characters of specific value between the form on wood of coniferous trees often referred to *Polyporus benzoinus* and the form on hardwoods commonly known as *P. resinosus*. I have again investigated this subject and can only repeat my former conclusion, that the two are not specifically distinct. The pileus of *P. benzoinus* is often marked with metallic blue zones (one to several), but this is not always true. For example, a specimen collected by Benbow in Idaho in 1917 on *Abies grandis* (Missouri Botanical Garden Herbarium No. 58364) shows no such zones. Yet, on the whole, it may be desirable to recognize this form on the wood of conifers as a variety. Lloyd maintained there was a spore difference, the spores of *P. resinosus* being 8–10 × 2 μ and those of *P. benzoinus* 4–6 × 2 μ. I find no such difference in the specimens I have examined. I have noted that in a few collections (Kellerman, Ohio Fungi No. 105) the spores of the form on hardwoods are apparently very slightly longer and narrower in proportion than are those of the form on wood of coniferous trees, but I have seen no spores more than 7 μ long in the former, and many spores are as short as they are in the latter.

In both species the basidia may protrude rather prominently from the general level of the hymenium at the time of spore production, are quite narrow (3–4 μ), and have rather prominent, divergent sterigmata. But where the hymenium is well formed and the basidia not separated by sterile filaments, as they are likely to be in very young portions of the hymenium, this tendency is not well marked in either form. Snell *et al.* (205, p. 280) intimate that these two forms probably cannot be separated in culture by comparative growth responses at identical temperatures.

Murrill regards *Boletus fuliginosus* Scop. as a synonym for *Polyporus resinosus*, and Lloyd prefers *P. fuscus* Pers. ex Fries. The species is an old one, long recognized in Europe, and the status of these names is difficult to determine. I have therefore preferred to retain the name under which it has been commonly known in this country, although Romell in one of his last papers (188, p. 16) concluded that the original *Boletus resinosus* of Schrader was probably the same as *Fomes pinicola*.

Polyporus resinosus produces a general delignifying, straw-colored decay of both sapwood and heartwood, in which the annual rings of the wood soon separate and the tangential surface of the wood shows fine transverse white flecks, as in *P. anceps*. The infested wood, at least at times, is strongly permeated with an anise-like odor, and the fungus gives the same odor in culture, though the sporophores in nature do not.

> 5b. *Spores ellipsoid to ovoid or globose*
> > 6a. *Tubes up to 0.5 cm. long* (see also *Tyromyces avellanei-albus*, p. 426, and *T. pseudolacteus* and *Rigidoporus surinamensis subauberianus*, p. 428)

75. Polyporus canadensis Overh.

Mycologia 33: 97. 1941

(Figs. 521–522 and Plate 128)

Sporophore imbricate-sessile with a tendency to be substipitate, watery-tough when fresh, drying rigid and brittle, the cluster 6 × 10 × 5 cm., composed of about six partially confluent pilei; pileus 3–5 × 3–7 × 0.3–0.8 cm., white or watery white when fresh, drying pallid, densely soft-tomentose with erect tomentose tufts that roughen the surface of dried specimens; context duplex, the upper softer layer consisting of the tomentose covering, white, 2–4 mm. thick, drying fragile, with a sweet odor when fresh; pore surface white, drying somewhat yellowish, the tubes 2–4 mm. long, fragile when dried, the mouths angular, very thin-walled but entire, subshining, averaging 4–6 per mm.; spores very minute, subglobose or broadly ellipsoid, smooth, hyaline, uniguttulate, 2–3 × 1.5–2 μ; basidia 3.5–4 μ in diameter; cystidia present as inconspicuous paraphysis-like organs slightly larger than the basidia, bluntly pointed at the tips, 4–5 μ in diameter; context hyphae somewhat agglutinated, sparingly branched, thin-walled, with cross walls and clamps, mostly 4–6 μ in diameter. (Compare no. 63, *Polyporus guttulatus*, and no. 83, *P. borealis*.)

Habitat: On stump of *Picea*.

Distribution: Specimens have been examined only from the type locality, Ottawa, Ontario, Canada.

Illustrations: Overholts, Mycologia 33: 99, figs. 7, 11.

Superficially, except for the small pores, this fungus resembles *Polyporus borealis*. The minute spores, definitely attached to basidia as well as free-floating in abundance, make it a very distinctive species. The habit recalls, also, that of *P. osseus*, from which the species is quite different in every other character. It is possible that other collections may show the fungus to be more definitely stipitate.

76. Polyporus abieticola Overh.

Mycologia 33: 93. 1941

(Figs. 542–543)

Sporophore sessile or strongly decurrent on the substratum, scarcely imbricate; pileus 0.5–2 cm. long, 1–7 cm. broad, 2–10 mm.

thick, watery and rather coriaceous when fresh, bending without breaking, pale watery buff to watery brown, very compactly tomentose, the margin rather thick, triangular in vertical section; context homogeneous, tough, not brittle on drying, pallid, 1–5 mm. thick, taste mild; tubes 1–3 mm. long, the pore surface pallid or straw color, the mouths subcircular or circular, rather thick-walled, entire, averaging 3–4 per mm.; spores ellipsoid to subglobose, smooth, hyaline, minute, 2.5–3 × 2–2.5 μ; basidia about 4 μ in diameter, 4-spored; cystidia none; context hyphae long and flexuous, sparingly branched, the walls partly or almost completely thickened, with no cross walls or clamps, 2–3 μ in diameter.

HABITAT: On dead wood of *Abies balsamea.*

DISTRIBUTION: Specimens have been examined only from Me. and, in Canada, from Quebec.

ILLUSTRATIONS: Overholts, Mycologia 33: 92, fig. 4.

There are so few species with the minute spores of this one that not many comparisons can be made. The fungus differs from *Polyporus canadensis* in not drying fragile and in not being at all fragile when fresh; the hyphae are of the type of those of more coriaceous species of the genus, without either cross walls or clamps and with thickened walls. The spores are entirely different from those of *P. anceps*, which the species perhaps resembles most closely, and the dendritic hyphae of that species are lacking. In 1940 a collection on *Abies balsamea* was made at Kokadjo, Maine, by H. G. Eno, and in 1942 another collection, also from Maine and on the same substratum, was received from F. H. Steinmetz.

77. POLYPORUS FUMIDICEPS (Atk.) Sacc. & Trott.

Syll. Fung. 21: 278. 1912

(Figs. 122, 640, and Plate 130)

Tyromyces fumidiceps Atk., Ann. Mycol. 6: 61. 1908.

Sporophore sessile, soft, watery, and rather fragile when fresh, drying rigid; pileus 1–4 × 2–6 × 0.5–1 cm., not pure white but gray to vinaceous-buff, avellaneous, or wood-brown, minutely pubescent or sparingly short hirsute-tomentose, or glabrous; context white, with a strong fragrant odor when fresh, 2–5 mm. thick; pore surface white or pallid, the tubes 2–5 mm. long, sometimes pale olive-green within on drying, the mouths angular, thin-walled, entire to slightly lacerate, averaging 4–5 per mm.; spores ellipsoid to subglobose, smooth, hyaline, 2.5–3.5 $\times$ 2–2.5 μ; cystidia none; hyphae rather thick-walled, mostly considerably branched with numerous hyphal complexes, a few larger ones unbranched, with cross walls and clamps, 3–6 μ in diameter. (Compare no. 73, *Polyporus albellus*, and no. 86, *P. gqlactinus.*)

HABITAT: On dead wood of deciduous trees, noted on *Acer*, *Betula*, *Fagus*, *Fraxinus*, *Salix*, and *Ulmus*; a single collection on *Thuja*.

DISTRIBUTION: Specimens have been examined from N.Y., Pa., N.J., Del., Md., Tenn., Ohio, and Mo.; in Canada from Quebec and Ontario.

ILLUSTRATIONS: Overholts, Ann. Mo. Bot. Gard. 2: pl. 23, fig. 6.

This species is separated from the *Polyporus albellus* group by the minute ellipsoid or subglobose spores. It is separated from *P. galactinus* by the nearly glabrous, gray pileus, the longer tubes, and the somewhat smaller spores. *P. smaragdinus* Lloyd (111, p. 818), described from collections by Brenckle in Arkansas, seems to be closely related, though it differs in having a browner pileus and in being larger.

The sweet odor sometimes persists for several months in dried plants, or it may become rather rancid. The species is occasionally met in the Mississippi and Ohio River Valleys, particularly on old logs along overflow river bottoms, but it is only rarely sent in by correspondents.

78. POLYPORUS COMPACTUS Overh.

Torrey Bot. Club Bul. 49: 170. 1922

(Figs. 131, 136, 592, and Plate 129)

Sporophore resupinate to narrowly reflexed or cushion-shaped; pileus not more than 1 cm. broad, and 1.5 cm. thick, in resupinate condition 3–8 mm. thick, white or gray, corky-watery when fresh, firm and compact when dry, glabrous or practically so, the margin rounded and obtuse; context light wood color, friable but compact when dry, odor disagreeable, taste mild; pore surface white, the tubes oblique, less than 2 mm. long, often lacking or poorly developed, the mouths subcircular, entire, averaging 3–4 per mm.; basidiospores ellipsoid or ovoid, often with a slightly truncate apex, hyaline, 7.5–9 × 4.5–6 μ; chlamydospores abundant on the hymenium and the hyphae of the context, subglobose to broadly ellipsoid, colorless or somewhat greenish or yellowish under the microscope, 7.5–9 × 6–7.5 μ or 6–7.5 μ in diameter; basidia large, pyriform, 9–10 μ in diameter; cystidia mixed with the basidia as pointed, narrow, flask-shaped organs 3–4 μ in diameter; hyphae of two kinds: (a) large, hyaline, unstaining hyphae often thick-walled, abruptly breaking up at one end into from several to many smaller branches that gradually taper out to the extremity, with no cross walls or clamps, 3–5 μ in diameter in the larger portions, and (b) small deeply staining and much-branched hyphae bearing at least some of the chlamydospores, with a few cross walls and clamps, 2–3.5 μ in diameter.

HABITAT: On dead standing trunks or on stumps of *Quercus*, especially *Q. alba*, and occasionally on *Fagus*, *Liquidambar*, and *Robinia*.

DISTRIBUTION: Specimens have been examined from Me., Pa., N.J., Md., Tenn., Ohio, and Ill.; in Canada from Ontario.

ILLUSTRATIONS: Overholts, Torrey Bot. Club Bul. 49: pl. 9, figs. 5–6.

Occasional collections of this species have been made since it was described, but all specimens are imperfectly developed. That the fungus is of some economic importance is brought out by the fact that it has frequently been cultured from butt-decayed oaks by W. A. Campbell and others.

79. POLYPORUS AMYGDALINUS Berk. & Rav.
Grevillea 1: 49. 1872
(Plate 128)

Sporophore sessile, dimidiate, applanate, soft and fleshy-watery when fresh, rigid but not hard on drying and then very light in weight; pileus 5–15 × 6–20 × 1–3 cm., or, if on top of a log, forming a mass as much as 30 cm. broad, densely tomentose-velutinous, probably white or pale buff when fresh, dirty white or cinereous on drying, azonate, the margin sometimes thick and obtuse; context white, soft, drying spongy, 1–2 cm. thick; pore surface white, cinereous or somewhat yellowish on drying, the tubes 1–2 mm. long, the mouths angular, thin-walled, uneven in side view, entire or denticulate, averaging 3–4 per mm., visible to the unaided eye; spores narrow-ellipsoid or very narrowly ovoid, smooth, hyaline, 3–3.5 × 1.5–2 μ; cystidia none; hyphae a mixture of considerably branched, nonstaining, narrow ones 3–5 μ in diameter, and wider ones 6–10 μ in diameter, heavily stained in eosin and looking like latex hyphae, with cross walls and clamps present and rather large, but staining poorly and quite inconspicuous; sections and context tissue lemon-yellow in KOH.   (Compare no. 28, *Polyporus sulphureus.*)

HABITAT: On dead wood of deciduous trees, noted on *Quercus.*

DISTRIBUTION: Specimens have been examined from Fla., Ala., and La.; type collected in S.C. by Ravenel.

This species is likely to be mistaken for *Polyporus sulphureus*, especially in the dried condition, but the spores are entirely different, the pileus when fresh is not bright-colored, and dried specimens are even lighter in weight than in that species.   The taste and the odor of fresh specimens are said to be amygdaline, but they do not persist in dried plants.   Our knowledge of this plant was extremely fragmentary until R. P. Burke rediscovered it near Montgomery, Alabama, in 1916.   Humphrey collected it in Louisiana in 1909, and Murrill in Florida in 1923.   Humphrey's specimen is at Beltsville, Maryland.   Burke's specimens are in the Missouri Botanical Garden, St. Louis, Missouri, in the New York Botanical Garden, and in the Lloyd Herbarium.

Nothing is known about the decay caused by this fungus.   In culture it produces a characteristic growth and becomes beautifully orange—entirely different from *Polyporus sulphureus*, which it might be expected to resemble in color.   Cultures are distinctly odorous, with a pleasant amygdaline fragrance.

80. POLYPORUS RIGIDUS Lév.

Ann. Sci. Nat. Bot. III, 2: 189. 1844

(Fig. 93 and Plate 131)

Polystictus rigidus (Lév.) Sacc., Syll. Fung. 6: 271. 1888.
Polyporus undatus Pers., Myc. Eur., Sec. 2, p. 90. 1825.
Polyporus Broomei Rabenh., Fungi Eur., no. 2004. 1876.

Sporophore sessile or more often largely or entirely resupinate, sometimes laterally connate, cartilaginous to fleshy-leathery when fresh, rigid and hard when dry; pileus dimidiate, 0–1.5 × 1–2 × 0.2–0.5 cm., somewhat flesh-colored or nearly white when fresh, isabelline or pale hazel in dried plants, convex, radiate-rugose and finally somewhat rough-tomentose to villose-tomentose, rather strongly zoned, the zones sometimes darker and more conspicuous in dried plants, usually drying rough-tomentose, the margin rather thin, somewhat deflexed on drying; context nearly white, 1–3 mm. thick, drying very hard; pore surface more or less flesh-colored and remaining somewhat so in dried plants or becoming somewhat smoky or gray, the tubes 1–3 mm. long, the mouths angular, thin-walled, entire, typically gray-pruinose, scarcely visible to the unaided eye, averaging 6–9 per mm.; spores globose or subglobose, smooth, hyaline, 4.5–6 × 4–5 μ or 4–5 μ in diameter; cystidia scarcely noteworthy, a few pointed organs sometimes present in the hymenium; hyphae sparingly branched, hyaline, mostly with very much thickened or completely thickened walls, with a few cross walls but no clamps, 5–10 μ in diameter or somewhat narrower. (Compare no. 81, *Polyporus zonalis*.)

HABITAT: On dead wood of deciduous trees, noted on *Acer, Carya, Fagus, Fraxinus, Liriodendron, Ostrya, Platanus, Populus, Quercus*, and *Ulmus*.

DISTRIBUTION: Specimens have been examined from Pa., N.J., Md., W. Va., Fla., Ala., La., Ohio, Ind., Mich., Iowa, and Mo.; in Canada from Ontario.

In vertical sections of the pileus there is a marked distinction between the context, with its large, thick-walled hyphae, and the trama of the tubes, with hyphae of much smaller diameter.

This species is closely related to *Polyporus zonalis* and perhaps should be considered a variety of it. But, particularly as it is found in the Mississippi and Ohio River Valleys, it is quite distinct in its semiresupinate habit and its considerably smaller and thinner pilei, which are much less zoned and more strongly tomentose and which usually dry rough. Fresh plants vary in the color of the hymenial surface, but some flesh color can usually be discerned, and the pileus, if developed, dries pale hazel, similar to the color in *Stereum rameale*. Plants growing mostly resupinate on old logs can be separated from the substratum in large sheets. These or their fragments curl badly on drying, with the substral surface becoming rough and taking on a peculiar ochraceous-bay coloration.

The rot associated with this species is similar to that caused by *Polyporus zonalis*—a pocket rot, with the pockets either outlined in large reticulations or else large (1 cm. or more long) and lens-shaped.

81. POLYPORUS ZONALIS Berk.

Ann. and Mag. Nat. Hist. 10: Suppl., p. 375. 1843

(Figs. 88, 99–101, 118, and Plate 132)

Rigidoporus surinamensis (Miq.) Murr., Torrey Bot. Club Bul. 34: 473. 1907.

Sporophore sessile or effused-reflexed, leathery when fresh, very hard and rigid when dry; pileus dimidiate or flabelliform, 1–7 × 2–9 × 0.1–0.5 cm., minutely pubescent to glabrous, at first white, becoming pale ochraceous to rufescent, isabelline, or ochraceous bay at maturity and on drying, multizonate with narrow concolorous or slightly darker zones, or sometimes with chestnut or dark zones, sometimes entirely bay-red behind, conspicuously radiate-striate or radiate-rugose, the margin thin, entire, strongly incurved on drying; context 0.25–1 mm. thick, pallid to concolorous; pore surface more or less flesh-colored and usually remaining so in dried plants, the tubes 2–4 mm. long, the mouths angular, thin-walled, entire, averaging 8–9 per mm.; spores globose, smooth, hyaline, 4–5 μ in diameter; basidia pyriform, 8–10 μ in diameter; cystidia none; hyphal pegs absent; hyphae closely compacted, hyaline, simple, thick-walled, sometimes with a few cross walls but no clamps, up to 9 μ in diameter.

HABITAT: On dead wood of deciduous trees, noted on *Carya*, *Citrus*, *Nyssa*, *Populus*, *Quercus*, and *Ulmus*.

DISTRIBUTION: Specimens have been examined from Fla., Ala., La., and Miss.

ILLUSTRATIONS: Lloyd, Synop. Apus, fig. 675.

The species is well characterized by its usually small size (less than 5 cm. broad), the multizonate pileus with ochraceous zones or shades, which dries very hard and with margin deflexed, and the very small pores. The context is usually much less than 1 mm. thick, and the large thick-walled hyphae of which it is mostly composed are an aid in separating the species from small, zonate forms of *Polyporus lignosus* of the tropics.

One variation is probably more puzzling than others. Several collections have been noted in which the pilei are covered with a very fine film of grayish pubescence, so as to give them quite a different color.

Investigations carried on by me in 1931 in Louisiana seem to point to the probability that this species is the cause of a widespread and serious heart rot of various living trees. The rot constantly associated with sporophores of this species showed either large and distinct reticulations in the wood or lens-shaped pockets 1 cm. or more long and nearly as broad. This is the same type of rot that is produced by *Polyporus rigidus* and *Poria undata,* and is additional evidence that these three are all variations of one species. Typical *Polyporus zonalis* is a common species in the Gulf States; the other two range farther north.

6b. *Tubes becoming more than 0.5 cm. long* (see also *Trametes Humeana* and *Polyporus iowensis,* p. 426; *P. lignosus* and *Tyromyces magnisporus,* p. 427; and *Tyromyces Tigertianus,* p. 428)

82. POLYPORUS SPRAGUEI Berk. & Curt.
Grevillea 1: 50. 1872
(Figs. 145, 255, 633, and Plate 132)

Tyromyces Spraguei (Berk. & Curt.) Murr., North Amer. Flora 9: 33. 1907.

Sporophore sessile or rarely effused-reflexed, watery-corky, somewhat flexible when fresh, typically drying very hard and rigid; pileus 4–12 × 4–15 × 0.6–3 cm., white or whitish to cinereous or pale "mouse gray," frequently somewhat reddish on the extreme margin when fresh and growing, and in early stages distilling watery drops from the margin and upper surface, not much changed on drying, appressed-tomentose or glabrous, often rugose or tuberculate, the margin often blackening when dried and in young specimens becoming green where handled; context white, watery-tough when fresh, very hard when dry, zonate, 0.3–2.5 cm. thick, sometimes pleasantly scented, taste bitter but usually not strongly so; pore surface white or whitish, often discolored on drying, the tubes 0.2–1 cm. long, the mouths rather thin-walled, entire, averaging 3–5 per mm.; spores ovoid to subglobose, smooth, hyaline, 4.5–7 × 4–5 μ;

basidia 6–8 μ in diameter; cystidia none; hyphae of two types, sometimes the one and sometimes the other predominating, one large, thick-walled, with narrow staining lumina, sparingly branched or simple, with a few conspicuous cross walls and clamps, 4–9 μ in diameter, the other smaller, thin-walled, often collapsing, frequently with oil globules, not much branched, with occasional clamps, 3–4 μ in diameter; tramal hyphae very small, about 2 μ in diameter. (Compare no. 61, *Polyporus durescens*.)

HABITAT: On dead wood and at the bases of living deciduous trees, especially *Quercus*, also noted on *Betula*, *Castanea*, *Fagus*, *Juglans*, *Liquidambar*, *Platanus*, *Prunus*, and *Ulmus*; reported on *Diospyros* (Ind., Weir [231]).

DISTRIBUTION: Specimens have been examined from N.H., Vt., Mass., Conn., N.Y., Pa., N.J., D.C., Va., W. Va., N.C., Ga., La., Tenn., Ohio, Ind., Ill., Mich., Mo., Nebr., and Ark.; in Canada from Ontario; also reported from Iowa (Wolf [234]) and Wash. (Zeller [236]).

In the Appalachian states this species seems to prefer oak logs, stumps, and trees. In the past I have confused with it the related species *Polyporus durescens*, which is extremely similar and becomes equally hard on drying, though perhaps never blackening. The best distinguishing characters are the very different spores, the much larger basidia, and either the absence of odor or the pleasant smell. The hyphae also seem to be different, for clamps are entirely lacking in *P. durescens*, whereas in *P. Spraguei*, though not abundant, they are very conspicuous and well formed. *P. sordidus* Cooke is said to be a synonym. See further discussion under no. 61, *P. durescens*.

The fungus produces a reddish-brown, general carbonizing decay of the heartwood (Weir [231]), quite similar to that of *Polyporus sulphureus* and of *Daedalea quercina*.

83. POLYPORUS BOREALIS Fries

Syst. Myc. 1: 366. 1821

(Figs. 132–135, 555, 572, 599, 626, and Plate 128)

Spongipellis borealis (Fries) Pat., Essai Tax. Hym., p. 84. 1900.
Polyporus pacificus Kauffman, Mich. Acad. Sci. Arts and Letters Papers 11: 178. 1930.

Sporophore sessile or substipitate, occasionally varying to multiplex as in *Polyporus frondosus* or *P. Berkeleyi*, soft but tough and watery when fresh, bending double without breaking, rigid on drying; pileus 3–15 × 4–15 × 0.5–2.5(–4) cm., or rarely in multiplex clusters 10 cm. or more broad, white when fresh, yellowish in age and on drying, hispid to tomentose, often radiate-fibrillose, drying rough; context white, usually duplex, firm and fibrous (hard when dry) next the hymenium, soft and floccose above, 0.3–2 cm. thick, not bitter; pore surface white, yellowish on drying, the tubes 3–15 mm. long, the mouths angular to daedaloid, dentate or uneven, thin-walled, averaging 2–3 per mm.; a stemlike and sometimes rooting base present in plants growing in a multiplex fashion from buried wood; spores ellipsoid, broadly ellipsoid, or ovoid, smooth, hyaline, 4.5–7 × 3.5–5 μ; cystidia abundant or scarce, hyaline, ventricose or fusoid, thick-walled above, thin-walled below, 24–40 × 7–10 μ, projecting 5–20 μ beyond the basidia; hyphal pegs none; hyphae of lower context simple or nearly so, mostly very thick-walled, with very occasional cross walls and clamps, 4.5–9 μ in diameter, hyphae of upper context much agglutinated, thin-walled, with occasional clamps, 3–4 μ in diameter. (Compare no. 63, *Polyporus guttulatus*.)

HABITAT: On logs and stumps, from buried roots of coniferous trees, and occasionally on living trunks, noted on *Abies*, *Picea*, *Pinus*, and *Tsuga*; reported on *Acer* (Vt., Murrill, and Spaulding [209]) and on *Populus* (Wis., Neuman [148]).

DISTRIBUTION: Specimens have been examined from Me., N.H., Vt., Mass., Conn., N.Y., Pa., N.J., Va., N.C., Tenn., Ohio, Mich., Colo., Mont., Idaho, Ore., Wash., and Alaska; in Canada from Nova Scotia, New Brunswick, Prince Edward Island, and British Columbia; reported from Wis. (Dodge [40]) and Mont. (Weir [227]).

ILLUSTRATIONS: Atkinson, Cornell Agr. Exp. Sta. Bul. 193: figs. 56–59; *idem*, Mushrooms, fig. 9; Kauffman, Mich. Acad. Sci. Arts and Letters Papers 11: pls. 24–26 (as *Polyporus pacificus*); Lloyd, Synop. Apus, figs. 668–670; Shope, Mo. Bot. Gard. Ann. 18: pl. 20.

This is a rather rare plant in most localities, quite northern in its range, but extending southward in the mountains of the Allegheny region, and usually found on hemlock, often near the base of the trunk or even on the roots. A characteristic feature of dried specimens is the rough upper surface and the very hard and distinct lower layer of the duplex context.   Among related species the plant is most certainly recognized by the cystidia in the hymenium.   A distinct stem is developed, though rarely, in sporophores of multiplex habit, and such sporophores were the basis of *Polyporus pacificus*, the types of which I have examined through the courtesy of Dr. E. B. Mains.   With the exception of the more centrally stipitate habit, the superficial characters of *P. pacificus* indicate *P. borealis*, and the microscopic characters confirm the similarity.   The spores are as in *P. borealis*, and the cystidia are exactly the same as in that species.   Instead of being "abundant," they are, I should say, only somewhat so, or, in some sections, not at all abundant.   Rather than being always "acutely pointed," large numbers of them are rather obtuse—at least not at all sharply pointed.   They are not "thin-walled," but have the peculiar characteristic of having their walls completely thickened at the apex of the cystidium, while in the basal part a lumen is present and the walls are thin.   All of these characters are those of *P. borealis*.   The sclerotium described as present in the types of *P. pacificus* is probably the rooting stemlike base, occasioned by the growth of the plant from deeply buried wood.

The decay produced is of the general delignifying type, with numerous small white flecks through the wood.   Miss C. W. Fritz (55, p. 230) reports that this species forms chlamydospores in cultures.

84. POLYPORUS ROBINIOPHILUS (Murr.) Lloyd

Letter 42: 12. 1912

(Figs. 68–69, 544, 663, and Plate 131)

Trametes robiniophila Murr., North Amer. Flora 9: 42. 1907.

Sporophore sessile, somewhat watery but firm when fresh, corky when dry, often in imbricate clusters as much as 10 cm. or more thick; pileus 3.5–15 × 4–20 × 1–5 cm., white, becoming cinereous, smoky, or yellowish on drying, glabrous or nearly so, frequently uneven or nodulose, sometimes subzonate or furrowed toward the margin; context white, soft and punky and often with a pleasant odor when dry, 0.5–3 cm. thick; pore surface white, often discoloring on drying, the tubes 0.3–1 cm. long, the mouths angular, averaging 4–6 per mm., the dissepiments rather thin but entire; spores ovoid to subglobose, smooth, hyaline, 6–9 × 5.5–7 μ; basidia 9–12 μ in diameter; cystidia often abundant as rather prominent fusoid organs in the hymenium, 3–9 μ in diameter; hyphae long and flexuous, simple, with completely thickened walls, with no cross walls or clamps, 6–12 μ in diameter, sometimes with smaller hyphae intermixed. (Compare no. 10, *Fomes geotropus*, and no. 6, *Trametes suaveolens*.)

HABITAT: On trunks of deciduous trees, especially *Robinia*, noted also on *Acer*, *Broussonetia*, *Celtis*, *Liriodendron*, *Morus*, *Paulownia*, and *Quercus*.

DISTRIBUTION: Specimens have been examined from Pa., Md., D.C., Va., W. Va., Ga., Miss., Tenn., Ky., Ohio, Ind., Mich., Wis., Mo., Kans., and Texas; reported from N.Y. (Lowe [125]) and Ill. (McDougall [128]).

ILLUSTRATIONS: Hesler, Tenn. Acad. Sci. Jour. 4: fig. 1; Lloyd, Synop. Apus, fig. 653 (as *Trametes*); McDougall, Ill. State Acad. Sci. Trans. 12: fig. 5; *idem*, Mushrooms, opp. p. 115; Overholts, Wash. Univ. Studies 3: pl. 4, fig. 17.

In the Ohio River Valley this is a common species on black locust, but it seems to be better developed when growing on hackberry than on any other host. The consistency of the plant allies it to *Trametes*, but neither the spores nor the tubes are of the *Trametes* type.

The construction of the hymenial layer shows much variation. The basidia, when seen with sterigmata, are clavate and 9–10 μ in diameter. They are rarely seen in good condition. More rounded or pyriform organs, 10–12 μ in diameter, that may be immature basidia are usually numerous in the hymenium. Mixed with these at most stages are more fusoid bodies, varying from 3 to 9 μ in diameter, that would seem to be sterile. In most specimens the context is almost entirely composed of large-diameter hyphae with entirely thickened walls, but sometimes one finds with these a considerable number of small, staining, much-branched hyphae which apparently disintegrate at maturity.

The fungus produces a white or pale-brownish general delignifying heart rot in the trunk of its hosts, the sounder wood being separated from the decayed wood by a narrow darker line (Kauffman and Kerber [107]).

85. Polyporus Calkinsii (Murr.) Sacc. & Trott.

Syll. Fung. 21: 280. 1912

(Fig. 85)

Tyromyces Calkinsii Murr., North Amer. Flora 9: 32. 1907.

Sporophore sessile, somewhat watery but corky and flexible when fresh, rigid but compressible when dry; pileus dimidiate, convex to subungulate, 3–12 × 4–18 × 0.6–4 cm., often imbricate, white when fresh, gray to ochraceous or partly ochraceous on drying, without an evident cuticle, slightly rough-tomentose to glabrous, azonate; context white, 0.5–2 cm. thick, firm-corky, usually with a fragrant odor in dried specimens; pore surface white, discolored darker on drying and sometimes slightly smoky, the tubes 2–8 mm. long, the mouths circular to angular, rather thick-walled, entire, averaging 4–5 per mm.; spores globose, hyaline, 3.5–4 μ in diameter; cystidia none; hyphae mostly thick-walled, the larger ones simple, the smaller ones branched, breaking at the occasional or rare clamps, up to 8 μ in diameter.

Habitat: On dead wood and growing from wounds in living trees, noted on *Liquidambar* and *Magnolia*.

Distribution: Specimens have been examined only from Fla.

I am thoroughly convinced that Lloyd is right in referring Murrill's *Tyromyces nivosellus* (from Cuba and Puerto Rico), and possibly *T. Palmarum* (from Cuba and Jamaica), as synonyms of this species. The plants of *Polyporus Calkinsii* are similar to those of *P. palustris*, but if our present ideas of spore form in the two species are correct, they are quite distinct. *P. palustris* is found on wood of coniferous trees. At times the hymenium of *P. Calkinsii* is rather dark, but scarcely enough so to suggest *P. fumosus*, from which this species is very distinct in the absence of a dark line separating tubes from context and in the absence of abundant and conspicuous clamps on the hyphae. *P. submurinus* is quite similar to *P. Calkinsii* in appearance, but has cylindric spores.

In a Puerto Rico collection in my herbarium I find spores as described by Lloyd (116, p. 307).

86. POLYPORUS GALACTINUS Berk.

London Jour. Bot. 6: 321. 1847

(Figs. 119–121, 618, and Plate 130)

Spongipellis galactinus (Berk.) Pat., Essai Tax. Hym., p. 84. 1900.

Sporophore sessile, soft and watery when fresh, rigid when dry; pileus (2–)3–8 × 4–12 × 1–3 cm., white or grayish white when fresh, conspicuously strigose-tomentose at the base, short-tomentose on the margin, drying yellowish and rough-tomentose; context white, very soft and watery when fresh, hard and sometimes resinous when dry, usually not strongly duplex, 0.3–2 cm. thick, strongly zonate, with a peculiar fragrant odor when fresh; pore surface white or yellowish, the tubes 5–10 mm. long, the mouths thin-walled, angular, entire or denticulate, averaging 4–6 per mm.; spores ellipsoid, smooth, hyaline, uniguttulate, 2.5–3 × 2–2.5 μ; cystidia none, or represented by narrow pointed paraphysis-like structures in the nonsporulating hymenium; hyphal pegs rare, slender, pointed; hyphae simple or sparingly branched, strongly agglutinated and difficult to separate, thin-walled, with some cross walls and clamps, 3–6 μ in diameter. (Compare no. 64, *Polyporus immitis*; no. 72, *P. tephroleucus*; no. 73, *P. albellus*; no. 77, *P. fumidiceps*; no. 89, *P. fissilis*; and *P. iowensis*, p. 426.)

HABITAT: On dead wood of deciduous trees, noted on *Acer, Betula, Fagus, Liquidambar, Platanus, Prunus, Quercus, Salix,* and *Ulmus.*

DISTRIBUTION: Specimens have been examined from Me., Mass., N.Y., Pa., Del., Md., D.C., Va., W. Va., N.C., Ala., La., Tenn., Ky., Ohio, Ind., Mich., Minn., Mo., and Ark.; in Canada from Nova Scotia and Quebec; reported from Iowa (Wolf [234]) and Ore. (Kauffman [103]).

ILLUSTRATIONS: Lloyd, Synop. Apus, figs. 643–646; Overholts, Mo. Bot. Gard. Ann. 2: pl. 24, figs. 12, 15, 17.

This is a species that reaches its best development in the Ohio and Mississippi River Valleys, is found only occasionally in the Eastern states, and is practically unknown from the West. In the first of these regions it is a rather common and characteristic species, easily recognized by the hairy (strigose-tomentose) pileus, the pleasant odor, the zonate context of fresh specimens, and the small, ellipsoid spores. Dried specimens are often resinous in appearance, and this also seems to be more or less characteristic.

In many specimens the hymenium collapses quickly in drying, and such specimens frequently do not yield spores. The species is easily separated from *Polyporus albellus* by the hairy covering and the different spores. *P. spumeus* var. *malicola* is distinct in the larger spores. Dodge's report of *P. galactinus* on apple trees (41, pp. 12–14) in New England should be referred, rather, to *P. spumeus* var. *malicola*.

I have re-examined all the collections in my own herbarium that seemed likely to be in a sporulating condition and fail to find that I have confused any collection with *Polyporus immitis* Peck, which I must admit is distinct in the very different spores, as has been pointed out by Kauffman (104).

87. POLYPORUS SPUMEUS Sow. ex Fries

Syst. Myc. 1: 358. 1821

(Figs. 114, 126, 552, and Plate 132)

Boletus spumeus Sow., Col. Fig. English Fungi, pl. 211. 1799.
Spongipellis occidentalis Murr., North Amer. Flora 9: 38. 1907.

Sporophore sessile, often imbricate, soft and watery when fresh, rigid and friable when dry; pileus 5–20 × 5–20 × 2–6 cm., white or somewhat yellowish, villose-strigose or matted strigose-tomentose, gray and almost glabrous in extreme age; context white, 0.5–3 cm. thick, more or less duplex, not drying resinous; pore surface white or yellowish, the tubes 1–2 cm. long, the mouths angular, averaging 2–4 per mm., the dissepiments thin and acute, entire or slightly dentate, often collapsing; spores broadly ellipsoid or subglobose, smooth, hyaline, 6–8(–10) × 4.5–6 μ or 5–7 μ in diameter; cystidia none, but sometimes isolated basidia, 6–8 μ in diameter, project so as to give the appearance of obtuse, peglike cystidia; hyphae of the lower context not at all agglutinated, thick-walled, those of the upper context thinner-walled and often collapsing, often tortuous, somewhat branched, with rather frequent but not conspicuous cross walls and clamps, 5–8 μ in diameter. (Compare no. 72, *Polyporus tephroleucus*; no. 73, *P. albellus*; no. 88, *P. delectans*; and no. 89, *P. fissilis*.)

HABITAT: Growing from wounds in living deciduous trees or rarely on hardwood logs, noted on *Acer, Aesculus, Fagus, Populus, Salix, Tilia,* and *Ulmus*; reported also on *Carya* (Wis., Neuman [148]), on *Celtis* (Mo., Maneval [131]), and on *Fraxinus* (Mich., Kauffman [101]).

DISTRIBUTION: Specimens have been examined from N.H., Vt., Mass., N.Y., Pa., W. Va., Ohio, Ind., Mich., Minn., Iowa, Mo., Colo., Mont., Wash.; in Canada from Quebec, Manitoba, and British Columbia; reported from Tenn. (Kauffman [100]), Wis. (Neuman [148]), and S. Dak. (Brenckle [25]).

ILLUSTRATIONS: Berkeley, Outl. British Fung., pl. 16, fig. 4; Hornemann, Flora Danica, pl. 1794 (as *Boletus*); Lloyd, Synop. Apus, figs. 641–642; Overholts, Mo. Bot. Gard. Ann. 2: pl. 24, figs. 10, 14a; Shope, Mo. Bot. Gard. Ann. 18: pl. 28, fig. 2.

I have discussed (150, pp. 701–704) the early history of this species and its relation to *Polyporus delectans,* from which it is usually easily distinguished by the smaller pores. After considerable weathering *in situ* the tomentum of the pileus wears away in part, often leaving the surface with a definite membranous cuticular crust. The species is easily separated from *P. fissilis* by the much larger spores, the lack of agglutination in the hyphae of the lower context, and the lack of zonation in the context. Zonation is well marked in *P. fissilis* and is associated with a resinous lower context in dried plants.

Var. MALICOLA Lloyd

Synop. Apus, p. 305. 1915

(Figs. 115, 146, 550, 556)

Sporophore usually much thinner than in the species, frequently drying yellowish and when dried showing a hard and resinous lower context with the hyphae much agglutinated; spores 4–5 × 3.5–4 μ.

HABITAT: On wounded areas or in hollows of living trees, especially apple (*Pyrus malus*), but occasionally on other hosts, including *Acer, Carya, Fraxinus,* and *Populus.*

DISTRIBUTION: Specimens have been examined from Me., Vt., Conn., N.Y., Pa., N.J., Tenn., and Ohio; in Canada from Quebec and Ontario.

ILLUSTRATIONS: Dodge, Mycologia 8: pl. 175 (as *Spongipellis galactinus*).

The variety *malicola* may be more closely related to *Polyporus fissilis* than to *P. spumeus*. It might even be considered a valid species, but the differentiation would have to be solely on grounds of coloration and the thinness of the pileus.

88. POLYPORUS DELECTANS Peck

Torrey Bot. Club Bul. 11: 26. 1884

(Figs. 113, 632, and Plate 129)

Spongipellis delectans (Peck) Murr., North Amer. Flora 9: 38. 1907.
Trametes Krekei Lloyd, Letter 69: 12. 1919.

Sporophore sessile or effused-reflexed, rarely varying to almost entirely resupinate, tough, spongy and watery when fresh, rigid when dry; pileus 3–15 × 5–20 × 1.5–5 cm., whitish or slightly yellowish, drying yellowish or ochraceous, glabrous or finely tomentose, even; context white, more or less duplex and rather friable when dry, 0.5–2 cm. thick; pore surface white or yellowish, the tubes 0.5–2 cm. long, the mouths circular to subangular or sinuous, averaging 1–2 per mm., the dissepiments slightly dentate, thin and acute, sometimes collapsing on drying; spores ellipsoid to subglobose, smooth, hyaline, 5–8 × 4–6 μ, usually with some (immature?) spores of smaller sizes; cystidia none; hyphae of lower context in part thick-walled, nearly simple, 5–8 μ in diameter, and in part thin-walled, branched, 4–6 μ in diameter, hyphae of upper context all thin-walled, sparingly branched, 4–6 μ in diameter, all hyphae with cross walls and clamps. (Compare no. 87, *Polyporus spumeus*, and no. 90, *P. obtusus*.)

HABITAT: Growing on old logs of deciduous trees, or more rarely from wounds in living trees, noted on *Acer*, *Carya*, *Fraxinus*, *Juglans*, *Populus*, and *Quercus*.

DISTRIBUTION: Specimens have been examined from Vt., Conn., N.Y., Pa., Del., Md., D.C., Va., Tenn., Ohio, Ind., Mich., Wis., Mo., Nebr., and Ore.; in Canada from Quebec and Ontario; reported from Iowa (Wolf [234]).

ILLUSTRATIONS: Lloyd, Synop. Apus, fig. 667; Overholts, Mo. Bot. Gard. Ann. 2: pl. 24, fig. 14b.

The species differs from *Polyporus spumeus* and *P. galactinus* in the larger pores, and is distinct from *P. albellus* in both the larger pores and the very different spores, not to mention other characters. Microscopically, it is similar to *P. obtusus*, and specimens may easily be taken to be small-pored, undersized examples of that species. Apparently the best separating character is the thinner-walled hyphae of the upper context, for in *P. obtusus* the upper-context hyphae are thick-walled, like those of the lower context. *Trametes Krekei* is a semiresupinate form of this species.

The fungus sometimes grows from wounded areas on living trees, but more often it is found on fallen timbers. It is probably always a saprophyte, and produces a general delignifying decay in which the annual layers of the wood separate easily and the whitened wood is marked with small, transverse, white flecks, slightly longer than broad, but scarcely exceeding 1 mm. in any direction.

89. POLYPORUS FISSILIS Berk. & Curt.
Hooker's Jour. Bot. 1: 234. 1849
(Figs. 117, 129, 624, and Plate 129)

Spongipellis fissilis (Berk. & Curt.) **Murr.**, North Amer. Flora 9: 39. 1907.
Polyporus fusco-mutans Lloyd, Myc. Notes 67: 1158. 1922.

Sporophore sessile, soft and watery-cartilaginous when fresh, drying hard; pileus 4–10 × 6–17 × 1–7 cm., white to reddish-discolored, sometimes somewhat reddish on drying, azonate, subglabrous to sodden-tomentose or coarsely fibrillose, roughly tomentose to nearly glabrous behind; context white or somewhat flesh-colored, fibrous, tough, strongly zonate, 0.5–6 cm. thick, taste bitter or astringent, drying hard and resinous; pore surface white or pallid flesh color, discolored to deep reddish brown where handled and usually becoming waxy and darker on drying, the tubes 4–10 mm. long, the mouths angular, thin-walled, entire or dentate, averaging 1–3 per mm.; spores ovoid or ellipsoid, smooth, hyaline, 3.5–4.5 × 3–3.5 μ; cystidia none; hyphal pegs none; hyphae much agglutinated, hyaline, the walls much thickened, with clamps and cross walls present but often difficult to distinguish, mostly 4–6(–8) μ in diameter. (Compare no. 87, *Polyporus spumeus*, and no. 133, *P. croceus*.)

HABITAT: Growing from wounds in living deciduous trees, perhaps occasionally on logs, noted on *Acer*, *Carya*, *Fraxinus*, *Liquidambar*, *Nyssa*, *Platanus*, *Pyrus*, and *Quercus*.

DISTRIBUTION: Specimens have been examined from Pa., Md., Va., W. Va., N.C., Ga., Fla., Ala., La., Miss., Tenn., Ky., and Ohio; in Canada from Ontario; reported from N.Y. (Lowe [125]).

ILLUSTRATIONS: Dodge, Mycologia 8: pl. 176 (as *Spongipellis*); Lloyd, Myc. Notes 68: fig. 2291 (as *Polyporus fusco-mutans*).

Extensive notes made by G. F. Jones on specimens collected at Oberlin, Ohio, indicate a prevailing fleshy tint to the pileus, context, and hymenium, with the context being decidedly duplex and the odor "not disagreeable when fresh." Dried plants have a pleasant odor.

The species is rather rare and not closely related to any other. It is probably nearest to *Polyporus croceus*, from which the very different colors will separate it. Spores and hyphae are almost entirely as in that species. *P. fissilis* is easily separated from *P. spumeus* by the smaller spores and the agglutinated hyphae of the lower context. The tubes in dried plants are usually waxy-firm and indentable with the thumbnail, but the context is very much harder. *P. fusco-mutans* Lloyd is apparently this species. I have a specimen from Mr. Leeper, who collected Lloyd's types, and have examined the types in the Lloyd Herbarium. Lloyd's description of the context as "cutting like Swiss cheese" is at variance with what I found in cutting the type, but otherwise the specimens accord well. Specimens collected in Louisiana in 1931 and in Pennsylvania in 1932 have a cheesy-soapy consistency. The sporophores collected in 1932 were usually aborted and formed no pores.

As here interpreted, the species is an important heart-rotting organism of living *Quercus* and *Liquidambar* in Louisiana, and probably in other Southern states. The advanced stages of decay show a soft spongy or pulpy wood mass of cinnamon-speckled appearance. The trees soon become hollow, and masses of a cheesy or soapy consistency are frequently found inside the hollows.

90. POLYPORUS OBTUSUS Berk.

Ann. and Mag. Nat. Hist. 3: 390. 1839

(Figs. 127–128 and Plate 131)

Boletus unicolor Schw., Schr. Nat. Ges. Leipzig 1: 97. 1822.
Spongipellis unicolor (Schw.) Murr., North Amer. Flora 9: 37. 1907.

Polyporus tomentoso-quercinus Johnson, Minn. Acad. Nat. Sci. Bul. 1: 338.
1878.

Sporophore sessile, spongy to firm, drying corky; pileus 3–20 ×
4–30 × 3–8 cm., convex to ungulate, white when fresh, gray to
yellowish on drying, often brownish in herbarium specimens, hirtose-
tomentose or weathering to an obscure, matted tomentum, the
margin thick and rounded; context white, spongy to soft-corky,
usually rather strongly duplex in consistency in dried plants, 1–3
cm. thick; pore surface white, yellowish or bay on drying, the tubes
1.5–3 cm. long, the mouths circular to angular or sinuous, sometimes
compound, 1 mm. or more in diameter, the walls usually rather thick
and even but sometimes strongly dentate; spores broadly ellipsoid,
some varying to subglobose, smooth, hyaline, 5–7 × 4–5 μ; cystidia
none or not noteworthy; hyphae simple or at times considerably
branched, all thick-walled, with rather abundant cross walls and
conspicuous thick-walled clamps, 4–7 μ in diameter. (Compare no.
87, *Polyporus spumeus*, and no. 88, *P. delectans*.)

HABITAT: On trunks and branches of living deciduous trees, nearly
always on *Quercus*, noted also on *Acer*, *Juglans*, and *Liquidambar*;
reported on *Carya* (Wis., Neuman [148]), on *Fagus* and *Robinia*
(Rhoads [182]), and on *Pyrus* (Mo., Maneval [131]).

DISTRIBUTION: Specimens have been examined from Pa., N.J.,
Md., D.C., Va., N.C., Ga., Fla., Ala., La., Miss., Tenn., Wis., Minn.,
Iowa, Mo., Kans., Ark., Okla., N. Mex., Ariz., and Ore.; in Canada
from Ontario.

ILLUSTRATIONS: Lloyd, Synop. Apus, fig. 666; Neuman, Wis.
Geol. and Nat. Hist. Survey Bul. 33: pl. 2, fig. 11 (as *Daedalea
obtusa*); Overholts, Wash. Univ. Studies 3: pl. 3, fig. 13; von Schrenk
and Spaulding, U. S. Dept. Agr. Pl. Ind. Bul. 149: fig. 5; Spaulding,
Mo. Bot. Gard. Ann. Rept. 16: pls. 13–14.

It seems likely that the fact that the context hyphae are all
thick-walled and that even the clamp connections are thick-walled
may prove a useful character in separating small-pored forms of this
species from large-pored forms of *Polyporus delectans*. In mounts of
that species the lower context shows some thick-walled hyphae,
but also an abundance of thin-walled ones that are considerably
branched and bear most of the clamps, and the upper context shows

hyphae that are all thin-walled.   The length of the tubes, however, is perhaps the best separating character, for even in the more applanate fruiting bodies occasionally met in *P. obtusus* the tubes are 1.5 cm. or more long and the mouths 1 mm. or more in diameter.

Neuman (148) places the species in *Daedalea*.   Murrill (139, p. 37) lists three specific names that antedate the one used here, but it seems totally unnecessary to displace a good name, and one by which the fungus has always been known.   Lowe (125, p. 71) includes this species in his New York manual, but admits there is no record of a New York collection; hence it must be doubted that it occurs in that state, though it may be looked for in the western part.

3b. *Pileus thin and coriaceous, usually less than 1 cm. thick*
4a. *Pores large, averaging not more than 2 per mm.* (see also
Trametes corrugata, p. 154)

91. POLYPORUS BASILARIS Overh.

In Bailey, Torrey Bot. Club Bul. 68: 112. 1941
(Fig. 320 and Plate 128)

Sporophore annual or reviving with only marginal growth, sessile or decurrent on the substratum, frequently poorly developed and nodulose in furrows on the trunk, imbricate where well developed, tough and leathery when fresh, rigid and hard on drying; pileus applanate or somewhat convex, 1–4 $\times$ 2.5–6 $\times$ 0.4–0.8 cm., dirty grayish, becoming grayish brown or blackish on drying, at first with a short velvety pubescence, later nearly glabrous or fibrillose-striate, not incrusted, with one or two broad zones or depressions; context white, tough, drying hard, zonate, 1–5 mm. thick; pore surface white when fresh, unchanged in drying or becoming only isabelline or dirty buff, the tubes 1–3 mm. long, the mouths circular then subangular to irregular, thick-walled, entire, averaging 3–4 per mm.; spores oblong-ellipsoid or narrow-ellipsoid, smooth, hyaline, 4–5 $\times$ 2.5–3.5 μ; basidia 4–5 μ in diameter; cystidia none; context hyphae hyaline, flexuous, sparingly branched, the walls not conspicuously thickened, with conspicuous though not abundant clamps, 3–7 μ in diameter.

HABITAT: On the lower portion of the trunks of *Cupressus macrocarpa.*

Distribution: Specimens have been examined only from Calif.

Illustrations: Bailey, Torrey Bot. Club Bul. 68: 117, fig. 3.

The species has the aspect of a trametoid and overdeveloped *Polyporus versicolor*, but the spores are quite different. It is distinct from *Fomes annosus* in the less globose spores, in the clamped context hyphae, and in being associated with a very different rot.

Harold E. Bailey (3) has studied this species in the limited range of *Cupressus macrocarpa* Hartw. in California. He reports that the brown carbonizing heart rot associated with the species is rather common. It begins in scattered areas in the wood, and these regions then often coalesce, until the greater portion of the heartwood in the lower trunk is involved, with irregular areas of undecayed wood running through the mass. In fact, except that extensive holes do not seem to occur in the wood, the picture is much like that presented by the pin rot of incense cedar.

92. Polyporus versatilis (Berk.) Rom.
Svenska Vet.-Akad. Bihang till Handl. 26, Afd. III, No. 16, p. 35. 1901
(Figs. 290, 321–322, and Plate 132)

Trametes versatilis Berk., Hooker's Jour. Bot. 1: 150. 1842.
? *Polyporus cladotrichus* Berk. & Curt., Linnean Soc. Bot. Jour. 10: 309. 1868.

Sporophore sessile or sometimes mostly or entirely resupinate; pileus dimidiate or elongate, 0–5 × 1.5–6 (or confluent laterally to 15) × 0.4–1 cm., at first villose with long silky or stiff suberect fasciculate fibers, these soon matted into a strigose-hirsute pubescence or tomentum and finally weathering into a fibrillose-striate tomentum, white, gray, blackish, or cinereous, often somewhat brownish on drying, azonate or nearly so, the margin thin and acute; context practically none, the entire pileus formed of the pubescence, which becomes more matted and interwoven next the tubes, with a total thickness of 2–5 mm., the deeper layers whitish to wood color; pore surface dark purple or lavender when fresh, often avellaneous to brown in weathered specimens, the tubes 2–5 mm. long, the mouths angular, thin-walled, uneven and often denticulate, averaging 1–2.5 per mm., sometimes radially elongate, and rarely sublamellate; spores cylindric, smooth, hyaline, 8–10 × 3–4 μ; cystidia present as numerous, small, fusoid-pointed organs 3–6 μ in diameter, slightly capitate-incrusted but incrustation soon dissolving in KOH; main hyphae simple, mostly thick-walled, with no cross walls or clamps, 2.5–5 μ in diameter.

HABITAT: On dead wood of deciduous and coniferous trees, noted on *Juniperus*, *Pinus*, *Prosopis*, *Quercus*, and *Taxodium*.

DISTRIBUTION: Specimens have been examined from N.C., Fla., La., Texas, and N. Mex.; reported from Ala. (Lloyd [111, p. 703]).

ILLUSTRATIONS: Lloyd, Myc. Notes 50: figs. 1049–1051 (as *Polystictus*).

Collectors' notes in a number of instances ascribe a purple shade to the hymenium, and I observed a sordid lavender in fresh collections made in Louisiana. Apparently the species is not uncommon in Louisiana, for it was collected there several times by Langlois; it is found occasionally in the other Gulf States.

The cystidia in the hymenium are a constant and characteristic feature of the species. They are exact counterparts of those found in *Polyporus pargamenus* and *P. abietinus*, and in sections mounted in KOH are easily seen to be similarly incrusted, though the KOH shortly dissolves the crystalline material. The present species differs from both of these, however, in the hispid pileus, the larger spores, and the size of the pores, which average 1–2.5 per mm. Spores are produced in the marginal tubes, as in most *Trametes* species. A collection at the New York Botanical Garden from Honduras, made by Peck in 1907, yields abundant spores. I can find no essential differences between *P. versatilis* and *P. cladotrichus*, although material labeled as the latter species is rare in herbaria. Lloyd (111, pp. 703–704) discusses the variations in the two species and says that *P. cladotrichus* is a synonym.

93. POLYPORUS PINSITUS Fries

Elench. Fung., p. 95. 1828
(Figs. 19–20, 27, and Plate 132)

Coriolus pinsitus (Fries) Pat., Essai Tax. Hym., p. 94. 1900.

Sporophore sessile or effused-reflexed, pliant when fresh, more or less flexible when dry, reviving; pileus dimidiate, 1–7 × 1–8 × 0.05–0.1(–0.2) cm., white to cinereous, avellaneous, or smoky brown, uniformly and conspicuously hirsute-tomentose, not becoming glabrous, concentrically multizonate with nearly or quite concolorous and persistently hairy zones, the margin thin; context white, fibrous, less than 1 mm. thick; pore surface white, yellowish, smoky brown, or almost black, the tubes less than 1 mm. long, the mouths thin-walled, angular, occasionally with a subconcentric or linear arrangement and then usually elongated in one direction, usually unequally dentate and somewhat fimbriate or denticulate, averaging 0.5–2 (rarely 3) per mm.; spores cylindric or allantoid, hyaline, 5–8 × 2.5–3.5 μ; cystidia none, or in some specimens represented by hyaline hairs projecting 8–12 μ and 2–4 μ in diameter on the projecting portion; hyphal pegs present but not abundant; many hyphae large, simple, with partially thickened walls, with no cross walls or clamps, 5–8 μ in diameter, others smaller and arising from hyphal complexes with much branching. (Compare no. 103, *Polyporus versicolor*, and no. 122, *P. pavonius*.)

HABITAT: On dead wood, usually of red cedar (*Juniperus*), noted also on *Acer*, *Fraxinus*, *Gleditsia*, *Prosopis*, and *Taxodium*; reported on *Chamaecyparis* (Weir [230]).

DISTRIBUTION: Specimens have been examined from N.C., S.C., Ga., Fla., Ala., La., Tenn., Ky., Mo., Ark., Okla., and Texas; reported also from Va. (Weir [230]), and Kans. (Bartholomew [4]).

ILLUSTRATIONS: Lloyd, Myc. Notes, Polyp. Issue No. 2: fig. 262; *idem*, Myc. Notes 57: fig. 1405 (as *Polystictus*).

The only species with which this is likely to be confused is *Polyporus pavonius*, which is, however, usually quite distinct, with entirely dissimilar spores and with small tube mouths. Yet occasional specimens are troublesome, and, in the absence of spores, the best separating character seems to be the regularly dentate pore mouths of *P. pinsitus*. This is a very pronounced character when the mouths of the tubes are viewed from a lateral position.

There is no basis for a constant distinction between this species and *Polyporus sericeo-hirsutus* Klotzsch as that species has been known in this country. The hymenium, in particular, is extremely variable, the pores ranging from rather large *Hexagona*-like ones to small ones that are either angular, somewhat elongate, or rather daedaloid. The color of the mouths varies from pure white to very dark smoky. *P. pinsitus* shows a preference for red cedar, though it occurs also on a variety of other substrata. It is a common species in tropical America and the Gulf States, but rare northward in the Mississippi River Valley. *P. barbatulus* Fries has also been indicated as a synonym on several occasions.

94. POLYPORUS BIFORMIS Fries

In Berkeley, Ann. and Mag. Nat. Hist. 3: 392. 1839

(Figs. 50–52 and Plate 128)

Coriolus biformis (Klotzsch) Pat., Essai Tax. Hym., p. 94. 1900.
Coriolus molliusculus (Berk.) Murr., Northern Polypores, p. 8. 1914.

Sporophore sessile or more often effused-reflexed or largely resupinate, usually imbricate and often laterally connate, coriaceous or soft and pliant and watery when fresh, rigid on drying, reviving; pileus 1–5(–9) $\times$ 1.5–6(–15) $\times$ 0.2–1.5 cm., white to alutaceous, often drying yellowish or ochraceous bay, fibrillose-tomentose when fresh, usually rough with appressed radiating fibrils on drying and then appearing nearly glabrous; context white, 1–5 mm. thick; pore surface white to yellowish, the tubes 2–5 mm. long, the mouths circular, angular, or daedaloid, averaging 1–2 per mm., usually soon lacerated and breaking up into teeth at an early stage; spores oblong or cylindric, slightly curved, smooth, hyaline, 6–8 $\times$ 2–2.5 μ; basidia 4–5 μ in diameter; cystidia and hyphal pegs none; hyphae mostly long, thick-walled, simple or sparingly branched, with occasional cross walls and clamps, often breaking at the nodes, 3–6 μ in diameter, but a few hyphae thin-walled, with cross walls and clamps, 3–4 μ in diameter. (Compare no. 1, *Trametes sepium*, and no. 105, *Polyporus pubescens*.)

HABITAT: On dead wood of deciduous trees, noted on *Acer*, *Alnus*, *Arbutus*, *Betula*, *Carya*, *Fagus*, *Fraxinus*, *Juglans*, *Liquidambar*, *Platanus*, *Populus*, *Prunus*, *Quercus*, *Ulmus*, and *Umbellularia*; rarely on wood of coniferous trees, noted on *Pinus*, *Pseudotsuga*, and *Tsuga*; reported on *Betula* (Mich., Kauffman [101]).

DISTRIBUTION: Specimens have been examined from N.H., Vt., R.I., N.Y., Pa., N.J., Del., Md., D.C., Va., W. Va., N.C., Ga., Fla., Ala., La., Tenn., Ohio, Ind., Ill., Mich., Wis., Iowa, Mo., Kans., Nebr., Ark., Okla., Texas, N. Mex., Ariz., Mont., and Calif.; in Canada from Quebec, Ontario, and Manitoba; reported from S.C. (Murrill) and Ore. (Kauffman [106]).

ILLUSTRATIONS: Hard, Mushrooms, fig. 341 (as *Polystictus*); Lloyd, Myc. Notes 42: fig. 817 (as *Polystictus*); Overholts, Wash. Univ. Studies 3: pl. 3, fig. 16.

The species reaches its best development in the hardwood regions of the Ohio and Mississippi River Valleys. Elsewhere it is not common. The appressed-fibrillose pileus and the large pores whose walls become dentate and then irpiciform serve to distinguish it from its allies. The fibrillose pileus, the lack of cystidia, and the context hyphae with clamps distinguish thin forms from *Polyporus pargamenus*. Most frequently, in early stages of growth, the pore surface is decidedly daedaloid.

Murrill (140, p. 8) took up the specific name *molliusculus* to replace *biformis*, in the genus *Coriolus*. He did this after Lloyd (111, pp. 422, 446) had pointed out that the plant Klotzsch named *Polyporus biformis* was only *P. pargamenus*. Since the name Klotzsch used has priority, a strict adherence to the rules of botanical nomenclature would require two changes: (1) *P. biformis* should supplant *P. pargamenus*, and (2) some other name should be given to the plants that have always passed as *P. biformis*. Whether this new name should be based on *Boletus cervinus* Schw. or on *P. populinus* Schulz. or on *P. molliusculus* Berk. is, to some extent, a matter of opinion. As the alternative to these changes, I propose to leave the plants as they have been known for the last hundred years, but to follow Lloyd's suggestion and credit *P. biformis*, as so used, to Berkeley. (See also Murrill, *Mycologia* 12: 7. 1920.)

According to Murrill (139, p. 26), the synonymy of this species also includes *Polyporus carolinensis* Berk., *P. chartaceus* Berk., and *P. scarrosus* Berk. & Curt. *P. pachylus* Cooke, described from "British North America," is said probably to belong here, also.

Weir (230) reports this species as attacking both sapwood and heartwood of living trees of *Quercus rubra* and *Fagus atropunicea*. On its usual eastern hosts it produces a soft, wet, straw-colored decay of the sapwood.

95. POLYPORUS TULIPIFERAE (Schw.) Overh.

Wash. Univ. Studies 3, 1: 29. 1915

(Figs. 15–18, 28, and Plate 132)

Boletus Tulipiferae Schw., Schr. Nat. Ges. Leipzig 1: 99. 1822.
Irpiciporus lacteus (Fries) Murr., sensu North Amer. Flora 9: 15. 1907.

Sporophore effused-reflexed or resupinate, rarely strictly sessile, thin and coriaceous, reviving; pileus 0–1.5 × 1–4 × 0.1–0.6 cm., white, often yellowish on drying, villose or villose-tomentose, or occasionally short hirsute-tomentose, sometimes partially subglabrate, azonate or subzonate; context white, 0.5–2 mm. thick; pore surface white or yellowish, the tubes 1–3(–5) mm. long, the mouths angular to sinuous and irregular, sometimes concentrically arranged, usually soon breaking up into teeth, averaging 2 per mm.; spores oblong-ellipsoid when young, cylindric when mature, hyaline, 4.5–6 × 2–3 μ; cystidia scattered, often obliquely projecting, rarely completely imbedded, hyaline, incrusted, usually conspicuous but sometimes rare, 35–45 × 6–8 μ, projecting 15–25 μ; hyphae sparingly branched, some with walls considerably thickened and without cross walls, others less thickened and with occasional inconspicuous cross walls but no clamps, 3–4(–6) μ in diameter. (Compare no. 98, *Polyporus pargamenus*.)

HABITAT: On dead wood, usually of deciduous trees, noted on *Acer, Aesculus, Ailanthus, Alnus, Amelanchier, Betula, Caragana, Carpinus, Carya, Castanea, Celtis, Cornus, Corylus, Fagus, Forsythia, Fraxinus, Gleditsia, Gymnocladus, Juglans, Liquidambar, Liriodendron, Maclura, Magnolia, Morus, Populus, Prunus, Pyrus, Quercus, Rhus, Ribes, Robinia, Rubus, Salix, Sassafras, Sorbus, Symphoricarpos, Tilia,* and *Vitis*; occasionally on wood of coniferous trees, noted on *Abies, Pinus,* and *Tsuga*; reported on *Picea* (Weir [223]) and *Platanus* (Weir [230]).

DISTRIBUTION: Specimens have been examined from every state in the Union except Miss., Okla., Texas, Ariz., Utah, Nev., Colo., and Calif.; known in Canada from Quebec, Ontario, Manitoba, Alberta, and British Columbia.

ILLUSTRATIONS: Baxter, Mich. Acad. Sci. Arts and Letters Papers 14: pl. 36 (as *Irpex*); Hard, Mushrooms, fig. 376 (as *Irpex*); Overholts, Wash. Univ. Studies 3: pl. 3, fig. 11.

Apparently *Irpex lacteus* Fries is a synonym, and one which antedates the Schweinitzian name, for it was published first (as *Sistotrema lacteum* Fries in *Obs. Myc.* 2: 266. 1818). Fries later transferred this species from *Sistotrema* to *Hydnum* (*Syst. Myc.* 1: 412. 1821) and still later to *Irpex* (*Epicr. Syst. Myc.*, p. 522. 1836–1838; *Hym. Eur.*, p. 621. 1874). If the specific epithet were to be transferred to *Polyporus* now, it would be invalid because antedated by *P. lacteus* Fries (*Syst. Myc.* 1: 359. 1821), a name commonly carried in the European literature for a species very different from the one here discussed. A transfer in the application of a name in this way is extremely undesirable, and for that reason I have retained the name *P. Tulipiferae* for the present species. Since 1874 this species has generally been included in *Irpex*, but usually it is truly polyporoid, although becoming toothed at an early stage. Occasionally, entirely poroid specimens occur, and, very rarely, the hymenium is so completely irpiciform in some portions that there is no suggestion of pores. *I. sinuosus* Fries and *I. pallescens* Fries are sometimes referred to synonymy here. A specimen in my herbarium under the first of these names, collected by Lowag and determined by Litschauer, is identical in all respects. The types of *Sistotrema spathulatum* Schw. are in good condition, showing both spores and incrusted cystidia typical of this species.

Sometimes this species simulates irpiciform specimens of *Daedalea unicolor*, from which it can always be easily separated by the numerous incrusted cystidia in the hymenium. Poorly developed specimens resemble *Poria versipora* at times, but that species has numerous cross walls and clamps on the hyphae and lacks cystidia.

The fungus produces a white delignifying decay of the sapwood. Black lines have been noted in connection with it. Wilson (233) declares it is sometimes parasitic on *Prunus* in Iowa, and Weir (230, p. 185 [using the name *Polystictus lacteus* (Fries)]) reports that it affects both sapwood and heartwood of plum, cherry, peach, apple, *Acer*, *Ailanthus*, *Platanus*, and *Quercus*.

96. POLYPORUS UNDOSUS Peck

N. Y. State Mus. Ann. Rept. 34: 42. 1881
(Figs. 94–95, 116, and Plate 132)

Tyromyces undosus (Peck) Murr., North Amer. Flora 9: 34. 1907.
Tyromyces Pseudotsugae Murr., Mycologia 4: 95. 1912.

Sporophore sessile or more typically effused-reflexed, watery-tough when fresh, rigid when dry; pileus 1–3 × 2–3 × 0.5–1 cm., dimidiate or laterally connate, pure white when fresh, gray to slightly rufescent on drying, covered with a short, compact, villose tomentum, azonate or nearly so; context white, less than 1 mm. thick; pore surface white, discoloring slightly on drying, the tubes 4–10 mm. long, the mouths angular, thin-walled, dentate and fimbriate, typically averaging 1–2 per mm., rarely half that size; spores cylindric or allantoid, smooth, hyaline, 4–6 × 1–1.5 μ; cystidia none; hyphal pegs present but not conspicuous; hyphae hyaline, sometimes quite irregular, thick-walled with very narrow lumina, 5–8 μ in diameter, sometimes much branched or forming dense hyphal complexes, with rather abundant cross walls and clamps but these not conspicuous because of the irregular outlines of the hyphae, sometimes becoming strongly yellowish green in KOH solution next the substratum. (Compare no. 3, *Trametes variiformis*, and no. 94, *Polyporus biformis*.)

HABITAT: Usually on dead wood of coniferous trees, noted on *Abies, Picea, Pinus, Pseudotsuga, Thuja*, and *Tsuga*; rarely on wood of deciduous trees, noted on *Acer, Betula, Fagus*, and *Quercus*.

DISTRIBUTION: Specimens have been examined from Me., N.H., Vt., N.Y., Va., W. Va., N.C., Tenn., Mont., and Wash.; in Canada from Ontario and British Columbia.

ILLUSTRATIONS: Lloyd, Synop. Apus, fig. 657; Lowe, Mich. Acad. Sci. Arts and Letters Papers 19: pl. 14, figs. 4–5.

I have compared side by side the types of *Polyporus Pseudotsugae* Murr. described from Seattle, Washington, on *Pseudotsuga*, with those of Peck's species, and find them identical. The spores of *P. Pseudotsugae* are not "ovoid, 5 × 3.5 μ," as stated, but are allantoid, and those of *P. undosus* are not elliptical, 3 × 4 μ, as given by Lloyd, but are cylindric or allantoid.

Usually the pileus is narrowly reflexed, and the margin more or less deflexed. The hyphae are very characteristic, their walls being irregular and much thickened and leaving only very narrow lumina, the contents of which stain deeply in eosin, while the walls do not take the stain at all. The species is rarely collected. A form with pores only half the usual size has come to me from British Columbia.

The fungus apparently produces a brown, carbonizing, checked rot of the sapwood.

4b. *Pores smaller, 2–5 or more per mm.*
  5a. *Pores averaging 2–4 per mm.*
    6a. *Context hyphae without cross walls*
      7a. *Cystidia present*

97. Polyporus abietinus Dicks. ex Fries

Syst. Myc. 1: 370. 1821

(Figs. 1-4, 48, and Plate 128)

Boletus abietinus Dicks., Plant Crypt. Brit., fasc. 3: 21. 1793.
Coriolus abietinus (Dicks. ex Fries) Quél., Ench. Fung., p. 175. 1886.
Daedalea unicolor violacea Clements, Crypt. Form. Colo., no. 170. 1905.

Sporophore sessile, often attached by a point, effused-reflexed or rarely resupinate, coriaceous when fresh, rather rigid when dry, quickly reviving; pileus 0-4 × 1-4 × 0.1-0.2 cm., white, gray, or cinereous, sometimes grayish black at the base, strigose, villose, or strigose-tomentose, more or less zonate; context white to gray or brownish, not more than 1 mm. thick, with a definite cuticular layer as seen in vertical section; pore surface white, bay, brownish, or violaceous, the tubes 1-3 mm. long, the mouths angular, averaging 2-4 per mm., rather thin-walled, usually slightly dentate and uneven, sometimes becoming irpiciform; spores cylindric or allantoid, hyaline, 4-6 × 1.5-2.5 μ; basidia 3.5-5 μ in diameter; cystidia or cystidioles present but often rather inconspicuous, hyaline, usually incrusted at the apex in lactic-acid mounts, 3-6 μ broad, projecting 5-15 μ; hyphal pegs present; hyphae often thick-walled, simple or nearly so, with no cross walls or clamps, 3-4.5(-6) μ in diameter.

Habitat: On dead wood of coniferous trees, noted on *Abies*, *Chamaecyparis*, *Cupressus*, *Juniperus*, *Larix*, *Libocedrus*, *Picea*, *Pinus*, *Pseudotsuga*, *Sequoia*, *Thuja*, and *Tsuga*; one collection on *Betula* (Newfoundland) and one on *Prunus* (Vt.); reported on *Populus* (Weir [223]) and on *Quercus* (Calif., Rhoads [183]).

Distribution: Specimens have been examined from every state in the Union except Ill., N. Dak., Kans., Nebr., Okla., and Nev.; known also from Alaska; in Canada from Nova Scotia, Newfoundland, Quebec, Ontario, Manitoba, Alberta, and British Columbia.

Illustrations: Humphrey, U. S. Dept. Agr. Bul. 510: pl. 5, figs. 3-4 (as *Polystictus*); Overholts, Mo. Bot. Gard. Ann. 2: pl. 23, fig. 2 and text figs. 1-2; Rhoads, N. Y. State Coll. Forestry Tech. Publ. 11: pl. 4; Shope, Mo. Bot. Gard. Ann. 18: pl. 18, figs. 2, 4, 6.

The coniferous habitat, the thin, grayish, coriaceous pileus, somewhat zoned and quite pubescent, and the typically subresupinate habit are the marks of the species.

Wherever conifers occur this species is just as common as *Polyporus versicolor*, although the surface characters of the pileus are much less variable. In young, growing specimens the pore surface usually has a violaceous or lavender color. Only one related species, *P. pargamenus*, shows this character. That species exhibits a further similarity in having the same type of inconspicuous cystidium. Both are nearly white on the pileus, but *P. pargamenus* does not assume the blackish discoloration so characteristic of old specimens of *P. abietinus*, particularly of its variety *Abietis*. *P. pargamenus*, however, usually inhabits hardwoods and can generally be recognized by its larger size, the velvety tomentum of the pileus, and the more toothed pore surface. Only occasionally, except in the variety, is *P. abietinus* more than 1 cm. in length, whereas *P. pargamenus* is frequently 5 cm. or more, and is rarely as small as 1 cm. Rhoads (184, pp. 41–44) discusses these differences at some length. In addition, Snell *et al.* (205, p. 279) record that *P. abietinus* can be distinguished in culture from *P. pargamenus* by a difference in growth rate at specified temperatures.

I have a collection from Wyoming (Solheim No. 1612) that differs microscopically from all other collections I have examined. In addition to having an "avellaneous" pore surface and slightly longer tubes, sections of the hymenium show cystidioles that at their largest are about twice the size usually seen in this species; the body of the cystidiole is as much as 8 μ in diameter and attenuated at the tip, the attenuated portion bearing a crystalline mass up to 8 μ in diameter which is composed of rather coarse crystals similar to those of *Poria corticola* (Fries) Cooke. There are other cystidioles in which this crystalline mass is of the usual size.

The incrustations on the apexes of the cystidia are more likely to be retained in sections of the hymenium mounted in lactic acid than in sections mounted in KOH, which often dissolves them. Old specimens weather out to a dull gray or leaden color on the pileus, and the pore surface becomes quite dark, varying from brown to dark lavender.

Var. ABIETIS (Lloyd) Overh.

Pa. Agr. Exp. Sta. Tech. Bul. 298: 21. 1933

(Figs. 5, 10)

Lenzites Abietis Lloyd, Myc. Notes 62: 909. 1920.

Characters as in the species, but the pileus measuring up to 5 × 7 × 0.5 cm. and usually weathering more strongly grayish black or blackish, the context more brown, and the hymenial region completely or partially lamellate or the lamellae broken up into flattened *Irpex*-like teeth.

HABITAT AND DISTRIBUTION: That of the species.

ILLUSTRATIONS: Lloyd, Myc. Notes 62: fig. 1607 (as *Lenzites*); Overholts, Mo. Bot. Gard. Ann. 2: pl. 23, fig. 1 (as *Polyporus abietinus*); Shope, Mo. Bot. Gard. Ann. 18: pl. 18, fig. 3.

Peck (164, p. 38) discusses the variations in hymenial configuration, and I (150, p. 686) have recorded observations on this point. The lamellate variety seems to be of common occurrence, and is likely to be referred to the genus *Lenzites*. It is somewhat similar to *L. abietinella*, but differs in having much smaller spores. It would hardly be confused with *L. trabea*, which usually grows on hardwoods, is brown rather than gray, and exhibits no strong pubescence on the pileus. *L. saepiaria* has a distinctly brown or rusty pileus, and the context is much thicker and rusty brown. The toothed variety is seldom met, but sometimes the lamellate hymenium gives way to an irpiciform condition that Peck designated at one time as var. *irpiciformis*; I am persuaded that *Irpex fusco-violaceus* (Ehrenb. ex Fries) Fries is the same plant. Recent European authorities, except Bourdot and Galzin, are not in accord with that idea. Pilát writes me that the common designation for this variety in Europe is *Trametes abietina* var. *lenzitoidea* Murr.

Polyporus parvulus Schw. (not Klotzsch) was described on *Pinus* from the Pennsylvania Pocono region. I have not seen the type, if it exists. Murrill refers the species in synonymy here. Saccardo and Cuboni renamed it *P. pusio*, since the name chosen by Schweinitz was preoccupied.

The species and its variety produce a peculiar delignifying rot of the sapwood, which in the last stages of decay is markedly honeycombed and extremely light in weight. As a decay organism the fungus is of more importance than any other on coniferous slash, particularly on the smaller branches (83, pp. 49, 52; 208). Neuman (148, pp. 7–11) reports it as more or less parasitic in character, and Weir (230, p. 184) says that on living *Abies grandis*, *A. balsamea*, *Tsuga heterophylla*, and *Thuja plicata* "the sap-wood is decayed and the adjacent heartwood discolored." I have studied the species over a wide range of territory and have seen no evidence of parasitism; only rarely has the fungus been noted growing from wounds.

98. POLYPORUS PARGAMENUS Fries

Epicr. Syst. Myc., p. 480. 1836–1838

(Figs. 6–9, 39–40, 642, and Plate 131)

Polyporus pseudopargamenus Thuem., Myc. Univ., no. 1102. 1878.
Coriolus prolificans (Fries) Murr., North Amer. Flora 9: 27. 1907.
Polystictus lavendulus Lloyd, Myc. Notes 66: 1121. 1922.

Sporophore sessile, often narrowed at the base, quite flexible when fresh, rigid or somewhat flexible on drying, reviving; pileus 1–7 × 1–7 × 0.1–0.5 cm., general color whitish or cinereous, brownish or rarely blackish behind with age, villose or velvety-pubescent, zonate at least on the margin, but often inconspicuously so; context white, usually less than 1 mm. thick, rarely 1–2 mm.; pore surface white, bay, or violaceous, the tubes 1–3 mm. long, the mouths angular, thin-walled, averaging 2–4 per mm. in poroid forms but usually soon extensively irpiciform; spores cylindric or slightly curved, hyaline, 5–6.5 × 2–2.5 μ; cystidia present but usually inconspicuous, hyaline, often incrusted at the tips, 4–5 μ broad, projecting 5–15 μ; hyphal pegs present, broad, obtuse; hyphae nearly simple, flexuous, mostly with thickened walls, with occasional or rare cross walls and inconspicuous clamps on the smaller hyphae, 3–7 μ in diameter. (Compare no. 94, *Polyporus biformis*; no. 97, *P. abietinus*; and no. 103, *P. versicolor*.)

HABITAT: On dead wood, usually of deciduous trees, noted on *Acer, Alnus, Betula, Carya, Castanea, Cornus, Fagus, Fraxinus, Gleditsia, Liquidambar, Liriodendron, Nyssa, Oxydendron, Populus, Prunus, Quercus, Salix, Sassafras,* and *Tilia*; rarely on wood of coniferous trees, noted on *Gingko, Juniperus, Larix, Pinus,* and *Tsuga*; reported on *Carpinus, Cercis, Fraxinus, Ilex, Juglans, Maclura, Persea, Platanus, Rhododendron, Rhus,* and *Ulmus* (Rhoads [184]).

DISTRIBUTION: Specimens have been examined from every state in the Union except Kans., Nebr., Okla., Ariz., and Calif.; in Canada from Nova Scotia, Quebec, Ontario, Manitoba, Alberta, and British Columbia; reported from Kans. and Okla. (Rhoads [184]).

ILLUSTRATIONS: Boudier, Icones, pl. 159 (as *Polyporus biformis*); Hard, Mushrooms, fig. 345 (as *Polystictus pergamenus*); Humphrey, U. S. Dept. Agr. Bul. 510: pl. 5, fig. 1–2 (as *Polystictus*); Overholts, Mo. Bot. Gard. Ann. 2: pl. 23, fig. 9; Rhoads, N. Y. State Coll. Forestry Tech. Publ. 11: pls. 1, 2 (*pars*), 3; von Schrenk and Spaulding, U. S. Dept. Agr. Pl. Ind. Bul. 149: fig. 7 (as *Polystictus pergamenus*).

This is one of the most common species in America. My own distribution records taken in conjunction with those published by Rhoads (184) leave but three states—Nebraska, Arizona, and California—from which the fungus is not yet known. Rhoads lists, moreover, a total of sixty-five species of woody plants on which it has been found. Often the zonations on the pileus are sufficiently varied in coloration to suggest *Polyporus versicolor*, but the hymenium usually becomes toothed at an early age and a lavender color is frequently present when the plants are in good growing condition. The species is thinner than *P. hirsutus*, which, moreover, lacks the irpiciform pore surface and the zonate pileus. Typical *P. abietinus* is usually much smaller and has a strigose rather than a velvety pubescence. The pileus of old specimens of the present species is often covered with a growth of green algae. As in some other related species, the margin of the pileus occasionally puts out a new growth the second year. When this happens, the specimens are likely to become black at the base.

This species is very infrequent on conifers. I have seen it, however, growing in company with *Polyporus abietinus*, but there was no difficulty in separating it from that species on the basis of the different pubescence. The pileus is often attenuate to a narrow point of attachment to the substratum. *P. elongatus* Berk. is said to be based on this type of sporophore. In sections of the hymenium mounted in water or lactic acid nearly all of the cystidia are capitate-incrusted; when sections are mounted in KOH solution this incrustation largely or entirely disappears.

The fungus produces both oidia and chlamydospores in pure culture.

Polyporus prolificans Fries is sometimes given as a synonym for this species. Further synonymy is said to include *P. laceratus* Berk., *P. Menandianus* Mont., *P. subflavus* Lév., and *P. ilicincola* Berk. & Curt.—all described from the United States. Var. *unifasciata* Peck is a white form of this species.

The large spores reported by Lloyd for *Polystictus lavendulus* are undoubtedly foreign. In the types of that species they are rather numerous along the hymenium, and many of them are two-celled. A good sporulating surface is not present, but cystidia occur as in *Polyporus pargamenus*.

Weir (230) reports this species as producing a heart rot of living trees in several species of *Quercus* and in *Acer saccharum, Betula lutea, Fraxinus americana, Nyssa sylvatica*, and *Populus tremuloides*, and Elliott (44) classes it as a parasite of the peach in Arkansas. Wood decayed by this fungus (184) is soft and spongy, whitish or straw color, indicating a general delignifying type of rot; there is some tendency for small pockets to be formed, similar to those produced by *Polyporus abietinus*.

99. POLYPORUS SUBCHARTACEUS (Murr.) Overh.

Wash. Univ. Studies 3, 1: 32. 1915
(Figs. 37–38, 665, and Plate 131)

Coriolus subchartaceus Murr., North Amer. Flora 9: 24. 1907.

Sporophore sessile, broadly attached, tough and flexible when fresh, drying rigid or very slightly flexible, reviving; pileus 1–5 × 1–8 × 0.4–0.8 cm., gray or cinereous or with a tinge of yellowish on drying, villose-tomentose to slightly hispid-tomentose, indistinctly zonate; context white, 2–4 mm. thick, firm on the lower two thirds, the upper third softer by reason of the rather conspicuous tomentose covering (hence context slightly duplex); pore surface bay or typically lavender-violaceous, sometimes darker and more avellaneous, occasionally paler, the tubes 1–3 mm. long, the mouths rather thick-walled, entire at first then lacerate but never irpiciform, averaging 2–3 per mm.; spores cylindric or slightly curved, smooth, hyaline, 7–9 × 2–3 μ; cystidia usually abundant and quite conspicuous, hyaline, incrusted at the apex but the incrustation soon dissolving in KOH, 4–5 μ in diameter, projecting up to 15 μ. (Compare no. 98, *Polyporus pargamenus*; no. 104, *P. hirsutus*; and no. 110, *P. velutinus*.)

HABITAT: On dead wood of *Populus*; perhaps occasionally on other substrata.

DISTRIBUTION: Specimens have been examined from Me., Conn., N.Y., Wis., Minn., Utah, Colo., Wyo., Mont., and Idaho; reported from Manitoba (Bisby et al. [12]).

Although it is at times treated as a thick form of *Polyporus pargamenus*, I am now convinced that this species is worthy of recognition. The spores are constantly larger than in that species, and the pileus is thicker. Indeed, as Shope (200) has pointed out, the pileus is so thick and the tomentum is so well developed that the context, when seen in lateral views of vertical sections, appears duplex—a character that cannot be recognized in *P. pargamenus* without considerable magnification. The cystidia are as a rule much better developed in this species than in *P. pargamenus*, and are occasionally very conspicuous. The hymenial region is never irpiciform, but varies in color as in that species. Apparently the fungus is confined to dead *Populus* wood, but many collections of both *P. subchartaceus* and *P. pargamenus* are not in sporulating condition, and the final evidence for distinguishing them is wanting. For example, certain collections on *Salix* and on *Alnus* seem to be as near to *P. pargamenus* as to *P. subchartaceus*, but they are not sporulating.

The rot produced is a general delignifying decay of the sapwood.

100. POLYPORUS SECTOR Ehrenb. ex Fries

Syst. Myc. 1: 505. 1821

(Figs. 64–65 and Plate 132)

Boletus sector Ehrenb., Horae Phys. Berol., p. 86. 1820.
Coriolus sector (Ehrenb. ex Fries) Pat., Essai Tax. Hym., p. 94. 1900.
Polyporus floridanus Berk., Ann. and Mag. Nat. Hist. 10: 376. 1843.

Sporophore sessile or effused-reflexed, dimidiate to flabelliform, sometimes attached by a narrowed base, coriaceous when fresh, more or less flexible in dried plants, reviving; pileus 0–9 × 1–10 × 0.1–0.3 cm., typically isabelline or cinereous, varying to cinnamon and darker with age, never pure white, zonate with nearly concolorous zones, typically villose-tomentose and velvety to the touch, becoming glabrous in zones and fibrillose with age, usually radiate-rugose or radiate-striate, the margin very thin, entire to dentate or somewhat fimbriate; context pallid brown, less than 1 mm. thick; pore surface wood-brown to smoky brown or hair-brown, concolorous with the context, the tubes usually about 1 mm. long, rarely considerably longer, the mouths nearly always dentate or irpiciform, angular to irregular, averaging 3–4 per mm.; spores cylindric or allantoid, hyaline, 6–7 × 2 μ; cystidia present as fusiform, hyaline, slightly projecting organs, often capitate-incrusted, 3–5 μ in diameter; hyphae up to the tomentose layer closely compacted, rather thick-walled, hyaline to light brown, mostly simple, with no cross walls or clamps, 3–7 μ in diameter. (Compare no. 120, *Polyporus tenuis*.)

HABITAT: On dead wood of deciduous trees, noted on *Liquidambar*, *Myrica*, *Nyssa*, and *Quercus*; reported also on *Chamaecyparis* (N.C., Weir [230]).

DISTRIBUTION: Specimens have been examined from S.C., Ga., Fla., Ala., La., and Texas; reported also from N.C. (Weir [230]).

This species is the tropical analogue of *Polyporus pargamenus* and is practically the same throughout, except for the darker hymenium and the sometimes darker pileus. Occasionally the pileus exhibits some color contrast, but usually it is about unicolorous. At times the pileus is inclined to be slightly sericeous on the margin, and the plants then resemble *Stereum sericeum* above, but they are fibrillose at the base. Sometimes the hymenium is as dark as in *P. adustus*.

101. POLYPORUS ACULEIFER (Berk. & Curt.) Overh.

Sci. Surv. Porto Rico and the Virgin Isl. 8: 160. 1926

(Fig. 78 and Plate 128)

Trametes aculeifera Berk. & Curt., Linnean Soc. Bot. Jour. 10: 319. 1868.
Funalia aculeifer (Berk. & Curt.) Murr., North Amer. Flora 9: 79. 1908.

Sporophore often poorly developed and resupinate or semiresupinate; pileus up to 1 cm. broad and long or resupinate for several centimeters, white to yellowish, the surface usually beset with concolorous hydnoid processes 1–2 mm. long which are sometimes almost lacking but at other times are so numerous that the surface appears hydnoid, or the entire fructification in an abnormal nodulose condition and covered by these blunt spines; context white, soft and watery when fresh, 0.5–3 mm. thick; pore surface white or yellowish, the tubes up to 3 mm. long, the mouths where best developed angular and thin-walled, sometimes with hydnoid processes, averaging 2–3 per mm.; spores ovoid or ellipsoid, smooth, hyaline, 4–5 × 2.5–3 μ; cystidia not abundant, of erratic distribution, hyaline, cylindric, capitate-incrusted, 5–6 μ in diameter, projecting 12–18 μ; some unincrusted hyphal organs also present, enlarged to 6–8 μ in diameter at the apex and projecting somewhat further than the cystidia; main context hyphae with semi-thickened walls, simple, with no cross walls or clamps, 4–6 μ in diameter, intermixed with a few thin-walled, sparingly branched or simple hyphae with very occasional inconspicuous clamps.

HABITAT: On dead wood, noted only on *Citrus*.

DISTRIBUTION: Specimens have been examined only from Fla.

Adequate, representative collections of this species always show some trace of the white hydnoid processes on the pileus, by which the species can be easily recognized. The color of these processes and of the sporophore readily separates this fungus from similar species, e.g., from *Polyporus hydnoides*, in which hydnoid hairs are present. The microscopic features are characteristic. Dried sporophores are uniformly yellowish and have somewhat the aspect of specimens of *P. biformis*, but the spores are very different and the pores are not so large. The species also has a resemblance to *Poria corticola*. It is evidently rare in tropical America, and only a few collections have been made. I have an ample one from Florida, which was made by L. W. Nuttall in 1923, on dead *Citrus* trunks.

102. POLYPORUS TRICHOMALLUS Berk. & Mont.

Ann. Sci. Nat. Bot. III, 11: 238. 1849

(Figs. 275–276 and Plate 132)

Trichaptum trichomallum (Berk. & Mont.) Murr., Torrey Bot. Club Bul. 31: 608. 1904.

Sporophore sessile or somewhat decurrent, flexible when fresh, nearly rigid on drying; pileus dimidiate to elongate, 3–10 × .5–15 (or laterally confluent to larger sizes) × 0.3–1.5 cm., upper surface composed of a dense mat of forked brownish or blackish stiff hairs 5 mm. or more long, azonate, the margin thin; context almost none, being merely a thin, membranous, umber layer bearing the mat above and the tubes below; pore surface fuliginous or dark smoky brown, the tubes 0.5–4 mm. long, the mouths angular to irregular and sinuous, thin-walled, entire, averaging 2–3 per mm. in shorter diameter; spores oblong-ellipsoid or short-cylindric, smooth, hyaline, 5–7 × 3–3.5 μ; cystidia abundant, especially in the nonsporulating hymenium, as narrow, elongated or somewhat fusiform organs with capitate-incrusted apexes 3–4 μ in diameter; hyphae long and flexuous, simple, pale brown in KOH, rather thin-walled, or some with walls partially thickened, with no or with very occasional clamps on the narrower ones, 2.5–4.5 μ in diameter.

HABITAT: On dead wood of deciduous trees.

DISTRIBUTION: Specimens have been examined only from Fla.

ILLUSTRATIONS: Lloyd, Synop. Polystictus, fig. 356 (as *Polystictus*).

Not previously reported from the mainland, this species was collected by Long in 1914 and by L. W. Nuttall in 1923. It differs from *Polyporus hydnoides* in having practically no context and in having larger, thin-walled tubes. In *P. hydnoides* the context is usually about 1 mm. thick, and the pores average 3–4 per mm. The Nuttall collection has a sporulating hymenium, but most of the spores are still attached to the basidia; at maturity they may be somewhat longer. The cystidia are as in *P. versatilis*, to which this species is evidently closely related. Often the marginal pores are subangular, though varying in size, while the older pores are decidedly daedaloid. The characteristic mat of fibers making up the pileus covering and the practical absence of a context are precisely as shown in Lloyd's figure of *P. leoninus*, a companion species from the Orient (see Lloyd, *Synop. Polystictus*, fig. 352 [as *Polystictus*]).

7b. *Cystidia lacking* (see also *Polyporus occidentalis*, p. 427)

103. POLYPORUS VERSICOLOR L. ex Fries

Syst. Myc. 1: 368. 1821

(Figs. 11–13 and Plate 132)

Boletus versicolor L., Sp. Plant., p. 1176. 1753.
Coriolus versicolor (L. ex Fries) Quél., Ench. Fung., p. 175. 1886.
Polyporus hirsutulus Schw., Amer. Phil. Soc. Trans. II, 4: 156. 1832.
Polystictus Macounii Lloyd, Letter 53: 9. 1914.

Sporophore sessile or effused-reflexed, usually imbricate, coriaceous when fresh, more rigid or subflexible when dry, reviving; pileus 2–5(–7) × 2–7(–10) × 0.05–0.3(–0.5) cm., variable in color and usually marked by many narrow multicolored zones ranging from white to yellow, brown, reddish, greenish, bluish, and blackish, rarely more uniformly colored but always zonate where well developed unless growing in sheltered situations, silky-villose or velvety, rarely almost hirsute, the alternate zones finally partially or entirely glabrous; context white, rarely more than 1 mm. thick; pore surface white, yellowish, or in dried plants brownish or rarely somewhat smoky, often glistening, the tubes up to 2 mm. long, the mouths angular, thin-walled, entire, averaging 3–5 per mm., visible to the unaided eye; spores cylindric or allantoid, smooth, hyaline, 4–6 × 1.5–2 μ; cystidia none; hyphal pegs occasional, broadly conoidal; hyphae mainly straight, the walls thickened, simple, with no cross walls or clamps, 3–10 μ in diameter, many of the larger sizes; hyphal complexes often abundant, with hyphae mostly 3–4 μ in diameter. (Compare no. 98, *Polyporus pargamenus*; no. 104, *P. hirsutus*; no. 105, *P. pubescens*; and no. 110, *P. velutinus*.)

HABITAT: On dead wood or on wounded areas, usually of deciduous trees, noted on *Acer, Ailanthus, Alnus, Amelanchier, Arbutus, Betula, Carpinus, Carya, Castanea, Castanopsis, Catalpa, Cornus, Corylus, Crataegus, Eucalyptus, Fagus, Fraxinus, Gleditsia, Gossypium, Hamamelis, Ilex, Juglans, Ligustrum, Liquidambar, Liriodendron, Maclura, Magnolia, Melia, Nyssa, Pasania, Paulownia, Platanus, Populus, Prunus, Pyrus, Quercus, Rhus, Salix, Sassafras, Syringa, Tilia, Ulmus, Umbellularia, Viburnum,* and *Vitis*; occasionally on wood of coniferous trees, noted on *Abies, Cupressus, Gingko, Juniperus, Larix, Libocedrus, Picea, Pinus, Pseudotsuga, Taxodium, Thuja,* and *Tsuga*; reported on *Cercis* (Mo., Maneval [131]), on *Ostrya* (Mich., Kauffman [101], and Vt., Spaulding [209]), and on *Sequoia* (Calif., Rhoads [183]).

DISTRIBUTION: Specimens have been examined from every state in the Union except R.I., Nev., and Wyo.; known also from Alaska; in Canada from Newfoundland, Quebec, Ontario, Manitoba, and British Columbia.

ILLUSTRATIONS: Elliott, Phytopathology 8: 616, fig. 2 (as *Coriolus*); Hard, Mushrooms, fig. 343 (as *Polystictus*); Hesler, Tenn. Acad. Sci. Jour. 4: fig. 3; Jaccottet, Champ. Nature, pl. 58; Marshall, Mushroom Book, opp. p. 112; Michael, Führ. f. Pilzfr. 2: fig. 32; Moffatt, Chicago Acad. Sci. Nat. Hist. Survey Bul. 7, 1: pl. 17, fig. 1;

Shope, Mo. Bot. Gard. Ann. 18: pl. 16, fig. 2; von Schrenk, Mo. Bot. Gard. Ann. 1: pl. 8; Sowerby, Col. Fig. English Fungi, pl. 229 (as *Boletus*); Stevens, Phytopathology 2: pl. 10 (as *Polystictus*); White, Conn. State Geol. and Nat. Hist. Survey Bul. 3: pl. 36 (as *Polystictus*).

Numerous variations in this species have been assigned varietal and specific names, none of which seem worth retaining. *Polystictus Macounii* Lloyd is a large form from Canada with a somewhat attenuate base. If maintained in *Polyporus* it would have to be renamed (not *Polyporus Macounii* Peck). *Polystictus azureus* Fries is a name often applied to a form that shows a predominance of bluish or ashy-blue coloration. *Polystictus ochraceus* Pers. ex Fries is a thick, pale-colored, velvety form less zoned than usual. Lloyd (111, p. 979) regarded it as distinct, but to me it suggests only *Polyporus versicolor* growing in a less exposed situation and developing neither the color nor the zones usually characteristic of that species. Miss J. S. Bayliss (*Jour. Econ. Biol.* 3: 16. 1908) has shown that when grown in diffuse light this species produces neither the range of colors nor the zonation characteristic of it when grown in more intense illumination. *Polyporus hirsutulus* Schw. is similar to *Polyporus versicolor*, but thinner and smaller in all ways. Some investigators have thought it closer to *Polyporus hirsutus*, but I cannot agree. It is merely a very small, densely pubescent form of *Polyporus versicolor*.

Several varieties of this species were recognized by Peck, including the varieties *caesius, griseus, opacus, villosus, daedaloides*, and *fumosiporum*, each descriptive of some minor variation. A thick, strongly zonate form with a thin hazel zone underlying the pubescence occurs on the West Coast and was erroneously regarded as *Polyporus zonatus* Fries in my earlier papers.

This species usually causes a general delignifying decay of the sapwood. Von Schrenk (218) describes it as a heart-rotting organism on lilac; Stevens (210) records a similar disease of *Catalpa* due to it; Elliott (44) describes its supposedly parasitic action on peach trees in Arkansas; Weir (230) says that it "causes a heart and sapwood rot in living trees of various species." Miss Bayliss (*op. cit.*, pp. 3 and 4) reports that this species forms conidia and oidia in culture, and Miss Clara Fritz (55, p. 277) reports chlamydospores, but failed to obtain either conidia or oidia. Scheffer (192) discusses the effects of this fungus on the chemical and physical properties of the sapwood of red gum.

104. POLYPORUS HIRSUTUS Wulf. ex Fries

Syst. Myc. 1: 367. 1821

(Figs. 14, 26, 31–32, 49, 60–61, and Plate 130)

Boletus hirsutus Wulf., in Jacq., Collect. ad Bot. 2: 149. 1788.
Boletus nigromarginatus Schw., Schr. Nat. Ges. Leipzig 1: 98. 1822.
Coriolus nigromarginatus (Schw.) Murr., Torrey Bot. Club Bul. 32: 649. 1905.

Sporophore sessile or effused-reflexed, coriaceous when fresh, drying rather rigid, reviving; pileus 1.5–6 × 1.5–10 × 0.15–1 cm., grayish to yellowish or brownish but nearly unicolorous in any one specimen except perhaps for one or more marginal darker zones, hirsute or tomentose, usually rather strongly zoned or furrowed, sometimes with the margin darker than the center, sometimes with the margin brown and the center blackish; context white, 1–6 mm. thick; pore surface white to yellowish or smoky, the tubes 1–4 mm. long, the mouths subcircular, the walls typically thick and entire but occasionally thin and somewhat sinuous or lacerate, averaging 3–4 per mm.; spores cylindric or allantoid, smooth, hyaline, 4.5–7 × 2–2.5 μ; cystidia none; hyphal pegs present but not abundant, conoidal to cylindric; hyphae mostly a mixture of thin-walled and thick-walled ones, nearly simple, with no cross walls or clamps, 3–6(–8) μ in diameter, a few hyphae somewhat smaller and much branched, but well-developed hyphal complexes apparently not formed. (Compare no. 103, *Polyporus versicolor*; no. 105, *P. pubescens*; and no. 110, *P. velutinus*.)

HABITAT: On dead wood, usually of deciduous trees, noted on *Acer, Aesculus, Alnus, Amelanchier, Betula, Carpinus, Carya, Castanea, Catalpa, Celtis, Citrus, Cornus, Crataegus, Fagus, Fraxinus, Gleditsia, Juglans, Liquidambar, Liriodendron, Magnolia, Nerium, Nyssa, Ostrya, Persea, Platanus, Populus, Prunus, Quercus, Rhododendron, Robinia, Salix, Sambucus, Sassafras, Sideroxylon, Sorbus, Tilia, Ulmus,* and *Xanthoxylon*; occasionally on wood of coniferous trees, noted on *Abies, Ginkgo, Picea,* and *Thuja*; reported on *Pinus* and *Pseudotsuga* (Calif., Rhoads [183]), on *Pyrus* (Mo., Maneval [131]), and on *Tsuga* (N.Y., Rhoads [181]).

DISTRIBUTION: Specimens have been examined from every state in the Union except Del., S. Dak., Okla., Nev., and Wyo.; in Canada from Nova Scotia, Quebec, Ontario, Manitoba, Alberta, and British Columbia.

ILLUSTRATIONS: Overholts, Wash. Univ. Studies 3: pl. 3, fig. 14; Owens, Prin. Plant Path., fig. 152 (as *Polystictus*).

Polyporus hirsutus is cosmopolitan and just as abundant as *P. versicolor*. Often there is a dark-brown or blackish zone on the margin of the pileus. The species differs from all relatives in the much thicker-walled tubes, which in most specimens make the pore surface very even. The context is thicker than in *P. versicolor* and *P. pargamenus*, and the plant is much more leathery than in *P. pubescens*. The species differs from *P. velutinus* in the more hirsute pubescence and the usually thicker-walled tubes, but the two are extremely easy to confuse until their limits are learned. Var. *albiporus* Peck is based on the white-pored form of the species. *Polystictus hirsutus* var. *calvens* Clements seems referable to *Polyporus adustus*.

Weir (230) reports that this species decays both heartwood and sapwood of plum, cherry, prune, peach, and apple, and of species of *Acer, Alnus, Betula, Castanea,* and *Quercus.* It usually causes a general delignifying decay of the sapwood, the wood finally becoming light and spongy. Black lines have been noted associated with the decay at times, but they do not seem to be a constant feature. The species is one of the most important decay fungi of hardwood slash.

105. POLYPORUS PUBESCENS Schum. ex Fries

Syst. Myc. 1: 367. 1821

(Figs. 41–45, 571, and Plate 131)

Boletus pubescens Schum., Enum. Plant. Saell. 2: 384. 1803.
Coriolus pubescens (Schum. ex Fries) Murr., Torrey Bot. Club Bul. 32: 645. 1905.
Polyporus subluteus Ell. & Ev., Amer. Nat. 31: 339. 1897.
Trametes merisma Peck, N. Y. State Mus. Bul. 139: 31. 1910.
Trametes quercina Lloyd, Myc. Notes 66: 1114. 1922.

Sporophore sessile, or in circular clusters attached at the center, often imbricate, coriaceous or tough and watery when fresh, drying rigid, reviving; pileus 1.5–5 × 2.5–8 × 0.3–1 cm., white or grayish yellow when fresh, often grayish or yellowish (rarely umber) in herbarium specimens, villose-tomentose (or occasionally almost hirsute at the base) to finely appressed tomentose or becoming subglabrous, often radiate-lineate toward the margin; context white, 1–5 mm. thick; pore surface white when fresh, drying yellowish or umber at times, the tubes 1–4(–6) mm. long, the mouths angular, averaging 3–4 per mm., the walls thin (except in immature plants), often dentate; spores cylindric or allantoid, smooth, hyaline, 5–8 × 2–2.5 μ; cystidia none; hyphal pegs present but rare; hyphae generally simple, straight, with entirely thickened walls, with no (or extremely few) cross walls or clamps, 4–8.5 μ in diameter; hyphal complexes present and distinct, the hyphae 3–4 μ in diameter. (Compare no. 98, *Polyporus pargamenus*; no. 103, *P. versicolor*; no. 104, *P. hirsutus*; and no. 110, *P. velutinus*.)

HABITAT: On dead wood of deciduous trees, noted on *Acer, Alnus, Betula, Eucalyptus, Fagus, Ostrya, Populus, Prunus, Pyrus, Quercus, Salix, Sassafras,* and *Ulmus*; reported on *Fraxinus* (Mich., Kauffman [101]).

DISTRIBUTION: Specimens have been examined from Me., N.H., Vt., Mass., Conn., N.Y., Pa., N.J., W. Va., N.C., Tenn., Ohio, Ind., Mich., Wis., Minn., S. Dak., Iowa, Nebr., Wyo., Mont., Idaho, and Calif.; in Canada from Newfoundland, Quebec, Ontario, Manitoba, Saskatchewan, and British Columbia; reported from Kans. (Bartholomew [4]) and from Ore. (Zeller [236]).

ILLUSTRATIONS: Hard, Mushrooms, fig. 339; Neuman, Wis. Geol. and Nat. Hist. Survey Bul. 33: pl. 4, fig. 21 (as *Polystictus velutinus*); Overholts, Wash. Univ. Studies 3: pl. 3, fig. 15.

Beech is the favorite host of this species through the Ohio River Valley, but in the East, where that host is lacking, alder and birch more often support it. Well-developed plants are nearly pure white, but often turn yellow on drying; in these characters the species differs from *Polyporus hirsutus*. Fresh specimens are usually more or less watery.

A form is occasionally collected that is very finely villose-tomentose and becomes practically glabrous, with a very smooth pileus, but that otherwise does not differ. Peck designated it var. *glaber*. American collections referred to *Polyporus fibulus* Fries belong here. *P. subluteus* Ell. & Ev. is a thick form of the species. *P. Sullivantii* Mont. is said to be referable here also. *Trametes merisma* Peck is an anomalous form with a very rough upper surface. A thickened and somewhat trametoid form of the species, not referable to the variety, was designated *T. quercina* by Lloyd. The sum of these variants renders the species rather difficult to recognize at times. Frequently it assumes some of the characters of *P. subchartaceus*, and at other times it approaches the plants here referred to *P. velutinus*. To separate it from *P. subchartaceus* it is often necessary to demonstrate the absence from the hymenium of the capitate-incrusted cystidia; it differs typically from *P. velutinus* in the pale hymenium and in the lack of the uniform velvety pubescence of the pileus. However, intermediates occur that are difficult to assign to any one of the three species.

The statement (125, p. 62) that "*P[olyporus] velutinus* is the thin form" of this species does not represent the true state of affairs. Neither is Neuman's illustration (as cited above) of *Polystictus velutinus* adequate to fill my conception of that species, for it shows a rather characteristic specimen of *Polyporus pubescens*.

Both *Polyporus pubescens* and its variety produce a soft, white, delignifying decay of the sapwood.

Var. GRAYII Cooke & Ell.

Ell. & Ev., North American Fungi, no. 1933. 1888
(Figs. 46–47)

Coriolus Lloydii Murr., North Amer. Flora 9: 23. 1907.
Coriolus concentricus Murr., North Amer. Flora 9: 23. 1907.

Pileus glabrous or very finely villose-scrupose at the base, typically radiately rugose, zonate, white or whitish, but drying uniformly ochraceous-tan or pale tawny or gilvous, more compact and trametoid than in the species, and the pores more regular and constantly thicker-walled.

HABITAT AND DISTRIBUTION: That of the species, but the variety is collected only rarely, though known from New Hampshire to Tennessee and northward into Canada.

The variety grades into the species by way of certain intermediates in which the pileus becomes glabrous and reddish or tawny only at the base or in rather broad zones. Such intermediates represent the conception of *Polyporus zonatus* Fries as held by Romell, Karsten, and Bresadola. Were it not for these intermediate specimens the variety might well be regarded as a distinct species.

106. POLYPORUS MAXIMUS (Mont.) Overh.

Sci. Survey Porto Rico and the Virgin Isl. 8, 1: 164. 1926

(Figs. 62–63 and Plate 130)

Irpex maximus Mont., Ann. Sci. Nat. Bot. II, 8: 364. 1837.
Coriolus maximus (Mont.) Murr., Torrey Bot. Club Bul. 34: 467. 1907.

Sporophore sessile or umbonate-affixed, leathery when fresh, rigid when dry; pileus 3–15 $\times$ 5–25 $\times$ 0.3–0.8 cm., white to ashy, cinereous, pale tan, or wood-brown, with a dense tomentose or hirsute-tomentose covering that may eventually disappear in zones or spots or patches and show a hard pale-chestnut or bay layer beneath, conspicuously concentrically zonate, the zones becoming glabrous first, the margin thin, entire or lobed; context white or pallid, soft-punky to subcorky, bounded above by a thin chestnut line, the tomentum in a loose layer on its outer surface, 1–5 mm. thick; pore surface whitish, becoming yellowish, avellaneous, or bay on drying, the tubes 1–2.5 mm. long, the mouths daedaloid or more often irpiciform, averaging about 3 per mm., the walls thick and rigid though finely and characteristically denticulate or irpiciform, so that the pore surface feels rough and has a hydnoid appearance; spores oblong-ellipsoid or cylindric, smooth, hyaline, 4–5 $\times$ 2–2.5 μ; cystidia none; hyphal pegs abundant, conspicuous; context tissue homogeneous below, bordered above by a definite, narrow, compact zone 75–100 μ broad; hyphae mostly simple, thick-walled, with no cross walls or clamps, 4–6 μ in diameter (in occasional specimens reaching 10 μ), but some hyphae somewhat smaller and very much branched, the long branches attenuate. (Compare no. 104, *Polyporus hirsutus*, and *P. occidentalis*, p. 427.)

HABITAT: On dead wood of deciduous trees, noted on *Ulmus*.

DISTRIBUTION: Specimens have been examined only from Fla. and La.

The covering and zonation of the pileus of this fungus are often exactly comparable to what we find in both *Polyporus hirsutus* and *P. occidentalis*, and since these species are all quite similar in size and thickness it is helpful to know that *P. hirsutus* does not have the abundant hyphal pegs of the other two species and that neither *P. hirsutus* nor *P. occidentalis* have the hard, clearly differentiated bay layer under the tomentum of the pileus that shows up in *P. maximus,* in lateral view of a vertical section, as a narrow dark line. Moreover *P. maximus* eventually becomes glabrous, first in zones (as in *P. versicolor*), and then in large patches, and the pore surface is always partially hydnoid and feels rough and harsh. *P. hirsutus* often has dark pore mouths that are regular and entire, whereas *P. maximus* has light pore mouths that are typically daedaloid or, more often, irpiciform. *P. occidentalis* has more even, brown pore mouths and an umber-brown context. The species is largely tropical, and barely enters our southernmost limits.

107. POLYPORUS CONCHIFER (Schw.) Fries

Elench. Fung., p. 96. 1828

(Figs. 33–36 and Plate 129)

Boletus conchifer Schw., Schr. Nat. Ges. Leipzig 1: 98. 1822.
Poronidulus conchifer (Schw.) Murr., Torrey. Bot. Club Bul. 31: 426. 1904.
Boletus virgineus Schw., Schr. Nat. Ges. Leipzig 1: 98. 1822.

Sporophore sessile or attached by a lateral tubercle and appearing substipitate, coriaceous when fresh, scarcely rigid on drying, often preceded by a discoid or saucer-shaped to cup-shaped sterile structure 0.5–2 cm. in diameter and zonate on the upper surface; pileus 1–3 × 1–5 × 0.1–0.3 cm., white, yellowish, or rarely somewhat isabelline, dimidiate to reniform, more or less zonate at least on the margin, glabrous or slightly velutinous, sometimes somewhat radiately wrinkled, often retaining the saucer-shaped sterile structure on its upper surface at the base of the pileus; context white, less than 1 mm. thick; pore surface white or yellowish, the tubes less than 2 mm. long, the mouths angular, thin-walled, entire or becoming slightly dentate, averaging 2–3(–4) per mm.; spores cylindric, smooth, hyaline, 5–7 × 1.5–2.5 μ; cystidia none; hyphal pegs present; many hyphae straight, hyaline, simple, with walls partially or entirely thickened, 4–8 μ in diameter, others smaller, 2–4 μ in diameter, and much branched to form hyphal complexes, with cross walls and clamps entirely lacking.

HABITAT: Usually on dead elm (*Ulmus*) branches, noted also on *Acer, Betula, Ostrya, Prunus, Quercus,* and *Salix.*

DISTRIBUTION: Specimens have been examined from Me., N.H., Vt., Mass., Conn., R.I., N.Y., Pa., N.J., Del., Md., Va., Ga., Ala.,

Ky., Ohio, Ind., Ill., Wis., Minn., N. Dak., Iowa, Mo., Kans., Nebr., and Ark.; in Canada from Nova Scotia, Quebec, Ontario, and Manitoba; reported also from W. Va. (Gould [58]), Tenn. (Hesler [71]), Mich. (Kauffman [101]), and Mont. (Weir [227]).

ILLUSTRATIONS: Farlow, Icones Farl., pl. 94 (bottom, as *Polystictus*; sterile cups only); Lloyd, Myc. Notes, Polyp. Issue No. 3: fig. 366 (as *Polystictus*); Moffatt, Chicago Acad. Sci. Nat. Hist. Survey Bul. 7, 1: pl. 16, fig. 2; Overholts, Wash. Univ. Studies 3: pl. 3, fig. 10.

The small, cuplike body at the base of the pileus will usually identify the species, although at times it is scarcely more than a brown circular area, or it may entirely disappear, or fail to develop. Frequently it bears tubes on its lower surface. The species is gregarious, however, and usually some of the specimens will have the cup well developed. The sterile cups alone are often found on dead elm branches. Specimens without the cups have some resemblance to thin forms of *Polyporus pubescens*, but may ordinarily be distinguished by the thinner pileus and its small, tubercular point of attachment. Occasionally specimens show a fine, soft tomentum on the upper surface of the pileus.

Miss Freda Detmers (39) reports this fungus as somewhat parasitic on species of *Ulmus*, but Weir's observations (230) agree with my own, that the fungus is never parasitic, will not directly attack a living branch, and is not known to decay the heartwood.

The decay produced is of the general delignifying type.

108. POLYPORUS VOLVATUS Peck

N. Y. State Mus. Ann. Rept. 27: 98. 1877

(Figs. 147–148 and Plate 132)

Cryptoporus volvatus (Peck) Hubbard, Canad. Ent. 24: 250. 1892.
Polyporus obvolutus Berk. & Cooke, Grevillea 7: 1. 1878.
Polyporus inflatus Ell. & Martindale, apud Ellis, in Amer. Nat. 18: 722. 1884.

Sporophore sessile or attached by a point, globose or compressed-globose, 1.5–8.5 cm. broad and long, 1–3.5 cm. thick, tough-corky to woody, drying rigid, the surface slightly incrusted with a thin resinous crust, whitish or yellowish when fresh, often drying ochraceous to nearly bay or rarely somewhat chestnut, sometimes tinged with red, glabrous, the margin thick and rounded, extending downward and backward and forming a veil-like covering over the pore surface; context 0.2–1 cm. thick; pore surface pure white to brownish, the tubes 2–5 mm. long, the mouths circular, thick-walled, entire, averaging 3–4 per mm.; the covering over the hymenium becoming perforated near the base with an opening (rarely 2 openings) 5–10 mm. long and 3–5 mm. wide which allows the spores to escape; spores flesh-colored in mass, hyaline under the microscope, elongate-ellipsoid or short-cylindric, 8–12 × 3–5 μ, in fresh specimens collecting in a pinkish heap on the volva; basidia 9–10 μ in diameter; cystidia none or scarcely noteworthy; hyphae hyaline, flexuous, thick-walled, sparingly branched, with no cross walls or clamps, 3–5(–9) μ in diameter.

HABITAT: Usually on dead standing or fallen coniferous trees, sometimes on living trees, noted on *Abies, Larix, Libocedrus, Picea, Pinus,* and *Pseudotsuga;* reported on *Tsuga* (Wash., Zeller [235]).

DISTRIBUTION: Specimens have been examined from Me., N.H., Vt., Mass., N.Y., Pa., N.J., Del., Md., D.C., Va., W. Va., Mich., Minn., S. Dak., Nebr., Utah, Nev., Colo., Mont., Idaho, Ore., Wash., and Calif.; in Canada from Ontario, Manitoba, and British Columbia.

ILLUSTRATIONS: Lloyd, Myc. Notes, Polyp. Issue No. 2: fig. 261; *idem,* Synop. Apus, fig. 652; Peck, N. Y. State Mus. Ann. Rept. 27: pl. 2, figs. 3–6; *idem,* Torrey Bot. Club Bul. 7: 104, figs. 1–3; Schmitz, Phytopathology 12: 495, fig. 1; Shope, Mo. Bot. Gard. Ann. 18: pl. 16, fig. 1; Zeller, Mycologia 7: pl. 159 (as *Cryptoporus*).

The development of this species, and especially the development of the aperture through the volva, are described by Zeller (235). He cultured the fungus on sterile wood substrata and found that it produced conidiospores, but his cultures never developed mature fruiting bodies.

No other species has a similar peculiar volval overgrowth on the pore surface. The sporophores first appear in May and become less frequent after July. *Pinus rigida* is the common host in Pennsylvania. Schmitz (194) thinks the species is an important one in the decay of coniferous slash. He is also of the opinion (193) that it may possibly be parasitic on living conifers. I have observed it only on standing dead trees, on which it seems to fruit the season following their death.

6b. *Context hyphae with cross walls or clamps* (see also
Tyromyces Pini-glabrae, p. 428)

109. POLYPORUS CUNEATUS (Murr.) Zeller

Mycologia 21: 101. 1929

(Figs. 154–155, 631, and Plate 129)

Coriolellus cuneatus Murr., North Amer. Flora 9: 28. 1907.
Coriolus washingtonensis Murr., Mycologia 4: 92. 1912.

Sporophore sessile or resupinate, sometimes narrowed at the
base and somewhat poculiform, sometimes broadly attached, watery-
tough when fresh, rather soft and flexible when dry, frequently
moss-covered; pileus 0–2 × 1–6 × 0.2–0.4 cm., often laterally connate
when reflexed, white or cream-colored in fresh plants, often yellowish
or tan on drying, finely villose-tomentose or fibrillose-tomentose and
soft and velvety to the touch, azonate, the margin rather thick;
context white, 0.5–3 mm. thick, soft-fibrous on drying, taste mild;
pore surface white or yellowish on drying, the tubes 1–2(–3) mm.
long, the mouths subangular or subrotund, rather thick-walled, entire
or dentate, finely pubescent, averaging 2–3 per mm.; spores ellipsoid
or subglobose, smooth, hyaline, 3.5–5 × 3–4 μ; cystidia present as
roughly capitate-incrusted tips of projecting hyphae 4–5 μ in diameter
and as inflated ellipsoid cells 18–20 × 7–9 μ, both types often rare in
sporulating portions of the hymenium; tramal tissue loosely con-
structed; hyphae mostly simple, hyaline or pale brown in KOH,
thin-walled, with cross walls but no clamps, 2.5–4 μ in diameter.
(Compare no. 1, *Trametes sepium*, and no. 71, *Polyporus carbonarius*.)

HABITAT: On bark of logs of coniferous trees, noted on *Larix*,
Sequoia, and *Thuja*, usually *T. plicata*.

DISTRIBUTION: Specimens have been examined from Colo., Mont.,
Idaho, Ore., Wash., and Calif.; in Canada from Manitoba and
British Columbia.

ILLUSTRATIONS: Lloyd, Myc. Notes 43: fig. 848 (as *Polystictus*
or *Trametes*).

The species is very similar in appearance to *Trametes sepium*,
but is of somewhat different texture, with different spores and
hyphae. *Coriolus washingtonensis* differs only in a more coarsely

pubescent pileus, and so cannot be regarded as separate. Its types have yellowed more than is usual, and the pilei are more distinct and less connate, but there is no specific difference.

110. POLYPORUS VELUTINUS Fries

Syst. Myc. 1: 368. 1821

(Figs. 29–30 and Plate 132)

Trametes pusilla Lloyd, Myc. Notes 54: 774. 1918.

Sporophore sessile, often imbricate, rather thin and pliant when fresh, rigid when dry, reviving; pileus 2–7 × 2–7 × 0.2–0.6 cm., white to gray, avellaneous, ochraceous, or brownish, zonate or multizonate with nearly concolorous zones or these showing some color variation, with a short, soft, villose tomentum typically giving to the pileus a velvety surface, sometimes becoming partly glabrous at the base and there somewhat reddish, the margin rather thin and entire; context white, 1–4 mm. thick; pore surface whitish or more often varying to slightly smoky or dark smoky, the tubes 0.5–3 mm. long, the mouths subcircular to angular, rather thick-walled, entire, averaging 3–4 per mm., visible to the unaided eye; spores cylindric or slightly curved, hyaline, 5–8 × 2.5–3 μ; cystidia none; hyphal pegs present but not abundant; hyphae hyaline, flexuous, with completely or partially thickened walls, 4–12 μ in diameter, with cross walls and clamps on some of the smaller stainable hyphae 3–4 μ in diameter. (Compare no. 98, *Polyporus pargamenus*; no. 103, *P. versicolor*; no. 104, *P. hirsutus*; and no. 105, *P. pubescens*.)

HABITAT: On dead wood of deciduous trees, noted on *Alnus*, *Betula*, *Fagus*, *Fraxinus*, *Populus*, *Pyrus*, and *Salix*; one collection said to be on *Tsuga heterophylla*.

DISTRIBUTION: Specimens have been examined from Me., N.H., Vt., Mass., Conn., N.Y., Wis., Minn., S. Dak., Iowa, Ariz., Utah, Colo., Wyo., Mont., Idaho, and Wash.; in Canada from Nova Scotia, Quebec, Ontario, Manitoba, and British Columbia; reported from Mich. (Povah [174]) and Wash. (Weir [230]).

The group relationships of this species, heretofore unrecognized in the recent American literature, are clear enough; the specific relationships are not so definite. The species partakes mainly of the upper-surface characters of *Polyporus versicolor*, but is less strongly zoned, with less color in the zones, and, in addition, the pileus typically has a velvety feel that is not found in that species. Both pileus and context are often thicker than in *P. versicolor*. Under the lens the pubescence at times recalls that of *P. hirsutus*, although the pileus is considerably less hirsute and more narrowly zonate; as in that species, the pore surface is usually dark, and the walls of the tubes are rather thick. The fungus is much more pubescent and velvety than is usual in *P. pubescens*. Consequently, it is rather intermediate between *P. versicolor* and *P. hirsutus*. I am compelled to admit collections that look superficially somewhat like *P. subchartaceus*, but lack the characteristic cystidia of that species. The context hyphae of *P. velutinus* run consistently larger than do those of any of these related species. In older, weathered specimens the pubescence may disappear, often doing so almost entirely at the base of the pileus, after which the upper surface is bay or hazel in color. *Trametes quercina* Lloyd may be more closely related to this complex than to *P. pubescens*.

It may well be questioned whether my interpretation of the specific name is correctly attributed to Fries. These plants might better be referred to *Polyporus zonatus* Fries, but not in the sense of Romell and Karsten.

A re-examination of the Minnesota types of *Trametes pusilla*, kindly sent by Mr. John Stevenson, convinces me that they are small specimens of the present species. Except for size, I can match them over and over in my herbarium. There is in the Lloyd Herbarium, also, a gathering by R. Latham, from New York. Part of this collection is like the type of *T. pusilla*; the remainder may be a different species.

Weir (230) reports that this species (as *Polyporus zonatus*) occasionally causes a heart rot of living trees of *Populus* and *Salix*; more often it is limited to the sapwood, causing a soft white decay.

111. POLYPORUS LINEATUS Overh.

Mycologia 33: 101. 1941

(Fig. 565)

Sporophore largely resupinate; pileus narrowly reflexed, 2–8 mm. long, 1–3.5 cm. wide, 1–3 mm. thick, laterally confluent and somewhat imbricate, the upper surface pallid to "cinnamon-buff," perhaps paler when young, sparingly and compactly tomentose, the margin strongly lineate-radiate with agglutinated fibrils; context white, 1–2 mm. thick in fresh specimens, soft and fibrous, never fragile; pore surface white but discoloring somewhat yellowish on drying, the tubes 1–3 mm. long, the mouths circular to somewhat elongate, rather thick-walled, entire, averaging 2–4 per mm.; spores cylindric, smooth, hyaline, straight, 4–5 × 1 μ; cystidia none; context hyphae rather flaccid, with partially thickened walls and easily stained lumina, with cross walls and clamps, 4–5 μ in diameter.

HABITAT: On log of *Pinus rigida*.

DISTRIBUTION: Specimens have been examined only from the type locality, Houserville, Centre Co., Pa.

ILLUSTRATIONS: Overholts, Mycologia 33: 99, fig. 12.

In general appearance the species shows some resemblance to *Polyporus biformis*, especially the dried specimens. However, the pileus is thinner, the pores smaller, and the spores both narrower and shorter. The pileus is tough and coriaceous when fresh, hence the species is unrelated to the *P. albellus* group.

The rot associated with this fungus is of the brown carbonizing type.

112. POLYPORUS BALSAMEUS Peck

N. Y. State Mus. Ann. Rept. 30: 46. 1878

(Figs. 96–97, 106–107, 547, 621, 649, and Plate 128)

Coriolus balsameus (Peck) Murr., North Amer. Flora 9: 21. 1907.
? *Polyporus crispellus* Peck, N. Y. State Mus. Ann. Rept. 38: 91. 1885.

Sporophore sessile or effused-reflexed, usually imbricate, watery-tough or somewhat cartilaginous when fresh, drying rigid, reviving; pileus 1–5 × 2–6 × 0.1–0.5 cm., decidedly appressed-fibrillose and considerably radiate-striate when dry, whitish or alutaceous and with water-soaked zones in fresh specimens, usually light brown and more conspicuously zoned when dry, with a few broad, light-brown zones, the margin even or undulate; context white, 0.5–3 mm. thick, not bitter; pore surface white, drying gray or yellowish, the tubes 1–3 mm. long, the mouths thin-walled, entire or slightly dentate, averaging 3–4 per mm.; spores oblong to oblong-ellipsoid, sometimes with a curved apiculus, smooth, hyaline, 3–4.5 × 2–2.5 μ; basidia 5–6 μ in diameter; cystidia present, very abundant in the non-sporulating hymenium, less conspicuous among the spore-bearing basidia, projecting but usually not conspicuous, sometimes incrusted at the apex, hyaline, narrowly conic, 4–7 μ in diameter; hyphal pegs present; hyphae simple or nearly so, very thick-walled and with small central lumina, with very occasional cross walls and clamps, 4–7(–9) μ in diameter. (Compare no. 35, *Polyporus floriformis*; no. 58, *P. anceps*; and no. 127, *P. semisupinus*.)

HABITAT: Usually on trunks or stumps of coniferous trees, noted on *Abies, Picea, Thuja,* and *Tsuga*; one specimen on *Acer rubrum.*

DISTRIBUTION: Specimens have been examined from N.H., N.Y., Pa., N.C., Tenn., and Mich.; in Canada from Nova Scotia, Quebec, Ontario, and British Columbia; also reported from Wis. and Minn. (Hubert [85]).

ILLUSTRATIONS: Hubert, Phytopathology 19: 729, fig. 3; *idem,* Outline Forest Path., fig. 89; McCallum, Canada Dept. Agr. Bul., N.S. 104: pl. 7, figs. 2–3.

The type specimens (New York State Museum, Albany) show the following microscopic characters: spores oblong or short-cylindric, 3–4 × 2 μ; cystidia occasional or rather abundant as hyaline, pointed organs 4–7 μ in diameter and protruding up to 10 μ, often difficult to locate where the hymenium is well developed; hyphal pegs narrow and cylindric or somewhat tapering at the apex, 7–12 μ in diameter at the base; context hyphae mostly of large diameter, 4–8 μ, and mostly with thickened walls. I have verified each of these characters several times, and believe that one cannot refer to this species collections that are not in substantial agreement with them. On that basis, I must exclude Boutlou's West Virginia collection in the Lloyd Herbarium at Beltsville, Maryland, which is referred here by Lloyd and is extremely similar to the present species in external appearance. But the spores are narrow-cylindric, 6 × 2 μ, and cannot be considered to represent the mature spore form of this species. The hyphal pegs are also entirely different, being low-conoidal and about as broad as high.

Young specimens that are full of water are rather cartilaginous in appearance when dried, the walls of the hyphae appear somewhat gelatinized, and clamps seem to be more numerous and conspicuous.

The flesh of the sporophore is not styptic or bitter; otherwise the species is similar to some European interpretations of *Polyporus stypticus*. *P. floriformis* is also similar to *P. balsameus* in some respects. However, one lot of collections referable to either *P. balsameus* or *P. floriformis* shows cystidia in the hymenium and a pileus that in dried plants is brownish and zoned. These seem the salient characters of *P. balsameus*. Other collections do not have cystidia, the pileus is not at all brown, and dried plants are more cartilaginous in appearance. It is impossible to macerate the context of *P. floriformis* by chewing, but *P. balsameus* context macerates easily. The characters of these other collections agree quite well with those of European collections of *P. floriformis* that I have examined.

Polyporus crispellus has long been a species of doubtful affinities. A study of the types shows it to have cystidia and spores like those of *P. balsameus*, and it seems unlikely that Peck's species can be anything else. Dr. Clara Fritz (55, p. 252) reports chlamydospores in cultures of *P. balsameus*.

This species causes a brown cubical rot in the butt and roots of coniferous trees, particularly in *Abies balsameus* (85, 98, 127).

113. POLYPORUS SUBCARTILAGINEUS Overh.

Mycologia 33: 90. 1941

Sporophore broadly effused, the margin only narrowly reflexed to form a pileus up to 1 cm. long, 2–5 mm. thick, laterally elongated to as much as 8 cm., coriaceous-tough, drying rigid and brittle and requiring several minutes to become soaked, at first white, in drying becoming brown or rufescent-tinted, softly and compactly tomentose, curling away from the substratum and showing on the exposed ventral surface a hard, dry, more or less resinous-gelatinized layer; context tough, almost cartilaginous in fresh condition, about 1 mm. thick, pallid, the taste mild; pore surface creamy white when fresh, the tubes 1–3 mm. long, the walls thin, unequal, fragile in the dried condition, the mouths averaging 2–3 per mm.; spores ellipsoid to elongate-ellipsoid or short-cylindric, smooth, hyaline, $4.5–6.5 \times 2–3\,\mu$; cystidia none; context hyphae somewhat gelatinized, with small staining lumina, hyaline, with few or no cross walls and clamps, $3–6\,\mu$ in diameter.

Habitat: On logs of *Picea* and *Prunus serotina*.

Distribution: Specimens have been examined in the United States only from Pa.; in Canada from Quebec.

Illustrations: Overholts, Mycologia 33: 92, fig. 1.

The diagnostic features of this species seem to be the subcartilaginous consistency of the sporophores, the rufescent coloration assumed by the pileus but not by the pore surface on drying, the spores, which are broader than in other similar species that assume a similar rufescent coloration, and the narrowly reflexed pileus. The species is most like *Polyporus cutifractus*, but seems to differ in the constant lack of well-developed cystidia, in the slightly larger spores, and perhaps in geographical range.

114. Polyporus amorphus Fries

Syst. Myc. 1: 364. 1821

(Figs. 151–152, 159, and Plate 128)

Tyromyces amorphus (Fries) Murr., Mycologia 10: 109. 1918.

Sporophore sessile, effused-reflexed, or occasionally resupinate, coriaceous when fresh, rigid when dry; pileus 0–2 × 1–5 × 0.1–0.3 cm., sometimes laterally confluent, whitish or cinereous, unchanged on drying, hirsute, villose, or sparingly tomentose, marked with one or more narrow concentric zones in well-developed specimens; context white, 1–2 mm. thick, drying to a thin resinous layer; pore surface typically pinkish red to orange or brick-red, rarely nearly or quite white, red where bruised if light-colored, the tubes less than 2.5 mm. long, the mouths angular, thin-walled, averaging 2–4 per mm.; spores allantoid, hyaline, 3–4 × 0.7–1 μ; cystidia none; hyphal pegs occasional; hyphae rather flexuous, not much branched, the walls greatly thickened, with only very occasional cross walls and clamps, 3–5 μ in diameter; context apparently duplex, as seen in vertical cuts through the pileus and hymenium of dried plants, in reality composed of a thick compact tomentose layer and a thin context layer that is red in fresh plants and in KOH, and light resin-colored and extremely hard in dried specimens, the layers not being sharply differentiated under the microscope. (Compare no. 116, *Polyporus dichrous*.)

HABITAT: On dead wood of coniferous trees, rarely on chips and needles of pine on the ground, noted on *Abies*, *Larix*, *Picea*, *Pinus*, *Pseudotsuga*, and *Tsuga*.

DISTRIBUTION: Specimens have been examined from Me., N.Y., Pa., Md., D.C., Va., N.C., Miss., Tenn., Ohio, Ark., Mont., Idaho, and Wash.; in Canada from British Columbia; reported from S. Dak. (Brenckle [25]).

ILLUSTRATIONS: Murrill, Mycologia 10: pl. 6, fig. 5 (as *Tyromyces*); Overholts, Mycologia 9: pl. 12.

The species is characterized by the soft coriaceous consistency, the thin, white, hairy pileus, the thin, white context, and the pinkish or reddish pore surface with somewhat merulioid pores.

Polyporus dichrous is similar to this species, but the furrows are lacking on the pileus and the hymenium is much darker, being dark reddish purple or reddish black. The depth of color developed on the pore surface varies with the position of growth. In specimens not exposed to strong light the pore surface is paler than it would be otherwise and changes immediately to red where wounded. Resupinate specimens are likely to be referred to *Merulius* on first examination.

The light resin-colored context contrasted with the white, thick, overlying tomentose layer, as seen with a hand lens in lateral views of vertical sections of dried sporophores, is a distinct aid in recognizing this species. Though the pore surface is somewhat soft in fresh sporophores, the tissue is not gelatinous. Schweinitz' record, if based on the specimen (No. 361) now in his herbarium, is in error, that plant being *Polyporus dichrous*.

The decay produced by this species has been described in detail by me (152) as a cellulose-destroying rot of the sapwood.

5b. *Pores averaging 5 or more per mm.*
6a. *Context hyphae with cross walls or clamps*

115. POLYPORUS OCHROTINCTELLUS (Murr.) Overh.

Sci. Survey Porto Rico and the Virgin Isl. 8, 1: 165. 1926
(Figs. 80, 230, and Plate 131)

Coriolus ochrotinctellus Murr., North Amer. Flora 9: 22. 1907.

Sporophore sessile and broadly attached, or narrowed to a lateral stemlike attachment, or rather definitely stipitate; pileus dimidiate to spathulate, reniform, or flabelliform, 2–7 × 2–10 × 0.2–0.4 cm., rigid when dry, isabelline-ochraceous to bright ochraceous tan in herbarium specimens, entirely glabrous or rarely very minutely villose-tomentose, more or less zonate with concolorous or slightly darker zones, sometimes somewhat radiate-rugose; context white, 0.5–4 mm. thick; pore surface nearly concolorous with pileus, the tubes 0.5–3 mm. long, the mouths angular, thin-walled, always entire, averaging 4–8 per mm.; stem lateral when present, not over 2 cm. long and about 0.5 cm. thick, usually very short or obsolete; spores allantoid, smooth, hyaline, 3–5 × 1–1.5 μ; cystidia none; hyphal pegs rather numerous; hyphae rather thin-walled, sparingly branched, with cross walls and clamps in the thinner-walled ones, 3–4 μ in diameter.

HABITAT: On dead wood, noted on *Quercus.*

DISTRIBUTION: Specimens have been examined from Fla. and Miss.

This species is easily recognized by the rather bright ochraceous pileus, by the strong tendency (usually) of the pileus to become stipitate, and, particularly, by the allantoid spores, the hyphal pegs in the hymenium, and the characteristic hyphae. It is distinct from *Polyporus Hollickii* (Murr.) Lloyd, from Jamaica, in the very different spores and in the hyphae. Lloyd reports the species as *P. subfulvus* Berk., which, however, was only a manuscript name, though the species had been earlier known, according to Lloyd, as *P. ochrotinctus.*

116. POLYPORUS DICHROUS Fries

Syst. Myc. 1: 364. 1821

(Figs. 150, 671, and Plate 129)

Sporophore sessile or effused-reflexed, often imbricate, very coriaceous when fresh, rigid when dry, reviving; pileus 0.5–4 × 1–8 × 0.1–0.5 cm., white or whitish, rarely ochraceous in herbarium specimens, villose-tomentose or compactly tomentose, then velvety to nearly glabrous, the margin often narrowly sterile below and white; context white, 1–4 mm. thick; pore surface waxy and separable from the context in a thin elastic layer when fresh or when soaked, pale buff to flesh color, reddish purple or purplish black, the tubes less than 1 mm. long, the mouths circular to angular, rather thin-walled, entire, averaging 5–8 per mm., in vertical microscopic sections showing a context of closely interwoven hyphae of the usual type, separated from the hymenium by a narrower darker zone, the entire hymenial region composed of strongly gelatinized nonstaining hyphae, contrasting sharply with the context; spores allantoid, 3–4.5 × 0.5–1 μ; basidia 2.5–3 μ in diameter; cystidia none; context hyphae somewhat branched, the walls partially thickened, with conspicuous clamps and cross walls, 3–6 μ in diameter. (Compare no. 114, *Polyporus amorphus*; no. 117, *P. conchoides*; and no. 118, *P. adustus*.)

HABITAT: On dead wood, usually of deciduous trees, noted on *Acer, Alnus, Betula, Carpinus, Carya, Castanea, Cephalanthus, Cornus, Crataegus, Fagus, Fraxinus, Gleditsia, Liquidambar, Liriodendron, Maclura, Nyssa, Populus, Prunus, Pyrus, Quercus, Salix*, and *Ulmus*; rarely on logs of coniferous trees, noted on *Abies, Juniperus, Picea, Pinus, Thuja*, and *Tsuga*; reported on *Tilia* (Mich., Kauffman [101]) and on *Larix*, occasionally on old dead sporophores, such as *Polyporus dryophilus* (Rhoads [181]) and *Fomes applanatus*.

DISTRIBUTION: Specimens have been examined from Me., N.H., Vt., Mass., Conn., N.Y., Pa., N.J., Del., Md., Va., W. Va., N.C., S.C., Ga., Fla., Ala., La., Tenn., Ky., Ohio, Ind., Ill., Mich., Iowa, Mo., Kans., Ark., Okla., N. Mex., Ariz., Mont., Idaho, Wash., and Calif.; in Canada from Ontario, Manitoba, and British Columbia; reported from Wis. (Dodge [40]) and from N. Dak. and S. Dak. (Brenckle [25]).

ILLUSTRATIONS: Moffatt, Chicago Acad. Sci. Nat. Hist. Survey Bul. 7, 1: pl. 16, fig. 1.

Fresh specimens are easily recognized by the pure-white pileus and the flesh-colored or reddish-purple tubes that peel off in a thin elastic layer or that can be readily scraped off with the thumbnail in young specimens. When the pileus is viewed from above, the appearance is much like that of *Polyporus semipileatus*, but a glance at the pore surface corrects any impression that it may be that species. The pore surface is a different shade of red than in *P. amorphus*, and may become reddish black, or, rarely, entirely black in old dried specimens. Such dark specimens may easily be confused with *P. adustus*, but the gelatinous appearance (2, pl. 13, fig. 63 [as *Gloeoporus conchoides*]; 154, pl. 4, fig. 8) of the tube tissue as seen in vertical or cross section, coupled with the fact that when the specimen is fresh or soaked the layer of tubes can be peeled off in a thin, rubbery sheet, is highly characteristic. Fresh young specimens frequently have a pale-buff pore surface. There are often rather numerous fusoid crystals 18–24 $\times$ 10–14 μ imbedded in the tube tissue. These are lacking in *P. adustus*.

The types of *Polyporus nigropurpurascens* Schw. are quite fragmentary, but it is likely that they belong here.

The rot produced by this fungus is probably of the brown carbonizing type, as is indicated by the reaction the fungus gives when subjected to the "oxidase" test. The decay usually seen associated with it is white, but careful dissection often shows a small amount of definitely brown rot in the vicinity of the sporophores. The inference is that the fungus decays extremely slowly and usually becomes surrounded by the decay produced by other species of fungi.

117. Polyporus conchoides (Mont.) Lloyd

Synop. Apus, p. 331. 1915

(Figs. 157–158)

Gloeoporus conchoides Mont., Plant Cell. Cuba, p. 385. 1838–1842. (Not *G. conchoides* of earlier American authors.)

Sporophore sessile or effused-reflexed, often imbricate, very flexible and tough when fresh, drying almost inflexible; pileus 1.5–7 $\times$ 3–12 $\times$ 0.05–0.2 cm., cinnamon-rufous in water-soaked condition, grayish cinnamon to cream color or white when dry, rather distinctly multizonate when fresh, nearly azonate when dry, covered with a fine, soft, short, villose-scabrous tomentum that becomes more conspicuous as the plants dry, the margin quite thin, usually deflexed on drying; context white or pallid, 0.5–2 mm. thick; pore surface more or less tinted with flesh color, becoming more prominently so or pale bay in dried plants, easily separated in a thin elastic layer from the context in fresh plants or when soaked, the tubes about 0.5 mm. long, the mouths circular, thick-walled, entire, averaging about 6–7 per mm., invisible or scarcely visible to the unaided eye; spores not found but probably quite minute; cystidia none; hyphae flexuous, thick-walled, considerably branched, with some cross walls but no clamps, 3–6 μ in diameter.

Habitat: On dead wood of deciduous trees.

DISTRIBUTION: Known only from tropical regions; apparently not yet collected on the mainland of the United States, but probably occurring in tropical parts of Florida.

This is a distinctive species, matched only by *Polyporus dichrous* in the thin, waxy tube layer that can easily be stripped from the overlying context if the plants are fresh or soaked. It usually differs from that species in that the hymenium is merely a distinct flesh color (dried plants), whereas in *P. dichrous* it is reddish purple to blackish. However, occasional specimens of *P. dichrous* have a pale-colored hymenium, but where the ranges of the two species overlap they may be easily separated by the presence of the clamp connections on the hyphae of *P. dichrous* and their entire absence from those of *P. conchoides*. Occasional cross walls occur in the hyphae of the latter species, especially at the origin of a lateral hyphal branch. Lloyd collected the species in Cuba and reports that the pore surface as well as the pileus is at first entirely white, the former becoming flesh-colored on drying. Dried specimens become water-soaked very readily, assuming immediately a watery-brown color, but if a dry cloth or a piece of blotting paper is closely pressed to the upper surface, water is quickly absorbed and the pileus becomes a peculiar gray or is tinted slightly pinkish or lavender. The specimens then reveal a thin, scurfy, uniform pubescence. The plants are very thin and flexible when fresh or when soaked.

118. POLYPORUS ADUSTUS Willd. ex Fries

Syst. Myc. 1: 363. 1821

(Figs. 72–74 and Plate 128)

Boletus adustus Willd., Florae Berol. Prod., p. 392. 1787.
Bjerkandera adusta (Willd. ex Fries) Karst., Soc. Fauna Flora Fenn. Meddel. 5: 38. 1879.
Polyporus Burtii Peck, Torrey Bot. Club Bul. 24: 146. 1897.
Polystictus hirsutus var. *calvens* Clements, Crypt. Form. Colo., no. 168. 1905.
Coriolus alabamensis Murr., North Amer. Flora 9: 19. 1907.

Sporophore sessile or effused-reflexed, tough to corky, rigid when dry, reviving, usually imbricate; pileus 1–6 × 3–10 × 0.1–0.8 cm., white or cinereous to smoke-gray or pale tan, rarely with reddish blotches or zones, finely tomentose to short villose-tomentose or nearly glabrous, or at times short strigose behind and the margin fibrillose or fibrillose-striate, the margin thin, even, often black in dried specimens, sterile below; context white or in dried specimens ochraceous or pale brown, 1–6 mm. thick, in large specimens separated from the tube layer by a narrow dark line; pore surface at first gray or grayish black, darker where bruised, often changing to black or rarely sordid brown in age and in herbarium specimens, the tubes 2 mm. long or less, the mouths very minute, subcircular then angular, averaging 5–7 per mm., scarcely visible to the unaided eye; tramal tissue decidedly brown under the microscope; spores oblong or oblong-ellipsoid, rarely slightly curved, smooth, hyaline, 3.5–5 × 2–3 μ; basidia quite small, 8–10 × 4–5 μ; cystidia and hyphal pegs none; hyphae hyaline, considerably branched, with cross walls and clamps, 3–6 μ in diameter. (Compare no. 116, *Polyporus dichrous*, and no. 119, *P. fumosus*.)

HABITAT: Usually on dead wood of deciduous trees, noted on *Acer, Aesculus, Ailanthus, Alnus, Betula, Carpinus, Carya, Celtis, Diospyros, Fagus, Fraxinus, Gleditsia, Halesia, Ilex, Juglans, Liquidambar, Liriodendron, Magnolia, Morus, Nyssa, Platanus, Populus, Prunus, Pyrus, Quercus, Rhus, Salix, Sambucus, Syringa, Tilia,* and *Ulmus*; occasionally on wood of coniferous trees, noted on *Abies, Juniperus, Picea, Pinus, Pseudotsuga, Thuja,* and *Tsuga*; also reported on *Larix* (Weir [222]) and on *Ostrya* (Mo., Maneval [131]).

DISTRIBUTION: Specimens have been examined from every state in the Union except Nev.; in Canada from Nova Scotia, Newfoundland, Quebec, Ontario, Manitoba, Saskatchewan, Alberta, and British Columbia.

ILLUSTRATIONS: Gillet, Champ. France 5: pl. 554 (57) (as var. *carpineus*); Humphrey, U. S. Dept. Agr. Bul. 510: pl. 5, figs. 5–6; Murrill, Mycologia 10: pl. 6, fig. 4 (as *Bjerkandera*); Shope, Mo. Bot. Gard. Ann. 18: pl. 23, fig. 1 (as *Polyporus crispus*).

This is a common species of wide distribution. It is not possible to draw a satisfactory line between it and *Polyporus fumosus*. Sporophores are usually smaller than those of *P. fumosus*, the context is considerably thinner, and the pores average considerably smaller. The hymenium is, at maturity, quite black, whereas in that species it becomes blackish only occasionally. Yet many collections partake of the characters of both species. In one form of the species the upper surface is short villose-tomentose; in another (apparently *P. crispus* Fries), it is almost strigose or becomes matted into a fibrillose condition. In thin specimens the narrow dark line at the tube bases is not apparent; in thicker ones it is quite evident.

In sections cut and stained in the usual way the tissue of the tube walls is seen to be very compact and distinctly brownish. The species is thus easily separated from dark-pored specimens of *Polyporus dichrous*, in which the tube tissue is distinctly gelatinized and entirely colorless. Moreover, vertical sections through the pilei and tubes of *P. dichrous* show a very distinct line separating the gelatinous tube tissue from the nongelatinous context. The color of the tramal tissue is also of some use in separating thin specimens of *P. fumosus* from *P. adustus*. The tube tissue of *P. fumosus* is colorless or nearly so in section. In general, the transition, seen in vertical sections through the pileus and hymenium, from the almost colorless context tissue to the decidedly colored tissue of the pores is reliable enough to serve as a diagnostic character in attempting to identify old or sterile specimens of this species.

Polyporus alabamensis (Murr.) Sacc. & Trott. is the fibrillose-strigose form referred sometimes to *P. crispus* Fries, a species that it seems hardly possible to maintain (150, pp. 688–695). Murrill's specimens are fertile and show all the characters of *P. adustus*, though the hymenium is only slightly darkened. *P. crispus* var. *microporus* Peck is not distinct even in having smaller pores than usual, according to the types in the New York State Museum, at Albany. Other names usually referred to synonymy are *Boletus isabellinus* Schw., *P. subcinereus* Berk., and *P. Halesiae* Berk. & Curt., all described from various parts of the United States and Canada. The variety *carpineus* (Sow. ex Fries) Peck is in no wise distinct.

The decay produced by this fungus is of the general delignifying type, affecting only the sapwood. No black lines are formed, and white flecks are present in the wood. Wilson (233, p. 20) reports that the species "may be a true parasite" in Iowa, but such a suggestion would seem to be in error.

119. POLYPORUS FUMOSUS Pers. ex Fries

Syst. Myc. 1: 367. 1821

(Figs. 75–77 and Plate 130)

Boletus fumosus Pers., Synop. Meth. Fung., p. 530. 1801.
Bjerkandera fumosa (Pers. ex Fries) Karst., Soc. Fauna Flora Fenn. Meddel. 5: 38. 1879.

Polyporus fragrans Peck, N. Y. State Mus. Ann. Rept. 30: 45. 1878.
Polyporus Amesii Lloyd, Synop. Apus, p. 309. 1915.

Sporophore sessile or effused-reflexed, watery and tough or leathery when fresh, rigid when dry, reviving; pileus 2–10 × 3–15 × 0.5–2 cm., white to ochraceous, smoky white, or pale sordid tan, sometimes with a reddish stain, finely tomentose to glabrous; context white or pallid, 2.5–10 mm. thick, zonate with a few very narrow zones in thicker plants, always separated from the tubes by a narrow dark line, anise-scented or with a disagreeable odor; pore surface white to grayish black, sometimes becoming black where bruised, the tubes 1.5–4 mm. long, angular and somewhat unequal when mature, averaging 3–4(–5) per mm.; tramal tissue hyaline or nearly so under the microscope; spores oblong-ellipsoid or oblong, smooth, hyaline, 4.5–6 × 2.5–3 μ; cystidia none; hyphal pegs none; hyphae simple or sparingly branched, rather thin-walled, with conspicuous clamps and cross walls, 3–6 μ in diameter. (Compare no. 118, *Polyporus adustus*.)

HABITAT: On dead wood of deciduous trees, noted on *Acer*, *Ailanthus*, *Carpinus*, *Castanea*, *Cephalanthus*, *Cornus*, *Platanus*, *Populus*, *Salix*, *Tilia*, and *Ulmus*; one collection noted on *Pinus*; reported on *Fraxinus*, *Tsuga*, and *Quercus* (Kauffman [101]).

DISTRIBUTION: Specimens have been examined from Me., Vt., Mass., N.Y., Pa., N.J., Del., Md., D.C., Fla., La., Tenn., Ky., Ohio, Ind., Mich., Wis., Minn., Iowa, Mo., Kans., Nebr., Texas, Ore., and Calif.; in Canada from Quebec, Ontario, and Manitoba; reported from W. Va. (Gould [58]), Ark. (Swartz [212]), and Mont. (Weir [227]).

ILLUSTRATIONS: Lloyd, Synop. Apus, figs. 647–648 (as *Polyporus holmiensis*); Overholts, Mo. Bot. Gard. Ann. 2: pl. 23, fig. 3.

This species is apparently just as widely distributed as *Polyporus adustus*, but is not so abundant. The wood of the elm tree seems to be a favorite habitat. Sporophores attain a larger size than do those of *P. adustus*, the context is considerably thicker, and it usually shows a more distinct narrow dark line separating it from the layer of tubes; the tube mouths are usually larger and sometimes quite pale, or darkening where bruised in fresh sporophores. The spores of the two species are somewhat different in shape. Those of *P. adustus* are inclined to be cylindric and narrow, those of *P. fumosus* broader and oblong-ellipsoid. The context of *P. fumosus* darkens slightly with KOH solution. *Daedalea puberula* Berk. & Curt., described from Pennsylvania, has been indicated as a synonym. Though Schweinitz probably collected *P. fumosus*, the single specimen preserved under that name in his herbarium is *Fomes annosus*.

The fungus produces a white rot of the sapwood of its hosts.

6b. *Context hyphae without cross walls* (see also *Coriolus membranaceus Taxodii*, p. 427, and *Hapalopilus subrutilans*, p. 428)

120. POLYPORUS TENUIS (Sacc.) Overh.

Sci. Survey Porto Rico and the Virgin Isl. 8, 1: 167. 1926

(Figs. 22–25 and Plate 132)

Polystictus tenuis Link ex Cooke, in Sacc., Syll. Fung. 6: 288. 1888.
Coriolus membranaceus (Berk.) Pat., Essai Tax. Hym., p. 94. 1900.

Sporophore sessile, effused-reflexed, or narrowed behind into a stemlike base, rarely in rosette-like clusters, flexible in thin specimens, rigid in thicker ones, reviving; pileus usually flabelliform but sometimes dimidiate, 0.5–5 × 0.7–8 × 0.05–0.2 cm., white to yellowish or isabelline, rarely white on drying, usually nearly glabrous, sometimes finely pubescent and rarely somewhat hispid-tomentose or hispid-fibrillose at the base or all over, more or less radiately striate, usually faintly zoned, sometimes conspicuously so, the margin rarely entire, more often lobed or fimbriate and very thin; context white, 1 mm. or less thick, often very thin; pore surface white to yellowish, the tubes less than 1 mm. long, the mouths sometimes regularly angular, frequently irregular and toothed and lacerate, the walls thin, finely denticulate, averaging 5–6 per mm.; spores oblong-ellipsoid or short-cylindric, smooth, hyaline, 4.5–6 × 2.5 μ; cystidia none; hyphal pegs present, not abundant; hyphae closely woven, mostly large, thick-walled, simple, with no cross walls or clamps, 5–9 μ in diameter, many narrower, much-branched hyphae interspersed. (Compare no. 103, *Polyporus versicolor*; no. 121, *P. Drummondii*; and no. 122, *P. pavonius*.)

HABITAT: On dead wood, noted only on *Taxodium*, but probably occurring on a variety of hardwoods.

DISTRIBUTION: Specimens have been examined from S.C., Ga., Fla., La., and Mo.

ILLUSTRATIONS: Lloyd, Myc. Notes 68: fig. 2388 (as *Polystictus*).

This is one of the most common polypores in the southern states. Whether it is specifically distinct from *Polyporus Drummondii* may well be questioned, and some collections are difficult to refer satisfactorily. The plant has also been known as *P. membranaceus* Swartz.

Boletus tenuis of Link I do not find published. In his "Praecursores" Cooke (*Grevillea* 14: 87) records it as in "Berl. Mag." (*Ges. Nat. Freunde Berlin Mag.*), but I failed to locate it there. It would seem that the name was probably a *nomen nudum* until the description was published by Saccardo, who states that it was furnished him, based on the original specimens, by Ascherson.

121. POLYPORUS DRUMMONDII Klotzsch

Linnaea 8: 487. 1833

(Figs. 53–57)

Coriolus Drummondii (Klotzsch) Pat., Essai Tax. Hym., p. 94. 1900.
? *Polyporus armenicolor* Berk. & Curt., Linnean Soc. Bot. Jour. 10: 315. 1868.

Sporophore sessile, imbricate, flabelliform and attenuate at the base so as to appear substipitate, very flexible when fresh, rigid when dry; pileus 1.5–6 × 1–6 × 0.05–0.1 cm., white or watery white and obscurely zonate when fresh, isabelline or pale coffee-brown to smoky avellaneous in dried specimens, and then very strongly radiate-striate and appearing fibrillose but in reality nearly glabrous and zonate or multizonate with darker zones, the margin very thin and somewhat lacerate; context white, less than 0.5 mm. thick; pore surface white when fresh, drying dark-discolored, the tubes 0.5–0.75 mm. long, the mouths angular and slightly radially elongate, very thin-walled, dentate-fimbriate, averaging 4–7 per mm.; spores not found, probably allantoid or cylindric, hyaline; cystidia none; hyphae nearly simple, mostly thin-walled and of large diameter, some with thickened walls, with no cross walls or clamps, 6–9 μ in diameter. (Compare no. 120, *Polyporus tenuis*.)

HABITAT: On dead wood, noted on *Taxodium*.

DISTRIBUTION: Specimens have been examined from Fla. and La.

This description is based on the very few collections at the New York Botanical Garden, one made in 1913 by W. H. Long, on logs of *Taxodium distichum* in Florida, and one made by me in Louisiana in 1931. Type fragments of this species are at the New York Botanical Garden and correspond exactly, so far as one can judge, to the other collections. If the species is to be maintained, it will probably be on the basis of the nearly white color when fresh (as noted in my 1931 collection), the change to brown, zonate, and strongly radiate-striate on drying, and the thin membranous margin. Perhaps it should be regarded as a brown form of *Polyporus tenuis*. Yet other collections from the same substratum (*Taxodium*), collected at approximately the same time, have shown no such color changes on drying; these are referred to *P. tenuis*. I am unable to separate from this species the specimens referred to *P. armenicolor* in the New York Botanical Garden. Lloyd lists that species in the stipitate section of the genus, although recognizing the similarity to the *P. versicolor* section.

122. POLYPORUS PAVONIUS (Hook.) Fries

Epicr. Syst. Myc., p. 477. 1836–1838

(Figs. 21, 84, 90, and Plate 131)

Boletus pavonius Hook., in Kunth, Synop. Plant. 1: 10. 1822.
Coriolus pavonius (Hook.) Murr., North Amer. Flora 9: 25. 1907.

Sporophore sessile or effused-reflexed, very flexible when fresh, flexible or rather rigid when dry, reviving; pileus dimidiate, 1.5–9 × 2–12 × 0.1–0.2 cm., white to yellowish, cinereous or avellaneous, villose or densely villose-tomentose and very velvety to the touch, narrowly multizonate with nearly concolorous zones that do not become glabrous, the margin very thin but entire; context white, very thin, scarcely more than 0.5 mm. thick; pore surface light-colored, white or deep cream color, the tubes 0.5–1 mm. long, the mouths angular, thin-walled, entire, usually glistening, averaging 5–6 per mm.; spores ellipsoid or broadly ellipsoid, smooth, hyaline, 5–6 × 3–4 μ; cystidia none; hyphal pegs short, domelike; many hyphae large, thick-walled, simple, with no cross walls or clamps, 5–9 μ in diameter, and many others smaller, originating in hyphal complexes, with no cross walls or clamps, 2–5 μ in diameter. (Compare no. 103, *Polyporus versicolor*; no. 104, *P. hirsutus*; and no. 120, *P. tenuis*.)

HABITAT: On dead wood, noted only on *Salix*.

DISTRIBUTION: Specimens have been examined from Fla. and La.

The species is usually easily recognized by the thin, multizonate pileus, which is villose-tomentose or inclining toward hirsute, yet soft and velvety to the touch, much thinner and softer than in *Polyporus hirsutus*, the closest relative. The pores are quite minute, barely or scarcely visible to the unaided eye, and nearly always light in color and glistening. The absence of the thin, dark layer underlying the tomentum renders the species easily distinct from thin plants of *P. maximus*. The very even and entire pore mouths are likewise a constant feature. This is a common species in tropical America, but only a few collections are known from the mainland of the United States.

123. POLYPORUS SUBECTYPUS (Murr.) Bres.

Studi Trentini, ser. 2, 7 (1): 80. 1926
(Figs. 66–67 and Plate 132)

Coriolus subectypus Murr., North Amer. Flora 9: 22. 1907.

Sporophore sessile, sometimes attached by a narrow base, coriaceous and flexible when fresh, almost inflexible when dry, reviving; pileus 3–7 × 4–11 × 0.3–0.5 cm., white to straw-colored or ochraceous tan, becoming only slightly if at all bay at the base, very finely tomentose or finely hirsute-tomentose, practically glabrous in age, multizonate with nearly unicolorous zones, the margin even, thin; context white, 1–2(–3) mm. thick, floccose; pore surface white, drying yellowish, the tubes 2–4 mm. long, the mouths angular, thin-walled, entire or slightly fimbriate-dentate, averaging 5–7 per mm.; spores cylindric, hyaline, 3.5–5 × 1–2 μ; basidia 4 μ in diameter; cystidia none; context hyphae long and subflexuous, simple or nearly so, much thickened, with no cross walls or clamps, 4–9 μ in diameter. (Compare no. 124, *Polyporus ectypus*.)

HABITAT: On dead wood of deciduous trees, noted on *Nyssa* and *Quercus*.

DISTRIBUTION: Specimens have been examined from Ga., Fla., and La.

The species approaches *Polyporus ectypus* in some respects, but is less conspicuously zonate and thinner, and lacks in dried specimens the decidedly bay color of the pileus. Abundant collections are at the New York Botanical Garden.

A number of attempts at sectioning the specimens in the collections at the New York Botanical Garden all failed to yield spores, and no hymenium was found. Murrill described the spores as ovoid, 5–6 × 3–4 μ. In a more recent Louisiana specimen I find spores in small numbers, measuring as I have indicated above. Good sporulating specimens may eventually show them to be somewhat longer.

124. POLYPORUS ECTYPUS Berk. & Curt.

Grevillea 1: 52. 1872

(Figs. 81–83 and Plate 129)

Coriolus ectypus (Berk. & Curt.) Pat., Essai Tax. Hym., p. 94. 1900.

Sporophore sessile or umbonate-affixed, leathery when fresh, rigid but not hard on drying; pileus 2–8 × 2–10 × 0.3–0.6 cm., dimidiate or reniform, drying isabelline or reddish isabelline or sometimes bay-red behind, zonate with concolorous or reddish zones, somewhat radiate, short hirsute-tomentose or finely villose-tomentose, often becoming glabrous in spots or zones, the margin thin; context punky to soft-fibrous, white, 2–5 mm. thick; pore surface yellowish or brownish on drying, the tubes 1–3 mm. long, the mouths becoming thin-walled, entire, angular, averaging 5–6 per mm.; spores short-cylindric, often slightly allantoid, smooth, 4.5–6 × 2–3 μ; cystidia none; hyphal pegs present; context hyphae mostly large, thick-walled, simple, with no cross walls or clamps, 4–10 μ in diameter, some smaller hyphae intermixed. (Compare no. 123, *Polyporus subectypus*.)

HABITAT: On dead wood, noted on *Acer, Carya, Fraxinus,* and *Quercus.*

DISTRIBUTION: Specimens have been examined from N.C., S.C., Ga., Fla., La., and Mo.

In some respects this species is similar to *Polyporus modestus,* but in others it is entirely different. *P. ectypus* is a true *Polyporus,* and though in age it may sometimes become red-stained on the upper surface, it is never rosy below at any stage. In consistency it is rigid and will not bend without breaking, whereas *P. modestus* is truly leathery and trametoid and bends readily without cracking. The large, thick-walled hyphae composing the context of *P. ectypus* contrast sharply with the smaller, thinner-walled, branched hyphae of *P. modestus*.

In some features *Polyporus pubescens* seems closer to *P. ectypus* than does any other species, particularly a specimen of *P. pubescens* verging toward *P. zonatus*; yet thicker specimens are totally dissimilar. When young, the pileus has a short, tomentose pubescence, very noticeable under a lens. With age this disappears, at first in zones, beginning at the base of the pileus and progressing toward the margin. Eventually the pileus may become almost glabrous, with the possible exception of one or two narrow zones near the margin, and may appear to have a very thin crust over the surface. The characteristic bay color of the pileus is a good mark of distinction among related species.

125. POLYPORUS MODESTUS Kunze

In Fries, Linnaea 5: 519. 1830

(Figs. 234–236)

Polyporus albo-cervinus Berk., Hooker's Jour. Bot. 8: 234. 1856.
Coriolus brachypus (Lév.) Murr., Torrey Bot. Club Bul. 32: 646. 1905.

Sporophore sessile or umbonate-affixed, occasionally with a lateral stemlike base, typically applanate, tough and leathery when fresh, more or less flexible in thin specimens when dry, often imbricate; pileus flabelliform to dimidiate, 1.5–7 × 1.5–8 × 0.1–0.4(–1) cm., rose-tinted or avellaneous to pinkish brown or isabelline, radiate-striate to nearly even, glabrous or very finely villose-tomentose, somewhat zonate or multizonate especially near the margin, the margin usually quite thin but always entire; context whitish to pinkish or pale cinnamon, usually about 1 mm. thick, rarely up to 3 mm., punky-fibrous, tough; pore surface typically pale rosy or pinkish, becoming darker in herbarium specimens but often retaining traces of rose or pink, the tubes usually 1 mm. long, rarely 3 mm., the mouths circular to subangular, rather thick-walled and always entire, averaging 4–6 per mm.; spores not found; cystidia and hyphal pegs none; hyphae interwoven, slightly colored under the microscope if from plants of dark context, sparingly branched, with walls slightly thickened, with no cross walls or clamps, 3–5 μ in diameter; entire sporophore becoming permanently dark with KOH solution. (Compare no. 13, *Fomes subroseus.*)

HABITAT: On dead wood.

DISTRIBUTION: Specimens have been examined only from Fla.

ILLUSTRATIONS: Lloyd, Synop. Stip. Polyp., fig. 433.

I have sectioned numerous specimens of this plant without finding a well-developed hymenium or spores. Usually the plant is less than 5 mm. thick, but occasionally it attains a thickness of 1 cm. Specimens are typically trametoid and leathery in texture, and in these characters they depart widely from *Polyporus ectypus.* The roseo-gilvoid tint that usually persists, at least in traces, on dried specimens is an additional diagnostic character. There are no thick-walled hyphae of large diameter in the context, as there are in many other thin, coriaceous species of similar morphology. The fungus as here treated is *Coriolus brachypus* of Murrill's work. *P. rubidus* Berk. of the Orient seems to be a similar species, and Bresadola's interpretation of *P. atypus* Lév. unquestionably belongs here. The species seems to be quite common in subtropical Florida and common in tropical America.

126. POLYPORUS SUPINUS Swartz ex Fries

Syst. Myc. 1: 376. 1821

(Figs. 91–92)

Boletus supinus Swartz, Flora Ind. Occid. III, p. 1926. 1806.
Fomitella supina (Swartz ex Fries) Murr., Torrey Bot. Club Bul. 32: 365. 1905.

Sporophore sessile, rarely effused-reflexed, dimidiate, leathery or corky when fresh, firm, rigid, and sometimes very hard when dry, reviving when wet, and occasionally persisting for two or three years; pileus 2–10 × 3–10 × 0.3–1.5(–3) cm., plane or convex, azonate or with one or two shallow furrows, at first minutely villose-tomentose and smooth to the touch, finally glabrous, whitish to isabelline or cinereous-ochraceous or olivaceous tan, often becoming bay-red and then blackish behind in larger specimens, very slightly incrusted in perennial plants, the margin thin or rather thick, entire; context usually duplex in color with a pale zone above and umber-brown to deep cinnamon or olivaceous below, sometimes colored uniformly, 2–10 mm. thick; pore surface usually isabelline, cinereous, or smoky, occasionally somewhat yellowish, the tubes 2–4 mm. long, often in 2–4 layers, the mouths circular, rather thick-walled, always entire, averaging 5–7 per mm.; spores cylindric, smooth, hyaline, 9–10 × 3 μ; cystidia none; hyphae in an upper zone more hyaline and of finer diameter, hyphae in a lower zone pale brown, with thin or only slightly thickened walls, with no cross walls or clamps, 5–9 μ in diameter; some hyaline hyphal complexes present, much branched, 3–4 μ in diameter; hymenium and context dark-spotted with KOH. (Compare no. 11, *Fomes Meliae*.)

HABITAT: On dead wood of deciduous trees or from wounds in living trees, noted on *Carpinus, Carya, Celtis, Fagus, Fraxinus, Gleditsia, Liquidambar, Nyssa, Platanus, Quercus,* and *Salix.*

DISTRIBUTION: Specimens have been examined from N.C., S.C., Ga., Fla., Ala., La., Miss., Ark., and Texas.

ILLUSTRATIONS: Lloyd, Synop. Apus, fig. 680.

In thin specimens the context is likely to be unicolorous, while in old, thick specimens the lower half is darker and, in addition, may be much harder than the upper. In the pileus there is wide variation from almost white to ochraceous tan or olivaceous umber.

In texture and general coloration this species is similar to *Fomes Meliae*, but can be distinguished by the fact that the pileus is usually thin and applanate and becomes reddish at the base; *F. Meliae* is narrowly reflexed, thicker, and triangular in section. *Polyporus supinus* is a very common species in the Gulf States. It has been known also as *P. phlebius* var. *cubensis* Berk. & Curt., *P. Valenzuelianus* Mont., and *P. hemileucus* Berk. & Curt.

Collections of this species are uniformly sterile. I have been able to locate spores in a single Puerto Rican collection by Britton and Marble. Occasionally basidia are present in other collections, but no spores. From a collection made in Louisiana in 1931 (Division of Forest Pathology Herbarium No. 50250, at Beltsville, Maryland) a culture was obtained which fruits prolifically in about three weeks and gives abundant spores. In this culture the spores are much less cylindric than those described above, being more elliptic or elongate-elliptic, 7–8 × 4–4.5 μ. There is no reason to doubt the authenticity of this culture, and the spore measurements given for it may be more typical, especially since the previous record was based on but a single collection.

127. Polyporus semisupinus Berk. & Curt.

Grevillea 1: 50. 1872

(Figs. 102, 108–109, 541, 589, 675, and Plate 132)

Tyromyces semisupinus (Berk. & Curt). Murr., North Amer. Flora 9: 34. 1907.
Polyporus pachycheiles Ell. & Ev., Acad. Nat. Sci. Phila. Proc. 1894: 322. 1894.

Sporophore sessile or distinctly substipitate at the base, sometimes in the form of a rosette, flexible, cartilaginous, and very tough when fresh, hard and rigid when dry, reviving; pilei mostly flabelliform or spathulate, 0.5–2 × 0.5–2.5 × 0.1–0.3 cm., white or nearly so in fresh plants, yellowish to tan or bay on drying, glabrous or at first silky-tomentose, sometimes distinctly zonate with resinous zones when dry; context white, 0.5–1.5 mm. thick, tasteless, not macerating when chewed; pore surface white, drying white or yellowish, the tubes 1–2.5 mm. long, the mouths glistening, angular or irregular, thin-walled, entire, averaging 4–7 per mm.; spores elliptic or ellipsoid, hyaline, 2.5–3 × 2–2.5 μ; basidia 7–8 × 3–4 μ; cystidia none; hyphal pegs present but not abundant, short conoidal, about as broad as long; main hyphae sparingly branched or simple, with partially or completely thickened walls, 3–5(–7) μ in diameter, the content not staining, with cross walls and clamps practically or entirely lacking or very occasional on the smaller, staining hyphae. (Compare no. 35, *Polyporus floriformis*.)

Habitat: On dead wood, usually of deciduous trees, noted on *Acer, Alnus, Betula, Fagus, Populus, Prunus,* and *Quercus*; rarely on wood of coniferous trees, noted on *Abies, Picea,* and *Pinus.*

Distribution: Specimens have been examined from Me., N.H., Vt., Mass., Conn., N.Y., Pa., N.J., Va., Mich., and Idaho; in Canada from Nova Scotia and Quebec; reported from Tenn. (Kauffman [100]) and Mont. (Weir [227]).

Illustrations: Lowe, Mich. Acad. Sci. Arts and Letters Papers 19: pl. 15, fig. 2.

This species seems to be quite distinct from *Polyporus semipileatus* Peck, with which Lloyd confused it (probably because of the similarity in names), in usually growing more reflexed, typically with a sub-stipitate base, and in having entirely different spores. It partakes considerably of the characters of *P. balsameus* and *P. floriformis*. It differs from *P. balsameus*, however, in the lack of cystidia in the hymenium, in the lack of the brown zonation characteristic of that species in dried plants, and in the more cartilaginous texture when fresh and the more resinous texture on drying, as well as in the typically hardwood substrata. And it differs from *P. floriformis* in the mild taste, in the slightly smaller and more globose spores, in the complete lack of clamps on the main context hyphae, some of which have the walls entirely thickened and do not stain in eosin, in the smaller basidia, and in the typically different kind of substratum. The plants are quite cartilaginous in appearance and often rather distinctly zonate, assuming a light bay color on drying. The texture is so excessively cartilaginous that small pieces cannot be macerated when chewed. The usual host appears to be *Alnus* or *Betula*.

The spores seem to vary somewhat in different collections, especially in shape. In some they are ellipsoid, only about $2.5 \times 2 \mu$; in others, somewhat more elongate, $3 \times 2 \mu$. This variation seems to be a factor characteristic of mature plants and therefore cannot be referred to the difference between mature and immature spores.

The types of *Polyporus pachycheiles* are sterile, but I consider that Murrill is correct in referring the species here.

Polyporus pallescens Karst., as described by Romell, is apparently another name applied to this fungus. Actually, it appears that Karsten never described this species, but he used the name on several occasions, and Romell in 1911 published the description (187, p. 19).

Polyporus semisupinus produces a soft white rot of the substratum.

128. POLYPORUS PLANELLUS (Murr.) Overh.

Wash. Univ. Studies 3, 1: 29. 1915

(Figs. 273, 296, and Plate 132)

Coriolus planellus Murr., Torrey Bot. Club Bul. 32: 649. 1905.
Polyporus planus Peck, N. Y. State Mus. Ann. Rept. 31: 37. 1879. (Not *P. planus* Wallr., 1833.)

Sporophore occasionally sessile, usually effused-reflexed or entirely resupinate, often narrowly attached and flabelliform, very thin and coriaceous, or in old plants thicker and rigid, rigid on drying; pileus 1–3.5 × 1–3 × 0.05–0.2 cm., finely and compactly tomentose, finally nearly glabrous or becoming glabrous in zones, multizonate, light brown to umber or tobacco-brown, some of the zones darker and eventually black, radiate-ridged; context paper-thin, whitish or pale cinnamon, with a narrow dark line above from which the brown tomentum arises; pore surface pallid to isabelline or cinereous, the tubes less than 1 mm. long, the mouths angular or radially elongate, often pruinose, rather thick-walled, entire, averaging 5–6 per mm., barely visible to the unaided eye; spores cylindric, smooth, hyaline, 9–12 × 3.5–5 μ; cystidia none; hyphae pale-colored or nearly hyaline under the microscope, long and flexuous, only slightly if at all branched, with no cross walls or clamps, the tips somewhat attenuate, 2.5–4.5 μ in diameter.

HABITAT: On dead limbs of deciduous trees, noted on *Acer, Carya, Ostrya, Populus,* and *Ribes*; one collection noted on *Thuja*; reported on *Quercus* (Wis., Neuman [148]).

DISTRIBUTION: Specimens have been examined from Me., N.H., Vt., Mass., N.Y., Wis., Minn., N. Dak., Iowa, Mo., Colo., Mont., and Idaho; in Canada from Manitoba.

ILLUSTRATIONS: Baxter, Mich. Acad. Sci. Arts and Letters Papers 24, 1: pl. 7 (as *Polyporus stereoides*); Shope, Mo. Bot. Gard. Ann. 18: pl. 22, fig. 1.

This is by no means a common species, though it is rather widely distributed. A single collection from Idaho (Epling No. 1312) departs from the usual thin, coriaceous form of the plant in being nearly 0.5 cm. thick and quite rigid, with almost a thin crust over the pileus. In all specimens in which the context is thick enough to be differentiated one finds, in looking at lateral views of pilei cut vertically, a distinct, thin, dark line underlying the tomentum. The decidedly brown color of the pileus, with a few black zones, is a characteristic feature of the species. The pore mouths, as seen in vertical sections of the tubes, are partially closed by flaring protrusions of brownish hyphae, many with knoblike outgrowths. Baxter (11h) has reported this as *Polyporus stereoides* Fries sensu Romell.

1b. *Context bright-colored*

129. POLYPORUS CINNABARINUS Jacq. ex Fries

Syst. Myc. 1: 371. 1821

(Figs. 239–240, 282, and Plate 128)

Boletus cinnabarinus Jacq., Flora Austr. 4: 2. 1776.
Pycnoporus cinnabarinus (Jacq. ex Fries) Karst., Rev. Mycol. 3, 9: 18. 1881.

Sporophore sessile or sometimes attached by an umbo, tough and leathery when fresh, drying rigid or somewhat flexible, sometimes reviving a second or third year; pileus 2–7 × 2–12 × 0.5–2 cm., orange to cinnabar-red when fresh and growing, often fading and paler with age, or becoming sordid red or blackish, compactly tomentose and somewhat uneven or weathering to glabrous; context red or yellowish red, floccose-fibrous to soft-corky, strongly zonate, 0.4–1.5 cm. thick, becoming black with KOH; pore surface cinnabar-red, the tubes 1–4 mm. long, occasionally in 2 or 3 layers, the mouths circular, angular, or daedaloid, averaging 2–4 per mm.; spores oblong or short-cylindric, often pointed at one end, smooth, hyaline, 4.5–6 × 2–3 μ; cystidia none or not noteworthy; hyphal pegs present only in old plants; some hyphae simple, others considerably branched, almost hyaline in KOH, long and flexuous, thick-walled, with occasional or rare cross walls or clamps, 4–6 μ in diameter.

HABITAT: On dead wood of deciduous trees, noted on *Acer*, *Alnus*, *Betula*, *Carya*, *Castanea*, *Fagus*, *Fraxinus*, *Juglans*, *Liriodendron*, *Nyssa*, *Populus*, *Prunus*, *Pyrus*, and *Quercus*; occasionally on wood of coniferous trees, noted on *Picea*, *Pinus*, *Thuja*, and *Tsuga*; reported on *Salix* (Weir [222]).

DISTRIBUTION: Specimens have been examined from Me., N.H., Vt., Mass., Conn., N.Y., Pa., N.J., Del., Md., D.C., Va., W. Va., N.C., S.C., Ga., Ala., La., Miss., Tenn., Ky., Ohio, Ind., Ill., Mich., Wis., Iowa, Mo., Kans., Ark., N. Mex., Colo., Wyo., Mont., Idaho, Ore., and Wash.; in Canada from Nova Scotia, New Brunswick, Prince Edward Island, Quebec, and Ontario; reported by Bisby *et al.* from Manitoba (12).

ILLUSTRATIONS: Hard, Mushrooms, fig. 338; Murrill, Mycologia 10: pl. 6, fig. 1 (as *Pycnoporus*); Shope, Mo. Bot. Gard. Ann. 18: pl. 24, fig. 1.

The chief distinction between this species and *Polyporus sangui-neus*, its only close relative, is that in *P. cinnabarinus* the pileus is typically somewhat rugose or uneven because of the unequal com-pacting of the tomentum over the surface, whereas in *P. sanguineus* the surface is smooth and even, as though seared over with a hot iron, and the pileus is very thin. It will also be noted that *P. sanguineus* does not occur in the northern states.

Spores are matured only in the oldest parts of the hymenium, after the tubes have attained considerable length—a fact that argues against including this species in the genus *Trametes*, where in many species spores are found only on the short tubes on the young, grow-ing margin. The young basidial layer is composed of ovoid to globose bodies 8–10 μ in diameter, or of narrow and more clavate or fusoid bodies 6–8 μ in diameter, and these have never been seen to produce spores. They are absent or much less conspicuous on spore-producing parts of the hymenium. Sections bleach out in KOH solution, and all parts become permanently dark where touched with a drop of this material.

Occasionally, when the plant is growing on top of a log, the pileus may be nearly circular and attached by a short, thick, stemlike tuber-cle; the measurements of such specimens may exceed those given above.

Weir (230) reports this species as attacking the heartwood of living *Betula occidentalis*. The fungus produces a white or straw-colored delignifying decay of the sapwood.

130. POLYPORUS SANGUINEUS L. ex Fries

Syst. Myc. 1: 371. 1821

(Figs. 280–281 and Plate 131)

Boletus sanguineus L., Sp. Plant., 2d ed., p. 1646. 1763.
Pycnoporus sanguineus (L. ex Fries) Murr., Torrey Bot. Club Bul. 31: 421. 1904.

Sporophore sessile or attenuate at the base and appearing substipi-tate, coriaceous when fresh and usually somewhat flexible when dry; pileus 2–7 $\times$ 2–8(–14) $\times$ 0.2–0.5 cm., bright red, rarely fading some-what, finely tomentose to glabrous, very smooth and even, the mar-gin very thin; context red or yellowish red, floccose, up to 2.5 mm. thick; pore surface red, the tubes 0.5–1.5 mm. long, the mouths angular, rather thin-walled, entire, averaging 2–4 per mm.; spores oblong or short-cylindric, hyaline, 4–5 × 2–3 μ; cystidia none; hyphal pegs rather abundant; hyphae flexuous, many entirely simple, others considerably branched, a few with cross walls and clamps, 4–7 μ in diameter.

HABITAT: On dead wood of deciduous trees, noted on *Fagus*, *Liquidambar*, *Nyssa*, *Platanus*, and *Quercus*.

DISTRIBUTION: Specimens have been examined from N.Y., Del., Md., D.C., Va., W. Va., N.C., S.C., Ga., Fla., Ala., La., Miss., Tenn., Ky., Ill., Mo., Kans., Nebr., Ark., Okla., Texas, and Ariz.; reported from Iowa (Fennell [48]).

This species differs from *Polyporus cinnabarinus* in usually having a much thinner and smoother pileus, as though it had been seared with a hot iron. Microscopically, the plants are much alike. I find hyphal pegs to be fairly abundant in the hymenium of the present species, whereas in *P. cinnabarinus* they are rather indefinite and seem to occur only in the older tubes. The two species are very closely related, however, and occasional collections are difficult to refer satisfactorily. The present species is most abundant in the Gulf States, but ranges north to central Illinois and Long Island. The tissue turns black in KOH, as it does in *P. cinnabarinus*.

131. POLYPORUS FIBRILLOSUS Karst.

Sydv. Finl. Polyp., p. 30. 1859
(Figs. 283–284, 548, and Plate 129)

Pycnoporellus fibrillosus (Karst.) Murr., Torrey Bot. Club Bul. 32: 489 1905.
Polyporus aurantiacus Peck, N. Y. State Mus. Ann. Rept. 26: 69. 1874.

Sporophore sessile, often narrowly attached, single or somewhat imbricate, soft and spongy when fresh, rigid and rather fragile when dry; pileus 2–8 × 4–12 × 0.5–3 cm., fiery red to orange-red or orange-brown, changing little on drying, fibrous-tomentose or somewhat fibrillose-scaly, usually somewhat zonate in large specimens; context pale saffron to saffron or bright rusty red, becoming cherry-red then quickly black in KOH, zonate, friable when dry, 0.3–2 cm. thick; pore surface cream color to light orange or brownish orange, not much discolored on drying, the tubes 2–6 mm. long, the mouths angular or sinuous, often unequal, averaging 1.5–2 per mm., the walls at first pubescent, soon slightly dentate and finally lacerate in old plants; spores oblong-elliptic or short-cylindric, pointed at one end, smooth, hyaline under the microscope, 5–9 × 2.5–4(–5) μ; cystidia present, not abundant, cylindric, hyaline, 3.5 μ in diameter, projecting up to 35 μ; hyphal pegs lacking; hyphae somewhat branched, thin-walled, with conspicuous cross walls but no clamps, 5–9 μ in diameter. (Compare no. 129, *Polyporus cinnabarinus*, and no. 132, *P. alboluteus*.)

HABITAT: On dead wood, usually of coniferous trees, noted on *Abies, Larix, Picea, Pseudotsuga,* and *Tsuga*; occasionally on hardwoods, noted on *Betula* and *Fagus*; reported on *Acer* (Idaho, Weir [222]) and on *Thuja* (Mich., Kauffman [101]).

DISTRIBUTION: Specimens have been examined from Me., N.H., Vt., Mass., Conn., N.Y., Pa., W. Va., Mich., Minn., Colo., Idaho, Ore., Wash., Calif., and Alaska; in Canada from Nova Scotia, Newfoundland, Prince Edward Island, Quebéc, Ontario, Manitoba, and British Columbia; reported from Wis. (Dodge [40]) and Mont. (Weir [227]).

ILLUSTRATIONS: Neuman, Wis. Geol. and Nat. Hist. Survey Bul. 33: pl. 11, fig. 35 (as *Polyporus aurantiacus*).

The spores of this species are quite variable in size, depending upon the age of the sporophores. The color change from red to black when KOH is applied takes place quickly. If the solution penetrates rapidly, no red is observed.

The species has no near relatives. The color, and to some extent the consistency when fresh, recalls *Polyporus alboluteus*, but the resemblance is not marked, and the consistency when dry is very different. It is not a common species.

The type of rot is not well known, but the fungus has been collected in juxtaposition to a brown cubical decay.

132. POLYPORUS ALBOLUTEUS Ell. & Ev.

Torrey Bot. Club Bul. 25: 513. 1898

(Figs. 237, 241, 262, 614, and Plate 128)

Fomes alboluteus Ell. & Ev., Acad. Nat. Sci. Phila. Proc. 1895: 413. 1895.
Aurantiporellus alboluteus (Ell. & Ev.) Murr., Torrey Bot. Club Bul. 32: 486. 1905.

Lenzites saepiaria var. *dentifera* Peck, N. Y. State Mus. Ann. Rept. 40: 73. 1887.

Sporophore effused-reflexed or resupinate, soft and spongy when fresh, drying rather soft; pileus 0–4 × 3–15 × 1–5 cm., orange, sometimes almost white after persisting through the winter, unchanged on drying; context orange or yellowish orange, soft and floccose, 0.5–3 cm. thick, cherry-red to deep red in KOH solution; pore surface yellowish to orange, the tubes 1–3 cm. long, the mouths large, 1–3 mm. or more broad, often splitting and the segments becoming spine-like; spores cylindric, smooth, hyaline, 7–10 × 3–4 μ; cystidia present, sometimes rather abundant, hyaline, thin-walled, projecting prominently 20–80 μ, cylindric, 6–9(–12) μ in diameter; hyphae somewhat branched, rather thin-walled and often collapsed, with occasional cross walls but no clamps, 4–10 μ in diameter; all tissue except the hymenial layer changing to deep cherry-red in KOH.

HABITAT: On logs of coniferous trees, noted on *Abies, Picea, Pinus,* and *Tsuga*; reported on *Larix* (Mont., Weir [227]).

DISTRIBUTION: Specimens have been examined from N.Y., Mich., Utah, Colo., Wyo., Mont., Idaho, Ore., Wash., and Calif.; in Canada from the Gaspé Peninsula, Ontario, and British Columbia.

ILLUSTRATIONS: Lloyd, Synop. Apus, fig. 678; Shope, Mo. Bot. Gard. Ann. 18: pl. 19, figs. 1–4.

This is an extremely well marked species, mostly confined to logs of coniferous trees in subalpine situations from the Rocky Mountains westward, extending up to the limits of tree growth in moist locations. In the eastern United States the species is almost unknown. The Lloyd Herbarium contains one collection from Michigan, and I have one collection from the Gaspé Peninsula, Quebec, collected on *Picea canadensis* in 1927 by A. W. McCallum. *Lenzites saepiaria* var. *dentifera* Peck, as recorded on spruce in the Adirondacks, is this species. The fungus persists in fairly good shape through the winter, though it is likely to bleach somewhat. It may be effused for several feet on the lower side of the log it inhabits, and peels off easily in a continuous felty layer. Sections in KOH have a characteristic appearance, with the tube tissue becoming cherry-red but the hymenial layer remaining uncolored.

Shope (200) reports the fungus as producing a white rot, and probably the rot is limited to the sapwood, though there is no information to this effect. I have specimens that show an association with a carbonizing decay.

133. Polyporus croceus Pers. ex Fries

Syst. Myc. 1: 364. 1821

(Figs. 285, 311, and Plate 129)

Boletus croceus Pers., Obs. Myc. 1: 87. 1796.
Polyporus Pilotae Schw., Amer. Phil. Soc. Trans. II, 4: 156. 1832.
Aurantiporus Pilotae (Schw.) Murr., Torrey Bot. Club Bul. 32: 487. 1905.
? *Polyporus Pini-canadensis* Schw., Amer. Phil. Soc. Trans. II, 4: 157. 1832.
Polyporus hypococcinus Berk., London Jour. Bot. 6: 319. 1847.
Polyporus castanophilus Atk., Jour. Mycol. 8: 118. 1902.

Sporophore sessile, watery and rather soft when fresh, drying rigid; pileus 5–20 × 6–30 × 1–10 cm., buff or orange, fading on drying if the specimens are young, darker and reddish-discolored, rusty red, or blackish in old specimens and on drying, appressed-tomentose or nearly glabrous, usually rough on drying, azonate, margin obtuse; context pale buff, carneous when dry, strongly zonate, 0.7–5 cm. thick, purple or dark in KOH; pore surface orange, saffron, or reddish yellow in fresh plants, brownish to blackish and resinous on drying, the tubes 0.5–2 cm. long, the mouths angular, rather thin-walled, averaging 2–4 per mm.; spores ovoid or ellipsoid, smooth, hyaline, 5–7 × 4–5 μ; cystidia and hyphal pegs none; hyphae simple or nearly so, very much agglutinated and extremely difficult to dissociate in dried specimens, mostly scabrous-walled and 3–5 μ in diameter, with some enlarged conducting hyphae mostly 6–13 μ in diameter, the hyphae in fresh plants with smoother walls and with clamps, 3–5 μ in diameter. (Compare no. 89, *Polyporus fissilis*.)

Habitat: On dead wood or living trees of chestnut (*Castanea*) and oak (*Quercus*).

Distribution: Specimens have been examined from N.Y., Pa., Del., W. Va., N.C., Fla., Tenn., Ohio, Ind., Ill., Mich., Wis., Minn., Iowa, Mo., and Ark.; in Canada from Ontario; reported from Va., S.C., and Tenn. (Long [117]) and from Ky. (Kauffman [100]).

There should be no difficulty in identifying this species. The yellowish-orange coloration of fresh plants is distinctive when taken into consideration along with the size of the plant and the substratum. The zonation of the context is a well-marked character in both fresh and dried plants. In drying, the tubes usually become quite resinous in appearance and darker. *Polyporus fissilis* is the only species with which this fungus is likely to be confused, and the microscopic features of the two are similar. But *P. croceus* has more color in fresh plants, and the dried plants are darker. The context of *P. fissilis* is white or only slightly flesh-colored and loses this color on drying, whereas the context of *P. croceus* is more deeply colored and remains distinctly colored on drying. Furthermore, the context of *P. fissilis* is duplex; that of *P. croceus* is more uniform. KOH darkens the context of *P. croceus* more than it does that of *P. fissilis*. I have found it useless to look for spores in old herbarium specimens; young, developing specimens yield them, however. Bresadola records spores as 4–6 × 3–4 μ in Javan plants.

The hyphae of the context are very difficult to make out from dried specimens, unless thoroughly soaked in alcohol and water and then crushed in KOH. Even then, they are likely to appear so agglutinated as to resemble amorphous masses. The large, conducting hyphae come out best in crushed mounts from the context, but do not show up well in sections. They take the eosin stain readily and are opaque when so stained, but the content is not granular.

What Schweinitz may originally have had as representing his *Polyporus Pini-canadensis* can only be conjectured. The fragment in the New York Botanical Garden labeled as from the type collection is *P. croceus*. The spores are uncertain, but the large conductive hyphae are distinctive. Schweinitz records the species as growing on hemlock, which is probably an error if his name is to be referred to synonymy here.

This fungus produces a characteristic piped, delignifying decay of the heartwood of its hosts. In the very advanced stages of decay the piped character is said to be more or less lost, the wood being reduced to an amorphous, brown, friable mass. Long's figures (117) indicate that the decay is primarily a butt rot, and on standing chestnut snags in Pennsylvania sporophores are usually not found more than ten feet from the ground.

1c. *Context brown*

2a. *Sporophore stipitate* (see also *Coltricia Mowryana*, p. 427)

134. POLYPORUS CINNAMOMEUS Jacq. ex Fries

Epicr. Syst. Myc., p. 429. 1836–1838

(Figs. 244–246 and Plate 128)

Boletus cinnamomeus Wulf., in Jacq., Collect. ad Bot. 1: 116. 1786.
Coltricia cinnamomea (Jacq. ex Fries) Murr., Torrey Bot. Club Bul. 31: 343. 1904.
Polyporus splendens Peck, N. Y. State Mus. Ann. Rept. 26: 68. 1874.
Polyporus subsericeus Peck, N. Y. State Mus. Ann. Rept. 33: 37. 1880.

Sporophore centrally stipitate; pileus pliant when fresh, rigid when dry, circular, often laterally confluent, convex to umbilicate or depressed, 1–5 cm. broad, 1–3 mm. thick, bright reddish cinnamon to amber-brown or tobacco-brown, usually with narrow inconspicuous zones, silky-fibrillose and more or less shining in growing plants, the fibers sometimes erect in the center, striate, the margin thin, often distinctly fimbriate, deflexed in drying; context rusty brown, less than 1 mm. thick, black where touched with KOH solution; pore surface yellow-brown to reddish cinnamon, the tubes 0.5–3 mm. long, not at all decurrent on the stem, the mouths rather thin-walled, angular, averaging 2–3 per mm.; stem central, reddish brown, velvety to villose, 1–4 cm. long, 1–3 mm. thick; spores ellipsoid or oblong-ellipsoid, smooth, hyaline or very pale brown under the microscope, $6–8 \times 4.5–6\ \mu$; cystidia none; hyphae simple or sparingly branched, thin-walled, red-brown, with abundant cross walls but no clamps, 4–7 μ in diameter.

HABITAT: On clay banks or along beaten paths in the woods, rarely on very rotten wood.

DISTRIBUTION: Specimens have been examined from Me., Vt., Mass., Conn., N.Y., Pa., N.J., Del., Md., D.C., Va., W. Va., N.C., Ga., Ala., La., Miss., Tenn., Ky., Ohio, Wis., Iowa, and Calif.; in Canada from Quebec, Ontario, and British Columbia; reported from Mich. (Kauffman [105]), Mo. (Maneval [131]), Colo. (Kauffman [102]), and Ore. (Kauffman [103]).

ILLUSTRATIONS: Lloyd, Myc. Notes, Polyp. Issue No. 1: fig. 200 (as *Polystictus*); Shope, Mo. Bot. Gard. Ann. 18: pl. 24, fig. 3.

When fresh and growing, this species is a dark rusty red throughout, the hymenium being more yellowish than the pileus and stem; old plants become dark rusty brown throughout. *Polyporus subsericeus* Peck was based on very thin, shining plants with a thin, fimbriate margin; specimens with a thicker and sometimes zonate pileus showing abundant coarse fibrils on the surface have been referred to *P. oblectans* Berk., which hardly seems to be distinct.

I have re-examined several collections of this species and find the spores uniformly very pale-colored or often practically hyaline under the microscope, which is opposed to my previous record of "brown." The most mature specimens I can find have very pale yellow-brown spores when seen in unstained mounts.

This is a common species in temperate parts of the United States. It differs from *Polyporus perennis* in the smaller size and the more silky, subshining pileus. *P. focicola* usually differs in having larger pores, but large-pored forms of *P. cinnamomeus* are best distinguished from that species by the broader and shorter spores.

Polyporus parvulus Klotzsch is regarded as a synonym by both Lloyd and Murrill. *P. simillimus* Peck might be referred to synonymy here about as well as under *P. perennis*. It is, in fact, intermediate in form and stature, and the lack of microscopic differences between the two species gives little basis for separation when intermediates are involved.

135. Polyporus perennis L. ex Fries

Syst. Myc. 1: 350. 1821

(Figs. 247–248, 266, and Plate 131)

Boletus perennis L., Sp. Plant., p. 1177. 1753.
Coltricia perennis (L. ex Fries) Murr., Jour. Mycol. 9: 91. 1903.
Polyporus simillimus Peck, N. Y. State Mus. Ann. Rept. 32: 34. 1879.
Polystictus proliferus Lloyd, Myc. Notes, Polyp. Issue No. 1: 8. 1908.
Polystictus decurrens Lloyd, Myc. Notes, Polyp. Issue No. 1: 12. 1908.

Sporophore stipitate, often confluent, thin and coriaceous when fresh, drying rather rigid; pileus orbicular to irregular, convex to depressed or umbilicate, 1.5–11 cm. broad, 1–4 mm. thick, grayish brown to cinnamon or rusty brown, often weathering to gray, finely velvety-tomentose, then radiate-striate, subshining at times, usually concentrically zonate, occasionally practically azonate. the margin sometimes quite thin or fimbriate; context brown, occasionally slightly more than 1 mm. thick, black in KOH solution; pore surface yellow-brown to cinnamon or gray, the tubes 1–3 mm. long, the mouths angular, sometimes somewhat decurrent on the stem, averaging 2–4 per mm.; stem usually central, brown, velvety, 1.5–7 cm. long, 1–10 mm. thick; spores oblong-ellipsoid or oblong, smooth, almost hyaline under the microscope, 6–9 × 3–5 μ; setae none; hyphae simple or very sparingly branched, thin-walled, with abundant cross walls but no clamps, 4–6 μ in diameter. (Compare no. 134, *Polyporus cinnamomeus*, and no. 136, *P. focicola.*)

HABITAT: On the ground in woods, often where fires have been kindled, or along clay banks, or in beaten forest trails, very rarely on rotten wood.

DISTRIBUTION: Specimens have been examined from Me., N.H., Vt., Mass., Conn., N.Y., Pa., N.J., Md., Va., N.C., Ga., Fla., Ala., Tenn., Ohio, Mich., Wis., Minn., Iowa, Mo., Ariz., Colo., Mont., Idaho, Ore., Wash., Calif., and Alaska; in Canada from Nova Scotia, Quebec, Ontario, and British Columbia; reported by Bisby *et al.* (12) from Manitoba.

ILLUSTRATIONS: Dufour, Atl. Champ. Comest. Vén., pl. 49, fig. 117; Hard, Mushrooms, fig. 346 (as *Polystictus*); Lloyd, Myc. Notes, Polyp. Issue No. 1: figs. 201 (as *Polystictus*) and 206 (as *Polystictus decurrens*); *idem*, Myc. Notes 62: figs. 1608–1609 (as *Polystictus*); Michael, Führ. f. Pilzfr. 2: fig. 30; Overholts, Wash. Univ. Studies 3: pl. 4, fig. 19; Shope, Mo. Bot. Gard. Ann. 18: pl. 26, fig. 3; Sowerby, Col. Fig. English Fungi, pl. 192 (as *Boletus*).

Sporophores on burned places are usually small (2–5 cm. broad) and soon become grayish, exhibiting the effect of a xerophytic habitat on this species. Larger specimens with brighter colors grow in forest trails or under conifers. The small plant seems to be an ecological variety of the species and usually has somewhat larger pores. Mature spores under a microscope have only a very faint tinge of brown, easily overlooked if the preparation has been stained with eosin.

The species intergrades with *Polyporus cinnamomeus* to some extent, but usually can be distinguished by its size and by the absence of a silky luster to the pileus. Yet some collections are difficult to refer satisfactorily. *P. cinnamomeus* does not grow on burned earth, but *P. perennis* often finds other habitats to its liking. It is a very elegant species when well developed, as it frequently is in mountainous regions, where it seems to thrive best. Plants of the lowlands are usually of the smaller type.

The species differs from *Polyporus circinatus* in its less obese form and in the absence of setae. *P. focicola* differs in the very much larger pores. *P. decurrens* Lloyd is only a form of this species with pores decurrent on the stem. *P. simillimus* Peck is a connecting form with *P. cinnamomeus*. It is a small form, the pileus 2.5 cm. or less in diameter, strongly zonate, and soon weathering to gray.

136. POLYPORUS FOCICOLA Berk. & Curt.

Linnean Soc. Bot. Jour. 10: 305. 1868

(Figs. 250–251, 265, and Plate 129)

Coltricia focicola (Berk. & Curt.) Murr., North Amer. Flora 9: 92. 1908.

Sporophore stipitate, coriaceous, drying rigid; pileus circular, convex-depressed to umbilicate or rarely infundibuliform, 2–5 cm. broad, 1–6 mm. thick, grayish brown to cinnamon or weathering to gray, finely tomentose to fibrillose, striate or wrinkled, somewhat zonate especially toward the margin; context brown, black in KOH solution, less than 0.5 mm. thick; pore surface yellow-brown, the tubes 1–4(–6) mm. long, the mouths circular to angular or very irregular, averaging 1 mm. or more broad, sometimes much lacerated next the stem, not at all decurrent; stem central, brown, minutely velvety, 1.5–4 cm. long, 2–5 mm. thick; spores oblong-ellipsoid or short-cylindric, smooth, almost hyaline under the microscope, 7–11 × 4–4.5 μ; cystidia none; hyphae brown to subhyaline, sparingly branched, with conspicuous cross walls but no clamps, 4–7 μ in diameter. (Compare no. 134, *Polyporus cinnamomeus*, and no. 135, *P. perennis*.)

HABITAT: On burned-over earth in woods.

DISTRIBUTION: Specimens have been examined from N.Y., Pa., N.J., Del., N.C., S.C., Ga., Fla., Ala., La., Miss., Tenn., Ky., Ohio, Ark., and Texas; in Canada from Quebec; reported from Mich. (Povah [174]).

ILLUSTRATIONS: Lloyd, Myc. Notes, Polyp. Issue No. 1: fig. 203 (as *Polystictus*).

Usually this is a short-stemmed species, the stem being only 1–2.5 cm. long. The pileus soon weathers to gray or ash color and is both zonate and radiate-striate.   The closest relatives are probably *Poly-porus perennis* and *P. cinnamomeus*, from which it differs in the large irregular pores and, especially, in the longer spores, which are much narrower in proportion to their length than they are in either of those species.

137. POLYPORUS TOMENTOSUS Fries

Syst. Myc. 1: 351. 1821

(Figs. 257, 260, 578, and Plate 128)

Coltricia tomentosa (Fries) Murr., Torrey Bot. Club Bul. 31: 346. 1904.
Polyporus aduncus Lloyd, Synop. Apus, p. 354. 1915.
Polyporus peakensis Lloyd, Myc. Notes 62: 933. 1920.

Sporophore stipitate or substipitate when terrestrial or on roots, sessile on stumps and trunks, subcoriaceous and often spongy and watery when fresh, rigid on drying; pileus circular to flabelliform or dimidiate, 3–18 cm. broad, 0.3–4 cm. thick, whitish (when young) to ochraceous, tan, or rusty brown, finely soft-tomentose to somewhat short hispid-tomentose, usually azonate or nearly so; context concolorous, 3–10 mm. thick, soft and spongy above, but with a narrow firm layer 1–3.5 mm. thick next the hymenium, black or cherry-red and then black in KOH solution; pore surface hoary or brown, darker where bruised, the tubes 1.5–7 mm. long, the mouths angular to somewhat irregular or daedaloid, thin-walled at maturity, entire or slightly dentate, slightly pubescent, averaging 2–4 per mm.; stem when present lateral, excentric, or central, often rudimentary, ochraceous to dark rusty brown, tomentose or soft velvety like the pileus, not more than 5 cm. long, 0.5–2 cm. thick; spores hyaline or very pale-colored under the microscope, ellipsoid or oblong-ellipsoid, smooth, 4–6 × 3–5 μ; setae rather abundant or scarce, dark brown, straight, pointed, 35–65 × 10–16 μ, projecting 15–50 μ; hyphae yellowish, simple or sparingly branched, with occasional cross walls but no clamps, 3–6 μ in diameter.

HABITAT: On stumps, trunks, or roots of living or dead coniferous hosts, or more frequently attached to buried wood of coniferous trees, occasionally on the ground under conifers, noted on *Picea, Pinus, Thuja,* and *Tsuga*; one collection at base of living *Acer* (Mich.); also reported on *Larix* and *Pseudotsuga* (Hubert [87]).

DISTRIBUTION: Specimens have been examined from Me., N.H., Vt., Mass., Conn., R.I., N.Y., Pa., N.J., Del., Md., D.C., W. Va., N.C., Ala., Tenn., Mich., Wis., Colo., Wyo., Mont., Idaho, Ore., Wash., and Calif.; in Canada from Nova Scotia, Prince Edward Island, Quebec, Ontario, and British Columbia; also reported from Minn. (Hubert [86]), Iowa (Wolf [234]), and Manitoba (Bisby *et al.* [14]).

ILLUSTRATIONS: Boyce, Forest Path., fig. 160 (as *Polyporus circinatus*); Fries, Icones Sel. Hym., pl. 180, fig. 1 (as *P. circinatus*); Hubert, Outline Forest Path., fig. 92 (as *P. circinatus*); Lloyd, Myc. Notes, Polyp. Issue No. 1: fig. 198 (as *Polystictus*); Marshall, Mushroom Book, opp. p. 112 (as *Polyporus circinatus*); Shope, Mo. Bot. Gard. Ann. 18: pl. 26, figs. 1–2 (as *Polyporus circinatus*).

Sections of this species become very much darker, or occasionally red, in KOH, and if the dried specimen is touched with KOH a cherry-red first develops, then, immediately, a black coloration; if the change is rapid, no red may be noticed. The hyphae of the lower context layer are usually somewhat more irregular, larger (3–6 μ in diameter), and somewhat thicker-walled than those in the upper tomentose layer. Young specimens are usually rather obese, yellowish, and azonate; older ones become thinner, darker, and often zonate, though the margin may remain yellowish. Collectors usually record the species as growing on the ground, and I have myself collected it there, with no indication of a woody substratum, but more frequently, when not on stumps or trunks, it is attached to buried wood.

Concerning this species and its relation to *Polyporus circinatus*, the following facts seem now to be established. Jørstad and Juul (*Det Norske Skogfors.* 6: 434 and 478. 1939) have shown that the setae of *P. circinatus* are curved or hooked at the tips; therefore that name replaces *P. dualis* Peck. Further, the forms with straight setae apparently belong to *P. tomentosus*. Now as to the disposition of these two species, those who so desire may recognize both. Or they may recognize but one species, which includes forms with hooked setae and forms with straight setae. Or they may designate one form as a variety of the other, viz., *P. tomentosus* var. *circinatus*. Since the curved setae are the only constant difference that anyone has pointed out between the two, and since it is usually held that species differ in more than one character, the most logical procedure is to accept

P. circinatus as a variety of *P. tomentosus*. It is only fair to make clear that this is not exactly Jørstad and Juul's handling of the situation. They agree that it is:

... best to place them under one species, *viz. P. tomentosus sensu lat.*, although we consider the forms having all or some of the setae curved as belonging to a separate variety *viz.*, var. *circinatus* (Quél.). As to the American stipitate form which is usually termed *P. circinatus* and has straight setae, it is our opinion that it appropriately may be regarded as a separate variety of *P. tomentosus*, and we suggest the name var. *americanus*.

According to this, then, the American plant with straight setae should be called *P. tomentosus* var. *americanus*, and the form with curved setae should be called *P. tomentosus* var. *circinatus*. More recently, Haddow (65) has investigated the situation and arrived at about the same conclusions, although he would follow the nomenclature of the present manual.

Var. CIRCINATUS (Fries) Sartory & Maire

Ass. France Sci. Congress de Montpellier, p. 779. 1922

(Figs. 252, 256, 258–259, 261, and Plate 128)

Trametes circinatus Fries, Svenska Vetensk.-akad. Handl. for 1848, p. 128. 1849.
Polyporus circinatus Fries, Monogr. Hymen. Suec. 2: 268. 1863.
Polyporus dualis Peck, N. Y. State Mus. Ann. Rept. 30: 44. 1878.

Characters exactly as in the species, but a large proportion of the setae strongly curved or hooked at the apex; spores ellipsoid or oblong-ellipsoid, smooth, hyaline, 5–7 × 3.5–4 μ.

HABITAT: As in the species.

DISTRIBUTION: Probably that of the species; records are at hand from Conn., N.Y., Pa., S.C., Tenn., Ariz., Mont., Idaho, and Calif.; in Canada from British Columbia.

ILLUSTRATIONS: Lloyd, Myc. Notes, Polyp. Issue No. 1: fig. 199 (as *Polystictus dualis*).

The species and its variety cause a pocket rot (86; 87, pp. 351–355 [see also C. M. Christensen, *Phytopathology* 30: 957–963. 1940—J. L. Lowe]) in the roots and butt of coniferous trees. The decay is somewhat similar to that produced by *Fomes Pini*, and has been designated "red root rot" and "pecky root rot." The pockets are lined with white fibers and have pointed ends rather than the more blunt ends of the rot produced by *Polyporus anceps.* Contrary to Hubert's statement (87, p. 355), sporophores are not uncommon on trunks and stumps in the Eastern states. In Pennsylvania, *Pinus rigida* is the common host. Faull (47) reports the fungus on spruce, hemlock, and eastern white pine in Ontario.

138. POLYPORUS MONTAGNEI Fries

Apud Montagne, in Ann. Sci. Nat. Bot. II, 5: 341. 1836
(Figs. 270–271, 594, and Plate 130)

Polystictus obesus Ell. & Ev., Torrey Bot. Club Bul. 24: 125. 1897.
Coltricia obesa (Ell. & Ev.) Murr., Torrey Bot. Club Bul. 31: 346. 1904.
Coltricia Memmingeri Murr., Torrey Bot. Club Bul. 31: 347. 1904.
Polystictus cuticularis Lloyd, Myc. Notes, Polyp. Issue No. 1: 12. 1908.

Sporophore stipitate, tough and spongy when fresh, drying rigid; pileus convex to plane or with depressed center, 2–10 cm. broad, 2–7 mm. thick, often connate, yellowish cinnamon to bright rusty brown or darker, at first with a soft-silky or fibrillose tomentum, becoming more compact and radiately ridged or uneven, often somewhat zonate; context brown, black in KOH solution, 1–5 mm. thick, sometimes somewhat duplex; pore surface white to alutaceous or umber, the tubes more or less decurrent, 1–5 mm. long, the mouths angular to daedaloid, 0.5–2 mm. broad; stem central or subcentral, often poorly developed, firm, tomentose, brown, 2–5 cm. long, 0.3–1.5 cm. or more thick; spores elongate-ellipsoid, very pale-colored or almost hyaline, smooth, 8–12 × 4.5–6 μ; setae none; hyphae thin-walled, sparingly branched, with abundant cross walls but no clamps, 7–15 μ in diameter, mostly 9–12 μ. (Compare no. 137, *Polyporus tomentosus*, and no. 140, *P. Schweinitzii*.)

HABITAT: On the ground, sometimes attached to buried wood of coniferous trees.

DISTRIBUTION: Specimens have been examined from N.H., Mass., N.Y., Pa., N.J., N.C., Tenn., and Mich.; in Canada from Ontario.

ILLUSTRATIONS: Lloyd, Myc. Notes, Polyp. Issue No. 1: fig. 205 (as *Polystictus cuticularis*).

This species resembles *Polyporus focicola* in the very large tubes, but differs in almost all other features. The pileus does not become gray as in that species, but remains a deep rich rusty brown; the context is much thicker and frequently duplex in dried specimens, with the hyphae very large, mostly 9–12 μ in diameter; the spores are larger and slightly more colored.   In color and form the sporophores are more similar to those of well-developed specimens of *P. tomentosus*, from which the large tubes and the absence of setae easily distinguish it.   Often the stem is not well developed, and the pileus is then scarcely elevated above the surface of the ground.

Though Lloyd in 1908 held that *Polyporus obesus* was distinct from *P. Montagnei*, he later (114, p. 162) gave up this contention. I see in Ellis and Everhart's species only a well-developed form of *P. Montagnei*; it represents small plants with a more slender stem than is often present and with spores (types) that are 8–12 $\times$ 5–8 μ, pale-colored, and almost hyaline.   *Coltricia Memmingeri* Murr. is even less distinct, being the short-stemmed form, in which the pileus often scarcely rises above the ground.   Many of Peck's determinations of *P. tomentosus* Fries belong here.   Some of Weir's determinations in the New York State Museum at Albany are *P. tomentosus*, and some are *P. Montagnei*.

139. Polyporus dependens Berk. & Curt.

Ann. and Mag. Nat. Hist. II, 12: 431. 1853

(Fig. 249 and Plate 129)

Coltriciella dependens (Berk. & Curt.) Murr., Torrey Bot. Club Bul. 31: 348. 1904.

Sporophore pendent from a short stem or attached at the vertex and not distinctly stipitate, gregarious or in clusters; pileus circular to irregular, 0.5–1.5 cm. broad and not more than 1 cm. high, rich coffee-brown or golden brown, covered with a soft, short, brown, fibrillose pubescence, subzonate or azonate; context brown, soft, fibrous, not more than 1 mm. thick; pore surface brown or yellowish brown, the tubes 2–8 mm. long, the mouths angular, usually pubescent, thin-walled, averaging 2–3 per mm.; stem usually dorsally attached, sometimes represented only by the attenuate apex of the pileus, less than 1 cm. long, 1–2 mm. thick, brown; spores inequilaterally ellipsoid, reddish brown, rough-walled, 8–10 $\times$ 4–5 μ; basidia about 6 μ in diameter; cystidia none; hyphae brown, thin-walled, sparingly branched, with cross walls but no clamps, 5–7 μ in diameter.

Habitat: On rotten logs of coniferous trees or, rarely, on wood of deciduous trees, noted on *Castanea, Juniperus, Liriodendron, Pinus,* and *Quercus.*

Distribution: Specimens have been examined from N.Y., N.J., Va., N.C., S.C., Fla., Tenn., and Ohio.

Illustrations: Baxter, Mich. Acad. Sci. Arts and Letters Papers 14: pl. 35 (as *Trametes*); Lloyd, Myc. Notes, Polyp. Issue No. 1: fig. 207 (as *Polystictus*).

This is a curious little species, which, with the rather large tubes, resembles in form a small wasp's nest. It is a rare species, and perhaps not more than a dozen collections are known. That the spores are rough-walled can be seen with the higher powers of the dry-objective lens, and comes out well under the oil-immersion lens. No related species has rough-walled spores. They have not been reported for this species by previous writers.

140. Polyporus Schweinitzii Fries

Syst. Myc. 1: 351. 1821

(Figs. 253–254, 272, 286, 557, 580, and Plate 132)

Polyporus hispidoides Peck, N. Y. State Mus. Ann. Rept. 33: 21. 1880.
Phaeolus sistotremoides (Alb. & Schw.) Murr., Torrey Bot. Club Bul. 32: 363. 1905.

Sporophore sessile or stipitate, spongy and watery or soft-corky when fresh, rigid and brittle on drying; pileus 5–25 cm. broad, 0.5–4 cm. thick, ochraceous to orange-colored or rusty brown, strigose-tomentose or woolly tomentose, weathering to compactly tomentose or nearly glabrous; context homogeneous or somewhat duplex, yellowish to reddish brown, 0.2–3 cm. thick; pore surface at first yellowish or greenish yellow, darker where bruised and on drying, the tubes 1–10 mm. long, the mouths soon irregular, thin-walled, entire to dentate, averaging 1–3 per mm., or here and there confluent and as much as 2 mm. in diameter; stem present or absent, central or excentric, concolorous with pileus, tomentose, soft as the pileus, 0–6 cm. long, 1–4 cm. thick; spores ellipsoid or ovoid, smooth, hyaline, 5.5–8 $\times$ 4–5 μ; cystidia present, never abundant and often rare, brown or hyaline, or brown at the base and hyaline at the tip, cylindric or subclavate, projecting 20–60 μ, fragile, sometimes knobbed at the apex; hyphae brown to chestnut, thin-walled, sparingly branched, with no cross walls or clamps, 6–12 μ in diameter; all parts becoming black, or cherry-red and then black, where touched with KOH solution. (Compare no. 137, *Polyporus tomentosus* and var. *circinatus*.)

HABITAT: Usually growing on or about trunks or roots of coniferous trees, noted on *Abies, Larix, Picea, Pinus, Pseudotsuga, Thuja*, and *Tsuga*; very rarely on deciduous trees, noted on *Betula, Halesia, Prunus*, and *Quercus*; reported on *Eucalyptus* (Calif., Rhoads [183]) and on *Taxus* (Mont., Weir [226]).

DISTRIBUTION: Specimens have been examined from Me., N.H., Vt., Mass., Conn., N.Y., Pa., N.J., Md., Del., D.C., Va., W. Va., N.C., S.C., Ga., Fla., Ala., La., Miss., Tenn., Mich., S. Dak., Mo., Ark., N. Mex., Ariz., Colo., Mont., Idaho, Ore., Wash., and Calif.; in Canada from Nova Scotia, Newfoundland, New Brunswick, Quebec, Ontario, and British Columbia; reported from Texas (Hepting and Chapman [70]) and Manitoba (Bisby *et al.* [14]).

ILLUSTRATIONS: Boyce, Osborn Bot. Lab. Bul. 1: fig. 21; *idem*, U. S. Dept. Agr. Tech. Bul. 286: pl. 7; *idem*, Forest Path., fig. 194; Fries, Icones Sel. Hym., pl. 179, fig. 3; Lloyd, Myc. Notes, Polyp. Issue No. 1: fig. 208; Lucand, Fig. Peint. Champ. France, pl. 172 (as *Merisma spongia*); Meinecke, Forest Tree Dis. Calif. Nev., pl. 13; Michael, Führ. f. Pilzfr. 3: fig. 40 (as *Polyporus sistotremoides*); Pilát, Bot. Centbl. Beih. 48: pl. 14 (as *Phaeolus*); von Schrenk, U. S. Dept. Agr. Veg. Phys. Path. Bul. 25: pl. 1, fig. 1; Shope, Mo. Bot. Gard. Ann. 18: pl. 25, figs. 1–2.

The change of color to red and then black when KOH is applied to any part of the fruiting body is a character shared by only a few species. Sometimes this change to black is so rapid that the red is not seen, especially in dried specimens if alcohol is first applied, but usually the cherry-red is very noticeable. Cystidia are at times difficult to locate in cross sections of the hymenium, and are never abundant. They are thin-walled and frequently collapsed. Small specimens of this species may be confused with *Polyporus tomentosus* var. *circinatus*, but the presence of setae in that variety renders such specimens easily distinct.

Boletus (or *Phaeolus*) *sistotremoides* Alb. & Schw. is indicated by Murrill as a synonym, and *Polyporus tabulaeformis* Berk. (from

Georgia) and *P. spectabilis* Fries (from North Carolina) have been referred to synonymy here. *P. hispidoides* Peck differs in no wise from the present species.

This fungus causes a serious carbonizing, cubical decay, known as "red-brown butt rot" or "cubical butt rot" (21; 22, pp. 26–27; 83, pp. 20–21, 24; 87, pp. 355–363; 215, pp. 18–24). The decay is usually limited to the lower part of the trunk, rarely extending upward farther than the first sixteen feet. The wood fractures into cubical blocks, and thin, inconspicuous sheets of white mycelium form in the fractures. The extent of development of these mats is usually a good diagnostic character in separating the decay caused by this fungus from that produced by *Polyporus sulphureus*, *Fomes officinalis*, and *F. pinicola*—the other mat-forming species of most importance in coniferous trees, all of which produce a similar carbonizing decay of the heartwood. Miss Clara Fritz reports (55, p. 237) that this species forms chlamydospores in culture.

Wean (220) discusses some of the phases of the parasitism of this species on seedlings of *Pinus Strobus* L., and Childs (33) describes the variations of the species in culture. Hepting and Chapman (70) discuss its importance in shortleaf and loblolly pine stands in Arkansas and Texas.

2b. *Sporophore sessile or effused-reflexed*
  3a. *Spores hyaline*
    4a. *Setae absent*

141. POLYPORUS HYDNOIDES Swartz ex Fries

Elench. Fung. I, p. 107. 1828
(Figs. 288–289 and Plate 130)

Boletus hydnoides Swartz, Nov. Gen. Sp. Plant. Prodromus, p. 149. 1788.
Pogonomyces hydnoides (Swartz ex Fries) Murr., Torrey Bot. Club Bul. 31: 609. 1904.

Sporophore sessile, dimidiate, reniform, or somewhat flabelliform, coriaceous when fresh, rigid on drying; pileus 3–10 × 3–15 × 0.3–1 cm., thin and applanate, covered with a dense coat of erect, dark-brown or black, fascicled or forked, coarse stiff hairs that may partially disappear with age, showing the isabelline, avellaneous, or smoky color of the pileus, azonate or only inconspicuously zoned after the hairs disappear; context yellowish brown or umber-brown, compact, 0.5–3 mm. thick; pore surface clay color to dark umber or yellowish brown, the tubes 1–3 mm. long, gray within, the mouths regular, thick-walled, circular, entire, averaging 3–5 per mm.; spores cylindric when mature, ellipsoid at earlier stages, smooth, hyaline, 9–12 × 3–4 μ; cystidia none; hyphae mostly flexuous, brown, some with walls partially thickened, simple, with no cross walls or clamps, 4–7 μ in diameter, some considerably branched and of smaller diameter, 2.5 μ. (Compare no. 92, *Polyporus versatilis*, and no. 102, *P. trichomallus*.)

HABITAT: On dead wood of deciduous trees, noted on *Carya*, *Gleditsia*, *Juglans*, *Liquidambar*, *Platanus*, *Prosopis*, *Quercus*, and *Ulmus*; also on *Casuarina equisetifolia* in Florida.

DISTRIBUTION: Specimens have been examined from Fla., La., and Texas.

This species is not uncommon in Florida and Louisiana, and it probably occurs in the other Gulf States as well. Even though the pores are almost invisible to the unaided eye, their walls are so thickened that they measure only 3–4 per mm. This species is most easily separated from such relatives as *Polyporus trichomallus* and *P. versatilis* by the small size of the pores. Furthermore, it does not have the cystidia characteristic of those species, and this, together with the distinctly brown context, indicates a lack of close relationship. Occasionally the pileus becomes almost completely denuded of the hairy covering. *P. Feathermanni*, originally described from Florida, is often cited as a synonym, as is also *Boletus hydnatinus* Bosc, described from "Carolina." I know of no other evidence that the fungus actually occurs in the Carolinas.

142. POLYPORUS NIDULANS Fries

Syst. Myc. 1: 362. 1821

(Figs. 277–278 and Plate 131)

Polyporus pallido-cervinus Schw., Amer. Phil. Soc. Trans. II, 4: 156. 1832.
Hapalopilus rutilans (Pers.) Murr., Torrey Bot. Club Bul. 31: 416. 1904.

Sporophore sessile or effused-reflexed, soft and watery when fresh, drying rigid; pileus 1.5–6(–8) × 2–8(–12) × 0.5–4 cm., usually umber

to cinnamon or tawny brown, sometimes somewhat reddish or purplish where bruised and on drying, finely pruinose to fibrillose or
glabrous, the margin often ochraceous, purplish or reddish where
bruised; context concolorous with pileus, soft and watery when fresh,
friable when dry, 2–30 mm. thick; pore surface hoary or yellowish
or reddish brown, the tubes 2–7 mm. long, the mouths angular or
sinuous, rather thin-walled but entire, averaging 2–4 per mm.; spores
ellipsoid to globose, smooth, hyaline, 3–4 × 2–3 μ; cystidia none;
hyphal pegs none; hyphae hyaline, more or less richly branched,
very thick-walled, often much contorted and irregular, with cross
walls and clamps, 5–9 μ in diameter; all portions of the plant turning
cherry-red or purple where touched with KOH solution. (Compare
no. 145, *Polyporus gilvus*; no. 148, *P. radiatus*; and no. 160, *P.
glomeratus*.)

HABITAT: Usually on dead wood of deciduous trees, noted on
*Acer, Alnus, Betula, Carya, Castanea, Fagus, Juglans, Populus,
Prunus, Pyrus, Quercus, Salix, Sorbus,* and *Vitis*; rarely on wood of
coniferous trees, noted on *Tsuga*.

DISTRIBUTION: Specimens have been examined from N.H., Vt.,
Mass., Conn., N.Y., Pa., N.J., Del., Md., D.C., Va., W. Va., N.C.,
La., Tenn., Ohio, Ind., Ill., Mich., Wis., Minn., Iowa, Mo., Kans.,
and Wash.; in Canada from Quebec, Ontario, and British Columbia;
reported from Manitoba (Bisby *et al.* [14]).

The general umber or cinnamon coloration of pileus, context, and
hymenium, with all parts turning cherry-red or wine-red where
touched with KOH solution, is usually enough to identify this species.
Fresh plants are quite soft and watery. When on small branches of
oak, birch, and other hosts, the sporophore is likely to be small,
while on larger branches and on trunks, especially of oak and hickory,
it is often large. The *Pyrus* host mentioned above was *P. americana,*
the mountain ash.

I have seen but a single specimen from west of Kansas in the
United States. Dr. G. H. Englerth, formerly of the Portland Office
of Forest Pathology, sent me a single specimen on *Tsuga heterophylla,*
from Verlot, Snohomish County, Washington.

The fungus produces a general delignifying decay of the outer
layers of the sapwood. Pilát's statement (171, vol. 52, p. 87) that
this fungus is "ein charakteristischer Parasit der Laubhölzer" and

"nur die kranken Äste infiziert" finds no confirmation in my experience.

143. POLYPORUS CROCATUS Fries
Epicr. Syst. Myc., p. 477. 1836–1838
(Fig. 299)

Polyporus byrsinus Mont., Plant Cell. Cuba, p. 391. 1838–1842.

Sporophore sessile, effused-reflexed, or resupinate, often coalesced in growth for a foot or more; pileus dimidiate to elongate, 0–6 × 3–15 × 0.1–0.3 cm., drying thin and flexible, light tan, buff tan, or rusty tan, conspicuously multizonate with narrow concolorous zones, compactly tomentose and soft to the touch, the margin thin and entire; context concolorous with the pileus, soft and fibrous, nearly homogeneous but showing a slightly denser zone where the tomentum begins to be evident, less than 0.5 mm. thick exclusive of the tomentum; pore surface paler than the pileus, smooth and velvety, the tubes less than 0.5 mm. long, the mouths circular, rather thick-walled, invisible to the unaided eye, averaging about 6 per mm.; spores elongate-ellipsoid or elongate-ovoid, smooth, hyaline, 8–11 × 5–6 μ; basidia 8–9 μ in diameter; cystidia and hyphal pegs none; hyphae brown, nearly simple, mostly with no cross walls or clamps, some 4–6 μ in diameter and thick-walled, others 2.5–4 μ with thinner walls; hymenium and context turning black where touched with KOH solution.

HABITAT: On dead wood of deciduous trees, noted only on *Populus*.

DISTRIBUTION: Specimens have been examined from Fla. and La.

ILLUSTRATIONS: Montagne, Plant Cell. Cuba, pl. 15, fig. 3 (as *Polyporus byrsinus*).

This species is easily recognized by the very thin, buffy-tan or pale-tan, tomentose, multizoned, flexible pileus with pores invisible to the unaided eye. In old plants I have noted a whitening of the hymenium, and from such specimens alone have I been able to obtain spores.

144. POLYPORUS VINOSUS Berk.
Ann. and Mag. Nat. Hist. II, 9: 195. 1852
(Figs. 330–332 and Plate 132)

Nigroporus vinosus (Berk.) Murr., Torrey Bot. Club Bul. 32: 361. 1905.

Sporophore sessile to effused-reflexed, dimidiate to broadly fan-shaped or reniform, rigid and brittle when dry; pileus 2–7 × 2–12 × 0.05–0.7 cm., dark avellaneous to vinaceous brown or vinaceous bay, often purplish black on drying and in age, at first velvety tomentose, then glabrous, soon zonate or multizonate with rather narrow zones, the margin thin, entire; context dark vinaceous brown or lavender-brown, sometimes paper-thin, usually less than 1 mm. thick, but rarely up to 2 mm. thick; pore surface vinaceous brown to sordid brown or smoky black, the tubes up to 1 mm. long, the mouths minute, invisible to the unaided eye, rather thick-walled, entire, averaging 7–8 per mm.; spores allantoid, smooth, hyaline, 3–4 × 1 μ; basidia 6–8 × 3.5–4 μ; cystidia none; hyphal pegs lacking or inconspicuous; hyphae brown to nearly hyaline, sparingly branched, some with thickened walls, with some cross walls and clamps, usually breaking at the clamps, 3–6 μ in diameter, some narrower.

HABITAT: On dead wood, noted on *Liquidambar*, *Pinus*, and *Quercus*.

DISTRIBUTION: Specimens have been examined from N.C., S.C., Fla., Ala., and La.

ILLUSTRATIONS: Lloyd, Synop. Apus, fig. 679.

There are two forms of this species, correlated with the maturity of the specimens. Younger plants are decidedly velvety-tomentose above and have a total thickness of as much as 7 mm. at the base of the pileus. As the plant ages, the tomentum disappears from the pileus, leaving it multizonate and very much thinner. The thicker and younger specimens are not so brittle; older specimens become very thin and brittle, especially on the margin of the pileus. The dark vinaceous color and the southern range are the chief diagnostic characters.

4b. *Setae present*

145. POLYPORUS GILVUS (Schw.) Fries

Elench. Fung., p. 104. 1828

(Figs. 292–293, 309, and Plate 130)

Boletus gilvus Schw., Schr. Nat. Ges. Leipzig 1: 96. 1822.
Hapalopilus gilvus (Schw.) Murr., Torrey Bot. Club Bul. 31: 418. 1904.

Sporophore sessile or effused-reflexed, leathery to corky when fresh, rigid on drying; pileus 1–7(–11) × 2–12(–15) × 0.2–1.5(–3) cm., ochraceous or bright rusty yellow when young, yellowish brown or dark rusty brown at maturity, finally weathering to blackish, velvety when young and on the growing margin, sometimes scabrous-fibrillose when older, becoming glabrous and somewhat rough and zonate when mature; context yellowish brown, 0.1–1(–2) cm. thick, black with KOH solution; pore surface grayish brown then reddish brown or dark brown, the tubes 1–5 mm. long, rarely in 2 to 5 annual layers, gray within, the mouths circular to subangular, pubescent when young, barely visible to the unaided eye, averaging 5–8 per mm.; spores oblong-ellipsoid, smooth, hyaline, 4–5 × 2.5–3.5 μ; setae rather abundant, brown, subulate, not bulbous-enlarged at the base, 20–30 × 3–6 μ, projecting 5–15 μ; hyphae simple or nearly so, the walls very slightly thickened in the larger ones, with rather frequent cross walls but no clamps, 3–6 μ in diameter. (Compare no. 146, *Polyporus licnoides*, and no. 148, *P. radiatus*.)

HABITAT: On dead wood of deciduous trees, noted on *Acer*, *Ailanthus*, *Alnus*, *Betula*, *Carpinus*, *Carya*, *Castanea*, *Catalpa*, *Cephalanthus*, *Cercis*, *Crataegus*, *Diospyros*, *Eucalyptus*, *Fagus*, *Fraxinus*, *Gleditsia*, *Juglans*, *Liquidambar*, *Liriodendron*, *Nyssa*, *Ostrya*, *Platanus*, *Populus*, *Prunus*, *Pyrus*, *Quercus*, *Robinia*, *Salix*, *Sassafras*, *Syringa*, *Ulmus*, and *Umbellularia*; occasionally on wood of coniferous trees, noted on *Juniperus*, *Pinus*, *Taxodium*, and *Tsuga*; reported on *Hamamelis* (Hirt [77]), on *Rhus* (Md., Rhoads [182]), and on *Tilia* (Mich., Kauffman [101]).

DISTRIBUTION: Specimens have been examined from Vt., Conn., N.Y., Pa., N.J., Del., Md., D.C., Va., W. Va., N.C., S.C., Ga., Fla., Ala., La., Miss., Tenn., Ky., Ohio, Ind., Ill., Mich., Wis., Minn., N. Dak., Iowa, Mo., Kans., Nebr., Ark., Okla., Texas, N. Mex., Ariz., Ore., and Calif.; in Canada from Ontario and Manitoba; reported from Mont. (Weir [227]).

ILLUSTRATIONS: Hirt, N. Y. State Coll. Forestry Tech. Publ. 22: pl. 1, figs. 1–2; Humphrey, U. S. Dept. Agr. Bul. 510: pl. 6, figs. 2–3; Lloyd, Synop. Apus, fig. 682 (as *Polyporus scruposus*); Moffatt, Chicago Acad. Sci. Nat. Hist. Survey Bul. 7, 1: pl. 15, fig. 2; Overholts, Wash. Univ. Studies 3: pl. 5, fig. 25.

Young specimens are frequently covered at first by a distinct ochraceous pubescence, and such plants are often rounded or obtuse on the margin. *Polyporus licnoides* of the southern states and tropical America is the closest relative, and the two at times intergrade. The pileus of *P. gilvus* is often rough and tuberculate, and only somewhat zonate, whereas that of *P. licnoides* is usually smoother, thinner, and marked with many narrow zones. The microscopic characters of the two are identical. *P. radiatus* differs in having somewhat larger pores, less abundant bulbous or broadly conical setae, and a somewhat different and more restricted habitat. *P. calvescens* Berk. and *P. Petersii* Berk. & Curt. are said to be near this species, and *P. pur-pureofuscus* Cooke and *P. scruposus* Fries are considered synonymous. *P. gilvus* is strangely rare in New England.

Specimens are often found which, on being cut vertically, show from two to several rather distinct tube layers, and such specimens are very likely to be referred to *Fomes*, which they markedly resemble. On the West Coast such perennial specimens reach considerably larger sizes, with a corresponding increase in thickness. The manner of growth of these layers has been observed and recorded by Hirt (77).

This species fruits readily in culture in about three weeks, forming a well-developed pad of tubes which, when the plate is inverted, give an abundant spore cast. These spores agree entirely with those from normal sporophores. Setae are likewise produced in the pore walls of such specimens.

The decay is similar to that caused by *Fomes conchatus*, being of the general delignifying type, with a tendency to assume a rusty-yellow coloration or to be shot through with rusty spots, particularly under the bark. In general, the wood is whitish or cream-colored when completely decayed, and very brittle. No black lines are formed. The decay is mostly confined to the sapwood. The species is rarely, if ever, truly parasitic (77, p. 40), though it often grows in the sapwood of wounds in living trees, and occasionally in the heart-wood.

146. POLYPORUS LICNOIDES Mont.

Plant Cell. Cuba, p. 401. 1838–1842

(Fig. 297 and Plate 130)

Hapalopilus licnoides (Mont.) Murr., Torrey Bot. Club Bul. 31: 417. 1904.

Sporophore sessile or effused-reflexed, leathery when fresh, quite rigid when dry; pileus thin, 2–6 × 2.5–10 × 0.2–0.7 cm., uniformly bright yellowish brown or cinnamon, at first with a short, compact, spongy tomentum, later more glabrate, often radiate-lineate, somewhat rugose, usually multizonate; context tawny, 1–6 mm. thick, black with KOH solution; pore surface dark gray-brown to dark rusty brown, the tubes 1–5 mm. long, the mouths rather thick-walled, entire, minute, averaging 6–8 per mm.; spores ellipsoid or oblong, [hyaline—J.L.L.], 3–4.5 × 2.5–3 μ; setae abundant, brown, subulate, not bulbous at the base, 30–40 × 5–7 μ, projecting up to 20 μ; hyphae simple or nearly so, the walls of the larger ones slightly thickened, with rather numerous but inconspicuous cross walls but no clamps, 3–6 μ in diameter. (Compare no. 145, *Polyporus gilvus*.)

HABITAT: On dead wood of deciduous trees, noted on *Quercus*; reported on *Taxodium* (Murrill).

DISTRIBUTION: Specimens have been examined from Ga., Fla.' La., and Texas.

ILLUSTRATIONS: Lloyd, Synop. Apus, fig. 684.

The species is very closely related to *Polyporus gilvus*, as is pointed out under that species. Spores are difficult to locate, and I have seen but a few free-floating ones, of the measurements given above. Romell records them as 3–4 × 2 μ. All the other microscopic features are identical with those of *P. gilvus*.

The straight, narrow-pointed tips of the setae easily separate this species from what I am calling *Fomes extensus* in this manual.

Var. **sublilacinus** (Ell. & Ev.) Overh., comb. nov.
(Fig. 298)

Mucronoporus sublilacinus Ell. & Ev., Torrey Bot. Club Bul. 27: 50. 1900.

Characters as in the species, but sporophore perennial for three or four years, the pileus thicker (up to 2 cm. or perhaps more), dark, weathered, hard and dead at the base, the margin and hymenium continuing growth.

HABITAT: As in the species, noted on *Acer*, *Melia*, and *Quercus*; reported as occurring on *Pinus* (types).

DISTRIBUTION: Specimens have been examined from Fla. and Ga.

The type collection of the variety was said to have been taken from pine logs in Louisiana, by Langlois. Lloyd (116, p. 387) regards the type specimen as a form of *Polyporus gilvus* rather than of *P. licnoides.* I find spores abundant in a collection from Jamaica, at the New York Botanical Garden, and they agree exactly with the few unsatisfactory spores I have been able to find in *P. licnoides.*

147. POLYPORUS IODINUS Mont.

Ann. Sci. Nat. Bot. II, 16: 108. 1841

(Figs. 323, 328–329, and Plate 130)

Cycloporellus iodinus (Mont.) Murr., North Amer. Flora 9: 85. 1908.

Sporophore sessile; pilei imbricate and laterally confluent, often narrowed at the base, dimidiate, somewhat flexible when dry, 1–5 × 1–6 cm. or confluent up to 10 cm., 0.05–0.3 cm. thick, typically bright rusty brown, sometimes dark rusty, rarely fading to sordid, completely covered by a compact, short, erect, rusty tomentum, multizonate or rarely azonate, the margin thin, entire or lobed; context rusty brown, firm, very different in texture from the soft overlying tomentum, from which it is separated by a dense black zone, not more than 1 mm. thick, usually less than 0.5 mm.; pore surface concolorous or darker than the pileus, sometimes almost black and sometimes with a slight umber-olivaceous tint, the tubes 0.5–2 mm. long, the mouths angular to irregular, sometimes arranged in concentric lines and so appearing irpiciform, but usually entire, rather thin-walled, averaging 4–7 per mm.; spores oblong-ellipsoid or short-cylindric, smooth, hyaline, 3.5–4.5 × 2–2.5 μ; setae rather abundant, projecting 12–25 μ beyond the hymenium, 6–7 μ in diameter; hyphae in the firm zone dark brown, rather thick-walled, rarely with indistinct cross walls but no clamps, 4–7 μ in diameter.

HABITAT: On dead wood, noted on *Quercus.*

DISTRIBUTION: Specimens have been examined from Fla. and La.

ILLUSTRATIONS: Lloyd, Synop. Polystictus, figs. 348–349 (as *Polystictus campyloporus*).

According to Lloyd (*Synop. Polystictus*, p. 59. 1910), *Polyporus (Polystictus) tabacinus* differs from *P. iodinus* in having smaller pores.

The number per millimeter is, however, not stated. No specimens of *P. tabacinus* from the southern United States had been seen by Lloyd.

This species is found only in subtropical stations. There are more than a half-dozen collections, made by Langlois, at Beltsville, Maryland, presumably mostly from Louisiana, and also one collection from Florida, by Stevenson, with the small pores of *Polyporus tabacinus* but not otherwise differing from the present species. Lloyd collected the fungus in Florida in 1897; a portion of this collection is in the New York State Museum at Albany.

148. POLYPORUS RADIATUS Sow. ex Frics

Syst. Myc. 1: 369. 1821

(Figs. 294, 658, and Plate 131)

Boletus radiatus Sow., Col. Fig. English Fungi, pl. 196. 1799.
Inonotus radiatus (Sow. ex Fries) Karst., Rev. Mycol. 3, 9: 19. 1881.
Polyporus aureonitens Pat., apud Peck, in N. Y. State Mus. Ann. Rept. 42: 25. 1889.

Sporophore sessile or somewhat decurrent on the substratum, often imbricate, rather firm though usually somewhat flexible when fresh, rigid when dry; pileus 1–6 × 2–7 × 0.3–2 cm., bright ochraceous orange or with a yellowish-green tinge at first, soon golden brown or yellowish brown or rusty brown, silky-tomentose or fibrillose-tomentose, then radiately fibrillose, usually radiately rugose on the margin, finally glabrous, usually zonate; context yellowish to rusty brown, black with KOH, corky, 2–5(–7) mm. thick; pore surface hoary brown to rusty brown, the tubes 1–8 mm. long, the mouths angular, averaging 4–5 per mm., the walls rather thin but entire; spores ellipsoid or elliptic, smooth, hyaline under the microscope or perhaps slightly yellowish, 4–6 × 3–4 μ; setae present but often rare, brown, subulate, usually bulbous-enlarged at the base, the tip scarcely projecting beyond the basidia, sometimes curved at the apex, 15–24 × 6–9(–12) μ; hyphae simple, thin-walled, brown, with cross walls but no clamps, 3–7 μ in diameter; all parts black where touched with KOH solution or, if the reaction is slow enough, a bright red intervening momentarily before the change to black. (Compare no. 145, *Polyporus gilvus*, and no. 160, *P. glomeratus.*)

HABITAT: On dead wood of deciduous trees, especially *Alnus*, *Betula*, and *Fagus*, otherwise noted only on *Acer*, *Hamamelis*, *Ostrya*,

Physocarpus, Pyrus, Salix, and *Viburnum*; reported on *Quercus* (Mo., Maneval [130]) and on *Ulmus* (Wis., Neuman [148]); one collection recorded on *Abies.*

DISTRIBUTION: Specimens have been examined from Me., N.H., Vt., Mass., Conn., N.Y., Pa., N.J., Va., N.C., Tenn., Ill., Mich., Wis., and Idaho; in Canada from Ontario and British Columbia; reported from Mo. (Maneval [131]), Mont. (Weir [227]), and Ore. (Kauffman [103]).

ILLUSTRATIONS: Lucand, Fig. Peint. Champ. France, pl. 123.

This species is usually smaller and thinner than *Polyporus cuticularis,* and the spores are entirely colorless, or in age show only a faint trace of color. It is more common in mountainous districts than is *P. cuticularis,* its favorite substrata being birch and alder. It differs from *P. glomeratus* notably in the lack of internal setae in the context and in the hyaline spores, as well as in the less yellowish pileus and the more distinctly sessile and less resupinate habit. It is an elegant species when in its prime, and its brighter coloration is one of the points in which it differs decidedly from *P. gilvus.* It appears later in the season than that species and disappears more quickly. The setae, at least a considerable proportion of them, have an abrupt bulbous enlargement at the base.

The type specimens of *Polyporus aureonitens* show a lack of internal setae, and therefore that species is to be referred here rather than to *P. glomeratus.* It represents an early and very bright-colored stage of the species. The specimens Schweinitz referred to the present species were entirely different, being radiate conditions of *P. versicolor,* according to a specimen now in his herbarium. *P. cucullatus* Berk. & Curt. is usually referred to synonymy here.

Wood decayed by this fungus is soft and spongy in texture and varies from nearly white in the earlier stages to straw color or decidedly rusty yellow in the advanced stages. The decay is of the general delignifying type.

Var. CEPHALANTHI Overh.

Torrey Bot. Club Bul. 65: 179. 1938

(Plate 131)

Polyporus illinoisensis Baxter, Mich. Acad. Sci. Arts and Letters Papers 24, 1: 180. 1939.

Sporophore mostly or entirely resupinate or nodulose-reflexed; spores broadly ellipsoid or subglobose, smooth, apparently slightly colored in mass though practically hyaline in KOH, 4–4.5 × 3.5–4 μ; setae not abundant, scattered, a large proportion with curved or hooked sharp-pointed tips, 20–32 × 8–12 μ, projecting up to half of their length; internal setae none; hyphae simple, with cross walls but no clamps, 4–5 μ in diameter.

HABITAT AND DISTRIBUTION: On dead *Cephalanthus* in swamps in La. and Ill.; reported from Mich. (Baxter [11h]).

ILLUSTRATIONS: Baxter, Mich. Acad. Sci. Arts and Letters Papers 24, 1: pl. 4, fig. 2.

The variety seems distinct enough for separate recognition. The smaller, more globose spores, the larger number of hooked or curved setae, the habitat, and the range would be almost sufficient basis for specific segregation were it not for the fact that one occasionally finds curved setae in *Polyporus radiatus*, and it is not a species of sharply limited host affinities. Dr. Baxter sent me an unnamed specimen of this fungus many years ago. I think I must have referred it to *P. radiatus* at that time; at least that is the name on the label at present. In the summer of 1931 I found it to be rather common in the partly dried-out swamps of Louisiana, and I reported it in my list of fungi from that region several years later. Undoubtedly the fungus occurs in the intervening states and in swamplands that support *Cephalanthus* through the Mississippi River Valley.

149. POLYPORUS DRYADEUS Pers. ex Fries

Syst. Myc. 1: 374. 1821

(Figs. 300, 616, and Plates 128 and 129)

Boletus dryadeus Pers., Obs. Myc. 2: 3. 1799.
Inonotus dryadeus (Pers. ex Fries) Murr., North Amer. Flora 9: 86. 1908.

Sporophore sessile, firm though somewhat watery when fresh, rigid when dry; pileus 6–40 × 8–35 × 2–10 cm., at first whitish or gray, then grayish brown, yellowish brown, or reddish brown, at first minutely tomentose, then glabrous and with a thin, easily indented crust at maturity, the margin obtuse, becoming thin and acute, distilling drops of water when young; context umber-brown or rusty brown, often yellowish under the crust, 1.5–4 cm. thick, firm-corky and shining brown when dry, black in KOH; pore surface grayish brown or darker, with a silvery sheen when fresh, the tubes 0.5–2 cm. long, the mouths angular, very thin-walled, entire, averaging 3–5 per mm.; spores globose or subglobose, smooth, hyaline or pale-colored, 5.5–8 μ in diameter, or 6–8 $\times$ 5–6 μ; basidia pear-shaped, 7–9 μ in diameter; setae rare or not abundant, brown, conical, very sharp-pointed and the tip frequently curved, 16–25 $\times$ 6–12 μ, enlarged and bulbous at the base; hyphae nearly simple, pale brown to very dark brown in KOH, with very occasional cross walls but no clamps, mostly 6–9 μ in diameter. (Compare no. 157, *Polyporus dryophilus.*)

HABITAT: Usually at the base of living oak trees (*Quercus*) or on the stumps of recently felled oaks; one collection said to be on *Aesculus*; also reported on *Acer* (Ore., Zeller [236]); in the Northwest occasionally on such coniferous hosts as *Abies, Picea, Tsuga,* and perhaps other genera.

DISTRIBUTION: Specimens have been examined from Pa., Md., D.C., W. Va., N.C., Ga., La., Tenn., Ky., Ohio, Ind., Ill., Mo., Texas, Ore., Wash., and Calif.; in Canada only from British Columbia; reported from N.Y. (Lowe [125]) and from Va., Ark., and Okla. (Long [118]).

ILLUSTRATIONS: Hubert, Outline Forest Path., fig. 98; Lloyd, Myc. Notes, fig. 383; Long, Jour. Agr. Res. 1: pl. 22, figs. 4–6; McDougall, Ill. State Acad. Sci. Trans. 12: fig. 7; Rankin, Man. Tree Dis., fig. 51.

The setae are short and conical, often with a subbulbous base, not deeply imbedded, and dark brown, and are therefore quite characteristic. *Polyporus dryophilus* differs in the well-marked central core of the pileus, as described under that species, in the dark-brown spores that are ellipsoid rather than exactly globose, as here, and in the lack of setae. The present species always fruits at or just above the ground line on its host, whereas *P. dryophilus* never fruits in that position, but always at some distance from the ground, although examples have been noted where the sporophores of that species were less than three feet from the ground. *P. dryadeus* may continue to fruit several seasons after the host is dead. It fruits sparingly over its range, but on the campus of Pennsylvania State College it has fruited yearly on one or more of several infected trees for a number of years.

Schweinitz' record of this species, if based on the specimen now so labeled in his herbarium, is in error, that being a specimen of *Polyporus gilvus.*

The fungus causes a serious delignifying, white or straw-colored, wet rot of both heartwood and sapwood, but, according to Long (118), the defect is limited to the roots and ends abruptly at the ground line. In this it differs from the rot of *Polyporus dryophilus,* which is distinctly a trunk rot and not a root rot.

3b. *Spores colored*
　4a. *Setae absent*
　　5a. *Sporophore without a central core* (see also *Inonotus ludovicianus melleus,* p. 427)

150. POLYPORUS CORROSUS (Murr.) Sacc. & Trott.

Syll. Fung. 21: 275. 1912
(Figs. 291, 308, and Plate 129)

Inonotus corrosus Murr., Torrey Bot. Club Bul. 31: 598. 1904.

Sporophore sessile or effused-reflexed, usually imbricate; pileus 1–4 × 1–10 × 0.5–2 cm., rusty brown to tan or ochraceous tan, spongy with a deep coat of compact tomentum that may disappear or become hardened and blackish except at the margin of the pileus, even or furrowed and irregular; margin thin to thick and rounded; context rusty brown or yellow-brown, duplex, with a thin, lower, firm layer and a spongy, thick, upper layer (really the tomentum), separated in well-developed specimens by a dark line, 0.3–1.5 cm. thick including the tomentum; pore surface yellow-tan to dark brown, the tubes 1–5 mm. long, the mouths circular, thick-walled, entire, averaging 6–8 per mm., invisible to the unaided eye; spores ellipsoid or subglobose, very dilute brown, 3–4 × 2–3 μ; setae none; hyphae chestnut-brown, rather thin-walled, with cross walls but no clamps, 4–6 μ in diameter, or some paler and smaller; all parts changing to red and then immediately or gradually to black with KOH solution. (Compare no. 151, *Polyporus fruticum.*)

HABITAT: On dead wood of deciduous trees.

DISTRIBUTION: Specimens have been examined only from Fla.

ILLUSTRATIONS: Lloyd, Synop. Apus, fig. 699 (as *Polyporus fruticum*).

This species is easily recognized by its small size, minute pores, small, yellowish-brown spores, lack of setae, and the very characteristic duplex context (see 154, pl. 4, fig. 2). Only a few collections are known from Florida, though it seems to be a frequent species in tropical America. For a further discussion of *Polyporus corrosus* see under *P. fruticum*.

151. POLYPORUS FRUTICUM Berk. & Curt.

Linnean Soc. Bot. Jour. 10: 310. 1868
(Figs. 287, 301, 333, and Plate 130)

Inonotus fruticum (Berk. & Curt.) Murr., Torrey Bot. Club Bul. 31: 601. 1904.
Inonotus amplectens Murr., Torrey Bot. Club Bul. 31: 600. 1904.

Sporophore usually circular and encircling branches of living trees, 1–5 cm. in diameter, 0.3–2.5 cm. thick; pileus surface tan or ochraceous to rusty tan, covered with a soft spongy coat of tomentum that extends to the tube layer, the margin rather thin and entire; context not differentiated from the tomentum, yellowish brown; pore surface brown or yellowish brown, the tubes 1–3 mm. long, the mouths angular, thin-walled, even or slightly dentate, averaging 2 per mm.; spores ellipsoid to oblong-ellipsoid or short-cylindric, pale yellowish brown, smooth, 4–5 × 3–3.5 μ; setae none; hyphae simple or sparingly branched, red-brown in KOH solution, with cross walls but no clamps, 4–8 μ in diameter. (Compare no. 150, *Polyporus corrosus*.)

HABITAT: On deciduous trees, noted on *Asimina* and *Citrus*.

DISTRIBUTION: Specimens have been examined from Ga. and Fla.

ILLUSTRATIONS: Lloyd, Synop. Apus, fig. 700.

The relations between this species and *Polyporus corrosus* are in doubt. Lloyd (116, p. 377) emphatically declares the two to be synonymous. The type specimen of *P. fruticum* was taken from living twigs and has pores averaging 2 per mm. The spores are like those of *P. corrosus*. But the pores of *P. corrosus* are very minute (invisible to the unaided eye), and the thick, felted tomentum is separated by a distinct black line from the underlying context.

Therefore the collections I have seen separate nicely into two species on the basis of the difference in habitat, the size of the pores, and the presence or absence of this black line. When one examines the types of *Inonotus amplectens*, one finds spores that are somewhat more cylindric than is usual for either *P. corrosus* or *P. fruticum*. Otherwise, there is no distinction between that species and *P. fruticum*.

152. POLYPORUS CUTICULARIS Bull. ex Fries

Syst. Myc. 1: 363. 1821

(Figs. 295, 564, 579, and Plate 129)

Boletus cuticularis Bull., Herb. France, pl. 462. 1790.
Inonotus perplexus (Peck) Murr., sensu Torrey Bot. Club Bul. 31: 596. 1904.

Sporophore sessile, usually imbricate, spongy, watery and tough when fresh, drying rigid; pileus 1–7 × 3–10 × 0.3–1 cm., yellowish brown to rusty brown, compactly woolly-tomentose or becoming fibrillose, often subzonate; context yellowish brown to rusty brown, 2–7 mm. thick; pore surface hoary brown to rusty brown or darker, the tubes 2–10 mm. long, the mouths angular, thin-walled, entire averaging 3–5 per mm.; spores ellipsoid to subglobose, smooth, yellowish brown (reddish brown in KOH), 5.5–8 × 4–5 μ; cystidia and hyphal pegs none; setae usually not abundant, sometimes absent, usually imbedded and inconspicuous, quite brown, sharp-pointed, 15–30 × 5–9 μ; context hyphae simple or somewhat branched, some thin-walled with occasional cross walls but no clamps, others with much thickened walls, 5–12 μ in diameter; tramal hyphae 3–4 μ in diameter; no imbedded setal hyphae. (Compare no. 148, *Polyporus radiatus*, and no. 157, *P. dryophilus* var. *vulpinus*.)

HABITAT: On dead wood of deciduous trees and from wounds in living trees, noted on *Acer, Carya, Celtis, Fagus, Fraxinus, Platanus, Populus, Quercus, Salix, Schinus, Tilia*, and *Ulmus*.

DISTRIBUTION: Specimens have been examined from Vt., Mass., Conn., N.Y., Pa., N.J., Del., D.C., Va., W. Va., N.C., S.C., Ga., Fla., Ala., La., Miss., Tenn., Ohio, Ind., Ill., Mo., Nebr., Ark., Texas, Ariz., Utah, Calif., and Alaska; in Canada from Quebec, Ontario, and Manitoba; reported also from Ky. and Mich. (Kauffman [100, 101]), and from Wis. (Neuman [148]).

ILLUSTRATIONS: Lloyd, Synop. Apus, figs. 693–694; Overholts, Wash. Univ. Studies 3: pl. 5, fig. 26.

The spores of this species are indistinguishable from those of *Polyporus dryophilus*, but are somewhat larger and more globose than those of *P. dryophilus* var. *vulpinus*. Specimens are usually much thinner and more applanate, and lack the mycelial core of *P. dryophilus*. The substratum is often stumps and logs; and the fungus is found only occasionally on living trees and usually not on *Quercus*. In addition, the pilei often grow in imbricate clusters. The species is distinct from *P. hispidus* in the usually smaller size, the fibrillose-tomentose rather than hispid pileus, and the very different, distinctly ellipsoid, and considerably smaller spores. Its closest relative is, perhaps, *P. radiatus*, from which it differs in the usually larger size and the dark brown spores. There seems also to be a difference in the size of the hyphae of the context that may be important. The setae are extremely similar to those of that species. Usually only the tip protrudes beyond the basidia, so that they are very inconspicuous.

There is some question whether *Polyporus perplexus* Peck is a synonym or whether it should be referred to *P. dryophilus* var. *vulpinus*. The type cannot be found, however, and the question cannot be definitely decided. *P. fuscovelutinus* (Pat.) Sacc. & Trott., described from Louisiana, is said not to be distinct. A specimen in the Schweinitz Herbarium under the name *P. cuticularis*, and presumably the basis for Schweinitz' report of this species, is *Fomes conchatus*.

153. POLYPORUS JUNIPERINUS (Murr.) Sacc. & Trott.

Syll. Fung. 21: 273. 1912

(Plate 130)

Inonotus juniperinus Murr., North Amer. Flora 9: 88. 1908.

Sporophore sessile and dimidiate to flabelliform and appearing substipitate, flexible and watery when fresh, drying rigid; pileus 3–7 × 3–4 × 0.4–2 cm., yellowish brown to dark brown, weathering to blackish, finely tomentose to glabrous, somewhat zonate and rugose in well-developed specimens, slightly incrusted with age; context umber-brown to yellow-brown, soft-corky, zonate in well-developed specimens, 3–7 mm. thick; pore surface brown, darkening on drying, the tubes 2–10 mm. long, the mouths angular, thin-walled, entire, averaging 4–5 per mm., barely visible to the unaided eye; spores subglobose, smooth, smoky brown, 6–8 μ in diameter; setae none; hyphae nearly simple, red-brown in KOH, rather thin-walled, with some cross walls but no clamps, 4–7 μ in diameter.

HABITAT: On buried roots of cedar (*Juniperus*).

DISTRIBUTION: Specimens have been examined only from Texas.

The species is not an entirely satisfactory one, in spite of the three collections at the New York Botanical Garden. One specimen resembles a thin, weathered form of *Polyporus cuticularis*; two others have well-developed tubes, but seem to have grown up in a circinate manner from buried wood. Murrill's spore record is in error. The spores are not rich chestnut-brown in KOH, as are those of such similar species as *P. dryophilus* and *P. hispidus*, but have a blackish tinge.

154. POLYPORUS LUDOVICIANUS (Pat.) Sacc. & Trott.

Syll. Fung. 21: 269. 1912
(Figs. 267–269 and Plate 130)

Xanthochrous ludovicianus Pat., Soc. Mycol. France Bul. 24: 6. 1908.
Inonotus ludovicianus (Pat.) Murr., Southern Polypores, p. 41. 1915.

Sporophore substipitate, forming large rosette-like clusters or imbricated masses of pilei 15–50 cm. broad; pileus usually flabelliform and attenuated to a stemlike base, watery and tough when fresh, drying rigid, 10–30 × 10–30 × 1–2.5 cm., covered with a rusty-red or rusty-brown tomentum, large specimens zonate or banded and drying rough or rugose with a very matted tomentum; context 0.5–2 cm. thick, brown, fibrous then friable; pore surface grayish brown to dark brown, the tubes 5–10 mm. long, the mouths thin-walled, entire, angular, averaging 2–3 per mm.; stem scarcely more than a lateral or downward prolongation of the pileus, confluent at the bases in large specimens; spores ellipsoid and flattened on one side, brown, smooth, 5–6 × 3.5–4 μ; setae none; main context hyphae chestnut-brown, the walls rough or scabrous, with no cross walls or clamps, 5–8 μ in diameter, a few hyphae smaller and paler, with some cross walls, 4 μ in diameter. (Compare no. 140, *Polyporus Schweinitzii*, and no. 152, *P. cuticularis*.)

HABITAT: Usually at the bases or on the roots of living hardwood trees, occasionally on logs or stumps, noted on *Liquidambar*, *Nyssa*, and *Quercus*.

DISTRIBUTION: Specimens have been examined from N.C., S.C., Ga., Fla., Ala., La., Ark., and Texas.

ILLUSTRATIONS: Overholts, Torrey Bot. Club Bul. 65: 177, fig. 8.

Lloyd's disposition of this name in synonymy under *Polyporus cuticularis* is erroneous, for adequate specimens had not been studied since Patouillard described the species in 1908. In fact, very few collections had been made until I visited Louisiana in 1931. During the summer, beginning in July, the species was found to be not uncommon, and magnificent specimens were obtained. As is indicated above, the sporophores reach sizes never closely approached by *P. cuticularis*. The spores are about the same as in that species or perhaps a trifle more narrow and more conspicuously flattened on one side, but setae are entirely absent.

The species causes an important pocket rot in the wood of its hosts, and it is to be regarded as one of the most important heart-rotting organisms of the southeastern United States. The decay is probably chiefly a butt rot, however, though it extends also into the roots. The pockets measure 4–10 × 1.5–3 mm. on the radial wood surface and 1–1.5 mm. wide on the tangential surface. Badly rotted wood, especially of *Liquidambar*, is very much honeycombed and very light in weight.

155. POLYPORUS PORRECTUS (Murr.) Sacc. & Trott.

Syll. Fung. 23: 374. 1925
(Figs. 274, 305, and Plate 131)

Inonotus porrectus Murr., Tropical Polypores, p. 68. 1915.

Sporophore sessile or more or less flabelliform and appearing substipitate, rigid and multiplex at times; pileus 4–9 × 4–9 × 0.5–1.5 cm., bright rusty brown to pale bay, very compactly tomentose or nearly glabrous, velvety to the touch, more or less radiate-rugose, multizonate, the margin thin, entire; context very bright yellow-brown, shining, 0.3–1 cm. thick; pore surface gilvous brown or dark gray-brown with a pale-tan, narrow, sterile margin at the edge of the pileus, the tubes 1–2 mm. long or eventually reaching a length of 4 mm., the mouths angular, rather thick-walled, entire, averaging 5–7 per mm.; spores globose, smooth, brown, 4–5 μ in diameter; setae none; hyphae straight, simple, brown, with cross walls but no clamps, 5–7.5 μ in diameter.

Habitat: On dead wood.

Distribution: Specimens have been examined only from La.

This species is characteristic in the bright-yellow context, the absence of setae, and the brown spores. *Fomes rheicolor* Lloyd is a synonym, and Lloyd's name antedates by three months that proposed by Murrill. I assume, however, that this is not *Polyporus rheicolor* of Berkeley, if one may judge from descriptions alone; hence Lloyd's name is untenable in *Polyporus*.

156. Polyporus texanus (Murr.) Sacc. & Trott.

Syll. Fung. 21: 272. 1912

(Plate 132)

Inonotus texanus Murr., Torrey Bot. Club Bul. 31: 597. 1904.

Sporophore sessile, somewhat soft-corky when fresh, rigid on drying; pileus strongly convex or ungulate, 2.5–7 × 4–9.5 × 1.5–5 cm., at first pale yellowish brown, then stained more reddish brown and finally blackish, finely tomentose, then fibrillose-glabrate and radiate, finally glabrous and imbricate-rimose, not incrusted, the margin obtuse; context bright yellow-brown to umber-brown, quite thin in comparison to the length of the tubes, fibrillose-corky, 2–4(–8) mm. thick; pore surface yellowish to dark brown, the tubes 0.5–3 cm. long, the mouths thin-walled and irregularly angular, entire, averaging 2–3 per mm.; spores ellipsoid to broadly ellipsoid, chestnut-brown, smooth, 7–10 × 5–7 μ; setae none; hyphae reddish brown in KOH, nearly simple or sparingly branched, rather thin-walled, with cross walls but no clamps, 5–8 μ in diameter. (Compare no. 157, *Polyporus dryophilus*, and no. 162, *P. Munzii*.)

Habitat: On trunks of living *Morus*, mesquite (*Prosopis*), and *Salix*; probably on a few other hosts also.

Distribution: Specimens have been examined only from Texas and Ariz.

Illustrations: Von Schrenk, Mo. Bot. Gard. Ann. 1: pls. 6–7.

Three collections of this species are at the New York Botanical Garden, and about the same number are at Beltsville, Maryland. Lloyd regards this species as a form of *Polyporus Rheades* (*P. dryophilus*) corresponding to *P. corruscans* of Europe. I cannot agree to this. There is no trace of a central core in the pileus. The color characters are those of *P. cuticularis* or *P. dryophilus*, but the pileus is much less tomentose and the long tubes, typically 1–1.5 cm., contrast strangely with the thin context, typically 2–4 mm. thick.

Von Schrenk (217) describes the decay produced by this fungus in *Prosopis glandulosa* Torr., in Texas, as a delignifying heart rot; the wood is "very brittle, but still remains fibrous, that is, it does not crumble into powder like charcoal." He also gives a revised description and a number of illustrations of the fungus and the decay.

5b. *Sporophore with a central core*

157. POLYPORUS DRYOPHILUS Berk.

London Jour. Bot. 6: 321. 1847

(Figs. 302–303, 312, 608–609, and Plate 129)

Inonotus dryophilus (Berk.) Murr., Torrey Bot. Club Bul. 31: 597. 1904.

Sporophore sessile, often imbricate, spongy and watery when young, firm when mature, crumbling when old, often subglobose or tubercular though more frequently triangular in section when well-developed; pileus 3–13 × 4–22 × 2.5–12 cm., at first whitish, slowly changing to brownish as it matures, later grayish brown to golden brown or reddish brown, finally blackish, at first somewhat tomentose or hirsute, then innately pubescent or scabrous, finally almost glabrous; context at first pale-colored but more brown next the tubes, finally brown, black (or red then black) in KOH solution, with a basal, globose, granular core 3–10 cm. thick permeated with white mycelial strands; pore surface cinnamon-brown or darker, the tubes 0.3–3 cm. long, the mouths angular, rather thick-walled, entire, averaging 2–3 per mm.; setae none; spores ellipsoid to broadly ellipsoid or subglobose, smooth, brown, 7–8 × 5–7 μ; basidia clavate, 7–8 μ in diameter; setae none; hyphae nearly simple, those in the lower context often much darker than those in the upper, the darkest considerably thickened, with rather frequent cross walls in most, and with very occasional clamps in the lighter-colored ones, mostly 4–9 μ in diameter, but some paler ones smaller. (Compare no. 149, *Polyporus dryadeus*; no. 152, *P. cuticularis*; and no. 161, *P. hispidus*.)

HABITAT: Usually on living (rarely on dead) deciduous trees, especially oaks (*Quercus*); also noted on *Acer*, *Fagus*, *Prunus*, and *Schinus*.

DISTRIBUTION: Specimens have been examined from N.H., Vt., N.Y., Pa., Va., N.C., Tenn., La., Ohio, Ill., Mich., Wis., Minn., S. Dak., Iowa, Mo., Texas, N. Mex., Ariz., Ore., and Calif.

ILLUSTRATIONS: Hubert, Outline Forest Path., fig. 99 (rot only); Long, Jour. Agr. Res. 1: pl. 21, figs. 1–3, 7–8; Lloyd, Myc. Notes 53: fig. 1129 (as *Polyporus Rheades*).

Polyporus hispidus differs prominently in the more hispid pileus, in the lack of a central core, and especially in the larger and more globose spores, which measure 7.5–10 $\times$ 6.5–9 μ. *P. cuticularis* has spores indistinguishable from those of the present species, but is thinner, lacks the central core, is more likely to grow imbricate, occurs on a variety of woody substrata but only rarely on living trees and usually not on *Quercus*, and, moreover, has setae in the hymenium. *P. dryophilus* differs decidedly from *P. dryadeus*, as is noted under that species.

In my earlier publications I recorded setae as sometimes present in this species, but in my recent studies of the hymenium I have failed to find them in a single instance, and I am forced to the tentative conclusion that I previously confused one or more collections of some other species with the present one.

The species is very important in producing a conspicuous pocket or piped decay of the heartwood of living *Quercus* trees which eventually results in the death of the trees (87, p. 367).

Var. VULPINUS (Fries) Overh.

Pa. Agr. Exp. Sta. Tech. Bul. 298: 23. 1933

(Figs. 304, 310, and Plate 129)

Polyporus vulpinus Fries, Svenska Vetensk.-akad. Handl. for 1852, p. 130. 1852.

Pileus more applanate and smaller than in the species, 1–5 $\times$ 1–10 $\times$ 1–2 cm., decidedly hirsute or strigose-tomentose, becoming matted-tomentose; color and consistency as in the species; context thin, the central core at the base of the pileus much smaller than in the species, practically lacking at times, usually only 0.5–1.5 cm. in diameter; spores oblong-ellipsoid, 4.5–7 $\times$ 3.5–4.5 μ; basidia clavate, 5–6 μ in diameter; setae none.

HABITAT: On various species of *Populus*.

Distribution: Probably coextensive with that of the species; noted also from Me., Conn., and Idaho, and in Canada from Ontario; reported from Montana (Weir [227]).

The variety resembles *Polyporus cuticularis* more than it does any other species, but differs in having a slight development of the central core characteristic of *P. dryophilus*, and somewhat smaller spores. It is restricted to dead *Populus* and causes a soft white rot which has little resemblance to the piped rot produced by the species in *Quercus* —a difference I regard as due to the very different structure of the wood in the two cases. The sporophores are more applanate and often decurrent on the wood, and thinner and smaller throughout, with the central core very much reduced in size though usually still recognizable. The spores are decidedly oblong-ellipsoid, measuring 4.5–7 $\times$ 3.5–4.5 μ and hence being narrower and shorter than those of the plant on *Quercus*. I believe that this variation is worthy of recognition. *P. vulpinus* Fries was originally described as occurring on *Populus*. *P. corruscans* Fries and *P. Rheades* are said to be synonyms for the oak-inhabiting form.

Although Lloyd cites and publishes photographs of a specimen from Persoon's Herbarium (111, figs. 333, 696 [as *Polyporus Rheades*]) of a plant representing Persoon's idea of *P. Rheades*, the photographs have much more resemblance to this form on *Populus*, and for that reason I have abandoned the name *P. Rheades* as I formerly used it. The central core of the species does not show in Lloyd's photographs. Lloyd (111, p. 755) suggests that *P. perplexus* Peck may be referable here rather than to *P. cuticularis*, and the idea is quite plausible.

158. Polyporus graveolens (Schw.) Fries

Elench. Fung., p. 79. 1828

(Figs. 315, 636, and Plate 130)

Boletus graveolens Schw., Schr. Nat. Ges. Leipzig 1: 97. 1822.
Globifomes graveolens (Schw.) Murr., Torrey Bot. Club Bul. 31: 424. 1904.
Polyporus conglobatus Berk., London Jour. Bot. 4: 303. 1845.

Sporophore a globose or cylindrical mass 5–20 cm. in diameter, composed of numerous small, very closely overlapping pilei arising from a central solid core; pilei 1–3 cm. long, laterally confluent, 3–8 mm. thick, leathery to rigid, at first pale brown behind, the margin whitish, then entirely rusty brown to cinnamon-brown or coffee-brown, and finally grayish black or blackish with age, slightly incrusted, pulverulent or glabrous, the margin deflexed and concealing the pores; context brown, floccose-fibrous, 1–4 mm. thick, at times odorous; pore surface at first gray, then gray-brown to umber, the tubes 1–4 mm. long, the mouths circular, entire, averaging 3–4 per mm.; spores cylindric, smooth, light brown when mature (hyaline when young), 9–12.5 × 3–4.5 μ; cystidia none, but incrusted ends of hyphae sometimes project from the hymenium; hyphae long and flexuous, simple or nearly so, pale brown under the microscope, some with walls completely thickened, others partially thickened, and others not at all thickened, with no cross walls or clamps, 4–9 μ in diameter.

Habitat: On logs or trunks of deciduous trees, noted on *Acer, Carya, Fagus, Liquidambar,* and *Quercus.*

Distribution: Specimens have been examined from N.Y., Pa., N.J., Del., Md., D.C., Va., W. Va., N.C., S.C., Ala., Tenn., Ky., Ohio, Ind., Ill., Iowa; reported from Wis. (Dodge [40]) and Mo. (Maneval [131]).

Illustrations: Graves, Mycologia 11: pl. 10, fig. 3 (as *Pyropolyporus*); Hard, Mushrooms, fig. 334 (upside down); Lloyd, Myc. Notes, Polyp. Issue No. 3, figs. 367–368 (as *Fomes*); *idem,* Synop. Stip. Polyp., fig. 455 (as *Fomes*); Overholts, Wash. Univ. Studies 3: pl. 5, fig. 24.

The species has had the reputation of giving off at a certain period of its development a very noticeable, sweet odor, which has caused it to be named "sweet knot." I have collected the species a number of times, and have recently had specimens under observation on the campus of Pennsylvania State College. In no instance has such an odor been detected. Neither is the fungus odorous when grown in pure culture. But many years ago when a fresh collection was shown to my father he at once recognized it as the "sweet knot" and described how on occasions he had seen the fungus placed in living rooms, where it soon scented the whole house. On one occasion there was no noticeable odor until the sporophore was broken, and then a very definite odor of apples or, according to some who were present, of ensilage, was noticeable.

I have collected the fungus on dead standing snags, on the dead tops of recently felled trees that were alive at the base, and also from wounded areas in living trees. In such situations it appears to have decayed both sapwood and heartwood, producing a general delignifying, straw-colored or yellowish-brown rot.

4b. *Setae present*

159. POLYPORUS FARLOWII Lloyd

Synop. Apus, p. 363. 1915

Pileus applanate, strongly hispid, brown to blackish, 5–18 × 5–10.5 × 2–3 cm.; context more or less woody, 0.5–2 cm. thick, "clay color"; tubes 1–14 mm. long, the mouths "Sayal brown," "warm sepia" to dark neutral gray in old specimens, averaging 1–4 per mm.; spores pale yellow or brown, 5.5–6.5 × 5.5 μ; setae present, scattered, brown, with partially thickened walls, sharp-pointed, not conspicuously enlarged at the base, 25–32 × 7–8 μ; hyphae pale brown to dark brown, with thickened walls, 3–4 μ in diameter.

HABITAT: On living trees of *Acer, Morus, Populus, Sambucus,* and *Schinus.*

DISTRIBUTION: Specimens have been examined from N. Mex. and Ariz.

ILLUSTRATIONS: Baxter, Mich. Acad. Sci. Arts and Letters Papers 24, 1: pl. 4, fig. 1; Lloyd, Synop. Apus, fig. 697.

I have not seen specimens of this species. The types are in the Royal Botanic Gardens, at Kew, England. They were collected in Arizona and by some means fell into Dr. Farlow's hands; he sent them to Cooke, who misdetermined them as *Polyporus endocrocinus.* Lloyd, coming across the specimens at Kew, gave them the name they bear here.

The foregoing account is taken largely from Baxter (11h, p. 179). It is not entirely certain that Baxter was dealing with the same plant as Lloyd, for he says "no brown setae." I have a slide of the type, and it is not difficult to show that setae are present, as described above. There is likewise a discrepancy as to spores in the two published descriptions. Lloyd says: "Spores colored, elliptical, 2.5 × 4.5–5." Certainly it might be surmised that the species is synonymous with *Polyporus Munzii.*

160. Polyporus glomeratus Peck

N. Y. State Mus. Ann. Rept. 24: 78. 1872

(Figs. 316, 638–639, and Plate 130)

Sporophore sessile, effused-reflexed or somewhat nodulose, usually imbricate, firm and watery when fresh, rigid when dry; pileus 2–4 × 2–10 × 0.4–2 cm., buffy brown to dark tawny, olive-ocher, or, in vigorously growing plants, greenish yellow, rough and more or less uneven, minutely velvety tomentose or becoming glabrous, at length with a thin but distinct crust; context tawny, 2–10 mm. thick, black in KOH; pore surface greenish yellow when fresh, becoming grayish or brown, the tubes 2–7 mm. long, the mouths angular, rather thin-walled, entire, averaging 3–6 per mm.; spores subglobose, smooth, greenish yellow or almost sulphur-yellow, 4.5–6 × 3.5–4.5 μ; setae absent or present but not abundant, 15–25 × 5–7 μ, slightly projecting, brown, and with large, thick (8–18 μ), cylindric seta-like hyphae present in the trama and the context; hyphae nearly simple, thin-walled, with rather frequent cross walls but no clamps, 4–6 μ in diameter.   (Compare no. 145, *Polyporus gilvus*, and no. 148, *P. radiatus*.)

HABITAT: On dead wood, usually of deciduous trees, especially *Acer* and *Fagus*, but also noted on *Populus*, *Salix*, and *Viburnum*; one collection on *Tsuga*; reported on *Betula* (Mont., Weir [227]).

DISTRIBUTION: Specimens have been examined from N.H., Vt., R.I., N.Y., Pa., Del., N.C., Ky., Ohio, Ind., Ill., Mich., Wis., Wyo., and Mont.; in Canada from Ontario, Manitoba, and Alberta.

ILLUSTRATIONS: Overholts, Torreya 17: pl. 1.

A more extended account of this species has been given by me in an earlier paper (153). It was long unrecognized as distinct from *Polyporus radiatus*, and Lloyd was the first to point out its most characteristic feature, viz., the conspicuous dark hyphae with enlarged, seta-like apices completely buried in the trama and in the context tissue. By crushing out a small bit of the context in KOH on a slide, or by making thin vertical sections of context or tubes (154, pl. 2, figs. 1–2), one can easily observe these bodies. The peculiar yellowish or yellowish-green color of the pileus and the colored spores are additional diagnostic characters.

Wood decayed by this fungus is soft and fibrous; the rot is a general delignifying decay of the sapwood, usually with considerable rusty yellow in its coloration. Campbell and Davidson (30) report that this species forms sterile conchs, not unlike those produced by *Poria obliqua*, on living beech and red maple. They report also the presence on these hosts of definite cankers that are to be attributed to this fungus.

161. POLYPORUS HISPIDUS Bull. ex Fries

Syst. Myc. 1: 362. 1821

(Figs. 314, 319, 586, 619, 623, 637, and Plate 130)

Boletus hispidus Bull., Herb. France, pl. 210. 1785.
Polyporus endocrocinus Berk., London Jour. Bot. 6: 320. 1847.
Inonotus hirsutus Scop. ex Murr., Torrey Bot. Club Bul. 31: 594. 1904.

Sporophore sessile, at first soft and spongy, then tough and firmer' watery when fresh, rigid on drying; pileus convex or plane, 5–30 × 8–25 × 2–10 cm., yellowish brown to rusty red or in age almost blackish, covered with a dense hirsute or hispid tomentum that may in part weather away; context usually bright rusty yellow above and toward the margin, dark reddish brown next the hymenium, but in small plants and in age becoming uniformly dark rusty brown, 1–7 cm. thick; pore surface rusty yellow to brown or with an olivaceous tinge, becoming darker where bruised and on drying, the tubes 0.5–2.5 cm. long, the mouths angular, thin-walled, denticulate or entire, averaging 2–4 per mm.; spores broadly ellipsoid to globose, smooth, chestnut-brown, 7.5–10 × 6.5–9 μ; setae apparently absent in some specimens, rare or rather abundant in others, 20–24 × 6–8 μ; main hyphae mostly chestnut-brown, simple, with some cross walls but no clamps, 5–9(–12) μ in diameter, others of somewhat smaller diameter, lighter in color, and with some branching; all parts black, or red then quickly black, in KOH. (Compare no. 157, *Polyporus dryophilus*.)

HABITAT: On living trunks of deciduous trees, noted on *Carya* *Fraxinus*, *Juglans*, *Morus*, *Quercus*, *Salix*, and *Schinus*; rarely on coniferous trees, noted on *Abies* and *Pinus*.

DISTRIBUTION: Specimens have been examined from Mass., Conn., N.Y., Pa., N.J., Del., Md., D.C., Va., W. Va., N.C., Ga., Fla., Ala., La., Tenn., Ohio, Ind., Mo., Kans., Texas, N. Mex., Ore., and Calif.; reported from Mich. (Baxter [5]) and Iowa (Wolf [234]).

ILLUSTRATIONS: Baxter, Mich. Acad. Sci. Arts and Letters Papers 3: pl. 8; Sleeth and Bidwell, Jour. Forestry 35: 779.

This species is related somewhat to *Polyporus dryophilus* and to *P. cuticularis*, especially the latter, from which it differs in the larger size, in the habit of growing at considerable heights and from wounds in living trees, and in the larger and more constantly globose spores. It differs from *P. dryophilus* in the more hispid pileus, the absence of a central core, and the considerably larger and more globose spores. The setae are much narrower and less conical than those of *P. dryadeus*.

I have examined some sporophores thoroughly, and not found setae. In others they are present, often only one or two to a pore in thin sections, but sometimes much more abundant. Lloyd says, "Setae rare and uncertain," and in my previous work I had recorded their absence from the hymenium of this species. Considering the variation in this respect, the spores become the most marked and certain character of the species. The hyphae differ considerably in young and old plants. In young specimens there is a preponderance of hyphae of the smaller diameters with unthickened walls. In the older sporophores the walls of the hyphae become partially thickened and sometimes somewhat scabrous, and very dark in KOH solution.

Polyporus Munzii Lloyd may belong here, having spores 6.5–8 × 4.5–6 μ, but often lacking setae, as sometimes happens in *P. hispidus*. *P. Patouillardii* Rick, as doubtfully reported from California by Lloyd on *Salix*, presumably belongs here, also.

The decay produced by this fungus is of the general delignifying type, the wood being uniformly soft and spongy throughout, and straw-colored to pale yellowish brown. No black zones are present (5, 6). The fungus inhabits the heartwood of living trees and, as has been reported, always or nearly always fruits in connection with large cankered areas on the trees. Sleeth and Bidwell (202) believe these cankers are caused by the fungus. I was loath to agree at first, but in view of other similar developments (see under *Polyporus glomeratus*, *Fomes igniarius*, *Daedalea unicolor*, and so on), it now seems that this idea must be accepted. The loss due to decay by this species was found to be as much as 33 per cent of the board-foot volume of the trees on a selected one-tenth-acre plot (202). The fungus is common in the Allegheny region.

162. POLYPORUS MUNZII Lloyd

Myc. Notes 67: 1163. 1922

(Figs. 672–673 and Plate 132)

Inonotus Schini Brown, Ariz. Agr. Exp. Sta. Bul. 132: 448. 1930.

Sporophore sessile, probably fleshy-tough when fresh, becoming corky at maturity and rather hard and rigid on drying; pilei simple or somewhat imbricate, plane or somewhat convex, 5–17 × 4–23 × 1.5–10 cm., at first orange-citrine, becoming snuff-brown or rusty brown with age, with a short velvety tomentum when young, more glabrate with age, scarcely zonate; context rusty brown to "Vandyke brown," 1–2 cm. thick, zonate in dried specimens; pore surface hoary to dark brown, the tubes 5–20 mm. long, the mouths angular, rather thick-walled, entire, averaging 2–3 per mm.; spores ellipsoid and often somewhat flattened on one side or subglobose, smooth, dark brown in KOH, 6.5–8 × 4.5–6 μ; basidia 5–7 μ in diameter, with rather thick sterigmata; setae very rare, narrow-fusoid, 20–24 × 6–8 μ, sharp-pointed, projecting beyond the basidia for not more than one third their length; no imbedded setal hyphae; context hyphae simple, straight, mostly with partially thickened walls, with very occasional cross walls but no clamps, 4–8 μ in diameter; all parts quickly black in KOH solution.

HABITAT: On trunks or branches of living trees of *Morus, Populus, Salix,* and *Schinus.*

DISTRIBUTION: Specimens have been examined only from Ariz., Utah, and Calif.

This species belongs to a group that includes *Polyporus ludovicianus, P. cuticularis, P. texanus,* and *P. hispidus.* The spores are too large and not of the correct shape for the first of these species, which, in addition, fruits at the base of living trees. The sporophores are much too large to be referred to *P. cuticularis.* The present species seems to be distinct from *P. texanus* in size and in the very different nature of the pileus surface. The microscopic characters ally it with that species, but the spores seem to be considerably darker when mounted in KOH. Nor have I ever seen setae in *P. texanus.* Nevertheless, *P. Munzii* and *P. texanus* may represent the same species. *P. Munzii* differs from *P. hispidus* in the smaller and darker spores, the less strongly developed pubescence, and the lack of the peculiar grained appearance of the context of that species. I am much indebted to Professor J. G. Brown for sending me authentic specimens and to Dr. P. A. Munz for a part of the type collection. Apparently the type collection is a mixture, for a portion of a sporophore of *Fomes fomentarius* was included in it.

The fungus produces a brown heart rot of its host, probably quite similar to that caused by *Polyporus cuticularis* and *P. hispidus*.

OMITTED SPECIES

(Entries not in brackets were included by Dr. Overholts,
but were not fully described; those in brackets have been
added to cover species recently proposed.—J.L.L.)

Polyporus albidus Schaeff. ex Fries. All that is known concerning this species in America is given by Lowe (123, p. 141). A number of collections at the New York State Museum at Albany, New York, referred by Peck to *P. epileucus* and var. *candidus*, may belong here. If they do, the species is best characterized by the soft and chalky-friable nature of the context and upper surface of the pileus. Lowe says that in its microscopic characters it is about the same as *P. immitis*, which, however, does not have the distinctive chalkiness.

[*Polyporus Arnoldae* Murr., *Torrey Bot. Club Bul.* 65: 653. 1938. According to Murrill, this species is similar to *P. albiceps*, except that it is deeply umbilicate, very thin, and not pure white. No spores were found on the type material, but they are described as being ellipsoid, 5–6 × 3–4 µ.]

[*Tyromyces avellaneialbus* Murr., *Torrey Bot. Club Bul.* 65: 657. 1938. The type material of this species appears to agree with *Polyporus fumidiceps*.]

[*Grifola cristatiformis* Murr., *Lloydia* 6: 227. 1943. This species is said by its author to differ from *Polyporus cristatus* in the color of the pore surface, which is described as "grayish-ocher to isabelline-avellaneous, at length fulvous."]

[*Polyporus Gratzianus* Murr., *Florida Acad. Sci. Jour.* 8: 197. 1945. The type material of this species does not appear to differ from *P. biennis*. Dr. Murrill maintains that it is a distinct species.]

[*Trametes Humeana* Murr., *Torrey Bot. Club Bul.* 65: 656. 1938. This species is very similar to *Polyporus fissilis*, except that the context is punky when dry.]

Polyporus iowensis Lloyd. This species was described from Iowa by Lloyd (*Myc. Notes* 75: 1363. 1925). It was included in the Iowa species by Wolf (234, p. 63), and was redescribed by Lowe (123, p. 145) on the basis of specimens collected in Michigan. In none of these descriptions is it evident that the characters are sufficiently distinctive to separate the species from *P. galactinus*.

[*Tyromyces leucomallellus* Murr., *Torrey Bot. Club Bul.* 67: 63. 1940. Sporophore is quite similar to that of *Polyporus fragilis*, except that it is much softer, being comparable in this respect to *P. leucospongia*.]

Polyporus lignosus Klotzsch. This species, represented in the key but not further accounted for, may occur in the area covered by the present manual. It is a common and very destructive tropical species. It is described by Lloyd (115, p. 230).

[*Inonotus ludovicianus melleus* Murr., *Torrey Bot. Club Bul.* 66: 34. 1939. This is a variety of *Polyporus ludovicianus*, differing, according to its author, from the species by being "honey-yellow banded with darker zones, tubes not stuffed when young, and spores somewhat smaller ($5 \times 3\ \mu$)."]

[*Tyromyces magnisporus* Murr., *Torrey Bot. Club Bul.* 67: 64. 1940. This is a *Trametes*-like plant similar to *Polyporus robiniophilus*, but with much more slender hyphae, 2–$3\ \mu$ in diameter, and spores often truncate at one end.]

[*Coriolus membranaceus Taxodii* Murr., *Torrey Bot. Club Bul.* 65: 657. 1938. This is a variety of *Polyporus tenuis* on cypress, with dark gray zones and margin.]

[*Coltricia Mowryana* Murr., *Torrey Bot. Club Bul.* 67: 228. 1940. This species is somewhat similar to *Polyporus Montagnei*, but differs in having smaller pores, 3 per mm., and occasional setae.]

[*Tyromyces Newellianus* Murr., *Torrey Bot. Club Bul.* 67: 64. 1940. The type material of this species appears to be *Polyporus fragilis*. Dr. Murrill disagrees: "*Polyporus fragilis* has a whitish tomentose surface; spores averaging $5 \times 2\ \mu$; and always grows on coniferous wood. *T. Newellianus* is ochraceous, not tomentose, with spores 3–$4 \times 1\ \mu$, and always occurs on hardwood."]

Polyporus occidentalis Klotzsch. This species is illustrated in Figs. 58, 59, and 229, and on Plate 131, but Dr. Overholts did not describe it. The fungus is a common and widely distributed one. It must not be confused with *P. occidentalis* (Murr.) Sacc. & Trott., which was placed in synonymy under *P. spumeus* by Dr. Overholts.

[*Tyromyces Pini-glabrae* Murr., *Torrey Bot. Club Bul.* 67: 65. 1940. The type material of this species appears to be young specimens of *Polyporus amorphus*. Dr. Murrill agrees.]

[*Tyromyces pseudolacteus* Murr., *Torrey Bot. Club Bul.* 67: 65. 1940. The type material of this species which was seen was sterile; it appears to agree with *Polyporus fumidiceps*. Dr. Murrill maintains that it is a distinct species.]

[*Polyporus Rhoadsii* Murr., *Torrey Bot. Club Bul.* 65: 653. 1938. This species is similar to *P. varius*, except that it has an ochraceous squamulose surface and spores 6 × 3 μ.]

[*Polyporus Stewartae* Coker, *Elisha Mitchell Soc. Jour.* 64: 295. 1948. This species is somewhat similiar to *P. cristatus*, but has a buffy-red upper surface and somewhat longer and narrower spores, 5–8 × 3–4.5 μ.]

[*Coriolus subabietinus* Murr., *Torrey Bot. Club Bul.* 65: 658. 1938. The type material of this species is sterile, and the plant is of unknown affinities.]

[*Abortiporus subabortivus* Murr., *Torrey Bot. Club Bul.* 65: 655. 1938. The type material of this species is very similar to *Polyporus Berkeleyi*, but has smaller (6 × 5 μ) oval spores. Dr. Murrill maintains that it is very distinct from *P. Berkeleyi*.]

[*Coriolus sublimitatus* Murr., *Torrey Bot. Club Bul.* 65: 658. 1938. The type material of this species is sterile, and the plant is of unknown affinities.]

[*Scutiger subrubescens* Murr., *Torrey Bot. Club Bul.* 67: 277. 1940. The type material of this species does not appear to differ from *Polyporus confluens*. Dr. Murrill believes it is a distinct species.]

[*Hapalopilus subrutilans* Murr., *Torrey Bot. Club Bul.* 65: 655. 1938. The type material of this species is less similar to *Polyporus rutilans* than to *P. ectypus* and *P. subectypus*, from which it differs in the ellipsoid spores, 3.5–4 × 2–2.5 μ.]

[*Rigidoporus surinamensis subauberianus* Murr., *Lloydia* 5: 156. 1942. The type material of this species appears to be a variety of *Polyporus zonalis* with a strong odor when fresh.]

[*Coriolus tenuispinifer* Murr., *Torrey Bot. Club Bul.* 65: 658. 1938. The type material of this species is a sterile, unidentified species of *Coriolus* parasitized by an imperfect fungus which has formed long brown spines.]

[*Tyromyces Tigertianus* Murr., *Lloydia* 6: 228. 1943. The type material of this species appears to be *Trametes Humeana*.   Dr. Murrill believes it is a distinct species.]

[*Scutiger Tisdalei* Murr., *Lloydia* 6: 227. 1943.   The type material of this species appears to be a noncystidiate condition of *Polyporus biennis*.   Dr. Murrill does not agree, maintaining that it is a distinct species.]

[*Polyporus Westii* Murr., *Torrey Bot. Club Bul.* 65: 651. 1938. The type material of this species resembles *P. melanopus*, but the sporophore grew on top of a log and the base is not so distinctly darkened.]

BIBLIOGRAPHY

1. ABBOTT, F. H.   The red rot of conifers.   Vermont Agr. Exp. Sta. Bul. 191. 1915.

2. AMES, ADELINE.   A consideration of structure in relation to genera of the Polyporaceae.   Ann. Mycol. 11: 211–253. 1913.

3. BAILEY, H. E.   The biology of *Polyporus basilaris*.   Torrey Bot. Club Bul. 68: 112–120. 1941.

4. BARTHOLOMEW, E.   The fungous flora of Kansas.   46 pp.   1927.[1]

5. BAXTER, D. V.   The heart rot of black ash caused by *Polyporus hispidus* Fr.   Mich. Acad. Sci. Arts and Letters Papers 3: 39–50. 1924.

6. —— The biology and pathology of some of the hardwood heart-rotting fungi. I.   Amer. Jour. Bot. 12: 522–552. 1925.

7. —— (Same title.) II.   *Ibid.* 12: 553–576. 1925.

8. —— *Fomes fraxineus* Fr. in culture.   Mich. Acad. Sci. Arts and Letters Papers 4, 1: 55–66. 1925.

9. —— Some porias from the region of the Lake States.   *Ibid.* 6: 67–76. 1927.

10. —— (Same title.) II.   *Ibid.* 9: 39–46. 1929.

11. —— Some resupinate polypores from the region of the Great Lakes.
    a.   III.   *Ibid.* 15: 191–228. 1932.
    b.   IV.   *Ibid.* 17: 421–439. 1933.
    c.   V.   *Ibid.* 19: 305–332. 1934.
    d.   VI.   *Ibid.* 20: 273–281. 1935.
    e.   VII.   *Ibid.* 21: 243–267. 1936.
    f.   VIII.   *Ibid.* 22: 275–295. 1937.
    g.   IX.   *Ibid.* 23: 285–305. 1938.
    h.   X.   *Ibid.* 24, 1: 167–188. 1939.
    i.   XI.   *Ibid.* 25, 1: 145–170. 1940.
    j.   XII.   *Ibid.* 26, 1: 107–121. 1941.
    k.   XIII.   *Ibid.* 27, 1: 139–161. 1942.
    l.   XIV.   *Ibid.* 28, 1: 215–233. 1943.

[1] Though the letter of transmittal in the front of this publication indicates that it is a special research bulletin of the Kansas Agricultural Station, the publication bears no bulletin number.

m. XV. *Ibid.* 29, 1: 85–109. 1944.

n. XVI. *Ibid.* 30, 1: 175–191. 1945.

12. BISBY, G. R., A. H. R. BULLER, AND J. DEARNESS. The fungi of Manitoba. 1929.

13. —— —— —— Additions to the fungous flora of Manitoba. Canad. Pl. Dis. Survey 13: 93–102. 1933.

14. —— —— —— W. P. FRASER, AND R. C. RUSSELL. The fungi of Manitoba and Saskatchewan. 1938.

15. BONDARZEW, A., AND R. SINGER. Zur Systematik der Polyporaceen. Ann. Mycol. 39: 43–65. 1941.

16. BOSE, S. R. Cytology of secondary spore formation in *Ganoderma*. Phytopathology 25: 426–429. 1935.

17. —— Moisture-relation as a determinant factor in the transformation of the basidia of certain Polyporaceae. Mycologia 35: 33–46. 1943.

18. BOURDOT, H., AND A. GALZIN. Hyménomycètes de France. 1927.

19. BOYCE, J. S. The dry-rot of incense cedar. U. S. Dept. Agr. Bul. 871. 1920.

20. —— Decays and discolorations in airplane woods. *Ibid.* 1128. 1923.

21. —— A study of decay in Douglas fir in the Pacific Northwest. *Ibid.* 1163. 1923.

22. —— Decay in Pacific Northwest conifers. Osborn Bot. Lab. Bul. 1. 1930.

23. —— Decay and other losses in Douglas fir in western Oregon and Washington. U. S. Dept. Agr. Tech. Bul. 286. 1932.

24. —— Forest pathology. 1938.

25. BRENCKLE, J. F. North Dakota fungi. II. Mycologia 10: 199–221. 1918.

26. BURT, E. A. *Merulius* in North America. Mo. Bot. Gard. Ann. 4: 305–362. 1917.

27. CAMPBELL, W. A. The cultural characteristics of *Fomes connatus*. Mycologia 29: 567–571. 1937.

28. —— *Daedalea unicolor* decay and associated cankers of maples and other hardwoods. Jour. Forestry 37: 974–977. 1939.

29. —— AND R. W. DAVIDSON. A *Poria* as the fruiting stage of the fungus causing the sterile conks on birch. Mycologia 30: 553–560. 1938.

30. —— —— Sterile conks of *Polyporus glomeratus* and associated cankers on beech and red maple. *Ibid.* 31: 606–611. 1939.

31. —— —— Cankers and decay of yellow birch associated with *Fomes igniarius* var. *laevigatus*. Jour. Forestry 39: 559–560. 1941.

32. CAMPBELL, A. H., AND R. G. MUNSON. Zone lines in plant tissues. III. The black lines formed by *Polyporus squamosus* (Huds.) Fr. Ann. Appl. Biol. 23: 453–464. 1936.

33. CHILDS, T. W. Variability of *Polyporus Schweinitzii* in culture. Phytopathology 27: 29–50. 1937.

34. CLEMENTS, F. E. Minnesota plant studies. IV. Minnesota mushrooms. 1910.

35. COKER, W. C. New or noteworthy Basidiomycetes. Elisha Mitchell Sci. Soc. Jour. 43: 129–145. 1927.

36. COOKE, M. C. Praecursores ad monographia polypororum. Grevillea 13: 80–87, 114–119; 14: 17–21, 77–87, 109–115; 15: 19–27, 50–60. 1885–1886.

37. COOKE, W. B. A nomenclatorial survey of the genera of pore fungi. Lloydia 3: 81–104. 1940.

38. —— Resupinate pore fungi in Oregon. Amer. Midland Nat. 27: 677–695. 1942.

39. DETMERS, FREDA. A preliminary report on a serious twig blight of American elm. Phytopathology 12: 47. 1922. (Abstract.)

40. DODGE, B. O. A list of fungi, chiefly saprophytes, from the region of Kewaunee County, Wisconsin. Wis. Acad. Sci. Arts Letters Trans. 17, 2: 806–845. 1914.

41. —— Fungi producing heart-rot of apple trees. Mycologia 8: 5–15. 1916.

42. DONK, M. A. Revision der niederländischen Homobasidiomycetae Aphyllophoraceae. II. Nederl. Mycol. Ver. Meded. 22: 1–278. 1933.

43. EADES, H. W. British Columbia softwoods; their decays and natural defects. Canada Dept. Int. Forest Serv. Bul. 80. 1932.

44. ELLIOTT, J. A. Wood-rots of peach trees caused by *Coriolus prolificans* and *C. versicolor*. Phytopathology 8: 615–617. 1918.

45. FAIRMAN, C. E. Hymenomycetae of Orleans County, N. Y. Rochester Acad. Sci. Proc. 2: 154–167. 1892.

46. FAULL, J. H. *Fomes officinalis* (Vill.), a timber-destroying fungus. Roy. Canad. Inst. Trans. 11: 185–209. 1916.

47. FAULL, J. H. Forest pathology, *in* Ontario Min. Lands and Forests Rept. for 1921: 259–266. 1921.

48. FENNELL, R. E. The Polyporaceae of Iowa. Iowa Acad. Sci. Proc. 31: 193–204. 1924.

49. FRIES, E. Systema mycologicum, Vol. I. 1821.

50. —— Elenchus fungorum, Vol. I. 1828.

51. —— Epicrisis systematis mycologici. 1836–1838.

52. —— Genera hymenomycetum. 1836.

53. —— Novae symbolae mycologicae. K. Vetenskaps-soc. Upsala, Nova Acta Reg. Soc. Sci. Upsaliensis III, 1: 17–136. 1855.

54. —— Hymenomycetes Europaei. 1874.

55. FRITZ, CLARA W. Cultural criteria for the distinction of wood-destroying fungi. Roy. Soc. Canada Trans., Ser. III, Vol. 17, Sect. V, pp. 191–288. 1923.

56. —— AND G. H. ROCHESTER. Red stain in jack pine. Canada Dept. Int. Forest Serv. Circ. 37. 1933.

57. GILLET, C. C. Les Champignons (Fungi, Hyménomycètes) qui croissent en France, Vols. I–IV. 1878–1890.

58. GOULD, C. Some Polyporaceae of southern West Virginia. South. Appalachian Club Jour. 1: 3–6. 1936.

59. GRAFF, P. W. North American polypores.—I. *Polyporus squamosus* and its varieties. Mycologia 28: 154–170. 1936.

60. GRAVES, A. H. Notes on diseases of trees in the southern Appalachians. I. Phytopathology 3: 129–139. 1913.

61. —— (Same title.) II. *Ibid.* 4: 5–10. 1914.

62. HADDOW, W. R. Studies in *Ganoderma*. Arnold Arboretum Jour. 12: 25–46. 1931.

63. —— On the classification, nomenclature, hosts, and geographical range of *Trametes Pini* (Thore) Fries. Brit. Mycol. Soc. Trans. 22: 182–193. 1938.

64. —— The disease caused by *Trametes Pini* (Thore) Fries in white pine (*Pinus Strobus* L.). Roy. Canad. Inst. Trans. 22, 1: 21–80. 1938.

65. —— On the history and diagnosis of *Polyporus tomentosus* Fries, *Polyporus circinatus* Fries, and *Polyporus dualis* Peck. Brit. Mycol. Soc. Trans. 25: 179–190. 1941.

66. HEDGCOCK, G. G. Notes on some diseases of trees in our national forests. II. Phytopathology 2: 73–80. 1912.

67. —— AND W. H. LONG. Preliminary notes on three rots of juniper. Mycologia 4: 109–114. 1912.

68. —— —— Heart-rot of oaks and poplars caused by *Polyporus dryophilus*. Jour. Agr. Res. 3: 65–78. 1914.

69. HEPTING, G. H., AND DOROTHY J. BLAISDELL. A protective zone in red gum fire scars. Phytopathology 26: 62–67. 1936.

70. —— AND A. D. CHAPMAN. Losses from heart rot in two shortleaf and loblolly pine stands. Jour. Forestry 36: 1193–1201. 1938.

71. HESLER, L. R. A preliminary report on polypores of eastern Tennessee. Tenn. Acad. Sci. Jour. 4: 3–10. 1929.

72. —— Notes on southern Appalachian fungi. *Ibid.* 6: 107–122. 1936.

73. —— A preliminary list of the fungi of the Great Smoky Mountains National Park. Castanea 2: 45–58. 1937.

74. HILBORN, M. T. The biology of *Fomes fomentarius*. Maine Agr. Exp. Sta. Bul. 409. 1942.

75. —— AND D. H. LINDER. The synonymy of *Fomes fomentarius*. Mycologia 31: 418–419. 1939.

76. —— AND F. H. STEINMETZ. Some epixylous fungi of Maine. Plant Dis. Rep. 20: 306–309. 1936.

77. HIRT, R. R. The biology of *Polyporus gilvus* (Schw.) Fries. N. Y. State Coll. Forestry Tech. Publ. 22. 1928.

78. —— *Fomes Everhartii* associated with the production of sterile rimose bodies on *Fagus grandifolia*. Mycologia 22: 310–311. 1930.

79. HOPP, H. Appearance of *Fomes igniarius* in culture. Phytopathology 26: 915–917. 1936.

80. —— Sporophore formation by *Fomes applanatus* in culture. *Ibid.* 28: 356–358. 1938.

81. —— The formation of colored zones by wood-destroying fungi in culture. *Ibid.* 28: 601–620. 1938.

82. HUBERT, E. E. The diagnosis of decay in wood. Jour. Agr. Res. 29: 523–567. 1924.

83. —— Manual of wood rots. 65 pp. [About 1927.]

84. —— Red-ray-rot in *Pinus ponderosa*. Northwest Sci. 2: 45–47. 1928.

85. HUBERT, E. E.   A butt-rot of balsam fir caused by *Polyporus balsameus* Pk.   Phytopathology 19: 725–732. 1929.

86. —— A root and butt rot of conifers caused by *Polyporus circinatus* Fr. *Ibid.* 19: 745–747. 1929.

87. —— An outline of forest pathology.   1931.

88. HUMPHREY, C. J.   Timber storage conditions in the eastern and southern states with reference to decay problems.   U. S. Dept. Agr. Bul. 510. 1917.

89. —— AND SIMEONA LEUS.   A partial revision of the *Ganoderma applanatum* group, with particular reference to its Oriental variants. Philippine Jour. Sci. 45: 483–589. 1931.

90. —— AND SIMEONA LEUS-PALO.   Studies and illustrations in the Polyporaceae.   III. Supplementary notes on the *Ganoderma applanatum* group.   *Ibid.* 49: 159–184. 1932.

91. JOHNSON, H. W., AND C. W. EDGERTON.   A heart rot of *Magnolia* caused by *Fomes geotropus*.   Mycologia 28: 292–295. 1936.

92. KALCHBRENNER, C.   Icones selectae hymenomycetum Hungariae, Pars I–IV.   1873–1877.

93. KARSTEN, P. A.   Sydvestra Finlands Polyporeer.   47 pp.   1859.

94. —— Symbolae ad mycologiam fennicam.   VI.   Soc. Fauna Flora Fenn. Meddel. 5: 15–46. 1879.

95. —— (Same title.) VII.   *Ibid.* 6: 1–6. 1881.

96. —— (Same title.) XXIX.   *Ibid.* 16: 84–106. 1889.

97. —— Enumeratio boletinearum et polyporearum fennicarum.   Rev. Mycol. 3, 9: 16–19. 1881.

98. KAUFERT, F.   Heart rot of balsam fir in the Lake States, with special reference to forest management.   Minn. Agr. Exp. Sta. Tech. Bul. 110. 1935.

99. KAUFFMAN, C. H.   The fungi of North Elba.   N. Y. State Mus. Bul. 179: 80–104. 1915.

100. —— Tennessee and Kentucky fungi.   Mycologia 9: 159–166. 1917.

101. —— Unreported Michigan fungi for 1915 and 1916, with an index to the hosts and substrata of basidiomycetes.   Mich. Acad. Sci. Ann. Rept. 19: 145–157. 1917.

102. —— The mycological flora of the higher Rockies of Colorado.   Mich. Acad. Sci. Arts and Letters Papers 1: 101–150. 1923.

103. —— The fungus flora of Mt. Hood, with some new species. *Ibid.* 5: 115–148. 1925.

104. —— *Polyporus anceps* and *Polyporus immitis.* Mycologia 18: 27–30. 1926.

105. —— A study of the fungous flora of the Lake Superior region of Michigan, with some new species. Mich. Acad. Sci. Arts and Letters Papers 9: 169–218. 1929.

106. —— The fungous flora of the Siskiyou Mountains in southern Oregon. *Ibid.* 11: 151–210. 1930.

107. —— AND H. M. KERBER. A study of the white heart-rot of locust, caused by *Trametes robiniophila.* Amer. Jour. Bot. 9: 493–508. 1922.

108. KUNZE, G., *in* E. Fries, Ecologae fungorum. Linnaea 5: 512. 1830.

109. LINNAEUS, CARL VON. Species plantarum, 1st ed., II, 1171–1186. 1753.

110. —— Systema plantarum, ed. novissima, cur. J. J. Reichard, Part IV. 1780.

111. LLOYD, C. G. Mycological notes, Nos. 1–75. 1898–1925.

112. —— Synopsis of the genus *Hexagona.* *In* Mycological writings 3: 1–46. 1910.

113. —— Synopsis of the section *Ovinus* of *Polyporus.* *Ibid.,* pp. 71–94. 1911.

114. —— Synopsis of the stipitate polyporoids. *Ibid.,* pp. 93–208. 1912.

115. —— Synopsis of the genus *Fomes.* *Ibid.* 4: 209–288. 1915.

116. —— Synopsis of the section *Apus* of the genus *Polyporus.* *Ibid.,* pp. 289–392. 1915.

117. LONG, W. H. Three undescribed heart-rots of hardwood trees, especially of oak. Jour. Agr. Res. 1: 109–128. 1913.

118. —— *Polyporus dryadeus,* a root parasite on the oak. *Ibid.* 1: 239–250. 1913.

119. —— A preliminary note on the cause of "pecky" cypress. Phytopathology 4: 39. 1914. (Abstract.)

120. —— A preliminary report on the occurrence of western red-rot in *Pinus ponderosa.* U. S. Dept. Agr. Bul. 490. 1917.

121. —— Investigations of the rotting of slash in Arkansas. *Ibid.* 496. 1917.

122. Long, W. H.   Two pocket rots of hardwood trees.   Torrey Bot. Club Bul. 66: 625–627. 1939.

123. Lowe, J. L.   Notes on some species of *Polyporus*.   Mich. Acad. Sci. Arts and Letters Papers 19: 141–148. 1934.

124. —— The Polyporaceae of New York State (pileate species).   N. Y. State Coll. Forestry Tech. Publ. 41. 1934.

125. —— The Polyporaceae of New York State (except *Poria*).   *Ibid.* 60. 1942.

126. —— The Polyporaceae of New York State (the genus *Poria*).   *Ibid.* 65. 1946.

127. McCallum, A. W.   Studies in forest pathology.   I. Decay in balsam fir (*Abies balsamea* Mill.).   Canada Dept. Agr. Bul., N.S. 104. 1928.

128. McDougall, W. B.   Some fungi that are rare or have not previously been reported from Illinois.   Ill. State Acad. Sci. Trans. 12: 104–107. 1919.

129. Mains, E. B.   Michigan fungi.   I.   Mich. Acad. Sci. Arts and Letters Papers 20: 81–93. 1935.

130. Maneval, W. E.   Parasitic and wood-destroying fungi of Boone County, Missouri.   Mo. Univ. Studies 1, 1: 63–111. 1926.

131. —— A list of Missouri fungi.   *Ibid.* 12, 3: 1–150. 1937.

132. Meinecke, E. P.   Forest tree diseases common in California and Nevada.   U. S. Dept. Agr., Forest Service.   1914.

133. —— Quaking aspen: A study in applied forest pathology.   U. S. Dept. Agr. Tech. Bul. 155. 1929.

134. Mounce, Irene.   Studies in forest pathology.   II. The biology of *Fomes pinicola* (Sw.) Cooke.   Canada Dept. Agr. Bul., N.S. 111. 1929.

135. —— Microscopic characters of sporophores produced in culture as an aid in identifying wood-destroying fungi.   Roy. Soc. Canada Trans., Ser. 3, Vol. 26, Sect. V, pp. 177–181. 1932.

136. —— and Ruth Macrae.   The behavior of paired monosporous mycelia of *Fomes roseus* (Alb. and Schw.) Cooke and *Fomes subroseus* (Weir) Overh.   Canad. Jour. Res., C, 15: 154–161. 1937.

137. —— —— Interfertility phenomena in *Fomes pinicola*.   *Ibid.* 16: 354–376. 1938.

138. MURRILL, W. A.   The Polyporaceae of North America.
    a.   I.   The genus *Ganoderma*.   Torrey Bot. Club Bul. 29: 599–608. 1902.
    b. II. The genus *Pyropolyporus*.   *Ibid.* 30: 109–120. 1903.
    c. III. The genus *Fomes*.   *Ibid.* 30: 225–232. 1903.
    d. IV. The genus *Elfvingia*.   *Ibid.* 30: 296–301. 1903.
    e.   V. The genera *Cryptoporus, Piptoporus, Scutiger* and *Porodiscus*.   *Ibid.* 30: 423–434. 1903.
    f. VI. The genus *Polyporus*.   *Ibid.* 31: 29–44. 1904.
    g. VII. The genera *Hexagona, Grifola, Romellia, Coltricia,* and *Coltriciella*.   *Ibid.* 31: 325–348. 1904.
    h. VIII. *Hapalopilus, Pycnoporus,* and new monotypic genera.   *Ibid.* 31: 415–428. 1904.
    i. IX. *Inonotus, Sesia* and monotypic genera.   *Ibid.* 31: 593–610. 1904.
    j.   X. *Agaricus, Lenzites, Cerrena,* and *Favolus*.   *Ibid.* 32: 83–103. 1905.
    k. XI. A synopsis of the brown pileate species.   *Ibid.* 32: 353–371. 1905.
    l. XII. A synopsis of the white and bright-colored pileate species.   *Ibid.* 32: 469–493. 1905.
    m. XIII. The described species of *Bjerkandera, Trametes,* and *Coriolus*.   *Ibid.* 32: 633–656. 1905.

139. —— Polyporaceae.   North Amer. Flora 9, 1–2: 1–131. 1907–1908.

140. —— Northern polypores.   1914.

141. —— Southern polypores.   1915.

142. —— Tropical polypores.   1915.

143. —— Western polypores.   1915.

144. —— Some described species of *Poria*.   Mycologia 11: 231–244. 1919.

145. —— Corrections and additions to the polypores of temperate North America.   *Ibid.* 12: 6–24. 1920.

146. —— Fungi from Hedgcock.   *Ibid.* 12: 41–42. 1920.

147. —— Light-colored resupinate polypores.
    a.   I. *Ibid.* 12: 77–92. 1920.
    b. II. *Ibid.* 12: 299–308. 1920.
    c. III. *Ibid.* 13: 83–100. 1921.
    d. IV. *Ibid.* 13: 171–178. 1921.

148. NEUMAN, J. J.   The Polyporaceae of Wisconsin.   Wis. Geol. and Nat. Hist. Survey Bul. 33. 1914.

149. ODELL, W. S.   List of mushrooms and other fleshy fungi of the Ottawa district.   Canada Dept. Mines, Museum Bul. 43. 1926.

150. OVERHOLTS, L. O.   Comparative studies in the Polyporaceae.   Mo. Bot. Gard. Ann. 2: 667–730. 1915.

151. —— The Polyporaceae of the middle-western United States.   Wash. Univ. Studies 3, 1: 3–98. 1915.

152. —— An undescribed timber decay of pitch pine.   Mycologia 9: 261–270. 1917.

153. —— The structure of *Polyporus glomeratus* Peck.   Torreya 17: 202–,206. 1917.

154. —— Research methods in the taxonomy of the Hymenomycetes. Internl. Cong. Plant Sci. Proc. 2: 1688–1712. 1929.

155. —— Diagnoses of American porias—III.   Some additional brown species, with a key to the common brown species of the United States and Canada.   Mycologia 23: 117–129. 1931.

156. —— The Polyporaceae of Pennsylvania.   I. The genus *Polyporus*. Pa. Agr. Exp. Sta. Tech. Bul. 298. 1933.

157. —— (Same title.)   II. The genera *Cyclomyces*, *Daedalea*, *Favolus*, *Fomes*, *Lenzites*, and *Trametes*.   *Ibid.* 316. 1935.

158. —— (Same title.)   III. The genus *Poria*.   *Ibid.* 418. 1942.

158a. —— New species of polypores.   Mycologia 44: 224–227. 1952.

159. OWENS, C. E.   Studies on the wood-rotting fungus, *Fomes Pini*.   I. Variations in morphology and growth habit.   Amer. Jour. Bot. 23: 144–149. 1936.

160. —— (Same title.)   II. Cultural characteristics.   *Ibid.* 23: 235–254. 1936.

161. PALISOT DE BEAUVOIS.   Flore d'Oware et Benin, I, 1.   1804.

162. PATOUILLARD, N.   Les Hyménomycètes d'Europe.   1887.

163. —— Essai taxonomique sur les familles et les genres des Hyménomycètes.   1900.

164. PECK, C. H.   Report of the Botanist.   N. Y. State Mus. Ann. Rept. 42: 38. 1889.

165. PERCIVAL, W. C.   A contribution to the biology of *Fomes Pini* (Thore) Lloyd.   N. Y. State Coll. Forestry Tech. Publ. 40. 1933.

166. PERSOON, C. H.   Neuer Versuch einer systematischen Eintheilung der Schwämme.   Römers Neues Mag. Bot. 1: 109. 1794.

167. —— Synopsis methodica fungorum. 1801.

168. —— Icones pictae rariorum fungorum. 1805.

169. —— Mycologia Europaea, Vols. 1–3. 1825.

170. PIEPER, E. J., C. J. HUMPHREY, AND S. F. ACREE. Synthetic culture media for wood-destroying fungi. Phytopathology 7: 214–220. 1917.

171. PILÁT, A. Monographie der europäischen Polyporaceen. Bot. Centbl. Beih. 48: 404–436. 1931; and 52: 23–95. 1934.

172. —— Polyporaceae. I–III. *In* Kavina, C., and A. Pilát, Atlas des champignons de l'Europe, Tome 3. 1936–1942.

173. POVAH, A. H. Some non-vascular cryptogams from Vermilion, Chippewa County, Michigan. Mich. Acad. Sci. Arts and Letters Papers 9: 253–272. 1929.

174. —— Fungi of Rock River, Michigan. *Ibid.* 13: 173–189. 1931.

175. —— The fungi of Isle Royale, Lake Superior. *Ibid.* 20: 113–156. 1935.

176. QUÉLET, L. Enchiridion fungorum. 1886.

177. RANKIN, W. H. Manual of tree diseases. 1918.

178. RAVENEL, H. W. Fungi caroliniani exsiccati, Fasc. III. 1855.

179. REA, C. British basidiomycetae, pp. 574–619. 1922.

180. RHOADS, A. S. The black zones formed by wood-destroying fungi. N. Y. State Coll. Forestry Tech. Publ. 8. 1917.

181. —— Some new or little known hosts for wood-destroying fungi. Phytopathology 7: 46–48. 1917.

182. —— (Same title.) II. *Ibid.* 8: 164–167. 1918.

183. —— (Same title.) III. *Ibid.* 11: 319–326. 1921.

184. —— The biology of *Polyporus pargamenus* Fries. N. Y. State Coll. Forestry Tech. Publ. 11. 1918.

185. RIDGWAY, R. Color standards and color nomenclature. 1912.

186. ROMELL, L. Hymenomycetes Austro-Americani. I. Svenska Vet.-Akad. Bihang till Handl. 26, Afd. III, No. 16, pp. 1–61 [sep. pag.]. 1901.

187. —— Hymenomycetes of Lappland. Arkiv för Bot. 11, 3: 1–35. 1911.

188. —— Remarks on some species of *Polyporus*. Svensk Bot. Tidskr. 20: 1–24. 1926.

189. ROSEN, H. R. A pink-colored form of *Polyporus sulphureus* and its probable relationship to root-rot of oaks. Mycologia 19: 191–194. 1927.

190. ROSTKOVIUS, F. W. T., *in* Sturm, Deutsch. Flora, Bd. 4. 1838.

191. SCHAEFFER, J. C. Fungorum qui in Bavaria et Palatinatu circa Ratisbonam nascuntur icones, Vols. I–IV. 1762–1774.

192. SCHEFFER, T. C. Progressive effects of *Polyporus versicolor* on the physical and chemical properties of red gum sapwood. U. S. Dept. Agr. Tech. Bul. 527. 1936.

193. SCHMITZ, H. Studies in wood decay. II. Enzyme action in *Polyporus volvatus* Peck and *Fomes igniarius* (L.) Gillet. Jour. Gen. Physiol. 3: 795–800. 1921.

194. —— Note concerning the decay of western yellow pine slash caused by *Polyporus volvatus* Peck. Phytopathology 12: 494–496. 1922.

195. —— Studies in wood decay. V. Physiological specialization in *Fomes pinicola* Fr. Amer. Jour. Bot. 12: 163–177. 1925.

196. —— AND L. W. R. JACKSON. Heartrot of aspen with special reference to forest management in Minnesota. Minn. Agr. Exp. Sta. Tech. Bul. 50. 1927.

197. —— AND F. KAUFERT. Studies in wood decay. VIII. The effect of the addition of dextrose and dextrose and asparagine on the rate of decay of Norway pine sapwood by *Lenzites trabea* and *Lentinus lepideus*. Amer. Jour. Bot. 25: 443–448. 1938.

198. DE SCHWEINITZ, L. D. Synopsis fungorum in America Boreali media degentium. Amer. Phil. Soc. Trans. II, 4: 141–318. 1832.

199. SEAVER, F. J., AND P. F. SHOPE. Some Rocky Mountain basidiomycetes. Colo. Univ. Studies 23: 189–197. 1936.

200. SHOPE, P. F. The Polyporaceae of Colorado. Mo. Bot. Gard. Ann. 18: 287–456. 1931.

201. ŠKORIĆ, V. *Poria obliqua* (Pers.) Bres. Prinos poznavanju biologije i patološkog djelovanja gljive. Ann. Exp. for., Zagreb, 1937. 31 pp. 1937. (*Reviewed in* Rev. Appl. Mycol. 16: 506. 1937.)

202. SLEETH, B., AND C. B. BIDWELL. *Polyporus hispidus* and a canker of oaks. Jour. Forestry 35: 778–785. 1937.

203. SMITH, E. C. *Trametes hispida*, a destructive parasite in apple orchards. Mycologia 22: 221–222. 1930.

204. SNELL, W. H. Studies of certain fungi of economic importance in the

decay of building timbers. U. S. Dept. Agr. Bul. (Prof. Paper) 1053. 1922.

205. —— W. G. Hutchinson, and K. H. N. Newton. Temperature and moisture relations of *Fomes roseus* and *Trametes subrosea*. Mycologia 20: 276–291. 1928.

206. Spaulding, P. A disease of black oaks caused by *Polyporus obtusus* Berk. Mo. Bot. Gard. Ann. Rept. 16: 109–116. 1905.

207. —— The timber rot caused by *Lenzites sepiaria*. U. S. Dept. Agr. Pl. Ind. Bul. 214. 1911.

208. —— Decay of slash of northern white pine in southern New England. U. S. Dept. Agr. Tech. Bul. 132. 1929.

209. —— Some wood-inhabiting fungi of Vermont. Vermont Bot. and Bird Club Joint Bul. 14: 28–50. 1930.

210. Stevens, N. E. *Polystictus versicolor* as a wound parasite of catalpa. Mycologia 4: 263–270. 1912.

211. Stevenson, J. A., and Edna M. Ermold. Natural history of Plummers Island, Maryland. V. Fungi. Biol. Soc. Wash. Proc. 49: 123–132. 1936.

212. Swartz, D. Studies of Arkansas fungi. Amer. Midland Nat. 14: 714–719. 1933.

213. Verrall, A. F. Variation in *Fomes igniarius* (L.) Gill. Minn. Agr. Exp. Sta. Tech. Bul. 117. 1937.

214. von Schrenk, H. Two diseases of red cedar, caused by *Polyporus juniperinus* n. sp. and *Polyporus carneus* Nees. U. S. Dept. Agr. Veg. Phys. Path. Bul. 21. 1900.

215. —— Some diseases of New England conifers. *Ibid.* 25. 1900.

216. —— A disease of the white ash caused by *Polyporus fraxinophilus*. U. S. Dept. Agr. Pl. Ind. Bul. 32. 1903.

217. —— Two trunk diseases of the mesquite. Mo. Bot. Gard. Ann. 1: 243–252. 1914.

218. —— A trunk disease of the lilac. *Ibid.* 1: 253–262. 1914.

219. —— and P. Spaulding. Diseases of deciduous forest trees. U. S. Dept. Agr. Pl. Ind. Bul. 149. 1909.

220. Wean, R. E. The parasitism of *Polyporus Schweinitzii* on seedling *Pinus Strobus*. Phytopathology 27: 1124–1142. 1937.

221. Weir, J. R. Two new wood-destroying fungi. Jour. Agr. Res. 2: 163–166. 1914.

222. WEIR, J. R.   Notes on wood destroying fungi which grow on both coniferous and deciduous trees.   I.   Phytopathology 4: 271–276. 1914.

223. —— (Same title.) II.   *Ibid.* 7: 379–380. 1917.

224. —— An unusual host of *Fomes fomentarius* Fries.   *Ibid.* 4: 339. 1914.

225. —— Some observations on abortive sporophores of wood-destroying fungi.   *Ibid.* 5: 48–50. 1915.

226. —— New hosts for some forest tree fungi.   *Ibid.* 5: 71–72. 1915.

227. —— Montana forest tree fungi.   I. Polyporaceae.   Mycologia 9: 129–137. 1917.

228. —— *Polyporus dryadeus* (Pers.) Fr. on conifers in the Northwest.   Phytopathology 11: 99. 1921.

229. —— Nature and cause of diseases and defects.   Pp. 19–55 *in* Trade course in log scaling for Idaho woods.   Idaho Voc. Ed. Bul. Vol. 5, No. 5. 1922.

230. —— The genus *Polystictus* and decay of living trees.   Phytopathology 13: 184–186. 1923.

231. —— Butt rot in *Diospyros virginiana* caused by *Polyporus Spraguei*.   *Ibid.* 17: 339–340. 1927.

232. WHITE, J. H.   On the biology of *Fomes applanatus* (Pers.) Wallr.   Roy. Canad. Inst. Trans. 12: 133–174. 1919.

233. WILSON, G. W.   The Polyporaceae of Fayette, Iowa.   Iowa Acad. Sci. Proc. 16: 19–22. 1909.

234. WOLF, MARGARET M.   The Polyporaceae of Iowa.   Iowa Univ. Studies Nat. Hist. 14: 1–93. 1931.

235. ZELLER, S. M.   Notes on *Cryptoporus volvatus*.   Mycologia 7: 121–125. 1915.

236. —— Contributions to our knowledge of Oregon fungi. I.   *Ibid.* 14: 173–199. 1922.

237. —— Contribution to our knowledge of Oregon fungi. III.   *Ibid.* 21: 97–111. 1929.

238. —— The brown-pocket heart rot of stone-fruit trees caused by *Trametes subrosea* Weir.   Jour. Agr. Res. 33: 687–693. 1926.

PLATES AND EXPLANATIONS

(The specimen numbers, unless otherwise indicated, are those on the collections in the Overholts Herbarium.)

PLATE 1

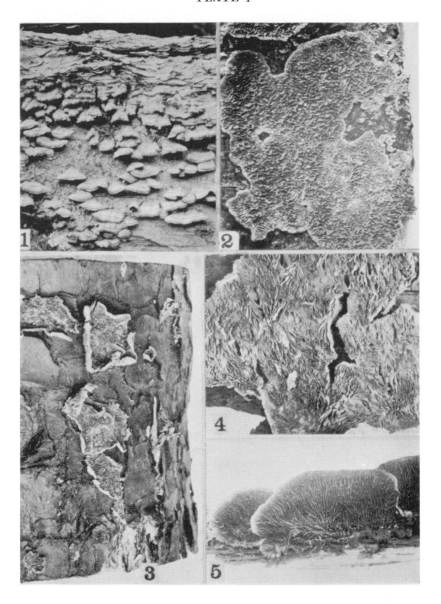

Figs. 1–4. *Polyporus abietinus*: Fig. 1, typical appearance, on *Pinus* bark;
Fig. 2, large- and irregular-pored resupinate form, often with violaceous
or lavender coloration, × 1.2; Fig. 3, usual effused-reflexed form with
poroid hymenium, phot. by A. S. Rhoads, × 0.8; Fig. 4, lamellate-
irpiciform resupinate type, phot. by A. S. Rhoads, × 0.8

Fig. 5. *Polyporus abietinus* var. *Abietis*: typical hymenial view, No. 9434,
× 0.8

PLATE 2

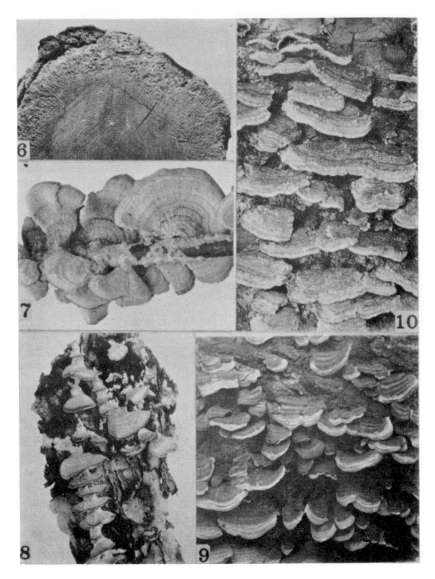

FIGS. 6–9. *Polyporus pargamenus*: Fig. 6, white sap rot produced in *Quercus alba* log, × 0.4; Fig. 7, upper-surface view of typical sporophores encircling small twig, Pa. State College Herb., × 0.8; Fig. 8, upper-surface view of small sporophores on bark of log, Pa. State College Herb., × 0.8; Fig. 9, upper-surface view of densely imbricate sporophores, Pa. State College Herb., × 0.8

FIG. 10. *Polyporus abietinus* var. *Abietis*: upper-surface view of old sporophores, × 0.8

PLATE 3

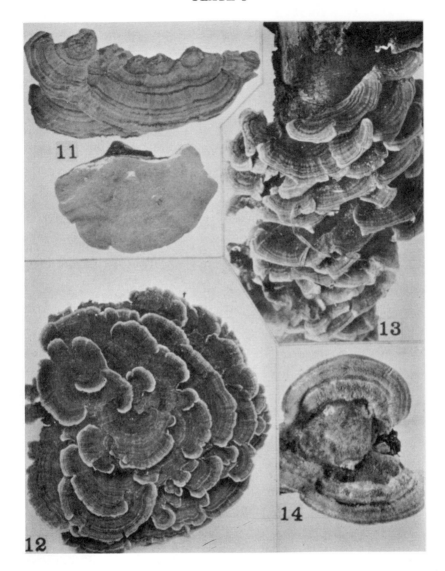

FIGS. 11–13. *Polyporus versicolor*: Fig. 11, upper- and lower-surface views
of thick and strongly zonate form, No. 3001, × 0.8; Fig. 12, upper-
surface view of typical dark-colored rosette form, Mo. Bot. Gard. Herb.,
× 0.4; Fig. 13, usual imbricate sporophores, No. 11323, × 0.8

FIG. 14. *Polyporus hirsutus*: upper-surface view of sporophore, Pa. State
College Herb., × 0.8

PLATE 4

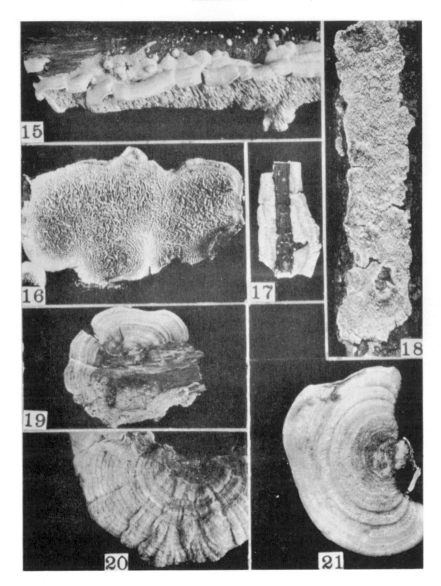

FIGS. 15–18. *Polyporus Tulipiferae*: Fig. 15, usual effused-reflexed form, Pa. State College Herb., × 0.8; Fig. 16, pore-surface view of resupinate form, Pa. State College Herb., × 0.8; Fig. 17, upper-surface view of sporophore reflexed on two sides of small twig, × 0.8; Fig. 18, resupinate sporophore developed in oblique situation, Pa. State College Herb., × 1.1

FIGS. 19–20. *Polyporus pinsitus*: upper-surface views, × 0.8

FIG. 21. *Polyporus pavonius*: upper-surface view, × 1.1

PLATE 5

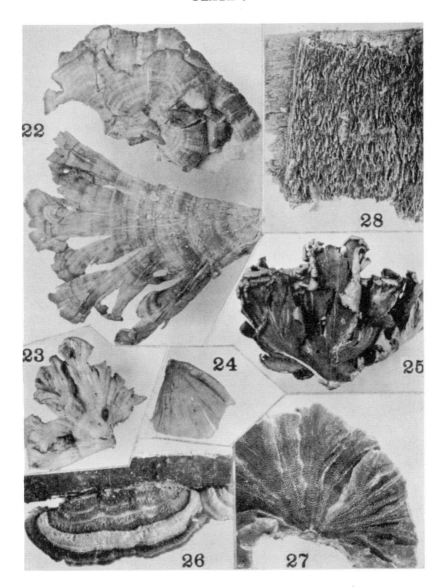

FIGS. 22–25. *Polyporus tenuis*: Fig. 22, upper-surface views of large specimens, N. Y. Bot. Gard. Herb., × 0.8; Figs. 23–24, upper-surface views
of small specimens, N. Y. Bot. Gard. Herb., × 0.8; Fig. 25, lower-
surface view, N. Y. Bot. Gard. Herb., × 0.8

FIG. 26. *Polyporus hirsutus*: typical upper-surface view of brown-margined
form, Pa. State College Herb., × 0.8

FIG. 27. *Polyporus pinsitus*: lower-surface view, No. 8686, × 1.1

FIG. 28. *Polyporus Tulipiferae*: resupinate, hydnoid form, No. 14295, × 1.5

PLATE 6

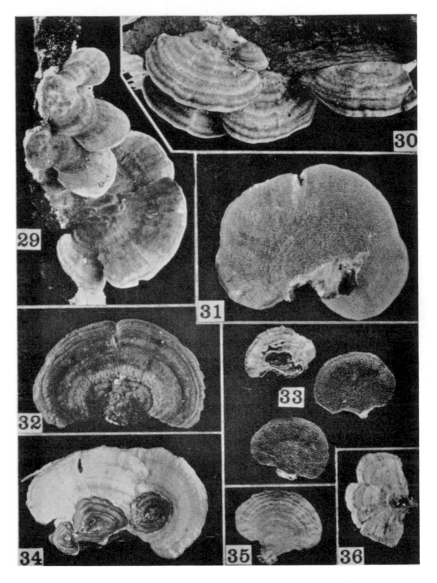

FIGS. 29–30. *Polyporus velutinus*: upper-surface views, Nos. 12828 and 3803, × 1.1

FIGS. 31–32. *Polyporus hirsutus*: lower- and upper-surface views of typical specimens, × 0.8

FIGS. 33–36. *Polyporus conchifer*: Figs. 33–34, views showing remnants of brown sterile cup, zoned within, on base of sporophore; Figs. 35–36, sporophores with the sterile cup lacking or inconspicuous; all × 0.8

PLATE 7

Figs. 37–38. *Polyporus subchartaceus*: lower- and upper-surface views of typical *Populus* form of species, Nos. 9493 and 9974, × 1

Figs. 39–40. *Polyporus pargamenus*: Fig. 39, upper-surface view of nearly azonate specimen, No. 5559 (sent in by P. J. Anderson as No. 2763), × 0.8; Fig. 40, lower-surface view of typical specimens, showing hydnoid pore surface, phot. by C. S. Parker, × 0.8

Figs. 41–43. *Polyporus pubescens*: Fig. 41, imbricate, typically sessile specimens, Pa. State College Herb., × 0.8; Fig. 42, upper-surface view of typical specimen on *Fagus*, × 0.8; Fig. 43, effused-reflexed specimen, No. 14870, × 0.8

PLATE 8

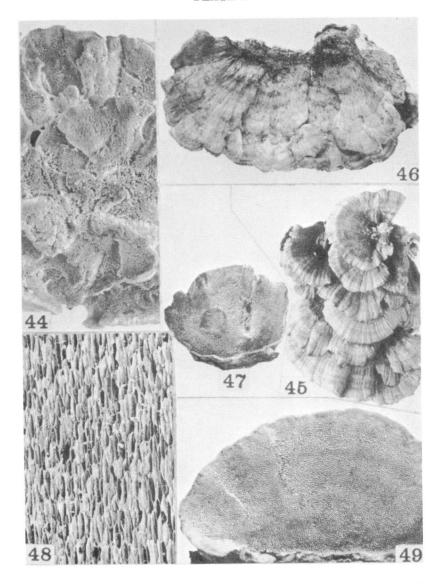

FIGS. 44–45. *Polyporus pubescens*: Fig. 44, pore-surface view of typical specimen, Pa. State College Herb., × 0.8; Fig. 45, upper-surface view of
strongly radiate-striate, imbricate specimens, No. 2632, × 0.8

FIGS. 46–47. *Polyporus pubescens* var. *Grayii*: Fig. 46, upper-surface view,
No. 253, × 0.8; Fig. 47, lower-surface view, No. 3564, × 1.1

FIG. 48. Hemlock wood completely decayed by *Polyporus abietinus*, Pa.
State College Herb., × 0.8

FIG. 49. *Polyporus hirsutus*: pore-surface view, No. 350, × 1.5

PLATE 9

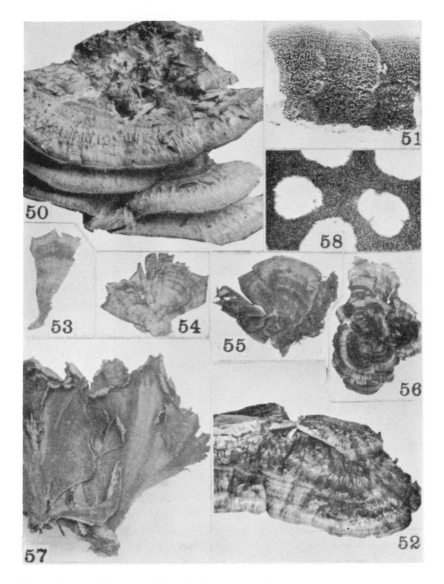

FIGS. 50–52. *Polyporus biformis*: Fig. 50, well-developed imbricate cluster of more than usual size, No. 8775, × 0.8; Fig. 51, pore-surface view of usual sporophore with subdaedaloid hymenium, No. 173, × 1; Fig. 52, typical specimen with matted-fibrillose upper surface, × 0.8

FIGS. 53–57. *Polyporus Drummondii*: various specimens in N. Y. Bot. Gard. Herb., filed as *P. armenicolor*, × 0.8

FIG. 58. *Polyporus occidentalis*: cross section of a few tubes, showing hyphal pegs, × 50

PLATE 10

Fig. 59. *Polyporus occidentalis*: upper-surface view of typical specimen, N. Y. Bot. Gard. Herb., × 0.6

Figs. 60–61. *Polyporus hirsutus*: upper-surface views of typical specimens, × 0.8

Figs. 62–63. *Polyporus maximus*: Fig. 62, upper-surface view of typical specimen, showing beginning of shedding of tomentum; Fig. 63, pore-surface view, showing irregular pores

PLATE 11

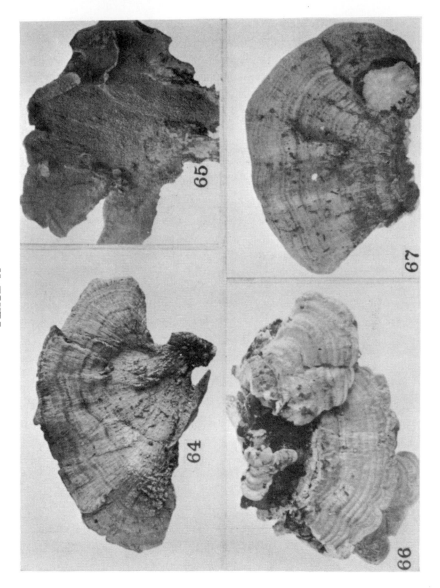

FIGS. 64–65. *Polyporus sector*: Fig. 64, upper-surface view of well-developed specimen, No. 8878, × 0.8; Fig. 65, pore-surface view of specimen in Lloyd Herbarium, × 0.8

FIGS. 66–67. *Polyporus subectypus*: Fig. 66, upper-surface view, No. 12391, × 0.8; Fig. 67, upper-surface view, N. Y. Bot. Gard. Herb., × 0.8

PLATE 12

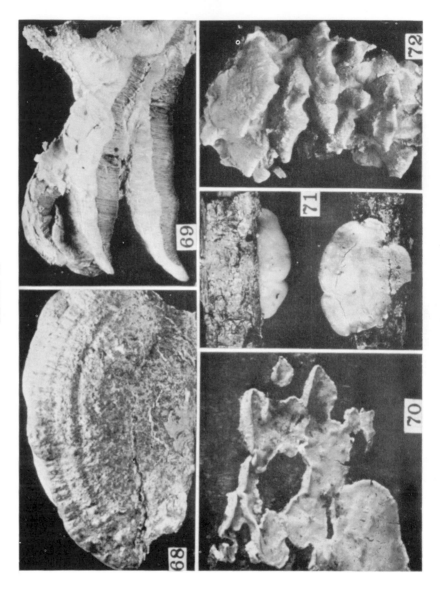

FIGS. 68–69. *Polyporus robiniophilus*: Fig. 68, upper-surface view of typical sporophore, × 0.8; Fig. 69, sectional view through imbricate sporophore, × 0.8

FIGS. 70–71. *Polyporus semipileatus*: Fig. 70, typical effused-reflexed specimen, No. 9891, × 0.8; Fig. 71, upper- and lower-surface views of fresh specimen, No. 14201, × 1

FIG. 72. *Polyporus adustus*: typical thin imbricate specimen, × 0.8

PLATE 13

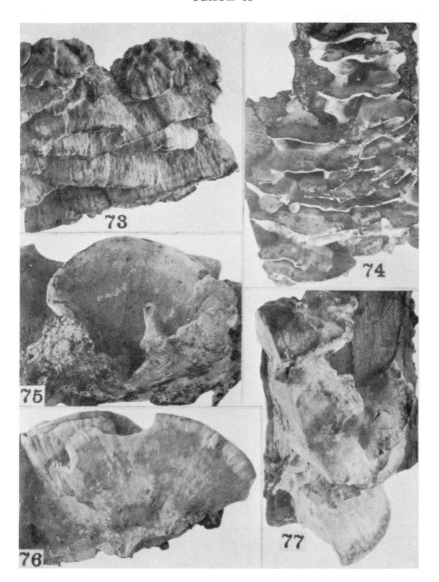

FIGS. 73–74. *Polyporus adustus*: Fig. 73, closely imbricate specimens, with
fibrillose pileus, × 0.8; Fig. 74, imbricate specimens with finely tomentose pileus, Pa. State College Herb., × 0.8

FIGS. 75–77. *Polyporus fumosus*: Fig. 75, pore-surface view, No. 3562, × 1.1;
Fig. 76, upper-surface view, No. 3562, × 0.8; Fig. 77, front-dorsal view,
Pa. State College Herb., × 1.1

PLATE 14

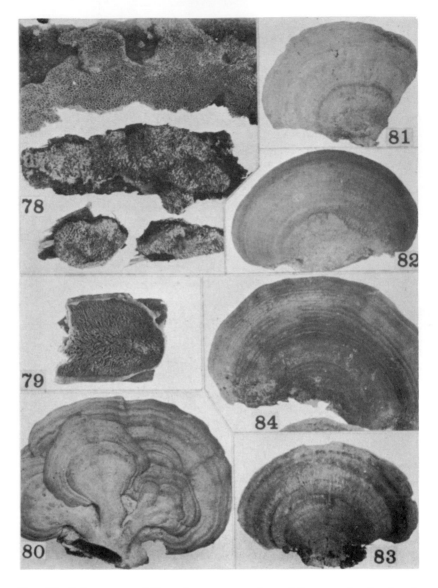

FIG. 78. *Polyporus aculeifer*: *above*, pore surface; *below*, poorly developed pileate specimens, with stiff hydnoid processes; No. 8675, × 1.5

FIG. 79. *Polyporus semipileatus*: nearly resupinate sporophoie, with barely reflexed margins, × 0.8

FIG. 80. *Polyporus ochrotinctellus*: upper-surface view, N. Y. Bot. Gard. Herb., × 0.8

FIGS. 81–83. *Polyporus ectypus*: upper-surface views of three specimens, N. Y. Bot. Gard. Herb., × 0.8

FIG. 84. *Polyporus pavonius*: upper-surface view, N. Y. Bot. Gard. Herb., × 0 8

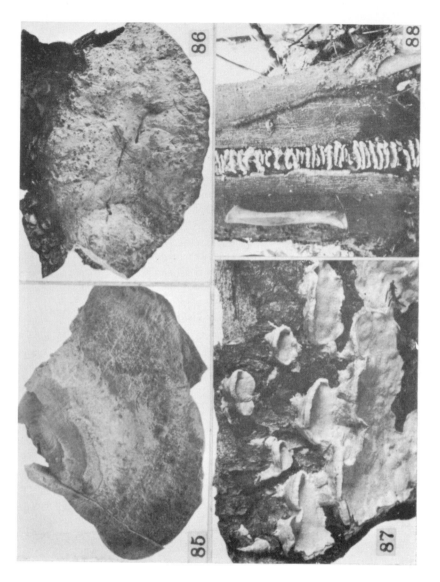

PLATE 9

FIG. 85. *Polyporus Calkinsii*: upper-surface view, No. 9972, × 0.8

FIG. 86. *Polyporus palustris*: upper-surface view, No. 15372, × 0.8

FIG. 87. *Polyporus anceps*: typical semiresupinate or effused-reflexed sporophores, No. 11062, × 0.8

FIG. 88. *Polyporus zonalis*: imbricate series of sporophores on dead strip in living *Celtis*, × 0.1

PLATE 16

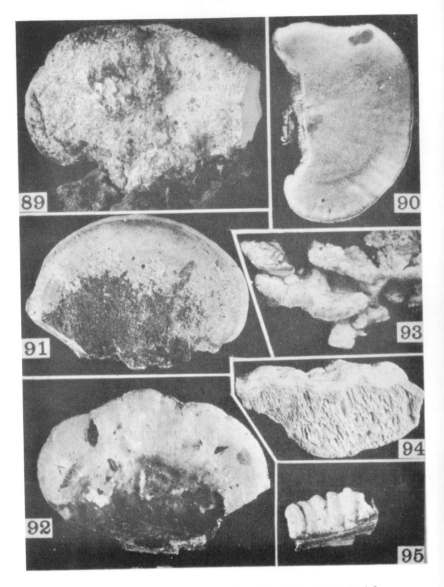

FIG. 89. *Polyporus durescens*: upper-surface view, No. 14699, × 0.8

FIG. 90. *Polyporus pavonius*: typical pore-surface view, × 1.5

FIGS. 91–92. *Polyporus supinus*: typical upper-surface views of sporophores, the bottom one becoming reddish at the base, Nos. 11761 and 8455, × 0.8

FIG. 93. *Polyporus rigidus*: typical pileate sporophores, No. 10367, × 0.8

FIGS. 94–95. *Polyporus undosus*: Fig. 94, front-dorsal view of decurrent sporophore, No. 10606; Fig. 95, upper-surface view, No. 10627

PLATE 17

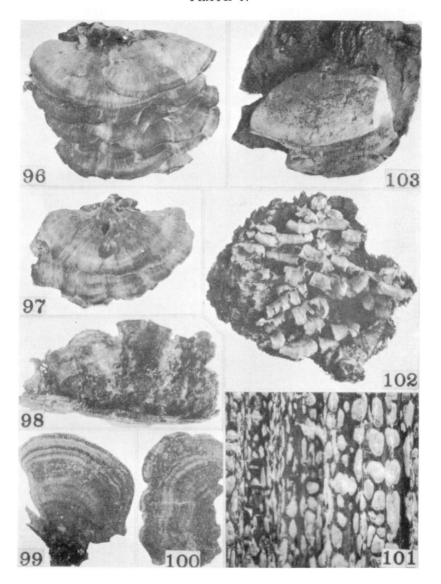

FIGS. 96–97. *Polyporus balsameus*: upper-surface views, Nos. 14345 and 11057, × 0.8

FIG. 98. *Polyporus cutifractus*: upper-surface view, No. 11158, × 0.4

FIGS. 99–101. *Polyporus zonalis*: Figs. 99–100, upper-surface views of two sporophores, No. 12375 and N. Y. Bot. Gard. Herb.; Fig. 101, large pocket rot produced on *Quercus* heartwood; all × 0.8

FIG. 102. *Polyporus semisupinus*: upper-surface view of typical sporophores, N. Y. State Mus., × 0.8

FIG. 103. *Polyporus caesius*: upper-surface view, No. 11652, × 0.8

PLATE 18

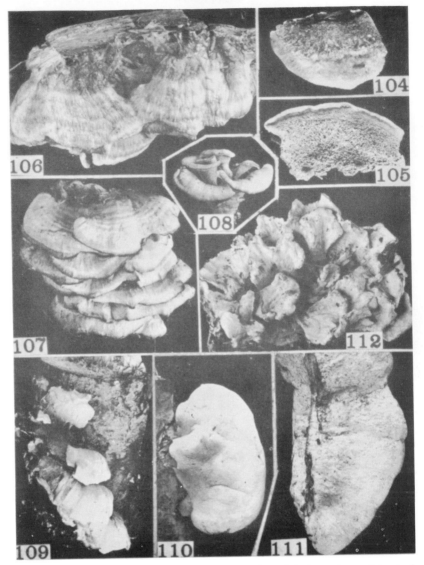

FIGS. 104–105. *Polyporus caesius*: upper- and lower-surface views of typical specimens, × 0.8

FIGS. 106–107. *Polyporus balsameus*: upper-surface views, Nos. 13442 and 14345, × 0.8

FIGS. 108–109. *Polyporus semisupinus*: Fig. 108, rosette type of substipitate sporophore, No. 12691; Fig. 109, more sessile form, No. 12676

FIG. 110. *Polyporus albellus*: upper-surface view of typical specimen in fresh condition, Pa. State College Herb., × 0.8

FIG. 111. *Polyporus immitis*: upper-surface view of typical specimen, No. 12558, × 0.8

FIG. 112. *Polyporus floriformis*: unusually well-developed sporophore cluster, No. 13390, × 0.8

PLATE 19

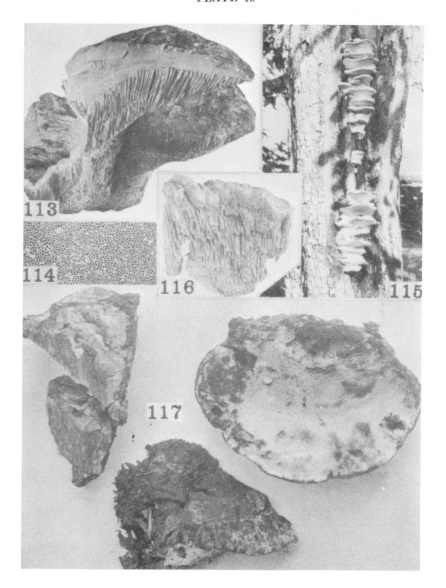

Fig. 113. *Polyporus delectans*: lateral view of vertical section, No. 145, × 0.6

Fig. 114. *Polyporus spumeus*: pore surface magnified, No. 10390, × 1.5

Fig. 115. *Polyporus spumeus* var. *malicola*: imbricate sporophores on living trunk of apple tree, phot. by R. P. Marshall

Fig. 116. *Polyporus undosus*: part of type collection, N. Y. State Mus., × 0.8

Fig. 117. *Polyporus fissilis*: vertical section, lower-surface view, and upper-surface view of sporophores (type specimens of *P. fusco-mutans* Lloyd), phot. by Burt Leeper

PLATE 20

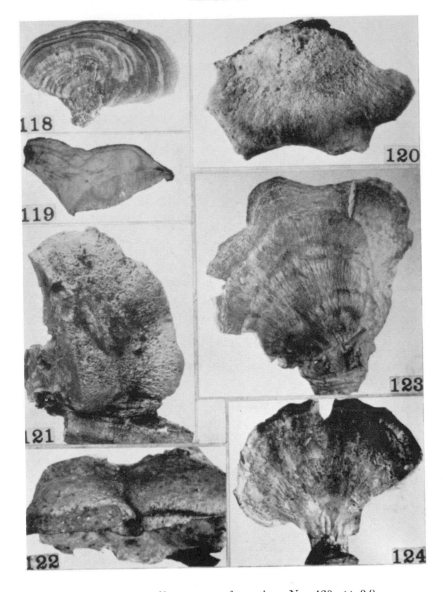

FIG. 118. *Polyporus zonalis*: upper-surface view, No. 430, × 0 8

FIGS. 119–121. *Polyporus galactinus*: Fig. 119, lateral view of specimen cut vertically, × 0.8; Fig. 120, upper-surface view, showing tomentum, No. 14959, × 0.8; Fig. 121, upper-surface view, No. 2549, × 0.8

FIG. 122. *Polyporus fumidiceps*: front-dorsal view, No. 10432, × 0.8

FIGS. 123–124. *Polyporus guttulatus*: Fig. 123, upper-surface view of typical sporophore, No. 10497, × 0.6; Fig. 124, upper-surface view, N. Y. State Mus., × 0.8

PLATE 21

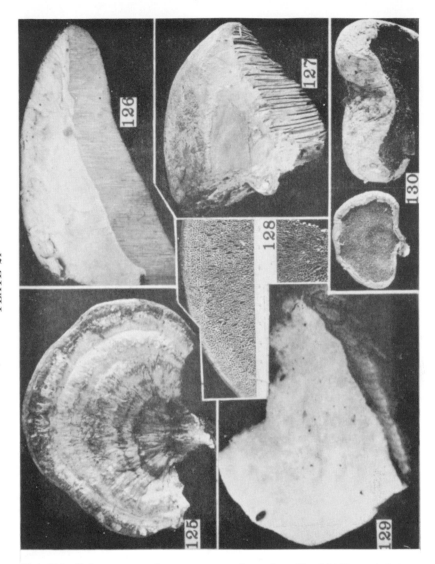

FIG. 125. *Polyporus guttulatus*: upper-surface view, No. 13448, × 0.7

FIG. 126. *Polyporus spumeus*: lateral view of specimen cut vertically, × 1

FIGS. 127–128. *Polyporus obtusus*: Fig. 127, specimen cut vertically, No. 2735, × 0.7; Fig. 128, pore-surface view with ruler, showing method of measuring pore diameters, No. 14655, × 0.5

FIG. 129. *Polyporus fissilis*: dorsolateral view of specimen cut vertically, × 0.7

FIG. 130. *Polyporus leucospongia*: specimens showing lower surface (*left*, No. 644) and marginal view (*right*, No. 643), both emphasizing the heavy cottony tomentum on margin and pileus, × 0.7

PLATE 22

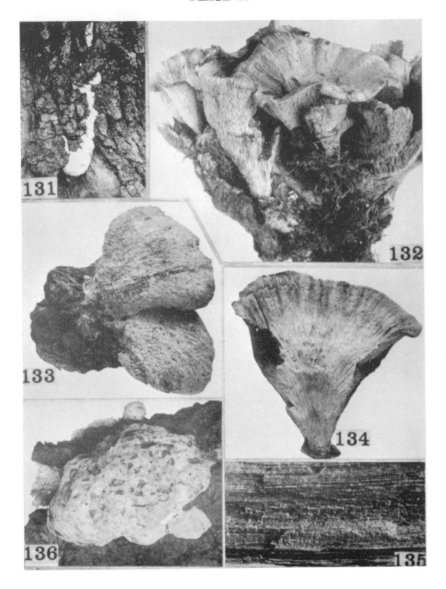

Fig. 131. *Polyporus compactus*: typical habit on edge of wounded area on living *Quercus*, phot. by W. A. Campbell

Figs. 132–135. *Polyporus borealis*: Fig. 132, rosette form of species (type specimen of *P. pacificus* Kauff.); Fig. 133, typical small specimen, No. 12692, × 0.8; Fig. 134, typical substipitate sporophore, No. 3508, × 0.8; Fig. 135, wood rotted by *P. borealis*, showing characteristic white cross flecks

Fig. 136. *Polyporus compactus*: type specimen, showing large nodulose form, × 0 8

PLATE 23

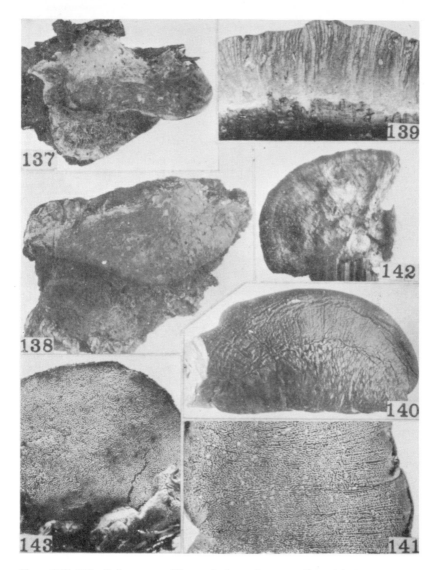

FIGS. 137–138. *Polyporus mollis*: typical specimens, collected in Michigan by
Povah in 1930, × 0.8

FIGS. 139–141. *Polyporus lapponicus*: Fig. 139, upper-surface view, with
pileus costately ribbed, No. 9054; Fig. 140, upper-surface view of smooth
form, No. 10203, × 0.8; Fig. 141, pore-surface view, showing irregular
pores, No. 9054, × 0.8

FIGS. 142–143. *Polyporus fragilis*: Fig. 142, upper-surface view, No. 11365,
× 0.8; Fig. 143, pore-surface view, showing daedaloid pores, No. 10593,
× 1.5

PLATE 24

Fig. 144. *Polyporus durescens*: upper-surface view, No. 14699, × 0.8

Fig. 145. *Polyporus Spraguei*: thin specimen, Pa. State College Herb., × 0.8

Fig. 146. *Polyporus spumeus* var. *malicola*: upper-surface view of single pileus, phot. by R. P. Marshall, × 0.8

Figs. 147–148. *Polyporus volvatus*: Fig. 147, upper-surface views; Fig. 148, lower-surface view, showing volval aperture; all in Pa. State College Herb., × 0.8

Fig. 149. *Polyporus subpendulus*: type specimens, × 1.5

PLATE 25

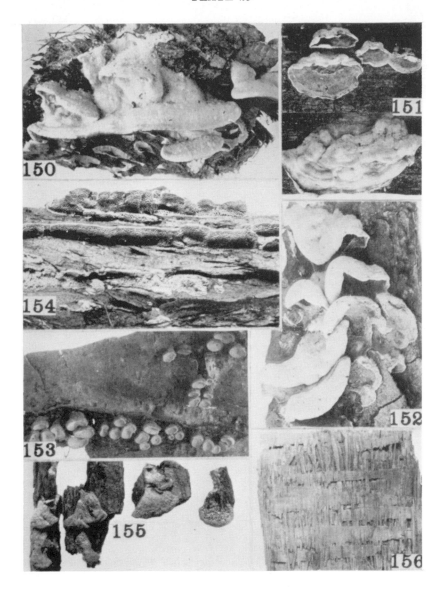

FIG. 150. *Polyporus dichrous*: typical specimens, No. 2751, × 0.8

FIGS. 151–152. *Polyporus amorphus*: Fig. 151, typical specimens, No. 3940, × 0.8; Fig. 152, specimen in Pa. State College Herb., phot. by E. T. Harper, × 0.8

FIG. 153. *Polyporus pocula*: typical specimens, No. 12396, × 1.5

FIGS. 154–155. *Polyporus cuneatus*: Fig. 154 (type specimens of *Coriolus washingtonensis*), × 0.8; Fig. 155, type specimens of *P. cuneatus*, × 0.8

FIG. 156. Wood completely decayed by *Polyporus Berkeleyi*, showing prominent medullary rays, × 0.8

PLATE 26

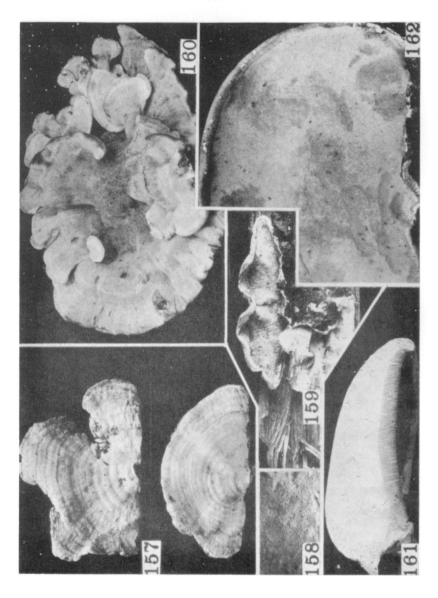

FIGS. 157–158. *Polyporus conchoides*: Fig. 157, upper-surface view of two specimens, × 0.8; Fig. 158, small portion of pore surface, No. 15714, × 1.5

FIG. 159. *Polyporus amorphus*: No. 4643, × 0.8

FIG. 160. *Polyporus Berkeleyi*: typical sporophore except for the excessive marginal proliferation, × 0.4

FIGS. 161–162. *Polyporus betulinus*: Fig. 161, lateral view of vertical section; Fig. 162, pore-surface view, showing deflexed margin; both × 0.8

PLATE 27

FIGS. 163–164. *Polyporus betulinus*: Fig. 163, unusual specimen in N. Y. State Mus., × 0.7; Fig. 164, upper- and lower-surface views of small specimens, No. 4525, × 0.7

FIG. 165. *Polyporus sulphureus* var. *cincinnatus*: typical sporophore on buried roots of living *Quercus*, × 0.3

FIG. 166. End view of log rotted by *Polyporus sulphureus*, showing the characteristic white mycelium in the larger cracks, × 0.1

FIG. 167. *Polyporus Berkeleyi*: typical sporophore, No. 14511, × 0.3

PLATE 28

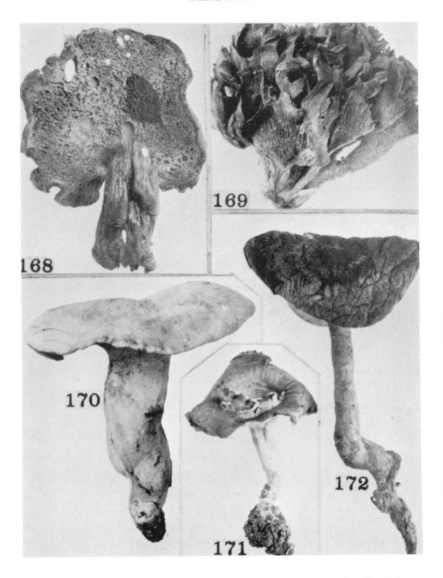

FIG. 168. *Polyporus griseus*: lower-surface view of specimen in N. Y. State Mus., × 0.8

FIG. 169. *Polyporus fimbriatus*: typical sporophore, No. 14706, × 0.8

FIG. 170. *Polyporus ovinus* (reproduced from Lloyd, *Synop. Ovinus*, fig. 497)

FIG. 171. *Polyporus Peckianus*: typical sporophore, No. 6021 (collected by A. W. McCallum as No. 100), × 0.8

FIG. 172. *Polyporus radicatus*: typical small sporophore with radicating stem, No. 71, × 0.8

PLATE 29

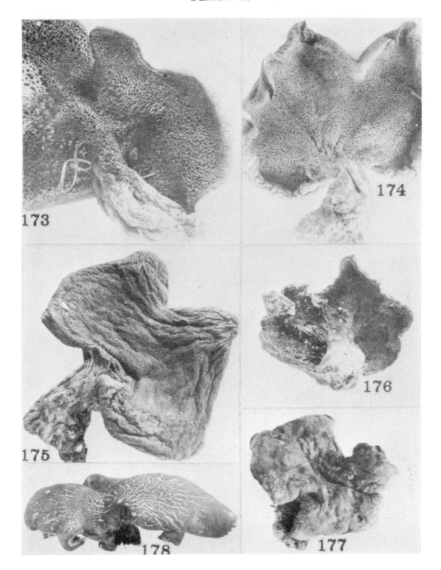

Figs. 173–175. *Polyporus Pes-Caprae*: Fig. 173, pore-surface view (type specimen of *P. retipes*), × 0.5; Fig. 174, lower-surface view (type specimen of *Scutiger oregonensis*), × 0.4; Fig. 175, upper-surface view of same specimen, × 0.4; all in N. Y. Bot. Gard. Herb.

Figs. 176–177. *Polyporus confluens*: lower- and upper-surface views (type specimens of *Scutiger Whiteae*), × 0.7

Fig. 178. *Polyporus cristatus*: small specimen, unusually short-stemmed, showing typical pileus areolations, No. 8739, × 0.7

PLATE 30

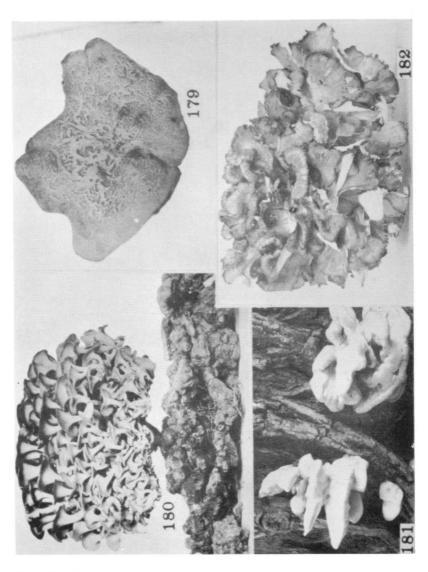

Fig. 179. *Polyporus ovinus*: upper-surface view, showing areolate pileus, No. 8735, × 0.7

Fig. 180. *Polyporus umbellatus*: typical specimen with multiplex sporophore arising from black underground sclerotium, phot. by Burt Leeper, reduced

Fig. 181. *Polyporus sulphureus*: young specimens on *Salix* trunk, No. 9887, × 0.2

Fig. 182. *Polyporus frondosus*: typical multiplex sporophore, × 0.2

PLATE 31

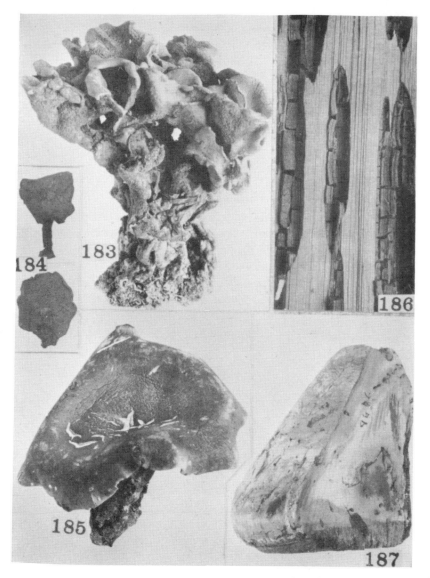

Fig. 183. *Polyporus illudens*: type specimen, No. 14302, × 0.8

Fig. 184. *Polyporus cryptopus*: upper- and lower-surface views of specimens in Lloyd Herb., × 0.8

Fig. 185. *Polyporus cristatus*: typical sporophore except for nearly even pileus, No. 8739

Figs. 186–187. *Polyporus amarus*: Fig. 186, radial view of typical pocket rot produced in incense-cedar wood, × 0.8; Fig. 187, sporophore cut vertically, U. S. Forest Path. Herb. No. 9666, × 0.4

PLATE 32

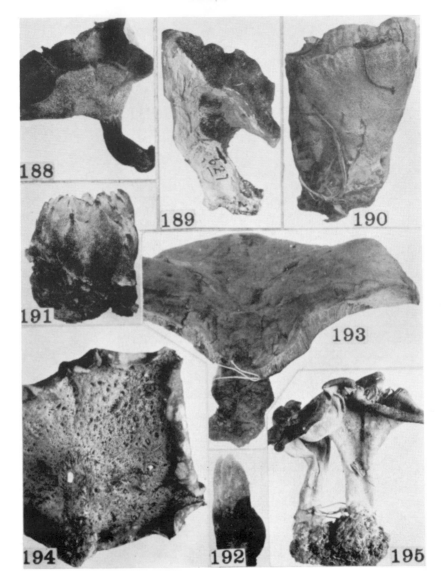

FIGS. 188–189. *Polyporus melanopus*: typical sporophores, Nos. 8524 and 12074 (collected by C. W. Fritz as No. 627), × 0.8

FIGS. 190–193. *Polyporus biennis*: Figs. 190–192, phases of the distorted, nonpileate type of sporophore, × 0.8; Fig. 193, typical pileate specimen, N. Y. Bot. Gard. Herb., × 0.8

FIG. 194. *Polyporus cristatus*: lower-surface view, × 0.8

FIG. 195. *Polyporus Peckianus*: typical sporophores, No. 6021, × 0.8

PLATE 33

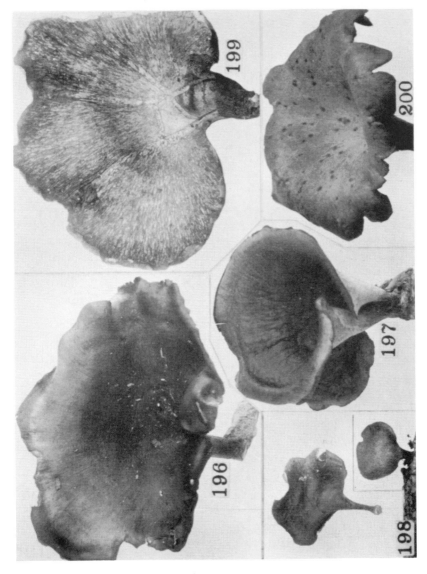

FIGS. 196–197. *Polyporus picipes*: typical small sporophores, No. 915, × 0.6, and No. 681, × 0.8

FIG. 198. *Polyporus Blanchetianus*: typical specimens, N. Y. Bot. Gard. Herb., × 0.8

FIGS. 199–200. *Polyporus varius*: Fig. 199, typical specimen, with thick, radiate-lineate pileus and short, thick stem, Lloyd Herb., × 0.8; Fig. 200, less typical form, Lloyd Herb., × 0.8

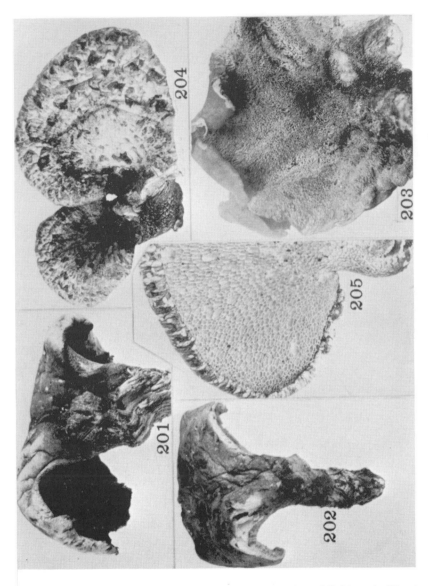

PLATE 34

FIGS. 201–203. *Polyporus hirtus*: Fig. 201, specimen from Michigan in Lloyd Herb., × 0.5; Fig. 202, typical specimen, No. 11052, × 0.5; Fig. 203, pore-surface view, Lloyd Herb., × 0.5

FIGS. 204–205. *Polyporus squamosus*: Fig. 204, upper-surface view of small specimen in Pa. State College Herb., × 0.5; Fig. 205, pore-surface view of portion of specimen, phot. by E. T. Harper, × 0.5

PLATE 35

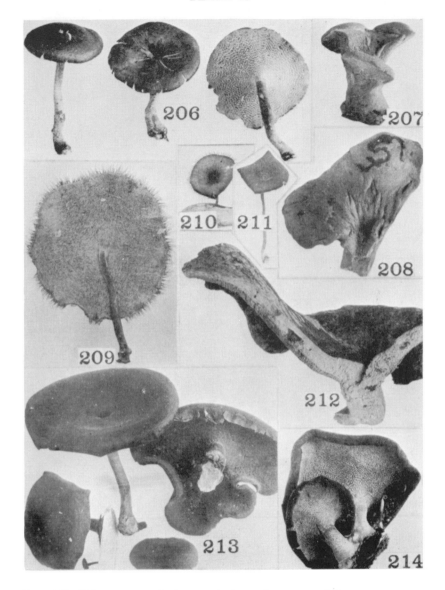

Fig. 206. *Polyporus arcularius*: typical specimens, × 0.8

Figs. 207–208. *Polyporus fractipes*: typical sporophores, Nos. 3643 and 457, × 1.5

Figs. 209–211. *Polyporus Tricholoma*: Fig. 209, sporophore, × 1; Figs. 210–211, small specimens, × 0.8; all in N. Y. Bot. Gard. Herb.

Fig. 212. *Polyporus virgatus*: half of typical sporophore, No. 303, × 0.8

Figs. 213–214. *Polyporus brumalis*: typical sporophores, × 0.8

PLATE 36

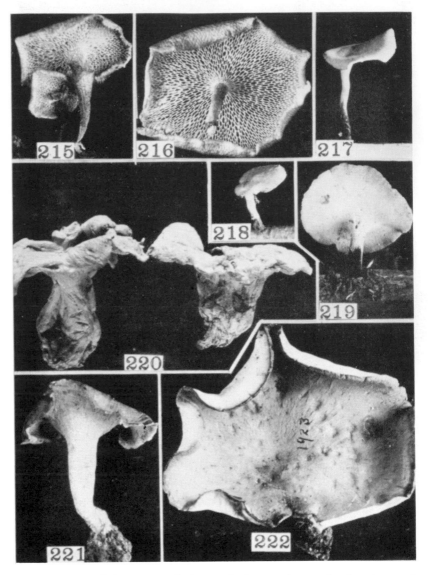

FIGS. 215–216. *Polyporus arcularius*: typical sporophores, showing stem and radiating pores, Nos. 9363 and 487, × 1

FIGS. 217–219. *Polyporus elegans*: small sporophores, × 0.8

FIG. 220. *Polyporus fractipes*: type specimen, × 0.8

FIG. 221. *Polyporus Peckianus*: No. 6021, × 0.8

FIG. 222. *Polyporus varius*: upper-surface view, No. 12110 (collected by E. H. Moss as No. 1923), × 0.8

PLATE 37

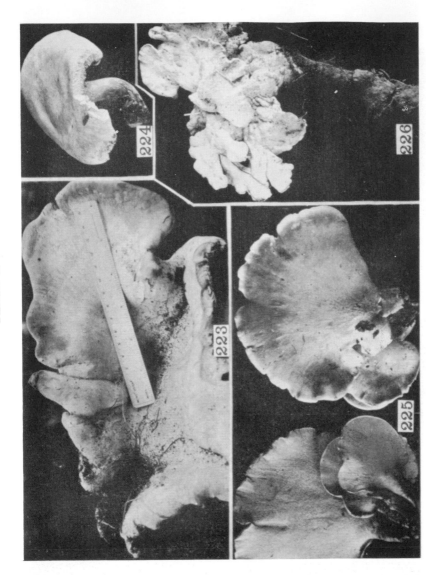

Fig. 223. *Polyporus admirabilis*: upper-surface view of specimen in Pa. State College Herb., phot. by C. S. Parker, × 0.4

Fig. 224. *Polyporus albiceps*: typical sporophore in N. Y. State Mus. Herb., × 0.5

Fig. 225. *Polyporus osseus*: lower- and upper-surface views of typical specimens, No. 12438, × 0.4

Fig. 226. *Polyporus sulphureus* var. *cincinnatus*: typical sporophore, showing the rootlike prolongation ending in a pseudo-sclerotium, No. 13769, × 0.3

PLATE 38

FIGS. 227–228. *Polyporus submurinus*: Fig. 227, type specimen; Fig. 228, specimen from Jamaica; both in N. Y. Bot. Gard. Herb., × 0.8

FIG. 229. *Polyporus occidentalis*: upper-surface view of small sporophore, × 0.8

FIG. 230. *Polyporus ochrotinctellus*: specimens in N. Y. Bot. Gard. Herb. larger one being the type collection, × 0.8

PLATE 39

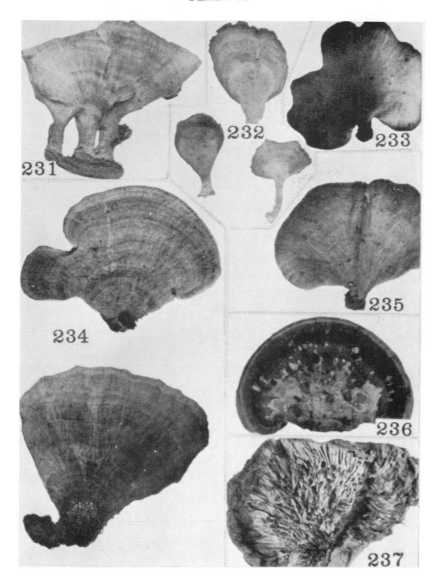

Figs. 231–232. *Polyporus mutabilis*: typical small sporophores, N. Y. Bot. Gard. Herb., × 0.8

Fig. 233. *Polyporus elegans*: sporophore with reduced stem, No. 4120, × 0.8

Figs. 234–236. *Polyporus modestus*: upper-surface views, × 0.8

Fig. 237. *Polyporus alboluteus*: lower-surface view of resupinate specimen, showing fimbriate pore mouths, × 0.8

PLATE 40

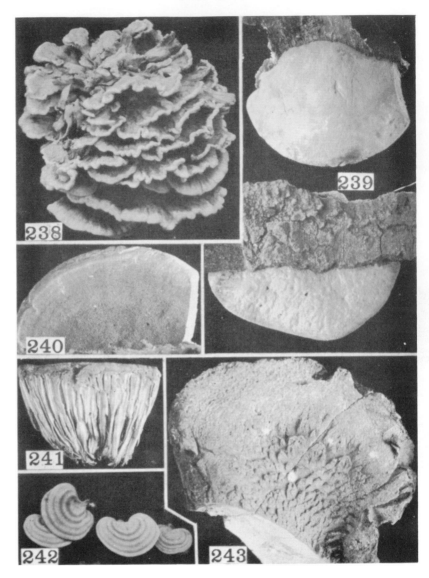

FIG. 238. *Polyporus sulphureus*: typical sporophore, × 0.2

FIGS. 239–240. *Polyporus cinnabarinus*: Fig. 239, upper-surface views, × 0.8; Fig. 240, lower-surface view

FIG. 241. *Polyporus alboluteus*: specimen showing tubes cut vertically, No. 1833, × 0.8

FIG. 242. *Polyporus mutabilis*: upper-surface view of fresh sporophores, showing strongly zonate pileus, × 0.4

FIG. 243. *Polyporus Ellisii*: upper-surface view, No. 15780, × 0.8

PLATE 41

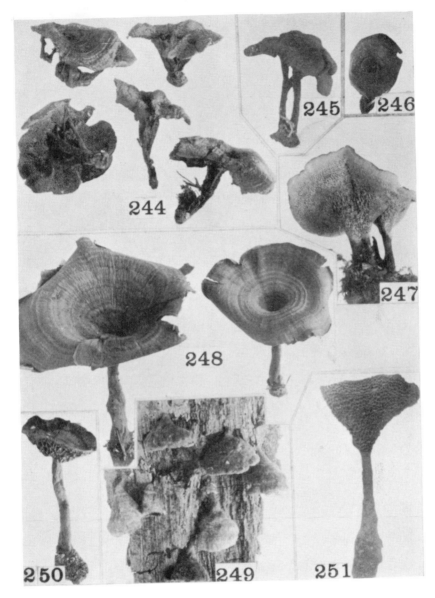

Figs. 244–246. *Polyporus cinnamomeus*: typical sporophores in various views, × 0.8

Figs. 247–248. *Polyporus perennis*: Fig. 247, pore-surface view, × 0.8; Fig. 248, upper-surface views, showing strongly zonate pilei, × 0.8

Fig. 249. *Polyporus dependens*: typical sporophores, No. 14912, × 1.5

Figs. 250–251. *Polyporus focicola*: specimens showing habit and large pores, both in Lloyd Herb., × 0.8

PLATE 42

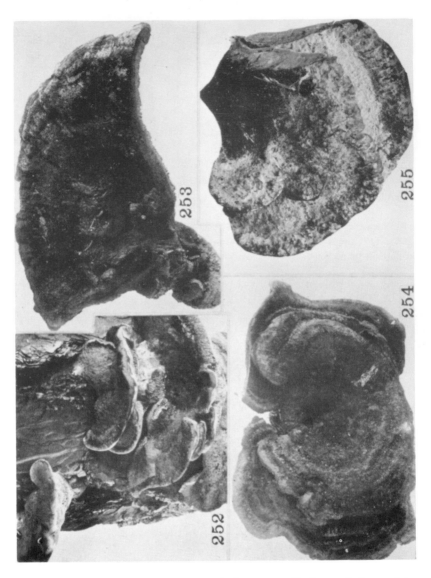

FIG. 252. *Polyporus tomentosus* var. *circinatus*: sessile form of the variety on pine trunk, No. 16291, × 0.5

FIGS. 253–254. *Polyporus Schweinitzii*: Fig. 253, typical sporophore cut vertically, Pa. State College Herb., × 0.5; Fig. 254, upper-surface view, Pa. State College Herb., × 0.3

FIG. 255. *Polyporus Spraguei*: front-dorsal view of typical sporophore, No. 15992 × 0.7

PLATE 43

FIGS. 256–260. *Polyporus tomentosus* and var. *circinatus*: Fig. 256, var. *circinatus* on living *Picea*, phot. by A. W. McCallum; Fig. 257, stipitate form of species, No. 5214, × 0.8; Figs. 258–259, wood rotted by var. *circinatus*, × 0.8; Fig. 260, upper-surface view of stipitate form of species, No. 16046, × 0.4

PLATE 44

FIG. 261. *Polyporus tomentosus* var. *circinatus*: photomicrographic view of cross section of tubes, showing the hooked setae characteristic of the variety

FIG. 262. *Polyporus alboluteus*: portion of resupinate sporophore, No. 1807, × 0.8

FIG. 263. *Polyporus osseus*: Front-dorsal view of sporophore cluster, Pa. State College Herb., × 0.8

FIG. 264. *Polyporus frondosus*: typical small sporophore cluster after drying, No. 11823, × 0.5

FIG. 265. *Polyporus focicola*: upper-surface view of confluent and weathered sporophores, No. 8460, × 0.8

FIG. 266. *Polyporus perennis*: typical small sporophores, phot. by C. S. Parker, × 0.8

FIG. 267. Radial (*lower*) and tangential (*upper*) sections of wood rotted by *Polyporus ludovicianus*, × 0.8

PLATE 44

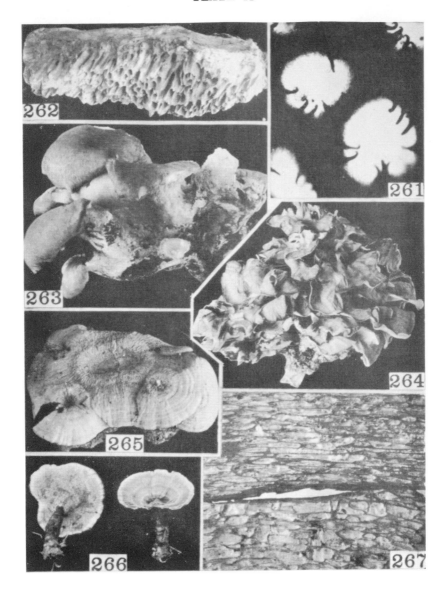

PLATE 45

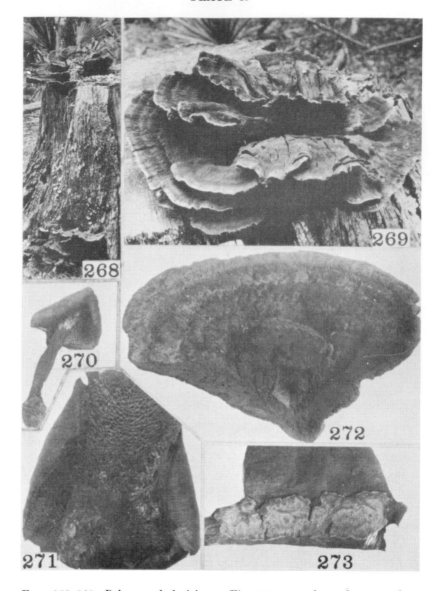

FIGS. 268–269. *Polyporus ludovicianus*: Fig. 268, sporophore clusters at base and on top of old *Quercus* stump; Fig. 269, sporophore cluster on top of stump, × 0.3

FIGS. 270–271. *Polyporus Montagnei*: Fig. 270, small sporophore; Fig. 271, typical sporophore showing large pores; both in Lloyd Herb., × 0.8

FIG. 272. *Polyporus Schweinitzii*: subsessile sporophore, No. 5590, × 0.6

FIG. 273. *Polyporus planellus*: resupinate specimen, Lloyd Herb., × 0.8

PLATE 46

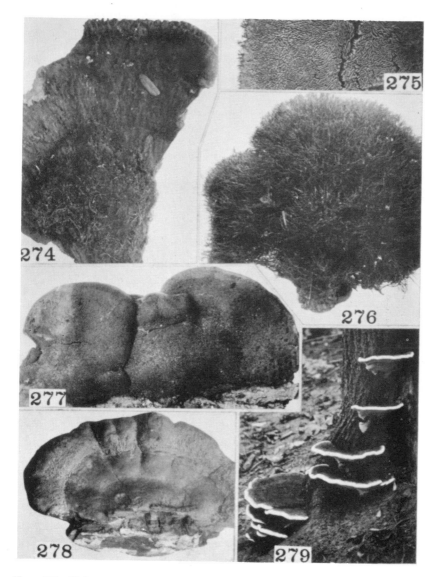

Fig. 274. *Polyporus porrectus*: upper-surface view, No. 9912, × 0.8

Figs. 275–276. *Polyporus trichomallus*: Fig. 275, pore-surface view, showing the strongly daedaloid pores, No. 8669, × 0.8; Fig. 276, upper-surface view, showing the coarse, strigose fibers, No. 8669, × 0.8

Figs. 277–278. *Polyporus nidulans*: lower- and upper-surface views of typical large sporophores, phot. by A. S. Rhoads, × 0.8

Fig. 279. *Polyporus resinosus*: habit of sporophores, phot. by J. B. Mac-Curry

PLATE 47

FIGS. 280–281. *Polyporus sanguineus*: upper-surface views of typical sporophores, No. 3963 and specimen in N. Y. Bot. Gard. Herb., × 0.8

FIG. 282. *Polyporus cinnabarinus*: typical sporophores on *Quercus* log, phot. by A. S. Rhoads, reduced

FIGS. 283–284. *Polyporus fibrillosus*: upper- and lower-surface views of typical sporophores, Nos. 11427 and 9462, × 1.1

FIG. 285. *Polyporus croceus*: pore-surface view, phot. by Burt Leeper, × 0.8

FIG. 286. Typical decay produced by *Polyporus Schweinitzii*, Mo. Bot. Gard. Herb., × 0.5

FIG. 287. *Polyporus fruticum*: specimen in N. Y. Bot. Gard. Herb. (type specimer of *P. amplectens*)

PLATE 48

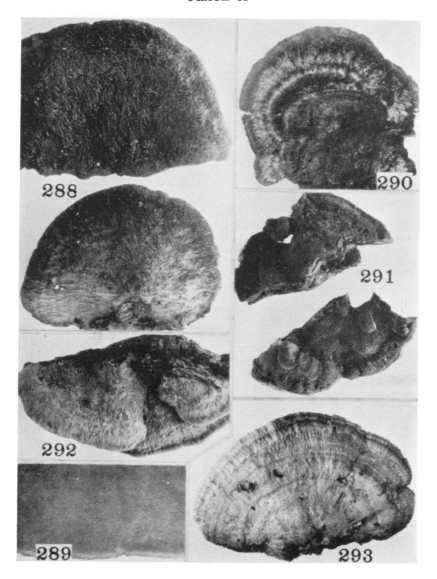

FIGS. 288–289. *Polyporus hydnoides*: Fig. 288, upper-surface views of typical specimens, the lower specimen being partly denuded, Nos. 164 and 8668, × 0.8; Fig. 289, pore-surface view, No. 164, × 1.1

FIG. 290. *Polyporus versatilis*: typical sessile sporophore, Lloyd Herb., × 0.8

FIG. 291. *Polyporus corrosus*: typical small sporophores, No. 8696, × 1.1

FIGS. 292–293. *Polyporus gilvus*: upper-surface views of typical sporophores, × 0.8

PLATE 49

FIG. 294. *Polyporus radiatus*: typical sporophores, × 0.8

FIG. 295. *Polyporus cuticularis*: dorsal view of typical sporophores, × 0.8

FIG. 296. *Polyporus planellus*: typical sessile sporophores, phot. by P. F. Shope, × 1.1

FIG. 297. *Polyporus licnoides*: upper-surface views of typical sporophores, Nos. 8671 and 8692, × 0.8

FIG. 298. *Polyporus licnoides* var. *sublilacinus*: upper-surface views of specimens in N. Y. Bot. Gard. Herb., × 0.8

PLATE 50

FIG. 299. *Polyporus crocatus*: upper-surface view, N. Y. Bot. Gard. Herb., × 0.7

FIG. 300. *Polyporus dryadeus*: half of typical sporophore, No. 7736, × 0.4

FIG. 301. *Polyporus fruticum*: small sporophore encircling twig and leaves, N. Y. Bot. Gard. Herb., × 0.7

FIGS. 302–303. *Polyporus dryophilus*: Fig. 302, front-dorsal view of typical sporophore, No. 2979, × 0.5; Fig. 303, lateral view of vertical section, showing central core permeated by whitish fibers, Mo. Bot. Gard. Herb., × 0.5

FIG. 304. *Polyporus dryophilus* var. *vulpinus*: imbricate specimens, No. 11234, × 0.5

PLATE 51

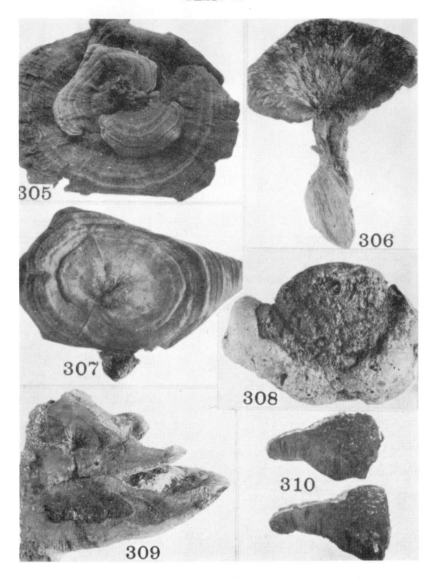

FIG. 305. *Polyporus porrectus*: upper-surface view, No. 15522, × 0.8

FIGS. 306–307. *Polyporus dealbatus*: Fig. 306, upper-surface view of specimen in U. S. Forest Path. Herb., × 1; Fig. 307, specimen in N. Y. Bot. Gard. Herb., × 0.8

FIG. 308. *Polyporus corrosus*: upper-surface view of specimen in N. Y. Bot. Gard. Herb., × 0.8

FIG. 309. *Polyporus gilvus*: unusually thick sporophores as seen in lateral view of vertical section, No. 5596, × 0.8

FIG. 310. *Polyporus dryophilus* var. *vulpinus*: lateral views of vertical sections, showing the thinner pilei with greatly reduced central core, × 0.8

PLATE 52

Fig. 311. *Polyporus croceus*: lateral view of vertical section, phot. by Burt Leeper, × 0.3

Fig. 312. Tangential section of wood block of *Quercus* decayed by *Polyporus dryophilus*, × 0.5

Fig. 313. *Polyporus giganteus*: upper-surface view of small dried specimen, No. 14102, × 0.3

Fig. 314. *Polyporus hispidus*: portion of specimen in Pa. State College Herb., × 0.3

Fig. 315. *Polyporus graveolens*: typical sporophore, × 0.8

PLATE 53

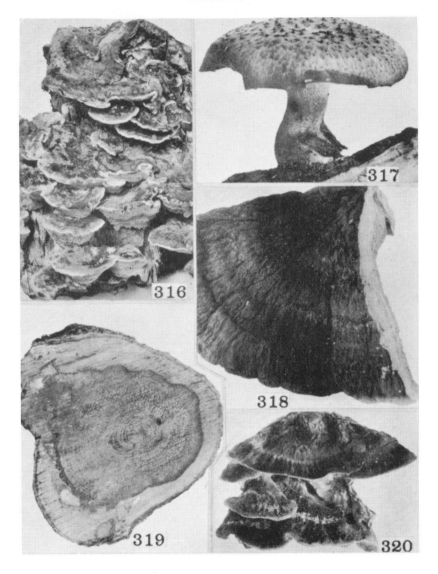

FIG. 316. *Polyporus glomeratus*: typical imbricate sporophores, No. 3555, × 0.7

FIG. 317. *Polyporus McMurphyi* (reproduced from photograph of the type specimen in N. Y. Bot. Gard. Herb.), × 0.7

FIG. 318. *Polyporus resinosus*: upper-surface view of portion of sporophore, No. 5862, × 0.3

FIG. 319. Cross section of *Quercus* trunk rotted by *Polyporus hispidus*, × 0.3

FIG. 320. *Polyporus basilaris*: type specimens, × 0.7

PLATE 54

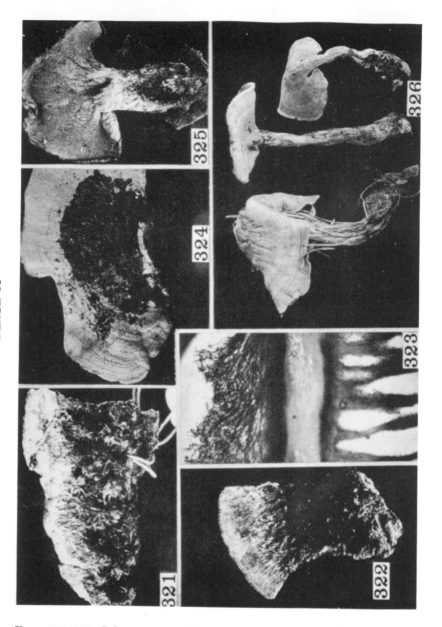

FIGS. 321–322. *Polyporus versatilis*: upper-surface views of typical sporophores, N. Y. Bot. Gard. Herb., × 0.7

FIG. 323. *Polyporus iodinus*: photomicrograph of vertical section through sporophores, showing the various regions, × 27

FIG. 324. *Trametes corrugata*: upper-surface view of typical specimen, showing the red (dark) area at base of pileus, × 0.7

FIG. 325. *Polyporus fagicola*: lower-surface view of sporophore with much stouter stem than in typical specimens, × 0.7

FIG. 326. *Polyporus dealbatus*: specimens in N. Y. Bot. Gard. Herb., × 0.7

PLATE 55

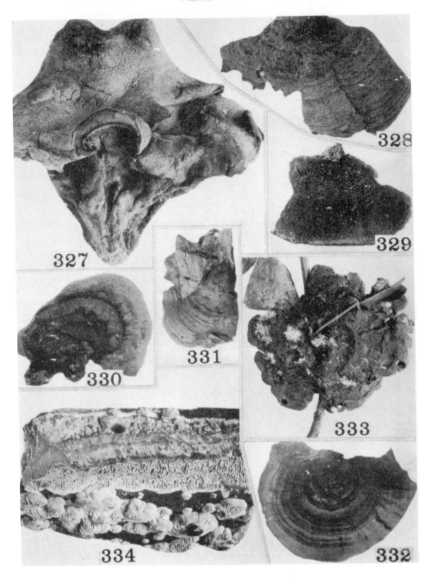

FIG. 327. *Polyporus sylvestris*: type specimen, × 0.8

FIGS. 328–329. *Polyporus iodinus*: upper- and lower-surface views of typical sporophores, No. 10708, × 1

FIGS. 330–332. *Polyporus vinosus*: typical sporophores, × 0.8

FIG. 333. *Polyporus fruticum*: Venezuelan specimen encircling living branch, × 0.8

FIG. 334. *Trametes malicola*: typical sporophores, No. 3646, × 1.1

PLATE 56

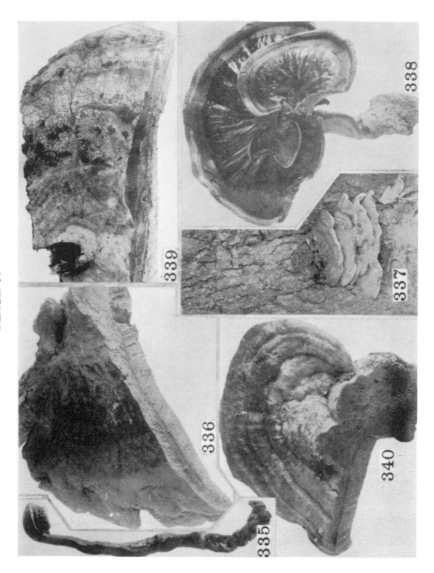

Figs. 335–338. *Polyporus lucidus*: Fig. 335, small, laterally stalked sporophore, Pa. State College Herb., × 0.5; Fig. 336, typical large, sessile
sporophore cut vertically, No. 2781, × 0.4; Fig. 337, sessile form of species on living *Quercus*, showing habit of growth in clusters at ground
line, phot. by C. S. Parker, reduced; Fig. 338, typical stipitate sporophore, × 0.7

Figs. 339–340. *Polyporus lucidus* var. *zonatus*: Fig. 339, portion of sporophore, No. 9240, × 0.7; Fig. 340, upper-surface view of substipitate
sporophore, No. 9130, × 0.4

PLATE 57

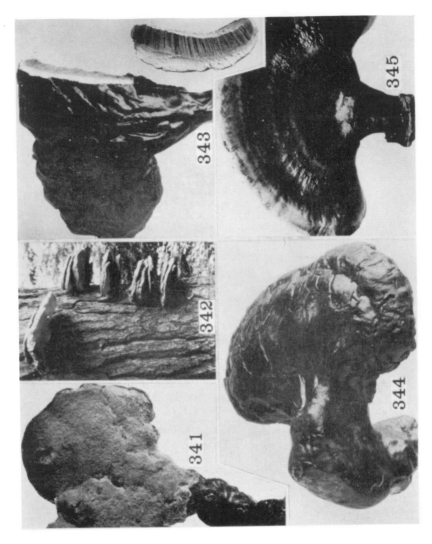

FIGS. 341–345. *Polyporus Tsugae*: Fig. 341, lower-surface view, No. 11750, × 0.5; Fig. 342, habit of typical sporophores on *Tsuga* trunk; Fig. 343, upper-surface view of sporophore and specimen cut vertically, showing context white except near the tubes, Pa. State College Herb., × 0.7; Fig. 344, typical blackish sporophore, No. 13404, × 0.7; Fig. 345, broadly flabelliform sporophore, No. 12445, × 0.4

PLATE 58

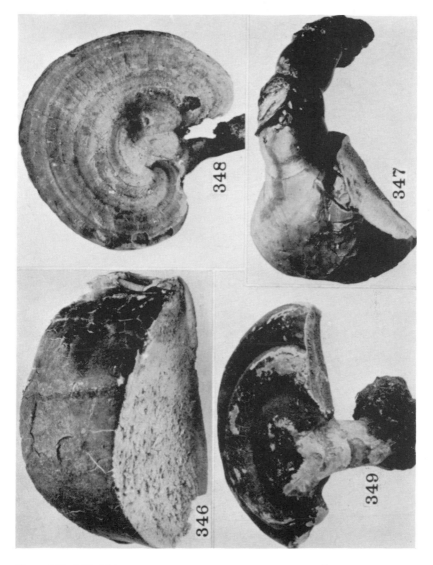

Figs. 346–347. *Polyporus oregonensis*: Fig. 346, typical thick sporophore, No. 6620, × 0.5; Fig. 347, sporophore of thin type, more comparable to eastern specimens of *Polyporus Tsugae*, No. 9949, × 0.7

Figs. 348–349. *Polyporus Curtisii*: typical sporophores, Pa. State College Herb. and No. 3796, × 0.5

PLATE 59

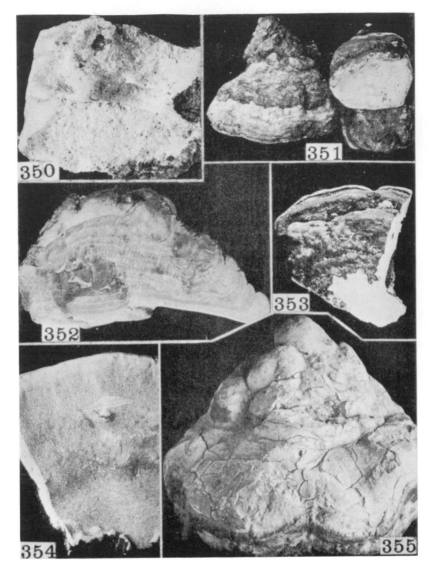

FIG. 350. *Fomes Meliae*: typical subresupinate sporophore, No. 11899, ×
1.1

FIG. 351. *Fomes fomentarius*: small sporophores, phot. by C. S. Parker,
× 0.5

FIG. 352. *Fomes pinicola*: lateral view of vertical section, showing annual
tube layers, × 0.5

FIGS. 353–354. *Fomes annosus*: Fig. 353, typical pileate sporophore, No.
4508, × 0.8; Fig. 354, pore-surface view, No. 11922, × 1.1

FIG. 355. *Fomes officinalis*: typical small sporophore, No. 4008, × 0.5

PLATE 60

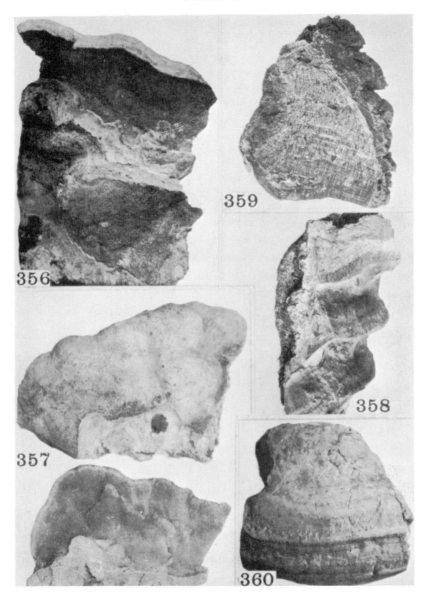

FIGS. 356–358. *Fomes Meliae*: Fig. 356, specimen in Lloyd Herb., × 0.7; Fig. 357, specimens in N. Y. Bot. Gard. Herb. (type specimens of *Trametes subnivosa*), × 0.7; Fig. 358, typical specimen, No. 8366, × 1.1

FIG. 359. *Fomes igniarius*: lateral view of vertical section, showing the characteristic white incrustation of old tube layers, No. 5887, × 0.7

FIG. 360. *Fomes officinalis*: specimen in N. Y. State Mus. Herb. (type specimen of *F. albogrisea*), × 0.7

PLATE 61

FIG. 361. *Fomes tenuis*: pore-surface view, No. 11868, × 1.5

FIG. 362. *Fomes robustus*: typical resupinate sporophore, × 0.8

FIG. 363. *Fomes tenuis*: upper-surface view of unusually well-developed pileate specimen, No. 13972, × 1.1

FIGS. 364–365. *Fomes scutellatus*: typical sporophores in various views, Nos. 11552 and 7324, × 1.1

FIG. 366. *Lenzites trabea*: upper- and lower-surface views of typical sporophores, No. 13441, × 1.1

PLATE 62

FIGS. 367–368. *Fomes extensus*: upper-surface views of typical sporophores, Nos. 10693 and 9927, × 0.8

FIGS. 369–370. *Fomes texanus*: typical sporophores, Nos. 2604 and 14284, × 0 8

PLATE 63

FIGS. 371–373. *Fomes robustus*: Fig. 371, lateral view of vertical section showing well-layered tubes, No. 4174, × 0.6; Fig. 372, lateral view of vertical section through old resupinate sporophore from lower side of *Tsuga* branch, × 0.6; Fig. 373, upper-surface view of typical young applanate sporophore, No. 5529, × 0.3

FIG. 374. *Fomes annularis*: front-lateral view of sporophore cut vertically, No. 5602, × 0.5

FIG. 375. *Fomes roseus*: typical sporophore, Lloyd Herb., × 0.6

PLATE 64

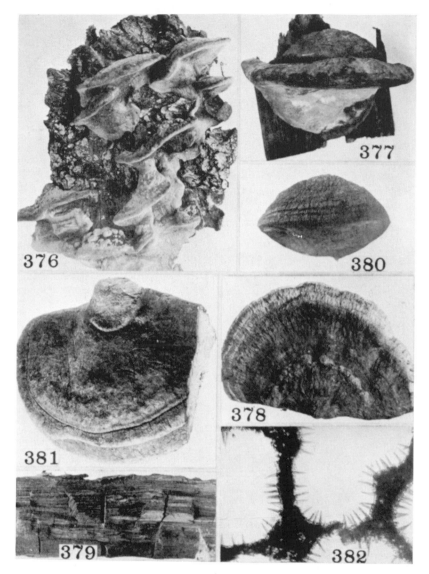

FIGS. 376–379. *Fomes subroseus*: Fig. 376, typical thin, applanate sporophores, No. 4731, × 0.8; Fig. 377, thick sporophore, No. 3559, × 0.8; Fig. 378, upper-surface view of thin sporophore, No. 6179, × 0.8; Fig. 379, wood rotted by *F. subroseus*, No. 3780, × 0.8

FIGS. 380–381. *Fomes roseus*: typical sporophores, Lloyd Herb. and No. 6026, × 0.8

FIG. 382. *Fomes tenuis*: photomicrograph of cross section of tubes, showing the numerous slender setae, No. 15119, × 114

PLATE 65

Fig. 383. *Fomes pinicola*: upper-surface view of typical sporophore, No. 5437, × 0.4

Figs. 384–386. *Fomes rimosus*: upper-surface views of typical sporophores, N. Y. Bot. Gard. Herb. and Pa. State College Herb., all about × 0.3

PLATE 66

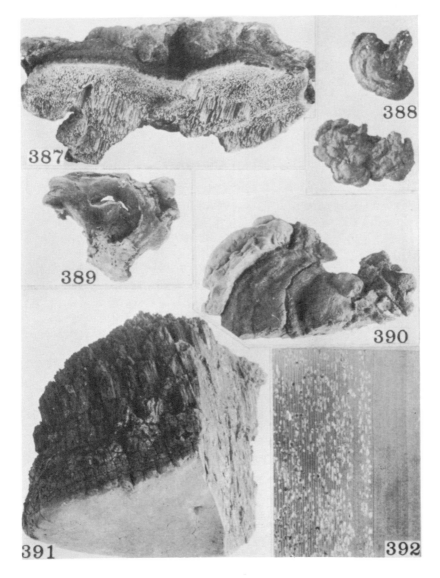

FIG. 387. *Fomes Pini* var. *Abietis*: typical sporophore, No. 642, × 0.8

FIGS. 388–390. *Fomes Ribis*: views of small and medium-sized sporophores, Nos. 8869 and 4521, × 0.8

FIG. 391. *Fomes praerimosus*: typical sporophore, No. 14536, × 0.8

FIG. 392. Pocket decay in pine heartwood, caused by *Fomes Pini*, × 0.8

PLATE 67

FIGS. 393–395. *Fomes Pini*: Fig. 393, upper-surface view of medium-sized sporophore, Mo. Bot. Gard. Herb., × 0.6; Fig. 394, large specimen with rimose surface, Mo. Bot. Gard. Herb., × 0.4; Fig. 395, rather small specimen, No. 12523, × 0.5

FIG. 396. *Fomes pinicola*: typical sporophore cut vertically but showing upper surface, No. 2005, × 0.5

PLATE 68

FIGS. 397–398. *Fomes marmoratus*: typical sporophores, Nos. 3695 and 9575, × 0.7

FIGS. 399–401. *Fomes nigrolimitatus*: Fig. 399, nearly resupinate sporophore, No. 1844, × 0.7; Fig. 400, sessile sporophore, No. 11668, × 0.9; Fig. 401, pocket decay produced by this species, No. 12503, × 1.1

PLATE 69

FIGS. 402–403. *Fomes Everhartii*: Fig. 402, upper-surface view of young sporophore, × 0.8; Fig. 403, small sporophore cut vertically, × 0.8

FIG. 404. *Fomes ohiensis*: upper-surface views of unusually large sporophores, No. 12985, × 1.1

FIG. 405. *Fomes lobatus*: typical sporophore, showing new (upper) pileus growing out of pileus of previous year, No. 239, × 0.8

FIG. 406. *Fomes Langloisii*: probably co-type specimen, Lloyd Herb., × 0.8

PLATE 70

FIGS. 407–408. *Fomes fomentarius*: typical sporophores, × 0.7

FIG. 409. *Fomes igniarius* var. *laevigatus*: nearly resupinate specimen with narrowly reflexed pileus, No. 4940, × 0.7

FIGS. 410–412. *Fomes juniperinus*: Figs. 410 and 412, pore-surface and front view of small specimen, × 0.7; Fig. 411, upper-surface view of large sporophore, Pa. State College Herb., phot. by P. F. Shope, × 0.5

PLATE 71

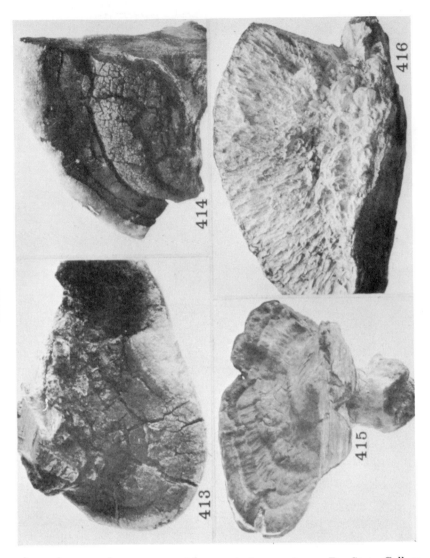

FIGS. 413–414. *Fomes fraxinophilus*: typical sporophores, Pa. State College Herb. and No. 122

FIG. 415. *Fomes lobatus*: typical substipitate sporophore, first year, No. 355, × 0.5

FIG. 416. *Fomes geotropus*: upper-surface view of specimen with unusually rough pileus, No. 11891, × 0.7

PLATE 72

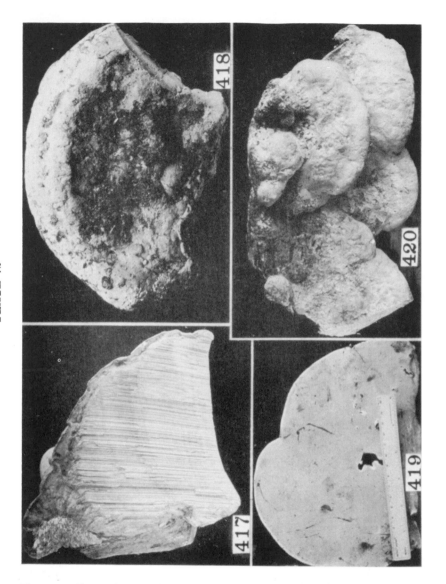

Fig. 417. *Fomes fomentarius*: lateral view of vertical section, showing the thin context and the typical elongated tubes without definite evidence of layering, No. 14867, × 0.6

Fig. 418. *Fomes geotropus*: upper-surface view of typical sporophore, No. 10713, × 0.5

Fig. 419. *Fomes applanatus*: pore-surface view of medium-sized sporophore, phot. by C. S. Parker, × 0.3

Fig. 420. *Fomes connatus*: typical sporophores, first year, Pa. State College Herb., × 0.6

PLATE 73

FIGS. 421–423. *Fomes Ellisianus*: Fig. 421, upper-surface view of typical old
sporophore, No. 5622, × 0.8; Figs. 422–423, upper- and lower-surface
views of smaller specimens, N. Y. State Mus. Herb., × 0.8

FIG. 424. *Fomes igniarius*: small specimens representative of variety on
Arctostaphylos, No. 7488, × 0.8

FIG. 425. *Fomes Everhartii*: portion of typical sporophore, No. 9133, × 0.8

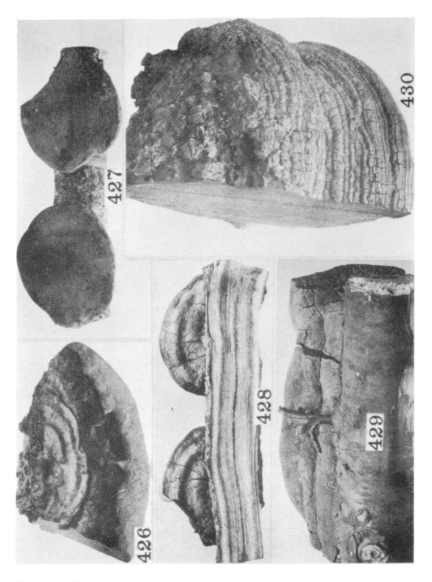

Fig. 426. *Fomes annosus*: upper-surface view of well-developed pileate sporophore, No. 11922, × 0.8

Figs. 427–429. *Fomes pomaceus*: Fig. 427, pore-surface view, × 0.8; Fig. 428, upper-surface view of pendent sporophores, × 0.8; Fig. 429, nearly resupinate sporophore on lower side of branch, Pa. State College Herb., × 0.8

Fig. 430. *Fomes igniarius*: typical ungulate sporophore cut vertically, No. 3352, × 0.5

PLATE 75

FIGS. 431–432. *Fomes densus*: typical sporophores with narrowly reflexed pilei, No. 965 (Fig. 431), × 0.8

FIG. 433. *Fomes fraxineus*: imbricate sporophore cluster (type specimen of *Polyporus induratus*), × 0.5

FIG. 434. *Fomes dependens*: typical sporophore, No. 10072, × 0.7

PLATE 76

FIGS. 435–438. *Fomes igniarius*: Fig. 435, type of sporophore usually referred to var. *nigricans*; Fig. 436, typical form of species; Figs. 437–438, intergrading forms; all upper-surface views of typical sporophores, × 0.7

PLATE 77

FIG. 439. *Fomes Calkinsii*: main portion of sporophore of typical form, No. 13644, × 0.8

FIGS. 440–442. *Fomes conchatus*: typical specimens of pileate form of species, × 0.8

FIG. 443. *Fomes dependens*: upper-surface view of typical sporophore, N. Y. Bot. Gard. Herb., × 0.8

PLATE 78

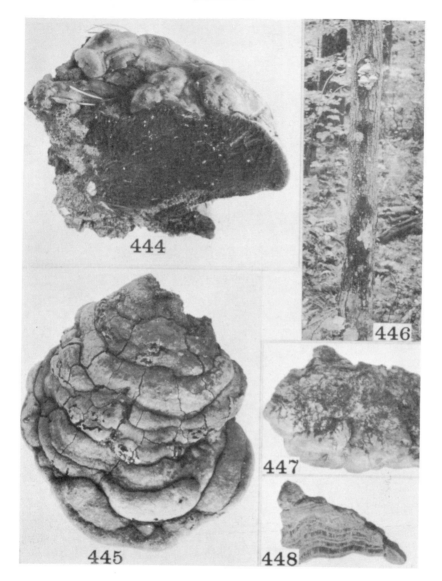

FIG. 444. *Fomes Brownii*: typical sporophore cut in half, showing the characteristic thick context, No. 5607, × 0.5

FIG. 445. *Fomes Calkinsii*: upper-surface view of unusually furrowed pileus, No. 10703, × 0.8

FIGS. 446–448. *Fomes connatus*: Fig. 446, typical sporophores on small red maple; Fig. 447, upper-surface view of small, moss-covered sporophore, × 0.5; Fig. 448, lateral view of vertical section through sporophore, showing the prominent tube layers, × 0.5

PLATE 79

FIGS. 449–452. *Fomes applanatus*: Fig. 449, upper-surface view of typical sporophore, × 0.5; Fig. 450, lateral view of vertical section through sporophore, showing three yearly layers of tubes, × 0.8; Fig. 451, thick, ungulate sporophore with whitened context, No. 13183, × 0.4; Fig. 452, habit of typical specimens, phot. by L. W. R. Jackson

PLATE 80

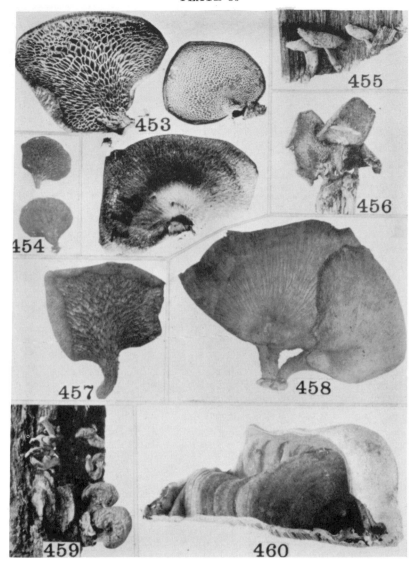

FIG. 453. *Favolus alveolaris*: typical sporophores, the lower-surface views showing large pores radiating from the reduced stem, No. 492, × 1.1

FIG. 454. *Favolus floridanus*: type specimen, N. Y. Bot. Gard. Herb., × 0.8

FIGS. 455–456. *Favolus Rhipidium*: typical sporophores in different views, Nos. 8474 and 10716, × 1.1

FIGS. 457–458. *Favolus brasiliensis*: lower- and upper-surface views of typical specimens, N. Y. Bot. Gard. Herb., × 0.8

FIG. 459. *Favolus Rhipidium*: typical sporophores, Nos. 14710 and 14095, × 1.1

FIG. 460. *Fomes annosus*: specimen developed in underground passageway in mine, No 5732, × 1

PLATE 81

FIGS. 461–462. *Daedalea farinacea*: typical semiresupinate sporophores, Nos. 12119 and 564, × 1.1

FIGS. 463–464. *Daedalea ambigua*: Fig. 463, typical daedaloid hymenium, N. Y. Bot. Gard. Herb., × 0.8; Fig. 464, pore-surface view, No. 10385, × 1.5

FIG. 465. *Cyclomyces Greenei*: small sporophore, No. 16524, × 1

FIG. 466. *Favolus cucullatus*: pore-surface view, N. Y. Bot. Gard. Herb., × 1.1

PLATE 82

FIGS. 467–472. *Daedalea confragosa*: Figs. 467–468, typical upper-surface views, the first (Pa. State College Herb.) more characteristic of the species on willow, the second (No. 12484) more typical on other substrata; Fig. 469, poroid hymenial surface occasionally developed, No. 3435, × 1.1; Fig. 470, hymenial surface that combines pores and gills, No. 531, × 0.8; Figs. 471–472, gilled hymenial surfaces, Lloyd Herb. and No. 9857, × 0.8

PLATE 83

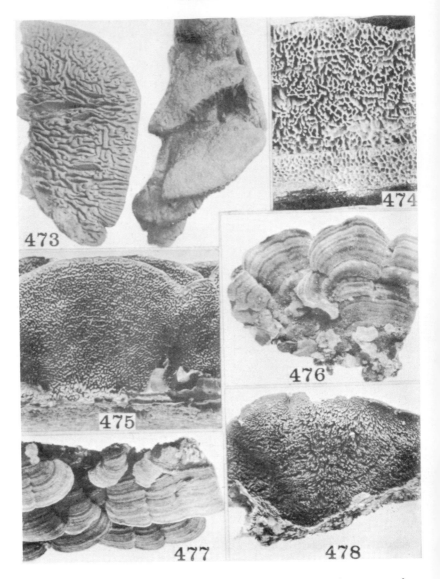

FIGS. 473–474. *Daedalea juniperina*: Fig. 473, lower- and upper-surface views of typical sporophore, Lloyd Herb., × 0.8; Fig. 474, resupinate form of species with more angular pores, No. 14282, × 0.8

FIGS. 475–478. *Daedalea unicolor*: Fig. 475, pore surface slightly daedaloid, Pa. State College Herb., × 1.5; Figs. 476–477, upper-surface views of typical specimens, × 0.8; Fig. 478, lower-surface view, showing toothed hymenial surface, No. 6162, × 1.5

PLATE 84

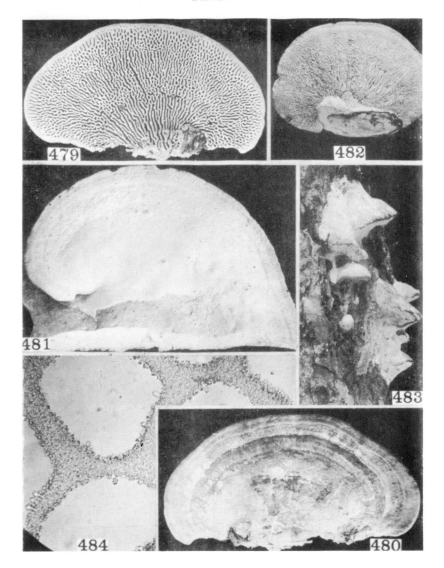

FIGS. 479–480. *Daedalea quercina*: typical lower- and upper-surface views, No. 11188, × 0.4

FIGS. 481–482. *Daedalea ambigua*: Fig. 481, upper-surface view, No. 10720, × 0.6; Fig. 482, lower-surface view, Pa. State College Herb., × 0.6

FIGS. 483–484. *Fomes connatus*: Fig. 483, typical sporophores, × 0.6; Fig. 484, photomicrograph of cross section of tubes, showing inconspicuous cystidia, No. 9105, × 390

PLATE 85

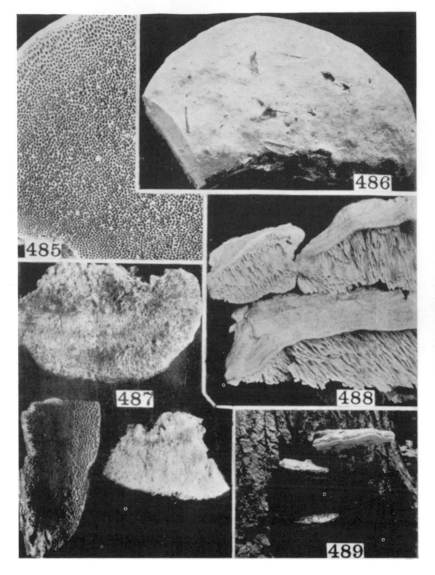

FIGS. 485–486. *Trametes suaveolens*: Fig. 485, pore-surface view, No. 2585, × 1.5; Fig. 486, upper-surface view, No. 2585, × 0.8

FIG. 487. *Trametes hispida*: typical small sporophores, hirsute and with large pores, × 0.8

FIG. 488. *Trametes heteromorpha*: typical sporophores, phot. by J. R. Weir, × 0.8

FIG. 489. *Polyporus Tsugae*: habit, phot. by L. W. R. Jackson

PLATE 86

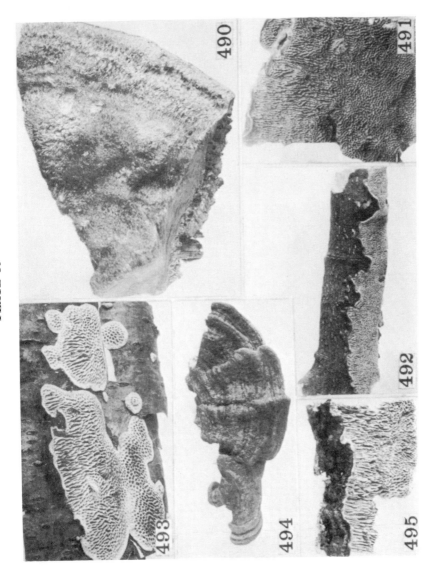

Fig. 490. *Trametes hispida*: upper-surface view of portion of large sporophore, × 0.8

Figs. 491–495. *Trametes mollis*: various views of sporophores, all (except Fig. 494) mostly resupinate, × 0.8

PLATE 87

FIGS. 496–497. *Trametes rigida*: Fig. 496, resupinate specimen, No. 15205, × 0.8; Fig. 497, pileate and nearly resupinate specimens, Nos. 420 and 10702, × 1

FIG. 498. *Trametes malicola*: pore-surface view, No. 9886, × 0.8

FIGS. 499–500. *Trametes Trogii*: Fig. 499, upper-surface view of typical sporophores, No. 5047, × 0.8; Fig. 500, pore-surface view, No. 4575, × 1.1

PLATE 88

FIGS. 501–503. *Trametes heteromorpha*: Fig. 501, typical pileate specimen (*above*) and typical resupinate specimen (*below*), phot. by J. R. Weir, × 0.8; Fig. 502, resupinate specimen with regular pores, Lloyd Herb., × 0.8; Fig. 503, resupinate specimen with larger and more irregular pores, Lloyd Herb., × 0.8

FIGS. 504–505. *Trametes variiformis*: Fig. 504, specimen with narrowly reflexed pilei, No. 12564, × 1.1; Fig. 505, resupinate specimen, No. 5076 × 1.1

PLATE 89

Figs. 506–507. *Trametes sepium*: typical small sporophores, × 0.8

Figs. 508–510. *Trametes serialis*: Fig. 508, resupinate sporophore with un-
dulate-nodulose surface, No. 7431, × 1; Fig. 509, sessile sporophores,
No. 7743, × 1.5; Fig. 510, pore-surface view, No. 10384, × 1

Fig. 511. *Trametes hispida*: large-pored form of species, × 0.8

PLATE 90

FIG. 512. *Trametes carbonaria*: typical resupinate form of species, × 0.8

FIGS. 513–516. *Trametes americana*: Fig. 513, upper-surface view of thick sporophore, No. 5471, × 1; Fig. 514, pore-surface view of form with somewhat irregular pores, No. 5471, × 1; Fig. 515, three sporophores from a single collection, showing transition from pores to gills, N. Y. Bot. Gard. Herb., × 0.8; Fig. 516, upper-surface view of typical thin sporophores, Nos. 11196 and 5663, × 1

PLATE 91

FIGS. 517–518. *Lenzites betulina*: upper- and lower-surface views of typical sporophores, No. 10743, × 0.8

FIGS. 519–520. *Trametes cubensis*: Fig. 519, specimen with somewhat corrugated upper surface, red just at base, Lloyd Herb., × 0.8; Fig. 520, zonate and more pubescent specimen, No. 16420, × 0.8

PLATE 92

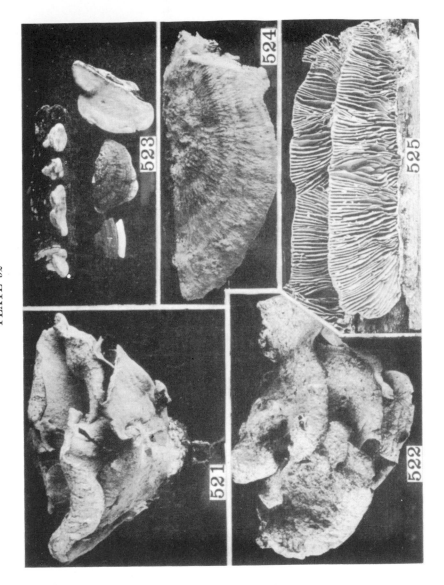

FIGS. 521–522. *Polyporus canadensis*: type specimens, × 0.8

FIG. 523. *Fomes ohiensis*: typical sporophores in various views, Nos. 38, 209, and 113

FIG. 524. *Trametes Trogii*: upper-surface view of typical sporophore, No. 16833, × 0.8

FIG. 525. *Lenzites betulina*: gill-surface view, Pa. State College Herb., × 0.8

PLATE 93

FIGS. 526–527. *Lenzites striata*: Fig. 526, lower-surface view, Lloyd Herb., × 0.8; Fig. 527, front view of imbricate sporophores, Lloyd Herb., × 0.8

FIGS. 528–529. *Hexagona variegata*: Fig. 528, pore-surface view, No. 10131, × 1.1; Fig. 529, upper-surface view, No. 10131, × 1.1

FIGS. 530–532. *Daedalea Berkeleyi*: Figs. 530, 532, lower-surface views of typical sporophores; Fig. 531, upper-surface view; all No. 14085, × 0.8

PLATE 94

FIGS. 533–536. *Lenzites saepiaria*: upper- and lower-surface views of typical sporophores, that in Fig. 533 (in Pa. State College Herb.) on branch of *Tsuga* and causing heartrot; all × 0.8

FIGS. 537–538. *Lenzites trabea*: upper- and lower-surface views, × 0.8

FIGS. 539–540. *Lenzites striata*: lower- and upper-surface views of typical sporophores, Nos. 10119 and 12088 (collected by C. W. Fritz as No. 688) × 0 8

PLATE 95

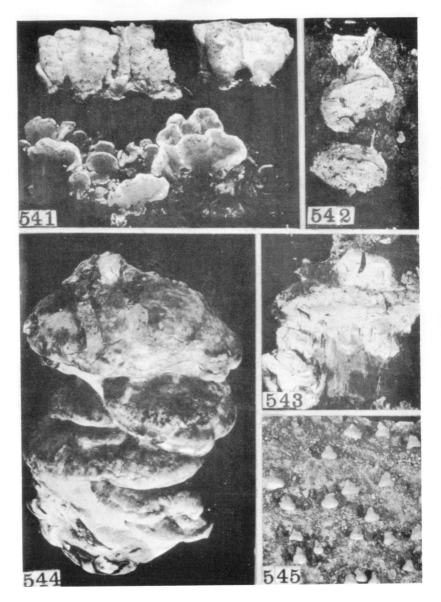

FIG. 541. *Polyporus semisupinus*: lower- and two upper-surface views, No. 18553, × 0.8

FIGS. 542–543. *Polyporus abieticola*: part of type collection, × 0.8

FIG. 544. *Polyporus robiniophilus*: on *Robinia*, LaFollette, Tenn., August, 1932, Oberlin College Herb., × 0.6

FIG. 545. *Polyporus pocula*: No. 23482, × 1.6

PLATE 96

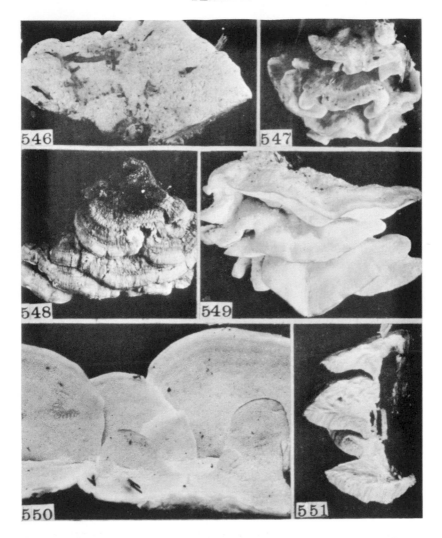

FIG. 546. *Polyporus immitis*: No. 19531, × 0.7

FIG. 547. *Polyporus balsameus*: specimens when fresh, No. 18572, × 0.7

FIG. 548. *Polyporus fib. illosus*: on *Betula*, Boothbay Harbor, Maine, Oberlin College Herb., × 0.4

FIG. 549. *Polyporus immitis*: No. 18521, × 0.7

FIG. 550. *Polyporus spumeus* var. *malicola*: pore-surface view, No. 18508, × 0.7

FIG. 551. *Polyporus tephroleucus*: lateral view of vertical section, No. 17349, × 0.7

PLATE 97

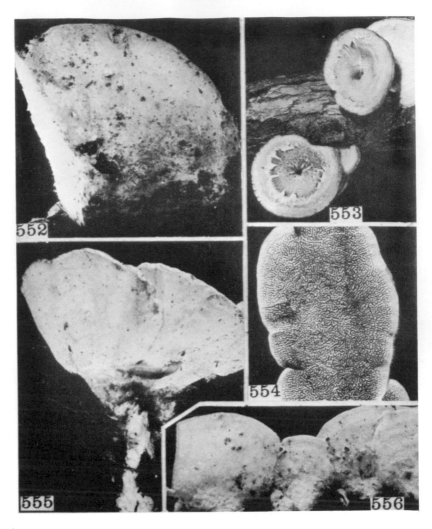

FIG. 552. *Polyporus spumeus*: No. 17340, × 0.7

FIG. 553. *Polyporus arcularius*: No. 22732, × 0.4

FIG. 554. *Daedalea unicolor*: specimen showing typical daedaloid pore surface, Pennsylvania State College campus, September 21, 1935, × 1.4

FIG. 555. *Polyporus borealis*: at base of living *Tsuga canadensis*, Tionesta Forest, Kane, Pa., 1936, × 0.4

FIG. 556. *Polyporus spumeus* var. *malicola*: upper-surface view, No. 18508. × 0.7

PLATE 98

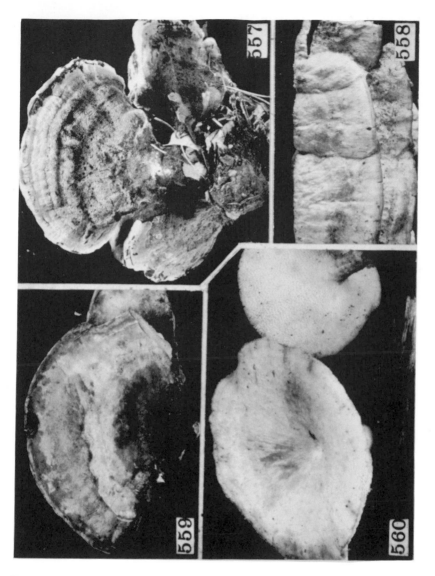

Fig. 557. *Polyporus Schweinitzii*: collected at Pine Hall, Centre County, Pa., 1936, × 0.4

Fig. 558. *Polyporus tephroleucus*: upper-surface view, No. 17349, × 0.8

Fig. 559. *Fomes fraxineus*: on *Fraxinus americanus*, collected in 1928, Oberlin College Herb., Lorain No. 3247 (Overholts Herb. No. 17423)

Fig. 560. *Polyporus fagicola*: No. 22754, × 0.8

PLATE 99

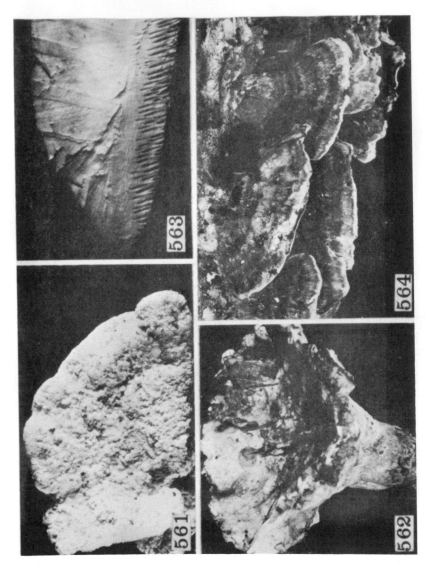

FIG. 561. *Polyporus immitis*: upper-surface view, No. 19531, × 0.8

FIG. 562. *Polyporus Pes-Caprae*: No. 21879, × 0.4

FIG. 563. *Trametes suaveolens*: lateral view of vertical section, showing the unequal bases of the tubes, No. 17342, × 1.5

FIG. 564. *Polyporus cuticularis*: × 0.8

PLATE 100

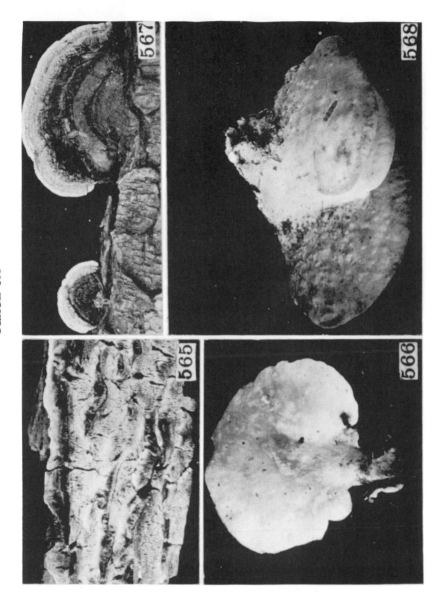

FIG. 565. *Polyporus lineatus*: No. 8023, × 1.1. A more extensive view of the same sporophore is shown in Fig. 634.

FIG. 566. *Polyporus osseus*: upper-surface view, No. 18609, × 0.8

FIG. 567. *Lenzites saepiaria*: on *Pinus rigida*, Colyer, Centre County, Pa., April 12, 1937, × 0.8

FIG. 568. *Trametes suaveolens*: upper-surface view, No. 17342, × 0.8

PLATE 101

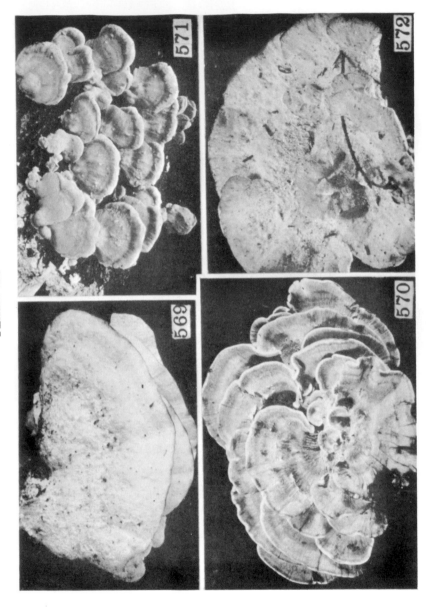

FIG. 569. *Polyporus immitis*: upper-surface view, No. 18521, × 0.7

FIG. 570. *Polyporus giganteus*: collected on Pennsylvania State College campus, August 12, 1938, × 0.2

FIG. 571. *Polyporus pubescens*: upper-surface view, No. 17274, × 0.7

FIG. 572. *Polyporus borealis*: collected in Tionesta Forest, Kane, Pa., August 14, 1936, × 0.5

PLATE 102

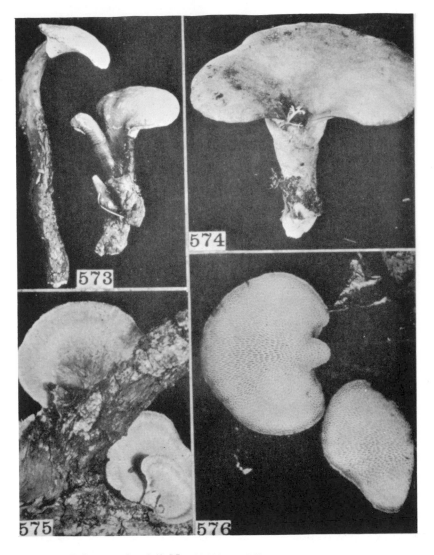

FIG. 573. *Polyporus Curtisii*: No. 15434, × 0.7

FIG. 574. *Polyporus hirtus*: collected at Laurentides National Park, Quebec, Canada, August 27, 1938, × 0.7

FIGS. 575–576. *Favolus alveolaris*: Fig. 575, collected at Poe Paddy Park, Centre County, Pa., May 29, 1937; Fig. 576, lower-surface view of same specimen, × 0.7

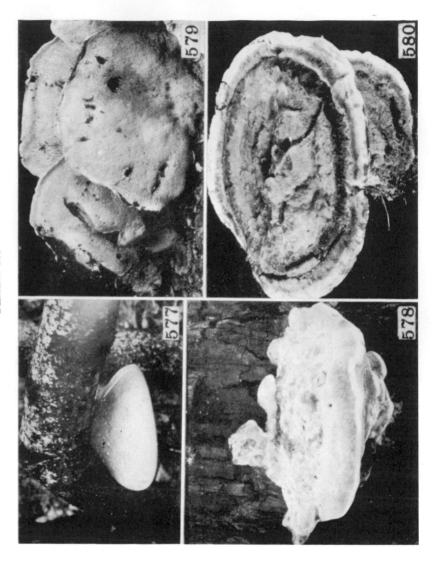

PLATE 103

FIG. 577. *Polyporus betulinus*: No. 17341, × 0.5

FIG. 578. *Polyporus tomentosus*: on *Pinus rigida*, Pennsylvania State College campus, October 13, 1939, × 0.7

FIG. 579. *Polyporus cuticularis*: lower-surface view, × 1.1

FIG. 580. *Polyporus Schweinitzii*: collected at Alan Segar Monument, Huntingdon County, Pa., July 30, 1937, × 0.5

PLATE 104

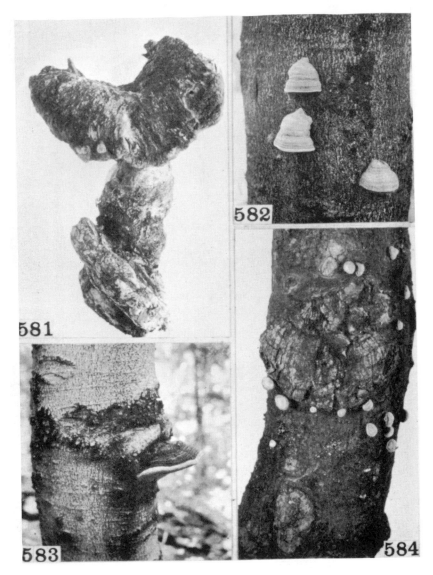

Fig. 581. *Polyporus montanus*: No. 12553, × 0.8

Fig. 582. *Fomes fomentarius*: on *Fagus*, Mt. Jewett, McKean County, Pa., July 7, 1938, × 0.2

Fig. 583. *Fomes igniarius*: on *Fagus*, Green Mountain National Forest, Vt., July 16, 1938, phot. by W. A. Campbell

Fig. 584. *Polyporus pocula*: on *Pinus Strobus*, No. 23492, × 0.8

PLATE 105

Fig. 585. *Polyporus Tsugae*: on dead *Tsuga canadensis*, Tionesta Forest, Kane, Pa., phot. by W. A. Campbell

Fig. 586. *Polyporus hispidus*: on *Quercus*, showing large open canker from which the sporophores are always produced on this host, 1939, phot. by W. A. Campbell

Fig. 587. *Fomes applanatus*: on *Fagus*, Black Forest, Potter County, Pa., 1936, × 0.4

Fig. 588. *Polyporus frondosus*: at base of living *Quercus*, Pennsylvania State College campus, September 25, 1937, phot. by W. A. Campbell

PLATE 106

FIG. 589. *Polyporus semisupinus*: No. 19459, × 0.8

FIG. 590. *Fomes applanatus*: on *Fagus*, Kane, Pa., phot. by W. A. Campbell

FIG. 591. *Polyporus sulphureus*: on *Quercus*, Huntingdon Furnace, Huntingdon County, Pa., 1932

FIG. 592. *Polyporus compactus*: on *Quercus*, Pennsylvania State College campus, 1939, phot. by W. A. Campbell

PLATE 107

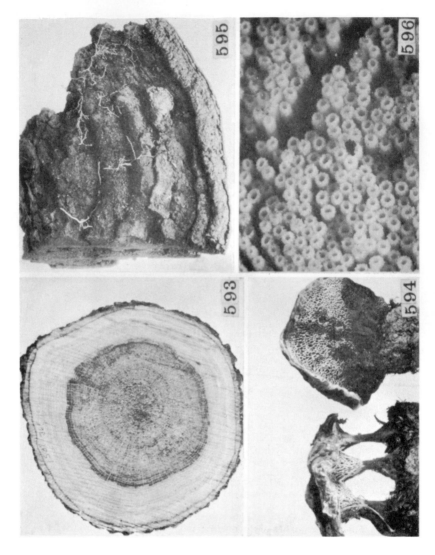

Fig. 593. Cross section of trunk rotted by *Fomes Everhartii*

Fig. 594. *Polyporus Montagnei*: No. 22700, × 0.7

Fig. 595. *Fomes extensus*: on dead *Castanea dentata*, Gatlinburg, Tenn., collected by L. R. Hesler, No. 6343, × 0.7

Fig. 596. *Fistulina hepatica*: pore-surface view, showing the isolated tubes, on *Castanopsis*, collected at Inverness, Calif., phot. by Lee Bonar

PLATE 108

FIG. 597. *Fomes Everhartii*: phot. by W. A. Campbell

FIG. 598. *Polyporus montanus*: on ground under *Picea sitchensis*, Queen Charlotte Islands, British Columbia, collected by Irene Mounce, September 21, 1925, × 0.5

FIG. 599. *Polyporus borealis*: on *Tsuga canadensis*, Buckstown, Somerset County, Pa., collected by A. G. Lisi, June 28, 1934

FIG. 600. *Polyporus giganteus*: collected at Pine Hall, Centre County, Pa., July 5, 1939, × 0.1

PLATE 109

Fig. 601. *Polyporus picipes*: upper-surface view, × 0.4

Figs. 602–604. *Fomes Ellisianus*: Fig. 602, pore-surface view, × 1.4; Figs. 603–604, upper-surface views, showing blackened and rimose character, on *Shepherdia argentea*, all collected in Piute County, Utah, 1945, by A. S. Rhoads, × 0.5

PLATE 110

FIG. 605. *Fomes officinalis*: collected in British Columbia in 1943, length 14 in., greatest width 9 in., approximate age 50 years, specimen received from D. C. Buckland

FIGS. 606–607. *Polyporus biennis*: Fig. 606, upper-surface view; Fig. 607, pore-surface view, No. 24730, × 1.6

FIGS. 608–609. *Polyporus dryophilus*: Fig. 608, No. 24229, × 0.4; Fig. 609, on *Quercus Prinus*, Stone Valley, Huntingdon County, Pa., September, 1945, × 0.4

PLATE 111

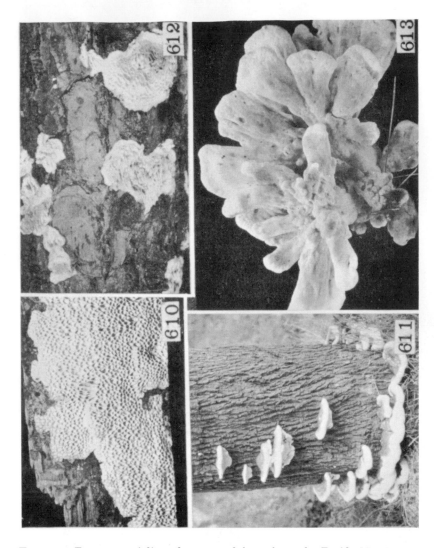

FIG. 610. *Trametes serialis*: a large-pored form from the Pacific Northwest, on *Picea sitchensis*, No. 24837, × 0.7

FIG. 611. *Polyporus lucidus*: on dead *Fraxinus americana*, Honesdale, Wayne County, Pa., August, 1945, about × 0.1

FIG. 612. *Trametes heteromorpha*: No. 24420, × 0.7

FIG. 613. *Polyporus sulphureus* var. *cincinnatus*: No. 18479, × 0.4

PLATE 112

Fig. 614. *Polyporus alboluteus*: entirely resupinate form, No. 24367, × 0.7

Fig. 615. *Polyporus immitis*: No. 24744, × 0.6

Fig. 616. *Polyporus dryadeus*: around stump of *Quercus* tree that died during preceding winter, Pennsylvania State College campus, June 17, 1945

Fig. 617. *Polyporus frondosus*: collected on Pennsylvania State College campus, October 7, 1944, × 0.2

PLATE 113

FIG. 618. *Polyporus galactinus*: No. 19457, × 0.8

FIG. 619. *Polyporus hispidus*: No. 19446, × 0.5

FIG. 620. *Fomes nigrolimitatus*: radial and tangential views of early (*left*) and late (*right*) stages of decay produced by this species, × 0.8

FIG. 621. *Polyporus balsameus*: No. 19458, × 0.8

PLATE 114

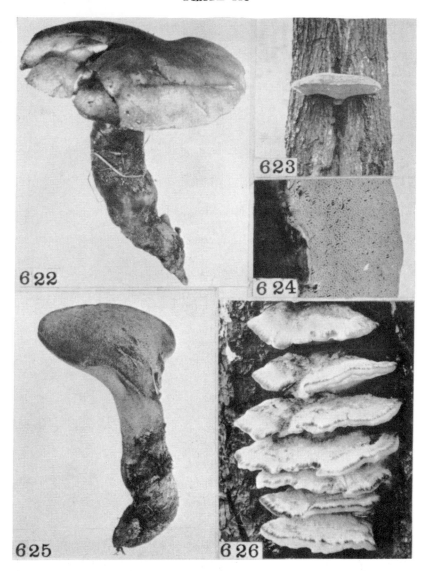

FIG. 622. *Polyporus radicatus*: No. 24733, × 0.5

FIG. 623. *Polyporus hispidus*: specimen on living *Quercus*, showing usual location with reference to accompanying lesion on tree, Bear Meadows, Centre County, Pa., 1945

FIG. 624. *Polyporus fissilis*: No. 19222, phot. by A. S. Rhoads, × 0.8

FIG. 625. *Fistulina pallida*: No. 22327, × 0.8

FIG. 626. *Polyporus borealis*: fresh specimens on living *Picea*, phot. by Bureau of Plant Industry, Soils and Agricultural Engineering, U.S.D.A.

PLATE 115

FIGS. 627–628. *Polyporus albiceps*: upper- and lower-surface views of specimen collected at West Winfield, Armstrong County, Pa., by Miss Marie Knauz, Carnegie Museum Herb., Pittsburgh, Pa., × 0.8

FIGS. 629–630. *Polyporus decurrens*: upper- and lower-surface views of specimen collected in California by Miss Elizabeth Morse and E. R. Schneider in 1933, No. 17563, × 0.8

FIG. 631. *Polyporus cuneatus*: × 0 8

PLATE 116

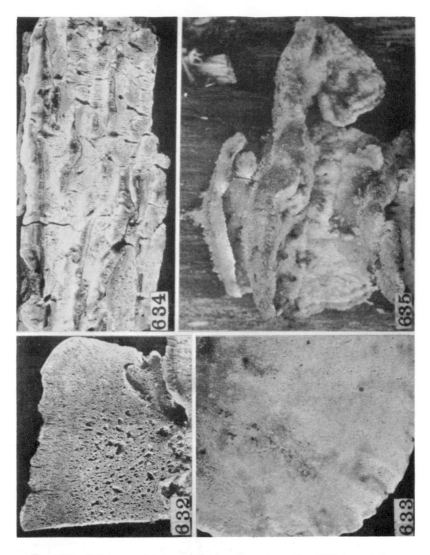

FIG. 632. *Polyporus delectans*: pore-surface view, No. 17518, × 0.8

FIG. 633. *Polyporus Spraguei*: pore-surface view, No. 24477, × 1.5

FIG. 634. *Polyporus lineatus*: part of type collection, No. 8023, × 1.1

FIG. 635. *Polyporus fragilis*: Lowe No. 4562, × 0.8

PLATE 117

FIG. 636. *Polyporus graveolens*: on *Quercus alba*, Pennsylvania State College campus, September 15, 1940, × 0.4

FIG. 637. *Polyporus hispidus*: specimen in usual position with reference to cankered area, phot. by W. A. Campbell

FIGS. 638–639. *Polyporus glomeratus*: sterile knots on *Acer rubrum* from which Campbell and Davidson report isolations of *P. glomeratus*, Fig. 639 showing the sterile fungous tissue usually present; Fig. 638, phot. by W. A. Campbell

PLATE 118

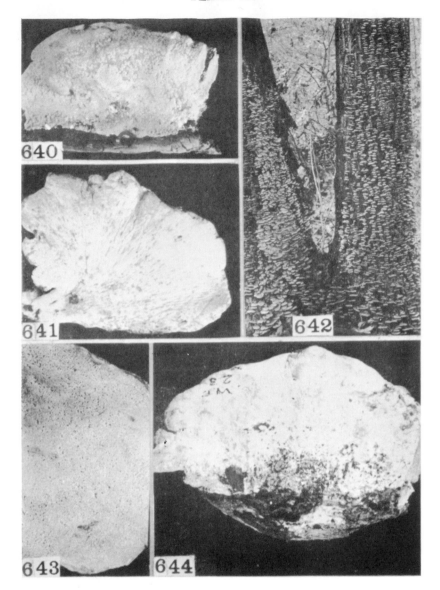

Fig. 640. *Polyporus fumidiceps*: upper-surface view, No. 12751, × 0.8

Fig. 641. *Polyporus guttulatus*: upper-surface view of dried specimen, showing the depressed spots, No. 22650, × 0.8

Fig. 642. *Polyporus pargamenus*: typical growth form on dead standing *Quercus*, phot. by A. S. Rhoads

Figs. 643–644. *Polyporus guttulatus*: Fig. 643, pore-surface view, No. 22650 (collected by G. H. Englerth as No. W.P. 23), × 1.6; Fig. 644, upper-surface view of same specimen, × 0.8

PLATE 119

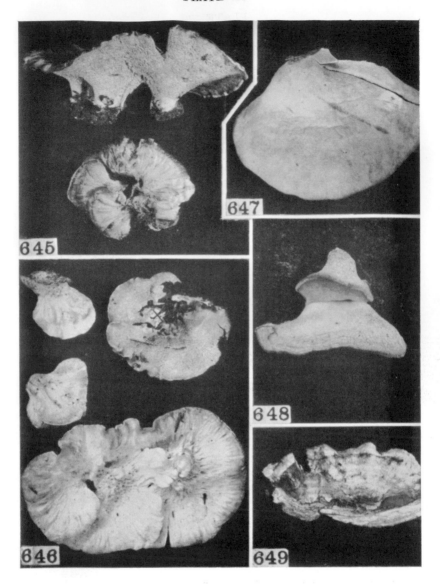

FIGS. 645–646. *Polyporus scrobiculatus*: type collection, No. 20376

FIGS. 647–648. *Polyporus albellus*: upper-surface views, Nos. 2956 and 17347, × 0.7 and × 0.6

FIG. 649. *Polyporus balsameus*: No. 24046, × 0.7

PLATE 120

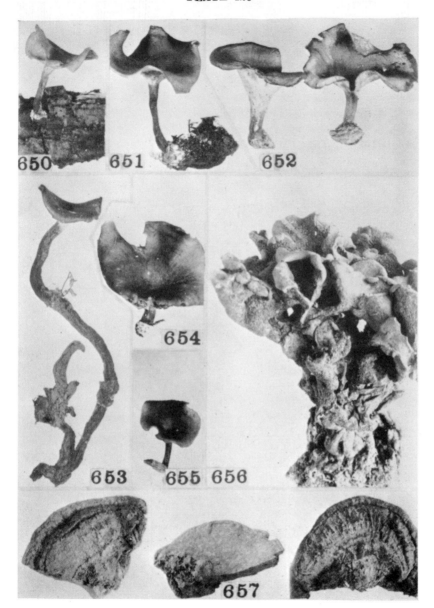

FIGS. 650–655. *Polyporus picipes*: a variety of collections illustrating a small form of the species; in order, Nos. 24127, 24109, 24570, all from British Columbia; No. 14484, from Sullivan County, Pa.; Nos. 24546 and 24117, from British Columbia; all × 0.8

FIG. 656. *Polyporus illudens*: type specimen, No. 14302, × 0.8

FIG. 657. *Fomes torulosus*: three specimens, the central one in lower-surface view, the other two in upper-surface view, No. 524, × 1

PLATE 121

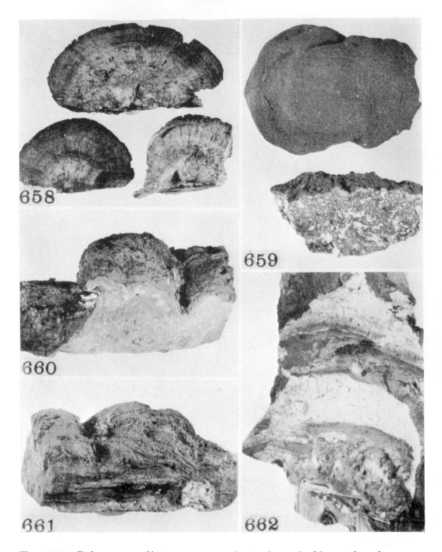

Fig. 658. *Polyporus radiatus*: upper-surface view of old weathered sporo-phores, No. 11297, × 0.7

Fig. 659. *Polyporus tuberaster*: sclerotium, specimen above showing ex-ternal view, that below showing bonelike internal structure, Nos. 12857 and 12814, × 0.7

Figs. 660–661. *Fomes repandus*: front-dorsal view and dorsal view, with sporophore cut to show thickness, No. 11648, × 0.7

Fig. 662. *Polyporus anceps*: on *Pinus rigida*, Pa., × 0.7

PLATE 122

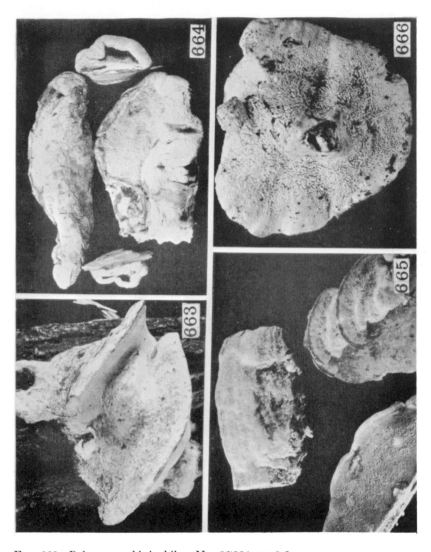

FIG. 663. *Polyporus robiniophilus*: No. 17324, × 0.3

FIG. 664. *Polyporus leucospongia*: No. 25025, × 0.5

FIG. 665. *Polyporus subchartaceus*: Nos. 9492 and 10293, × 0.7

FIG. 666. *Sistotrema confluens*: specimen revealing daedaloid nature of lower surface, especially near the margin, No. 17266, × 1.7

PLATE 123

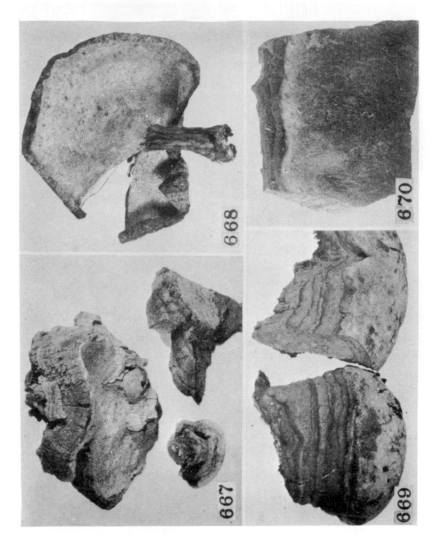

Fig. 667. *Fomes occidentalis*: type collection. No. 21572, × 0.7

Fig. 668. *Polyporus brumalis*: No. 24456, × 0.7

Fig. 669. *Fomes robustus*: No. 24475, × 0.7

Fig. 670. *Fomes repandus*: No. 3878, × 0.7

PLATE 124

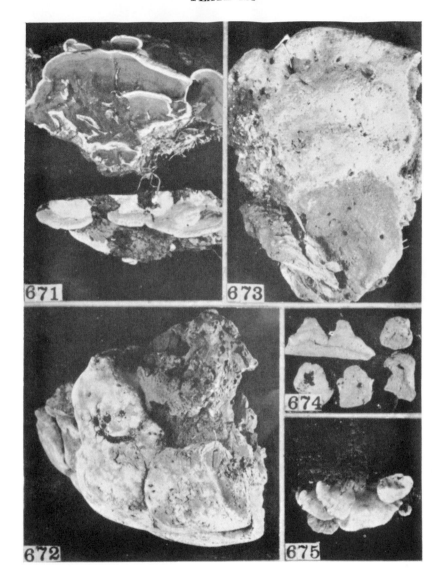

Fig. 671. *Polyporus dichrous*: lower-surface view (*above*) and upper-surface view (*below*), No. 2751, × 0.7

Figs. 672–673. *Polyporus Munzii*: upper-surface views, Nos. 21367 and 21312, × 0.4

Fig. 674. *Polyporus perdelicatus*: No. 23441, × 1.5

Fig. 675. *Polyporus semisupinus*: No. 19410, × 0.7

PLATE 125

Hymenial features of various species of polypores

Cyclomyces Greenei, No. 5389
Daedalea ambigua, No. 929
Daedalea confragosa, No. 5581
Daedalea farinacea, No. 4004
Daedalea juniperina, Mo. Bot. Gard. Herb.
Daedalea quercina, No. 10799
Daedalea unicolor, No. 10921
Favolus alveolaris, No. 7950
Favolus brasiliensis, No. 17053
Favolus cucullatus, N. Y. Bot. Gard. Herb.
Favolus Rhipidium, No. 10716
Fomes annosus, No. 5732
Fomes applanatus, No. 58

Fomes Brownii, No. 15776
Fomes Calkinsii, No. 15703
Trametes americana, No. 5733
Trametes carbonaria
Trametes cubensis, No. 15724
Trametes heteromorpha, No. 6033
Trametes hispida, No. 1774
Trametes malicola, No. 831
Trametes mollis, No. 18312
Trametes rigida, No. 17441
Trametes sepium, No. 988
Trametes serialis, No. 7431
Trametes suaveolens, No. 3530
Trametes Trogii, No. 5119
Trametes variiformis, No. 12559

PLATE 125

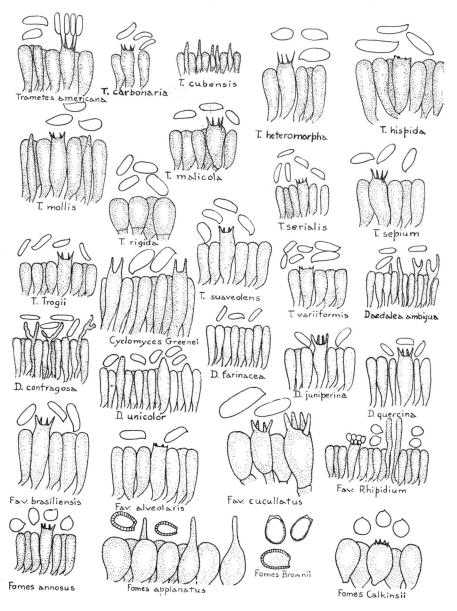

Trametes americana
T. carbonaria
T. cubensis
T. heteromorpha
T. hispida
T. mollis
T. malicola
T. serialis
T. sepium
T. rigida
T. Trogii
T. suaveolens
T. variiformis
Daedalea ambigua
Cyclomyces Greenei
D. farinacea
D. confragosa
D. juniperina
D. quercina
D. unicolor
Fav. brasiliensis
Fav. alveolaris
Fav. cucullatus
Fav. Rhipidium
Fomes annosus
Fomes applanatus
Fomes Brownii
Fomes Calkinsii

PLATE 126

Hymenial features of various species of *Fomes*

Fomes conchatus, No. 10964
Fomes connatus
Fomes densus, No. 4216
Fomes dependens
Fomes Ellisianus, No. 5622
Fomes fomentarius, No. 8375
Fomes fraxineus, No. 414
Fomes geotropus
Fomes igniarius, No. 3519
Fomes juniperinus, No. 2330
Fomes Langloisii, type specimen
Fomes Meliae, on *Fraxinus*, No. 1910
Fomes nigrolimitatus, No. 11668
Fomes officinalis, No. 4008

Fomes ohiensis, No. 4269
Fomes Pini, No. 3183
Fomes pinicola
Fomes pomaceus, No. 427
Fomes praerimosus, type specimen
Fomes repandus, No. 3878
Fomes Ribis, No. 8869
Fomes robustus, No. 3638
Fomes roseus, U. S. Forest Path. Herb., No. 11252
Fomes scutellatus, No. 7324
Fomes extensus, No. 9927
Fomes subroseus

PLATE 126

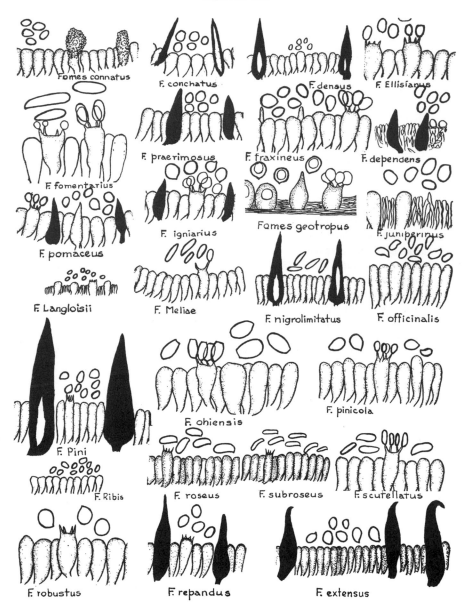

Fomes connatus

F. conchatus

F. densus

F. Ellisianus

F. praerimosus

F. fraxineus

F. dependens

F. fomentarius

F. igniarius

Fomes geotropus

F. juniperinus

F. pomaceus

F. Langloisii

F. Meliae

F. nigrolimitatus

F. officinalis

F. Pini

F. ohiensis

F. pinicola

F. Ribis

F. roseus

F. subroseus

F. scutellatus

F. robustus

F. repandus

F. extensus

PLATE 127

Hymenial features of various species of polypores and views of clamp
connections

Fomes Everhartii, No. 2685
Fomes tenuis, No. 11681
Fomes texanus, No. 2333
Fomes torulosus, specimen collected by C. W. Edgerton, Lloyd Herb.
Hexagona variegata, No. 10131
Lenzites abietinella, type specimen
Lenzites betulina, No. 4713
Lenzites saepiaria, No. 7140
Lenzites striata, specimen collected in Puerto Rico in 1913
Lenzites trabea, No. 10967
[Clamp connections: *a*, sectional view; *b*, external side view of a small one; *c*,
external top view; *d*, side view of a large one—J.L.L.]

PLATE 127

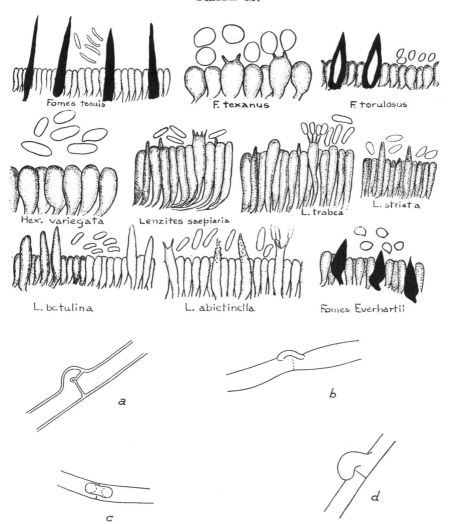

Fomes tenuis   F. texanus   F. torulosus

Hex. variegata   Lenzites saepiaria   L. trabea   L. striata

L. betulina   L. abietinella   Fomes Everhartii

a   b

c   d

Clamp connections

PLATE 128

Hymenial features of various species of *Polyporus*

Polyporus abietinus, No. 13217
Polyporus aculeifer, No. 10039
Polyporus admirabilis, No. 12740
Polyporus adustus, No. 284
Polyporus albellus, No. 13412
Polyporus alboluteus, No. 9348
Polyporus amorphus, No. 4643
Polyporus amygdalinus, No. 14268
Polyporus anceps, No. 8509
Polyporus arcularius, No. 10696
Polyporus balsameus, No. 13442
Polyporus basilaris, type specimen
Polyporus Berkeleyi, No. 12234
Polyporus betulinus, No. 6155
Polyporus biennis, No. 9119

Polyporus biennis, chlamydospores, No. 4241
Polyporus biformis, No. 241
Polyporus borealis, No. 14892
Polyporus brumalis, No. 17480
Polyporus caeruleoporus, No. 7517
Polyporus caesius, No. 11652
Polyporus canadensis, No. 16860
Polyporus cinnabarinus, No. 47
Polyporus cinnamomeus, No. 16331
Polyporus dryadeus, No. 7736. Setae not filled in.
Polyporus tomentosus, No. 16046
Polyporus tomentosus var. *circinatus*, No. 16291

PLATE 128

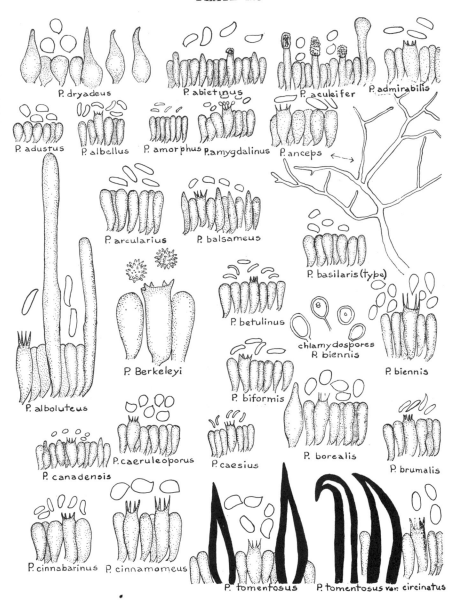

P. dryadeus P. abietinus P. aculeifer P. admirabilis

P. adustus P. albellus P. amorphus P. amygdalinus P. anceps

P. arcularius P. balsameus

P. basilaris (type)

chlamydospores
P. biennis

P. Berkeleyi P. betulinus P. biennis

P. alboluteus P. biformis

P. caeruleoporus P. borealis

P. canadensis P. caesius P. brumalis

P. cinnabarinus P. cinnamomeus

P. tomentosus P. tomentosus var. circinatus

PLATE 129

Hymenial features of various species of *Polyporus*

Polyporus compactus, No. 8309
Polyporus conchifer, No. 577
Polyporus confluens, No. 11061
Polyporus corrosus, No. 8696
Polyporus cristatus, No. 972
Polyporus croceus, No. 11722
Polyporus cryptopus, type specimen
Polyporus cuneatus, No. 14095
Polyporus Curtisii, No. 3796
Polyporus cuticularis, No. 5410
Polyporus cutifractus, collected by Murrill, Seattle, 1911
Polyporus dealbatus, collected by Murrill and House, North Carolina, 1908
Polyporus decurrens, No. 17563
Polyporus delectans, No. 250

Polyporus dependens, No. 17591
Polyporus dichrous, No. 16341
Polyporus dryadeus, No. 2759
Polyporus dryophilus, No. 13251
Polyporus dryophilus var. *vulpinus*, No. 15912
Polyporus durescens, No. 19080
Polyporus ectypus, No. 12960
Polyporus elegans, No. 13394
Polyporus Ellisii, No. 15780
Polyporus fagicola, No. 108
Polyporus fibrillosus, No. 19462
Polyporus fimbriatus, No. 14706
Polyporus fissilis, No. 14481
Polyporus floriformis, No. 14962
Polyporus focicola, No. 15204
Polyporus fractipes, No. 503

PLATE 129

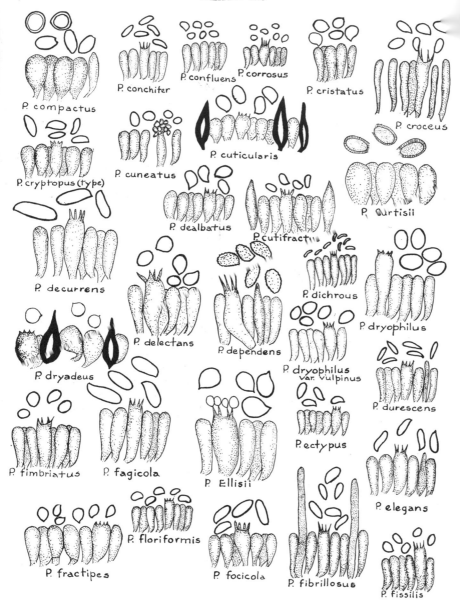

P. compactus

P. conchifer

P. confluens

P. corrosus

P. cristatus

P. croceus

P. cryptopus (type)

P. cuneatus

P. cuticularis

P. curtisii

P. dealbatus

P. cutifract...

P. decurrens

P. dichrous

P. delectans

P. dependens

P. dryophilus

P. dryadeus

P. dryophilus var. vulpinus

P. durescens

P. ectypus

P. fimbriatus

P. fagicola

P. Ellisii

P. elegans

P. floriformis

P. fractipes

P. focicola

P. fibrillosus

P. fissilis

PLATE 130

Hymenial features of various species of *Polyporus*

Polyporus fragilis, No. 19553
Polyporus frondosus, No. 16140
Polyporus fruticum, No. 11817
Polyporus fumidiceps, No. 18175
Polyporus fumosus, No. 3562
Polyporus galactinus, No. 14959
Polyporus giganteus, No. 4621
Polyporus gilvus, No. 12965
Polyporus glomeratus, No. 18649
Polyporus graveolens, No. 515
Polyporus griseus, collected in Massachusetts
Polyporus guttulatus, No. 11043
Polyporus hirsutus, No. 8070
Polyporus hirtus, No. 11052
Polyporus hispidus, No. 7894.   Setae not filled in.

Polyporus hydnoides, Mo. Bot. Gard. Herb., No. 714450
Polyporus illudens, No. 14302
Polyporus immitis, No. 12558
Polyporus iodinus, No. 10708
Polyporus juniperinus, type specimen
Polyporus lapponicus, No. 10203
Polyporus leucospongia, No. 5426
Polyporus licnoides, No. 15633
Polyporus lucidus, No. 3962
Polyporus ludovicianus, No. 15498
Polyporus McMurphyi, No. 15045
Polyporus maximus, No. 9737
Polyporus melanopus, No. 14737
Polyporus mollis, No. 13238
Polyporus Montagnei, No. 16727
Polyporus montanus, No. 12553

PLATE 130

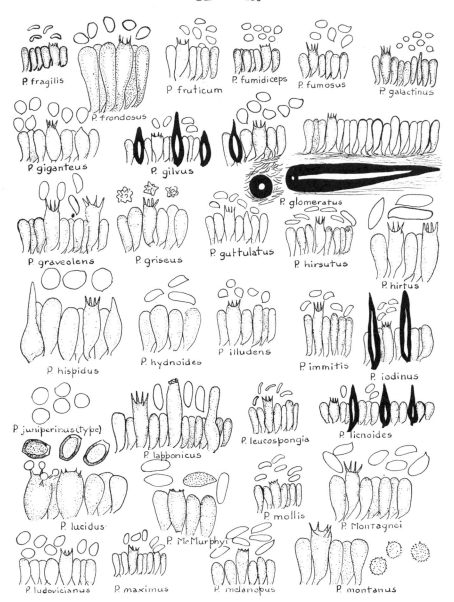

P. fragilis

P. fruticum

P. fumidiceps

P. fumosus

P. galactinus

P. frondosus

P. giganteus

P. gilvus

P. glomeratus

P. graveolens

P. griseus

P. guttulatus

P. hirsutus

P. hirtus

P. hispidus

P. hydnoides

P. illudens

P. immitis

P. iodinus

P. juniperinus (type)

P. lapponicus

P. leucospongia

P. licnoides

P. lucidus

P. McMurphyi

P. mollis

P. Montagnei

P. ludovicianus

P. maximus

P. melanopus

P. montanus

PLATE 131

Hymenial features of various species of *Polyporus*

Polyporus mutabilis, No. 14199
Polyporus nidulans, No. 379
Polyporus obtusus, No. 14655
Polyporus occidentalis, No. 15756
Polyporus ochrotinctellus, N. Y. Bot. Gard. Herb.
Polyporus oregonensis, No. 14177
Polyporus osseus, No. 19378
Polyporus ovinus, No. 16478
Polyporus palustris, No. 14703
Polyporus pargamenus, No. 11956
Polyporus pavonius, No. 12017
Polyporus Peckianus, No. 6021
Polyporus perdelicatus, collected on *Tsuga* by Murrill, Washington, 1911
Polyporus perennis, No. 13457

Polyporus persicinus, No. 14628
Polyporus Pes-Caprae, No. 15039
Polyporus picipes, No. 142
Polyporus pocula, No. 10409
Polyporus porrectus, No. 15522
Polyporus pubescens, No. 14870
Polyporus radiatus, No. 6147
Polyporus radiatus var. *Cephalanthi*, No. 14072. Setae not filled in.
Polyporus radicatus, No. 71
Polyporus resinosus
Polyporus rigidus, No. 5731
Polyporus robiniophilus, No. 16252
Polyporus sanguineus, No. 16718
Polyporus subchartaceus, Nos. 1756, 8039, 9974

PLATE 131

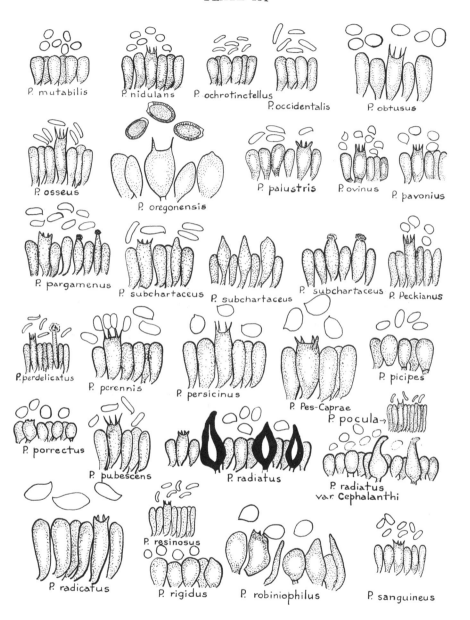

P. mutabilis

P. nidulans

P. ochrotinctellus

P. occidentalis

P. obtusus

P. osseus

P. oregonensis

P. palustris

P. ovinus

P. pavonius

P. pargamenus

P. subchartaceus

P. subchartaceus

P. subchartaceus

P. Peckianus

P. perdelicatus

P. perennis

P. persicinus

P. Pes-Caprae

P. picipes

P. porrectus

P. pubescens

P. radiatus

P. pocula→

P. radiatus var. Cephalanthi

P. resinosus

P. radicatus

P. rigidus

P. robiniophilus

P. sanguineus

PLATE 132

Hymenial features of various species of *Polyporus*

Polyporus pinsitus, No. 8686
Polyporus planellus, No. 7935
Polyporus Munzii, No. 15914
Polyporus Schweinitzii, No. 5379
Polyporus sector, No. 8878
Polyporus semipileatus, No. 12314
Polyporus semisupinus, No. 18553
Polyporus Spraguei, No. 11641
Polyporus spumeus, No. 17771
Polyporus squamosus, No. 11592
Polyporus subectypus, No. 14911
above, Britton 6588 below
Polyporus submurinus, type specimen
Polyporus subpendulus, type specimen
Polyporus sulphureus, No. 3831
Polyporus sylvestris, type specimen
Polyporus tenuis, No. 16506

Polyporus tephroleucus, No. 10872
Polyporus texanus, type specimen
Polyporus Tricholoma, No. 9746
Polyporus trichomallus, No. 8669
Polyporus Tsugae, No. 2965
Polyporus tuberaster, material received from Dr. Irene Mounce
Polyporus Tulipiferae, No. 13496
Polyporus umbellatus, No. 18246
Polyporus undosus, No. 13947
Polyporus varius, No. 13277
Polyporus velutinus, No. 3453
Polyporus versatilis, No. 14744
Polyporus versicolor, No. 11323
Polyporus vinosus, No. 9741
Polyporus volvatus, No. 16473
Polyporus zonalis, No. 15477

PLATE 132

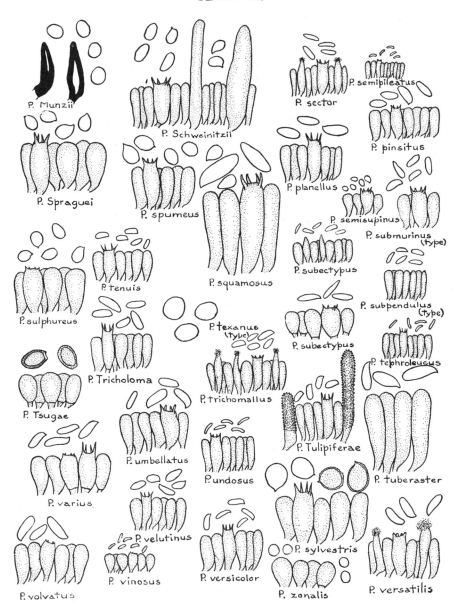

P. Munzii

P. Schweinitzii

P. sector

P. semipileatus

P. pinsitus

P. Spraguei

P. spumeus

P. planellus

P. semisupinus

P. submurinus (type)

P. subectypus

P. tenuis

P. squamosus

P. sulphureus

P. texanus (type)

P. subpendulus (type)

P. subectypus

P. Tricholoma

P. trichomallus

P. tephroleucus

P. Tsugae

P. umbellatus

P. Tulipiferae

P. varius

P. undosus

P. tuberaster

P. velutinus

P. sylvestris

P. volvatus

P. vinosus

P. versicolor

P. zonalis

P. versatilis

GLOSSARY

Aculeate. Slender and with a sharp point; spinelike.

Allantoid. Elongate and curved; sausage-shaped.

Alutaceous. Light tan.

Alveolar. With large pores or pits, resembling a honeycomb.

Anastomosing. Running together irregularly.

Anoderm. Without a crust.

Anomalous. Not closely related to other forms.

Applanate. Horizontally expanded; plane.

Appressed. Pressed closely to the surface.

Areolate. Cracked or torn into small areas.

Avellaneous. Light wood brown.

Azonate. Without zones or concentric markings.

Bay. Red-brown approaching but lighter than chestnut.

[*Broad.* Horizontal dimension parallel to the substratum.—J.L.L.]

Capitate. Abruptly enlarged at the apex.

Carbonizing decay. A decay characterized by loss of cellulose and pentosans, leaving lignin in the form of a brown carbonous mass. (See further on p. 20.)

Cartilaginous. Of the texture of cartilage.

Chestnut. Dark red-brown.

Cinereous. Ash-colored; dirty white.

Cinnabar. Deep bright red.

Clamp. (See *Clamp connection.*)

Clamp connection. A by-pass around a cross wall in a hypha. (See Plate 127.)

Clavate. Club-shaped; gradually enlarged upward.

Conchate. Shell-shaped.

Concolorous. Of the same color.

Connate. United.

Context. The inner substance of the pileus or stem.

Coriaceous. Leathery in texture.

Crateriform. Crater-like; cup-shaped.

Cuneate. Wedge-shaped.

Cystidia. Sterile structures of varying shape and form between the basidia or buried in the tramal tissue. (See also explanation on p. 15.)

Daedaloid. With elongated and sinuous mouths.

Decurrent. Extending down the stem; also applied to the tubes, which in some sessile forms of polypores extend down upon the substratum.

Decurved. Curved under.

Delignifying decay. A decay characterized by loss of all components, leaving affected wood light-colored and fibrous. (See further on p. 20.)

Dentate. Toothed.

Denticulate. Minutely toothed; very finely dentate.

Dimidiate. Semicircular.

447

Dissepiments. The walls of the tubes.

Distorted. Twisted out of regular shape; deformed.

Drab. Dark gray with shades of yellow.

Duplex. Double; a term applied to the substance of the pileus when it is soft above and firm next the tubes.

Echinulate. Minutely roughened; set with short, sharp points.

Effused. Spread out over the substratum without regular form.

Effused-reflexed. Spread out over the substratum and turned back at the margin to form a pileus.

Ellipsoid. Curved and longer than broad, with the ends rounded.

Epixylous. Growing on wood.

Excentric. Not in the center.

Farinaceous. Mealy; with the odor or taste of meal.

Faveolate. With pores resembling the cells of a honeycomb.

Ferruginous. Rusty red.

Fibrillose. Covered by or composed of minute fibers.

Fibrils. Minute fibers.

Filiform. Threadlike; long and slender.

Fimbriate. Fringed.

Flabelliform. Fan-shaped.

Floccose. Downy-woolly.

Friable. Easily crumbling.

Fuliginous. Sooty brown or dark smoke-colored.

Fulvous. Reddish yellow; pale.

Fuscous. Dusky; grayish brown.

Fusiform. Spindle-shaped; thick in the center and tapering at both ends.

Gilvous. A bright yellowish brown.

Glabrate. Becoming glabrous.

Glabrous. With neither hairs nor scales; smooth.

Gregarious. Growing close to each other but not tufted.

Guttate. Having droplike spots.

Guttulate. A term applied to spores containing an oily, nucleus-like globule.

Hirsute. Covered with stiff hairs.

Hirtose. Hairy; hirsute.

Hispid. Covered with rough hairs or bristles.

Hyaline. Colorless; transparent.

Hydnoid. Toothed or spinelike.

Hymenium. The spore-bearing surface; in the polypores composed mainly of basidia that line the inner surface of tubes and bear the spores.

Hyphal complex. A type of hyphae characterized by profuse branching. (See further on p. 18.)

Hyphal peg. A sterile organ, formed of closely compacted hyphae, that projects into the lumen of the tube. (See further on p. 17.)

Imbricate. Overlapping.

Incised. Deeply cut.

Incrusted. Covered with a thin, hard crust; covered with crystals.

Indurated. Hardened.

Inflexed. Bent inward; incurved.

Infundibuliform. Funnel-shaped.

Insertion. The manner or place of attachment of a stem to the pileus.

Interspaces. Spaces between the lamella-like plates on the under surface of the pileus of a few polypores.

Inverted. Attached by a dorsal, stem-like prolongation of the pileus.

Involute. Rolled inward.

Irpiciform. Broken up into teeth.

Isabelline. The color of unbleached linen.

Labyrinthiform. With intricate and winding passageways.

Laccate. Looking as though varnished.

Lacerate. Irregularly torn.

Lamella. A leaflike plate occurring on the under surface of the pileus; a gill.

Lamellate. Composed of lamellae or gills.

Latericeous. Brick-red.

Ligneous. Of a woody texture.

[*Long.* The horizontal dimension at right angles to the substratum.—J.L.L.]

[*Lumen.* The cell cavity (and its contents).—J.L.L.]

Membranaceous. Very thin.

Membranous. Very thin.

Merismoid. Applied to a pileus that is subdivided into many smaller pilei.

Multizonate. With many zones.

Nodulose. Covered with nodules or rounded knobs.

Obese. Stout and fleshy.

Obsolete. Imperfectly or scarcely at all developed.

Ochraceous. Yellow tinged with red or brown.

Ovoid. Egg-shaped.

Pallid. Pale; light-colored, but not white.

Paraphysis. A type of sterile organ in the hymenium. (See also explanation on p. 14.)

Pellicle. The thin, cuticle-like covering of the pileus in a few species.

Pelliculose. Provided with a cuticle or pellicle.

Pendent. Suspended at the apex; hanging down.

Pileate. Having a pileus or cap.

Pileolus. A small pileus or cap.

Pileus. The cap or shelflike part of a fungus bearing the hymenium on the lower side.

Piped rot. A decay characterized by yellow or white stripes in the wood.

Polyporoid. Of the consistency or structure of species of the genus *Polyporus.*

Poroid. With pores.

Pruinose. Covered with a bloom or powder.

Puberulent. Covered with fine soft hairs; minutely pubescent.

Pubescence. Hairiness.

Pubescent. Covered with hairs.

Punctiform. Like a point or dot; extremely small.

Punky. Having the consistency of punk; soft and tough.

Radiate-lineate. Marked with radiating lines.

Radicating. With a long root.

Reflexed. Turned back to form a pileus.

Reniform. Kidney-shaped.

Resupinate. Spread out upon the substratum with neither pileus nor stem.

Reticulate. Covered with a network of interlacing lines.

Rimose. Becoming deeply cracked and roughened.

Rivulose. Marked with small irregular lines.

Rufescent. Reddish.

Rugose. Covered with wrinkles.

Rugulose. Covered with fine wrinkles.

Scabrous. With a rough surface.

Sclerotium. A dense mass of hyphae or mycelium of definite form.

Scrupose. Rough with minute hard points.

Scutate. Circular; shield-shaped.

Sessile. Without a stem, the pileus being attached at one side.

Setae. Brown sterile organs in the hymenial layer. (See also explanation on p. 15.)

Sodden. Saturated with water.

Spathulate. Shaped like a spatula or spoon.

Sporophore. The fruiting body.

Squamose. Covered with scales.

• *Squamulose.* Covered with small or minute scales.

Squarrose. Covered with large, erect, pointed scales.

Sterigma (pl. *sterigmata*). Projection on a basidium to which the basidiospore is attached.

Stipe. Stem.

Stipitate. Having a stipe or stem.

Striations. Radiating or parallel lines.

Strigose. Covered with rough, stiff hairs.

Sub-. Almost; somewhat; slightly.

Substratum. The substance or material on which a plant grows and to which it is attached.

Subulate. Awl-shaped.

Subzonate. Marked with obscure, indefinite zones.

Sulcate. Grooved or furrowed.

Superimposed. Overlapping.

Tawny. Yellowish brown or rusty brown.

Terrestrial. Growing on the ground.

Tessellate. With checkered areas over the surface.

Testaceous. Brown mixed with yellow or red, close to brick color.

[*Thick.* The vertical dimension of a sporophore.—J.L.L.]

Tomentose. Covered with dense, matted wool or hair.

Trama. The tissue composing the walls of the tubes or the context of the pileus.

Trametoid. With the consistency or structure of species of the genus *Trametes.*

Tubercular. Like a tubercle.

Tumid. Thick; swollen.

Turbinate. Top-shaped; shaped like an inverted cone.

Umber. Pale smoky in color, or smoky-brown.

Umbilicate. With a rounded, central depression.

Umbo. An elevation on the surface of the pileus.

Umbonate-affixed. Attached to the substratum by an umbo.

Umbrinous. Olive-brown.

Undulate. With the surface alternately concave and convex; wavy.

Ungulate. With the pileus steep in front; hoof-shaped.

Velutinous. Velvety.

Vertex. The apex or highest point.

Villose. Covered with soft, weak hairs.

Vinaceous. Dark wine color.

Virgate. Giving the appearance of bearing many small twigs.

Zonate. Having concentric bands or zones.

INDEX

(Boldface type indicates technical descriptions.)

UNIVERSITY OF MICHIGAN STUDIES

SCIENTIFIC SERIES

Orders should be directed to the University of Michigan Press

Vol. I. The Circulation and Sleep. By John F. Shepard. Pp. ix + 83, with an Atlas of 83 plates, bound separately. Text and Atlas, $2.50.

Vol. II. Studies on Divergent Series and Summability. By Walter B. Ford. Pp. xi + 194. $2.50.

Vol. III. The Geology of the Netherlands East Indies. By H. A. Brouwer. Pp. xii + 160. $3.00.

Vol. IV. The Glacial Anticyclones: The Poles of the Atmospheric Circulation. By W. H. Hobbs. Pp. xxiv + 198. $2.75.

Vols. V-VI. Reports of the Greenland Expeditions of the University of Michigan (1926–33). W. H. Hobbs, Director.

> Vol. V. Aërology, Expeditions of 1927 and 1927–29. Pp. x + 262. $6.00.

> Vol. VI. Meteorology, Physiography, and Botany. Pp. vii + 287. $5.00.

Vol. IX. The Genus Diaporthe Nitschke and Its Segregates. By Lewis E. Wehmeyer. Pp. xii + 349. $3.50.

Vol. X. The Distribution of the Currents of Action and of Injury Displayed by Heart Muscle and Other Excitable Tissue. By F. N. Wilson, A. G. Macleod, and P. S. Barker. Pp. vii + 59. $1.50.

Vol. XI. The Asymptotic Developments of Functions Defined by Maclaurin Series. By W. B. Ford. Pp. viii + 143. $2.00.

Vol. XII. The Geology and Biology of the San Carlos Mountains, Tamaulipas, Mexico. Edited by Lewis B. Kellum. Pp. xi + 341. $5.00.

Vol. XIII. Marine Algae of the Northeastern Coast of North America. By W. R. Taylor. (*Out of print.*)

Vol. XIV. A Revision of Melanconis, Pseudovalsa, Prosthecium, and Titania. By Lewis E. Wehmeyer. Pp. viii + 161. $2.50.

Vol. XV. Aquatic Phycomycetes, Exclusive of the Saprolegniaceae and Pythium. By Frederick K. Sparrow, Jr. Pp. xix + 785. $5.00.

Vol. XVI. Beams on Elastic Foundation. By M. Hetényi. Pp. ix + 255. $4.50.

Vol. XVII. North American Species of Mycena. By Alexander H. Smith. Pp. xviii + 521. $6.00.

Vol. XVIII. Plants of Bikini and Other Northern Marshall Islands. By W. R. Taylor. Pp. xvi + 227. $5.50.

Vol. XIX. The Polyporaceae of the United States, Alaska, and Canada. By Lee Oras Overholts. Pp. xiv + 466. $7.50.